Introduction to Corrections

Second Edition

Michael L. Birzer
Cliff Roberson
Washburn University

COPPERHOUSE PUBLISHING COMPANY
P.O. Box 5463, Incline Village, Nevada 89450
All Copperhouse titles are now distributed by
Atomic Dog Publishing

Atomic Dog is a higher education publishing company that specializes in developing and publishing HyBred Media™ textbooks that combine online content delivery, interactive media, and print. You can contact Atomic Dog as follows:

1148 Main Street, Third Floor
Cincinnati, OH 45202
800-310-5661   Fax 513-842-3384
e-mail copperhouse@atomicdogpublishing.com
www.atomicdog.com

Your Partner in Education
with
"QUALITY BOOKS AT FAIR PRICES"

Copyright © 2004 by Copperhouse Publishing Company

All rights reserved. No portions of this book may be reprinted or reproduced in any manner without prior written permission of the publisher; except for brief passages which may be quoted in connection with a book review and only when source credit is given.

Library of Congress Control Number: 2003107119
ISBN 1-928916-26-0

10   9   8   7   6   5   4   3   2   1

Printed in the United States of America

Dedications

For Michael Birzer
To my loving wife Gwynne, and my parents Leo and Lou who taught me well.

For Cliff Roberson
To Geneva, Nikkie, Isaiah, Treavor, and Amy—my grandchildren.

Contents

Preface   *xiii*

Chapter 1

Corrections: Introduction and Overview   1

1-1 The Criminal Justice Enterprise   3
 1-1a First Response to Crime   *3*
 1-1b The Government's Response to Crime   *4*
 1-1c Prosecution and Pretrial Services   *4*
 1-1d Adjudication Procedures   *5*
 1-1e Sentencing Sanctions   *5*
 1-1f Corrections   *5*
1-2 The Correctional Enterprise   6
1-3 Careers in Corrections   8
1-4 Trends and Challenges   9
1-5 Looking Ahead: A Preview of This Book   14
1-6 Additional Resources   17
Summary   19
Discussion Questions   19
Chapter Quiz   20
Endnotes   21

Chapter 2

Corrections: The Beginning   23

2-1 History and Philosophy   25
 2-1a Beginning of Legal Punishments   *25*
 2-1b Middle Ages   *28*
2-2 The Early Reformers   29
 2-2a Voltaire (Francois Marie Arouet) (1694–1778)   *29*
 2-2b Cesare Beccaria (1738–1794)   *29*
 2-2c Cesare Lombroso (1835–1909)   *30*
 2-2d Jeremy Bentham (1748–1832)   *31*
 2-2e John Howard (1726–1790)   *32*
 2-2f William Penn (1644–1718)   *32*
2-3 Purpose of Criminal Sanctions   33

    2-3a Retribution   34
    2-3b Deterrence   35
    2-3c Incapacitation   36
    2-3d Rehabilitation   37
2-4 Purposes of Punishment   37
    2-4a English Statement of Purposes   37
    2-4b Guiding Principles   38
    2-4c Social Purposes of Punishment   39
2-5 Crime and Offenders   39
    2-5a Magnitude of the Problem   39
    2-5b Demographics   40
    2-5c Disproportionate Minority Confinement   40
2-6 Locations of Confinements   44
    2-6a Types of Crime   44
    2-6b Time Served   46
    2-6c Overcrowding   46
2-7 Changes to the "Justice" Correctional Philosophy   47
Article—Rehabilitation: Holding Its Ground in Corrections   49
Summary   57
Discussion Questions   58
Chapter Quiz   58
Endnotes   59

Chapter 3

The Sentencing Process   63

3-1 Determinate and Indeterminate Sentencing   68
    3-1a Mandatory Prison Terms   70
    3-1b Flat Time with Mandatory Supervision   71
    3-1c Sentencing Guidelines   71
    3-1d Three Strikes Legislation   73
    3-1e United States Sentencing Commission   75
    3-1f Good-Time Policies   77
    3-1g Emergency Overcrowding Provisions   79
    3-1h National Conference on Corrections   79
    3-1i Judicial Process for Misdemeanants   80
    3-1j Judicial Process for Felons   80
    3-1k Presentence Investigations   80
    3-1l Suspended Sentences   83
3-2 Alternative Sentencing and Diversion   83
3-3 Judicial Process for Juveniles   84
    3-3a Juvenile Court Procedures   84
    3-3b Detention Hearings   85
    3-3c Citation   86
    3-3d Venue   87
    3-3e Intake   87
    3-3f Adjudicatory Hearings   88
    3-3g Disposition Hearings   88
    3-3h Uniform Juvenile Court Act   89
Summary   92
Discussion Questions   94
Chapter Quiz   95
Endnotes   96

Chapter 4

The Correctional Client 97
4-1 Prisonization 99
4-2 The Career Criminal 99
4-3 Prison Violence 100
4-4 The Young Criminal 101
4-5 The Professional Criminal 103
4-6 The Drug Criminal 103
4-7 The Elderly Criminal 105
4-8 The Female Criminal 106
4-9 Gender Bias 106
4-10 Noncitizen Offenders 107
4-11 The Federal Inmate 108
Article—Golden Years Behind Bars: Special Programs and Facilities for Elderly Inmates 110
Summary 119
Discussion Questions 120
Chapter Quiz 120
Endnotes 122

Chapter 5

Alternatives to Incarceration 125
5-1 Diversion 127
    5-1a Purpose and Objectives 127
    5-1b Targets for Diversion 127
    5-1c Evaluating Diversion 128
5-2 Shock Incarceration 129
    5-2a Boot Camp Programs 129
    5-2b Characteristics of Shock Incarceration 129
    5-2c Profiles of Selected Programs 130
    5-2d Evaluation of Boot Camp Programs 132
    5-2e Catalyst for Change 133
5-3 Rehabilitative Programming 134
5-4 Attitude Change 137
5-5 Recidivism 139
Article—Community Service: A Review of the Basic Issues 140
Summary 150
Discussion Questions 151
Chapter Quiz 152
Endnotes 153

Chapter 6

Probation 155
6-1 What Is Probation? 157
6-2 History of Probation 158
6-3 Status of Probation 159
6-4 Extent of Probation 161
6-5 Criteria for Granting Probation 161

6-6 Conditions of Probation   163
6-7 Probationers' Rights   164
    6-7a Search of Probationers   164
    6-7b Right to Confidentiality   164
    6-7c Revocation of Probation   164
6-8 Functions of Probation   167
    6-8a The Probation Officer   169
6-9 Probation Offices   171
6-10 Future of Probation   171
Article—Guiding Philosophies for Probation in the 21st Century   172
Summary   184
Discussion Questions   186
Chapter Quiz   186
Endnotes   187

Chapter 7

Jails and Misdemeanants   189

7-1 Jails   191
    7-1a History of Jails   191
    7-1b Jail Standards   192
    7-1c Role of Jails   193
    7-1d The Revolving Door   194
    7-1e Female Jail Inmates   195
7-2 Jail Procedures   196
    7-2a Intake   196
    7-2b Classification   196
    7-2c Orientation   197
    7-2d Court Liaison   197
    7-2e Release   197
7-3 State Jail Felony   197
7-4 Issues in Jails   199
    7-4a Overcrowding   199
    7-4b Controversies   201
    7-4c Jail Suicides   202
7-5 Jail Designs   208
    7-5a Traditional Jails   208
    7-5b Direct-Supervision Jails   208
Summary   210
Discussion Questions   211
Chapter Quiz   211
Endnotes   212

Chapter 8

Doing Time   215

8-1 Prisonization   217
8-2 Inmate Social System   221
    8-2a Prison Subculture   222
8-3 Gangs in Prison   224
8-4 Prison Routine   227
    8-4a Classification   227

    8-4b Shakedowns   228
    8-4c Sexual Activity   228
    8-4d Inmates and Guards   229
    8-4e Controlled Movement   229
    8-4f Counts   230
8-5 Special Issues in Doing Time   230
    8-5a AIDS   230
    8-5b Mental Health Issues   231
    8-5c Sex Offenders   232
Summary   236
Discussion Questions   238
Chapter Quiz   238
Endnotes   239

Chapter 9

Institutional Procedures   241

    9-1 Why Prisons?   243
        9-1a Diagnostic Process   243
        9-1b Inmate Orientation Process   244
        9-1c Custody Levels   245
        9-1d Discipline   246
        9-1e Disciplinary Hearing Procedures   246
        9-1f Grievances   248
    9-2 Rules of Conduct   249
    9-3 Release from Confinement   250
    9-4 Release on Parole   250
    9-5 History of Parole   252
    9-6 Good-Time Credit   253
    9-7 Supervised Release   253
    9-8 Parole Today   254
    9-9 Parole Services   255
    9-10 Revocation of Parole   256
    9-11 Discharge from Parole   257
    9-12 Costs of Prisons   266
Article—Is Further Prison Expansion Worth the Costs?   268
Summary   271
Discussion Questions   272
Chapter Quiz   273
Endnotes   274

Chapter 10

Juvenile Corrections   275

    10-1 History of Juvenile Justice   277
    10-2 Establishment of Juvenile Court   278
    10-3 Present Role of Juvenile Justice   280
    10-4 Juvenile Diversion   280
    10-5 Waiver of Juvenile Court Jurisdiction   281
    10-6 Juvenile Trials   282
    10-7 Disposition   282
    10-8 Institutionalization   283

10-9 The Right to Treatment   283
10-10 Types of Cases Handled by the Juvenile Courts   283
    10-10a Violent Youths   283
    10-10b Property Cases   284
10-11 Types of Institutions   285
10-12 Conditions of Confinement in Juvenile Facilities   285
10-13 Disproportionate Minority Youth Confinement   288
10-14 Group Home Programs   289
10-15 Juvenile Release Decisions   292
10-16 Parole   293
Summary   294
Discussion Questions   295
Chapter Quiz   295
Endnotes   296

Chapter 11

Women and Corrections   297
11-1 Women's Prisons in the United States   299
11-2 The Early Years   300
    11-2a Separate Quarters   301
    11-2b Women's Reformatories   301
    11-2c Racial Disparities   302
    11-2d The End of the Reformatory Era   303
11-3 Women Offenders   304
11-4 Issues   306
    11-4a Substance Abuse Treatment   308
    11-4b Parenting Programs   308
    11-4c Educational Programs   312
    11-4d Mental Health Programs   313
    11-4e Medical Treatment   314
11-5 Women Correctional Officers   316
11-6 Problems Facing Women Correctional Officers   316
    11-6a Job-Related Issues   317
11-7 History of Women in Corrections   319
11-8 Progress of Women in the Correctional Field   320
11-9 Affirmative Action Goals   323
Summary   324
Discussion Questions   327
Chapter Quiz   327
Endnotes   328

Chapter 12

Capital Punishment   333
12-1 Capital Cases   335
12-2 The Death Penalty and the Courts   339
    12-2a The Courts and Executing the Mentally Impaired   341
    12-2b Who Decides the Death Penalty?   342
12-3 Status of Capital Cases   343
12-4 Statutory Changes   345
12-5 Methods of Execution   346

12-5a History 346
12-5b Present Day 348
12-6 Automatic Review 350
12-7 Characteristics of Prisoners under Sentence of Death 350
12-8 Criminal History of Inmates under Sentence of Death 352
12-9 Is the Death Penalty Biased? 353
12-10 Is the Death Penalty Broken? 354
Summary 362
Discussion Questions 363
Chapter Quiz 363
Endnotes 364

Chapter 13

Prisoners' Rights 367
13-1 Hands-off Period 369
13-2 Rights Period 369
13-3 Categories of Involvement 370
  13-3a Due Process Rights 370
  13-3b Torts 370
  13-3c Conditions of Confinement 371
  13-3d Habeas Corpus 371
13-4 Prison Litigation Reform Act 372
13-5 Back to Basics 373
13-6 Historical Background of the "Cruel and Unusual" Clause 374
13-7 Significant Cases Involving Prisoners' Rights 377
  13-7a Large v. Superior Court of County of Maricopa 714 P2d 399 (1986) 377
  13-7b Bounds v. Smith 97 S.Ct. 1491 (1977) 377
  13-7c Hutto v. Finney 98 S.Ct. 2565 (1978) 377
  13-7d Estelle v. Gamble 97 S.Ct. 285 (1976) 378
  13-7e Helling v. McKinney 113 S.Ct. 2475 (1993) 378
  13-7f Jones v. N.C. Prisoners' Labor Union 97 S.Ct. 2532 (1976) 378
  13-7g Meachum v. Fano 96 S.Ct. 2532 (1976) 378
  13-7h Vitek v. Jones 100 S.Ct. 1254 (1987) 378
  13-7i Turner v. Safety 107 S.Ct. 2254 (1987) 379
  13-7j Wolff v. McDonnell 94 S.Ct. 2963 (1974) 379
  13-7k Procunier v. Martinez 416 U.S. 396 (1974) 379
  13-7l McKune v. Lile 536 U.S. 24 (2002) 380
13-8 Deliberate Indifference 380
  13-8a Farmer v. Brennan 511 U.S. 825 (1994) 381
13-9 *Warner v. Orange County Probation Department*, CA 2, No. 95-7055 decided 9/9/96, affirming 870 F.Supp. 69 386
Summary 390
Discussion Questions 391
Chapter Quiz 391
Endnotes 392

Chapter 14

Innovations in Corrections 395
14-1 Alternatives to Confinement 397
  14-1a Electronic House Arrest 397
14-2 Other Innovations 400

      14-2a Mobile Intervention Supervision Team 400
      14-2b Operation Night Light 401
Article—Using Day-Reporting Centers As an Alternative to Jail 402
Article—Intensive Supervision: A New Way to Connect with Offenders 408
Article—Inmate Involvement in Prison Governance 413
Summary 423
Discussion Questions 424
Chapter Quiz 424
Endnotes 425

Chapter 15

Corrections As a Career Field 427

15-1 Parole and Probation Officers
    and Correctional Treatment Strategies Specialists 431
      15-1a Nature of Work 432
      15-1b Correctional Treatment Specialists 433
      15-1c Caseloads 433
      15-1d Changes in Work 434
      15-1e Working Conditions 434
      15-1f Training, Other Qualifications, and Advancement 435
      15-1g Job Outlook 435
Article—The Multifaceted Role of the Juvenile Probation Officer 436
15-2 Codes of Ethics 438
Article—Success in the Organization: A Primer for Probation Officers Seeking Upward
  Mobility 439
15-3 A Career As a Correctional Officer 448
      15-3a Federal Bureau of Prisons 448
      15-3b Kansas Department of Corrections 448
      15-3c California Department of Corrections 449
      15-3d Texas Department of Criminal Justice—Corrections Officer 450
      15-3e New York State Department of Corrections 450
Summary 451
Discussion Questions 452
Chapter Quiz 453
Endnotes 454

Appendix A 455
Appendix B 483
Glossary 493
Index 503

Preface

> *Prison is, in practice, the ultimate power the democratic state exercises over a citizen, yet we lack a jurisprudence of imprisonment.*
>
> —Norval Morris, *The Future of Imprisonment*

Introduction to Corrections, 2nd edition is designed to be comprehensive, yet affordable. The text discusses the stages of criminal justice administration that occur after an individual has been convicted of a crime. The title is really a misnomer. The text is about *punishment* and the use of punishment/sanctions to prevent and/or control crime.

This text is written for an introductory corrections course that focuses on both adult corrections and juvenile court dispositions. The main focus of the book is about how the current correctional subsystems function within the larger umbrella of our criminal justice system. It provides a complete overview to the corrections field and considers all types of custody, including probation and parole. As expected, the text covers everything from historical precedents to the latest programs and practices. Pursuant to our times, special attention is given to elderly inmates, violent juveniles, alternative penalties, and private correctional facilities. We have also made it a point in the second edition to critically examine several disturbing complexities, such as the disproportionate confinement of minorities in our nation's correctional institutions, the lingering debate over capital punishment, and the issues centering on women inmates. In addition, included are articles from leading professional journals on corrections. These articles are designed to provide the reader with insight from different viewpoints regarding critical issues affecting modern corrections.

The state of Texas, along with several other states, has concluded that the term "inmate" is politically incorrect. In fact, in Texas, the state office that Cliff Roberson was associated with has changed its name from "Inmate Legal Services" to "State Counsel for Offenders." The problem is that the term "offenders" does not describe an individual who is confined. Most offenders receive probation and therefore are not confined. Accordingly, in this text the authors have retained the use of the term "inmate" to refer to an individual who is incarcerated.

Textbooks are biased to a certain degree based on the background, experiences, and philosophy of the authors. In light of this, we have attempted to remove most biases from this text. Cliff Roberson's background as a prosecutor, defense counsel, and judge, and Michael Birzer's background as an educator and law enforcement officer, which included assignments in an adult detention facility, have allowed us to research the corrections area from the perspective of different viewpoints. Additionally, Cliff Roberson had the unique opportunity to teach criminological theory courses to inmates in a federal medium security institution on three separate occasions. This experience provided him with an opportunity to have frank discussions with the inmates on crime causation and correctional policies. Therefore, this text is designed to provide the reader with *real world* insight based on our teaching and practical experiences.

Acknowledgments

While we are listed as the only authors of the text, it could not have been possible without the help, assistance, and guidance of numerous others including Tom Romaniak, Christine Abshire, Cathy Lowe-Anderson, Rick Anderson, Ken Kerle, Kay Welchhans, Rachelle Carlson, and Professors Harvey Wallace, Gary Bayens, David McElreath, and Ron Tannehill. We also send a special thanks to the guru of corrections, Professor emeritus Ted Heim. We also thank our reviewers Stephen S. Owen from Radford University and David Ruiz from Centralia College. Finally, Michael Birzer extends a warm thank you to those fine professors from Oklahoma State University (Professors Robert Nolan, John Cross, and Gary Conti) who shaped his scholarship in the spirit of a critical and reflective thinker, and a special thank you to Professors Delores Craig and Michael Palmiotto from Wichita State University who were instrumental in encouraging his graduate studies.

We view this work as a living and breathing document, thus, any suggestions or comments you have that could improve future editions are especially welcome. Any suggestions, comments, or questions, may be addressed to the authors at

Washburn University
Department of Criminal Justice
1700 SW. College
Topeka, Kansas 66621

Michael Birzer, Ed.D.　　　　　　　　　　**Cliff Roberson, LLM, Ph.D.**
Washburn University　　　　　　　　　　　*Washburn University*

About the Authors

Michael L. Birzer is an assistant professor of criminal justice at Washburn University in Topeka, Kansas. He earned both his bachelor's and master's degrees in the Administration of Justice from Wichita State University and his doctorate in adult education from Oklahoma State University. Prior to his entry into academia, he served 18 years with the Sedgwick County Sheriff's Department in Wichita, Kansas, where he rose to the rank of lieutenant. He has an interest in both quantitative and qualitative research designs in the study of criminal justice. His writing and research interests have not only centered on corrections but also a wide range of policing and social justice issues. A few of his recent publications include "Criminal justice education: Where have we been and where are we headed?" co-authored with Michael Palmiotto, which appeared in *Justice Professional*, 15 (3) 2002; "Learning strategies of selected urban police related to community policing," co-authored with Robert Nolan, which appeared in *Policing: An International Journal of Police Management and Administration*, 25 (2), 2002, and "Writing partnership between police practitioners and researchers," which appeared in *Police Practice and Research: An International Journal*, 3 (2), 2002.

Cliff Roberson is a professor of criminal justice at Washburn University. His previous academic experience includes professor of criminology and director of the Justice Center at California State University–Fresno; professor of criminal justice and dean of arts and sciences at the University of Houston–Victoria; association vice-president for academic affairs at Arkansas Tech University; and Director of Programs for the National College of District Attorneys, University of Houston.

His nonacademic legal experience includes Trial and Legal Services Supervisor, Office of State Counsel for Offenders, Texas Board of Criminal Justice; private legal practice; judge pro-tem in the California courts; trial and defense counsel and military judge as a Marine judge advocate; and director of the Military Law Branch, U.S. Marine Corps. Cliff is permitted to practice before the U.S. Supreme Court, federal courts in California and Texas, Supreme Court of Texas, and the Supreme Court of California.

His educational background includes: Ph.D. in Human Behavior, U.S. International University; L.L.M. in Criminal Law, Criminology, and Psychiatry, George Washington University; J.D. American University; B.A. in Political Science, University of Missouri; and one year of post-graduate study at the University of Virginia School of Law. Cliff has authored or co-authored 40 books and other texts.

Chapter 1

Corrections: Introduction and Overview

Mark C. Ide

Key Terms

American Correctional Association	jail	prison privatization
American Jail Association	juvenile correctional facilities	probation
arraignment	parole	qualified immunity
correctional subsystem	plea	reintegration
incarceration	prison	State Department of Corrections

Outline

1-1 The Criminal Justice Enterprise
   1-1a First Response to Crime
   1-1b The Government's Response to Crime
   1-1c Prosecution and Pretrial Services
   1-1d Adjudication Procedures
   1-1e Sentencing Sanctions
   1-1f Corrections

1-2 The Correctional Enterprise
1-3 Careers in Corrections
1-4 Trends and Challenges
1-5 Looking Ahead: A Preview of This Book
1-6 Additional Resources
Summary
Discussion Questions
Chapter Quiz
Endnotes

Learning Objectives

After studying this chapter, the reader will be able to:

- Identify the major scope and aims of the book.
- Identify the organizational theme of the book.
- Articulate the meaning of the term "system" in describing the criminal justice process.
- Recognize the field of corrections as comprising not only a profession but also an important subsystem of the criminal justice profession.
- View the correctional field as an important career and social phenomenon that has the potential to change the lives of not only convicts but also those employees within the walls of the correctional facility.
- Identify and discuss issues and challenges that face the field of corrections now and in the future.

Crime continues to be a major problem in the United States. As we enter into the twenty-first century, the criminal justice system continues to grapple with and debate how to effectively deal with crime and disorder problems in our society. Americans suffered 11.6 million serious criminal offenses in 2000.[1] Likewise, a very small group of offenders commit the vast majority of crimes and studies show that most felony offenders are recidivists, meaning that most are repeat offenders. In fact, we know that 70 percent of the inmates in the nation's jails or prisons are not there for the first time.[2] Not only has crime remained an area of national concern but also after the tragic events on September 11, 2001, America has become more aware of the threat of terrorism. Even in light of these bleak concerns, there have been laudatory improvements made in the criminal justice system. Improvements in such areas as community-based courts, community-oriented probation, community-based corrections, restorative justice, and community-oriented policing strategies are just a few of the changes taking place. These strategies represent new and innovative approaches in dealing with crime and disorder problems as well as in dealing with the offenders.

It cannot be denied that the progress made in the criminal justice enterprise is grounds for optimism in many respects, but there is still a long way to go. The police are constantly urged to do more, the courts are hindered by full and overburdened dockets, the nation's prisons are vastly overcrowded, and probation and parole caseloads are overwhelming. Clearly, crime represents a complex and perplexing problem with no easy solutions or explanations in our society.

The American criminal justice system is composed of three components, the police, courts, and corrections. In fact, these three areas make up the subsystems of the entire criminal justice enterprise. The following overview is provided to describe as closely as possible the intricate workings of the three components of the criminal justice system and, more importantly, an understanding of how the correctional enterprise fits into the criminal justice system as a whole.

1-1 The Criminal Justice Enterprise

1-1a First Response to Crime

The criminal justice system begins with the private sector's response to crime (i.e., individuals, families, neighborhood associations, business and industry). A crime is committed and citizens take part in the criminal justice system by reporting the crime to the police and by being a reliable participant in the process (for example, acting as a witness or juror in a criminal proceeding and cooperating with the police during the investigation of a crime).

1-1b The Government's Response to Crime

After a citizen calls the police to report a crime, the government response is initiated. The police make a report and conduct a preliminary investigation. The goal is to gather enough evidence to identify and apprehend the offender. In some cases an offender is apprehended at the scene of a crime, but in most cases they are arrested after considerable police investigation. Once an offender has been identified and apprehended the case advances to the next stage in the criminal justice system.

1-1c Prosecution and Pretrial Services

After law enforcement makes an arrest, they present information about the case and the accused to a state or federal prosecutor. The prosecutor will decide if formal charges will be filed with the court. If no charges are filed, the accused must be released. The prosecutor can also drop the charges if the evidence or elements of the crime are not present or after making efforts to prosecute (*nolle prosequi*).

Once the accused is charged with a crime, he or she must be taken before a judge or magistrate within a reasonable time and without unnecessary delay. At the initial appearance, the judge or magistrate informs the accused of the charges that have been brought against him or her. The judge or magistrate then decides if there is enough probable cause to detain the accused. In some jurisdictions pretrial release (bail or release on own recognizance) is decided upon and arranged at the initial court appearance. Also during the pretrial stage, the matter of legal council (attorney) is discussed. If the defendant cannot afford an attorney, one will be appointed by the court.

A preliminary hearing is held during the pretrial stage. The main objective at this hearing is to determine if there is enough probable cause to bind the accused over for trail. If the judge does not find probable cause, the accused is released. However, if the judge finds probable cause or the accused waives his or her right to a preliminary hearing, the case may be bound over for trial.

In the federal system and some state systems, the government prosecutor presents evidence before a grand jury and there is no preliminary hearing. The grand jury decides if there is enough evidence for the case to proceed to trail. If the grand jury decides there is enough evidence, an indictment is issued.

1-1d Adjudication Procedures

Once the accused has been bound over for trial or once the accused is indicted by a grand jury, he or she is formally arraigned at the **arraignment** or the proceeding during which the accused is informed of the charges and advised of his or her rights as a criminal defendant. The accused is requested to enter a **plea** to the charges. There are four pleas that an offender can enter into: (1) guilty; (2) not guilty; (3) nolo contendere, and (4) not guilty by reason of insanity. If the accused pleads guilty or nolo contendere (accepts penalty without admitting guilt), the judge may accept or reject the plea. If the judge accepts the guilty or nolo contendere plea, no trial is held and the defendant can then be sentenced. The judge may not accept the plea if there is reason to believe that the rights of the accused were violated or that the accused was coerced into a confession. In this situation, the case may proceed to trial. If the accused pleads not guilty, a trial date is set. The accused has the right to have a judge hear the evidence and decide guilt or innocence (bench trial), or have a jury of his peers hear the evidence and decide upon guilt or innocence (jury trial). The trial results in an acquittal or conviction on the original charges or lesser-included offenses. In a finding of guilty other than by a plea, the accused has only a limited right to appeal.

1-1e Sentencing Sanctions

The next step in the criminal justice process after a guilty plea is entered is the sentencing stage. In most cases the judge decides on the sentence. In some states the sentence is decided by a jury. Prior to sentencing and after conviction, the judge may order a pre-sentence report completed on the defendant by a **probation** agency or a court services officer. A pre-sentence report contains information about the offense, the offender, and the history of prior offenses, and may include a sentence recommendation. Many courts also take into consideration victim impact statements. There are a number of sentencing choices including: the death penalty, **incarceration** in **jail** or **prison,** probation, fines, and restitution. Many states now have sentencing guidelines that mandate prison sentences for certain types of crimes, thus leaving the judge minimal or no discretion.

1-1f Corrections

Offenders sentenced to incarceration spend time in a prison or jail. Offenders sentenced to less than a year usually complete their time in a local jail, while sentences longer than a year will be served at a state or federal prison. Offenders sentenced to prison may be held in prison facilities with different levels of custody (which usually depend on the severity of the crime) such as minimum security, medium security, or maximum security. In some cases the offender may be sentenced to serve time at a community corrections facility.

After the prisoner serves some of his or her time, he or she may become eligible for **parole.** Parole is a post-sentencing process that usually occurs when an inmate is released early from prison and is required to report to a parole officer for the rest of his or her original prison sentence. The parole officer monitors the offender's progress after release from prison. If the offender violates the conditions of his or her parole, he or she can be sent back to prison to serve the remainder of the original prison sentence. In some cases the offender has been sentenced under what is referred to as a determinant sentence (e.g., a determinant sentence of 60 months in prison) and does not have the option for parole. In determinant sentencing, the offender serves his or her prison sentence outright without the option of parole. In a determinant sentence, after the offender serves the entire sentence, he or she is released from the custody of the correctional system with no requirement of reporting to a parole officer.

1-2 The Correctional Enterprise

The American criminal justice system is truly a system with three mutually related subsystems (i.e., police, courts, and corrections), with each subsection impacting the rest of the system. For example, if the police make an exerted effort to target illegal drug crimes, and as a result arrests increase 20 percent, the increased arrests will impact the courts and ultimately jails and prisons. The correctional enterprise is a vast enterprise, in terms of the number of people it processes and services, the number of inmates it cares for, the cost of maintenance to keep the facilities in shape, the number of personnel it requires for inmate care, and the awesome burden to the taxpayer. In recent years, there have been some changes in the American correctional system. These changes have been in the areas of tougher sentencing policies, public attitudes toward corrections, growing inmate populations, substandard prison facilities, an inmate population that is increasingly growing older, and more serious levels of violent crime.

In part, tougher sentencing policies are the result of growing concern of the general public for the criminal justice system to do something about crime. Because of tougher sentencing policies the inmate populations in our nation's jails and prisons have soared to astronomical levels. For example, between 1984 and 1994, according to the Federal Bureau of Justice Statistics, the number of convicts admitted to the nation's state and federal prisons in just one year swelled 120 percent, from 246,260 to 541,434, boosting the total incarcerated 116 percent, from 419,346 to 904,647.[3] As indicated in Table 1-1, by midyear 2001, the nation's prison population was at 1,965,495.

TABLE 1-1 Incarceration in the United States

Prison Population	Number
Federal Prisons	140,741
State Prisons	1,187,322
Jails	631,240
TOTAL	1,965,495

Source: Bureau of Justice Statistics, *Prisoners and Jail Inmates at Midyear 2001* (Washington, DC, June 2001)

Often when the media portray the criminal justice system to the American public, it is usually the police and the courts that receive the glamorous, and at times not so glamorous, headlines. While these two subsystems are important, the correctional enterprise makes up the other vital subsystem and is often not given the same attention (at least through the media) as the police and the courts. Correctional facilities frequently invoke images of small, dirty cells with two, three, or four inmates stuffed together in a less than adequate facility, expected to do their time in harmony, and waiting in hope of someday reentering mainstream society. We rarely hear the stories of the staff within the prison walls who perform an invaluable, yet at times difficult service to society.

The **correctional subsystem** is charged with providing care in both community and institutional settings. Prisons are federal or state penal institutions in which offenders serve court-imposed sentences in excess of one year. Legislators and the general public are increasingly requiring greater levels of accountability and efficiency as more tax money has been poured out to support prison operations and programs. For the most part, both state and federal prisons have been blessed with better management, and often better education and employment training programs, than jails.[4] Correctional administrators have the unenviable but important task of ensuring the smooth operation of the prison facility, often under much public and political scrutiny. There have been a number of innovative advancements within the correctional enterprise, which have been proposed in part to improve the operations of correctional institutions. For example, there has been a move to evolve toward business management practices that include greater responsiveness to constituent concerns and sensitivity to the communities that surround their correctional facilities.[5]

1-3 Careers in Corrections

The field of corrections offers its own distinct career paths. Most state correctional facilities require the applicant to possess at least a high school diploma. Many prisons, including the federal prison system, require a college degree or a minimum amount of college hours to be eligible for employment. Those prison employees who hold graduate degrees improve their chances to obtain key positions in prison management and administration. There are over 365,755 employees working in adult correctional systems in state and federal systems and the District of Columbia.[6] There are an additional 39,376 employees working in the **juvenile correctional facilities** across the United States. Career opportunities in the correctional field depend on the applicant's background, education, and past work performance. It is projected that jobs in the nation's correctional facilities will continue to be abundant in the future.

We suggest that students who are interested in a career in corrections begin to make contacts with recruiters as soon as possible for several reasons. First, students will better understand the qualifications for employment in the correctional field so that they can begin to work toward meeting the qualifications. Second, students can obtain advice on certain courses that may improve their chances for a job with a particular facility. Finally, students may attract the attention of a recruiter, which may be helpful when they initiate an application with the correctional agency. We also recommend that students interested in the correctional field become familiar and perhaps join the various correctional and/or jail associations. For example, the **American Correctional Association** (ACA) is the oldest and largest international correctional association in the world. ACA serves all disciplines within the corrections profession and is dedicated to excellence in every aspect of the field, from professional development and certification to standards and accreditation. Students are encouraged to explore the ACA website (www.aca.org) as it is a viable resource for research, data, and other information regarding corrections.

One other noted organization is the **American Jail Association** (AJA). The AJA is a national nonprofit organization dedicated to supporting those who work in and operate the nation's jails. The AJA as an organization focuses exclusively on issues specific to operations of local jails. Students are encouraged to visit the AJA website (www.corrections.com/aja/).

A complete examination of careers in the correctional profession is covered in Chapter 15 of this text, however job opportunities are provided here to give the reader a brief overview of the possibilities before proceeding in the book.

- **State Department of Corrections Job Opportunities**
  Warden
  Chief Administrative Officer
  Corrections Officer
  Director of Classification
  Director of Vocation
  Director of Education
  Parole Officer
  Substance Abuse Counselors
  Mental Health Workers
  Religious Staff
- **Federal Bureau of Prisons Job Opportunities**
  Correctional Officer
  Treatment Specialists
  Safety Specialists
- **Juvenile Correctional Facilities Job Opportunities**
  Child Welfare Caseworker
  Juvenile Detention Officer

There are two categories of facilities that typically house inmates: detention and correctional facilities. Detention facilities, or jails as they are sometimes called, are primarily designed to house defendants that are being processed, awaiting trial, or awaiting transfer to a correctional facility after conviction. Inmates serving one year or less will serve their time in jails. On the other hand, correctional facilities house inmates who have been sentenced to a specific amount of time. These inmates usually serve their sentences at state and federal prisons. Those offenders serving misdemeanor sentences of not more than one year may serve time in a detention facility or jail. Our primary treatment in the *Introduction to Corrections (2nd Edition)* will focus on correctional facilities.

1-4 Trends and Challenges

The following section is presented early in the book so the student can begin to think about trends and challenges that face the correctional profession and begin to reflect critically on the issues presented prior to studying the rest of the book. The objective here is to give the student an idea of the perplexing issues, arguments, and viewpoints that center on the correctional enterprise.

In 1967, the President's Commission on Law Enforcement and Administration of Justice Task Force Report on Corrections, noted:

> The task of corrections . . . includes building or rebuilding ties between the offender and community, integrating or reintegrating the offender into the community life, restoring family ties, obtaining employment and education, securing in the larger sense a place for the offender in the routine functioning of society. This requires not efforts directed toward the individual offender, which has been almost the exclusive focus of rehabilitation, but also mobilization and change of the community and its institutions.[7]

The commission's language and use of the word "**reintegration**" of the offender back into society left those in the criminal justice and corrections profession somewhat puzzled, particularly at a time when deterrence, incapacitation, and punishment seemed to be the prevailing thought in corrections. Nevertheless, a slow shift in corrections began to emerge. Reintegration stresses adaptation to the community by requiring the offender to participate in programs aimed at providing job skills, personal skills, and motivational skills, or to refine these skills. All of which are done in the community setting.[8] In fact, the language of the president's commission in 1967 was clearly a call for a new and innovative model of corrections "rehabilitation." Rehabilitation is a systematic attempt to change criminal offenders so that deviant propensities, especially those that are damaging or destructive to others, are reduced or eliminated from their lives.[9]

It has been approximately thirty-five years since the president's commission report. Since that time, we have seen the evolution of community-based correctional programs designed to reintegrate offenders back into the community. In recent years, community-based corrections have increasingly come under attack for failing to provide the assurance that the criminal offender will not offend again while under the supervision of the reintegration process. However, research is somewhat mixed regarding this matter.[10] Some community correctional programs are successful while others fail miserably. Determining the success or failure of a community-based corrections sanction can be problematic, that is, it depends on the manner in which researchers and evaluators define success and failure. Many researchers solely rely on arrests, convictions, and reimprisonment, yet these measures may not provide the most valid measure of success or failure.[11]

There has been a shift in the rehabilitation or reintegration model to a "crime control model" of criminal justice. In essence, the get tough on crime mentality has slowly emerged, in part because of the politicalization of crime, that is, politicians and policymakers have inflamed the passions of Americans about crime and disorder. However, media sensationalism, the war on drugs, new laws designed to mandate incarceration and extended confinement for certain types of crimes, and the increase in the number of persons being returned to prison as parole violators are also factors in the exploding prison industry.

Many who support the "crime control model" are quick to point out that these get-tough policies and America's high rate of incarceration have contributed significantly to the drop in the crime rates that America has been experiencing. However, criminologists are quick to caution that America's growing jail and prison population poses serious future consequences. For example, incarceration can have severe social consequences for communities and the families that make up those communities. When a parent is imprisoned, it can result in serious dysfunction for the family. The offenders' children often suffer financial hardships, reduced parental supervision and discipline, and a general deterioration of the family structure.[12] These factors are commonly used to explain why the children of offenders are more likely to become involved in criminal or delinquent behavior.

The prison boom has had profound economic consequences as well. Every year we are spending more and more to incarcerate offenders. Every dollar spent on corrections is a dollar that is not available for other public services. If state and federal budgets increasingly go into additional spending for the maintenance of large populations of inmates, and to build more jails and prisons, assuredly other important public programs will be reduced. We have seen this general trend evolve for several years. For example, the Justice Policy Institute recently reported that the state of Florida provides more funds for nearly 60,000 prisoners than it does for over 200,000 university students.[13] Or consider this, in the 1970s California built 21 new prisons but added only one university to the public university system.[14] From 1984 to 1994, prison spending in California increased 209 percent compared with a 15 percent increase in higher education.[15] A similar pattern has emerged in New York, where state support for public universities dropped 29 percent while funding for prisons increased 76 percent.[16]

As you have now read, there are many factors that present real and immediate challenges for the corrections profession, and the criminal justice system as a whole. Moreover, it should be clear that America's get-tough policies directly impact corrections. In addition to the pressures of overcrowded facilities, prison administrators must operate within a tight budget (which is becoming more and more challenging) assigned by an overseeing government entity. For example, the Federal Bureau of Prisons (BOP) is part of the United States Department of Justice. The BOP operates about

100 federal prisons and is accountable to the Department of Justice. At the state level, most prisons are controlled by, and accountable to, the executive branch of the state government. Prison administrators are held accountable to run their institution smoothly within a given budget. Some states that have led the growth in prison populations are finding their budgets devastated. For example, the Texas legislature is considering slashing the 2004–2005 budget for state prisons by $44 million. This move is prompted by the Texas governor asking state agency heads to scour their operations to identify as many ways to save money as they can before lawmakers return to write the state's 2004–2005 budget.[17]

The costs to incarcerate offenders increases every year and is now the largest single budget expenditure for many states, and from 1982 to 1999 out of the direct expenditures for each of the major criminal justice functions (police, corrections, judicial) the expenditures for corrections has the largest change of 442 percent[18] In Ohio, prison spending has swelled by nearly $1 billion since 1985 in inflation-adjusted figures. Furthermore, it costs more than $22,000 to keep one person in an Ohio prison for a year.[19] A recent report by the Michigan Department of Corrections reveals that the average cost of incarcerating one inmate is about $28,000 per year. Incarceration costs are further exacerbated by habitual violator statutes that lock up offenders for many years. The life expectancy for inmates is about the same for a new prison, thus, we are locking up an increasingly larger permanent population, which must be housed in more secure and more expensive institutions. Rising prison costs will continue to seriously hamper state budgets now and in the future.

Across the nation, state and local governments are increasingly contracting with private firms to deliver services that were once performed by public employees. Public prisons are no different. In the 1980's, **prison privatization** expanded, and the prison industry became, for some, a capital investment. The major reason for this was cost. There is a perception by many government officials that private companies can provide services cheaper and better than public institutions. Thirteen private corrections firms operate about 200 private prison facilities across the United States. Private prisons are run by private business firms with the objective to make a profit.

The privatization of the corrections industry in the United States is alive and well. Privately run correctional facilities are usually lower level security institutions. Only 1 in 25 (4%) private facilities is a maximum-security institution.[20] The main reason for this is that minimum-security prisons are cheaper to build, maintain, and operate compared to a maximum-security institution.

The trend in private corrections has many observers concerned. One concern is the poorer quality correctional officer applicants that private facilities may attract. Because private prisons are profit driven, they may pay their employees less. Thus, less qualified employees may be attracted to the corrections field, or perhaps those that have been turned down at government-run institutions. Lower pay may force private facilities to lower their standards to attract employees. Moreover, the private prison industry may not provide the quality of training to correctional officers of the government-operated facilities.

It has been suggested that private correctional officers employed by a private prison, because of lower selection standards, may be an invitation to civil rights violations, excessive use of force, and a variety of other abuses. For example, the February 21, 2002, edition of the *Albuquerque Journal* reported that a former corrections officer at the privately run prison in Hobbs, New Mexico, has confirmed that he and other guards beat inmates and tried to cover up the incidents at the request of the assistant warden.[21] Or, consider the article that appeared in the February 2, 2002, edition of the *Arkansas Democrat Gazette* reporting that two guards at a privately run youth services center were suspended because they stood by and watched while a group of boys being housed in the serious offender unit beat up another boy also housed in the facility.[22] The guards were shown on video watching the beating. On March 15, 2002, *The Philadelphia Inquirer* reported that a prison guard employed by a private prison firm was fired amid allegations that he took money to allow male inmates at the prison to have sex with female visitors.[23] The *Las Vegas Review* on January 28, 2002, reported that a privately run juvenile prison in Nevada was set to close due to a wide variety of problems. The problems were reported as financial problems, allegations of sexual misconduct by members of its staff, including two prison guards who were sentenced to probation for having sexual relations with teenagers they were paid to supervise.[24] Reports such as these appear to be the crux of a lively legal debate regarding private correctional facilities.

One concern about privatization of prisons lies in the question of what is the private contractor's responsibility when the inmates of their facility claim to have suffered violations of their constitutional rights. Individual officials of government agencies have **qualified immunity,** or protection against being held individually responsible, when the institution or organization they work for violates an individual's rights. This immunity is qualified and does not cover an individual's actions that are illegal or in violation of the institution's or facility's official policy and procedures. On the other hand, private correctional facilities are not government agencies.

In light of this, are employees of private correctional institutions provided qualified immunity? The United States Supreme Court in *Richardson et al. v. McKnight* held that prison guards employed by a private prison firm are not entitled to a qualified immunity from suit by prisoners charging a constitutional tort action for physical injuries inflicted by prison guards.[25] Some have argued that private correctional facilities do not have the right to detain people because the U.S. Supreme Court has ruled that detention is a power reserved for the government.

Many observers find the trend of introducing profit into the prison industry downright disturbing. The concern here is clear, as discussed previously, private correctional institutions are profit driven, and thus they make money off of every offender they incarcerate. In essence, the more inmates housed in private facilities, usually means more profit. Likewise, and perhaps more importantly, many observers question the practice and appropriateness of granting authority for detaining and supervising offenders to a group of private persons.

In no way do the issues and concerns presented above represent an exhaustive list of those that face the correctional field. We offer the above issues to give the student some idea of what prison personnel have to deal with. There are no easy solutions. However, the good news is that the correctional field is stable in employment, and qualified men and women who desire to make a difference will most likely have minimal difficulty finding enjoyment in the correctional field, whether it is as a correctional officer, probation officer, parole officer, or in the juvenile system.

1-5 Looking Ahead: A Preview of This Book

The objective of this book is to introduce the student to the exciting field of corrections. It is written in a straightforward manner and it is our intent to spark critical thinking about the American correctional enterprise. Not only do we discuss what is right with the correctional system but we also shed light on the imperfections of the prison enterprise. Throughout the book, a broad and comprehensive overview of the corrections enterprise is presented.

The second edition has been updated to include the most recent data on American prisons. Furthermore, the second edition includes additional coverage of the most pressing issues and developments in corrections. For example, we examine the important issue of disproportionate minority confinement in our prison system, which is increasingly becoming an area of concern, and we have expanded our coverage of the death penalty debate including a discussion of the recent development on capital punishment in the state of Illinois by Governor George H. Ryan.

There have been a few organizational changes in the second edition. The student will note that the chapter in the first edition titled "Special Applications of Detention and Corrections" has been changed, and we now feature a new topic and chapter titled "Women and Corrections" (Chapter 11). The material that was formally covered in "Special Applications of Detention and Corrections" has been incorporated in relevant chapters throughout the book, which we feel, will be more student-friendly.

Chapter 2 provides the student with fundamental information on the history of corrections, such as the beginning of legal punishment, the early reformers, the purpose of criminal sanctions, the purpose of punishment, crime factors in our society, characteristics of inmates, and the demographic makeup of American prisons.

Chapter 3 provides an introduction to the sentencing process and the variety of sentences that are used as sanctions by the judiciary. Extensive coverage will be given to sentencing guidelines and its impact on prison overcrowding. There is also updated coverage of alternative sentencing and diversion programs, which are, in part, aimed to ease prison overcrowding and criminal court dockets. We also present an overview of the judicial process for juveniles.

While the first three chapters impart basic, fundamental knowledge, subsequent chapters enter into an examination of the specific components and programs of the correctional system. Thus, the correctional client will be examined in Chapter 4, including a discussion and profile of the criminal offender and prisonization. We then turn to an analysis of alternatives to incarceration, such as community service, boot camps, shock incarceration, and rehabilitative programming, which have increasingly undergone rapid developments in the last decade (Chapter 5).

When an offender has been found guilty of a crime, the judge may decide on a community sentence if the crime is not serious and the offender is a good candidate for reform. The judge may place the offender on probation. Probation is the release of a prison-bound convict into the community, usually with terms, conditions, and stipulations (e.g., that the convict must not commit other crimes, must not leave the county without permission, must maintain employment, must not use alcohol or drugs, must make restitution payments to the victim, and so on). In Chapter 6, the student will be introduced to probation. Probation will be examined from its historical roots to the more contemporary issues and concerns.

Jails differ from prisons in the general scope and purpose. As students of criminal justice and corrections it is important to have an understanding of the contrasting nature of jails and prisons (Chapter 7). The one thing that jails and prisons do have in common is that they both house persons either waiting for trial or those offenders who have been found guilty of a crime and sentenced to serve time in an institution. In the prison environment there is an elaborate inmate social system in place. Likewise, it should come as no surprise that both prisons and jails have their fair share of organized gangs and drug activity operating within the walls. Chapter 8 will examine these issues along with the dilemmas of "doing time," the environment of incarceration, and the life of the inmate while in prison.

Some inmates may be released early from prison and placed on parole or supervised conditional release before expiration of the sentence of imprisonment. In Chapter 9 the nature of parole is discussed. We will examine the history of parole and contemporary themes that center on parole services, parole revocation, good time credit, and supervised release policies.

In Chapters 10 and 11, we discuss two important issues pertaining to corrections. In Chapter 10, we explore the conditions of confinement in juvenile corrections from its inception to recent developments. Did you know that until the early nineteenth century, women convicts were imprisoned in institutions designed primarily for male prisoners? In some prisons they were housed in separate quarters. In Chapter 11, we examine the issue of women and corrections. First, we look at women as prisoners, and then we examine the current state of women in the correctional field.

A judge's most difficult sentencing alternative for those convicted of a capital crime is the imposition of the death sentence. Legal execution has existed since the beginning of civilization and continues to be one of the most perplexing issues facing both the criminal justice profession and society. Capital punishment is a controversial issue and one that constantly challenges the judiciary. Chapter 12 examines the death penalty from both viewpoints (for the death penalty and against the death penalty). A discussion is then initiated on the equity of the death penalty. Chapter 12 also examines the issues surrounding the studies revealing that minorities may be disproportionately sentenced to death. Timely discussion of the commuting of all death sentences in the state of Illinois, and some of the issues regarding statutory changes and methods of execution will also be featured in Chapter 12.

Inmates may file two types of lawsuits. In the first, the attack is on general policies or conditions in the institution. This type of lawsuit does not directly attack the actions by individual correctional officers, however the outcome may affect the officer's job. The second type of lawsuit directly attacks the actions (or failures) of the correctional officer, claiming the officer failed to follow the policies and procedures of the institution in a way that violated the rights of inmates. Regardless of the severity or the horrendous nature of the crime that an inmate has been convicted of, he or she still maintains some basic rights while incarcerated. Due process rights, torts, conditions of confinement, habeas corpus, Prison Litigation Reform Act, and significant cases involving prisoner rights will all be analyzed in Chapter 13.

The last two chapters present the innovations in the field of corrections and corrections as a profession. In 1985, Federal District Court Judge Jack Weinstein imposed an unusual sentence on Maureen Murphy, who had been convicted of insurance fraud. Instead of being confined to prison, the judge ordered her confined to her own home. Home confinement or house arrest is just one of several innovative approaches that are being experimented with in recent years. In Chapter 14, we examine such innovations as house arrest, electronic monitoring, and the legal and policy issues that underscore alternative confinement methods. Chapter 14 also introduces evaluations of alternative confinement and the legal issues involved with these alternatives.

We conclude the book with Chapter 15, which examines corrections as a career field. Students who desire a career in corrections (probation officer, parole officer, correctional officer, or other positions in corrections) will find this chapter of particular interest. Often, the popular perception of the corrections officer is one who controls prisoners by using brute force tactics such as a club or other impact weapon. In reality, correctional officers rarely carry weapons while inside of the prison. Rather, modern correctional officers rely more on effective communication skills to control inmates. In Chapter 15 we examine what it is like to work in a prison, including general working conditions and the nature of the job. An attempt is made to portray the most accurate description of working in the correctional profession short of actually visiting a prison, probation office, or a parole office. The chapter serves to orient the student to the training and qualifications for positions in the corrections field. We walk the student through what he or she can expect during the application and selection process for the various positions in the correctional profession. The chapter concludes with an examination of the current job market and future outlook for employment in the correctional enterprise.

1-6 Additional Resources

As you read through and study the book, we realize that many students find it helpful to refer to additional resources for a better understanding of the material. In the following section we list several websites that students may find of interest as they study the material in the book. The websites are not only an excellent supplement to the subject matter presented in the book, but will also allow students of corrections to begin to explore the world of corrections via the world wide web. Students are encouraged to log onto and browse a few of the web pages listed below.

- Bureau of Justice Statistics: An easy and excellent resource to a wide range of government statistics on crime and criminal justice. (http://www.ojp.usdoj.gov/bjs/)
- Alcatraz Island: This website offers a look at the historic and infamous federal prison. (http://www.nps.gov/alcatraz/)
- National Institute of Corrections: An organization that provides assistance to federal, state, and local correctional personnel. (http://www.nicic.org/)
- Prisoner Activist Resource Center: Updates on prison activists who are striving for change in the U.S. Correctional Institutions. (http://www.prisonactivist.org/)
- American Civil Liberties Union: The ACLU is an organization that leads the way for prisoners' rights. (http://www.aclu.org)
- Center on Juvenile and Criminal Justice: A private non-profit organization with the mission to reduce society's reliance on the use of incarceration as a solution to social problems. (http://www.cjcj.org/)
- Office of Juvenile Justice and Delinquency Prevention: This agency is a division of the U.S. Department of Justice. (http://ojjpd.ncjrs.org/)
- American Jail Association (AJA): The AJA as an organization that focuses exclusively on issues specific to operations of local jails. (www.corrections.com/aja/)
- AFSCME—Corrections United: An excellent website for numerous links to correctional websites and Private Prison Watch, which provides updated news and data on private prisons. (http://www.afscme.org/)

Summary

We believe in this book we are taking you on an exciting, yet informative voyage through the world of corrections. We hope that the book will accomplish, at a minimum, the following four objectives: (1) to assist the neophyte student of corrections in gaining the knowledge and tools necessary to complete advanced courses in corrections; (2) to spark interest in students who are not focusing their studies specifically in corrections and may be taking an introductory course in corrections as an elective course, or perhaps as part of the required core curriculum at their college or university; (3) to provide a comprehensive overview and introduction to the student or reader who is just curious about corrections; and (4), to serve as a reference and resource for those persons who are currently working in the corrections field. By the end of studying *Introduction to Corrections (2nd ed.)*, you will understand corrections as an important part (subsystem) of the larger criminal justice system. More importantly, you will understand corrections to be a vital and human system that employees thousands of dedicated men and women, who perform and carry out what is at times a very difficult job under the most vexing conditions.

Discussion Questions

1. Explain how the corrections subsystem fits into the whole system of criminal justice.
2. Describe the differences between jails and prisons.
3. Discuss what the 1967 President's Commission meant when they used the term reintegration of inmates back into the community.
4. Discuss the concept of incapacitation.
5. Discuss a few of the career opportunities in the corrections field.
6. Discuss the legal issues that center on the privatization of corrections.

Chapter Quiz

True/False

1. The American criminal justice system has been described as three mutually reinforcing areas.
2. The system begins with the prosecution.
3. The correctional industry is charged with providing care in only institutional settings.
4. The American Jail Association is an organization that provides networking and support for correctional professionals and other correctional related services.
5. There are three categories of inmate housing facilities: (1) detention facilities; (2) drug treatment facility; and (3) prisons.

Multiple Choice

1. The 1967 President's Commission advocated which one of the following positions regarding punishment?
   a. non rehabilitation
   b. deterrence and incapacitation
   c. Reintegration should become increasingly important.
   d. The commission did not address issues of punishment and left this to the discretion of the correctional administrators
2. The problem of determining the failure or success of community-based corrections sanctions can be problematic because
   a. there has been little research conducted in this area, which leaves researchers with little direction.
   b. due to the nature of recidivism, community corrections sanctions are difficult to measure.
   c. success and failure may be defined differently by different researchers.
   d. due to the nature of the data success and failures of community corrections sanctions cannot be measured with a certainty.
3. The "get tough" crime stance throughout the 1980s and into the twenty-first century has slowly emerged in part, because
   a. rehabilitation philosophies have become dominant.
   b. policy-makers and politicians have inflamed the passions of Americans about crime.
   c. of increases in the population of America.
   d. we have built more prisons than we have prisoners to fill them.

4. Which one of the following is NOT a plea that a defendant can enter into?
   a. guilty
   b. not guilty by reason of insanity
   c. *nolo contendere*
   d. *nolle prosequi*

5. Individual officials of government agencies have protection against being held individually responsible when a prison he or she is employed by violates an individual's rights is referred to as:
   a. *nolle prosequi.*
   b. qualified immunity.
   c. deliberate indifference.
   d. *habeas corpus.*

Endnotes

1. Uniform Crime Report (Washington, DC: Federal Bureau of Investigation, *Uniform Crime Reports,* 2000).
2. Jeffrey Reiman, *The Rich Get Richer and Poor Get Prison: Ideology, Class and Criminal Justice.* (Boston: Allyn and Bacon, 2001).
3. Bureau of Justice Statistics, Criminal Victimization, End of the Year 1994 (Washington, DC: U.S. Department of Justice, 1994).
4. Richard Hawkins and Geoffrey P. Alpert, *American Prison Systems: Punishment and Justice* (Englewood Cliffs, NJ: Prentice Hall, 1989).
5. Edward E. Rhine, *Best Practices in Corrections* (Lanham, MD: American Correctional Association, 1998).
6. Gary F. Cornelius, *The Correctional System: A Practical Guide* (Durham, NC: Carolina Academic Press, 2001).
7. President's Commission on Law Enforcement and Administration of Justice, *The Challenge of Crime in a Free Society: A Report.* (Washington, DC: U.S. Government Printing Office, 1967).
8. National Advisory Commission on Criminal Justice Standards and Goals, *Corrections* (Washington, DC: U.S. Government Printing Office, 1973).
9. Andrew Von Hirsh, *Doing Justice: The Choice of Punishment* (New York: Hill and Wang, 1976), 12.
10. Peter R. Jones, "The Risk of Recidivism: Evaluating the Public Safety Implications of a Community Corrections Program," *Journal of Criminal Justice,* 19 (1991): 4–66.

11. Ibid.
12. Joann B. Morton, and Deborah M. William. "Mother/Child Bonding: Incarcerated Women Struggle to Maintain Meaningful Relationships with Their Children," *Corrections Today*, 60 (7): 98–105.
13. Ambrosio, Tara-Jen, and Vincent Schiraldi. *From Classrooms to Cell Blocks: A National Perspective* (Washington, DC: Justice Policy Institute, 1997).
14. Fox Butterfield, "Crime Keeps on Falling, but Prisons Keep on Filling," *New York Times*, 28 September 1997.
15. Alida V. Merlo, and Peter J. Benkos. *What's Wrong with the Criminal Justice System: Ideology, Politics and the Media* (Cincinnati: Anderson Publishing Co., 2000).
16. Ibid.
17. John Moritz, "Prison System to Propose $44 million Budget Cut," *Fort Worth Star Telegram*, 11 September 2002, metro 8.
18. U.S. Department of Justice, *Justice Expenditures and Employment, 1999* (Washington, DC: Bureau of Justice Statistics, 2002).
19. Amy Hanauer, "All That Cash for College; Headed for Ohio's Prisons," *Akron Beacon Journal*, 15 September 2002, B 3.
20. Byron R. Johnson, and Paul P. Ross. "The Privatization of Correctional Management: A Review," *Journal of Criminal Justice*, 18 (1990): 351–358.
21. "Wachenhut Guard Admits Beating Inmates Up, Cover Up," *Albuquerque Journal*, 21 February 2002.
22. "Two Cornell Guards Beat Up Three Boys," *Arkansas Democratic Gazette*, 2 February 2002.
23. "Allegations of Sex for Cash at Jail; Guard Fired," *The Philadelphia Inquirer*, 15 March 2002.
24. "Prison for Juveniles Set to Close," *Las Vegas Review Journal*, 28 January 2002.
25. *Richardson et. al. v. McKnight*, 88 F. 3d 417.

Chapter 2

Corrections: The Beginning

The pillory was once used as a form of punishment.

Key Terms

blood feuds	holy inquisition	rehabilitation
Code of Draco	ideology	retribution
Code of Hammurabi	incapacitation	trials by ordeal
deterrence	penal servitude	values
disproportionate minority confinement	penitentiary	wergeld

Outline

2-1 History and Philosophy
   2-1a Beginning of Legal Punishments
   2-1b Middle Ages
2-2 The Early Reformers
   2-2a Voltaire (Francois Marie Arouet) (1694–1778)
   2-2b Cesare Beccaria (1738–1794)
   2-2c Cesare Lombroso (1835–1909)
   2-2d Jeremy Bentham (1748–1832)
   2-2e John Howard (1726–1790)
   2-2f William Penn (1644–1718)
2-3 Purpose of Criminal Sanctions
   2-3a Retribution
   2-3b Deterrence
   2-3c Incapacitation
   2-3d Rehabilitation
2-4 Purposes of Punishment
   2-4a English Statement of Purposes
   2-4b Guiding Principles
   2-4c Social Purposes of Punishment
2-5 Crime and Offenders
   2-5a Magnitude of the Problem
   2-5b Demographics
   2-5c Disproportionate Minority Confinement
2-6 Locations of Confinements
   2-6a Types of Crime
   2-6b Time Served
   2-6c Overcrowding
2-7 Changes to the "Justice" Correctional Philosophy
Article—Rehabilitation: Holding Its Ground in Corrections
Summary
Discussion Questions
Chapter Quiz
Endnotes

Learning Objectives

After studying this chapter, the reader will be able to:

- Explain how the criminal justice system is fragmented.
- List the major goals of punishment.
- Explain the beginning of legal punishments.
- Explain the purposes of punishment.
- Contrast the different ideologies based on political beliefs.
- Identify and explain the four popular goals of punishment.
- Identify the early reformers involved in corrections.
- Explain the social purposes of punishment.
- Identify the criminogenic factors in society.

The criminal justice system is traditionally considered to have three subsystems: law enforcement, the judicial system, and corrections. This text focuses on corrections. While this text deals only with corrections, it is important to remember that corrections is a subpart of the broader criminal justice system and can be understood only as a part of the whole. It is also important to remember that before an individual comes under correctional control, he or she has already moved from citizen, to suspect, to arrestee, to defendant and finally to convict.[1] In other words, the individual has already experienced the other two subsystems of the criminal justice system: law enforcement and the judiciary.

Recall from Chapter 1, corrections, like other subsystems in the criminal justice field, is fragmented. This fragmentation makes administrative coordination and linkage to the other criminal justice components difficult. The following list illustrates the fragmentation of the subsystem.

- By jurisdiction: federal, state, or local
- By location: institutional or community-based
- By age: adult or juvenile
- By other factors: size of institution, sex of inmates, types of offenses, and special programs

Box 2-1

The Justification of Punishment

The problem of punishment causes constant, anguished reassessment, not only because we keep speculating on what the effective consequences of crime should be, but also because there is a confusion of the ends and means. We are still far from the answer to the ultimate questions: What is the right punishment? On what grounds do we punish others?[2]

2-1 History and Philosophy

2-1a Beginning of Legal Punishments

In ancient societies, the remedy for wrongs committed against one's person or property was personal retaliation against the wrongdoer. Unlike modern society, in the early primitive societies, personal retaliation was encouraged. From the concept of personal retaliation developed **blood feuds,** which occurred when the victim's family or tribe took revenge on the offender's family or tribe. Often, blood feuds escalated and resulted in continuing vendettas between families or tribes. In many cases, for religious reasons, individuals were expected to avenge the death of a kinsman. The duty of retaliation was imposed by universal practice upon the victim or in case of death, the nearest male relative.

To lessen the costly and damaging vendettas, the custom of accepting money or property in place of blood vengeance developed. At first, the acceptance of payments instead of blood vengeance was not compulsory. The victim's family was still free to choose whatever form of vengeance they wished. Often the relative power of the families or tribes decided whether payment or blood vengeance was used.

The acceptance of money or property as atonement for wrongs became know as *les salica* or **wergeld.** This practice of atonement is still used in some regions, such as the Middle East. The amount of payment was based on the rank or position of the victim. The tradition of accepting money for property damages was the beginning of the development of a system of criminal law.

One problem with the acceptance of payment as complete satisfaction for the wrong was the concept that punishment of an individual wrongdoer should also include some religious aspects. To many, crime was also a sin against the church or the state. Accordingly, the concept developed that punishment in the form of *wergeld* (payment to the victim) should also be supplemented with *friedensgeld* (payment to the church or the crown).

Fines and other forms of punishment replaced personal retaliation as tribal and community leaders began to exert their authority during the negotiations or proceedings concerning the damages caused and the wrongs committed. The wrongdoers were not required to attend the proceedings. If, however, they failed to follow the recommendations of the leaders, they were banished or exiled, and thus considered "outlaws."

Because criminal law requires an element of public action against the wrongdoer, the banishment or pronouncement of outlawry was the first criminal punishment imposed by society.[3] With its roots in the *les salica* or *wergeld* system, the development of this custom of punishment is considered by many present-day researchers the beginning of criminal law as we know it today. Subsequent legal codes and punishments for different crimes have either stressed or refined the vengeance principle. The concept that a society expresses its vengeance within a system of rules was present in the customs of ancient societies.

The two earliest codes involving criminal punishments were the Sumerian and Hammurabic (**Code of Hammurabi**) codes. The punishment phases of these codes contained the concept of personal vengeance. The listed punishments in the codes were harsh, and in many cases, the victim or nearest relative was allowed personally to inflict punishment. Permitted punishments included mutilation, whipping, or forced labor. At first, the punishments were applied almost exclusively to slaves and bond servants and demonstrated the dominance over those being punished. Later they were extended to all offenders.

The practice of **penal servitude** also developed. Penal servitude involved the use of hard labor as punishment and was generally reserved for the lower classes of citizens. Penal servitude included the loss of citizenship and liberty (i.e., civil death). With civil death, the offender's property was confiscated in the name of the state and his wife was declared a widow. The criminal was labeled an outlaw and banished from society. Later, the use of penal servitude by the Romans was encouraged by the need for workers to perform hard labor.

Box 2-2

The Case against Socrates

Socrates was charged in 399 B.C. with the offense of impiety (corrupting young minds and of believing in new gods). He was tried before a jury of 500 members. The trial lasted only one day. When the ballots were counted, 280 jurors had voted to find Socrates guilty, 220 jurors for acquittal. During the punishment phase of the trail, the prosecution proposed the death penalty. Socrates had a right to propose an alternative penalty. He stated:

> Shall I [propose] imprisonment? And why should I spend my days in prison, and be the slave of the magistrates? Or shall the penalty be a fine and imprisonment until the fine is paid? There is the same objection. I should have to lie in prison, for money I have none, and cannot pay. And if I say exile, I must indeed be blinded by the love of life, if I am so irrational as to expect that when you, who are my own citizens, cannot endure my discourses and arguments, and have found them so grievous and odious that you will have no more of them, that others are likely to endure them.

The jury condemned him to death by a narrow 30 vote margin. He committed compulsory suicide by drinking poison, the Athenian method of execution.[4]

The fact that early punishments were considered synonymous with slavery is evident in the practice of shaving the heads of those punished as a "mark of slavery." Other marks of slavery used on punished wrongdoers included branding on the forehead or use of a heavy metal collar that could not be easily removed.

The Greek code, **Code of Draco,** used the same penalties for both citizens and slaves and incorporated many of the concepts used in primitive societies (e.g., vengeance, outlawry, and blood feuds). The Greeks apparently were the first society to allow any citizen to prosecute an offender on behalf of the victim. This practice appears to indicate that both the lawmakers and the public were beginning to realize that crimes affected not only the victim, but society in general.

2-1b Middle Ages

During the Middle Ages, rapid changes were made in the social structure of societies. In addition, the growing influence of the church on everyday life helped create a divided system of justice. The offender, in committing a crime, also committed a sin. Accordingly, he or she had two debts to pay—one to the victim and one to the church. **Trials by ordeal** were used by the churches as substitutes for jury trials. In a trial by ordeal, the accused was subjected to dangerous or painful tests with the belief that God would protect the innocent but allow the guilty to suffer agonies and die. The brutality of the trial by ordeal ensured that most would die and thus be considered guilty. The practice of trial by ordeal was finally abolished in 1215.

It was also during the Middle Ages that the churches expanded the concept of a criminal offense to include new prohibited areas, most of which are still present in our modern-day codes. For example, sexual offenses were now covered by law. People found guilty of sex offenses, which included either public or "unnatural" acts, were severely punished. Heresy and witchcraft were also included in the new prohibited areas of conduct. The church inflicted cruel punishments and justified the punishments as necessary to save the souls of the unfortunate sinners. For example, the zealous movement to stamp out heresy resulted in the Inquisition, a tribunal established by the church in which unlimited punishments could be used for the suppression of heresy. During the Inquisition alleged heretics and witches were searched for (or some would say hunted) rather than waiting for charges to be brought forward.

Whipping was the usual method of punishing persons for minor offenses. Whipping was inflicted on women while kneeling and on men while lying on the ground. Generally the victims were stripped to the waist and the blows inflicted on their backs.[5]

The **holy inquisition** was a court set up by the Roman Catholic Church to inquire into cases of heresy. Since the word "inquisition" means an inquiry, all modern courts of law are essentially inquisitions. During the holy inquisition, use of the term was extended to cover crimes of witchcraft and ecclesiastical offenses committed by members of the church. For example, Jews found guilty by an inquisition of deserting their faith were sentenced to be stoned to death.

The holy inquisition flourished in all European countries, but its barbarities were the greatest in Spain and the Spanish dominions. The sentences of the court were generally pronounced on Sunday in a church and consisted of burning, scourging, imprisonment, penances, humiliation, and/or fines.[6]

2-2 The Early Reformers

2-2a Voltaire (Francois Marie Arouet) (1694–1778)

Voltaire was one of the most enlightened and versatile eighteenth-century philosophers. His writings alerted the public to the abuses of criminal law in France. He opposed the use of torture and other violent punishments and believed that the fear of shame could be used as a deterrent to crime. For his theories, Voltaire was imprisoned in the Bastille in 1726 and released only on the condition that he leave France and never return. Voltaire clearly established by his writings that the pen was mightier than the sword.

2-2b Cesare Beccaria (1738–1794)

Cesare Beccaria was one of the first theorists to espouse the concept of punishment as a deterrent to crime. Cesare Beccaria wrote an essay on penal reform that was originally published in January 1764. It was first published anonymously because its contents challenged the cherished beliefs of those in position to determine the fate of people convicted of crimes. The 17-page essay is still regularly quoted over 300 years later. It was, however, his only notable publication.

Both his mother and father were members of the aristocracy, and both had achieved distinction in various fields. His mother, worried that her son could not withstand the rigors of business or commerce, obtained for him a professorship with prestige and yet little responsibility. At the university, he tended to be lazy and easily discouraged. He preferred to drink beer at the local pub and discuss literary and philosophical subjects other than work.

Beccaria's interest in penology and crime was aroused by his discussions and debates with two stimulating and keen brothers, Pietro and Alessandro Verri. They encouraged him to consolidate his ideas and to put them in an essay that was later entitled "On Crimes and Punishment."

According to Beccaria, laws are conditions whereby free and independent men unite to form society. Punishments were established to deal with those who transgress the laws. The right to punish transgressors is an essential consequence of the nature and scope of society. The primary purpose of punishment should be to insure the continued existence of society. Furthermore, the amount and nature of the punishment inflicted against the offender should vary in proportion to the degree to which an act of an individual endangers the existence of society. According to Beccaria, the essential end of punishment is not to torment the offenders nor to undo the crime already committed. It is rather to prevent offenders from doing further harm to society and to prevent others from committing crime. To be effective as a deterrent to crime, punishment should be prompt and inevitable and applied equally to all for similar crimes. It should not be cruel or severe, but the punishment must be certain. According to him, it is the strength of the association of crime and punishment that is the most effective deterrent.[7]

2-2c Cesare Lombroso (1835–1909)

More has been written about Cesare Lombroso than any other criminologist. He is considered by many as the "father of modern criminology." According to him, criminals are distinguished from noncriminals by the manifestation of multiple physical or psychological anomalies and that the criminal is defective and his or her criminal misconduct is not the result of a rational choice on the part of the criminal. Lombroso contended that punishment should have two objectives—to protect society and to improve the criminal. The fundamental principle regarding punishment should be to study and treat, not so much the abstract crime, but the criminal. Accordingly, punishment should fit the needs of the offender. He also contended that the length of imprisonment should depend on the time needed to improve the criminal.[8] Table 2-1 compares Beccaria's and Lombroso's views on crime and punishment.

TABLE **2-1** Comparisons between Beccaria and Lombroso

	Beccaria	Lombroso
To determine punishment focus on:	Crime (price tag approach)	Criminal (need to correct the criminal)
Causes of crime:	Free will	Lack of free will

2-2d Jeremy Bentham (1748–1832)

Many consider Jeremy Bentham to be the greatest leader in the reform of English criminal law. Bentham believed that punishments should be designed to negate any pleasure or gain that a criminal would achieve from the criminal act. He advocated a system of graduated penalties that are closely associated with the crime committed. He contended that the main objective of any intelligent person is to achieve the most pleasure and experience the least pain. He applied his "hedonistic calculus" to his efforts to reform criminal law and the punishments used to punish offenders. Included within the concept of hedonistic calculus was the doctrine of utilitarianism. This doctrine holds that the aim of all action should be to obtain the greatest pleasure for the largest number of citizens. Accordingly, the law should be used to inflict enough pain on criminals that they will cease to commit crime and thus "good" would be achieved. Like Beccaria, he advocated that punishment should be used as a deterrent to crime.

During the later years of Bentham's life, he designed the ultimate prison, the Panoptical. While it was never constructed, the debate over it raged for many years. The crux of the debate centered mainly on philosophical grounds. The Panoptical focused on the personality of the prisoner and its success was largely dependent upon knowledge of the prisoners as individuals. Inmates were to be known by the warden so that they could be controlled with both body and mind. In contrast to the Panoptical, was the philosophy that punishment should not be designed to gain knowledge and understanding of the individual prisoner, but rather to deter offenders from re-offending by making punishment immediate, public, and necessary. The Panoptical was designed to be a rational, humane environment for offenders. It was the answer to the human warehouses that existed at the time. The prison was designed as a circular building with a glass roof. Every cell would be visible from a central point.

A prison inspector could be kept from the sight of the prisoners by the use of blinds. When a prisoner thought that he was fit and healthy enough to be observed, the prisoner could show himself by raising the blinds. The manager of the prison would be liable if too many of his prisoners died. The prisoners could be contracted out, with the manager receiving a percentage of the money earned by the prisoners. In addition, the manager would be held liable if prisoners under his supervision later committed additional crimes after their release.

Bentham died in 1832. According to the instructions in his will, his body was dissected. The skeleton was dressed in his usual attire and is on display at the University College in London. For over 150 years, the fully dressed skeleton has attended the college faculty assemblies. Speakers at the assembly traditionally first voice recognition to Mr. Bentham and then to other members of the assembly and guests.[9]

2-2e John Howard (1726–1790)

Until he was appointed Sheriff of Bedfordshire, England in 1773, John Howard showed no interest in prisons or prison reform. As sheriff, he was appalled by the conditions of the hulks being used to hold prisoners. *Hulks* were decrepit transport or warships used to house prisoners in eighteenth-century England. He pressed for legislation to alleviate the abuses and to improve sanitary conditions. In addition, he traveled extensively in France and Italy and wrote about the conditions of their prisons.

As a direct result of Howard's actions, the English Parliament passed the Penitentiary Act in 1799. That act provided four principles for reform: secure and sanitary structures, systematic inspections of the prisons, abolition of fees, and a reformatory regime. The Penitentiary Act resulted in the first **penitentiary** in England, located at Wyndomhan in Norfolk. Ironically, John Howard died in 1790 of jail fever (typhus) in the Russian Ukraine.

2-2f William Penn (1644–1718)

William Penn, the founder of Pennsylvania and leader of the Quakers, brought to America the concept of humanitarian treatment of offenders. William Penn was an English Quaker who fought for religious freedom and individual rights. He obtained a charter from King Charles II in 1681 and founded the Quaker settlement that later became Pennsylvania.

At the time, the American colonies were governed under the codes established by the Duke of York, and earlier, the Hampshire Code. The Quakers advocated eliminating the harsh principles of criminal law in favor of more humane treatment of offenders. The Quakers, though very religious, eliminated most of the religious crimes and created a criminal code that was very secular. The Quaker Code, enacted in 1682, remained in force until its repeal in 1718, the day after the death of William Penn. The code was replaced by the English Anglican Code, which was even worse than the former codes of the Duke of York. The English Anglican Code restored the death penalty for many crimes and restored mutilation, branding, and other brutal forms of corporal punishment.

Throughout much of the sixteenth and seventeenth centuries sanctions for criminal behavior tended to be public events that were designed to shame the person and deter others. Evidence suggests that the prisons of this period were badly maintained and often controlled by negligent prison wardens. Prison reformers of the time made a significant impact on the state of incarceration. Reformers such as Jeremy Bentham, William Penn, and John Howard pointed out that prison was meant to be the punishment itself, not the sickness or death which could result. These reformers condemned the prison system as disorganized, barbaric and filthy. The ideas of prison reform became increasingly popular thanks to these energetic reformers.

2-3 Purpose of Criminal Sanctions

In discussing the purpose of criminal sanctions, various ideologies become evident. For purposes of studying this chapter, **ideology** refers to the belief system adopted by a group and consists of assumptions and **values**. The assumptions are beliefs about the way the world is constituted, organized, and operated. Values, however, are beliefs about what is moral and desirable.[10] There are numerous methods to classify ideologies. Three popular classifications based on political theories that influence our corrections system are conservative, liberal, and radical.

The conservative ideology tends to accept the concept that human beings are rational, possess free will, and voluntarily commit criminal misconduct. Accordingly, criminals should be held accountable for their actions. Punishment should be imposed to inflict suffering on the criminal because the suffering is deserved and because it will deter future crime. The punishment imposed should fit the crime. This ideology, because of its view on the causes of human behavior, generally does not accept the concept of rehabilitation as an attractive objective of punishment.

The liberal ideology tends to view human behavior as greatly influenced by social circumstances including one's upbringing, material affluence, education, peer relationships, and so on. Accordingly, human behavior is more than a simple product of free choice. All of the social influences are important factors in shaping our conduct. Viewing criminal behavior as a product of both social circumstances and individual actions, liberals are more likely to support rehabilitation as the proper form of criminal punishment. Most liberals tend to be receptive to a wider range of goals for criminal punishment, including **deterrence.**

The radical ideology rejects both the conservative and liberal ideologies and views crime as a reflection of the status of our present social system. Crime is only a natural consequence of our social system. According to the radicals, fundamental changes in the socioeconomic basis of society are required in order to control crime.

The ultimate purpose of criminal sanctions is generally considered to be the maintenance of our social order. Herbert Packer contends that the two major goals of criminal sanctions are to inflict suffering upon the wrongdoers and to prevent crime.[11] According to Robert Dawson, the major purpose of the criminal justice system is to identify, in a legally acceptable manner, those persons who should be subjected to control and treatment in the correctional process.[12] According to Dawson, if corrections does not properly perform its task, the entire criminal justice system suffers. An inefficient or unfair correctional process can nullify the courts, prosecutors, and police alike. Conversely, the manner in which the other agencies involved perform their tasks has an important impact upon the success of the process: a person who has been unfairly dealt with prior to conviction is a poor subject for rehabilitation.

The four popular goals of criminal sanctions are **retribution,** deterrence, **incapacitation,** and **rehabilitation.** From the 1940s to the 1980s, rehabilitation was considered by most as the primary goal of our system. Since the 1980s, retribution has received popular support. Each of these four commonly accepted goals are discussed.

2-3a Retribution

Retribution generally means "getting even." Retribution is based on the ideology that the criminal is an enemy of society and deserves severe punishment for willfully breaking its rules. Retribution is often mistaken as revenge. There are, however, important differences between the two. Both retribution and revenge are primarily concerned with punishing the offender and neither is overly concerned with the impact of the punishment on the offender's future behavior or the behavior of others. Unlike revenge, however, retribution attempts to match the severity of the punishment to the seriousness of the crime. Revenge acts on passion, whereas retribution follows specific rules regarding the types and amounts of punishment that may be inflicted. The biblical response of an "eye for an eye" is a retributive response to punishment. While the "eye for an eye" concept is often cited as an excuse to use harsh punishment, it is less harsh than revenge-based punishment, which does not rule out "two eyes for an eye" punishment. Sir James Stephen, an English judge, expressed the retributive view by stating that "the punishment of criminals was simply a desirable expression of the hatred and fear aroused in the community by criminal acts."[13] This line of reasoning conveys the message that punishment is justifiable because it provides an orderly outlet for emotions that, if denied, may express themselves in less socially acceptable ways. Another justification under the retribution ideology is that only through suffering punishment can the criminal atone for his sin. In one manner, retribution treats all crimes as if they were financial transactions. You got something or did something, therefore you must give equivalent value (suffering).

Retribution is also referred to as "just deserts." The just deserts movement reflects the retribution viewpoint and provides a justifiable rationale for support of the death penalty. This viewpoint has its roots in a societal need for retribution and the individual need for retaliation and vengeance. The transfer of the vengeance motive from the individual to the state has been justified based on theories involving theological, aesthetic, and expiatory views. According to the theological view, retaliation fulfills the religious need to punish the sinner. Under the aesthetic view, punishment helps reestablish a sense of harmony through requital, and thus resolves the social discord created by the crime. The expiatory view is that guilt must be washed away, or cleansed, through suffering. There is even a utilitarian view that punishment is the means of achieving beneficial social consequences through the application of a specific form and degree of punishment deemed most appropriate to the particular offender after careful individualized study of the offender.[14]

2-3b Deterrence

Deterrence is a punishment viewpoint that focuses on future outcomes rather than past misconduct. It is also based on the theory that creating a fear of future punishments will deter crime. There is substantial debate as to the validity of this concept. Specific deterrence works only on the offender, whereas general deterrence works on others who might consider similar acts. According to this viewpoint, the fear of future suffering motivates individuals to avoid involvement in criminal misconduct. This concept assumes that the criminal is a rational being who will weigh the consequences of his or her criminal actions before deciding to commit them.

One of the problems with deterrence is determining the appropriate magnitude and nature of punishment to be imposed in order to deter future criminal misconduct. For example, an individual who commits a serious crime and then feels badly about the act may need only slight punishment to achieve deterrent effects, whereas a professional shoplifter may need severe fear-producing punishments to prevent future shoplifting.

Often, increases in crime rates and high rates of recidivism cast doubt that the deterrence approach is effective. Recidivism may cause some doubt as to the efficacy of specific deterrence, but it says nothing about the effect of general deterrence. In addition, unless we know what the recidivism rates would be if we did not attempt to deter criminal misconduct, the assertions are unfounded. Are we certain that the rates would not be higher had we not attempted to deter criminals?

2-3c Incapacitation

Incapacitation is the idea that we incarcerate offenders for a period of time to protect society from a particular threat. At least while the prisoner is in confinement, he is unlikely to commit crimes on innocent persons outside of prison. To this extent, confinement clearly helps reduce criminal behavior outside of prison. Under this incapacitation viewpoint, there is no hope for the individual as far as rehabilitation is concerned, therefore the only solution is to incapacitate the offender. Marvin Wolfgang's famous study of crime in Philadelphia indicated that while chronic offenders constituted only 23 percent of the offenders in the study, they committed over 61 percent of all the violent crimes.[15] Accordingly, the supporters of the incapacitation viewpoint contend that incapacitating the 23 percent would have prevented 61 percent of the future violent crimes. This approach has often been labeled the "nothing else works" approach to corrections. According to this viewpoint, we should make maximum effective use of the scarce prison cells to protect society from the crimes of such dangerous and repetitive offenders. This approach is present in California's "Three Strikes and You're Out" statute.

There are two variations in the incapacitation viewpoint. *Collective incapacitation* refers to sanctions imposed on offenders, such as violent offenders, without regard to their personal characteristics. *Selective incapacitation* refers to the incapacitation of certain groups of individuals who have been identified as high-risk offenders, such as robbers with a history of drug use. Under selective incapacitation, offenders with certain characteristics or history would receive longer prison terms than others convicted of the same crime. The purpose of incapacitation is to prevent future crimes, and the moral concerns associated with retribution are not as important as the reduction of future victimization.[16] As Herbert Packer states, "Incapacitation is a mode of punishment that uses the fact that a person has committed a crime as a basis for predicting that he will commit future crimes."[17] Packer also states that the logic of the incapacitative position is that, until the offender stops being a danger, we will continue to restrain him. Accordingly, one can conclude from this theory that offenses regarded as relatively trivial may be punished by imprisonment for life if the offender is still construed a danger.

2-3d Rehabilitation

The rehabilitation approach pronounces that punishment should be directed toward correcting the offender. This approach is also considered the "treatment" approach in that the criminal misconduct is considered a manifestation of a pathology that can be handled by some form of therapeutic activity. While this viewpoint may consider the offender "sick," it is not the same as a medical approach. Under the rehabilitation viewpoint, we need to teach the offenders to recognize the undesirability of their criminal behavior and make significant efforts to rid themselves of that behavior. The main difference between the rehabilitation approach and the retribution approach is that under the rehabilitation approach the offenders are assigned to programs designed to prepare them for readjustment or reintegration into the community, whereas the latter approach is more concerned with the punishment aspects of the sentence. Packer sees two major objections to making rehabilitation the primary justification for punishment. First, we do not know how to rehabilitate offenders. Second, we know little about who is likely to commit crimes and less about what makes them apt to do so. As long as we are ignorant in these matters, Packer contends that punishment in the name of rehabilitation is gratuitous cruelty.[18] The role of rehabilitation has not changed and even today, there is still some support for rehabilitation by correctional officials and the general public.

2-4 Purposes of Punishment

2-4a English Statement of Purposes

The United States is not the only country that has had problems determining the proper purpose of punishment. It appears that most other countries have the same problem. An examination of the English Statement of Purposes, as follows, indicates that the English have similar problems. The English Prison Service (EPS) has approximately 43,000 confined prisoners. The EPS declares that it "serves the public by keeping in custody those committed by the courts," and that its duty is to "look after them with humanity and help them lead law-abiding and useful lives in custody and after release." The purposes are divided into a series of goals:

- To keep prisoners in custody
- To maintain order, control, discipline, and a safe environment
- To provide decent conditions for prisoners and meet their needs, including health care
- To provide positive regimes to help prisoners address their offending behavior
- To allow prisoners as full and responsible a life as possible
- To help prisoners prepare for their return to the community[19]

Box 2-3

The Chinese Proverb

There is an old Chinese proverb that states: "It is better to hang the wrong fellow than no fellow." This proverb indicates that certainty of punishment is important. When a crime is committed, someone must be punished.

2-4b Guiding Principles

Certain principles guide the decision as to how to sanction a person convicted of criminal behavior. The principles are simple, yet subject to interpretation according to the philosophy of the individuals involved. The generally accepted principles include:

1. *Parsimony.* The least restrictive sanction necessary to achieve the defined purposes should be imposed. The debate regarding this principle centers on what is the purpose of criminal sanctions.
2. *Dangerousness.* Should the likelihood of future criminal activity be considered? The controversy on this point is whether we should use predictions of future misconduct as a basis for present criminal sanctions. Numerous studies indicate that predictions of dangerousness are unreliable. The studies indicate that we tend to

overpredict future dangerousness in individuals. There is also the philosophical and due process concerns of punishing a person for conduct not yet committed.
3. *Just Deserts.* Any sanction imposed should not be greater than that which is deserved by the last crime, or series of crimes, for which the defendant is being sentenced.[20]

2-4c Social Purposes of Punishment

C. Ray Jeffery, a noted criminologist, contends that the more glaring defect in most analyses of punishments is that the analyses view punishments always in the context of what it means to the individual offender and never in terms of what it means to society. The purpose of punishment, according to Jeffery, should be to establish to the public social disapproval of the act. To him, the use of punishment by society is done for society's sake and not for the individual's. He also contends that punishment serves an important social function in that it creates social solidarity and re-enforces social norms.[21]

Punishment has been presented throughout history as meaning many things to many different people. Regardless, there has been one consistent theme presented throughout our nation's history, the idea that punishment exists to make the offender suffer for his or her crime. Even in light of the philosophies that advocate incapacitation, rehabilitation, or other punitive sanctions, to respond punitively to the criminal is almost always latent in our consciousness. This is evident in our policies, practices, and in our escalation of the prison and jail industry.

2-5 Crime and Offenders

2-5a Magnitude of the Problem

This section presents statistics regarding prisoners confined in correctional institutions to provide the reader with an understanding of the magnitude of the corrections problem.[22] By midyear 2001 the nation's prisons and jails incarcerated 1,965,495 persons. Inmates in the custody of the 50 states, the District of Columbia, and the federal government accounted for two-thirds of the incarcerated population (1,334,255 inmates). The other third were held in local jails (631,240).

From the end of 1995 to midyear 2001, the six-month growth rate for states combined dropped from 4.8 percent in the first half of 1995 to −0.1% in the last half of 2000. The rate of incarceration in prisons and jails increased from 1 in every 166 U.S. residents to 1 in 145. State, federal, and local government had to accommodate an additional 69,074 new inmates per year (or the equivalent of 1,328 new inmates per week). By the end of 2001 in the largest state prison systems, the total number of inmates declined: Texas (down 3,661), California (down 525), and New York (down 2,553).

As of June 2001, the states with the highest incarceration rates per 100,000 population were Louisiana (795), Texas (731), Mississippi (689), and Oklahoma (669). Maine (126) had the lowest rate, followed by Minnesota (131), North Dakota (158), and Rhode Island (179).[23]

2-5b Demographics

The demographic characteristics of the nation's prison population are changing. From July 1, 2000, to June 30, 2001, the number of women under the jurisdiction of state and federal prison authorities grew from 93,681 to 94,336, an increase of 0.7 percent. At midyear 2001 California, Texas, and the federal systems housed nearly 4 of every 10 female prisoners.

Since 1990 the annual rate of growth of female inmates has averaged 7.5 percent higher than the 5.7 percent average increase of male inmates. While the number of male prisoners has grown 80 percent since 1990, the number of female prisoners has increased 114 percent. By June 2001, women accounted for 6.7 percent of all prisoners, up from 5.7 percent in 1990.

The Bureau of Justice Statistics reported that as of June 30, 2001, the number of white men incarcerated in state or federal prisons and local jails was 684,800; the number of black men was 803,400; and the number of Hispanic men was 283,000. White women accounted for 67,700; black women 69,500; and Hispanic women 19,900.[24] Table 2-2 shows the number of sentenced prisoners in 2000.

2-5c Disproportionate Minority Confinement

The disproportionate representation of minorities in the U.S. criminal justice system is well documented. By the early 1990s, 29 percent of black men could expect to spend some time in a state or federal prison during their lifetime. At the end of the 1990s and the beginning of the twenty-first century, the **disproportionate minority confinement** in our nation's jails and prisons has grown to disturbing proportions. The incarceration rate of blacks is six times that of whites and for Hispanics it is two times higher than the rate for whites. Based on the latest available estimates of the U.S. resident population for July 1, 2000, there are 4,668 black inmates per 100,000 black U.S. residents compared to 705 white inmates per 100,000 white U.S. residents. There were 1,668 Hispanic inmates per 100,000 population compared to 705 white inmates.

TABLE 2-2 Number of Sentenced Prisoners under State or Federal Jurisdiction, by Gender, Race, Hispanic Origin, and Age, 2000

Number of Sentenced Prisoners

Age	Males				Females			
	Total[a]	White[b]	Black[b]	Hispanic	Total[a]	White[b]	Black[b]	Hispanic
Total	1,237,469	436,500	572,900	206,900	83,668	34,500	37,400	10,000
18–19	33,000	8,400	16,300	6,800	1,200	600	500	100
20–24	199,600	56,500	98,100	38,700	7,800	3,300	3,000	1,200
25–29	232,100	67,100	119,100	41,300	14,700	5,300	6,600	2,000
30–34	234,000	81,900	109,400	40,000	21,000	8,300	9,900	2,300
35–39	212,700	79,200	101,700	30,400	18,200	7,600	8,600	2,000
40–44	149,400	58,300	64,600	24,800	10,200	4,100	4,800	1,100
45–54	128,800	60,300	49,200	17,800	8,300	3,800	3,100	1,100
55 or older	42,300	23,700	11,300	6,600	1,900	1,300	600	200

Note: Based on custody counts form National Prisoners Statistics (NPS-1A) and updated from jurisdiction counts by gender at yearend. Estimates by age derived from the Surveys of Inmates in State and Federal Correctional facilities, 1997. Estimates were rounded to the nearest 100.
[a]Includes American Indians, Alaska Natives, Asians, Native Hawaiians, and other Pacific Islanders.
[b]Excludes Hispanics.
Source: Bureau of Justice Statistics, NCJ 188207.

When total incarceration rates are estimated separately by age group, black males in their twenties and thirties are found to have high rates relative to other groups. According to the Bureau of Justice Statistics among the more than 1.96 million offenders incarcerated as of June 2001, an estimated 601,800 were black males between the ages of 20 and 39. Expressed in terms of percentages, 13.4 percent of black non-Hispanic males age 25 to 29 were in prison or jail, compared to 4.1 percent of Hispanic males and about 1.8 percent of white males in the same age group. A black male in the United States in 1997 had greater than a one in four chance of going to prison in his lifetime, a Hispanic male had a one in six chance, and a white male had a one in 23 chance of spending time in prison.[25]

Although incarceration rates usually drop with age, the percentage of black males age 45 to 54 in prison or jail in 2001 was an estimated 3.4 percent, nearly twice the highest rate (1.9 percent) among white males age 30 to 34. A discussion on the disproportionate confinement of minorities in our prisons and jails would not be complete without some attempt to examine why this disturbing trend is occurring.

In every state, the proportion of blacks in prison exceeds, sometimes by a significant amount, their proportion in the general population. For example, the Bureau of Justice Statistics in 1996 reported that in Minnesota and Iowa, blacks constitute a share of the prison that is twelve times greater than their share of the state population. In eleven states, Kansas, Montana, Nebraska, New Hampshire, Oregon, Rhode Island, South Dakota, Utah, Washington, Wisconsin, and Wyoming, the percentage of the prison population that is black is more than six times greater than the percentage of the state population that is black.

Most agree that the war on drugs has had the most profound effect on the disproportionate confinement of minorities, especially African Americans.[26] In 1992, the United States Public Health Service estimated that 76 percent of illicit drug users were white, 14 percent black, and 8 percent Hispanic. However, African Americans make up 35 percent of all drug arrests, 55 percent of all drug convictions, and 74 percent of all sentences for drug offenses.[27] From 1986 to 1991, the number of white drug offenders incarcerated in state prisons increased by 110 percent, but the number of black drug offenders increased by 465 percent.[28]

Many have criticized the sentencing disparities between crack and powder cocaine. Crack cocaine, which is more likely to be used by African Americans, will trigger felony charges for amounts 100 times less than powdered cocaine, which is more likely to be used by whites. The sentencing disparity between the two forms of cocaine dates back to 1988 when Congress established a special sentencing exception for cocaine base or crack cocaine. That same year Congress increased the penalties for the sale of crack cocaine so that a dealer with five grams of crack cocaine received the same punishment as a dealer who had 500 grams of powder cocaine. Federal sentencing guidelines further illustrate the clear disparity in sentencing between crack and powder cocaine. Five grams of crack cocaine would land the defendant a mandatory minimum of five years in federal prison compared to 500 grams of powder cocaine. Some researchers justify this disparity based on the concept that crack cocaine is more lethal while others claim that this is yet another instance of discrimination against minorities.

Some scholars have been critical of the war on drugs due to its alleged disproportionate targeting of minorities. Criminologist Donald Yates argues that the current U.S. drug war, fought by both civilian and national forces, is not a neutral war. It is a war on the poor and minorities. The police's drug enforcement measures are directed at the inner city, poor neighborhoods, and African American and Latino drug users. Yates goes on to assert that U.S. drug polices are biased.[29] One possible reason for the high arrest rates for crack cocaine is that in many inner-city neighborhoods crack is visibly sold in the open neighborhood or on a street corner. This practice makes it very easy for the police to conduct surveillance and subsequently make arrests. On the other hand, powder cocaine is usually not sold in this manner and dealers may be more discrete.

Not only has the war on drugs had a significant impact on the disproportionate minority confinement, but also criminal justice policy on street gangs has been suspected of disproportionately targeting minority groups. Many believe the United States' criminal justice policy today remains uneven in the pressures it exerts on gang units in this country.[30] According to criminologist Donald Yates, street gangs, mostly of young African American, Latinos, and other young people of color are said to be the targets of the most intense and persistent law enforcement efforts. By contrast, rich, powerful Mafia and other organized criminal syndicated gangs have largely escaped any comparably sized police scrutiny and pursuit, according to some. Because street gangs consist mostly of the poor and of people of color, there are allegations that criminal justice authorities treat street gang structures more harshly than syndicated gangs, clearly inviting an analysis of racial status, and to a lesser degree, class status as guiding principles in setting contemporary gang policy.[31]

It may very well be that the overwhelming targets of the war on drugs and street gangs have been disproportionately young minority males. As a result, not only did overall incarceration rates skyrocket throughout the 1990s, but more disturbing is the evidence of the disparity of who is disproportionately being incarcerated (minorities), even in light of the fact that drug use by race does not reflect the disparities evident in the criminal justice system. The disparities in the crack/powder disparity have been challenged on constitutional grounds in the federal court system but have failed.[32]

Between 1993 and 1995, 24 states and the federal government adopted some form of "three strikes you're out" legislation, under which repeat offender's face life sentences for a third felony conviction.[33] In California the three strikes law is applied to blacks 42 percent more than would be expected from the imprisonment rate alone. Blacks in California are 31 percent of the population and represent 44 percent of those convicted on a third strike resulting in a 25 years to life sentence.

The debate over the problem of disproportionate minority confinement goes well beyond the correctional system and may stem from fundamental criminal justice policy. It is important to point out that many social scientists believe that racial disparities in the criminal justice system are primarily the result of indirect discrimination, for example, the impact of race-linked poverty, education, and neighborhood where the arrest took place. Whether this is the case or not, correctional administrators must work with others who have a stake in criminal justice policy to address the disturbing problem of potential disproportionate minority confinement.

2-6 Locations of Confinements

State and federal prisons house two-thirds of all people incarcerated in the United States—the other third are in local jails. About two-thirds of the growth in the prison populations during the 12 months ending June 30, 2001, was accounted for by the federal system (10,258 additional inmates). During this 12-month period, several states experienced growth, including Mississippi, (12.5 percent), West Virginia (8.7 percent), and Vermont and Nebraska (each 7.7 percent). At midyear 2001 the ten jurisdictions with the largest prison populations had under their jurisdiction 844,535 inmates, or 60 percent of the nation's total prison population. Texas (164,465), California (163,965), and the federal system (152,788) accounted for a third of the prison population.[34]

2-6a Types of Crime

Between 1990 and 1999 the distribution of the four major offense categories—violent, property, drug, and public order offenses—changed slightly among the state prisoners. The percent held for property and drug offenses dropped while the percent held for public order offenses rose.[35]

In absolute numbers, an estimated 570,000 inmates were held for violent offenses, 161,800 for robbery, 141,500 for murder, 115,110 for assault, and 109,000 for rape and other sexual assaults. In addition, 245,000 inmates were held for property offenses, and 120,6000 for public order offenses.[36]

Overall, the largest growth in state inmates between 1990 and 1999 was among violent offenders. During the 9-year period, the number of violent offenders grew 254,100, while the number of drug offenders grew 101,500. As a percentage of total growth, violent offenders accounted for 51 percent of the growth; drug offenders 20 percent; property offenders 14 percent; and public order offenders 15 percent.[37]

Prisoners sentenced for drug offenses comprised the largest group of federal inmates (62 percent) in 1999, up from 53 percent in 1990. As of September 30, 1999, federal prisons held 68,360 sentenced drug offenders, compared to 30,470 at year end 1990. Figure 2-1 shows how the proportion of offenders incarcerated in federal prisons for drug offenses has increased in the past three decades.

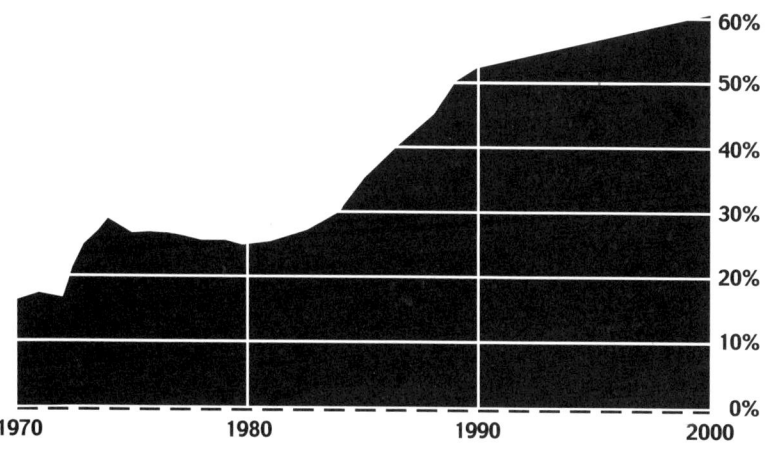

Figure 2-1
Percent of Federal Inmates Committed for Drug Offenses
In Federal prisons, the rising proportion of offenders committed for drug offenses exceeded to 60 percent in 2000.
Source: Bureau of Prisons, May 2002

Between 1990 and 1999, the number of federal inmates held for immigration offenses increased 488 percent, and the number held for weapons offenses increased 209 percent. The number of immigration offenders rose from 1,728 in 1990 to 15,613 in 2000; weapons offenders rose from 3,073 to 9,494. By September 1999, weapons offenders represented 10.3 percent of federal inmates and immigration violators 13.6 percent. Overall, from 1990 to 1999 the percentage of violent federal inmates declined from 17 percent to 11 percent.[38]

Although the latest data is not yet released on immigration related arrests since September, 11, 2001, it is likely to reveal significant increases due to the U.S. Patriot Bill which was passed as a result of the September 11 terrorist attack. The U.S. Patriot Bill grants the government more authority under federal law for detaining and questioning immigration law violators. A New York *Newsday* report published on September 16, 2002, revealed that over 2,000 people have been arrested in the terrorism investigation since September 11, 2001 and immigration and civil liberties lawyers estimate nearly all of them are Islamic, Middle Eastern, or South Asian.

Drug offenders continue to make up a significant proportion of the prison population. Approximately 169,860 inmates are in federal and state prison for drug offenses. The number of offenders incarcerated for a drug offense accounted for the largest percentage of total growth (61 percent).

These statistics suggest what social scientists have thought for some time: that there is a strong association between drug use and drug-related offenses.

2-6b Time Served

Average sentence length and time served for state inmates has remained relatively unchanged. Data on prison admissions and releases collected annually in the National Corrections Reporting Program (NCRP) suggest that growth in the state prison populations has not been the result of longer sentences. (Each year participating states provide information on sentencing and time served for persons entering or leaving prison. Thirty-eight states and the District of Columbia submitted data, accounting for nearly 93 percent of all admissions and 85 percent of all releases nationwide during the year.) Between 1985 and 1995, years in which comparable data are available, the mean maximum sentences of prisoners actually declined from 78 months to 67 months.

The median sentence length (the fiftieth percentile) of prisoners admitted from court remained constant at 48 months. Moreover, despite the increasing use of mandatory minimums and sentencing enhancements during the period, the percent of inmates who received a maximum sentence of 10 years or longer actually declined (from 19.7 percent in 1985 to 17.7 percent in 1995).

Average prison sentences imposed by judges in the state courts for murder and manslaughter were 269 months, or 22 years. Federal inmates convicted of murder or manslaughter were sentenced to an average of 153 months. When examining violent offenders sentenced to state prisons their average sentence is about 118 months or 11 years, compared with 100 months for federal offenders.[39] Property offenders sentenced to state prison averaged 57-month sentences compared to 37-month sentences on average for federal offenses. Although average state sentences seem longer and more severe than average federal sentences, federal prisoners must serve at least 85 percent of their sentences. This means the federal prisoners often serve substantially greater portions of their sentences compared with state prisoners.

2-6c Overcrowding

The exact extent of crowding in the nation's prisons is difficult to determine because of the absence of uniform measures for defining capacity. Most jurisdictions are operating above capacity. Prisons generally require reserve capacity to operate efficiently. Dormitories and cells need to be maintained and repaired periodically, special housing is needed for protective custody and disciplinary cases, and space may be needed to cope with emergencies. State prisons are generally operating at 17 to 29 percent above capacity, while the federal system is operating at 25 percent above capacity.

Recently, the National Prison Project released a report indicating that overcrowded and dangerous prisons are commonplace in the United States. The report found that 40 states are now under court order to reduce overcrowding and other unconstitutional prison conditions. These states have been found in violation of the Eighth Amendment (forbidding cruel and unusual punishment).[40] Many prison and jail administrators are faced with the perplexing problem of what to do about overcrowding and it appears that there are no easy solutions.

In Atlanta, Georgia, the governor was quoted as saying that the prison population estimates for the 2000 decade don't look good.[41] Likewise, the *Daily Texan* reported that a jailbreak by two convicted killers on January 31, 2002, in Dallas raised questions about overcrowding and security in Texas jails, which saw more than 140 escapes in 2001.[42] Oklahoma prisons, glutted by an influx of nonviolent drug offenders, are reaching the breaking point and may have to be taken over by the federal courts. In January 1993, the Oklahoma Corrections Department predicted that without strict limits, the growing rate of incarceration would bankrupt the state by the turn of the century. A task force that studied the State of Oklahoma's correction system recommended reducing penalties for many crimes and shorten the prison length of the average prison sentence which would result in a reduction in prison overcrowding and a savings of $100 million to $150 million per year. The task force, created by legislative mandate, found that Oklahoma classifies many crimes as felonies that are treated only as misdemeanors in other states boarding Oklahoma. In addition, the sentences imposed for all crimes in Oklahoma tend to be more severe than the sentences imposed in other states.[43]

2-7 Changes to the "Justice" Correctional Philosophy

The Violent Crime Control and Law Enforcement Act of 1994 was one of the most ambitious crime bills in our history.[44] The act allocated over $22 billion to expand prisons, impose longer sentences, hire more police officers, and to a very limited extent, fund prevention programs. The following year, however, the money allocated to prevention programs was eliminated. Such acts have great political appeal, but little support among criminal justice professionals. Most professionals feel that such efforts will do little to reduce crime. This approach has been labeled as the "enforcement model."[45] The popular criticisms of the present "enforcement model approach" are that it is racist, it costs too much, and it fails to prevent young people from entering, and continuing, lives of crime. The popularity of prison as a response to crime has resulted in changes in the public and professional perceptions of the role of corrections.

The various approaches to correctional philosophy fall into one of three categories: punishment, treatment, or prevention. Often, they overlap, as punishment and treatment can be argued as an approach to prevent crime. The 1960s was a period when treatment was the dominant approach. This changed in the late 1970s. Since that time, society in general has preferred the punishment approach. As will be discussed in Chapter 3, the punishment approach has resulted in overcrowded institutions and budgets are stripped of so-called "frills" needed for treatment and prevention programs. It appears that in the 1990s, the punishment approach may have reached its height, and the future may see the pendulum swing back toward the treatment or prevention emphasis. As shown in Box 2-4, the California Penal Code indicates a shift away from the punishment approach with its 1995 amendment. It is difficult, however, to predict the future of corrections.

Box 2-4

California Penal Code, Section 1170 (a)

(1) The Legislature finds and declares that the purpose of imprisonment for crime is punishment. This purpose is best served by terms proportionate to the seriousness of the offense with provisions for uniformity in the sentences of offenders committing the same offense under similar circumstances.

(2) Paragraph (1) shall not be construed to preclude programs, including educational programs, that are designed to rehabilitate nonviolent, first-time felony offenders. The Legislature encourages the development of policies and programs designed to educate and rehabilitate nonviolent, first-time felony offenders consistent with the purposes of imprisonment.

[Paragraph (2) added by legislature in 1995.]

[Paragraph (3) omitted.]

ARTICLE
Rehabilitation: Holding Its Ground in Corrections[46]

Introduction

During the Jacksonian era (1820–1830s), American penitentiaries failed miserably in their efforts to reform inmates. Yet, rehabilitation was an idea that would not die easily. In fact, prison administrators during the Reformatory era renewed the optimism and benevolence of rehabilitation in the 1870s. Among the many structural alterations that prisons underwent at that time were substantive changes in rehabilitation programs. Prison officials once again embraced the ideals of rehabilitation by offering educational and vocational training, especially at the Elmira Reformatory, where classification was introduced to facilitate individualized treatment (Rothman, 1971, 1980; Welch, 1996a).

It should be pointed out that during the Reformatory era, rehabilitation was not viewed in explicit medical terms. By the turn of the century, however, medical technology was rapidly improving, and it did not take long for corrections officials to take note of medical breakthroughs. In an effort to rehabilitate offenders, it made good sense to incorporate advances in medicine into correctional treatment. Taking a genuine medical approach to corrections, prisons began reorganizing programs and introducing a therapeutic staff, psychiatrists, psychologists, clinical social workers, and other specialists. Obviously, the role of the therapeutic staff was to facilitate the process of rehabilitation by transforming the offender into a socially amenable and law-abiding citizen. The newly created Federal Bureau of Prisons furthered efforts to integrate the medical model into corrections in the 1930s. Also during that period, classification became more refined and the medical model provided a state-of-the-art clinical orientation by developing diagnostic and treatment methods.

For decades now, the terms treatment and rehabilitation have been used to refer to a variety of programs that range from educational and vocational training to individual therapy and substance abuse counseling. According to the National Academy of Sciences, rehabilitation is defined as "any planned intervention that reduces an offender's further criminal activity" (Sechrest, White, & Brown, 1979). In this sense, the focus of rehabilitation remains on the psychological causes of crime excluding deterrence strategies (see Kratcoaki, 1994). Although the terms treatment and rehabilitation may have different meanings within the correctional community, in this article these terms are used interchangeably.

The Rehabilitation Controversy

The controversy over rehabilitation generally occurs on two fronts. First, there is discussion over theoretical issues—most importantly, their assumptions and propositions. Second, there remains considerable controversy over program-oriented issues surrounding the ways in which rehabilitation is designed, implemented, and evaluated.

Theoretical Issues

Correctional experts who support rehabilitation programs operate on two basic assumptions. First, that the offender's behavior is related to particular personal defects stemming from the offender's own psychological makeup or adverse conditions (or a combination of both). Second, that the offender can be effectively transformed into a law-abiding human being.

Rehabilitation has been attacked by various critics representing diverse philosophical viewpoints. Conservatives remain skeptical about the assumption that an offender's criminality stems from adverse social conditions or psychological defects (or a combination of both). For instance, if it is argued that living in poverty causes criminal behavior, then why are most impoverished people actually law-abiding citizens? Conservatives question such sweeping generalizations about poverty being a cause of crime (Wilson, 1975).

Critics also question whether offenders can be transformed into law-abiding citizens, thus raising an important issue regarding the medical model in corrections. Prisoners in many ways resemble involuntary patients in psychiatric facilities, because offenders are incarcerated against their will. Conventional wisdom leads us to believe that forcing an offender to become prosocial is problematic. An old tongue-in-cheek riddle among psychologists illuminates this dilemma: How many therapists does it take to change a light bulb? One, but the light bulb must be willing to change (Welch, 1996).

Even in cases where the offender is willing and capable of being rehabilitated, questions remain about the long-term effectiveness of such treatment. This is especially true when we acknowledge that ex-cons (e.g., drug peddlers) eventually return to the community. Typically, the neighborhoods to which they return are impoverished with high unemployment, inadequate housing, high rates of crime and violence, and high concentrations of illegal drug use. Critics argue that the long-term effectiveness of rehabilitation is strained unless comparable changes are also made in society (Currie, 1993, 1985; Reiman, 1995; Walker, 1994). Even so, from a basic logistical standpoint, it is certainly easier to try to correct offenders than it is to alter societal conditions.

Program Effectiveness: "What Works?" v. "Nothing Works!"

Since the 1960s, critics of correctional treatment have referred to the body of evaluation research that reports the weaknesses and limitations of rehabilitation programs. Yet, the evaluation study that delivered the hardest blow to rehabilitation was authored by Lipton, Martinson, and Wilks (1975). In a widely cited spin-off article, Martinson (1974, p. 25) concluded: "With few and isolated exceptions, the rehabilitative efforts that have been reported so far have had no appreciable effect on rehabilitation." Martinson entitled his article "What Works?: Questions and Answers About Prison Reform," but it quickly became known as the "nothing works" report.

Contrary to popular opinion, Lipton, Martinson, and Wilks (1975) did not make the sweeping claim that "nothing works." In fact, they cited positive outcomes in 48 percent of the programs evaluated. In the early 1970s, there had been growing disillusion surrounding rehabilitation, and for several years policy makers were "waiting for the other shoe to drop." The publication of Martinson's article was that "other shoe," and the fact that it became known as the "nothing works" report was testimony that the chapter on liberal-oriented rehabilitation was officially coming to a close. Though conservatives succeeded in driving rehabilitation out of prisons, many liberals also voiced their dissatisfaction with correctional programs. Among other things, liberals pointed to the criminal justice system as the problem, therefore arguing that the effectiveness of rehabilitation was irrelevant. Moreover, radicals also launched resounding attacks on rehabilitation by arguing that rehabilitation strategies represent attempts by those in power to "impose a repressive system of social control over the less powerful" (Michalowski, 1985). In this vein, Greenberg and Humphries (1980) noted that liberal interventions, namely rehabilitation, perpetuated class biases in criminal justice:

> Seen in this light, rehabilitation was not merely a laudable goal that scientific research had failed thus far to achieve, but something more insidious, an ideology that explained crime in highly individualistic terms and legitimated the expansion of administrative powers used in practice to discriminate against disadvantaged groups and to achieve covert organizational goals.

Liberals adamantly defended themselves against charges that rehabilitation represents a form of additional social control and pointed out that the demise of rehabilitation resulted from ideological shifts toward conservatism. Cullen and Gendreau suggested that "the rejection of rehabilitation has less to do with a careful reading of empirical literature and more to do with changes in the social fabric that triggered a corresponding shift in thinking about corrections" (1989, p. 24).

A principal method of assessing the effectiveness of rehabilitation programs was to examine the program evaluation reports. It was assumed that if the evaluation specialists found the program ineffective, their conclusion was uncritically accepted without further investigation. As advocates of rehabilitation programs aptly demonstrated, in many cases the evaluation research was at fault, not the program itself. Indeed, buried deep inside Martinson's (1974) article is the regrettable fact that many researchers had failed to follow rigorous scientific procedures while evaluating these programs.

As we take a closer look at the evaluation research of correctional rehabilitation, it is important to be aware that three outcomes are possible. First, that the program is indeed ineffective. Second, that the program is designed effectively, but suffers from faulty administration (perhaps due to unqualified or incompetent staff). Finally, that research methods used to evaluate rehabilitation programs are flawed. As a result, two types of errors might occur: concluding the program is effective when it is not, or concluding that the program is ineffective when it is not.

In the years leading up to the "nothing works" controversy, several social scientists focused on the research methods of previously published evaluation studies. Overall, most of the evaluation studies that were reexamined suffered from shoddy methodology, therefore, raising questions about their findings and conclusions about correctional programs. Perhaps even more relevant to the current debate on the merit of rehabilitation are the recently published evaluation studies that provide substantial support for the effectiveness of correctional treatment (Andrews, Zinger, Hoge, Bonta, Gendreau, & Cullen, 1990a; Gendreau, 1981; Gendreau & Ross, 1979, 1981, 1987; Greenwood & Zimring, 1985; Halleck & Witte, 1977; Palmer, 1983; Van Voorhis, 1987).

Eventually, even Martinson (1979) recanted some of his earlier conclusions. Moreover, his conversion was based largely on the fact that traditional research designs were too rigid to measure accurately the effectiveness of rehabilitation programs. Martinson later wrote that some programs were indeed beneficial and some treatment programs do have an appreciable effect on recidivism. "It is ironic, but instructive, that whereas Martinson's 1974 nothing works article is one the most cited of criminological writings, his revisionist 1979 essay earned scant attention." Once again, it is helpful to view these developments in the context of important social changes transpiring in the 1970s. The nation was struggling to reestablish the image of a strong government after the turbulent 1960s, and one method of achieving this was to mount a visible "tough on crime" campaign. The "tough on crime" ideology asserted that those who favored rehabilitation were "bleeding heart" liberals—suggesting that liberals were soft on crime.

The implications of this ideological shift are evident. Evaluation reports shape both public opinion as well as public policy, and the two often go hand-in-hand. Therefore, in light of what happened in the wake of the Martinson report, one could argue that rehabilitation was unintentionally sabotaged by evaluation researchers (including many academics), who relied on weak or faulty methodological procedures. In addition, proponents have argued that rehabilitation programs were further sabotaged (intentionally or unintentionally) because they were never fully implemented. The decline of rehabilitation was due to administrative or staff limitations. Yet each of these developments took place in a social context characterized by a shift in correctional ideology from liberal to conservative.

A case in point is the argument presented by conservative retributionist Ernest van den Haag, who asked this question: What is the likely effect of rehabilitation on the crime rate? Van den Haag relied on a set of principles and equations borrowed from econometrics deterrent theorists to support the following contention: because rehabilitation can affect criminals only after their first conviction, even total rehabilitation could reduce neither the rate of first offenses, nor the overall crime rate to the extent to which it depends on first offenses.

Though van den Haag recommends that the criminal justice system assert its emphasis on punishment to deter future crimes, his criticism of rehabilitation shows some valuable insight. With first-time offenders, he notes that rehabilitation comes too late. Indeed, to a certain point he is correct. But the answer does not rest in deterrence and the increased use of punishments. Perhaps a better approach is to prevent such crimes by improving societal conditions (e.g., reducing unemployment) and responding to the offenders' personal problems (e.g., substance dependency and substandard education).

Rehabilitation for the 1990s and Beyond

In light of the ongoing controversy over rehabilitation, we need to address some of the most basic applications of the rehabilitation ideal. Whereas some experts have suggested that various forms of counseling be made available in prison simply to undo the damage that incarceration has on the inmate, there are numerous programs which have become common features within prisons that rarely draw criticism—for example, educational programs. The reason why educational programs are not controversial is because they are based on the conventional wisdom that attributes some types of property crime to inadequate education. Most correctional facilities offer various educational programs ranging from literacy classes, high school equivalency diploma (GED) programs and, in some institutions, college courses. Most correctional facilities also offer vocational training to promote job skills. For example, many correctional systems employ inmates in prison industries, such as bakeries, furniture and sewing shops, cosmetology salons, as well as employing them as telephone operators for the state tourism department.

Educational and vocational programs continue to draw support from mainstream citizens, essentially because education in and of itself is valued in our society. Moreover, educational and vocational programs not only develop practical skills, but they also foster a sense of work-ethic that is central to American culture's emphasis on self-reliance.

However, social services advocates point out the paradox that such programs provide inmates with skills that might have helped to prevent them from turning to crime in the first place. Many social policy and prison experts also note that it is "almost as if Americans have concluded that the problems of the urban poor are intractable and therefore spent their money on a vast network of prisons, rather on than on solutions" (Butterfield, 1992). Again, it is ironic that citizens support the construction of prisons but oppose basic social and educational services for the poor, though such interventions are far cheaper than building prisons. For instance, in 1991 the United States allocated $26.2 billion for building and operating prisons, as well as for supervising parolees and probationers (according to the Edna McConnell Clark Foundation). The same year, $22.9 billion was spent on the main welfare program, Aid to Families With Dependent Children (according to the Department of Health and Human Services). Moreover, we are comparing the social services allocated to 13.5 million women and children on public assistance to the 1.1 million prisoners, mostly men. Critics argue that spending billions of dollars on prisons diverts funds from social services that might prevent crime (Butterfield, 1992).

According to Robert Gangi, the executive director of the Correctional Association of New York, "Prisons are becoming the place where we provide services to our poor people" (Butterfield, 1992, p. E-4). Indeed, "the prison system has become part of the welfare system," says penologist Mark Fleisher. Prisons offer housing that is typically better than that of the inner cities. For inmates from the urban ghettos, meals, medical care (especially for persons with AIDS), substance abuse treatment, and educational and vocational training are generally better in prison than in society at large.

Currently, most inmates lack even the most basic educational and vocational skills. Among the men incarcerated in state prisons, 21 percent have an eighth-grade education or less; roughly 41 percent attended some high school; approximately 27 percent are high school graduates; and barely 11 percent report some college or more. Moreover, in terms of employment, approximately 58 percent of these prisoners were working full-time jobs at the time of their arrest (Bureau of Justice Statistics, 1993).

Ideally, it would make good sense to ensure job placement for those returning to the community. However, such proposals remain unrealistic because we live in a society that does not provide full employment—even for its law-abiding citizens. One can imagine the public outcry if the government gave preference to unemployed ex-cons over the ranks of other unemployed citizens. Nevertheless, educational and vocational programs in correctional institutions remain because they symbolize an important form of rehabilitation.

Another form of rehabilitation that is an integral fixture in most correctional facilities is substance abuse counseling (for both drugs and alcohol). The fact is, the great majority of persons being sent to prison are convicted of drug-related offenses, and many more report drug and alcohol abuse histories. In federal prisons, for example, the number of drug offenders has more than doubled since 1981 and now accounts for 53 percent of the inmate population. It is projected that this figure will increase to 69 percent by the end of 1995 (Mauer, 1992). According to the Johnson Foundation (1993), two-thirds of homicides and serious assaults involve alcohol. Similarly, the Bureau of Justice Statistics (1993) reports that 31 percent of state inmates committed their offenses under the influence of drugs, and 17 percent committed their offenses to get money for drugs; further, 32 percent committed their offenses under the influence of alcohol.

Naturally, it is important to provide such services to those who are willing to take full advantage of treatment. However, most correctional administrators concede that their substance abuse programs are grossly under-funded by state and federal authorities. This problem is not surprising, because the vast majority of substance abuse programs outside of prison are also neglected by policy makers. A typical response to a drug addict who voluntarily requests treatment at a community substance abuse clinic is: "Come back in four to six months. That's when the program expects the soonest available bed." At this time, 70 percent of federal antidrug funding is still allocated to law enforcement and only 30 percent to treatment and prevention (Mauer, 1992). As a society, perhaps we need to provide more substance dependency treatment to offenders (as well as non-offenders), especially considering what we know about the association between crime, illegal drugs, and alcohol.

In sum, Cullen and Gilbert (1982) cite four reasons why rehabilitation should be reaffirmed in corrections:

1. Rehabilitation is the only justification of criminal sanctioning that obligates the state to care for an offender's needs or welfare.

2. The ideology of rehabilitation provides an important rationale for opposing the conservative assumptions that increased repression will reduce crime.

3. Rehabilitation still receives considerable support as a major goal of the correctional system.

4. Rehabilitation has historically been an important motive underlying reform efforts that have increased the humanity of the correctional system.

Conclusion

By focusing solely on the problems facing rehabilitation, the more basic assumptions of the liberal perspective are neglected. The liberal agenda recognizes the limitations of patching up offenders who have gone astray without seriously examining the deep underlying social and economic problems (Currie, 1985). Indeed, many liberals concede that if rehabilitation means equipping offenders with better coping and survival skills and returning them to their troubled environment (hoping that this intervention would keep them from engaging in future crimes) instead of attempting to alter some basic social conditions, then the foundation of liberalism is virtually ignored. It seems that over the past few decades, liberals adopted an individual-based form of intervention much like the conservatives because of the realization that it is probably easier to try to correct the offender than to alter social conditions. Certainly, this was found to be the case in the 1820s, when the Jacksonians resorted to building prisons because their efforts to reform society failed (i.e., closing brothels and taverns) (Rothman, 1971). Over time, the liberal approach has become more individual-oriented and less society-oriented (see Clear, 1994).

A popular myth today is that most citizens simply support the conservative "tough on crime" proposals to the exclusion of rehabilitation. Politicians have greatly misjudged the complexity of attitudes that citizens hold regarding punishment and rehabilitation. Numerous studies demonstrate that most citizens favor rehabilitation (especially educational, vocational, and substance abuse programs) in addition to a reasonable level of deserved punishment. Furthermore, many citizens have reasonably accurate impressions of the correctional system insofar as they know that prisons do not rehabilitate offenders—even those offenders who probably are good candidates for reform. Nevertheless, the rehabilitation debate is certainly not settled. It is important to note that the rehabilitative approach has proven to be fairly well-received, especially among citizens.

Cullen and Woznik insist that conservatives have enjoyed free reign of the criminal justice system. The conservative "tough on crime" agenda is characterized by liberals as a form of repression of the disadvantaged and less powerful. In reaction to the conservative criminal justice policies, Cullen and Wozniak propose an eight-point counterattack:

1. Expose the irrationality of "getting tough."
2. Punishing doesn't help: do conservatives really care about victims?
3. Oppose all prison construction.
4. Continue the struggle for offender rights.
5. Oppose determinate sentencing reform.
6. Reaffirm rehabilitation.
7. Promote the work ethic as an avenue of penal reform.
8. Appreciate the humane potential of religion.

In sum, the recommendations by Cullen and Woznik are anything but new—indeed, they were introduced nearly 15 years ago. Moreover, since that time, the law-and-order approach to corrections has deepened, even under a Democratic president. According to Currie, "It is painfully apparent that the decade-long conservative experiment in crime control has failed to live up to its promises." Conservatives are now left with the annoying question of why such an enormous investment in punishment has produced such little impact on crime. Perhaps now political leaders ought to reconsider the value of rehabilitation in corrections.

Source: Reprinted with permission from *Federal Probation*, Vol. 59, No. 4, (December), (1995).

Summary

The criminal justice system is traditionally considered to have three subsystems: law enforcement, judiciary, and corrections. Before an individual comes under the control of correctional agencies, he or she has already moved from citizen, to suspect, to arrestee, to defendant, and finally to convict.

In ancient societies, the remedy for wrongs done to one's person or property was personal retaliation against the wrongdoer. Blood feuds developed from the concept of personal retaliation. A blood feud occurred when the victim's family or tribe took revenge on the offender's family or tribe. To lessen the costly and damaging vendettas, the custom of accepting money or property developed. This practice is still used in some regions in the Middle East. Later, fines and other forms of punishment replaced personal retaliation.

The two earliest codes delineating criminal punishments were the Sumerian and Hammurabic codes. The punishment phases of these codes were based on the concept of personal vengeance. Early punishments were considered synonymous with slavery. Later, the Greek Code and the Code of Draco used the same penalties for both citizens and slaves.

During the Middle Ages, the growing influence of the churches helped create a divided system of justice. The offender, in committing a crime, had two debts to pay. One to the victim, and one to the church. It was also during the Middle Ages that the churches expanded the concept of crime to include new prohibited areas such as heresy, witchcraft, and sex offenses.

While there are numerous methods to classify punishment ideologies, the three popular classifications based on political theories are the conservative, liberal, and radical. The conservative ideology tends to accept the concept that human beings are rational, possess free will, and voluntarily commit criminal misconduct. The liberal ideology tends to view human behavior as greatly influenced by social circumstances, including one's upbringing, material affluence, education, peer relationships, and so on. The radical ideology rejects both the conservative and liberal ideologies. To the radicals, crime is a reflection of the status of our present social system.

The ultimate purpose of criminal sanctions is generally considered the maintenance of our social order. The four popular goals of criminal sanctions are retribution, deterrence, incapacitation, and rehabilitation. Retribution generally means getting even and is based on the ideology that the criminal is an enemy of society. Retribution is also referred to as the "just deserts" ideology. Deterrence is a punishment viewpoint that focuses on future outcomes rather than past misconduct. It is also based on the theory that creating fear of future punishments will deter crime. The incapacitation viewpoint is often labeled as the "nothing else works" concept. It is based on the concept that prisoners, while in prison, have less chance to commit crimes against the public. The rehabilitation approach emphasizes correcting the offender, and is also considered as the "treatment" approach.

State, federal, and local governments had to accommodate an additional 69,074 inmates per year as of 2001. This is the equivalent of 1,328 inmates per week. The nation's prison population has more than doubled since 1980. The states with the highest incarceration rates per 100,000 residents are Texas, Mississippi, and Oklahoma. Five states had prison incarceration rates below 200 per 100,000 population, led by Maine, Minnesota, and North Dakota. The incarceration rate of blacks is six times that of whites. State and federal prisons house two-thirds of all persons incarcerated in the United States. The other one-third are in local jails.

Discussion Questions

1. Explain how the concept of blood feuds developed.
2. Discuss the functions and purpose of the holy inquisition.
3. Compare and contrast the three political ideologies regarding punishment.
4. Compare and contrast the rehabilitation and deterrence approaches to punishment.
5. Explain the contributions to punishment reform of Jeremy Bentham.
6. Describe the demographics of the prison population.
7. List recent changes to the justice correctional philosophy.

Chapter Quiz

True/False

1. In ancient societies the remedy for wrongs against one's person or property usually was met with no retaliation against the wrong doer.
2. Penal servitude involved the use of rehabilitative philosophies in prisons.
3. During the middle ages, trials by ordeal were used by churches as substitutes for trials.
4. Jeremy Bentham is considered by many to be the greatest leader in the reform of English criminal law.
5. The conservative ideology tends to view human behavior as greatly influenced by social circumstances including one's upbringing, material affluence, and education and peer relationships.

Multiple Choice

1. _____ is based on the idea that the criminal is the enemy of society and usually means getting even.
   a. Deterrence
   b. Rehabilitation
   c. Retribution
   d. Incapacitation
2. The viewpoint of this punishment philosophy focuses on future outcomes rather than past misconduct and it is also based on fear of future punishment.
   a. retribution
   b. deterrence
   c. rehabilitation
   d. radicalism
3. The _____ approach pronounces that punishment should be directed toward correcting the offender.
   a. incapacitation
   b. rehabilitation
   c. deterrence
   d. retribution
4. In ancient societies when the victim's family took revenge on the offender's family, this was known as
   a. blood feuds.
   b. trials by ordeal.
   c. friedensgeld.
   d. penal servitude.
5. The disturbing problem of disproportionate minority confinement in American prisons can be attributed to all but which one of the following?
   a. crack v. powder cocaine sentencing disparities
   b. the war on drugs
   c. biased criminal justice policy
   d. population increases in minority communities

Endnotes

1. Lawrence F. Travis III, Martin D. Schwartz, and Todd R. Clear, *Corrections: An Issues Approach*, 3rd ed. (Cincinnati: Anderson, 1992), 50
2. Stephen Schafer, *Theories in Criminology* (New York: Random House, 1969), 291.
3. Albert Kocourek and John Wigmore, *Evolution of Law* II (Boston: Little, Brown and Company, 1915), 15.
4. John Swain, *The Pleasures of the Torture Chamber* (New York: Dorset Press, 1931), 157.

5. Ibid. 27.
6. Alexis M. Durham III, *Crisis and Reform: Current Issues in American Punishment* (Boston: Little, Brown and Company, 1994), 16–18.
7. Elio Monachesi, "Cesare Beccaria," in *Pioneers in Criminology,* 2nd ed. Hermann Hannheim, ed., (Monclair, NJ: Patterson Smith, 1973), 42–49.
8. Marvin Wolfgang, "Cesare Lombroso," in *Pioneers in Criminology,* 2nd ed., Hermann Hannheim, ed. (Montclair, NJ: Patterson Smith, 1973), 232–249.
9. Charles Milner Atkinson, *Jeremy Bentham: His Life and Work* (London: Smith, 1905).
10. Herbert L. Packer, *The Limits of Criminal Sanction* (Stanford, CA: Stanford University Press, 1968), 33.
11. Ibid.
12. Robert O. Dawson, *Sentencing: The Decision as to Type, Length, and Conditions of Sentence* (Boston: Little, Brown and Company, 1969).
13. Elmer H. Johnson, *Crime, Correction, and Society* (Homewoood, IL: Dorsey Press, 1974), 173.
14. Marianne W. Zawitz, ed., *Report to the Nation on Crime and Justice* (Washington, DC: Bureau of Justice Statistics, U.S. Government Printing Office, 1983), 35.
15. Durham, *Crisis and Reform,* 26.
16. Packer, *The Limits of Criminal Sanction,* 49.
17. Packer, *The Limits of Criminal Sanction,* 55–57.
18. Packer, *The Limits of Criminal Sanction,* 37.
19. As reported in *The Oxford History of the Prison,* eds. Norval Morris and David J. Rothman. (New York: Oxford, 1995), xi.
20. Norval Morris, *The Future of Imprisonment* (Chicago: University of Chicago Press, 1974), xi.
21. C. Ray Jeffery, "The Historical Development of Criminology," *Pioneers in Criminology,* 2d ed. Hermann Mannheim, ed., (Montclair, NJ: Patterson Smith, 1973), 487.
22. Thomas Bonczar, and Allen J. Beck, "Lifetime Likelihood of Going to State or Federal Prison." Bureau of Justice Statistics Special Report (March 2001): 1–13. Washington, DC: U.S. Department of Justice.
23. Ibid., 1–13.
24. Allen J. Beck, Jennifer C. Karberg, and Paige M. Harrison. NCJRS Report: Prison and Jail Inmates at Midyear 2001, NCJ–191702, April, 2002.
25. Bureau of Justice Statistics, *Prisoners in 2001,* July 2002.
26. Samuel Walker, Casia Spohn, and Miriam DeLone, *Race and Ethnicity and Crime in America: The Color of Justice,* 2nd ed. (Belmont, CA: Wadsworth, 2000).
27. Beck, Karberg, and Harrison, NCJRS Report.
28. Jerome G. Miller, *Search and Destroy: African American Males in the Criminal Justice System* (New York: Cambridge University Press, 1996).

29. Donald L. Yates, Prejudiced in the Criminal Justice System, in Richard H. Roper's and Dan J. Pence, *American Prejudice: Liberty and Justice for Some* (New York: Plenum, 1995).
30. Donald L. Yates, "Street vs. Mafia Gang Pursuit: The Social Racism of Contemporary Criminal Justice Gang Policy," *Free Inquiry of Sociology* 25 (1, May 1997): 37-45.
31. Ibid., 91.
32. David Cole, *No Equal Justice: Race and Class in the American Criminal Justice System* (New York: The New Press, 1999).
33. National Institute of Justice, Department of Justice, *Three Strikes You're Out: A Review of State Legislation*, (September 1997).
34. Allen J. Beck, Jennifer C. Karberg, and Paige M. Harrison. NCJRS Report: Prison and Jail Inmates at Midyear 2001, NCJ–191702, April, 2002.
35. Allen J. Beck, and Paige M. Harrison, "Prisoners in 2000," *Bureau of Justice Statistics* (August 2001).
36. Ibid.
37. Ibid.
38. Ibid.
39. Kathleen MaGire, and Ann L. Pastore. *Bureau of Justice Statistics Sourcebook of Criminal Justice Statistics* (Albany, NY: Hindelang Criminal Justice Research Center, State University of New York at Albany, 1997).
40. "Study: Prison Overcrowding Taking its Toll," *National Law Journal* (March 29, 1993): 9.
41. James Salzer. "Barnes Looking Into Issue of Prison Overcrowding" *The Athens Banner Herald*, 2 August 1999.
42. "Jailbreak Throws Spotlight on Prison Overcrowding," *The Daily Texan*, 31 January 2002.
43. Ray Carter, "Reduced Penalties Could Save Oklahoma $150 Million." The Journal Record Legislative Report, *Dolan Media Newswires*, 25 February 2003.
44. Joan Petersilia, "A Crime Control Rationale for Reinvesting in Community Corrections," *The Prison Journal*, Vol. 75, No. 4.
45. Ibid.
46. Michael Welch, Associate Professor, Administration of Justice, Rutgers University. Reprinted with permission from *Federal Probation*, Vol. 59, No. 4, December 1995.

Chapter 3
The Sentencing Process

Billy E. Barnes/PhotoEdit

Key Terms

adjudicatory hearing
alternative sentencing
consent decrees
deferred adjudication
determinate sentence
disposition hearing
emergency overcrowding
   provisions
good-time guidelines
informal probation
intake
mandatory prison terms
misdemeanants
parole guidelines
presentence investigation
   (PSI) report
presumptive sentence
pretrial diversion
sentence
sentencing guidelines
three strikes legislation
truth in sentencing laws

Outline

3-1 Determinate and Indeterminate
   Sentencing
   3-1a Mandatory Prison Terms
   *3-1b Flat Time with Mandatory
      Supervision*
   3-1c Sentencing Guidelines
   3-1d Three Strikes Legislation
   *3-1e United States Sentencing
      Commission*
   3-1f Good-Time Policies
   *3-1g Emergency Overcrowding
      Provisions*
   *3-1h National Conference
      on Corrections*
   *3-1i Judicial Process for
      Misdemeanants*
   3-1j Judicial Process for Felons
   3-1k Presentence Investigations
   3-1l Suspended Sentences

3-2 Alternative Sentencing
   and Diversion
3-3 Judicial Process for Juveniles
   3-3a Juvenile Court Procedures
   3-3b Detention Hearings
   3-3c Citation
   3-3d Venue
   3-3e Intake
   3-3f Adjudicatory Hearings
   3-3g Disposition Hearings
   3-3h Uniform Juvenile Court Act
Summary
Discussion Questions
Chapter Quiz
Endnotes

Learning Objectives

After studying this chapter, the reader will be able to:

- Identify who has the responsibility for determining the appropriate sentence in a criminal case.
- List the restrictions that are placed on judges regarding their sentencing discretion.
- Explain the differences between determinate and indeterminate sentences.
- Explain the use of sentencing guidelines.
- List the duties of the U.S. Sentencing Commission.
- Describe the function of good-time laws.
- List the conditions under which the Model Penal Code recommends the use of imprisonment as a prison sentence.
- Explain the procedures used in juvenile cases.
- List the essential components of a presentence investigation (PSI) report.
- Explain the two types of suspended sentences.

Before the correctional process may begin, the defendant must be convicted of a crime by a court with proper jurisdiction. Table 3-1 shows the felony convictions in state courts in 1998 by type of offense. In this chapter, we will examine the process by which a citizen becomes a client in the correctional process—the sentencing process. While there are some variations among the states, generally the processes are very similar. Sentencing is the formal process by which the courts deal with defendants convicted of crimes. A **sentence** is an authorized judicial decision that places some degree of penalty on a person convicted of a crime.[1] The responsibility for deciding the appropriate sentence is generally delegated to the judges. In a few states, such as Texas, the defendant can elect to be sentenced by a jury.

TABLE 3-1 Felony Convictions in State Courts
By Offense, United States, 1998[a]

Most Serious Conviction Offense	Felony Convictions Number	Percent
All Offenses	**927,717**	**100%**
Violent offenses	164,584	17.8
Murder, nonnegligent manslaughter[b]	9,158	1.0
Muder	6,944	0.7
Nonnegligent manslaughter	2,127	0.2
Sexual assault, rape	29,693	3.2
Rape	11,622	1.3
Other sexual assault	18,071	1.9
Robbery	38,784	4.2
Armed	11,977	1.3
Unarmed	10,358	1.1
Unspecified	16,450	1.8
Aggravated assault	71,060	7.7
Other violent[c]	15,889	1.7
Property offenses	283,002	30.5
Burglary	87,957	9.5
Residential	12,542	1.4
Nonresidential	20,419	2.2
Unspecified	54,996	5.9
Larceny	107,621	11.6
Motor vehicle theft	14,368	1.5
Other theft[d]	93,253	10.1
Fraud, forgery, embezzlement	87,424	9.4
Fraud, embezzlement	43,975	4.7
Forgery	43,449	4.7
Drug offenses	314,626	33.9
Possession	119,443	12.9
Trafficking	195,183	21.0
Marijuana	22,975	2.5
Other	54,633	5.9
Unspecified	117,575	12.7
Weapons offenses	31,904	3.4
Other offenses[e]	133,601	14.4

Note: These data are from the National Judicial Reporting Program (NJRP), a biennial survey of State felony courts. Data were collected by the U.S. Census Bureau for the U.S. Department of Justice, Bureau of Justice Statistics. The 1998 NJRP survey was based on a sample of 344 counties selected to be nationally represented. The sample included the District of Columbia and at least one county from every State except, by chance, Delaware, Montana, and Wyoming. Only offenses that State penal codes define as felonies are included. Excluded are Federal courts and State or local courts that did not adjudicate adult felony cases. Data specifying the conviction offense were available for the estimated total of 927,717 convicted felons. These data are estimates derived from a sample and therefore are subject to sampling variation.

TABLE **3-1 (continued)**

For survey sampling procedures and definitions of terms, see Appendix 11.
aDetail may not add to total because of rounding.
bIn a small number of cases where it was unclear whether the offense was murder or manslaughter, the case was classified under nonnegligent manslaughter.
cIncludes offenses such as negligent manslaughter and kidnapping.
dIncludes a small number of cases in which type of larceny was unspecified.
eComposed of nonviolent offenses such as receiving stolen property and vandalism.

Source: U.S. Department of Justice, Bureau of Justice Statistics, *Felony Sentences in State Courts, 1998,* Bulletin NCJ 190103 (Washington, DC: U.S. Department of Justice, October 2001), p. 2, Table 1.

The sentencing process involves selecting the appropriate sentence from an array of choices, including incarceration, fine, forfeiture, probation, and alternative corrective programs (see Box 3-1). Once the sentencing decision is made, the responsibility for administrating the decision is placed with the department of corrections.

Box 3-1

American Bar Association's Standards Relating to Sentencing Alternatives

The sentencing court should be provided in all cases with a wide range of alternatives, with gradations of supervisory, supportive, and custodial facilities at its disposal so as to permit a sentence appropriate for each individual case.

Until recent years, the determination as to whether a convicted defendant went to prison and for how long was left largely to the courts. Judicial decisions were made with few statutory guidelines except for the stated statutory maximum sentence that may be imposed on the conviction of an offense. In the last two decades, however, judges are becoming increasingly restricted regarding the types of sentences allowed, whether to suspend sentences, or grant probation. Concerns regarding disparate sentences and perceived abuses of power in sentencing have resulted in six common legislative strategies to maintain control over the sentencing process and "reduce judicial and correctional imperialism." The six strategies are as follows:

1. **Determinate sentencing.** Establishing set sentences whereby parole boards are also restricted from releasing prisoners before their sentences (minus good-time credit) have expired.
2. **Mandatory prison terms.** Statutes that require the courts to impose mandatory prison terms for convictions of certain offenses or for certain defendants.
3. **Sentencing guidelines.** Guidelines designed to structure sentences based on the offense severity and the criminal history of the defendant.
4. **Parole guidelines.** Guidelines designed to require parole decisions to be based on measurable offender criteria.
5. **Good-time guidelines.** Guidelines that allow for reducing prison terms based on an inmate's good behavior in prison.
6. **Emergency overcrowding provisions.** Regulations that allow early release of prisoners based on systematic provisions to relieve overcrowding.

3-1 Determinate and Indeterminate Sentencing

A determinate sentence is a sentence with a fixed period of confinement imposed by the judge of the sentencing court. The determinate sentence is based on the concept that each crime should have a price tag. You commit the crime, you pay the price. Its underlying ideology is based on retribution and incapacitation. A form of determinate sentencing now being used by the federal government and many states is the "presumptive" sentence.

Presumptive sentencing was brought about to reduce crime through a fair and effective sentencing system. This was to be accomplished by honest sentences, meaning that there was to be no more reduction of terms in prison by parole boards. The total sentence whether in months or years is to be served regardless of the prisoner's behavior.

A presumptive sentence is a sentence suggested by the legislative body based on certain factors pertaining to the crime and the criminal. The judge is expected to impose the presumptive sentence. If the presumptive sentence is not given, the judge must justify why it was not imposed. Generally, determinate sentencing is used in adult criminal courts. Figure 3-1 is an example of Minnesota's guidelines for presumptive sentences.

Italicized numbers within the grid denote the range within which a judge may sentence without the sentence being deemed a departure. Offenders with nonimprisonment felony sentences are subject to jail time according to law.

Severity level of conviction offense (common offenses listed in italics)		Criminal History Score						
		0	1	2	3	4	5	6 or more
Murder, 2nd degree (intentional murder; drive-by-shootings)	XI	306 *299-313*	326 *319-333*	346 *339-353*	366 *359-373*	386 *379-393*	406 *399-413*	426 *419-433*
Murder, 3rd degree Murder, 2nd degree (unintentional murder)	X	150 *144-156*	165 *159-171*	180 *174-186*	195 *189-201*	210 *204-216*	225 *219-231*	240 *234-246*
Criminal sexual conduct, 1st degree[2] Assault, 1st degree	IX	86 *81-91*	98 *93-103*	110 *105-115*	122 *117-127*	134 *129-139*	146 *141-151*	158 *153-163*
Aggravated robbery, 1st degree	VIII	48 *44-52*	58 *54-62*	68 *64-72*	78 *74-82*	88 *84-92*	98 *94-102*	108 *104-112*
Felony DWI	VII	36	42	48	54 *51-57*	60 *57-63*	66 *63-69*	72 *69-75*
Criminal sexual conduct, 2nd degree (a) & (b)	VI	21	27	33	39 *37-41*	45 *43-47*	51 *49-53*	57 *55-59*
Residential burglary Simple robbery	V	18	23	28	33 *31-35*	38 *36-40*	43 *41-45*	48 *46-50*
Nonresidential burglary	IV	12[1]	15	18	21	24 *23-25*	27 *26-28*	30 *29-31*
Theft crimes (Over $2,500)	III	12[1]	13	15	17	19 *18-20*	21 *20-22*	23 *22-24*
Theft crimes ($2,500 or less) Check forgery ($200-$2,500)	II	12[1]	12[1]	13	15	17	19	21 *20-22*
Sale of simulated Controlled substance	I	12[1]	12[1]	12[1]	13	15	17	19 *18-20*

☐ Presumptive commitment to state imprisonment. First Degree Murder is excluded from the guidelines by law and continues to have a mandatory life sentence. See section **II.E. Mandatory Sentences** for policy regarding those sentences controlled by law, including minimum periods of supervision for sex offenders released from prison.

▨ Presumptive stayed sentence; at the discretion of the judge, up to a year in jail and/or other non-jail sanctions can be imposed as conditions of probation. However, certain offenses in this section of the grid always carry a presumptive commitment to state prison. These offenses include Third Degree Controlled Substance Crimes when the offender has a prior felony drug conviction, Burglary of an Occupied Dwelling when the offender has prior felony burglary conviction, second and subsequent Criminal Sexual Conduct offenses and offenses carrying a mandatory minimum prison term due to the use of a dangerous weapon (e.g., Second Degree Assault). See sections **II.C. Presumptive Sentence** and **II.E.Mandatory Sentences**.

1   One year and one day
2   Pursuant to M.S.§ 609.342, subd. 2, the presumptive sentence for Criminal Sexual Conduct in the First Degree is a minimum of 144 months **(see II.C. Presumptive Sentence and II.G. Convictions for Attempts, Conspiracies, and Other Sentence Modifiers)**.

Effective August 1, 2002

Figure 3-1
Minnesota Guideline Grid, Presumptive Sentence Lengths in Months

The indeterminate sentence is based on the concept that the sentence should be tailored to the correction needs of the defendant. Generally indeterminate sentences include the pronouncement by the judge as to the minimum and maximum terms of confinement. For example, the judge may sentence the defendant to serve a period of confinement of not less than two years and not more than ten. The minimum term establishes the earliest release date (after adjustments for credits such as good time or time served while awaiting trial). The maximum term is the maximum length of time that the prisoner will be required to serve. The indeterminate sentence is based on the concept of rehabilitation. The defendant is to be released when he or she is rehabilitated. The decision as to when the defendant is rehabilitated is taken from the judge and transferred to an administrative agency. Most juvenile courts use indeterminate sentencing.

A discussion of determinant and indeterminate sentencing would not be complete without briefly mentioning truth in sentencing laws. **Truth in sentencing laws** arose when the public learned that many in the correctional system serve much less time than expected. Truth in sentencing requires offenders to serve a substantial proportion of their sentences. According to the Bureau of Justice Statistics, truth in sentencing requires that most offenders serving sentences for violent crimes serve about 85 percent of their sentence before being released on parole. The Violent Crime Control Act of 1994 requires states that wish to qualify for federal financial aid to change their laws so that offenders serve at least 85 percent of their sentences. For example, a defendant who has been sentenced to 120 months (10 years) in prison would be required to serve at least 102 months (8 years and six months) before being eligible for parole.

The federal government offered large grants to states that adopted truth in sentencing laws. By 1998, 29 states had adopted truth in sentencing laws that met the federal government's guidelines and another 13 states adopted their own versions. Critics argue that as more and more states adopt some form of truth in sentencing laws prison populations will increase to proportions that could literally cost millions to accommodate the building of new prison facilities and the maintenance of existing facilities.

3-1a Mandatory Prison Terms

The American criminal justice system traditionally permits judges to weigh all the facts of a case when determining an offender's sentence. But in the 1970s and 1980s, the U.S. Congress and many state legislatures passed laws that forced judges to give fixed prison sentences to those convicted of specific crimes, most often drug offenses. Members of congress and state legislators believed these harsh, inflexible sentences would catch those at the top of the drug trade and deter others from entering it. Mandatory prison terms are set forth in statutes that require prison terms always be imposed for convictions of certain offenses or offenders. As of 1996, 48 states had some form of mandatory prison term statutes. The statutes not only apply to drug offenses but also apply for certain crimes of violence such as crimes involving the use of a firearm, violations of drinking and driving statutes, and for habitual criminals. The states that have adopted mandatory sentencing have eliminated the judges' discretion regarding the imposition of probation in those cases.

Most mandatory sentencing statutes prescribe a minimum period of incarceration for offenders whose crimes fall within specific categories. This heavy-handed response to the nation's crime problem filled prisons with low-level offenders, usually drug offenders, resulting in over-capacity prison populations and increased costs for taxpayers. For example, the Federal Bureau of Prisons reported in 2001 that 55 percent, or 77,791 inmates, serving time in the federal prison system were serving time for drug offenses. Mandatory sentencing laws have also been criticized because many believe they disproportionately affect persons of color and, because of their severity, destroy families. A discussion on the disproportionate minority confinement was taken up in Chapter 2.

Mandatory sentences are usually justified on the basis of their deterrence effect. However, more than two decades after these laws were passed they do not appear to have had a significant deterrent effect. Moreover, these laws have failed to deter people from using or selling drugs.

3-1b Flat Time with Mandatory Supervision

As noted earlier, a determinate sentence is a "flat time" sentence set by the sentencing judge and is usually based on legislated guidelines. The defendant is given a finite sentence, and after good-time or program-credit calculations are made, the defendant knows his or her expected release date. Since parole is premised on indeterminate sentencing, which allows the correctional administration to set the release date, the move toward determinate sentencing, with mandatory supervision on release, is seen by many as the way to eliminate the parole system.

3-1c Sentencing Guidelines

To determine the appropriate sentence in most states, the judge is required to follow guidelines and statutory restrictions. Most states require that a **presentence investigation (PSI) report** be prepared and submitted to the court to assist judges in determining the appropriate sentences. The PSI contains a variety of information, such as statements describing the seriousness of the crime, the defendant's past criminal history, any history of substance abuse, and any aggravating or mitigating circumstances of the crime.

Sentencing guidelines are being used by the federal government and many states to enable judges to issue appropriate sentences. A report by the National Institute of Justice indicated that by the end of 1999, 18 states had developed and implemented some form of sentencing guidelines. The guidelines were developed in an attempt to reduce disparity among sentences, to limit discretion of judges, and to establish more detailed criteria for sentencing. In many states, a sentencing commission monitors the use of the guidelines and written explanations are required when a judge departs from the guideline ranges. Minnesota, for example, provides that while sentencing guidelines are advisory to the judge, departures from the guideline sentences established should be made only when substantial and compelling circumstances exist. In Pennsylvania, failure of the court to explain sentences deviating from the guidelines is grounds for vacating the sentence and resentencing the defendant. In addition, if the appellate court considers the guidelines inaccurate or inappropriate, the appellate court may vacate the sentence and order a resentencing.

The U.S. Sentencing Reform Act of 1984 advocated the "least restrictive alternative" in sentencing federal prisoners. For example, if a person is a nonviolent offender and has little to no criminal history, a least restrictive alternative to prison would be intensive supervised probation or community corrections with strict conditions. In 1984, the U.S. Sentencing Commission established federal sentencing guidelines that authorized prison terms for all felony convictions and these guidelines have governed federal sentencing decisions since 1989. The guidelines created 43 offense levels with each level reflecting increased severity of crime. In addition, offenders were divided into six categories based on their criminal history. The net result is a grid containing 258 cells, each of which has a sentencing range expressed in terms of months. The intent was to have the grids serve as an advisory to judicial decision making on sentencing. While the stated objective of the federal sentencing reform was to encourage alternative sanctions to prison, the guidelines are constructed in such a manner as to discourage judges from imposing alternative sanctions. Research indicates that since the adoption of the federal sentencing guidelines, the use of probation and other nonincarcerative sentences has declined.[2]

The sentencing court must select a sentence from within the guideline range. If, however, a particular case presents atypical features, the act allows the court to depart from the guidelines and sentence outside the prescribed range. In that case, the court must specify reasons for departure.[3]

According to the Bureau of Justice Statistics, in 1984, before the use of the guidelines, approximately 52 percent of felony federal offenders were sentenced to prison. In 1991, the percentage had increased to 71 percent and to 72 percent in 1999. Since their adoption, there has been widespread criticism of the guidelines among the federal district court judges, who call them unduly harsh and mechanical. Other judges feel that in addition to being harsh, the guidelines are inflexible. Most agree that the guidelines rely too heavily on imprisonment as a sanction.

Criticisms of sentencing guidelines are that the sentence uniformity appears to deteriorate after a few years' experience with sentence guidelines, and that guidelines violate constitutional separation of powers by permitting legislatures to set sentences, which is a judicial prerogative. Sentencing guidelines have also been criticized on the grounds that sentences for crack cocaine are more harsh when compared to sentences for powder cocaine. Thus, these punishments have been found to punish black offenders disproportionately over whites. Recall from Chapter 2 that first-time offenders who are caught in possession of five grams of cocaine receive a mandatory minimum term of five years in prison, compared with a first-time powder cocaine offender who must possess 500 grams of the substance to receive the same sentence.

3-1d Three Strikes Legislation

The nation was in horror as the story of Polly Klaas unfolded in the print and electronic media. On October 1, 1993, twelve-year-old Polly was kidnapped at knife point from her Petaluma, California, home while her parents were sleeping in a nearby room. Two other girls who were spending the night with Polly were left bound and gagged after a suspect described as a bearded stranger broke into the Klaas home. Nine weeks later a state parolee with a prior criminal record named Richard Allen Davis was arrested and charged with Polly's murder. Davis led police to Polly's strangled body, which was buried in a shallow grave near a freeway. The discovery distressed hundreds of residents who had launched a campaign to try to find the missing girl. Davis had a very lengthy criminal history and had been in and out of the criminal justice system for many years. Davis was subsequently convicted for the murder of Polly Klaas and sentenced to death. Many casual observers criticized the criminal justice system for failing to keep a dangerous man like Davis behind bars.

In the wake of the widely publicized Polly Klaas murder, California Governor Pete Wilson signed into law on March 7, 1994, one of the most punitive sentencing statutes in recent history. The law was dubbed "three strikes and you're out" because of its provision requiring 25 years to life prison terms for defendants convicted of any felony who were already convicted of two serious or violent felonies. The law was overwhelmingly affirmed by three-fourths of California voters through a statewide initiative.

Currently, "three strikes and you're out" laws have been adopted by 24 states.[4] **Three strikes legislation** represent a form of mandatory sentencing, requiring that judges sentence offenders with three felony convictions (in some states two or four convictions) to long prison terms, sometimes to life without parole.[5] The three strikes law promised to reduce violent crime by putting repeat offenders behind bars for life. The severe nature of the law was intended to maximize the criminal justice system's deterrent and incapacitation effect. In other words, persons would be deterred from committing crimes because of the fear of incarceration for a long period of time.

There is some research that indicates that the "three strikes" laws have not been as effective as originally intended. A study by the National Institute of Justice found that three strikes laws have had very limited effects in California.[6] The combination of three strikes and truth in sentencing laws has significantly affected the proportion of prison inmates over 50 years of age. In essence, offenders are spending a longer period of time in prisons. In Washington, there appears to be some reduction in the growth of parole entries and exits associated with three strikes laws. The lack of significant effects of three strikes laws nationally is attributed in large part to the fact that the laws are very rarely used in most states.[7] Other critics of the law argue that there is no proof yet that it is deterring crime and that factors other than three strikes can be attributed to the decrease in crime seen during the 1990s.[8]

Proponents of the three strikes law in California have pointed out that the recent drop in major crime in California from 1999 to 2001 far exceeds the reduction in the United States as a whole. They cite decreases not just in the rates of offenders, but also in actual numbers. For example, there were nearly 500 fewer homicide victims statewide in California in 1995 compared with 1993.[9] According to the FBI, major crime in California dropped 4.9 percent in 1994, the first year of three strikes, compared with 2 percent nationwide. The disparity was even more pronounced in the first six months of 1995, a 7 percent reduction in California compared with 1 percent for the nation.[10]

The three strikes law is currently the subject of much debate and scrutiny and more research is needed to evaluate its effectiveness. The implications of three strikes can be challenging and perplexing to those in the criminal justice system. This is particularly the case when nonviolent offenders are sentenced to lengthy sentences under three strikes laws. One such case occurred in Kansas when Gloria L. Van Winkle, a three-time drug offender, was sentenced to life in prison for possession of $40.00 worth of crack cocaine under the Kansas three strikes law. The law that Van Winkle was sentenced under dates to the early 1970s. Kansas eventually changed these laws in 1993 when sentencing guidelines were enacted that reserve the harsh penalties for serious violent offenders.[11] Another similar case occurred in California when a homeless person named Michael Riggs, stole a bottle of vitamin pills from a supermarket. This minor theft was a misdemeanor, but under California law it was elevated to a felony because Riggs had at least two prior felony convictions. This placed him under the California three strikes law that imposed a mandatory minimum of 25 years to life.[12] The U.S. Supreme Court denied hearing Riggs's appeal that the harsh sentence violated his Eighth Amendment Rights. If it would have been Riggs's first offense, he would have been sentenced to a fine or a jail term of six months or less.

3-1e United States Sentencing Commission

The United States Sentencing Commission is an independent agency in the judicial branch composed of seven voting and two nonvoting, ex officio members. Its principle purpose is to establish sentencing policies and practices for the federal criminal justice system that will ensure the ends of justice by promulgating detailed guidelines prescribing the appropriate sentences for offenders convicted of federal crimes. The guidelines and policy statements promulgated by the commission are issued pursuant to Section 994 (a) of Title 28, United States Code.

Box 3-2

National Crime Victimization Survey

The annual BJS Bulletin presents the findings from the National Crime Victimization Survey (NCVS), based on an ongoing survey of households, each year interviewing about 100,000 persons in 50,000 households. First fielded in 1973 and redesigned most recently in 1992, the survey can now trace a three-decade trend in criminal victimization in the United States. The NCVS estimates the total number of offenses committed by asking individuals from a large national sample about their experiences as victims during a given time period.

continues

Box 3-2 (continued)

According to the NCVS in 2001, U.S. residents age 12 or older experienced more than 24.2 million victimizations, a decrease from 25.9 million victimizations in 2000, and furthered a downward trend that began in 1994. Criminal victimizations are the lowest recorded since the 1973 estimate of 44 million victimizations when the NCVS was initiated.

Overall criminal victimizations in 2001 included about 18.3 million property crimes (burglary, motor vehicle theft, and theft), 5.7 million violent crimes (rape, sexual assault, robbery, aggravated assault, and simple assault), and personal thefts (pocket picking and purse snatching).

Box 3-3

Can Society Afford a Zero Crime Rate?

Mark A. Cohen, an economics professor at Vanderbilt University states that our society could not afford a zero crime rate, that it would bankrupt us. He also estimates that crime costs this country about $500 billion a year, making it a major industry. Cohen's comments are based on the concept that as a major industry, criminal justice supplies many people with employment (e.g., police officers, lawyers, judges, correctional officers, etc.) and that if this industry is eliminated, unemployment would rise, and with high unemployment, less taxes would be received by governments and more money would need to be spent on welfare. If the crime problem is solved, some economists predict that over 6 million people in the United States would lose their jobs.

Franklin Zimring, Director of the Earl Warren Legal Institute at the University of California at Berkeley, calls the $500 billion estimate a "phony number." He is worried that by fixing the cost of crime so high, it will make the building of prisons look like a cheap and politically palatable answer to crime. For example, in California in 1996, the state spent more to build and operate prisons than on its public colleges and universities. Prisons are the fastest growing item in almost all state budgets.

John J. DiIulio, professor of public affairs at Princeton University, contends that prisons do pay for themselves. He states that it costs $25,000 a year to keep a prisoner behind bars. He contends, however, that "society saves at least $2.80 in the social costs of crime for every one dollar spent on prisons."

Parole guidelines are procedures designed to limit or structure parole release decisions based on measurable offender criteria. In some states, the parole board has great latitude in making the parole release decisions. In other states, the parole guidelines are closely prescribed and provide only limited discretion to the parole boards.

States with Statutory Guidelines for Parole Decision
Federal System: Florida, and New York

States with Statewide Policies That Are Not Written into Statutes
Alaska, California (CYA), District of Columbia, Georgia, Maryland, Missouri, New Jersey, Oregon, Pennsylvania, Utah, and Washington

States Where Parole Guidelines Are Differently Applied
California (adults) and Minnesota

3-1f Good-Time Policies

Good-conduct time (i.e., good-time credit) has traditionally been used for inmates to reduce their time in custody. In most states, by law, good-conduct time applies only to an inmate's eligibility for parole or mandatory release. New York, in 1817, was the first state to pass a good-time statute. By 1916, every state had passed some kind of good-time statute. Most states provide for one day of credit for every two days of good time served. Many states have recently modified their good-time statutes. Generally, good-conduct time is awarded based on the law in effect when the crime was committed. Figure 3-2 shows the average time served, with time off for good behavior, for certain crimes. Some states now use programming time or earned time in lieu of good-time credit. The programming time or earned time allows administrators to consider matters other than time in awarding credit. For example, since January 1983, California eliminated automatic time off for good behavior. Prisoners sentenced after that date must earn all their good-time credit through work or school participation. The California approach has been criticized on the basis that it allows the prison guards and other prison personnel to become sentencers. This is based on the fact that the amount of time that a prisoner may earn in California is discretionary and has therefore enlarged the discretionary power of prison officials to affect the duration of confinement.

Good-time benefits, which have the effect of reducing prison sentence lengths, are given to inmates for institutional behavior that conforms to rules and regulations. Traditionally, good-conduct time is considered a privilege, not a right. Inmates must follow rules to get good-conduct time.

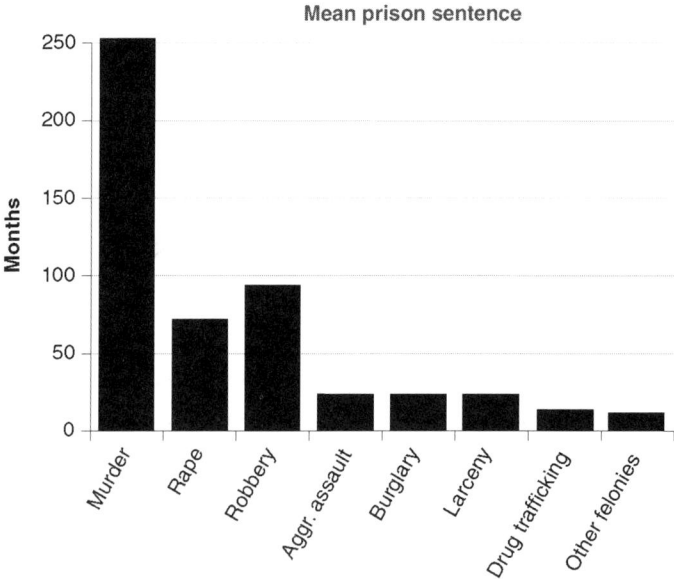

Figure 3-2
Average Time Served in Prison in 2001: Time Off for Good Behavior
Source: Bureau of Justice Statistics, *Prisoners in 2001*, July 2002.

Some or all of the good-conduct time awarded an inmate may be taken away for breaking rules. In some cases, previously forfeited good-conduct time may be restored to the inmate.

Texas has two principle good-time earning categories, state-approved trusty and line class, each having different time-earning levels with a specific number of days that can be earned for each month actually served. Besides behavior in prison, the amount of good time that can be earned is also affected by the circumstances of the inmate's offense as determined by the sentencing court and by the state laws relevant to good-conduct time that were in effect when the offense was committed. Likewise, good-time credit may apply to an offender's prison confinement in terms of eligibility for release to parole or mandatory supervision. For certain offenders serving sentences for assaultive offenses, good-conduct time is not used to calculate parole eligibility.

An article that appeared in the *Houston Chronicle,* on July 18, 1999, related that the Texas Department of Criminal Justice says that it is handling about 5000 cases from the state's 140,000 inmates at any given time. While some of them have legitimate concerns, they are not all valid lawsuits. Because most of these lawsuits involve civil rights, they end up in federal courts. Many steps have been taken to reduce the number of frivolous lawsuits. One of those steps involves an inmate who files a frivolous law suit can have his or her good-time credits toward early release wiped out.

A key purpose of good-time credit is to ensure conformity with prison rules and regulations. Moreover, it can be used as a direct incentive for compliant or even exemplary behavior. Even states that have "truth in sentencing laws" have not eliminated good-time credit all together. For example, Virginia now requires its inmates to serve 85 percent of their sentences. The other 15 percent of good-time credit was retained in order to encourage good behavior and compliance with rule and regulations. Good-time credit is an excellent prison management tool that assists in maintaining order behind bars.

3-1g Emergency Overcrowding Provisions

In some states, there are statutes that provide the governor with the authority to release prisoners prior to their normal release date in order to relieve crowded prison conditions. Some states allow parole boards to consider prison overcrowding conditions in determining the release date of certain classes of offenders, and offenders may be released earlier than normal to relieve crowded prison conditions. For example, in the early 1970s, Florida released thousands of prisoners early to make room for newly sentenced prisoners. Since the 1970 release, emergency overcrowding provisions have been used in other states, including Texas, New York, and Arizona, but not to the extent that it was used in the 1970s.

The sentencing judge should be guided by statutory statements of policy, the criteria in these rules, and the facts and circumstances of the case.

3-1h National Conference on Corrections

The National Conference on Corrections held in Williamsburg, Virginia, considered the problems and needs of judges in ascertaining appropriate sentences in criminal cases. The conference advocated eight points with regard to more appropriate sentencing:

1. It should be mandatory that trial judges have presentence reports in all felony cases. These reports should be prepared by qualified probation or corrections officers.
2. Diagnostic facilities should be made available to all judges. Diagnostic facilities generally provide the judges with psychological tests and counseling records.
3. Jury sentencing should be abolished.
4. Sentencing judges should be required to record the reasons for each sentence.

5. Sentencing judges should educate their communities on the philosophy of sentencing.
6. Defense counsels and prosecutors should be consulted before imposing the sentence.
7. Probation officers and judges should receive instructions in sentencing and perhaps attend sentencing courses.
8. Trial judges should be elected or appointed in as nonpolitical a way as possible.

3-1i Judicial Process for Misdemeanants

Misdemeanants are individuals convicted of minor crimes (misdemeanors). Their sentences are to jails for periods normally not to exceed one year, fines, community service, and/or attendance at some type of behavior-modification course. In studying corrections, we rarely consider the roles of our minor courts and their handling of misdemeanants. More citizens, however, get involved at this level than at the felony level. On any given day, it is estimated that approximately 500,000 individuals are confined in local jails. The lower courts of America are truly involved in an "assembly-line" type justice. The operation of jails, jail conditions, and jail problems are discussed in Chapter 7.

3-1j Judicial Process for Felons

In most states, sentences to prison or correctional institutions are decided by judges. Several states, such as Texas, allow the defendants to opt for jury sentencing. The incarceration of an individual in a state prison is a dramatic, but often overused sanction. The Model Penal Code addresses the problems involved in selecting the appropriate sentence. The code also provides that imprisonment should be used only when one of the following conditions exist:

1. There is undue risk that during the period of probation the defendant will commit another crime.
2. The defendant is in need of correctional treatment that can be provided most effectively by commitment to an institution.
3. A lesser sentence will depreciate the seriousness of the defendant's crime.

3-1k Presentence Investigations

In most states, a presentence investigation (PSI) report is mandatory for felony convictions. The presentence investigation report is an important document for trial judges in making their sentence determinations. In most cases, the PSI is prepared by the court's probation office. In some states, such as California, there are private companies that also prepare alternative PSIs for the judges to consider. The alternative PSIs are commissioned and paid for by the defense. Accordingly, they are generally used only in cases where the defendant or defendant's family can afford their costs.

A PSI generally includes the following items:

- A fact sheet showing the defendant's name and other identifying data; case number; the crime for which the defendant was convicted; the date of commission of the crime; the date defendant was convicted; the defendant's present custody status; and the terms of any agreement upon which a plea of guilty was based.
- The facts and circumstances of the crime and the defendant's arrest, including information concerning any codefendants and the status or disposition of their cases. The source of the information contained in this section should be stated in the report.
- A summary of the defendant's record of prior criminal conduct, including convictions as an adult and sustained petitions in juvenile delinquency proceedings. Records of an arrest or charge not leading to a conviction generally are not included.
- Any statement made by the defendant to the probation officer, or a summary thereof, including the defendant's account of the circumstances of the crime.
- Information concerning the victim of the crime, including the victim's statement or a summary thereof, the amount of the victim's loss, whether or not it is covered by insurance, and any information required by law.
- Any relevant facts concerning the defendant's social history, including family, education, employment, income, military status, medical/psychological history, record of substance abuse or lack thereof, and any other relevant information.
- Collateral information, including written statements from official sources, such as police officers, defense counsels, probation and parole officers, and interested persons, such as family members.
- An evaluation of factors relating to the sentence, including a reasoned discussion of the defendant's suitability and eligibility for probation. If probation is recommended, a proposed probation plan. If prison is recommended, a reasoned discussion of the aggravating and mitigating factors affecting the sentence length. In addition, a discussion of the defendant's ability to make restitution, pay any fine or penalty that may be imposed to satisfy any special conditions of probation.

- The probation officer's recommendation, including the length of any prison term that may be imposed, including the base term. In the case of multiple offenses, the recommendation shall also include whether the terms for each offense will be concurrent or consecutive.
- Detailed information on presentence time spent by the defendant in custody, including the beginning and ending dates of the period(s) of custody; the existence of any other sentences imposed on the defendant; the amount of good behavior, or work, or participation credit to which the defendant is entitled and whether a hearing has been requested regarding the denying of good behavior, work, or participation credit.
- A statement regarding mandatory and recommended restitution, restitution fines, other fines, and costs to be assessed against the defendant.

The source of all information is listed in the report. Any person who furnished information shall be identified by name or official capacity unless a reason is given for not disclosing the person's identity.

Box 3-4

Duty to Provide Corrected Presentence Report

In *State v. Utah*[13], Stephen Thomas Utah pleaded guilty to one count of forgery. At the sentencing hearing, Mr. Utah moved for the presentence report to be thrown out because it contained inaccuracies concerning his prior criminal record.

The district court refused to order a new presentence report. The court stated that it would not consider the disputed items in the report. Mr. Utah appealed. He contended that the district court was required to provide the Department of Corrections with an accurate presentence report. The state high court disagreed. The appellate court held that the presentence report is used primarily to aid the district court in sentencing. The court stated that any use by the Department of Corrections is secondary and not grounds for reversal of the sentence.

3-1 | Suspended Sentences

There are two types of suspended sentences, suspension of imposition of sentence and suspension of execution of sentence. In cases involving suspension of imposition of sentence, there is a judgment of guilt, but no sanction is imposed. For example, the defendant is found guilty, but imposition of sentence is suspended for a period of three years due to the offender having a clean record. In a case involving the suspension of execution of sentence, there is a judgment and a sentence pronounced, but the execution is suspended. If, within the time frame of the suspension, the defendant remains a noncriminal, the suspension expires along with the court's ability to impose a sanction for the attributable crime(s). If the defendant is rearrested within the suspension time frame, then the court can immediately impose the sentence for the suspended crime.

3-2 Alternative Sentencing and Diversion

Alternative sentencing involves the use of nontraditional programs in lieu of fines and custody. One of the most popular alternative sentencing procedures is the use of deferred adjudication. **Deferred adjudication** is a form of probation that is used without a finding of guilt. In deferred adjudication, the defendant pleads guilty and agrees to defer further proceeding. The defendant is then placed on probation or directed to attend counseling, behavior modification courses, and so on. After the defendant has successfully completed the requirements, the guilty or nolo contendere plea is withdrawn and the case is dismissed. When the charges are dismissed, the defendant does not have a criminal conviction for this misconduct. If the defendant fails to comply with the requirements, then the court sentences the defendant based on his or her original plea.

Pretrial diversion is a form of probation that is granted prior to trial. Under this process, the defendant agrees to waive time and to complete a program or process. Pretrial diversion is used primarily for offenders who need treatment or supervision and for whom criminal sanctions would be excessive. Like deferred adjudication, there is no finding of guilty and thus no conviction if the program is successfully completed. If the program is not successfully completed, the defendant is then brought to trial on the charges. One of the popular criticisms of pretrial diversion is based on research that indicates that many people are diverted that would not have been prosecuted because of the lack of evidence against them. Accordingly, if this is correct, such action increases the number of persons involved in the criminal justice system.

3-3 Judicial Process for Juveniles

3-3a Juvenile Court Procedures

In this section, juvenile court procedures and hearing requirements are examined. In addition, the rules required when a juvenile is taken into custody are covered. Generally, the commencement of proceedings in the juvenile court to declare a minor a ward of the court is by a verified petition (signed under oath) and contains the following:

(a) The name of the court to which it is addressed.
(b) The title of the proceeding.
(c) The code section and subdivision under which the proceedings are instituted. Any petition alleging that the minor has committed a crime shall state for each count whether the crime charged is a felony or a misdemeanor.
(d) The name, age, and address, if any, of the minor upon whose behalf the petition is brought.
(e) The names and residence addresses, if known to petitioner, of both of the parents and any guardian of the minor. If there is no parent or guardian residing within the state, or if his or her place of residence is not known to petitioner, the petition shall also contain the name and residence address, if known, of any adult relative residing within the county, or, if there are none, the adult relative residing nearest to the location of the court.
(f) A concise statement of facts, separately stated, to support the conclusion that the minor upon whose behalf the petition is being brought is a person within the definition of each of the sections and subdivisions under which the proceedings are being instituted.
(g) The fact that the minor upon whose behalf the petition is brought is detained in custody or is not detained in custody, and if he or she is detained in custody, the date and the precise time the minor was taken into custody.
(h) A notice to the father, mother, spouse, or other person liable for support of the minor child, that:
  (1) State law may make that person, the estate of that person, and the estate of the minor child, liable for the cost of the care, support, and maintenance of the minor child in any county institution or any other place in which the child is placed, detained, or committed pursuant to an order of the juvenile court;

(2) That the person, the estate of that person, and the estate of the minor child, may be liable for the cost to the county of legal services rendered to the minor by a private attorney or a public defender appointed pursuant to the order of the juvenile court;
(3) State law may make that person, the estate of that person, and the estate of the minor child, liable for the cost to the county of the probation supervision of the minor child by the probation officer pursuant to the order of the juvenile court; and
(4) That the above liabilities are joint and several (the costs or expenses may be added together).

(i) If a proceeding is pending against a minor child for a violation of the Penal Code, the parents or legal guardians of the minor will be notified that if the minor is found to have violated either or both of the following provisions that:
(1) Any community service that may be required of the minor may be performed in the presence, and under the direct supervision, of the parent or legal guardian pursuant to either or both of these provisions; and
(2) If the minor is personally unable to pay any fine levied for the violation of either or both of these provisions, then the parent or legal guardian of the minor shall be liable for payment of the fine pursuant to those sections. If the minor is ordered to make restitution to the victim, the parent or guardian will be notified that they may be liable for the payment of restitution.

3-3b Detention Hearings

Whenever a minor is taken into custody by a peace officer or probation officer, except when such minor willfully misrepresents himself as 18 or more years of age, such minor shall be released within 48 hours after having been taken into custody, excluding nonjudicial days, unless within said period of time a petition to declare him a dependent child or a ward of the court has been filed.

A proceeding in the juvenile court to declare a minor a dependent child of the court is commenced by the filing with the court, by the probation officer, of a petition. Petitions to declare minors wards of the court and criminal complaints are generally filed by the prosecutor, county attorney, or district attorney.

In many states, whenever a minor, who has been held in custody for more than six hours by the probation officer, is subsequently released and no petition is filed, the probation officer must prepare a written explanation of why the minor was held in custody for more than six hours. The written explanation is generally required to be prepared within 72 hours after the minor is released from custody and filed in the record of the case. A copy of the written explanation is also sent to the parents, guardian, or other person having care or custody of the minor.

If a minor has been taken into custody and not released to a parent or guardian, the juvenile court shall hold a hearing (which shall be referred to as a "detention hearing") to determine whether the minor shall be further detained. This hearing shall be held as soon as possible, but in any event before the expiration of the next judicial day after a petition to declare the minor a dependent child or ward of the court has been filed. If the hearing is not held within the period prescribed, the minor is required to be released from custody.

If a probation officer or prosecutor determines that a minor shall be retained in custody, he or she shall immediately file a petition pursuant with the clerk of the juvenile court, who shall set the matter for hearing on the detention hearing calendar. The probation officer or prosecutor shall then notify each parent or each guardian of the minor of the time and place of the hearing if the whereabouts of each parent or guardian can be ascertained by due diligence. Each person will be served with a copy of the petition and notified of the time and place of the detention hearing. In some cases, this notice may be given orally and shall be given in this manner if it appears that the parent does not read.

Upon his or her appearance before the court at the detention hearing, each parent or guardian and the minor, if present, shall first be informed of the reasons why the minor was taken into custody, the nature of the juvenile court proceedings, and the right of each parent or guardian and any minor to be represented at every stage of the proceedings by counsel.

In the hearing, the minor, parents, or guardians have a privilege against self-incrimination and have a right to confrontation by, and cross-examination of, any person examined by the court. Upon reasonable notification by counsel representing the minor and the parents or guardians, the clerk of the court shall notify such counsel of the hearings.

3-3c Citation

If an officer takes a minor into temporary custody for a criminal offense and determines that the minor should be brought to the attention of the juvenile court, he or she may release the minor after preparing a written notice to appear before the probation officer. The notice shall also contain a concise statement of the reasons the minor was taken into custody. The officer shall deliver one copy of the notice to the minor or to a parent, guardian, or responsible relative of the minor and may require the minor or his or her parent, guardian, or relative, or both, to sign a written promise that either or both will appear at the time and place designated in the notice. Upon the execution of the promise to appear, the officer may release the minor. The officer then files one copy of the notice with the probation officer.

In determining whether to hold in custody or to release the minor with a citation (written promise to appear), the officer should use the alternative that least restricts the minor's freedom of movement, provided that alternative is compatible with the best interests of the minor and the community.

3-3d Venue

Venue refers to the geographic location of the court in which the proceedings will be conducted. Under the U.S. Constitution, the accused in an adult criminal trial has the right to be tried in the county and judicial district where the crime occurred. In juvenile cases, most state statutes provide that in any proceedings involving a juvenile, the proceedings will be held in the county in which the juvenile resides. If the proceedings begin in a different county, the proceedings at the request of the juvenile may be transferred to the county of residence. If a juvenile changes residence during the proceedings, the court may transfer the proceedings to the county of the new residence of the juvenile. For most purposes, a juvenile is considered to reside in the county in which his or her parents or guardian reside.

3-3e Intake

The **intake** phase of the juvenile justice case has several purposes. It is used to screen cases in determining whether the juvenile needs the help of the court and to help control the use of detention. It also is used to screen cases in an effort to reduce the courts' caseload. Unlike dependency cases, intake has different functions in different states. In general, intake officers exercise a great deal of discretion during this phrase of the proceedings.

One of the first decisions that must be made during intake is whether the case comes under juvenile court jurisdiction. Next, the decision must be made on whether to assume jurisdiction, dismiss the case, or refer the youth to another agency. During this phase, the court may also use informal methods to handle the case, such as informal probation. If the youth is in detention and the case is not dismissed or referred, the decision must also be made as to whether the detention should continue until the adjudicatory hearing is held.

During this phase of the case, an intake officer generally reviews the case and makes the preliminary decisions noted above. Generally, the intake officer's recommendations are followed by the judge. In many states, the intake officer's duties are performed by a probation officer. The intake officer will normally recommend dismissal or informal probation for first-time offenders and for minor offenses unless the youth has committed a serious crime.

Under **informal probation,** the youth is released if he or she agrees to accept certain conditions that are spelled out by the court. Normally, the conditions are that if the youth stays out of trouble for a specified period of time, then the case is dismissed. If the youth violates the terms of the agreement or gets involved in other delinquent acts, the court may recall the case and hold the youth for further adjudication.

Consent decrees are also used in delinquency cases. These decrees are court orders that are agreed to by the youth and accepted by the court. A consent decree removes the need for an adjudicatory hearing. It is similar to a plea bargain in adult criminal court.

3-3f Adjudicatory Hearings

After the intake proceedings, the **adjudicatory hearing** is used in those cases not dismissed, referred to other agencies, or subject to consent degrees. The adjudicatory hearing is equivalent to a trial in adult court. While the adjudicatory hearings are less formal that adult trials, as will be discussed in the next chapter, the juvenile has certain due-process rights that must be provided to him or her during this hearing.

Unlike adult trials, the trials are closed to the public and in most states there are no rights to a jury trial. Procedural rights contained in the rules of evidence are required in the adjudicatory hearings and the question as to whether the juvenile committed the crime in question must be established beyond a reasonable doubt.

The order of proceedings during the adjudicatory hearing is generally similar to that of adult criminal cases. The prosecutor leads the presentation of the case, followed by the defense, and then any rebuttal by the prosecutor.

3-3g Disposition Hearings

The **disposition hearing** is similar to the sentencing phase of an adult criminal trial. In most states, after the court determines that the juvenile has committed the offense, the judge sets a date for the disposition hearing. At the disposition hearing, the rules of evidence are relaxed and the judge is permitted to receive a wide range of evidence regarding the youth. In most states, the probation officer is required to present a pre-disposition report to the court. This report generally contains a written description of the incident, the youth's prior conduct record, information on the youth's family, employment record of the youth, if any, and any other information that may assist the judge in making a disposition decision.

3-3h Uniform Juvenile Court Act

The provisions of the Uniform Juvenile Court Act's waiver of jurisdiction and discretionary transfer to adult criminal court provisions are set forth in this section. In addition, at the end of the section are several key court decisions regarding these transfer procedures.

Box 3-5

Indiana Juvenile Statutes (Indiana Juvenile Statutes, 31-6-4-13) Sec. 13.

- **(a)** This section applies only to a child alleged to be a delinquent child.
- **(b)** The juvenile court shall hold an initial hearing on each petition.
- **(c)** The juvenile court shall first determine whether counsel has been waived . . . or whether counsel should be appointed . . .
- **(d)** The court shall next determine whether the prosecutor intends to seek a waiver of jurisdiction [for purposes of referral to adult criminal court]. . . . If waiver is sought, the court may not accept an admission or denial of the allegations from the child . . . and shall schedule a waiver hearing and advise the child.
- **(e)** The juvenile court shall inform the child and his parents, guardians, or custodian, if that person is present, of:
  - (1) the nature of the allegations against the child;
  - (2) the child's right to:
    - (A) be represented by counsel;
    - (B) have a speedy trial;
    - (C) confront witnesses against him;
    - (D) cross-examine witnesses against him;
    - (E) obtain witnesses or tangible evidence by compulsory process;
    - (F) introduce evidence on his own behalf;

continues

Box 3-5 (continued)

      (G) refrain from testifying against himself; and
      (H) have the state prove that he committed the delinquent act charged beyond a reasonable doubt.
(f) If the child admits the allegations of the petition, the juvenile court shall enter judgment accordingly and schedule a dispositional hearing.

[Subparagraphs (e)(3) and (4), (f), (g), and (I) are omitted.]

Box 3-6

Waiver of Jurisdiction and Discretionary Transfer to Criminal Court

(a) The juvenile court may waive its exclusive original jurisdiction and transfer a child to the appropriate district court or criminal district court for criminal proceedings if:
    (1) the child is alleged to have violated a penal law of the grade of felony;
    (2) the child was 15 years of age or older at the time he is alleged to have committed the offense, and no adjudication hearing has been conducted concerning that offense; and
    (3) after full investigation and hearing the juvenile court determines that there is probable cause to believe the child before the court committed the offense alleged and that, because of the seriousness of the offense or the background of the child, the welfare of the community requires criminal proceedings.
(b) The petition and notice requirements of this code must be satisfied, and the summons must state that the hearing is for the purpose of considering discretionary transfer to criminal court.
(c) The juvenile court shall conduct a hearing without a jury to consider transfer of the child for criminal proceedings.
(d) Prior to the hearing, the juvenile court shall order and obtain a complete diagnostic study, social evaluation, and full investigation of the child, his circumstances, and the circumstances of the alleged offense.

(e) At the transfer hearing, the court may consider written reports from probation officers, professional court employees, or professional consultants in addition to the testimony of witnesses. At least one day prior to the transfer hearing, the court shall provide the attorney for the child with access to all written matter to be considered by the court in making the transfer decision. The court may order counsel not to reveal items to the child or his parent, guardian, or guardian ad litem if such disclosure would materially harm the treatment and rehabilitation of the child or would substantially decrease the likelihood of receiving information from the same or similar sources in the future.

(f) In making the determination required by Subsection (a) of this section, the court shall consider, among other matters:
  (1) whether the alleged offense was against person or property, with greater weight in favor of transfer given to offenses against people;
  (2) whether the alleged offense was committed in an aggressive and premeditated manner;
  (3) whether there is evidence on which a grand jury may be expected to return an indictment;
  (4) the sophistication and maturity of the child;
  (5) the record and previous history of the child; and
  (6) the prospects of adequate protection of the public and the likelihood of the rehabilitation of the child by use of procedures, services, and facilities currently available to the juvenile court.

(g) If the juvenile court retains jurisdiction, the child is not subject to criminal prosecution at any time for any offense alleged in the petition, or for any offense within the knowledge of the juvenile court judge as evidenced by anything in the record of the proceedings.

(h) If the juvenile court waives jurisdiction, it shall state specifically in the order its reasons for waiver and certify its action, including the written order and findings of the court, and shall transfer the child to the appropriate court for criminal proceedings. On transfer of the child for criminal proceedings, he shall be dealt with as an adult and in accordance with the Code of Criminal Procedure. The transfer of custody is an arrest. The court to which the child is transferred shall determine if good cause exists for an examining trial. If there is no good cause for an examining trial, the court shall refer the case to the grand jury. If there is good cause for an examining trial, the court shall conduct an examining trial and may remand the child to the jurisdiction of the juvenile court.

(i) If the child's case is brought to the attention of the grand jury and the grand jury does not indict for the offense charged in the complaint forwarded by the juvenile court, the district court or criminal district court shall certify the grand jury's failure to indict to the juvenile court. On receipt of the certification, the juvenile court may resume jurisdiction of the case.

continues

Box 3-6 (continued)

(j) The juvenile court may waive its exclusive original jurisdiction and transfer a person to the appropriate district court or criminal district court for criminal proceedings if:
   (1) the person is 18 years of age or older;
   (2) the person was 15 years of age or older, and under 17 years of age at the time he is alleged to have committed a felony;
   (3) no adjudication concerning the alleged offense has been made or no adjudication hearing concerning the offense has been conducted;
   (4) the juvenile court finds from a preponderance of the evidence that after due diligence of the state, it was not practical to proceed in juvenile court before the 18th birthday of the person because:
      (A) the state did not have probable cause to proceed in juvenile court and new evidence has been found since the eighteenth birthday of the person; or
      (B) the person could not be found; and
   (5) the juvenile court determines that there is probable cause to believe that the child before the court committed the alleged offense.
(k) The petition and notice requirements of this code must be satisfied, and the summons must state that the hearing is for the purpose of considering waiver of jurisdiction under Subsection (j) of this section.
(l) The juvenile court shall conduct a hearing without a jury to consider waiver of jurisdiction under Subsection (j) of this section.[14]

Summary

Before the correctional process may be involved, the defendant must be convicted of a crime by a court with proper jurisdiction. Sentencing is the formal process by which the courts deal with defendants convicted of crimes. A sentence is an authorized judicial decision that places some degree of penalty on a guilty person. The responsibility for deciding the appropriate sentence is generally delegated to the judges. Sentencing involves selecting the appropriate sentence from an array of choices, including incarceration, fine, forfeiture, probation, and alternative corrective programs. Once the sentencing decision is made, the responsibility for administrating the decision is placed with the departments of corrections.

Concerns regarding disparate sentences and abuses or perceived abuses in sentencing have resulted in six common strategies used by legislatures to maintain control over the sentencing process and reduce the discretion of the judiciary and correctional administrators.

A determinate sentence is a "flat-time" sentence with a fixed period of confinement imposed by the judge of the sentencing court. The defendant is given a finite sentence, and once good-time credit calculations are made, the defendant knows his or her expected release date. The increased use of flat-time sentencing is seen by many as a way to eliminate parole.

A form of determinate sentencing now being used by the federal government and many states is the presumptive sentence that is suggested by the legislative body based on certain factors regarding the crime and the criminal. The indeterminate sentence is based on the concept that the sentence should be tailored to the correctional needs of the defendant. Generally, indeterminate sentences allow the judge a greater degree of flexibility, which includes a pronouncement by the judge as to the maximum and minimum terms of confinement. In determining the appropriate sentence in most states, the judge must follow required guidelines and statutory restrictions. To assist judges in determining the appropriate sentences, most states require that a presentence investigation (PSI) report be prepared and submitted to the court. The PSI report is mandatory for felony convictions and is an important document for trial judges in making their sentence determinations. In most cases, the PSI is prepared by the court's probation office.

Truth in sentencing laws refer to the requirement that offenders must serve a substantial amount of their sentence. "Three strikes and you're out" laws require judges to sentence offenders with three felony convictions to long prison terms, sometimes to life without the possibility of parole. Many states are joining the growing movement to get tough on crime. Truth in sentencing and three strikes laws are two attempts to keep serious offenders in prison and increase public safety. Research is mixed on the effectiveness of truth in sentencing and three strikes laws in reducing crime.

Good-conduct time (good-time credit) has traditionally been used by inmates to reduce their time in custody. In most states, by law, good-conduct time applies only to an inmate's eligibility for parole or mandatory release. In most states, good-time credit is awarded based on an inmate's conduct, obedience to rules, willingness to work, and work or school record. Traditionally, good-conduct time is considered a privilege, not a right. Inmates must follow rules to get good-conduct time. Some or all of the good-conduct time awarded an inmate may be taken away for breaking rules. In some cases, previously forfeited good-conduct time may be restored to the inmate. In some states there are statutes that provide the governor with the authority to release prisoners prior to their normal release date in order to relieve crowded prison conditions.

The federal sentencing guidelines were enacted in 1984 and have governed federal sentencing decisions since 1989. The guidelines, which were promulgated by the Sentencing Commission, created 43 offense levels with each level reflecting increased severity of crime. In addition, offenders were divided into six categories based on their criminal history.

There are two types of suspended sentences, suspension of imposition of sentence and suspension of execution of sentence. Alternative sentencing involves the use of non-traditional programs in lieu of fines and custody. One of the most popular alternative sentencing procedures is the use of deferred adjudication where the defendant is placed on probation or directed to attend counseling, behavior modification courses, or similar incarceration options. After the defendant has successfully completed these requirements, the guilty or nolo contendere plea is withdrawn, and the case is dismissed. When the charges are dismissed, the defendant does not have a criminal conviction for this misconduct.

Parole guidelines are procedures designed to limit or structure parole release decisions, based on measurable offender criteria. In some states, the parole board has great latitude in making the parole release decisions. In other states, the parole guidelines are closely prescribed and provide only limited discretion to the parole boards.

Generally, a petition for the commencement of proceedings in the juvenile court to declare a minor a ward of the court is by a verified petition (signed under oath). The intake phase of the juvenile justice case has several purposes: it is used to screen cases in determining whether the juvenile needs the help of the court and to help control the use of detention; it is also used to screen out cases in an effort to reduce the court's caseload. Unlike dependency cases, intake has different functions in different states. In general, intake personnel exercise a great deal of discretion during this phase of the proceedings. After the intake proceedings, the adjudicatory hearing is used in those cases not dismissed, referred to other agencies, or subject to consent decrees. While the adjudicatory hearings are less formal than adult trials, the juvenile has certain due process rights that must be provided during this hearing. Unlike adult trials, the trials are closed to the public, and, in most states, there are no rights to a jury trial.

Discussion Questions

1. Explain the various restraints imposed on a judge's sentencing discretion.
2. Discuss the problems confronting a judge in determining the appropriate sentence to impose in a criminal case.
3. Explain the purposes of the presentence report.
4. Compare and contrast the different types of suspended sentences.
5. Describe the diversion process.
6. Explain the trial process in juvenile court.

Chapter Quiz

True/False
1. In the past, judicial decisions were made with few statutory guidelines except for the stated maximum sentence that may be imposed on the conviction of an offense.
2. Good-time guidelines are regulations that allow early release of prisoners based on systematic provisions to relieve overcrowding.
3. An indeterminate sentence is based on the concept that the sentence should be tailored to the needs of the defendant.
4. To assist judges in determining appropriate sentencing, most states require a presentence report.
5. Good-time credit has traditionally been used by inmates to reduce their time in custody.

Multiple Choice
1. Which one of the following is NOT one of the eight points the National Conference on Corrections advocated with regard to more appropriate sentencing?
   a. Jury sentencing should be abolished.
   b. Defense counsels should educate their communities on the philosophies of sentencing.
   c. Diagnostic facilities should be made available to all judges.
   d. Judges should not be influenced by favorable presentence reports.
2. Nontraditional programs in lieu of fines and custody are referred to as
   a. alternative sentencing.
   b. incapacitation.
   c. parole.
   d. community corrections.
3. This sentencing philosophy is based on the concept that the sentence should be tailored to the needs of the defendant. This sentence may preclude the announcement by the judge as to the maximum and minimum terms of confinement.
   a. determinate
   b. indeterminate
   c. truth in sentencing
   d. sentencing guidelines
4. A form of probation that is granted before a trial where the defendant agrees to waive his/her time and complete a program or process is called
   a. probation.
   b. parole.
   c. pretrial diversion.
   d. alternative sentencing.

5. A judge imposes a sentence of 15 years to life on a defendant. This exemplifies which type of sentencing philosophy?
   a. determinate
   b. indeterminate
   c. mandatory
   d. alternative

Endnotes

1. Richard W. Snarr, *Corrections* (Madison, WI: Brown & Benchmark, 1996).
2. Elaine Wolf, and Marsha Weissman, "Revising Federal Sentencing Policy: Some Consequences of Expanding Eligibility for Alternative Sanctions," *Crime and Delinqueny* 42 (2 April, 1996): 192–197.
3. United States Sentencing Commission. *Guidelines Manual* (November 1995).
4. M. G. Turner, B. K. Sundt, and B. K. Applegate. "Three Strikes and You're Out Legislation: A National Assessment," *Federal Probation* (September 1995): 16–18.
5. Michael Vitiello, "Three Strikes: Can We Return to Rationality?" *Journal of Criminal Law and Criminology*, 87: 395–463.
6. Elisa Chen, *Impacts of Three Srikes and Truth in Sentencing on the Volume and Composition of Correctional Populations* (Washington, DC: National Institute of Justice, 2000).
7. Ibid.
8. Andy Furillo. "The Future: Three Strikes Hinges on Issue of Deterrence," *The Sacramento Bee*, 1 April 1996.
9. Ibid.
10. Ibid.
11. *State of Kansas v. Gloria L. Van Winkle*, 254 Kan. 214; 864 P.2d729; 1993Kan. See also, "Her Conviction Was for Having Cocaine," *Kansas City Star*, 7 June 1999.
12. *Michael Wayne Riggs v. California*, 525 U.S. 1114; 119S. Ct. 890; 142 L. Ed. 2d 789; 1999 U.S. Lexis 743.
13. Decided by the Supreme Court of Iowa, No. 348/95-107, Dec. 20, 1995.
14. For juvenile procedures described in this section, the rules adopted in the state of California were used. While most states are generally the same, there are some minor variations.

Chapter 4

The Correctional Client

Mark C. Ide

Key Terms

career criminals
prisonization
professional criminals
UNICOR
white-collar criminals

Outline

4-1 Prisonization
4-2 The Career Criminal
4-3 Prison Violence
4-4 The Young Criminal
4-5 The Professional Criminal
4-6 The Drug Criminal
4-7 The Elderly Criminal
4-8 The Female Criminal
4-9 Gender Bias
4-10 Noncitizen Offenders
4-11 The Federal Inmate
Article—Golden Years Behind Bars: Special Programs and Facilities for Elderly Inmates
Summary
Discussion Questions
Chapter Quiz
Endnotes

Learning Objectives

After studying this chapter, the reader will be able to:

- Describe the concept of prisonization.
- Analyze the research on violent criminals.
- Explain the problem involved in confining elderly criminals.
- Explain the problems caused by the increase in female prisoners.
- Analyze the gender-based problems in the corrections field.
- Identify the issues involved with non-citizen prisoners.
- List the types of prisoners serving time in federal prisons.
- Diagram the organizational structure of the federal prison system.

This chapter examines the various types of individuals who are incarcerated. One of the characteristics of prison populations that should concern us is the increasing absolute numbers and the increases per 100,000 in the rate of incarceration. Included within the prison population are various groups of individuals who need special care and treatment.

4-1 Prisonization

Prisonization is the process by which prisoners learn the rules of socialization into the prison culture. Many see it as a criminalization process, whereby a novice criminal is transformed from a prosocial errant to a committed predatory criminal. During the prisonization process, the prisoner learns to exist in the prison community and its depersonalized and routinized life. During this process, the prisoner accepts that his name is replaced by a number, that the warden is all powerful, prison slang, and the other tricks of seasoned prisoners.

4-2 The Career Criminal

The term **career criminals** identifies those persons who make or attempt to make a living committing crime.[1] Generally, career criminals are property offenders. Most often they begin their criminal careers early in their juvenile years. Most of them view crime as a safe and enjoyable way to obtain a good life. They expect to return to a life of crime after they are released from confinement. The average career criminal is normally in and out of prison or jail all of his or her life. Most career criminals live, however, at or below the poverty level when not confined in prison.

The Rand Corporation conducted several studies on habitual offenders. The first study involved 49 prisoners in California institutions. The second study involved 624 prisoners from five California prisons. The individuals selected in both studies represented all male prisoners in terms of custody level, age, offense, and race. The studies focused on criminal activities of the prisoners during the three-year period prior to their current incarceration. A third study with a larger sample of prisoners from the states of Texas, California, and Michigan was also conducted.[2]

The first Rand study concluded that most career offenders are not specialized in their criminal activity. They engage in a variety of criminal activities. Most commit crimes at a fairly low rate and the rate of violent crime was low among these inmates. The other two studies tended to confirm these findings. The Rand investigators also concluded that many of the criminals had the self-concept that they could beat the odds, that they were better than the average criminal, that crime was exciting, and that regular work was boring. Most of the individuals involved had started their criminal careers at a young age, usually before age 16. Most were unmarried with few family obligations. Most had been employed only irregularly and for short times.

4-3 Prison Violence

Prison violence has increased dramatically in recent years.[3] Rapes, beatings, and killings have become common in many prisons. Given the nature of the prison environment, it is not a surprise that violence among inmates exists in our nation's prisons. Prison violence places prison administrators in a perplexing position as to what steps to take to ensure that prison violence is at least kept to a minimum. Likewise, the Supreme Court has ruled that under the Eighth Amendment, prison officials have a duty to protect inmates from violence at the hands of other inmates.

Researchers have attempted to identify the factors that restrain or encourage inmate aggression. Most of the studies on prison violence deal with characteristics of inmates rather than institutions. The situations in prisons, such as crowding, visiting patterns, involvement in prison programs, and stringency of rule enforcement, have indicated that an association exists between prison conditions and prison violence.

Researchers in California examined situational factors as predictors of types of individual aggressive incidents in a medium-security state prison in California. These researchers found that violent incidents comprised just over 50 percent of all infractions. A total of 82 involved aggressive behavior toward staff; 128 toward another inmate; 53 toward oneself; and 153 toward property. Support emerged for the position that background or personality factors, when used without situational factors, may not provide a complete understanding of prison violence. Violence toward staff was more likely to occur in areas in which inmates were active, but not in a highly structured situation; inmates were more likely to be alone during such incidents. Violence toward other inmates tended to occur anywhere prisoners were allowed to congregate. Violence toward self and property was less likely to occur anywhere outside of the cell or dorm area.[4]

Some researchers have examined the link between gender and prison violence. This research has revealed that women are much less likely to commit more serious kinds of misconduct than men while in prison.[5]

Research has also explored links between various forms of psychopathology and prison violence. In one study, data were drawn from a survey of mental disability among inmates housed in 53 correctional facilities in New York. Among the measures of psychiatric impairment, confusion and depression were most related to violent behavior. Being young increased the probability of violence toward other inmates and staff. Those inmates who were never married were more likely to be violent, but only toward property. This study concluded that the lack of a relationship between violent criminal history and prison violence suggests that there is more involved in the latter than the aggregation of violence-prone individuals.[6]

Many believe the most violent criminals, such as those serving a prison sentence for murder, are the most violent inmates in prison. However, research has proved and most correctional administrators and inmates agree that murderers are generally among the most docile, trustworthy, and nonviolent inmates.[7] This is also the case when assaultive behavior and rule infractions among inmates serving time for murder are examined. Studies reveal that capital murderers have very low incidents of assaultive behavior and rule infractions while in prison.[8]

Unfortunately, given the nature of the typical inmate population, violence in prison will always exist. For some time researchers have attempted to explain factors that cultivate prison violence. It is now clear that there are many significant factors explain inmate violence. These factors take into account not only individual characteristics but also situational factors. Despite the pervasive nature of inmate violence, prison administrators will continually have to monitor and attempt to minimize the many violence-inducing factors that are prevalent in the prison system. Furthermore, prison administrators have an important responsibility to ensure that prison staff maintain a level of control and provide inmates with an environment free of threat or occurrence of violence.

4-4 The Young Criminal

Under current law, prison authorities must keep juveniles out of the "sight and sound" of adult inmates. The definition of juvenile varies by age according to states' definitions. In addition, they must keep juveniles convicted of crimes in the usual sense (e.g., burglary, carjackings, etc.) in different institutions from those that detain youths charged with status offenses, such as truancy, which is the failure to go to school, and incorrigibility. These federal mandates were enacted in 1974 by President Ford. They are administered by the Office of Juvenile Justice and Delinquency Prevention, which is a Justice Department agency that also sponsors research on ways to fight juvenile crime. Each year, however, bills are introduced in the U.S. Congress to remove or eliminate these requirements.

As of July 1996, 40 states were in full compliance with the above mandates. States that are not in compliance are ineligible to receive certain federal grants. In all but one state, Wyoming, status offenders are kept separate from more serious juvenile offenders.

The first efforts to remove juveniles from adult prisons and jails began in 1825 with the founding of the New York House of Refuge, in Manhattan. The refuge was founded by a group of reformers who were appalled by the conditions that young prisoners were enduring in the prisons. According to one reformer, John Pintard, the conditions were designed to make "little devils into great ones and at the expiration of their terms turn out accomplished villains." Later efforts lead to the establishment of juvenile reformatories, followed by the creation of separate courts for juveniles. We still follow these models today.

Box 4-1

Hamparian's Research on the Violent Criminal

Donna Martin Hamparian studied 1,222 people born between 1956 and 1960. Her major findings are listed below:

- A relatively small number of violent juvenile offenders are responsible for most arrests for violent offenses.
- Violent juvenile offenders, as a group, do not specialize in the types of crimes they commit.
- Most violent juvenile offenders are repeat offenders.
- Most violent juvenile crimes do not involve the use of weapons.
- The frequency of arrests declines with age.
- Most adult crimes committed by juveniles are not violent crimes.
- Four out of ten adult offenders were arrested for at least one violent crime.
- Most violent juvenile offenders make the transition to adult offenders.
- Relatively few chronic offenders are responsible for a disproportional number of crimes.
- Incarceration does not slow the rate of arrest, in fact, the subsequent rate of arrest increases after each incarceration.

4-5 The Professional Criminal

Professional criminals or **white-collar criminals** are people of respectability and high social status who commit crime in the course of their occupations.[9] Examples of white-collar crimes include embezzlement by bankers, overcharging by doctors in billing under Medicare programs, and price-fixing in government contracts. It is estimated that white-collar crimes cost our society about $100 billion a year. Many white-collar criminals have extensive financial resources to employ when combating law enforcement efforts to control their activities.

4-6 The Drug Criminal

Drugs have increasingly become a focal point of crime in U.S. Society. Throughout the 1980s and 1990s, we have seen criminal justice policy declare war on drugs. In fighting the war on drugs, the nation's jails and prisons have become overcrowded, forcing politicians to declare emergency situations in many jails and prisons. At the same time, the war on drugs has cost literally billions of dollars and has focused on the poor and minority communities. In light of the epidemic proportions of drug offenders in our nation's jails and prisons, a brief discussion of the drug criminal is in order.

The number of drug arrests for drug abuse violations increased from 1999 to 2000 for both juveniles and adults. In 1999 there were 251,200 inmates in state or federal prison for drug crimes.[10] During 1999, U.S. attorneys evaluated 38,288 persons for prosecution based on referrals by federal law enforcement agencies and drug offense suspects. Thirty-one percent of these suspects were involved with marijuana; 28 percent with cocaine powder; 15 percent with crack cocaine; 15 percent with methamphetamine; 7 percent with opiates; and 3 percent with other illegal drugs.

At some point in your college education you will undoubtedly be asked by one of your professors the age-old question: Is drug use a gateway to other crimes? Or stated more simply, do drugs cause crime? There is some evidence that suggests that drugs may be a precursor to certain crimes. For example, the commonly portrayed images of the crazed drug addict who steals in order to support his drug addiction is possible evidence. However, other evidence suggests that there is no relationship between drugs and crime. The National Household Survey claims there were 12.6 million drug users in 1991. Few of them became addicts or career criminals and most of their drug use was recreational. Self-report studies of high-rate offenders indicate that many began their criminal activity before they began using drugs. For other offenders, drug use preceded criminal activity. Still others became involved in crime and drugs at about the same time.[11]

Typically, in jails and prisons there are those drug offenders who have been convicted of selling or manufacturing an illegal substance and those offenders who have been convicted of merely possessing an illegal substance. For quite some time researchers have been grappling with the question of just what is the relationship of drug abuse to other types of crime. The National Crime Victimization Survey asks victims of violent crimes such as rape, robbery, and assault about their perception of the offender's use of alcohol and drugs. In 30 percent of violent crime victimization, victims reported that they believed their assailants were under the influence of drugs or alcohol.[12] Data from the Bureau of Justice Statistics show that one-quarter of convicted jail inmates, one-third of state prisoners, and two-fifths of youths in long-term, state-operated facilities admit that they were under the influence of an illegal drug at the time of their offense.[13]

The Bureau of Justice Statistics has found that drugs and crime are related in three distinct ways. First, there are drug-defined crimes, such as possession and sale of drugs. Second are drug-related offenses, such as the drug addict who steals to support his habit. Third are interactional behaviors, in which drugs and crime are part of a deviant lifestyle resulting in commission of a crime.[14] The data tends to support the notion that there is some relationship between drugs and crime. Those high-rate offenders who are addicted or heavily dependent on drugs commit crimes at higher rates than when they are not so heavily involved. Heroin addicts, for example, commit four to six times as many crimes when addicted as during periods of low-level use.[15]

There are also those incarcerated offenders who are not users of drugs or drug addicts who are serving sentences for drug-related crimes to support their habit, but rather they are serving time for selling illegal drugs. These offenders range from the local street dealer who supplies six or seven persons with their drugs, or they may be the dealer who supplies a few street dealers with their drugs, or they could be a member of some large-scale drug cartel that supplies many dealers across the country with drugs. In the United States there are many traditional criminal organizations that specialize in drug trafficking in metropolitan areas throughout the country, for example, Chicago, East St. Louis, and Detroit. Generally, urban organizations want to monopolize the drug trade in their area. Drug offenders serving their sentences may also be members of an international drug cartel. For example, the offender may be a member of a

Colombian drug cartel. The Colombian drug cartels are the largest international drug organizations. Their organizational structure is like an onion with the leaders at the center, insulated but directing operations. The outer layers are involved in the direct selling of drugs, production, growing, and smuggling.

4-7 The Elderly Criminal

Jail and prison populations are becoming more middle aged. In 1996, 24 percent of jail inmates were between the ages of 35 and 44 compared to 12 percent in 1983. The percentage under age 25 dropped from 41 percent in 1983 to 31 percent in 1996. This is also the case for inmates incarcerated in state and federal prisons. In 2001 there were over 50,000 inmates in state or federal prisons who were 55 years of age or older. We tend to think of prisoners as being young. All indications are, however, that the number of elderly prisoners will continue to grow. For example during 2000 in Florida, the number of prisoners aged 50 and older increased by 51 percent while the total prison population increased by 25 percent. Elderly prisoners need a variety of special care and treatment considerations. Elderly inmates suffer from illnesses such as diabetes, pulmonary diseases, circulatory problems, arthritis, and Alzheimer's disease. By far the greatest number of elderly are arrested for larceny-thefts, mainly shoplifting. In addition, recent studies indicate increasing problems of deviant behavior among the elderly may be the cause of the increase in criminal activity. For example, alcoholism and alcohol-related offenses such as drunkenness make up a large portion of the arrests of older people.[16]

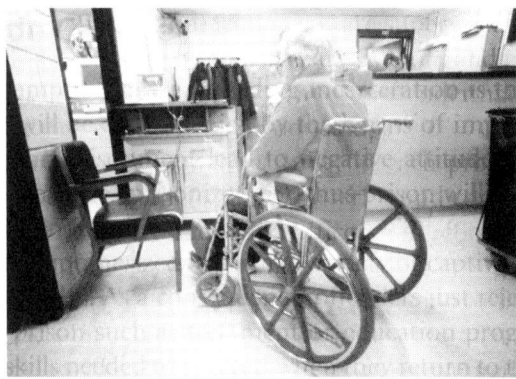

Elderly inmates may require long-term medical care while incarcerated.
Mark C. Ide

Housing requirements differ for elderly prisoners. Many need housing away from the general population to reduce the risk of victimization. Even the types of recreation programs need to be different to accommodate the elderly. Arts and crafts geared for the elderly are needed. The reading at the end of this chapter refers to a research study regarding the problems of the increasing number of elderly prisoners.

4-8 The Female Criminal

> The President's Commission on Law Enforcement and Administration of Justice did not include a single paragraph or statistic on the female offender, nor could any such material be found in its nine supportive Task Force Reports.[17]

Statistics indicate that the growth rate of female inmates has exceeded that for males. For example, the male population in prisons increased by 112 percent in the 1980s, and the female population increased by 202 percent during the same time.[18] A similar growth occurred from July 1, 2000, to June 30, 2001, during which time the number of women under the jurisdiction of state and federal prison grew from 93,681 to 94,336, an increase of 0.7 percent. The increases in arrest rates of females for index crimes over the past 20 years exceeds the increases in male arrest rates. Despite the increasing numbers of female offenders, women are still arrested for only about one in five index crimes. (Note: index crimes are murder, forcible rape, robbery, aggravated assault, burglary, larceny-theft, motor vehicle theft, and arson.) Three-fourths of the female arrests for index crimes are theft-related offenses. Women are also arrested for prostitution. However, the arrest rates for prostitution have decreased in the past 20 years. The most frequent non-index crimes for which women are arrested are driving under the influence, minor assaults, drug-abuse violations, fraud, and disorderly conduct.[19]

While one in every four people arrested in the United States is female, only one woman out of every 25 is eventually sent to prison. Approximately 70 percent of the women are given probation when convicted. About 10 females out of every 25 arrested serve some time in jails. A thorough discussion on female criminals is taken up in Chapter 11.

4-9 Gender Bias

Are men treated more harshly than women in the criminal justice system? This was a question that the Gender Bias Task Force of Texas examined. This task force was jointly sponsored by the State Bar Association, the

Dallas Bar Association, the Texas Women's Foundation, the Coastal Bend Women Lawyers Association and others. The final report of the task force concluded that there are disparities in treatment based on gender. They concluded that at every stage of the criminal justice process in all sorts of crimes, from investigation through arrest, bond, indictment, plea bargaining, trial, conviction, punishment, probation and parole, men are treated more harshly than women. This was true even when allowances were made for prior convictions, by tracking only first-time offenders, and for circumstances of the crime by using only similar circumstances.[20]

A similar study in California indicated that for every woman arrested for assault, seven men will be arrested; but by the punishment phases, 25 men will be sent to prison for every woman. For every woman arrested for aggravated assault, 10 men will be arrested, but by the punishment phase, 79 men will go to prison for every woman. The report also indicated that men are nine times more likely to go to prison for the same crime as women.[21]

4-10 Noncitizen Offenders

The percentage of state and federal prisoners who are noncitizens has increased in the past 20 years. For example, the number of noncitizens in federal prison increased from 4,088 in 1984 to 18,829 in 1994. The two states with the largest number of noncitizen inmates are Texas and California. While noncitizen inmates are from more than 75 different countries, approximately 50 percent are from Mexico. Approximately 55 percent of them were legally in the United States.

Approximately 35 percent of the noncitizens convicted in state courts were charged with violent offenses and 45 percent for drug offenses. Most convicted in federal court (85 percent) were for drug offenses.

The Immigration and Nationality Act of 1990 authorizes the U.S. Immigration and Naturalization Service (INS) to apprehend and deport criminal aliens. The number of criminal aliens in the United States is unknown. The INS must rely on federal, state, and local law enforcement agencies to notify them when those agencies come into contact with individuals believed to be criminal aliens. Once the alien is identified, INS issues a detainer. The alien is then deported after the criminal proceeding or sentence has been completed. In 1995, INS deported nearly 32,000 criminal aliens.

A recent report released in August 2002 by the Bureau of Justice Statistics reveals that the number of immigration defendants prosecuted rose from 6,605 in 1996 to 15,613 in 2000. The average time to be served by immigration offenders entering federal prison increased from about 4 months in 1986 to 21 months in 2000. Fifty-seven percent of suspected immigration offenders were Mexican citizens; 7% U.S. citizens; 3% Chinese; and 28% all other nationalities. Moreover, the Bureau of Justice report related that the number of immigration offenders serving a federal prison sentence increased from 12,593 during 1985 to 13,676 during 2000. These increases can best be attributed to changes in the federal sentencing law, which had a substantial impact on the processing of immigration offenders.

INS has several options for removing an illegal alien (including a criminal alien) from the United States. Fewer than three percent of those apprehended are actually deported. Most admit to their illegal status and agree to leave the United States voluntarily. Unlike deportation, voluntary departure does not require adjudication by an immigration judge. Aliens who voluntarily returned, at no expense to the United States, are not prohibited from legally entering at a later time. If, however, they have been convicted of a felony, they are prohibited from returning without special permission.

A deported alien may not be admitted to the United States for five years after deportation. Entry by a previously deported alien within five years of deportation is a felony. Entry by a previously deported alien with a criminal history (felony conviction) is a criminal offense with the maximum term of 20 years imprisonment.

A recent Supreme Court decision will impact the way the government handles criminal aliens after they have served their prison sentence. In June 2001, the Supreme Court ruled that after criminal aliens have served out their prison sentences, and their countries refuse to take them back, the government cannot continue to detain the criminal alien. In the past, the Immigration and Naturalization Service has held these ex-cons in detention centers and local jails, sometimes for months, even years, while trying to deport them.

4-11 The Federal Inmate

Federal inmates or those confined for drug violations, tax evasion, and robbing federally insured banks serve in correctional institutions for the commission of federal crimes. Because murder, rape, assaults, and other violent crimes are state and not federal crimes, offenders who commit those crimes will generally be in a state, not a federal, institution.

The federal prisons are controlled by the Federal Bureau of Prisons, which has a central office in Washington, DC and has five regional offices. The central office comprises the director and his/her staff and four operational divisions. The operational divisions are Correctional Programs,

Administration, Medical Services and Industries, Education and Vocational Training. In addition, at the central office, there is an Office of General Counsel and Office of Inspections. The five regional headquarters are located in Atlanta, Dallas, Philadelphia, Dublin (near San Francisco), and Kansas City. Each is headed by a regional director.

There are approximately 115 federal confinement facilities with approximately 100,000 inmates. All federal prisoners who are physically able are required to complete regular daily work assignments. The prisoners have the opportunity to participate in educational training, vocational training, work, religious practices, and counseling programs.

The federal classification system is based on the concept that prisoners should be placed in the least-restrictive institution possible that is nearest to their homes. Approximately one-third of the federal prisoners are classified as Security Level 1. This is the lowest level and permits inmates to be retained in open institutions, such as prison camps.

Box 4-2

The Ford Pinto Case

On September 13, 1978, Ford Motor Company was indicted by a grand jury in Elkhart, Indiana, on three counts of reckless homicide based on the deaths of three teenagers who were killed in the fiery crash of a Ford Pinto. The victims died of burns suffered when the Pinto burst into flames after being rear-ended. The Pinto was developed by Ford to sell for about $2,000. The design was completed on a rush schedule. For design reasons, the gas tank was placed behind, rather than over, the rear axle. This placement made it more probable that the car would explode and burn in a rear-end collision than similar-sized compact automobiles.

Evidence was presented that Ford was aware of the problem and that the car could have been modified for a cost of $15.30 per car, but that the executives at Ford decided to go ahead with the project to save money. The Ford Motor Company was acquitted on March 13, 1980. Had Ford been found guilty, the company could have been fined $175,000. A $175,000 fine for Ford would be comparable to the average wage-earner paying a fine of $3.25. It is estimated that approximately 500 people died because of this design.

No individuals were ever punished for their decisions. Compare this lack of punishment with the fact that individuals who kill store clerks in robberies are routinely given the death penalty.

The federal prison system uses Federal Prison Industries, Inc. to sell its products and services to other federal agencies. The Federal Prison Industries, Inc. goes by the corporate name of **UNICOR**. It is wholly owned by the federal government with the mission to support the Federal Bureau of Prisons through the gainful employment of inmates in work programs. Federal inmates may obtain gainful employment with UNICOR to earn money and obtain valuable on-the-job training, vocational education, and apprenticeship programs.

The federal system has implemented a mandatory literacy program for federal inmates who read below certain grade levels. Eventually, the federal system plans to require mandatory literacy training for inmates who read below the twelfth grade level. All promotions in UNICOR and work assignments are contingent upon an inmate's achievement of the desired level of literacy.

The federal system also has an adult basic education program that provides the inmates with the opportunity to obtain GED (high-school equivalency) certificates and take college courses. English as a Second Language is also provided for those inmates who need it. Most of these programs are funded in part by UNICOR.

The federal system operates four co-correctional facilities and one all-female institution. There are approximately 7,000 female inmates in the federal system.

ARTICLE

Golden Years Behind Bars: Special Programs and Facilities for Elderly Inmates[22]

Most researchers and policy makers deem the crimes of youthful offenders to be more serious and dangerous for society than the crimes committed by older people. However, in recent years, crime and the elderly has emerged as an issue of increasing importance. While we are more accustomed to seeing the elderly as victims, attention has begun to shift to how the elderly are increasingly the perpetrators of crime. A common portrayal of the elderly offender has been the "victimless" felon writing bad checks or the senior citizen who shoplifts in order to survive or attract attention. The elderly are not only committing more crimes, their offenses are also more serious, offenses which at one time were reserved exclusively for the young. As a result, elderly offenders are presenting complex challenges to our nation's prison systems.

Approximately 381,000 persons ages 50 and older are arrested annually in the United States (*Uniform Crime Reports, 1990*). Of these, 15 percent are arrested for serious felonies such as murder, forcible rape, robbery, aggravated assault, burglary, larceny, motor vehicle theft, and arson. As more of the older population commit violent offenses, the likelihood that they will become incarcerated becomes apparent. *The Corrections Yearbook* reported in 1992 that 709,587 inmates were confined to state prisons nationwide including the District of Columbia. Of these prisoners, 35,032 were over the age of 50, representing a 50 percent increase in four years. This age group comprises approximately five percent of the total inmate population.

The Corrections Yearbook further reported that the Federal Bureau of Prisons housed 66,472 prisoners, of which 6,554, or about 10 percent, were 50 years of age or older. By the year 2005, this over-50 prison population is expected to increase to 16 percent. Of course, as our state prison systems expand, so will our federal prisons. The number of inmates will continue to increase and will exceed 100,000 by 1995. By the year 2000, a projected 137,000 inmates will be in the federal system.

It appears that the population of older prisoners will continue to increase well into the 21st century. For example, Virginia currently has 15,000 prisoners in the general population, and 2,500 of these have special needs. This sector of the prison's population includes over 800 elderly inmates. By the year 2000, the prison population is expected to total 32,000, with 8,532 exhibiting special needs. Again, it is projected that approximately one-third of those in the special needs category will be classified as geriatric. Numerous other states also face similar increases.

Chaneles has estimated that by the year 2000, if present trends continue, the number of long-term prisoners over 50 will be approximately 125,000, with 40,000 to 50,000 over 65 years of age. This projection is based on new admissions and the fact that there are currently 13,937 natural lifers (life without parole), 52,054 lifers (parole possibilities), and 125,996 inmates serving 20 years or more. In addition, another 2,214 prisoners are currently serving time on death row. These groups comprise 22 percent of all inmates in state and federal prisons.

Research Rationale

While the number of older prisoners is now manageable in most states, the trend toward an aged inmate population is raising questions that will significantly affect correction programs in the coming decades. Older offenders pose unique and costly problems for corrections departments already struggling to cope with outdated and overcrowded facilities. Many states are faced with an increased number of aging prisoners who are in need of acute or chronic medical care. It is estimated that the average elderly prisoner suffers from three chronic illnesses. Many older offenders need corrective aids and prosthetic devices including eyeglasses, dentures, hearing aids, ambulatory equipment, and special shoes. Correctional systems are faced with making necessary adjustments to accommodate the special needs of aging inmates. Issues, such as providing special diets and round-the-clock nursing care, building new facilities or altering old ones, and restructuring institutional activities, are becoming more frequent topics of discussion.

Older prisoners differ from younger inmates not only in their need for medical care, but also in their psychosocial needs. Walsh found that older male inmates expressed a greater need for privacy and for access to preventive health care and legal assistance than younger men. Older inmates are often unable to cope with the fast pace and noise of a regular facility. Studies have also found that older inmates reported feeling unsafe and vulnerable to attack by younger inmates and expressed a preference for rooming with people their own age. Vega and Silverman also reported that abrasive relations with other inmates were the most disturbing incidents elderly prisoners had to cope with while incarcerated. Fifty-five percent of their respondents indicated that abrasive situations occurred daily. These factors, among others, often result in increasing stress for older inmates.

The physical condition and structure of institutions also create significant problems for elderly inmates. Prison systems are primarily designed to house young, active inmates. Older, frail offenders often find the prison environment cold and damp, and the stairs and distance to the cafeteria difficult to cope with. Inmates with limited mobility may find many prisons' physical designs too stressful to negotiate, and they simply withdraw into an isolated state.

The purpose of this research is to provide a comprehensive description of the special policies, programs, and facilities for geriatric inmates in United States prisons. Another goal is to determine the most pressing concerns correctional systems face in responding to the special needs of elderly prisoners. Other research questions focus on developing future programs and policies and identifying research topics useful for correctional officials in responding better to the needs of aging inmates. Implications for policy and practice are also addressed.

During the first half of 1990, a nationwide survey was conducted soliciting information from the 50 states and the District of Columbia. An open-ended questionnaire and comprehensive prison program checklist was mailed directly to the administrator of health services for each state correctional system. Those corrections officials who failed to respond to the mailed survey were interviewed by telephone. A follow-up phone inquiry was conducted in June 1992 to allow each correctional unit to report any recent changes in program or facility development. The results reported here are based on a 100 percent response rate.

Survey Results
Policies and Programs
A shortcoming of the studies of older prisoners is the failure of both researchers and correctional officials to agree on what constitutes "elderly." Some authors define "elderly" as 65 years of age and older, some suggest 60 years, while others have reported 55 years, and many use 50 years of age or

older. Likewise, states reporting special programs for aging inmates use a variety of ages to indicate special need. However, 50 years of age and older is the most common definition found in this study. Several correctional officials suggested that the typical inmate in his 50s has a physical appearance of at least 10 years older. In addition, the declining health of many inmates contributes to them being "elderly" before their time.

From responses to this survey, it is evident that most states do not have any specific written policies which address aged or infirm inmates. In practice, however, the needs of older inmates are addressed, to the extent possible, in the course of the classification process. Typically, all inmates, including the elderly, are screened in the admission process. Generally, housing and work assignments are made with regard to the inmate's health, security level, and location of family. In this regard, older inmates who possess numerous chronic health problems are granted special treatment based on their inferior health status.

For example, in Washington state, inmates with infirmities related to old age are likely to be transferred to the state penitentiary, where a number of cells in one unit have been designated for use by such inmates. Older inmates, who require long-term inpatient care, would be considered for transfer to the state reformatory, which has the largest inpatient unit in the system. Those who require special services, other than inpatient care, are transferred to the Special Needs Unit at Washington Correction Center.

A few states, such as Texas, Alaska, Mississippi, and South Carolina, make some policy decisions based solely on age. In Texas, the inmate is medically classified according to medical history, general health, physical findings, and age. Inmates 50 to 55 years of age receive a classification requiring lighter, slower duties. Inmates 55 and over are provided a classification that restricts the inmate from harder, heavier work and may allow for reduced work hours. Alaska reports occasionally providing a modification in sentencing for disease onset in the elderly. In Mississippi, inmates over 50 years of age are housed in geriatric units if their security classification permits. In South Carolina, inmates may retire from work at age 65. Numerous states also provide physicals annually for inmates over the age of 50, rather than every other year as they do for the general prison population.

Although most states do not have a policy based strictly on age, they do provide compassionate leave for those inmates who are terminally ill or not capable of physically functioning in the correctional system. Generally, the prognosis is six months or less to live, and specific criteria with regard to custody classification and medical requirements must be fulfilled. In some states, nursing home placement is a practical alternative. However, nursing home administrators may not be favorable to the notion of accepting ex-prisoners who have life histories of crime and violence, even if they are ill.

When compassionate leave is impossible due to the nature of the crime, correctional policy, or lack of available alternatives, prisons are developing policies and programs to better serve the terminally ill. For example, McCain

Correctional Hospital in North Carolina has incorporated the hospice concept into its geriatric/infirm facility. Family members are permitted to spend extended periods of time with the dying inmate, and hospice supervisors work closely with the inmate and his family.

Geriatric Facilities

An increasing number of states do routinely house older inmates apart from the general population and offer them unique programming or services. In specific states (including Alabama, Georgia, Illinois, Kansas, Kentucky, Maryland, Michigan, Minnesota, Mississippi, North Carolina, New Jersey, Ohio, South Carolina, Tennessee, Texas, Virginia, West Virginia, and Wisconsin) elderly inmates are housed in special units often described as "aged/infirm," "medical/geriatric," "disabled," or simply "geriatric." Most of these units frequently mix older inmates with younger disabled ones. Whenever possible, same-aged inmates are grouped together in dormitory style cells. Generally, those states reporting some form of special housing have one or two facilities within their prison systems where older inmates are grouped.

Special considerations are usually given to accommodate safely the handicapped and less physically able. Stairs are minimal, and distances from various facilities in the institution (e.g., canteen, recreation room) are reduced. Educational, vocational, recreational, and rehabilitative programs have been expanded to accommodate the elderly. A few facilities now employ psychologists and counselors with professional training in geriatrics, so there is a greater awareness of the unique social, psychological, and emotional needs of these inmates.

One of the first and more comprehensive facilities to accommodate elderly inmates was developed in South Carolina. In 1970, prison officials began providing special facilities for the elderly. The state, renowned for its harsh sentencing practices, has always had a large number of long-termers growing old behind bars. Due to the need for more space, the state's prison for the elderly moved into a former tuberculosis hospital at State Park in 1983. The majority of minimum custody inmates are housed at the State Park Correctional Center, which has 100 male beds and 11 female beds for handicapped elderly. South Carolina is the only state that reported housing its older female prisoners in a special geriatric facility.

Twenty-four-hour medical coverage is available at State Park. Thirteen nurses are on duty around the clock. A doctor is assigned to the facility full-time and writes an average of 925 prescriptions a month. In addition to providing two daily sick calls, pill line, and emergency and routine treatment, the medical staff provides educational programs geared to the needs of the residents. Those inmates on dialysis and chemotherapy are bused daily to a nearby hospital.

Some states are developing "nursing-home-like settings" within the prison environment, which provide a greater degree of shelter. For example, Mississippi has a geriatric unit that houses 85 offenders. In 1987, the old hospital was remodeled and specifically designed as a nursing home in a correctional setting. In this type of unit, 24-hour nursing care is provided and sick call is available weekly. A physician checks with the unit daily. In addition to the nursing staff, a psychiatric assistant provides recreational activities, and a case manager is also assigned to the unit.

Special Concerns

Rising medical costs in conjunction with health care mandates are having a tremendous impact on a significant number of states. Thirty percent of the states listed rising costs as the most pressing concern. An important issue for 26 percent of the state units is meeting the special needs of older inmates who are "aging in place" with numerous chronic health problems and limited Activities of Daily Living (ADL) functions. As one correctional health official stated, "a significant number of prisoners 50 years and over have a number of chronic illnesses that require long-term care. Another problem is lack of previous dental care requiring the provision of dental prosthesis and long-term dental care." Other problems listed by some states included a lack of community support and appropriate programming for the older inmates, in addition to the victimization of frail, aged inmates.

Planning for the Future

Numerous states indicate that they have future plans to implement special programming and/or facilities for the geriatric and handicapped prison population. Responses to the survey question ranged from immediate plans to establish new facilities, to ongoing discussions or research, to long-range plans to build or remodel facilities, to no plans whatsoever. For example, Maine, Maryland, Kentucky, and Montana currently have building plans in place or are converting current structures for their elderly and infirm inmates. Other states such as Arkansas, Nevada, New Jersey, Ohio, South Carolina, and Wyoming have long-range plans to build nursing-home-like facilities. Delaware, Georgia, Iowa, Michigan, and Washington have recently undergone major feasibility studies to determine better the needs of the ever-increasing number of older prisoners. Arizona, Tennessee, Texas, and Virginia have recently opened new geriatric/special needs units. Pennsylvania reported the development of new geriatric services and support systems, as well as special training for correctional staff. Finally, Texas is in the process of developing appropriate programming for its new geriatric unit.

Research Needs

As older prisoners become the focus of concern for many prison systems for the next generation, state prison officials do not have adequate research outcomes to help them solve the problem. Prison officials surveyed in this study stressed that indicators are needed to help identify more clearly "model programs" that are adequately meeting the special needs of the elderly inmate.

For example, while this survey discovered a variety of programs and facilities instituted in certain states, a need still exists to provide a systematic program evaluation of these efforts. Important questions remain regarding the effectiveness of such programs in meeting the needs of aging prisoners. Research, in this case, would emphasize the (1) living environment or custodial care, (2) humanitarian care, and (3) therapeutic care. An evaluation research design would focus on how effectively these programs currently meet the physical, medical, social, and mental needs of the aging prisoner.

Other research information desired by correctional officials includes: (1) What are the general health care needs of this special population? (2) What is the average annual medical cost for aged offenders? (3) What incarceration alternatives are available for frail, elderly inmates and what is the post-release success of elderly prisoners? (4) What is the nature of family relationships for those growing old in prison? (5) How will states determine who gets costly health care services and who does not? (6) What projections can be made utilizing data from states with life without parole concerning the size and cost of their older prison populations in the coming decades? (7) What are the typical coping strategies for those who enter prison later in life? Finally, correctional officials also expressed an interest in additional research information concerning sentencing and parole policies for the elderly.

Policy Implications

In many ways, geriatric programming in the prison setting is in a developmental stage. While it is obvious that correctional officials are becoming more sensitive to the special needs of aging inmates, barriers continue to exist that interfere with the ability of states to respond more effectively. For example, most states are faced with the rising costs of medical care and general overcrowding. In the past decade, the war on drugs and tough mandatory sentencing laws have doubled the number of inmates. Overcrowding, AIDS, and other issues have hindered many states from implementing special programming for the aging inmate. Currently, the prison system is demanding 1,100 new beds every week.

Although studies have found that older inmates prefer to be housed with people their own age, some correctional officials find no need for or responsibility to provide special consideration to older offenders. Others feel older inmates provide a sense of stability to the general prison population and should not be housed separately. From this perspective, older inmates should be given housing and work assignments based on their health and the type of custody they require. Other placement considerations should be work skills and family status. Placing an inmate in a special unit for the elderly, hundreds of miles away from family could be detrimental to the inmate.

Older offenders may also have a difficult time being assigned to facilities providing special needs because slots are limited. In particular, those states converting a small wing for older inmates may have a long waiting list. Also, there is still disagreement regarding the ethical obligation to provide inmates with such acute care as heart bypass surgery or kidney transplants when others in society may not have access to or the money for the same level of care. Thus, due to lack of space, philosophy, or costs, some elderly inmates may not benefit from socialized programming. Of course, health access and care may vary from state to state.

A major problem in meeting the special needs of older inmates is that, in many states, there are still few aging inmates. For example, in Vermont, North Dakota, South Dakota, Hawaii, and Maine, where there are few elderly inmates, separate facilities or programs cannot be justified. In such states, correctional units have little choice but to mainstream elderly inmates in the general prison system. This is particularly true for aging female inmates, as they typically make up a small portion of the total female population.

Another barrier to responding fully to the special needs of aging inmates is the lack of adequately trained prison staff. As one prison official confessed, "I know how to run prisons, not old-age homes." Moreover, not everyone who works in a correctional environment may have the aptitude or the essential skills needed to manage elderly people. Careful selection for sensitivity to the unique requirements of geriatric inmates should be an important consideration. Training, involving administrative personnel, line security staff, and health providers, should include an increased knowledge of growing old and how this knowledge specifically affects the elderly in a prison environment. Prison staff need to be specifically trained to understand more fully the social and emotional needs of the elderly, the dynamics of death and dying, procedures for identifying depression, and a system for referring older inmates to experts in the community.

While states are responding by providing special units for older inmates, programming for elderly inmates has not kept pace. Although older inmates may be grouped together in a special needs facility, they often have nothing to do to pass the time. Physical activities popular with younger inmates may not be well-suited to many elderly inmates. Vocational training programs, a primary activity for much of the prison population, serve no purpose for long-term older offenders who are unlikely to return to the workforce. In most prisons, counseling is geared to rehabilitating younger inmates rather than coping with issues such as chronic illness or death. Instead of preparing the inmate for reentry as a productive member of society, wellness programs that aim to keep the individual alert and active are needed. Walking, gardening, woodworking, ceramics, low-impact exercises, prison support groups, and other more passive recreational activities can prove successful among older inmates.

The diversity of the growing number of older offenders should also be recognized and incorporated into rehabilitative programs. For example, the elderly first offender should be integrated into prison life differently than the repeat offender. The first offender is likely to be more anxious, fearful, depressed, and suicidal than the chronic offender. Aging inmates coming into an institutional setting late in life with the realization that prison may be their final home may experience a tremendous shock to their system. Williams (1989) found that new offenders were more withdrawn and passed their time sleeping, watching television, or performing some other solitary activity. Other inmates, imprisoned for long periods of their lives may fear returning to the free world.

In other situations, locating family members who may accept an aging inmate as well as provide necessary care-giving tasks may be difficult. Some family members also may be aged and in poor health. The nature of the crime may have created a conflict among family members, resulting in a break in kinship ties. Such inmates may have few or no visits from close friends or relatives on the outside. The lack of a supportive social network may adversely affect the incarcerated elderly, because significant others are key factors that serve to buffer the negative effects of incarceration.

In order to transfer elderly offenders back to the community, housing and financial assistance must usually be secured for inmates who have been imprisoned for long terms and who have lost all contacts in the community. Parole decisions should be handled on a case-by-case basis. Prison staff should maintain good relationships with a variety of social service agencies, such as social security officials and nursing home personnel. Older offenders will need assistance in getting their social security reinstated and in determining if they are eligible for Medicaid. Intervals for parole review of older inmates should be more frequent, especially in cases where terminal illnesses have been diagnosed.

Correctional officials are just beginning to grapple with the large number of elderly prisoners. The increased probability of longer sentences due to the increased use of habitual offender statutes with life without parole and mandatory minimum sentencing will pose unique and costly problems for corrections departments in the future. Additional research is needed to assist correctional officials in their decision-making processes and in the implementation of quality programs and facilities. Prisons, like other social institutions in society, must be prepared for the "graying of America."

Summary

One of the characteristics of prison populations that concerns us is the increasing absolute numbers and the increases per 100,000 in the rate of incarceration. Included within the prison population are various groups of individuals who need special care and treatment. The term "career criminals" is used to identify those persons who make, or attempt to make, a living committing crime. Generally, career criminals are property offenders. They begin their criminal career early in their juvenile years. Most view crime as a safe and enjoyable way to obtain a good life. They expect to return to a life of crime after they are released from confinement. The average career criminal is normally in and out of prison or jail all of his or her life. Most career criminals live at or below the poverty level when not confined in prison.

Under current law, prison authorities must keep juveniles out of the "sight and sound" of adult inmates. The definition of juveniles varies by age according to the states' definitions. In addition, they must keep juveniles who have committed crimes in the usual sense in institutions different from those occupied by youths charged with status offenses, such as truancy and incorrigibility.

The professional criminal or white-collar criminal refers to a person of respectability and high social status who commits crime in the course of his or her occupation. Examples of white-collar crimes include embezzlement by bankers, overcharging by doctors in billing under Medicare Programs, and price-fixing in government contracts. It is estimated that white-collar crimes cost our society about $100 billion a year. Many white-collar criminals have extensive financial resources to employ when combating law enforcement efforts to control their activities.

Violent crime is normally committed by the young. Accordingly, we tend to think of prisoners as being young. All indications are, however, that the number of elderly prisoners will grow. Elderly prisoners need a variety of special care and treatment considerations. Elderly inmates suffer from illnesses such as diabetes, pulmonary diseases, circulatory problems, arthritis, and Alzheimer's disease. By far the greatest number of arrests for the elderly are larceny-thefts, mainly shoplifting. In addition, recent studies indicate the increasing problems of deviant behavior facing the elderly may be leading to, or associated with, criminal activity. For example, alcoholism and alcohol-related offenses, such as drunkenness make up a large portion of the arrests of older people.

Statistics indicate that the incarceration rate of female inmates has exceeded that for males. For example, the male population in prisons increased by 112 percent in the 1980s, and the female population increased by 202 percent during the same time. Similar growth has been noted for the 1990s. The increases in arrest rates of females for index crimes over the past 20 years exceeds the increases in male arrest rates. Despite the increasing numbers of female offenders, women are still arrested for only about one in five index crimes. Three-fourths of the female arrests for index crimes are theft-related offenses. Women are also arrested for prostitution. However, the arrest rates for prostitution have decreased in the past 20 years. The most frequent non-index crimes for which women are arrested are driving under the influence, minor assaults, drug abuse violations, fraud, and disorderly conduct.

While one in every four people arrested in the United States is female, only one woman out of every 25 is eventually sent to prison. Approximately 70 percent of the women are given probation when convicted. About 10 females out of every 25 arrested serve some time in jails.

Discussion Questions

1. Describe the career criminal's lifestyle.
2. Explain the problems caused by the aging of the prison population.
3. What special problems do female prisoners cause?
4. What types of individuals are considered "white-collar" criminals?
5. Is the criminal justice system gender-biased?

Chapter Quiz

True/False
1. Prisonization is the process in which prisoners learn the rules.
2. Career criminals are those individuals who attempt to make a living committing crime.
3. Most career criminals are property offenders.
4. The number of drug offenders in American prisons decreased throughout the 1990s.
5. The growth of female offenders in recent years has actually exceeded that for males.

Multiple Choice

1. The process by which prisoners learn the rules of socialization into the prison culture is called
   a. labeling.
   b. prisonization.
   c. nurturing.
   d. socialization.
2. Which one of the following statements is NOT true regarding the findings of the Rand Corporation study on habitual offenders?
   a. Career criminals are not specialized in their criminal activity.
   b. Many career criminals had a self-concept that they could beat the odds.
   c. Most career criminals were unmarried with few family obligations.
   d. The rate of violent crime was high among the career criminals.
3. Which one of the following is a major shortcoming of studies of older prisoners?
   a. There is much disagreement between researchers and correctional officials of what constitutes elderly.
   b. It is difficult to study older inmates because there aren't that many of them in prisons.
   c. Researchers lack access to prison systems limiting knowledge of older offenders.
   d. Elderly inmates are much less willing to talk with researchers for fear of being labeled a "snitch."
4. Embezzlement by bankers and overbilling by physicians under Medicare programs are examples of what typology of crime?
   a. blue collar crime
   b. white collar crime
   c. tort crimes
   d. crimes against persons
5. Which of the following is NOT true regarding juvenile offenders?
   a. They must by kept separate from adult inmates.
   b. The definition of juveniles varies by age according to states' definitions.
   c. Juveniles who commit crimes such as burglary must be kept separate from a juvenile who commits a status offense such as truancy and incorrigibility.
   d. Juvenile offenders can be housed on a temporary basis only with non-violent adult offenders.

Endnotes

1. Ruth Masters and Cliff Roberson, *Inside Criminology* (Englewood, NJ: Prentice-Hall, 1989), 366.
2. Peter W. Greenwood and Allan Abraham, *Selective Incapacitation*, prepared for the National Institute of Justice (Santa Monica, CA: Rand Corp., 1981) and Jan Chaiken et al. *Doing Crime* (Santa Monica, CA: Rand Corp., 1982).
3. R.C. McCorkle, "Living on the Edge: Fear in a Maximum Security Prison." *Journal of Offender Rehabilitation* 20: 73–91.
4. Pamela Steinke, "Using Situational Factors to Predict Types of Prison Violence," *Journal of Offender Rehabilitation* 17: 119–132.
5. Miles Harer, and Neal P. Langan, "Gender Differences in Predictors of Prison Violence: Assessing the Predictive Validity of a Risk Classification System," *Crime and Delinquency* 47 (4): 513–536.
6. Deborah R. Baskin, Ira Sommers, and Henry H. Steadman, "Assessing the Impact of Psychiatric Impairment on Prison Violence," *Journal of Criminal Justice* 19 (3): 271–280.
7. Jonathan R. Sorenson, and Rocky L. Pilgrim, "An Actual Risk Assessment of Violence Posed by Capital Murder Defendants," *The Journal of Criminal Law and Criminology* 90 (4, 2000): 1251–1270.
8. Ibid.
9. Edwin H. Sutherland, "White Collar Crime" (New York: Holt, Rinehart, and Winston, 1959).
10. Allen J. Beck and Paige M. Harrison, "Prisoners in 2000," Bureau of Justice Statistics, August 2001.
11. Samuel Walker, *Sense and Nonsense about Crime and Drugs: A Policy Guide*, 3rd ed. (Belmont, CA: Wadsworth, 1994).
12. Bureau of Justice Statistics, *Drugs and Crime Facts*, 1994.
13. Allen J. Beck and Paige M. Harrison, "Prisoners in 2000," *Bureau of Justice Statistics*, August 2001.
14. Bureau of Justice Statistics, *Drugs, Crime, and the Justice System*, 1999, p. 12.
15. Walker, *Sense and Nonsense*.
16. Sue Titus Reid, *Crime and Criminology*, 6th ed. (New York: Harcourt Brace Jovanovich, 1991), p. 70.
17. Edith Flown, "The Special Problems of the Female Offender," In L. E. Ohlin, ed. *We Hold These Truths* (Richmond, VA: Virginia Division of Justice and Crime Prevention, 1972).
18. Lawrence Greenfield and Stephanie Minor-Harper, *Women in Prison, 1990* (Washington, DC: Department of Justice, 1991).
19. William Sessions, *Uniform Crime Reports: 1994* (Washington, DC: Federal Bureau of Investigation, 1995).
20. *The Gender Bias Task Force of Texas Final Report* (Austin, TX: State Bar of Texas, Department of Research and Analysis, 1994).

21. *Committee on Gender Bias in the Courts, Final Report,* National Coalition of Free Men (1991).
22. Ronald H. Aday, PH.D. Gerontology Program Director, Middle Tennessee State University. Reprinted with permission of Dr. Aday. This article was originally printed in *Federal Probation,* 58 (2 June 1994). Footnotes and charts are omitted.

Chapter 5

Alternatives to Incarceration

Many boot camp programs include a spiritual component.
Mark C. Ide

Key Terms

boot camps
community service
  programs
diversion
intermediate sanctions
recidivism
restitution
risk management
shock incarceration

Outline

5-1 Diversion
  5-1a Purpose and Objectives
  5-1b Targets for Diversion
  5-1c Evaluating Diversion
5-2 Shock Incarceration
  5-2a Boot Camp Programs
  5-2b Characteristics of Shock
    Incarceration
  5-2c Profiles of Selected Programs
  5-2d Evaluation of Boot Camp
    Programs
  5-2e Catalyst for Change

5-3 Rehabilitative Programming
5-4 Attitude Change
5-5 Recidivism
Article—Community Service:
  A Review of the Basic Issues
Summary
Discussion Questions
Chapter Quiz
Endnotes

Learning Objectives

After reading this chapter, the reader will be able to:

- Explain why the processing of prisoners is often called "risk management."
- Explain why diversion is considered the "front door" program.
- Identify the concepts involved with "shock incarceration."
- Explain the three psychological principles involved in rehabilitative programs.
- List the advantages of using community service instead of prison as a sanction.
- Explain the dual focus involved in selecting people for community service.
- Analyze the organizational issues involved in community service.
- Explain the issues involved in the supervision of community service.

This chapter will explore many of the alternatives to incarceration. The primary alternative used in the United States today is probation. While probation is considered the backbone of our present corrections system (see Chapter 6), innovative programs and controls schemes have been developed as alternatives to incarceration and probation. These sanctions are often referred to as **intermediate sanctions.** Processing of offenders in the criminal justice system is referred to as **risk management.** Prior to the 1970s, most offenders were either confined to prison or placed on probation, with the majority being placed on probation. As explained in Chapter 1, probation is not as popular as it once was. Accordingly, to reduce the prison population, alternative sanctions had to be developed. Two of the most popular sanctions now in use are diversion and shock incarceration, each of which is discussed in this chapter.

5-1 Diversion

5-1a Purpose and Objectives

Diversion is designed to funnel offenders away from the criminal justice system and into community programs, which should be more beneficial to the offender and the community than incarceration. Diversion is frequently used to refer to the release of the accused from the normal path of the criminal justice process to an alternative path. Diversion is based on the assumption that the diverted individual will participate in some treatment program in return for the removal from the criminal justice system process before trial. Diversion is commonly referred to as the "front door" program because it limits the number of people entering jail or prison. Diversion programs attempt to deal with the problems that may have led the individual to the criminal behavior. Those arrested for drug offenses or driving under the influence, for example, may be diverted to an alcohol or drug abuse treatment program. Diversion can occur before or after charges are filed. However, once the accused has agreed to participate in the diversion program, formal prosecution is suspended pending program completion. If the accused completes all program requirements, the charges in most cases are dismissed. If an offender does not comply with the conditions of the diversion, the formal prosecution can be reinitiated.

5-1b Targets for Diversion

Typical targets for diversion are individuals with drug and alcohol problems. Many researchers contend that diversion actually widens the criminal justice system's net in that people who would not have been processed through the criminal court system are processed with the intention of referring them out to diversion programs. A major rationale for diversion is that the individual is more likely to be rehabilitated when not as directly involved with the criminal justice system. Generally, as a condition of diversion, the candidate must establish some plan for **restitution.** Restitution refers to compensating the victim for damages caused by the criminal activity.

The National Advisory Commission on Criminal Justice Standards and Goals, in its report, "Courts," suggested the following guidelines for using diversion:

> In appropriate cases, offenders should be diverted into noncriminal programs before formal trial or conviction. Such diversion is appropriate where there is a substantial likelihood that conviction could be obtained and the benefits to society from channeling an offender into an available noncriminal diversion program outweigh any harm done to society by abandoning the criminal prosecution.[1]

Diversion programs have been used extensively to divert juveniles out of the juvenile justice system. The diversion programs for juveniles include remedial education, foster homes, group homes, and local counseling facilities and centers.

5-1c Evaluating Diversion

Evaluations of diversion programs have shown a fair amount of success. Offenders who go through diversion programs generally have very low rates of subsequent offending. For example, in Brooklyn, New York, drug offenders who were diverted to a program called Drug Treatment Alternative to Prison (DTAP), were least likely to commit new crimes. The evaluation revealed that only 4 percent of offenders diverted to DTAP were rearrested.[2]

There is much optimism centering on diversion programs. However, even in light of the promising evaluations of diversion, researchers are still unsure whether the low rates of re-offending found in participants of diversion programs are due to the selection of the offenders for diversion programs, or are due to the effects of the diversion program. It may be that the offenders selected to complete diversion programs are the ones less likely to commit new offenses under any circumstances. Additional research is needed to more effectively evaluate the benefits of diversion programs.

5-2 Shock Incarceration

5-2a Boot Camp Programs

Since their inception in 1983, **shock incarceration**/probation programs, also known as **boot camps,** have enjoyed considerable support.[3] Like other intermediate sanctions, the programs are intended to alleviate institution overcrowding and reduce **recidivism** or repeat criminal behavior. In addition, because they are perceived as being "tough" on crime (in contrast to some other intermediate sentences such as probation), they have been enthusiastically embraced as a viable correctional option for delinquent youths. In addition, the presumed combination of cost savings and punitiveness has proven irresistible to politicians.

There has been a remarkable growth of boot camp prisons nationwide. In January 1984, there were only two states, Georgia and Oklahoma, with boot camp programs. By 1992, 25 states and the Federal Bureau of Prisons were operating a total of 41 programs. In 1994, five more states had either opened boot camp programs or were planning to open them. In 1984, Georgia's program capacity was 250 beds; by 1994 the capacity had expanded to over 3,000 beds. According to the Bureau of Justice Statistics, by the end of 1995, more than 55 jurisdictions had implemented some type of boot camp for offenders. These figures pertain only to those programs developed statewide and do not include the programs developed at the county level.

5-2b Characteristics of Shock Incarceration

As the name suggests, boot camp programs are modeled after military boot camp training. The term "boot camp" was coined by the military and usually consists of a six- to ten-week period of training designed to turn young men and women into disciplined soldiers. Participation in military drill and ceremony, physical training, and hard labor are mandatory in prison boot camps. Inmates begin their day before dawn and are involved in structured activities until "lights out," approximately 16 hours later.

The military-style training is generally supplemented with rehabilitative programming, such as drug treatment/education or academic education. The emphasis placed on such programs varies. New York, for example, has structured the program as a therapeutic community. Rehabilitative programming, therefore, plays a central role in the program. In other states, rehabilitative programming is peripheral to the military boot camp experience.

As the boot camp programs have developed, rehabilitative programming has come to play a more prominent role in the day-to-day routine. The earliest boot camp models devoted little time to such programs. Many of those pioneering programs have since been enhanced with additional therapeutic services. Programs developed in recent years have placed a greater emphasis on rehabilitative programming from the start.

The boot camp programs are designed for young, male offenders convicted of nonviolent offenses. Eligibility and suitability criteria were developed to restrict participation to this type of offender. For example, a March 1992 survey of shock incarceration programs revealed that the majority of programs (61.5 percent) then in operation limited participation to individuals convicted of nonviolent offenses. Fifty percent of the programs further restricted participation to individuals serving their first felony sentence. Most programs have minimum and maximum age limits. The minimum age limit was generally 16 years of age and the maximum 23 years of age. Female offenders are permitted to participate in about 50 percent of the programs. The number of beds available to females, however, has been limited. Several state courts have ruled that failure to include female offenders in the programs was gender discrimination.

5-2c Profiles of Selected Programs

New York State's Shock Incarceration program was established by enabling legislation in 1987. In 1987, the Monterey Shock Incarceration Correctional Facility became one of the largest in the nation with a capacity of 1,390 male inmates and 180 female inmates in four facilities located throughout the state. Female inmates are lodged in the largest of the facilities, Lakeview Shock Incarceration Correctional Facility, where 540 male inmates also participate in the six-month institutional phase of the program. In 1995, legislation mandated the creation of the Willard Drug Treatment Center, an 850-bed program for second felony offenders and parole violators, which operates under the shock model in a 90-day institutional phase and a one-year, graduated period of aftercare.[4] New York's program is a holistic model, addressing physical, mental, emotional, and spiritual dimensions of participants within the context of a therapeutic community and is molded after a strict and disciplined military protocol.

The Oregon Department of Corrections' boot camp for adult male and female felony offenders is located at Shutter Creek Correctional Institution in North Bend, Oregon. It was mandated by the 1993 Oregon legislature and was designed to ease prison crowding and impact criminal recidivism. The program is a two-phase program, six months in the institutional setting, followed by transitional leave and an aftercare program supervised by parole officers throughout the state. The program includes both male and female offenders from the age of juvenile remand through age 40, and has a program capacity of 150 males and 16 females. Shutter Creek Correctional Institution also houses 100 general population male inmates. Program eligibility requirements exclude those convicted of sex offenses and most first-degree crimes. Offenders with recent escape histories and unresolved detainers are also excluded. Eligibility screening is done on site and after being screened, inmates must volunteer to participate. Within the military framework, the heart of the program is the modified therapeutic community, centered on the concept of cognitive change: the idea that a change in thinking results in a change in behavior.[5]

The Arkansas Boot Camp program was created in 1989. The boot camp is located at the Wrightsville Correctional Institution in Wrightsville, Arkansas. Like many other boot camp programs the Arkansas program was created to relieve the skyrocketing cost of incarceration and overcrowding. The boot camp at Wrightsville is a regimented, military-style program. The boot camp program is intended to teach self-control, responsibility, and the skills and habits needed for a productive life to individuals who have shown they lack such skills. The drill and work portions of the program are designed to provide structure and discipline for individuals who may have been irresponsible and unmotivated in the past. The treatment portion of the program stresses internalizing positive values, developing internal controls, and setting positive goals, while providing the skills needed to pursue those goals.[6]

The Elayn Hunt Correctional Center in St. Gabriel, Louisiana, began its shock incarceration program in 1997. It has a capacity of 136 males and is available to females housed at the adjacent Louisiana Correctional Institute for Women. In the summer of 1997, the facility was expanded to accommodate 200 males. Initially, the target population was first-felony offenders committed to state custody for seven years or less for offenses carrying parole eligibility. In 1989, statutory eligibility was expanded to include second offenders who previously have not been incarcerated. One of the goals of the program is to prevent the process of deviant acculturation or "hardening" through lengthy involvement in the usual prison experience. The program is premised on a treatment model within a military setting. Louisiana's program is a two-part program, consisting of a period of 180 days of highly regimented, tightly structured incarceration, followed by at least six months of intensive parole supervision.

5-2d Evaluation of Boot Camp Programs

As noted earlier, a major goal of the programs was to reduce recidivism by means of rehabilitation and deterrence. Specific rehabilitative strategies include teaching accountability or responsibility, developing self-worth or self-esteem, and providing education or substance abuse education or treatment. In addition, the shock incarceration programs are designed to serve as specific deterrents.

The hope is that the rigor of the military-style training or the harsh reality of prison life will deter participants from future offending and thus reduce recidivism. An examination of a core element, military-style training, which includes military drill and ceremony, physical training, strict discipline, and physical labor, is necessary to determine if there is any value to the regimented military routine.

Research on specific deterrence has not been promising. Researchers have previously reported limited or no deterrent effect as the result of incarceration in a training school.[7] In addition, similar research on the Scared Straight program has failed to find evidence of a deterrent effect.[8] Realistically, it is unlikely that the boot camp experience will lead to increased perceptions of either the certainty or severity of punishment. In terms of general deterrence, there is no reason to believe that individuals on the street will be deterred by the threat of serving time in a boot camp prison. In fact, camp participants interviewed revealed that prior to arriving at the boot camp, they did not believe that they would have trouble meeting program requirements.

Political support for boot camp programs seems, in part, to be based on the idea that the regimented lifestyle and discipline of the boot camp will be transferred to life on the outside. Completing the highly structured and demanding program is further expected to inspire a sense of accomplishment that can be applied to other activities. This sense of accomplishment is reinforced in many programs by graduation ceremonies that are attended by family and friends.

Former shock incarceration participants reported that the program helped them to "get free" of drugs and to become physically fit. Other advantages mentioned by offenders included learning to get up in the morning and remain active all day. Thus, the military-style regimen appeared to promote physical health by ensuring a drug-free environment, balanced diet, and sufficient exercise.

Contrary to popular opinion, however, it is unlikely that the long hours of hard labor characteristic of shock incarceration will improve work skills or habits. The labor that is often required of shock incarceration participants is largely menial, consisting of picking up trash along highways, cleaning the facility, or maintaining grounds. Researchers have noted that for work programs to be successful, or promote rehabilitation, they must "enhance practical skills, develop interpersonal skills, minimize prisonization, and ensure that work is not punishment alone."[9] Considering the type of work generally required of inmates, it appears unlikely that it will be of much value in and of itself.

In short, the basic shock incarceration model may have some merit independent of rehabilitative programming. To summarize, positive by-products attributed to the core elements of shock incarceration alone may include physical fitness, drug-free existence, the experience of a structured life-style, and a sense of accomplishment.

5-2e Catalyst for Change

The basic shock incarceration experience is designed to induce stress. Incarceration, too, by its very nature, produces stress. Stress levels peak early during a period of incarceration and gradually taper off.[10] Research reveals that prison inmates are most receptive to personal changes (e.g., self-improvement classes, education, or training) during this initial period of high emotional stress. Within a period of several months, as stress levels taper off, however, desire to change does also. Inmates who, for example, enrolled in self-improvement classes dropped out in favor of institutional jobs. In one study, researchers concluded that the desire for change was related to the emotional distress experienced at the onset of the prison term. They argued further that treatment programs should begin as early in the prison term as possible to take advantage of the motivation to change.[11]

These research findings may prove relevant to shock incarceration. Not only are inmates incarcerated, but they are forced to participate in a physically demanding and stressful program. At the same time, most programs require participation in rehabilitative programming ranging from academic education, to drug treatment, to individual counseling. Generalizing from the findings then, the basic shock incarceration experience may make participants particularly receptive to the rehabilitative programming that is required of them. The program experience may initiate a period of self-evaluation and change.

The implications of this approach are twofold. First, the basic program may function predominantly as a catalyst for change. Therefore, shock incarceration programs that do not also offer rehabilitative programming will have no effect other than those previously discussed. Secondly, if shock incarceration programs, by definition, function primarily as catalysts due simply to the stress-inducing nature of the program, attention then must shift to the adequacy of rehabilitative programming.

5-3 Rehabilitive Programming

Over 20 years have passed since a researcher, referring to correctional treatment, suggested that "nothing appears to work." In response, prominent researchers in the field of corrections reviewed the extant literature on the effectiveness of treatment programs and concluded, on the contrary, that effective treatment existed and that, on average, appropriate treatment reduced recidivism by 50 percent.[12] The key, of course, was the word "appropriate."

Appropriate treatment was defined as treatment guided by three psychological principles:

1. Intensive treatment should be matched with high-risk offenders.
2. Treatment should address "criminogenic needs."
3. Treatment should follow general strategies of effective treatment (e.g., anticriminal modeling, warm and supportive interpersonal relations) and match the type of treatment (e.g., cognitive or behavioral) to individual characteristics.[13]

On the other hand, intervention strategies that have generally been found to be ineffective are those that are nondirective (use strategies that lack definite guidelines and are loosely organized), use behavior modification techniques that focus on incorrect targets (techniques that focus on the wrong problems or attaining the wrong goals), and emphasize punishment.[14]

The first principle suggests that more intensive treatment should be reserved for offenders who are considered higher risk. This is because high-risk offenders respond more positively to intensive treatment than do lower-risk offenders who perform just as well or better in less intensive treatment. Examination of the types of offenders targeted by this study's multi-site programs reveals that participants tend to be young, male, first-felony offenders. Many of these offenders were drug involved as well. Therefore, by virtue of age and gender, as well as the fact that many shock incarceration participants are drug involved and would otherwise serve prison time, they appear to be relatively high-risk offenders.

The second principle requires that treatment programs target the criminogenic needs of offenders. Criminogenic needs are dynamic needs of offenders that, when addressed, reduce the likelihood of recidivism.

Criminogenic needs may vary from individual to individual. Important criminogenic needs include substance abuse treatment, pro-social skill development, interpersonal problem-solving skills, and pro-social sentiment.

By and large, shock incarceration programs attempt to address criminogenic needs. According to the Bureau of Justice Statistics seven states incorporated substance abuse education/treatment; six states provided vocational training; six states included academic education; four states taught problem-solving or decision-making skills. Three states also provided intensive supervision upon release, which extended treatment/education to the community and sometimes provided job training and opportunities.

There are, however, additional program characteristics that may influence the effectiveness of programming. The length of the program itself is one. Four of the programs in the multi-site study were 90 days long. Others ranged from 90 to 180 days. It would appear that six months of substance abuse treatment and/or education is more likely to have a positive outcome than three months. In fact, researchers have reported that the length of drug treatment is related to successful outcome. This may be true of other program components as well. Programs that provide intensive supervision as treatment opportunities on release may more effectively address criminogenic needs.

Another important component that may influence programming is the voluntary nature of the program. In some programs, participation was completely voluntary. Offenders must volunteer to participate and can drop out of the program at any time. In others, participation was mandatory. Offenders were forced to participate and were not permitted to drop out voluntarily. It has been hypothesized that offenders who volunteer to participate in shock incarceration possess a greater sense of control than those for whom participation is mandatory. A sense of control may consequently lead to higher levels of commitment to the program.

The third principle, responsivity, outlines styles or modes of treatment used in effective treatment programs. Effective styles of treatment use firm but fair approaches to discipline, anti-criminal modeling, and concrete problem solving. Workers in these programs "relate to offenders in interpersonally warm, flexible, and enthusiastic ways, while also being clearly supportive of anti-criminal attitude and behavior patterns. Furthermore, effective programs must be cognizant that individual characteristics may interact with treatment style or mode of delivery. For example, highly anxious individuals are not as likely to benefit from stressful, interpersonal confrontation as would less anxious individuals.

What is most evident from the media reports and visits to boot camp prisons, though, is confrontation (e.g., drill sergeants screaming at inmates). Although staff and inmates directly involved in the programs say the discipline and staff authority is firm and relatively fair, outsiders who view the program, and some program dropouts, accuse the staff of domination and abusive behavior. Program staff generally attempt to act as anti-criminal models, reinforcing anti-criminal styles of thinking, feeling, and acting. However, few programs hire psychologists or others experienced in behavior modification techniques to be intimately involved in the training of staff.

There have been a number of abuses found in many boot camp prisons. For example, in 1999 five former inmates of the Custer boys boot camp, located in Sioux Falls, South Dakota, filed a lawsuit over alleged abuses at the facility. The suit accused the Custer program of strapping boys to a restraint board for hours, isolating them without clothes in a cold cell, and running an asthmatic boy without his medication until he dropped. Abuses such as these were apparently commonplace from 1996 to 1999.[15] In Phoenix, Arizona, a juvenile offender died while incarcerated in a boot camp prison facility. The youth died while attending a five-week boot camp, where the regimen included forced marches, wearing black uniforms in triple-digit temperatures, in-your-face discipline and a daily diet limited to an apple, a carrot, and a bowl of beans. Youths were kicked and forced to swallow mud at the boot camp facility. The youth died of heat exhaustion and vomited mud before he died.[16] In South Dakota's Plankinton boot camp a female offender who had been sentenced to the facility for shoplifting a Beanie Baby died after being forced to a 2.7 mile run in sweltering heat. Staff denied the inmate water but did administer a full course of ridicule: calling her a faker, laughing at her, dragging her, and dropping her limp hand onto her face. By the end, she was lying in a pool of her own urine, frothing from the mouth, gasping for breath, and twitching.[17]

Shock incarceration programs provide a combination of punitive and rehabilitative program elements that are expected (in many programs) both to deter and to rehabilitate. The basic program model contains the more punitive elements including hard work, physical training, and military drill and ceremony. These elements may have some positive value. For example, they may promote physical health, a drug-free environment, and a sense of accomplishment. However, it is unlikely that any of the individual programs' components will lead to increased discipline, accountability, or improved work habits as frequently hypothesized. Based on previous research on deterrence, it is also unlikely that they will have a deterrent effect. For example, Arizona's boot camp for criminals between the ages of 18 and 25, opened in January 1990, has not shown to be effective in rehabilitation or as a deterrent. Of the 1,253 offenders admitted during the first three years of the facilities' existence, 70 percent were back in custody within four to seven years; the total number of prisoners housed by the state's Department of Corrections grew by 41 percent; and the annual cost of operating the unit was 1.5 million more than that of a traditional prison in Arizona.[18]

Rehabilitative programming in shock incarceration programs has received increased emphasis over the years. If the basic military model is viewed primarily as a catalyst for personal change, rehabilitative programming is of great importance because the other benefits of the program are minimal and, most importantly, are not related to recidivism.

Examination of the three guiding principles of effective treatment, however, reveals that shock incarceration programs probably do not maximize their treatment potential. Although rehabilitative programming attempts to target criminogenic needs, the effects of such programming are mediated by the responsivity principle, which stipulates that treatment is most effective when counselors relate to offenders in a warm and supportive manner and provide anti-criminal modeling and problem solving. Thus, although staff may try to provide anti-criminal modeling, the authoritarian atmosphere may not be conducive to effective treatment. The following sections discuss the effectiveness of boot camp programs in changing inmate attitudes, reducing recidivism, and providing positive activities in the community upon release.

5-4 Attitude Change

A frequent assumption made regarding incarceration is that the pains of imprisonment will be accompanied by the harms of imprisonment. That is, the pains of imprisonment lead to negative attitudes toward prison, staff, and programs (i.e., prisonization), thus prison will have a detrimental impact on offenders.

Inmates are hypothesized to form a "society of captives" characterized by anti-staff attitudes. As a consequence, offenders just reject constructive aspects of the prison such as treatment or education programs that may give them the skills needed to succeed when they return to the community.

An equally destructive influence of incarceration may be the development (or exacerbation) of general antisocial attitudes. Reviews of the evaluation literature indicate a positive association between antisocial attitudes and criminal activities. Most theories of crime also recognize the significance of criminal cognitions or attitudes.

The impact of shock incarceration on inmate attitudes has not yet been fully explored. It has been hypothesized that the boot camp environment, with its strict rules, discipline, and regimentation, may increase the pains of imprisonment and as a result promote the development of increased anti-staff, anti-program, and antisocial attitudes. According to this view, the regimental routine may have a negative impact on participants. Offenders may leave the boot camp prison angry, disillusioned, and more negative than they would have been had they served time in a traditional prison.

On the other hand, the negative effect of the regimented routine may be offset or mediated by the rehabilitative programming required of inmates. In New York's boot camp program, with its emphasis on rehabilitation, inmates may have developed more antisocial or anti-program/staff attitudes. Changes in inmate attitudes, then, may vary as a function of the type of program. Offenders graduating from more treatment-oriented programs may not change at all or may change in a positive direction, while offenders graduating from programs that emphasize work and physical training may develop more negative attitudes over time.

The impact of boot camp prisons on inmate attitudes during incarceration (attitudes toward the program/staff and antisocial attitudes) was assessed in this phase of the evaluation. The attitudes of offenders serving time in the shock incarceration programs was compared with the attitudes of demographically similar offenders serving time in traditional prisons. Attitudes toward the shock incarceration program (or prison) and antisocial attitudes were assessed once after the offenders arrived at the boot camp (or prison) and again three to six months later, depending on the length of the shock incarceration program. Programs differed in critical dimensions, such as the emphasis placed on rehabilitation, the voluntary nature of the program, and program difficulty—dimensions that might be expected to influence attitudinal change.

The researchers concluded that boot camp entrants became more positive about the boot camp experience over the course of the programs. In contrast, prison inmates either did not change or developed more negative attitudes toward their prison experience. In addition, there was no evidence that attitudinal change varied as a function of the type of boot camp.

When the antisocial attitudes were measured, there were no differences between boot camp inmates and prison inmates. Both types of inmates became less antisocial during their time in confinement.

Changes in attitudes may also be related to the characteristics of the program, such as the amount of time devoted to rehabilitation versus work and physical training, the number of offenders dismissed from the program, and the voluntary nature of the program. Neither time devoted to rehabilitation nor voluntary exit was significantly related to program attitude. However, time devoted to rehabilitation, program rigor, and the voluntary nature appeared to lead to greater reductions in antisocial attitudes.

Despite differences among the programs in content and implementation, the results of this study were surprisingly consistent. Boot camp inmates became more positive about the program over time, while offenders serving prison time did not develop more positive attitudes. Both groups reflected less antisocial attitudes over time. This was true of enhanced boot camp programs that emphasized treatment as well as programs that emphasized military training, hard labor, and discipline.

The study finding that boot camp inmates and prison inmates become less antisocial during incarceration supports some current research indicating that prison may have positive influence on some inmates. However, it is important to remember that these offenders were different from the general prison population. By and large, they were young and had been convicted of relatively minor offenses.

5-5 Recidivism

One of the first questions asked about boot camp programs is, "Are they successful?" By successful, many people mean, "Do they reduce the criminal activity of offenders subsequent to release?" The researchers concluded that the impact of boot camp programs on offender recidivism is at best negligible. The results suggest that offenders who are released from shock incarceration programs appear to perform just as well as those who serve longer prison terms. Accordingly, longer prison terms do not serve as an additional deterrent.

Recent studies conducted by the Department of Justice, criminologists, and task forces in various states have shown that boot camps fare no better in rehabilitating criminals than traditional lock-ups.[19] After these studies came to light in the 1990s, and controversies surrounding deaths at a few boot camps, several states, including New Hampshire, Georgia, Illinois, Maryland, and California, have either closed or restructured their programs.[20] The researchers concluded that it would be irresponsible to continue placing offenders (particularly juveniles) in such programs without more carefully monitoring their effects at both the individual and system levels. If success is measured in terms of recidivism alone, there is little evidence that the in-prison phase of boot camp programs has been successful.

Are boot camp programs successful in achieving their objectives? Programs that clearly defined their major objectives, such as those that had two major objectives—reducing prison crowding and changing offenders were the most effective in reducing prison crowding. However, the programs were far less effectiveness in changing offenders.

Most evaluators of prison boot camp programs use the recidivism rate standard of 30 percent to gage the success or failure of a particular program. For example, using 30 percent as a reference, a boot camp program with a recidivism rate of 35 percent would be deemed not effective whereas a recidivism rate of 28 percent would be successful. Researchers studying Alabama's boot camp programs indicate that they have a 37 percent recidivism rate for boot camp graduates in one-year follow ups.[21] Similarly, Alabama parolees who did not participate in boot camp programs had a recidivism rate of 25.7 percent within one year of their release from prison. In Washington there are no differences in recidivism in those prisoners placed in boot camp programs and those inmates paroled through traditional mechanisms.[22] Overall, the evaluations of boot camp prisons show little evidence that they can significantly lower recidivism rates.[23]

ARTICLE
Community Service: A Review of the Basic Issues[24]

Introduction

It is clear that the use of community service as a sentencing alternative is a major judicial and correctional trend in the United States. In part driven by tax-limiting initiatives such as propositions 13 in California and 2.5 in Massachusetts, community service seemingly has high potential in the continued search for more effective and less costly methods of dealing with offenders. The trend toward community service is driven by economic considerations brought about by the efforts to balance the federal budget. These efforts forecast that there will be a reduction in federal funds available to states, counties, and municipalities that will impact the criminal justice systems generally and correctional systems specifically.

In addition to these economic influences, the prospects for community service were significantly bolstered by enactment of the Federal Comprehensive Crime Control Act of 1984, effective November 1, 1987, which states:

> If sentenced to probation, the defendant must also be ordered to pay a fine, make restitution, and/or work in community service.

Changes and directions in the federal correctional system—probation, parole, and institutions—have often established trends for corrections at state and local levels.

The definition of community service varies in the professional literature, but for purposes of this commentary, it is a court order that an offender perform a specified number of hours of uncompensated work or service within a given time period for a nonprofit community organization or tax-supported agency. It clearly is distinguished from monetary restitution to the victim or payment of a fine to a political jurisdiction: restitution and fine, as in the federal legislation noted above, also may be part of a court order. In a generic sense, community service has been labeled as "restitution"—a sanction imposed by an official of the criminal justice system requiring an offender to make a payment of money or service to either the direct or a substitute crime victim. Community service has had other labels, among them court referral, reparation, volunteer work, symbolic restitution, service restitution, and, for those individuals who perform community service without an adjudication of guilt, pretrial diversion and pretrial intervention.

More pragmatically, however, the specific use of community sanctions is of recent origin, emerging conceptually in England in the late 1960s and operationally in 1972, with Parliament granting the courts authority to order convicted offenders to perform community service. Within just a few years, the program was expanded in England and introduced into the United States and Canada.

Considerable literature on this sentencing and correctional alternative has been generated since that time, and at least two major bibliographies are now available which reflect that growing interest.

There are several issues that should be carefully reviewed prior to the decision to begin community service as a sentencing alternative or enhancement. The purpose of this article is to review the more significant issues and the options available to the judicial and correctional decision makers as each issue is examined. The issues include, but are not limited to, offender eligibility, criteria for selection, organizational models for community service, community service investigations, sentencing considerations, assignments to community service programs, supervision, and evaluation.

Judicial and Correctional Philosophy

Community service, as with any other sanction, should support the overall philosophical orientation of the criminal justice system and its judicial and correctional decision makers specifically. That philosophical orientation—whether it be rehabilitation, restitution, deterrence, retribution, punishment, or something else, singly or in combination—should be translated into community service program goals, objectives, and orientation. Simply stated, operational decisions should be developed from some shared understandings about community service as a sentencing alternative—an alternative to confinement, fines, restitution, and/or other traditional penalties, with special attention focused upon the offender and the community. Operationally, a community service program may be developed to increase the penalty to an appropriate level of deterrence (just desert). Such programs may marginally repay the community for criminal damages by helping the community meet its needs for unpaid workers (e.g., highway cleanup, school maintenance, etc.).

It is not our purpose to argue here what the purposes for community service should be, but it is important to emphasize the need for decision makers to specify why community service would be a useful sentencing alternative for them. If they state the goals that they seek, they can design programs to achieve these goals.

Offender Eligibility

Community service has been utilized mostly by the lower courts for individuals convicted of offenses considered less serious, especially misdemeanors, including traffic violations. An option to be considered is the use of community service for more serious offenders. Within the federal system, even apart from the Comprehensive Crime Control Act requirements, community service has been ordered for white-collar and corporate offenders, and even for corporations. The inclusion of felons, in addition to misdemeanants, appears a rational expansion of community service, providing that the threat to community safety is always considered and minimized. The issue of dangerousness clearly is a critical correctional issue.

Concerns about dangerousness may be reflected in mandated exceptions to the utilization of community service for people (1) committing certain types of offenses, (2) exhibiting particular traits or characteristics in their background, such as drug addiction, or (3) committing offenses with weapons or violence. Indeed, as the question of offender eligibility is considered, it may be appropriate to consider whether there is any reason why individuals entering into, or being processed through, the criminal justice system, who otherwise are deemed appropriate for a judicial or correctional release to the community, should be barred from community service. This would include adults and juveniles, felons, misdemeanants, probationers, parolees, individuals, corporations, those convicted of offenses and those diverted from the justice system.

Selection for Community Service

Selection for a **community service program** requires a dual focus: on the offender and on the community. In considering individuals, explicit and objective criteria are necessary to prevent in community service the sentencing disparities that have been so well documented nationwide in other sentencing options. It has been noted that "the lack of standards or guidelines means that similar offenders can receive very different community service sentences for the same offense from a given judge, from two judges in the same jurisdiction, or from judges in different jurisdictions."

Allegations that community service sentences are applied in an unfair or discriminatory fashion also flow from a lack of criteria. The question of equity assuredly will surface if the community service sanction is applied only to the poor and the minorities or, contrastingly, only to middle- or upper-income offenders.

In determining selection criteria, assigning an offender to community service requires attention to community safety, to the offender's attitude and special skills or talents, to the seriousness of the offense, to the availability of a suitable community service placement, and to the wisdom of selecting other sentencing alternatives. As the community is examined, several other important issues emerge, including the public's attitude toward specific offenses and offenders, as well as the impact of community service on perceptions of the justice system by the citizenry. It is important that the public see community service as both a benefit to the community and a reasonable judicial disposition of the offender.

The process by which the criteria are established may be as important as the criteria themselves. It has been suggested that a "core group of advocates" consisting perhaps of members of the judiciary, corrections, and the community, join together to establish the standards for selection to community service.

Organizational Issue

A community service program of any size requires some administrative structure. The two most common administrative entities are the probation agency and a volunteer bureau. There may also be a combined effort in which the probation agency has some oversight of those functions that are uniquely offender-connected within the volunteer bureau. In this case, the probation office and the private organization have mutually supportive and compatible roles. A third type of administrative entity is the private organization created solely for the purpose of overseeing community service activities. An example of this third type is the Foundation for People, a nonprofit corporation established in Los Angeles under the aegis of the Probation Office of the U.S. District Court for the Central District of California. One of its several activities is to work with the federal courts to arrange community service for white-collar offenders and assist in the vocational training, counseling, and job-placement of blue-collar offenders.

There are several important distinctions that enter into the issue of the probation agency, volunteer bureau, or other entity providing the organizational structure for community service. The probation agency and the volunteer bureau are established in the community and have important connections with other organizations that already play a role in community-based corrections, which could serve as the foundation for the community service function. Probation, as an established part of the criminal justice system, can provide a legitimacy and stability to a community service program and affect both judicial and community acceptance. Volunteer bureaus long have been involved in identifying and matching community needs with individuals able to offer a variety of services.

Regardless of the agency charged with the community service function, it is assumed in this writing that the order to community service is usually a condition of probation. However, it may be appropriate for community service to be ordered by the court without probation, particularly for less serious offenses, and in those smaller jurisdictions in which the court has continuous firsthand contact with the agency providing the community service function. The organization with the administrative responsibility must be able to provide some form of community service investigation, discussed below, as well as to supervise community service. Therefore, it must have the authority to insure compliance with the court order.

In making an organizational decision, there is a need to focus on two basic functions: developing a plan to join offenders with community service and supervising these offenders in that service obligation. These functions parallel the traditional investigation and supervision functions of probation, but this similarity is not to be interpreted as a preference for the probation agency option. Let us examine these functions separately.

The Community Service Investigation

The community service investigation is similar to a presentencing investigation and report. This investigation determines the appropriateness of community service as a sanction. A number of important issues surface in a community service investigation and report, especially in the development of a plan for community service. Some of the issues are:

- What constitutes an appropriate community service investigation?
- What is an appropriate format for a community service report?
- Should there be an investigation and report on all individuals eligible to receive a community service sentence or only on specific individuals? If the latter, is it at the direction of the court, the discretion of the probation agency or volunteer bureau, or upon request by the prosecutor, the defendant, or the defense attorney?

- Should a community service investigation and report be separate from, an adjunct to, or part of the formal presentence investigation and report? Indeed, for some minor offenses, would a community service investigation and report be an appropriate substitute for a presentence investigation and report? How much (additional) time should be allowed for the investigation, the preparation of a report, and the development of an appropriate plan?
- Does the community service investigation and report require a "specialist," familiar with the community and its needs, who is able to connect offender and community?
- Should the community service investigation and report be conducted before or after the imposition of a community service requirement?
- Should the agency responsible for the investigation and report also be charged with supervision of the community service?
- From an administrative perspective, how many community service investigations and reports are the equivalent of a presentence investigation and report?

Some Sentencing Considerations

The addition of community service as a sentencing alternative creates several unique issues for the court. Obviously, traditional considerations relating to the imposition of sentence remain, such as the concern for justice, equity, protection of the community, and rehabilitation. If there is an order of community service in lieu of confinement in a local custodial facility, a question of equivalence arises. How many hours of community service are the equivalent of a day in custody? Is it a day-for-a-day, two for one, three for one, or some other ratio? If it is a day-for-a-day, then is the equivalent of a 30-day jail sentence 30 eight-hour days of community service, or 90 eight-hour days? In the interest of fairness and equity, these ratios need to be established.

If on the other hand, the court wishes to impose community service instead of a fine—perhaps because the offender simply will be unable to pay a fine—what is the dollar equivalent of an hour of community service work? Is it minimum wage, the prevailing wage in the community, or is it equal to the offender's normal hourly rate—perhaps $4 an hour for one offender and $25 an hour for another? Is it more equitable to have a uniform "equivalency" or to have equivalency individualized? If the latter, one of these offenders could work off a $1,000 community service obligation with 250 hours of service; the other could accomplish the same in 100 hours.

Community service can be thought of as providing some of the equity that is credited to the day-fine principle pioneered in Scandinavia and now found in several other nations, including Austria and Germany. Under this principle, an offender is sentenced to a fine of his or her earnings for a given number of days, so that the amount of money involved varies with the size of the earnings. As administered in Sweden, the fine is collected by that country's equivalent of our Internal Revenue Service, which collects all taxes or other money owed to the government. This agency determines the amount of the fine from its records of the offender's past taxable earnings, deducts an amount for necessities and dependents, but imposes some fine-per-day of the penalty, even on those whose only income is from welfare. They collect almost every fine without jailing by allowing installment payments with interest for those who cannot pay immediately, but attaching salaries and even seizing possessions if there is a persistent failure to pay. Our courts, by imposing a penalty of a specified number of days of community service, are getting the same amount of service from each offender punished in this way, regardless of contrasts in the price that the services of different persons command per day when compensated in the free market.

It seems essential that the court fix both the precise number of hours of community service to be performed and the period of time during which the obligation is to be completed. Regardless of whether the number of hours was determined by the nature of the offense or the background of the offender, some other "arithmetic" needs to be completed. That arithmetic must focus on the balance between the number of hours to be performed and the length of time given for completion of community service. An order for 400 hours of community service approximately equals one day, or perhaps two evenings, of service per week for a year. Is that a reasonable assessment when examining all of the factors—the offense, the offender, the offender's family and employment obligations, the community's needs for the service to be performed, and the feeling that "justice was done"? Or would 400 hours of community service over two years be more appropriate, considering all of the variables?

One last numeric item: there seemingly should be both a minimum and maximum number of hours that can be ordered. It is assumed that there is some number of hours below which the administrative burden to the agencies involved in the delivery of community services would be inefficient and ineffective, and a number above which the offender could not hope to comply with the order. While we do not intend to be prescriptive here, the courts need to establish a meaningful range; perhaps from a 30-hour minimum, equivalent to one day a week for one month for a minor offense or offender, to as much as 400 hours per year for five years, a total of 2,000 hours of service, for the most serious offense or offender that still would permit imposition of a community-based correctional alternative.

Community Service Assignments

Following an investigation and report, and an order by the court for community service, there is a requirement to assign the offender to a specific community activity. As noted, this assignment may be made through a probation agency, volunteer bureau, or other organization designated to administer the community service effort. There are two basic perspectives about the assignment issue: the first argues for matching offenders with community service based on the skills or talents of the offender and the documented needs of the community. An often-cited example is the assignment of a physician ordered to perform community service to a program in which medical skills may be utilized, such as a public health or "free" medical clinic of some sort. This kind of matching of abilities and needs may or may not seem as appropriate. A second type of matching attempts to connect the community service assignment to the offense committed. For example, the assignment of an offender without medical service skills convicted of driving under the influence to a hospital emergency room—where there is considerable opportunity to see the harm done by drinking drivers—may not provide much relevant service, but it may serve as a good deterrent.

An alternative to these two types of matching is the more or less random assignment of offenders to community activities as offenders become available through the system and community needs are identified. Simply put, if two or three projects are identified as valid community needs requiring the services of 25 individuals, one assigns to these projects the next 25 offenders ordered to community service by the court, regardless of the number of hours ordered or the special abilities of the offenders. Offenders may be allowed to request participation in one or another of the community services identified. This method has the advantage of simplicity, and perhaps some basic equity, although it is clear that the hypothetical physician mentioned above is not providing the most meaningful service to the community, particularly if the community service project at that time is clearing trash from the side of the road.

All approaches require basic data about the offense, offender, and the community service requirements, but the matching approach—in contrast to randomness—requires considerably more data about these matters. Personal data about skills and abilities are needed, as is related information about employment schedules, indicating hours of the day and days of the week available for service, and special clothing or other needed equipment. Indeed, systems involved in matching also require considerable specificity about the nature of the tasks to be accomplished and the skills required of the offender for their accomplishment. A large matching system most likely would be computer-based, whereas a smaller system might simply use 3 × 5-inch index cards.

A number of other related issues surface about the assignment phenomena: what agencies are eligible to receive community service? Agencies with a religious orientation or involvement might be ineligible because of perceived violations of the doctrine of separation of church and state, while assignments to political organizations, public interest or pressure groups, or controversial collectivities of citizens create other problems. Then, too, there are special problems associated with organized labor and with some citizen perceptions that community service deprives "honest citizens" of employment opportunities. Even apart from the issue of legitimacy of organizations to receive services, there are questions as to whether such community services should be provided to individuals as opposed to organizations . . . for example, to individual victims of crime.

Supervision of Community Service

The supervision function, whether performed by a probation agency, volunteer bureau, or other organization, also raises some significant issues. Among them are questions that focus on disclosure about the offender, the offense, and personal background to the community organization receiving the offender's service. Is there a reverse side of that coin that assures the offender at least a minimum right to privacy? And during the time that the offender is performing community service, does the community service sponsoring agency—the volunteer bureau, for example—have some degree of liability for the offender's behavior? If the offender is injured while performing community service, are there disability rights vested in that service? And should individuals sponsoring community service activities have personal insurance to protect them against a variety of potential legal actions that may grow from the connection to community service? While the charging of fees to offenders for probation services has been emerging nationwide, would it be appropriate for similar charges to be extended for community service investigations and supervision? Finally, would it be appropriate for the tax-supported agencies or the nonprofit community organizations receiving community services to pay the court for the services received?

Apart from these issues, there are more traditional questions about community service supervision, ranging from the identification of those who provide it, the frequency of contact with the offender and the community service supervisor or agency, the nature and schedule of reports, reassignment determinations, and the overall relationship between probation supervision and community service supervision, particularly if two separate agencies are involved.

Under some circumstances, there may be important questions raised about compliance with the community service court order. What constitutes a violation: would it be a failure to complete all of the assigned hours in the prescribed time or, in the shorter time frame, a failure to appear to perform service on one or more occasions? Would a belligerent or disruptive attitude warrant cessation of a community service order? Probation and parole supervision long have had explicit conditions or standards of behavior. Is there a need for a parallel series of community service guidelines for those involved in both the supervision and performance of community service?

Evaluation of Community Service

At a minimum, two areas of community service need assessment: the first centers on measures of offender success and failure; the second upon some determination of cost-benefits. The cost-benefit analyses must consider both the criminal justice system and the community. In short, effectiveness and efficiency are required targets for analysis.

Definitions of success and failure for offenders involved in the many varieties of community corrections long have been troublesome. Although we do not address that conflicted arena here, we note that community service does not make those assessments simpler, but rather more complex. An overall evaluation should go beyond that which could be generated by data as to whether or not the offender completed the required number of hours of community service within the court-ordered period of time.

Several examples may illustrate the complexity. The first focuses on the definition of success and failure by asking how the two are related in probation and community service. Consider an offender who successfully completes a court-ordered community service obligation but is declared in violation of probation for behavior that is not related to the community service. How is the offender's overall performance to be assessed?

If costs are the focus of evaluation, two different sets of cost data may be examined. The first may be the value of services provided the community, calculated at some arbitrary hourly or daily rate such as the national minimum wage or an average local wage. The overall dollar value of the services provided are the number of hours of service multiplied by the value of those hours for a given period of time. A second set of data may be derived from the "savings" obtained by having offenders provide community service instead of being in local custody. This may be calculated as the daily custodial rate multiplied by the number of confinement days not served minus the cost of community service. It is probable that estimates of monies saved by the justice system from the non-incarceration of offenders who are performing community service may be markedly different from estimates of the value of the community service developed from hourly or daily wage comparisons, and that the two might be added. This difference would grow if calculated to include welfare assistance given to families of confined offenders. If community service serves as an alternative to the capital costs of constructing a custodial facility, the savings, even when prorated in some fashion, become enormous. If these community services generate activities and projects which otherwise might not have been accomplished—that is, things which the community could not have done without these court ordered services—perhaps some other dollar equivalents would be justified.

Finally, improvements in community feelings about "justice" generally, and the criminal justice system specifically, on one hand, or the improvement of the offender's personal feelings of self worth which may be generated from performing a service to the community on the other, cannot be measured readily, but nevertheless need assessment.

Summary

Community service, as a sentencing option, has an operational history of about 15 years. There is every reason to believe that its utilization in America and elsewhere will expand significantly during the next decade. Because it has evolved and grown so rapidly, there has not yet been adequate time or attention given to identifying the issues that surround its use or to develop standards for that use. Indeed, there is some evidence of a failure to understand that the many issues that have been or yet may be identified are completely interrelated.

The authors have not been prescriptive, but would argue that there is a mandate to examine carefully a number of issues about community service. Some of these have been identified—judicial and correctional philosophies, offender eligibility and selection criteria, organizational arrangements, community service investigations and supervision, sentencing considerations, community service assignments, and evaluation. If community service is to become a truly viable sentencing option, these areas need thoughtful consideration by those academicians, administrators, practitioners, and researchers concerned with criminal justice.

Summary

Diversion is designed to funnel the offender away from the criminal justice system and into community programs that should be more beneficial than incarceration. Diversion became popular in the late 1960s and 1970s and is frequently used to refer to the release of the accused pending trial. Diversion is based on the assumption that the diverted individual will participate in some treatment program in return for the removal from the criminal justice system process before trial. Diversion is commonly referred to as the "front door" program, because it limits the number of people entering jail or prison facilities.

Since their inception in 1983, shock incarceration/probation programs, also known as boot camps, have enjoyed considerable support. Like other intermediate sanctions, the programs are intended to alleviate institution overcrowding and reduce recidivism. In addition, because they are perceived as being "tough" on crime, in contrast to some other intermediate sentences such as probation, they have been enthusiastically embraced as a viable correction option for delinquent youths. In addition, the presumed combination of cost savings and punitive nature has proven irresistible to politicians.

As boot camp programs have developed, rehabilitative programming has begun to play a more prominent role in the day-to-day routine. The earliest boot camp models devoted little time to such programs. Many of those pioneering programs have since been enhanced with additional therapeutic services. Programs developed in recent years seemed to place a greater emphasis on rehabilitative programming from the start. Despite the excitement over boot camp prisons, the success of these institutions has been found by researchers to be minimal. Thus, the recidivism rates of boot camp programs are equal to those of state prisons.

It is clear that the use of community service as a sentencing alternative is a major judicial and correctional trend in the United States. In part, driven by tax-limiting initiatives such as Propositions 13 in California and 2.5 in Massachusetts, community service has a seemingly high potential in the continued search for more effective and less costly methods of dealing with offenders. The trend toward community service also is driven by economic considerations brought about by efforts to balance the federal budget. These efforts forecast that there will be a reduction in federal funds available to states, counties, and municipalities that will impact the criminal justice systems generally and correctional systems specifically.

Discussion Questions

1. Explain the concept behind shock incarceration.
2. How does shock incarceration differ from prison?
3. Explain the concept behind diversion.
4. What are the advantages of diversion for the defendant? Disadvantages?
5. How successful have shock incarceration programs been?
6. What are the three psychological principles considered in determining the appropriate treatment of an offender?

Chapter Quiz

True/False

1. Diversion programs are designed to funnel offenders away from the criminal justice system and into community programs, which should be more beneficial for the offender and the community when compared to incarceration.
2. Diversion programs can only take place after the offender has been officially charged with a crime.
3. Boot camp programs are an example of shock incarceration.
4. Boot camp programs are modeled after the military with the exception that inmates do not have to participate in military drill and ceremony.
5. Boot camp programs are designed primarily for middle-aged offenders convicted of violent crimes.

Multiple Choice

1. Typical targets for diversion programs are which type of offenders?
   a. first time violent offenders
   b. individuals with drug and alcohol problems
   c. repeat property offenders
   d. Diversion programs are only for those charged with driving under the influence and other minor traffic offenses.
2. In rehabilitative treatment, which one of the following is NOT one of the guiding psychological principles?
   a. Intensive treatment should be matched with high-risk offenders.
   b. Treatment should address criminogenic needs.
   c. Intensive treatment should be matched with very low risk offenders
   d. Treatment should follow general strategies of effective treatment.
3. Which one of the statements below is NOT true of shock incarceration programs?
   a. They are designed for middle-aged offenders convicted of violent crimes.
   b. They are designed for young offenders convicted of non-violent offenses.
   c. Female offenders are permitted to participate in about 50 percent of the programs.
   d. Most programs have minimum and maximum age limits.
4. Which one of the following statements has been hypothesized regarding antisocial attitudes between boot camp inmates and prison inmates?
   a. Prison inmates demonstrated more antisocial attitudes.
   b. Boot camp inmates demonstrated more antisocial attitudes.
   c. There were no differences in antisocial attitudes between boot camp inmates and prison inmates.
   d. It is not possible to measure a variable such as antisocial attitudes among inmates because they all have committed crimes.

5. What year did shock incarceration programs come into existence?
   a. 1930
   b. 1967
   c. 1983
   d. 1990

Endnotes

1. National Advisory Commission on Criminal Justice Standards and Goals, *Courts* (Washington, DC: Government Printing Office, 1973).
2. Paul Dynia and Hung-En Sung, "The Safety and Effectiveness of Diverting Felony Drug Offenders to Residential Treatment as Measured by Recidivism," *Criminal Justice Policy Review* 11(2000): 299–311
3. "Multisite Evaluation of Shock Incarceration: Evaluation Report," *National Institute of Justice Research Report,* November 1994.
4. Ibid. Note: this section is an abridgement of the report and the conclusions noted are those of the researchers.
5. American Correctional Association, *Excellence in Corrections* (Lanham, MD: American Correctional Association, 1998).
6. Ibid.
7. Ibid.
8. R. Lot, R. Regal, and R. Raymond, "Delinquency and Special Deterrence," *Criminology* 15 (4, 1978): 539–547.
9. J. O. Fickenauer, *Scared Straight! and the Panacea Phenomenon* (Englewood Cliffs, NJ: Prentice-Hall, 1992.)
10. P. Gendreau and R. R. Ross, "Revivication of Rehabilitation: Evidence from the 1980s," *Justice Quarterly* 4 (1987): 349–408.
11. E. Zamble and F. Porporino, "Coping, Imprisonment, and Rehabilitation: Some Data and Their Implications," *Criminal Justice Behavior* 17 (1, 1990) 53–70.
12. R. Martinson, "What Works? Questions and Answers About Prison Reform," *Public Interest* 35 (1974): 22–54.
13. The Associated Press State and Local Wire, "Custer Boot Camp Sued Over Alleged Abuses," 8 August 2001.
14. Alisa Blackwood, "Boy's Death Puts Spotlight on Boot Camps for Youth," *Chattanooga Times,* 8 July 2001: A11.
15. Christian Parenti, "When Tough Love Kills," *The Progressive* 64 (10, 2000) 31–34.
16. Misty Allen, "Boot Camps Fail to Pass Muster," *Governing* 11 (2, 1997): 41–41.

17. D. A. Andrews, I. Zinger, R. D. Hoge, J. Bonta, P. Gendreau and F. T. Cullen, "Does Correctional Treatment Work? A Clinically Relevant and Psychologically Informed Meta-Analysis," *Criminology* 28 (3, 1990): 369–404.
18. Deborah Sharp, "Correctional Options: Boot Camps, Punishment and Treatment," *Corrections Today* 57 (June 1995).
19. D. A. Andrews, J. Bonta, and R. D. Hoge, "Classification for Effective Rehabilitative: Rediscovering Psychology," *Criminal Justice and Behavior* 17 (1, 1990): 19–52.
20. F. Cullen and P. Gendreau, "The Effectiveness of Correctional Rehabilitation: Reconsidering the 'Nothing Works' Debate," in L. Goodstein and D. L. Mackenzie (eds.), *The American Prison: Issues in Research and Policy* (New York: Plenum Press, 1989.)
21. Jerald C. Burns and Gennaro F. Vito, "An Impact Analysis of the Alabama Boot Camp Program," *Federal Probation* 49 (1995): 63–67.
22. Carol Poole and Peggy Slavick, Boot Camps: A Washington State Update and Overview of National Findings. (Olympia, Washington State Institute for Public Policy, 1997).
23. Ronald Burns, "Boot Camps: The Empirical Record," *American Jails,* 10:42–49.
24. Robert M. Carter, Jack Cocks, and Daniel Glaser, "Community Service: A Review of the Basic Issues," *Federal Probation* (March 1987): 4–10. Reprinted with permission (notes omitted).

Chapter 6

Probation

Checking in with your probation officer is a must.
John Boykin/PhotoEdit

Key Terms

intensive supervision probation
jail therapy probation
regular probation
revocation of probation
shock probation
split sentencing
technical violation of probation

Outline

6-1 What Is Probation?
6-2 History of Probation
6-3 Status of Probation
6-4 Extent of Probation
6-5 Criteria for Granting Probation
6-6 Conditions of Probation
6-7 Probationers' Rights
    6-7a Search of Probationers
    6-7b Right to Confidentiality
    6-7c Revocation of Probation
6-8 Functions of Probation
    6-8a The Probation Officer
6-9 Probation Offices
6-10 Future of Probation
Article—Guiding Philosophies for Probation in the 21st Century
Summary
Discussion Questions
Chapter Quiz
Endnotes

Learning Objectives

After studying this chapter, the reader will be able to:

- Explain why probation is the most often used sanction for felony offenders.
- Identify what is involved with the granting of probation.
- List the four categories of probation.
- Explain the contributions of John Augustus to probation.
- Explain the philosophy involved in probation.
- Describe the criteria for granting probation.
- List the usual conditions placed on defendants when they are placed on probation.
- Analyze the issues involved in determining what constitutional rights individuals on probation retain.
- Explain the two questions involved in revoking probation based on new criminal activity.
- Explain the functions of probation.
- Identify the popular philosophies in contemporary probation.

6-1 What Is Probation?

Probation is the conditional release of a defendant and can be used to describe a sentence that has been given to a defendant in which the defendant is placed and maintained in the community under the supervision of an agent of the court. Probation can have several different meanings within our present criminal justice system.

1. Probation refers to a status or class (i.e., he or she is on probation and thus subject to certain rules and conditions that must be followed in order to avoid being institutionalized).
2. Probation also refers to an organization (i.e., the county probation department).

Once a defendant is found guilty, the most frequently used method of court disposition is probation. It is clear that not every defendant should be institutionalized. Nationwide, in 2001, 53% of all probationers had been convicted of a felony, 45% of a misdemeanor, and 1% of other infractions.[1]

Probation is a sentence that involves no confinement, or at most, only a short period of confinement under specific conditions. Under probation, the court retains authority over the case to supervise, modify the conditions, and resentence the defendant if the terms of probation are violated. Probation is a legal status created by the court. While the classic definition of probation as set forth above indicates that it does not involve commitment, it is being increasingly linked to a short period of commitment at a training school, boot camp, or other local custody facility.

Probation permits the defendant to remain in his or her community under the supervision of a probation officer. Probation usually involves:

1. A judicial finding that the defendant is guilty;
2. The imposition of conditions upon the defendant's continued freedom; and
3. The provisions or means for helping him or her meet these conditions and for determining the degree to which he or she needs them.

Probation is more than giving the defendant another chance. Its central thrust is to give him or her positive assistance in adjustment in the free community.[2]

Probation is generally classified into four different categories:
1. Regular probation
2. Intensive probation
3. Deferred adjudication probation
4. Pretrial diversion probation[3]

Deferred adjudication and pretrial diversion were discussed in Chapter 1. **Regular probation** is defined as the release of a convicted offender under conditions imposed by the courts for a specified period of time. **Intensive supervision probation** is for offenders who are too antisocial for the relative freedom afforded by regular probation yet not so seriously criminal to require incarceration. Approximately 40 states have some form of intensive supervision probation.[4]

6-2 History of Probation

John Augustus is considered the originator of the concept of probation. As early as 1841, Augustus, a private citizen, requested that Boston judges release young defendants under his supervision. It is estimated that over an 18-year period, he supervised about 2,000 individuals on probation. Most of these were youths age 16 to 19. He helped them get jobs and reestablish themselves in the community. Only a few of the individuals under his supervision became involved in subsequent criminal behavior.

John Augustus was born in Burlington, Massachusetts, in 1785. He moved to Lexington in approximately 1806 and established a shoe factory in his home. In 1820, he established another shoe factory in Boston. In 1829, he moved from Lexington to Boston. His Boston shop at 5 Franklin Street was near the police court. According to Augustus's records, he was frequently contacted at this shop by individuals seeking his help.

It appears that it was the Washington temperance movement that first led Augustus to visit the police court and later the municipal court in Boston. The movement resulted in the formation of the Washington Total Abstinence Society in Boston in 1841. The society's members pledged not only to refrain from using intoxicating drinks but also to restore to temperance those who were addicted to alcohol. The members visited the police court and attempted to rescue the drunks.

Augustus's first probation experience was in August 1841. Set forth below is his description of the experience:

> In the month of August 1841, I was in court one morning, when the door communicating with the lock-room was opened and an officer entered, followed by a ragged and wretched looking man . . . I imagined

from the man's appearance that his offence was that of yielding to his appetite for intoxicating drinks . . . the man was charged with being a common drunkard. The case was clearly made out, but before sentence had been passed, I conversed with him a few moments, and found that he was not yet past all hope and reformation, although his appearance and his looks precluded a belief in the mind of others that he would ever become a man again. . . . I bailed him, by permission of the Court. He was ordered to appear for sentence in three weeks from that time. He signed a pledge and became a sober man; at the expiration of this period of probation, I accompanied him into the court room; his whole appearance was changed and no one, not even the scrutinizing officers, could have believed that he was the same person who less than a month before, had stood trembling on the prisoner's stand. The Judge expressed himself much pleased with the account we gave of the man, and instead of the usual penalty, imprisonment in the House of Corrections, he fined him one cent and costs.[5]

Augustus continued to appear in court to receive on-probation alcoholics who seemed likely prospects for rehabilitation. From 1841 until his death in 1859, his home became a refuge for people he had bailed until more permanent places could be made for them.

Augustus's work inspired the Massachusetts legislature to authorize the hiring of a paid probation officer for Boston. By 1880, probation was extended to other jurisdictions within the state. Missouri and Vermont soon copied the Massachusetts procedures. The federal government established a probation system in 1925. By that date, most other states had also adopted similar systems.

6-3 Status of Probation

Probation is based on the philosophy that the average defendant is not a violent or dangerous criminal, but one that needs additional guidance in order to conform to society's demands. Probation generally involves the replacing of the defendant's commitment to a secure facility with a conditional release. Probation is essentially a contract between the defendant and the court. If the defendant complies with certain orders of the court (conditions of probation), the court will not require the defendant to be committed to a correctional facility. If the defendant later violates the terms of the contract, the court is no longer restricted by the contract and may commit the defendant to a correctional facility.

In some states, at the time the defendant is placed on probation, he or she is informed as to the terms of the commitment being probated. For example, the defendant may be committed to a state prison for ten years with the commitment probated for five years. If the defendant stays out of trouble for five years, then the commitment is never served. If the defendant's probation is revoked, then the defendant is committed to serve his or her 10-year term.

In most states, the defendant is placed on probation for a certain period of time. If the probation is revoked, then the defendant receives a commitment, the length of which is determined at a disposition hearing after the probation is revoked.

In some states, juries may recommend probation. However, even in those states where the juries may decide the punishment (e.g., Texas) only the judge may grant probation. Most states have restrictions on the granting of probation for certain serious or violent crimes. In addition, the death penalty may not be probated because the death penalty is limited to those cases in which the defendant is beyond rehabilitation and to probate the penalty would indicate that there is hope the defendant will be rehabilitated.

The length of the probation period may vary. A five-year period is common for adult felony cases. In fact, the Federal Criminal Code recommends that federal probation periods last for five years. In juvenile cases, the period of probation is usually until the juvenile reaches the age of majority or 21 years of age.

In many adult cases, the judge grants probation only if the defendant agrees to serve a period of local time (jail). For example, one judge, as a matter of policy, will not grant probation in felony cases unless the accused does at least 30 days in the local jail. This practice is known as **split sentencing.**

Shock probation is frequently used in the case of first-time young offenders. In these cases, the judge grants probation only after the accused has sampled prison life. Shock probation is designed to give defendants a "taste of the bars" before placing them on probation. Thus, the defendant is shocked by a brief period of confinement. For example, after a defendant has been in jail for a brief period of time (e.g., 30, 60, 90, or 120 days), he or she is brought back before the original sentencing judge who may grant probation if the defendant behaved while incarcerated.

Evaluations of shock probation have indicated that shock probation's rate of effectiveness may be as high as 78 percent.[6] A report on the use of shock incarceration in South Carolina indicated much success. Those offenders who were given shock probation had a recidivism rate of only 9 percent after one year.[7] Similarly, the use of long- and short-term shock incarceration in Arizona appeared effective in nearly two thirds of the cases processed. The State of Oklahoma started the Oklahoma Shock Incarceration Program (SIP) in 1991. Researchers examined data from 1991 through 1994 involving 1,546 male clients who participated in the shock incarceration program (SIP) and 2,936 inmates who had been incarcerated. Recidivism rates were substantially lower among SIP participants compared with the comparison sample of parolees during the same period.[8]

Advocates for shock probation argue that this option should be extended to those offenders who otherwise would not be good candidates for the standard probation based on the evaluations that have revealed relatively low recidivism rates for offenders given shock probation. Critics of shock probation claim that even a brief period of incarceration can reduce the effectiveness of probation, which is designed to provide the offender with non-stigmatized, community-based treatment.

6-4 Extent of Probation

There are approximately 1,900 probation agencies in the United States. About half are associated with a state-level agency and the remaining with county or city governments. Approximately 30 states have combined probation and parole agencies. While prison populations have been increasing at a rapid rate in the past 20 years, it appears that the number of people on probation has been increasing at an even faster rate. The Bureau of Justice Statistics reports that there are approximately 3,773,600 adults on probation in the United States as of January 1, 2000, a 41.3 percent increase of adults on probation since 1990. In 1999 alone, probation populations gained 10 percent or more in Idaho (up 17.7 percent), Vermont (up 17.1 percent), Arizona (up 11.2 percent), and Montana (up 10.2 percent). Among offenders on probation, slightly more than half (52 percent) have been convicted of a felony, 46 percent for a misdemeanor, and 2 percent for other infractions. Seventy-six percent of probationers were being actively supervised by the end of 2000; 9 percent were inactive cases and 9 percent had absconded.[9]

6-5 Criteria for Granting Probation

Listed below is the recommended criteria for granting probation developed by the American Law Institute's Model Penal Code. The criteria is also used in many juvenile cases:

1. The court shall deal with a person who has been convicted of a crime without imposing sentence of imprisonment unless, having regard to the nature and circumstances of the crime and the history, character, and condition of the defendant, it is of the opinion that his or her imprisonment is necessary for protection of the public because:

a. There is undue risk that during the period of a suspended sentence or probation the defendant will commit another crime.
   b. The defendant is in need of correctional treatment that can be provided most effectively by his or her commitment to an institution.
   c. A lesser sentence will depreciate the seriousness of the defendant's crime.
2. The following grounds, while not controlling the direction of the court, shall be accorded weight in favor of withholding sentence of imprisonment:
   a. The defendant's criminal conduct neither caused nor threatened serious harm.
   b. The defendant did not contemplate that his or her criminal conduct would cause or threaten serious harm.
   c. The defendant acted under a strong provocation.
   d. There were substantial grounds tending to excuse or justify the defendant's criminal conduct, though failing to establish a defense.
   e. The victim of the defendant's criminal conduct induced or facilitated its commission.
   f. The defendant has compensated or will compensate the victim of his criminal conduct for the damage or injury that he sustained.
   g. The defendant has no history of prior delinquency or criminal activity or has led a law-abiding life for a substantial period of time before the commission of the present crime.
   h. The defendant's criminal conduct was the result of circumstances unlikely to recur.
   i. The character and attitudes of the defendant indicate that he or she is unlikely to commit another crime.
   j. The defendant is particularly likely to respond affirmatively to probationary treatment.
   k. The imprisonment of the defendant would entail excessive hardship to the defendant or his or her dependents.
3. When a person has been convicted of a crime and is not sentenced to imprisonment, the court shall place him or her on probation if he or she is in need of the supervision, guidance, assistance or direction that the probation service can provide.[10]

6-6 Conditions of Probation

A probated disposition is an act of clemency on the part of the court. Accordingly, in most states, the court may place conditions that restrict an individual's constitutional rights. For example, a judge may require the defendant to voluntarily submit to searches and/or drug testing when requested by the probation officer. Generally, there are two sets of conditions that are imposed on a probationer: standard conditions that are imposed on every probationer, and special conditions designed for a particular defendant. Box 6-1 depicts the standard rules or conditions of probation used in the state of Texas. We use the Texas rules and conditions of probation because of the similarity to those used in other states.

Box 6-1

Texas Code of Criminal Procedure, Article 42.12

1. Commit no offense against the laws of the state of Texas or of any other state or of the United States.
2. Avoid injurious or vicious habits.
3. Avoid persons or places of disreputable or harmful character.
4. Report to the probation officer as directed.
5. Permit the probation officer to visit him at his home.
6. Regularly attend school or work faithfully at suitable employment as far as possible.
7. Remain within the country unless travel outside the country is approved by probation officer.
8. Pay any fines imposed and make restitution or reparation in any sum that the Court deems proper.
9. Support your dependents.
10. Participate in any community-based program as directed by the Court or probation officer.
11. Reimburse the county for any compensation paid to appointed defense counsel.
12. Compensate the victim for any property damage or medical expense sustained by the victim as a direct result of the commission of the offense.

6-7 Probationers' Rights

The courts have ruled that probationers (those on probation) have fewer constitutional rights than other citizens. The theory is that probation is an act of mercy by the courts, therefore certain conditions can be placed on individuals accepting probation.

The three major issues in probationers' rights are:
1. Search and seizure
2. Right of confidentiality
3. Revocation of rights

6-7a Search of Probationers

Courts have traditionally held that defendants on probation may be searched by their probation officers without the need for a warrant or probable cause. The basis of the search is that the defendant, by accepting the conditions of probation, has consented to waive his or her rights against unreasonable searches and seizures as a condition of being granted probation. Some states, however, limit the right to search without warrant or probable cause to only probation officers and not to other law enforcement members. The courts have also held that probationers' homes may be searched without a warrant. The courts have also indicated that probationers may be required to consent to future searches as a condition of probation.

6-7b Right of Confidentiality

The courts have held that the probation officer–client relationship is not a confidential relationship and therefore, the probation officer may testify as to matters related to him or her in confidence by the probationer.

6-7c Revocation of Probation

Revocation of probation may be administered by the court if the individual commits either a new crime or violates a technical condition of the probation. A **technical violation of probation** is a violation that does not involve criminal misconduct. For example, failure to report to the probation officer as required is considered a technical violation of the probation contract. As a general rule, the courts will seldom revoke probation for technical violations unless the violations are frequent or constitute a threat to society.

Probation officers are also given alternatives to handle technical violations without referral to the court. In many cases, a warning to the probationer by the probation officer is sufficient to correct the problem. A more controversial alternative is that of jail therapy. **Jail therapy** is the act of placing the probationer in jail, then without holding a hearing, releasing the probationer after a short stay.

In most states, the probation officer may modify or recommend the modification of the conditions of probation if it appears that the conditions are impossible to meet, unreasonable, or inappropriate. For example, federal policy places a duty on the probation officer to request modification of the probation conditions when necessary to reduce risk or to assist in the probationer's rehabilitation.[11]

Technical violations for which probation has been revoked include:

- Failure to pay off civil judgment for fraud
- Failure to make child support payments when probationer was able to do so
- Failure to report
- Associating with persons known not to be "law-abiding"

Even when the probationer commits a new crime, probation is not automatically revoked. Generally, probation officers are required to report to the court when the officer has knowledge that a probationer has committed a crime. In addition, in most cases the probation officer is required to make a recommendation regarding the issuance of a warrant and initiation of revocation proceedings. Federal policy provides:

> A violation of any federal, state, or local law that is punishable by any term of imprisonment must be reported immediately to the court or Parole Commission. In making a recommendation regarding issuance of a warrant, the officer must consider the risk posed by the new offense behavior. If it appears that the violation represents a significant threat to community safety or signals a risk of flight, the officer should recommend the issuance of a warrant.[12]

Two questions are apparent when considering revocation of probation based on new criminal activity. If the revocation of probation is based solely on the commission of a new crime, should the court await the disposition of the new charge before revoking probation? If the probationer is acquitted or the criminal proceedings on the new charge are terminated prior to the government obtaining a conviction, can the conduct still be the sole basis to revoke the probation? Both the American Bar Association Standards Relating to Probation and the National Advisory Commission Standards indicate that revocation of probation based solely on the commission of another crime should not occur until after the disposition of those charges. In most states, however, there are no statutory restrictions that require courts to delay revocation until the new charges are disposed of.

Disposition includes the court accepting a plea of guilty or nolo contendere and the finding by the court or jury of guilt. Disposition does not extend to final disposition because the appellate process can be quite lengthy. Both standards provide, however, that the court should have discretion to detain the probationer without bail while awaiting trial on the new charge involving a violent crime.

Revocation does not require the probationer to be found guilty in order to vacate the probation for criminal misconduct. In cases where the probationer is not convicted on the new charges, generally there are no constitutional or statutory grounds that prohibit the court from using the incident to revoke probation. In most cases, if the court or jury finds the probationer not guilty on the new charge or charges, the courts do not revoke probation solely on that misconduct. There are exceptions to this general rule, which are usually determined on a case-by-case basis. If the charges are dropped for other reasons, usually a case-by-case review is also used to determine if probation should be revoked.

Revocation of probation is possible after the term of probation has expired under certain circumstances. If a revocation warrant is issued prior to the expiration of the period of probation, the court may proceed within a reasonable time to revoke the probation. In addition, if the probationer has fled from supervision before the completion of the term of probation, when located, he or she generally is subject to revocation of probation. In many states, the statutes governing probation provide that the term of probation is tolled (ceases to expire) if the probationer is charged with new criminal misconduct, cannot be found, or flees the jurisdiction. In most states, the initiation of revocation proceedings also tolls the time period.

Before probation may be revoked, the probationer has certain procedural due process rights. Generally, when the probation officer makes the decision to revoke probation, the offender is notified and a formal hearing is scheduled. The rules for revoking probation and parole are generally the same. There are three major U.S. Supreme Court decisions that pertain to adult probation, but would presumably apply also to juvenile probationers.

Mempa v. Rhay, decided by the court in 1967, held that a probationer was constitutionally entitled to counsel in a revocation of probation hearing in which the imposition of the sentence had been suspended. Most lower courts interpreted this case to apply only in those situations that involved deferred sentencing and not in those cases in which the probationer was sentenced at the time of trial. Accordingly, some jurisdictions provide counsel at revocation hearings and other jurisdictions do not. While this case involved an adult criminal case, it appears to be applicable also to juvenile probation revocations.

In *Morrissey v. Brewer,* the Supreme Court required an informal hearing to determine if there was probable cause to believe that an individual on parole had violated the terms of his parole. If the informal hearing establishes probable cause of a parole violation, then a formal hearing needs to be held to determine if parole should be revoked. At the formal hearing, the parolee has procedural due process rights. The lower courts have applied the Brewer case to probation revocations. (The *Morrissey v. Brewer* case is reprinted in Chapter 9.)

In *Gagnon v. Scarpelli,* the Supreme Court held that both probationers and parolees have a constitutionally limited right to counsel in revocation proceedings.[13] In many states, probationers and parolees have a right to counsel by state statute or court decision. For example, a California court announced as a judicially declared rule of criminal process that a probationer is entitled to representation of retained or appointed counsel at formal proceedings for the revocation of probation.[14] The rule set forth in Gagnon is that a case-by-case determination of the need for counsel is the sound discretion of the state authority responsible for administrating the probation and parole system. If the probationers or parolees dispute the key issues, and the issues can only be fairly presented by trained counsel, the appointment of counsel for indigent probationers or parolees should be made. The court also noted that participation by counsel is probably undesirable and unnecessary in most revocation hearings.

In a criminal trial, the state must prove an accused is guilty beyond a reasonable doubt. Proof beyond a reasonable doubt requires that the jury or judge be fully satisfied, entirely convinced, or satisfied to a moral certainty. The standard of proof in a revocation hearing, however, is a preponderance of evidence. This is the same standard used in civil cases. A preponderance of evidence is defined as evidence that is of greater weight or more convincing than the evidence offered in opposition to it. This standard is much lower than required in a criminal trial. Figure 6-1 shows the outcomes for felony probationers who committed infractions.

6-8 Functions of Probation

A probation department's primary goal is to provide services designed to help defendants overcome their problems and their environments. For probation to be successful, the reasons for the defendant coming into contact with the justice system must be resolved, and the defendant must be reintegrated into the community. Probation is preferred over other forms of disposition for the following reasons listed on page 169.

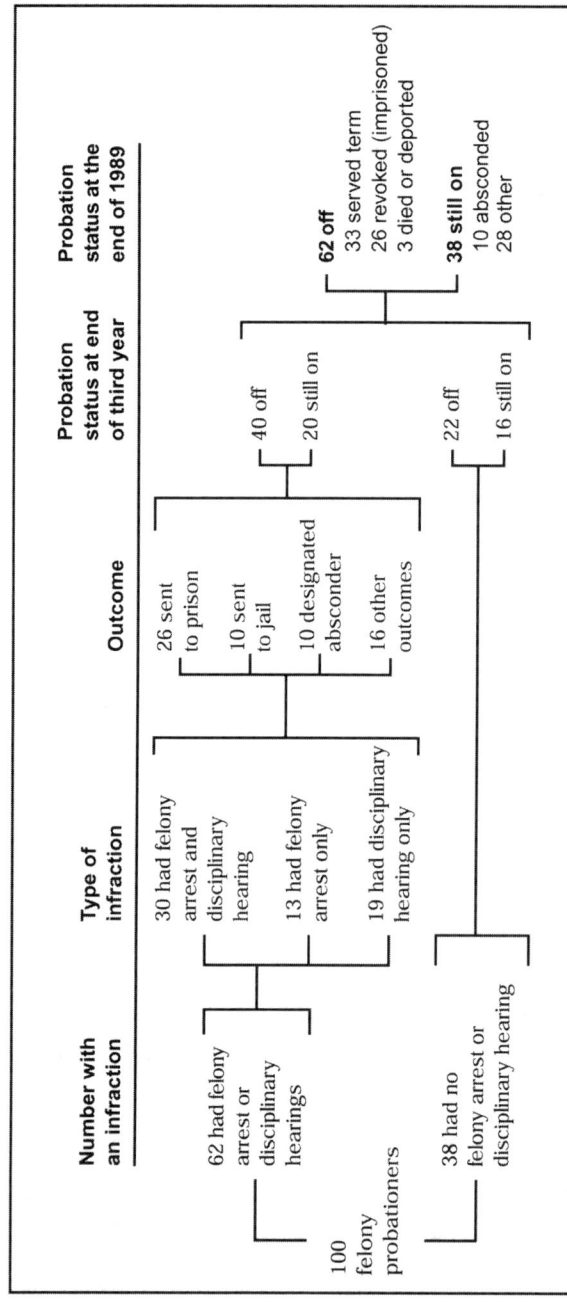

Figure 6-1
Probation Outcomes for 100 Felons 1986–1989

- It allows the defendant to remain in the community and function at a fairly normal level, while providing protection for the community against further law violations.
- It helps the defendant avoid the negative effects of institutionalization.
- Probation decreases the stigma of the labeling process, because the description of the crime is usually worded in a less severe manner than in those cases involving other dispositions.
- The rehabilitation program is facilitated by keeping the defendant in the community and living at home.
- Probation is much less expensive than institutionalization.

6-8a The Probation Officer

The probation officer plays a vital role in the criminal justice system. Probation officers have three basic functions, (1) to manage a specified case load of probationers; (2) to supervise adult probationers; and (3) to complete presentence investigations for the courts. On any given day a probation officer may write a presentence investigative report, write a probation report on a probationer, interview probationers, or make appropriate referrals to probationers.

Many probation departments divide the case load according to the risk a probationer poses to the community. Some offenders may be placed on minimal supervision status and have to mail in a report once a month. Offenders placed on medium status must personally report to their probation officer once a month, while offenders who have maximum or intensive supervision status must physically report to their probation officer several times a month. According to the Bureau of Justice Statistics, among offenders on probation, 95 percent are supervised on regular case loads, 4 percent are placed on intensive supervision, and about 1 percent are subject to specialized case loads where the offender may wear a monitoring ankle bracelet or be sent to a boot camp.

The probation officer maintains a file on each probationer. The file contains court documents that specify the terms and conditions of probation as ordered by the court. Probation officers add reports and other documented information to the probation file regarding the offender's conduct during the probationary period. Probation officers often find themselves overwhelmed with large cases loads, not to mention the numerous presentence investigation reports that they are required to complete in a short period of time. The probation officer performs many tasks and roles. The Texas Department of Criminal Justice divides the many tasks of the probation officer into ten distinct parts.

1. Information manger: The primary focus is the collection, classification, and analysis of data about the individual case and the community.
2. Evaluator: This involves assessing personal or community problems, weighing alternatives and priorities, and making decisions for action.
3. Enabler: The primary objective is to provide support and to facilitate change in the behavior patterns, habits, and perception of individual clients. The key assumption is that problems may be alleviated or crises may be prevented by modifying, adding, or extinguishing discrete bits of behavior; increasing insights; or changing values and perceptions.
4. Educator: Instruction is used in the sense of an objective rather than a method. The primary objectives are to convey and impart information and knowledge and to develop various kinds of skills. A great deal of social casework is simple instruction.
5. Broker: The primary objective is to steer (refer) clients to existing services that can be of benefit to them. The focus is on enabling or helping people to use the system and to negotiate its pathways. A further objective is to link elements of the service system with one another. The essential benefit of this objective is the physical hookup of the person with the source of help and the physical connection of elements of the service system with one another.
6. Advocate: The primary objective is to fight for the rights and dignity of people in need of help. The key assumption is that there will be instances when practices, regulations, and general conditions will prevent individuals from receiving services, using resources, or obtaining help. This position includes the notion of advocating changes in laws, rules, and regulations on behalf of a whole class of persons or segment of society. Advocacy aims at removing obstacles or barriers that prevent people from exercising their rights or receiving benefits and using the resources they need.
7. Mediator: The primary objective is to mediate between people and resource systems and among resource systems. The key assumption is that problems do not exist within people or within resource systems but rather in the interactions between people and resource systems and among systems. As opposed to the advocate, the mediator stance is one of neutrality.
8. Community Planner: This involves participating in and assisting neighborhood groups, agencies, community agents, or governments in the development of community programs to ensure that client needs are represented and met to the greatest extent feasible.

9. Detection: Detection involves identifying when a client is at risk or when the community is at risk from the client. The first objective for the officer is to identify individuals who are experiencing difficulty (at crisis) or who are in danger of becoming risks to the community. A second objective is to identify conditions in the community itself (such as lack of job or job training or the influx of easily available controlled substances) that may be contributing to personal problems of the client and that may raise his or her assigned risk level. A third objective is to determine when the community is at risk from the offender and steps are needed to protect the community.
10. Enforcer: This role requires the use of authority to revoke supervision because of changes in the status quo, which involves heightened community or individual risk outside the control of the officer.[15]

6-9 Probation Offices

Generally there is a probation office for each court. In large urban areas, the probation offices of several courts may be merged into one office. The individual in charge of a probation office is normally called the chief probation officer (CPO) whose duty it is to carry out policy and to supervise the probation officers (POs).

The probation officer's analysis of the defendant's personality and the development of a personality profile of the defendant occurs during the diagnosis functions. Diagnosis also involves the formulation of the treatment necessary to rehabilitate the defendant (i.e., the PO diagnoses that the defendant has a drinking problem). The treatment supervision refers to the duties of the PO after the defendant has been placed on probation. During the treatment supervision phase, the PO should evaluate the effectiveness of the treatment programs ordered by the court.

6-10 Future of Probation

Many individuals have voiced concerns regarding the placing of criminals on probation. Despite this, it appears that probation will continue as the most popular form of alternative sentencing available to judges. Part of the appeal of probation is its low cost and flexibility. There appears to be a trend to increasingly use probation in conjunction with community treatment programs in an effort to help rehabilitate the probationer and alleviate prison overcrowding.

ARTICLE
Guiding Philosophies for Probation in the 21st Century[16]

Opinion polls conducted over the past several decades have consistently shown that while crime is viewed as an important public concern, it has not been ranked by the majority of Americans as the most pressing problem facing the country. Other concerns, including the economy and unemployment, have traditionally eclipsed citizens' anxieties about crime. Yet in January 1994, the public, for the first time in nearly 60 years of opinion polling, ranked crime as the nation's most important problem.

Public anxieties about crime and violence have been fueled by media attention and political rhetoric. In the process, enormous attention has been focused on responding to the problem by proposing measures that include hiring thousands of additional police officers, banning assault weapons, imposing strict sanctions for repeat offenders, and expanding prison capacity.

Despite all the attention paid to the justice system's response to crime, there has been little public discourse about the role the probation system is to play in the process. On one hand, the failure to consider the future of probation is understandable since researchers, policy makers, and the public have tended to ignore this vital component of the justice system. Conversely, however, the failure to plan for the future of probation seems a crucial oversight since about two-thirds of all offenders under correctional supervision are on probation. As the nation augments its police forces, sanctions more offenders, and prisons experience increased overcrowding, many authorities have suggested that even more offenders will be channeled into the probation system. There is already evidence of this trend, between 1984 and 1990, probation caseloads rose from 1.74 million people to 2.67 million people—a 53.4 percent increase. Hence, some scholars have proposed that "probation crowding" presents more of an immediate threat to both the criminal justice process and to community protection than does prison crowding.

Given these developments, there is a pressing need to consider thoughtfully the role that probation will play in managing crime and criminal offenders. More than anything else, there is a need to identify the philosophies that will guide probation as we prepare for the next millennium. The purpose of this article is to explore the direction that probation might take in the near future. To accomplish this, we have drawn from the probation literature and have identified apparent trends for the probation profession.

The Need for Articulating a Coherent Mission and Philosophy for Probation

If there has been a recurrent theme in the probation literature over the past few decades, it has been the compelling need for the profession to articulate a distinct mission and for agencies to define their responsibilities in accomplishing that mission. Scores of critics have noted that in the absence of developing an overriding philosophy, probation's very survival is in jeopardy. Identifying the mission of probation represents a crucial, threshold issue. Both theoretically and practically, everything that an agency seeks to accomplish flows from its mission. Succinctly stated, organizational mission statements, philosophies, and goals imbue agencies with a source of legitimacy, provide employees with a sense of direction and a source of motivation, enable agencies to set goals and form guidelines, and provide the foundation on which to establish performance criteria. On a more practical level, Clear and Latessa's work suggests that organizational philosophies and priorities are important forces in shaping the actual work strategies employed by officers.[17]

Despite the need to develop a clear-cut mission for probation, there has been considerable disagreement about the role that probation should, or can, play in the criminal justice process. At the risk of oversimplification, authorities have proposed probation models that range from control to case management to offender rehabilitation. Yet despite all that has been written, probation continues to be plagued by an uncertain mixture of goals and philosophies that incorporate, to varying degrees, all of these elements. To understand where probation appears to be headed in the future, it is instructive to review briefly its historical evolution, identify predominant philosophies that seem to be guiding probation today, and then to note some of the calls that have been made for reform.

The Evolution of Probation Philosophies

From its inception, and until at least the mid-1960s, probation was guided by a casework-type philosophical ideology. Under this mandate, the purpose of probation was to identify causal factors of the offender's behavior and to intervene so that the offender could reform his or her conduct and avoid further contact with the legal system. In effect, the control of crime was to be attained through treatment.

Beginning in the 1960s, questions were raised about the efficacy of the rehabilitative model in corrections. The publication of Lipton, Martinson, and Wilks's celebrated study suggesting that "nothing works" all but sounded the death knell for the rehabilitative ideal in corrections.[18] In the wake of this now-famous study, authorities sought to identify other workable models for probation. Some, for example, suggested that probation officers should function as "resource brokers" for offenders under supervision. Under this mandate, probation officers were to assess offenders' needs and then channel them to social service agencies that could address those needs. Although mentioned infrequently in the literature, the brokerage approach seems to enjoy considerable support among probation officers today. Importantly, at the same time that probation was attempting to devise an appropriate alternative model, public support began to erode, skepticism about the ability of probation to control and rehabilitate offenders increased, and fiscal resources diminished.

Through the 1980s, a combination of factors contributed to an overcrowding crisis in prisons and jails across the nation. With the "war" on drugs, campaigns to crack down on drunk drivers, the enactment of harsher sentencing statutes, and efforts to constrict judicial discretion in sentencing, the per capita rate of offenders under correctional supervision rose to levels never encountered before in the history of the United States. As prison and jail populations swelled in response to the "get tough" approach on crime, even more offenders were subjected to probation supervision. Concurrently, highly publicized studies questioned whether probation was a viable sanction for felony offenders. In their study, for example, Petersilia et al. found that nearly two-thirds of those on felony probation were re-arrested.[19] In response, probation began to devise strategies to comport with prevailing public and political sentiments that suggested the need to protect society by closely monitoring and controlling probationers.

Popular Philosophies in Contemporary Probation

Although it would be impossible to identify any one philosophy that dominates probation today, it is possible to examine indicators of operant philosophies in contemporary probation. At perhaps the broadest level, one indicator of correctional philosophies may be found in those portions of each of the 50 states' legal codes that specify the approaches to be employed by departments when handling offenders. In their study of states' legal codes, Burton, Dunaway, and Kopache found that "by far, the major legislated correctional goal is rehabilitation." Burton and his colleagues qualified their findings in two ways, however. First, although rehabilitation is the most commonly prescribed correctional goal, recently enacted statutes tended to incorporate punitive goals. Second, Burton et al. noted that a majority of the states prescribed multiple goals—including reintegration, punishment, custody, public protection, and deterrence—for their correctional departments. In sum, Burton et al.'s research suggests that while state codes endorsed rehabilitation as their primary goal, most also included some form of goals oriented toward offender punishment and control.[20]

Another indicator of probation philosophies is reflected in a collection of studies that have asked probation officers what they perceive their primary responsibilities to be. If anything can be concluded from this body of research, it is that probation officers endorse dual goals. More specifically, although probation officers continue to endorse offender rehabilitation, they also express substantial support for offender control.

A final important indicator of contemporary probation philosophies is found in the variety of probation programs implemented across the country in the past decade. A number of intermediate sanctions have been introduced to the probation system. These programs include intensive supervised probation, house arrest, shock incarceration, boot camps, community service, restitution, and day fines. Of these, the program that has perhaps attracted the greatest amount of attention has been intensive supervision probation (ISP). Petersilia and her colleagues predicted, for instance, that "ISP will be one of the most significant criminal justice experiments in the next decade."[21] Although ISP has taken several forms, virtually all ISP programs emphasize the strict control of offenders through restricting liberty, mandatory treatment programs, and the establishment of employment requirements. In essence, ISP programs are engineered to control offenders through strict supervision. Today, every state, plus the federal probation system, has some form of ISP program.

Despite the popularity of ISP, questions remain about its use. First, and foremost, questions have been raised about the uncertainty of goals for ISP programs. Most ISP programs endorse formal goals that include reducing jail and prison overcrowding, employing cost-effective alternatives to imprisonment, preventing criminal behavior by probationers, and using appropriate intermediate punishments that are based in the community. Other than the last of these goals, others have questioned whether ISP programs, in general, are accomplishing their stated mission. Many ISP programs, because of rigorous eligibility requirements, have actually widened the net by subjecting less serious offenders to more restrictive probation conditions. Because of the close offender supervision provided by ISP, offenders are much more likely to be revoked from probation and sentenced to jail or prison time. Thus, there are indications that ISP may actually contribute to prison and jail overcrowding instead of reducing it. Doubts have also been raised about the claimed cost savings of ISP and whether ISP programs prevent crime and reduce recidivism.

Tonry has raised a valid question: If ISP has failed to accomplish its stated goals, then why does it continue to be endorsed as a viable correctional approach?[22] First, ISP strategies are in line with popular sentiments that offenders should be held accountable for their crimes. In essence, the strict supervision characteristic of ISP has provided probation with enhanced credibility. Second, ISP has provided probation employees with "more visibility, acknowledgment, and respect." Finally, ISP is in line with prevailing political ideologies that endorse punishment and fiscal responsibility. As Clear and Hardyman concluded, the public relations success of ISP has been phenomenal:

> While most observers had given probation up for dead only a few years ago, in its "new, improved" version it appears to have returned stronger than ever. Legislators are virtually falling over each other trying to sponsor legislation funding for intensive supervision alternatives to incarceration. The intensive supervision movement of the 1980s has helped revitalize probation, establishing it once again as a powerful cog in the machinery of justice.[23]

In summarizing the above information, it can be said that there are mixed goals operating in contemporary probation. State statutory provisions and probation officers themselves generally support dual goals revolving around offender rehabilitation and control. Yet at the same time, the focus on various forms of intermediate sanctions reveals an orientation toward sanctioning and controlling offenders. Taking all these factors into account, what is the mission of probation likely to be in the future?

Philosophies That Will Guide Probation in the 21st Century

Although varying in degree and prominence, probation has always been characterized by a dual emphasis on reform and control, and this will inevitably remain the case as we approach the 21st century. At the same time, however, there are many good reasons to suspect that future probation goals will contain strong themes of offender rehabilitation. Although states have embarked upon massive prison building projects during the past decade, there are questions whether they will be able to operate these facilities in the coming years, meaning that probation will become even more of a mainstay sanction in the future. Consider the remarks of Friel:

> States that recently initiated capital expansion programs are beginning to realize that while they may be able to build capacity, they may not be able to afford to operate these new facilities. Sure, construction is expensive, but if you issue 20- or 30-year bonds to cover the cost, the bill will not come due for a generation, even though the interest paid will double or triple the cost. But operational costs must come from appropriated funds. . . . The fiscal crisis for the states in the future will be operating their new prisons, not building the . . . [In the future] We will put the worst of the worst in prison for a long time. The second tier of offenders will go to prison as well, but will serve shorter sentences, and the rest will be supervised in the community by whatever means possible.[24]

In effect, Friel's predictions suggest that the economic strains of punitive sanctions will force the public to reassess justice policies, which, in turn, we believe, will lead to greater use of reform-oriented strategies.

A second reason why offender rehabilitation will supplant control ideologies is implicitly suggested in a recent study that questions conventional wisdom about the threat felony probationers present to community safety. In the past, research has suggested that a significant proportion of those placed on probation continue to commit crime. In perhaps the most often cited study on the topic, Petersilia and her colleagues reported that about two-thirds of offenders released on felony probation in California were rearrested during a 40-month follow-up. Other studies have found recidivism rates for probationers that range from about 20 percent to more than 50 percent. Yet in their study of arrestees in New Orleans from 1974 to 1986, Geerken and Hayes found that only eight percent of all adults arrested in that city for burglary or armed robbery involved offenders on probation. Based on their findings, Geerken and Hayes concluded that, "any restriction in probation and parole policy short of elimination, therefore, can only have a very minimal effect on the crime rate."[25] Suggestions, for example, that alternatives to incarceration be reserved for less violent, property offenders . . . or that probationers be supervised more intensively . . . can therefore also have little effect." Based on the evidence from this limited study, the implementation of additional "get tough" approaches like ISP would seem to contribute little to community protection.

A third reason to suspect that rehabilitation will become a guiding correctional philosophy lies in public attitudes. On one level, even recent popular publications have begun to question whether punitive measures are a rational approach to the country's crime problem. Perhaps most important, research questions the notion that the public has rejected offender rehabilitation in favor of offender control and surveillance. In their study of public attitudes, Cullen, Cullen, and Wozniak found that the public was reluctant to accept the idea that offenders should simply be warehoused.[26] Based on their findings, Cullen and his colleagues concluded:

> Although citizens clearly believe that the state has the legitimate right to sanction offenders on the basis of just deserts, they also believe that criminal penalties should serve utilitarian goals. Further, the evidence indicates that among the utilitarian goals, rehabilitation is supported as much as and usually more than either deterrence or incapacitation. It thus appears that the rehabilitative ideal has withstood the many attempts to discredit it and remains firmly anchored in the American value structure.

Another study by the Edna McConnell Clark Foundation revealed that when the public was informed about various sentencing options and their costs, they supported non-incarcerative options. More specifically, subjects in the study expressed support for sentencing options that stressed rehabilitation for a range of serious but nonviolent offenders.

Evidence of growing support for reformation ideologies is also evident in the academic criminal justice literature. Much of what has been written stems from dissatisfaction with the ability of the present system to respond effectively to the nation's crime problem. A sampling of conclusions in recent articles on the topic suggests that many criminal justice professionals cited the potential for intermediate sanctions for involving offenders in rehabilitative programs. With the corrections system overwhelmed by large numbers of drug-addicted offenders, many of whom are repeat offenders, and with the ever-growing inmate population outstripping even the most ambitious prison construction plans, a renewed and widespread interest in rehabilitation is emerging, even among many prosecutors.

> The findings reported . . . suggest that it is time to reconsider the respective roles of rehabilitation and surveillance in [ISP] programs. . . . Up to this point, our attention has been focused on evaluating the effectiveness of increased surveillance in community settings. It is now time to evaluate the effectiveness of increased offender treatment (e.g., substance abuse, employment, and family problems) in these same community settings, both alone and in combination with closer surveillance.

ISP programs may be important not for the surveillance and control afforded offenders, but for the relationships that develop as a result of closer contact. In our rush to embrace this new wave of intermediate sanctions, we have not adequately considered the implications of this basic change in the officer-offender relationship for subsequent offender recidivism. If Braswell is correct, closer contacts that lead to a strong relationship between offenders and probation officers have a greater deterrent effect than an equal number of surveillance contacts that do not involve such close interaction.

An analysis of the rehabilitative ideal and the ensuing policies indicates that, in spite of the fact that currently this orientation is on the decline, it has not vanished completely. This orientation has deep historical and traditional roots in Western, especially American, culture; and the fact that the alternative penal and control approaches do not show much better results in social control contributes to the tenacity of this penal idea and policy, not only among social scientists, but in the public opinion as well.

Using various alternative sanctions, correctional systems have been "turning up the heat" on probationers. But our study of these new sanctions found: no discernible improvement in the delivery of "better justice"; a doubling of the cost compared with regular probation; a reduction in public safety; an increase in the prison overcrowding problem; no effect on offender recidivism; and a belated rediscovery that only the inclusion of treatment services will have any positive effect on reducing recidivism. As to the so-called rediscovery of treatment services, it has been shown once again that ideology has little respect for evidence. From the late 1970s to 1990, about a dozen reviews have appeared in the literature indicating that treatment services can reduce offender recidivism and that punishment and sanctions cannot.

The above comments are consistent with recent research by Petersilia and Turner. In their study of 14 intensive supervision programs around the country, they found that offenders in ISP programs who received treatment had significantly lower recidivism rates when compared with those who did not, even when controlling for offender background characteristics.

The Emergence of Reform-Based Probation Ideology Tempered by Offender Control

We suggest that future probation goals are likely to have a strong emphasis on offender rehabilitation. This is not to say that concerns about controlling and punishing offenders will simply disappear. On the contrary, programs like ISP will continue to thrive, but there will be a more coherent "system" of punishments in the future. In their seminal work on the topic, Morris and Tonry proposed the creation of a graduated system of penalties. These authors noted the need to devise an orderly mix of alternative sanctions, suggesting that judges could select from predetermined possible sentences to meet the needs of individual offenders. It seems inevitable that such a system will slowly be realized in probation; the philosophy driving this system will be premised upon reforming the offender, rather than simply controlling, punishing, or monitoring law breakers.

In order for such a system to work, several modifications must be made to the existing system. First, sentences must be arrayed and ranked according to their severity. Byrne, for instance, has suggested a ranked system of alternative penalties, ranging from least to most severe, that include: (1) restitution, (2) day fine with restitution, (3) community service, (4) active probation, (5) intensive probation, (6) house arrest, (7) residential community corrections, (8) split sentences, (9) jail, and (10) prison. Second, the correctional and legal systems must come to a new understanding about the use of a graduated system of alternative sanctions. In the past, alternative sanctions have functioned as a net-widening device where offenders were subjected to stricter controls than would have been the case without an array of available intermediate punishments. For the future, there is a pressing need to begin to match punishments with various types of offenders and offenses. Some scholars have suggested the need for articulating "exchange rates," to identify the number of days under various forms of community supervision that would be equal to a single day of incarceration in a traditional correctional facility. For example, authorities would need to determine that "x" number of days of house arrest are equal to one day of incarceration, or that one year in prison is equal to "x" number of years on ISP. It is worth noting that the idea of using exchange rates is compatible with offender reformation: both ideologies are premised on a notion of individualized justice, in which sentences are meted out on the basis of the nature of the offense and the needs of individual offenders.

It is unclear how the idea of using "exchange rates" might be translated into practice so as to avoid grave sentencing disparities. Morris and Tonry have suggested that mandatory sentencing guidelines be created that govern judges' use of intermediate sanctions. Under this approach, exchange rates would be calculated for various offenses and judges would select from among the available alternative sanctions to fit the needs of the individual offender. Yet there are serious concerns about tying the use of intermediate sanctions to mandatory sentencing guidelines. In their study of criminal justice professionals' opinions about intermediate sanctions, DeJong and Franzeen found "a widespread disliking among criminal justice officials for mandatory sentencing of any kind, not only among judges, but among most probation officials and even several prosecutors as well."[27] The opposition to mandatory intermediate sanction guidelines is no doubt the product of professionals' experiences with the approach at both federal and state levels. DeJong and Franzeen found that criminal justice professionals attributed much of the present prison overcrowding problem to determinate sentencing; officials expressed concerns that mandatory guidelines would have the same effect by overloading any system devised for imposing intermediate sanctions.

One likely alternative to mandatory guidelines would be the development of voluntary or model guidelines to guide the imposition of intermediate sanctions. To be effective, this approach would necessitate informing and educating the judiciary, correctional officials, and the public. This would obviously be a massive undertaking, but there are clear indications that when properly informed, the public is supportive of alternative sanctions. While a voluntary system would invariably result in sentence disparities, it is difficult to imagine that the disparities would be any greater, and would most likely be less, than they are under the present system.

Implementing a graduated penalty system could have other benefits as well. Under such an approach, offenders could also be "educated" about the consequences of continued criminality. As it stands today, there is evidence that at least some offenders perceive sentences to ISP as harsher than sentences to prison. In one RAND study, offenders sentenced to prison were given the option of participating in ISP or going to prison. In the first year, one-third of those who had originally chosen the probation option changed their minds and asked to be sent to prison. A subsequent study in Texas found that "a preference for prison is more likely among offenders who are African-American, older, unmarried, and widely exposed to crime and institutional corrections, and who share beliefs that probation has grown stricter and that other offenders now prefer prison to probation." Implicitly, these findings suggest that at least some offenders perceive current punishment structures as inverted. Under a graduated system of penalties to which judges adhere, this phenomenon would likely disappear.

Summary and Conclusion

We acknowledge that our proposal suggesting reform-based philosophies will emerge to guide probation in the coming years is at odds with others who have written about the future of probation in America. On the fringes, writers have suggested ideas ranging from abolishing the terms "probation" and "treatment" to reorganizing probation work so that officers would provide the court with investigative services but would no longer supervise offenders.

Despite suggestions to the contrary, we believe that concerns with offender reform will command greater attention in the next decade. This prediction does not simply reflect hopeful speculation on our part but, we believe, it is anchored in recurring themes in the literature. First, there are indications that, more and more, the public has begun to question current crime control strategies. Importantly, much of the criticism is based upon economic concerns. Despite pouring billions of dollars into prison construction and incarcerating a growing proportion of the population, citizen fear has continued to rise. Friel has noted that 80 percent of the cost of corrections is consumed by prisons. Ironically, this component of the correctional system only handles about 25 percent of the offender population. The remainder is managed by probation, parole, and other community-based programs. Doubts have been raised about whether the public will be willing to continue to allocate a significant proportion of their tax dollars to institutional corrections. In the future, the public will not abandon the crime problem. Instead, it is likely that renewed interest will be generated in examining cost-effective programs that promise not only community protection but also hope for reforming those who have come into contact with the justice system.

Although important, economic considerations are not the only factors that support our predictions that reform-based ideologies will guide probation in the future. Research suggests that there continues to be strong public support for the idea that corrections should seek to rehabilitate offenders. Studies also suggest the emergence of a renewed and widespread interest in offender treatment among criminal justice professionals. In addition, states' statutory provisions, although articulating multiple goals, continue to endorse offender rehabilitation as a guiding correctional philosophy.

It is somewhat ironic to note that much of the interest generated for community corrections in the past decade is attributable to control-oriented programs, such as intensive supervision probation, house arrest, and electronic monitoring. Community corrections, including probation, have capitalized upon this exposure by emphasizing such issues as offender accountability, reduced correctional costs, and the promise to alleviate institutional overcrowding. In the process, probation has generated renewed public and political support. With this support, probation is poised, perhaps more powerfully so than was ever the case in the past, to harvest a larger share of the resources available to the justice system. The irony of the situation lies in the fact that research questions the efficacy of intermediate sanctions premised solely on the control of offenders. Evaluations, for example, of traditional ISP programs suggest that they may increase probation costs, exacerbate prison overcrowding, and do little to enhance community protection. At the same time, however, research suggests that when ISP is coupled with treatment programs, recidivism rates can be substantially reduced. Thus, policymakers and probation leaders are faced with a dilemma that is as old as the probation profession itself. On one hand, members of the profession must continue to attend diligently to the control aspects of their work. Control themes have been, and will continue to be, an important part of probation work. On the other hand, offender reform strategies will emerge as a guiding force for probation during the next decade. Although ISP and related programs will continue to grow in the coming years, we suggest that most, if not all, will incorporate treatment programs.

What do these predictions mean for those who work in probation? The simplest answer is that probation will both change and remain the same. There will be change in the sense that, as departments incorporate mission statements that emphasize offender reformation, agency goals, programs, and objectives will be modified to comport with this redirected orientation. Research suggests that despite past programmatic shifts, probation workers continue to support reform-based ideologies. Thus, in many ways, much about the probation profession and those who work in it will remain the same. Hopefully, those workers who support offender reform will be funneled into treatment-based programs. Because there will be a greater diversity of intermediate sanctions, those workers who are oriented toward offender control will likewise find a number of positions in the probation system that mesh with their interests.

Reprinted with permission from *Federal Probation*, pp. 4–10, March 1997.

CASE
State v. Fuller (Montana Supreme Court, No. 95-343, decided 4/16/96)

Question: May a state condition probation for a sex offender upon participation in a treatment program that requires total honesty and then prosecute the defendant on the basis of what he admits in treatment?

Facts: In suspending the defendant's 10-year prison term in favor of probation, the sentencing court ordered him to "follow all policies" of the treatment program on which his probation hinged. One of the policies was that participants reveal every sex crime they ever committed. The defendant complied, his revelations were relayed to the police, and new charges were brought.

Holding: No. The state may not condition probation upon participation in a treatment program that requires total honesty and then prosecute the defendant for any crimes that he admits in treatment.

In *Minnesota v. Murphy*, 465 U.S. 420 (1984), the U.S. Supreme Court held that the defendant needs to invoke his privilege against self-incrimination for it to apply. The ultimate result in *Murphy* was contrary to the result here, but the Montana Court explained that the cases are factually distinguishable. The difference, the court said while quoting *Murphy*, is that in *Murphy* the defendant was merely required to refrain from lying to a state agent, whereas this defendant was faced with a "required choice" between making incriminating statements and jeopardizing his conditional liberty by remaining silent.

It did not matter that, under the court's ruling in *State v. Imlay*, 813 P.2d 979 (1991), the lower court actually lacked power to revoke the defendant's probation for failure to admit to a criminal act. According to the majority, the defendant was faced with a credible threat, and he should not be required to have known that the threat was empty.

Justice Trieweiller, joined by Justice Gray, concurred in the majority opinion and accused the dissent of crediting the defendant with more knowledge of his rights than can be reasonably expected.

Justice Nelson, dissenting and joined by Chief Justice Turnage and Justice Erdmann, argued that the principle established in *Imlay* freed the defendant from the "classic penalty situation." The dissenters also said that this case cannot be distinguished from *Murphy*.

The Defendant Matthew C. Fuller appealed the denial of his motion to dismiss rape and sexual assault charges, to which he entered conditional guilty pleas. The events leading to the charges began in 1992, when Fuller was convicted of three counts of attempted sexual assault. The district court sentenced him to 10 years imprisonment, but suspended the sentence and imposed probation. One condition of the probation was that Fuller "obtain and/or continue his enrollment and participation in [an] outpatient Sex Offender Treatment Program" and "follow all policies of that program." This court later reversed the attempt convictions.

In the meantime, however, Fuller was accepted into a treatment program. Patients are not admitted into the program if they are in denial or do not honestly disclose their offense history. Further, patients will be terminated from the program for exhibiting dishonesty or denial during the treatment. The employees of the treatment center are required to report to the authorities any evidence they possess about past or present offenses committed by individuals in the program.

During treatment, Fuller disclosed several past offenses, including the three at issue here. Until these disclosures, there had been no investigation of the offenses. Fuller never asserted his Fifth Amendment privilege or refused to answer. Instead, he fully and honestly answered the questions put to him by the treatment program, in accordance with the district court's order. However, failure to invoke the privilege does not preclude the benefit if the defendant is placed in a situation in which he is not "free to admit, deny, or refuse to answer." *Minnesota v. Murphy*, 465 U.S. 420, 429 (1994) [citing *Garner v. United States*, 424 U.S. 648, 657 (1976)]. In such cases, the privilege is said to be "self-executing." The U.S. Supreme Court has applied this exception to different types of cases, including those in which the government prevents a voluntary invocation of the Fifth Amendment in by threatening to penalize the individual should he or she invoke it. This foreclosure of access to the Fifth Amendment is termed a "classic penalty situation."

Fuller claimed the state placed him in a classic penalty situation. Consequently, he says, his failure to invoke the Fifth Amendment should be excused, and the state is prohibited from using any disclosure made in treatment in a subsequent prosecution.

The district court ordered Fuller to enter and comply with the program. If he failed to comply, his probation would be revoked and he would be sent to prison. It is therefore undisputed that the state compelled Fuller to divulge past activities that it knew would be criminal. It is further undisputed that the information divulged by Fuller was self-incriminatory and was the sole trigger of his conviction of three additional crimes.

The state insists these circumstances did not rise to the level of a classic penalty situation because the district court never threatened to punish Fuller for exercising his Fifth Amendment privilege. At any time Fuller could have invoked his privilege against self-incrimination and the district court could not have lawfully punished him for its invocation and his consequent refusal to speak.

This decision is supported by the U.S. Supreme Court's interpretation of the Fifth Amendment as articulated in *Murphy*, even though it reached the opposite conclusion in that case. In *Murphy* the defendant's probation required that he participate in a sex offender treatment program, that he report periodically to his probation officer, and that he "be truthful with the probation officer in all matters." 465 U.S. at 422.

After Murphy left the treatment program, a counselor informed his probation officer that, while in treatment, Murphy had confessed to a rape and murder. When the probation officer confronted Murphy, he again confessed. This information was the basis for Murphy's conviction of murder, The Supreme Court found that Murphy was not placed in a classic penalty situation because the Minnesota probation revocation statute did not impermissibly foreclose a free choice to be silent. It therefore concluded that Murphy's Fifth Amendment privilege was not self-executing and, since he had not invoked it, that it was properly deemed to have been waived.

Summary

Probation refers to the conditional release of a defendant. Probation can have several different meanings within our present criminal justice system. Probation can be used to describe a sentence that has been given to a defendant in which the defendant is placed and maintained in the community under the supervision of an agent of the court. Probation refers to a status or class (i.e., he or she is on probation and thus subject to certain rules and conditions that must be followed in order to avoid being institutionalized). Probation also refers to an organization (i.e., the county probation department). It is a disposition that does not involve confinement, or at most involves only a short period of confinement, that imposes conditions. Under probation, the court retains authority over the case to supervise, modify the conditions, and resentence the defendant if the terms of probation are violated. Probation is a legal status created by the court. Although the classic definition of probation, as set forth above, indicates that it does not involve commitment, it is being increasingly linked to a short period of commitment at a training school, boot camp, or other local custody facility.

John Augustus of Boston is considered the originator of the concept of probation. As early as 1841, Augustus, a private citizen, requested that Boston judges release young defendants under his supervision. It is estimated that over an 18-year period he supervised about 2,000 individuals on probation. Most of these were youths age 16 to 19. He helped them get jobs and reestablish themselves in the community. Only a few of the individuals under his supervision became involved in subsequent criminal behavior.

There are about 1,900 probation agencies in the United States. Approximately 30 states have combined probation and parole agencies. On any given day there are approximately 1.8 million individuals on probation in the United States. Of those probationers, about 53 percent had been convicted of a felony, and 45 percent of a misdemeanor.

Judges use certain criteria when granting probation. For example, a judge may take into consideration whether a defendant is likely to commit another crime if probation is granted or whether a lesser sentence of probation will depreciate the seriousness of the crime. Judges may also impose conditions of probation such as requiring a defendant to voluntarily submit to random drug tests on a periodic basis.

While probationers have certain fundamental rights the courts have ruled that they have fewer constitutional rights than other citizens. For example, the courts have consistently ruled that defendants on probation may be searched by their probation officer without the need for a warrant. Furthermore, the courts have held that the probation officer–client relationship is not a confidential relationship and therefore, the probation officer can be called to testify about matters related to him or her in confidence by the probationer.

The court may revoke an individuals probation if he or she commits a new crime while on probation or violates any terms or conditions of the probation. For example, if the defendant fails to report to his or her probation officer or tests positive for an illegal substance the court may revoke probation and the individual would be sent to prison to serve the remainder of the sentence.

In many states, the probation officer may modify or recommend a modification of the conditions of probation if it appears that conditions are impossible to meet. Federal policy places a duty on the probation officer to request a modification of the probation conditions when necessary to reduce risk or to assist in the probationer's rehabilitation.

Probation is based on the philosophy that the average defendant is not a violent dangerous criminal, but one that needs additional guidance in order to conform to society's demands. Probation generally involves the replacing of the defendant's commitment to a secure facility with a conditional release. Probation is essentially a contract between the defendant and the court.

Discussion Questions

1. Describe the conditions that lead to the development of the concept of probation.
2. What are your opinions regarding the place that probation should take in the future of corrections?
3. Briefly summarize the rights of probationers.
4. Explain the differences between technical violations and substantive violations of the terms of probation.
5. Why is probation so popular with judges? prosecutors? defense counsel?
6. Explain the significance of the court's hold in *State v. Fuller*.

Chapter Quiz

True/False

1. Probation allows an offender early release from prison.
2. Probation permits the defendant to remain in his or her community under the supervision of a probation officer.
3. Evaluations of shock probation have shown minimal effectiveness.
4. John Augustus of Boston is considered the originator of the concept of probation.
5. Probation is based on the philosophy that the average defendant is a violent and dangerous criminal.

Multiple Choice

1. The length of probation can vary, however a _____-year period appears to be a common one for adult felony cases.
   a. one
   b. five
   c. six
   d. ten
2. Which one of the following is NOT one of the major issues in probationers' rights?
   a. search and seizure
   b. right of confidentiality
   c. revocation of rights
   d. work status
3. Which one of the following is NOT a function of probation?
   a. It helps the defendant avoid the negative effects of institutionalization.
   b. Probation is much less expensive than institutionalization.
   c. It allows the offender, after release from prison, to be supervised under a structured program for a specified period of time.
   d. Probation decreases the stigma of the labeling process.

4. Probation officers have three main functions, which one of the following is NOT a function?
   a. manage a caseload
   b. complete pre-sentence investigation reports
   c. supervise probationers
   d. investigating crimes that a probationer has committed while on probation
5. Regular probation is defined as
   a. an intensive supervision program for those who are too antisocial for the relative freedom.
   b. the release of a convicted offender under conditions imposed by the courts for a specified period of time.
   c. the early release of an offender from prison that requires him/her to report a probation officer.
   d. an intensive shock program for serious violent offenders.

Endnotes

1. Lauren E. Glaze, *Probation and Parole in the United States, 2001* (U.S. Department of Justice, Bureau of Justice Statistics, August 2002).
2. President's Commission on Law Enforcement and Administration of Justice, Task Force Report: Corrections (Washington, DC: Government Printing Office, 1967), 130.
3. Rolando del Carmen, Betsy Witt, Thomas Caywood, and Sally Layland, *Probation Law and Practice in Texas* (Huntsville, TX: Criminal Justice Center, Sam Houston State University, 1989).
4. Paul F. Cromwell and George G. Killinger, *Community-Based Corrections*, 3rd ed. (St. Paul: West, 1994).
5. John Augustus, First Probation Officer, reprint of *Report of the Labors of John Augustus, for the Last Ten Years, in Aid of the Unfortunate* (Boston: Wright & Hasty, 1852), New York: National Probation Association, 1939, p. 4.
6. South Carolina State Reorganization Commission, *An Evaluation of Omnibus Criminal Justice Improvements Act of 1986, Section 3, 4 and 5, second year report* (Columbia: South Carolina State Reorganization Commission, 1990).
7. Ibid.
8. Arizona Department of Corrections, *Offender Classification System (OCS): Classification Operating Manual* (Phoenix: Arizona Department of Corrections, 1991).
9. Bureau of Justice Statistics, *2000 Midyear Report*.
10. Model Penal Code and commentaries, Part I and II, the American Law Institute (1985).

11. Susan T. Marcus-Mendoza, "A Preliminary Investigation of Oklahoma's Shock Incarceration Program," *Journal of Oklahoma Criminal Justice Research Consortium* 2 (1995): 44–49.
12. Supervision of Federal Offenders, Monograph No. 109 (Washington, DC: Government Printing Office, 1991).
13. *Gagnon v. Scarpelli*, 411 U.S. 778 (1973).
14. *People v. Vickers*, 25 Cal. App. 3d 1080 (1972).
15. Ann Strong, *Case Classification Manual, Module One: Technical Aspects of Interviewing* (Austin: Texas Adult Probation Commission, 1981).
16. Richard D. Sluder, Allen D. Sapp, and Denny C. Langston, The authors are all with the Criminal Justice Department at Central Missouri State University. Dr. Sluder is assistant professor, Dr. Sapp is professor, and Dr. Langston is associate professor. The article in based on a paper presented at the March 1994 annual meeting of the Academy of Criminal Justice Sciences, Chicago, Illinois. The article is reprinted with permission from *Federal Probation*, June 1994. Note: many of the footnotes are omitted.
17. T. R. Clear and E. J. Latessa, "Probation Officers' Roles in Intensive Supervision: Surveillance Versus Treatment," *Justice Quarterly* 10 (3, 1993): 440–462.
18. Lipton, Martinson, and Wilks, "What Works? Questions and Answers About Prison Reform," *The Public Interest* 42 (1974,): 22–54.
19. Joan Petersilia, "Community Supervision: Trends and Critical Issues," *Crime and Delinquency* 31 (1985): 339–347.
20. V. S. Burton, Jr., R. G. Dunaway, and R. Kopache, "To Punish or Rehabilitate? A Research Note Assessing the Purposes of State Correctional Departments as Defined by State Codes," *Journal of Crime and Justice* 16 (1, 1993): 177–188.
21. J. Petersilia, S. Turner, J. Kahan and J. Peterson, *Granting Felons Probation: Public Risks and Alternatives* (Santa Monica, CA: Rand Corp., 1985).
22. M. Tonry, "Stated and Latent Functions of ISP," *Crime and Delinquency* 36 (1, 1990): 174–191.
23. T. R. Clear and P. L. Hardyman, "The New Intensive Supervision Movement," *Crime and Delinquency* 36 (1, 1990): 42–60.
24. C. M. Friel, "Crime, Justice, and the Paradigm Shifts of the 1990s," Presentation to the Southeast Region Summit on Violent Crime, July 8, 1992, Charlotte, NC.
25. M. R. Geerken and H. D. Hayes, "Probation and Parole: Public Risk and the Future of Incarceration Alternatives," *Criminology* 31 (4, 1993): 549–564.
26. F. T. Cullen, J. B. Cullen, and J. F. Wozniak, "Is Rehabilitation Dead? The Myth of the Punitive Public," *Journal of Criminal Justice* 16 (1993): 303–317.
27. W. DeJong and S. Franzeen, "On The Role of Intermediate Sanctions in Correctional Reform: The Views of Criminal Justice Professionals," *Journal of Crime and Justice* 16 (1, 1993): 47–73.

Chapter 7

Jails and Misdemeanants

Dennis MacDonald/PhotoEdit

Key Terms

booking
classification
court liaison
direct-supervision jails
jails
lockups
new-generation jails
orientation
revolving door concept
state jail felony

Outline

7-1 Jails
    7-1a History of Jails
    7-1b Jail Standards
    7-1c Role of Jails
    7-1d The Revolving Door
    7-1e Female Jail Inmates
7-2 Jail Procedures
    7-2a Intake
    7-2b Classification
    7-2c Orientation
    7-2d Court Liaison
    7-2e Release

7-3 State Jail Felony
7-4 Issues in Jails
    7-4a Overcrowding
    7-4b Controversies
    7-4c Jail Suicides
7-5 Jail Designs
    7-5a Traditional Jails
    7-5b Direct-Supervision Jails
Summary
Discussion Questions
Chapter Quiz
Endnotes

Learning Objectives

After studying this chapter, the reader will be able to:

- Identify the two features of the early English jails that are similar to our present jails.
- Explain the early history of jails.
- Explain the functions of jail standards and list the organizations that have developed jail standards.
- Analyze the present functions of our jails.
- Explain the "revolving door" concept involving our jails.
- Describe common jail procedures.
- Explain the many problems involved with the operation of our jails.

7-1 Jails

7-1a History of Jails

The word "jail" is derived from the Latin root *cavea*, meaning cavity, cage, or coop. It is also an alternate form of *gaol*, which is pronounced like the word jail and has a Norman-French origin. **Jails** were originally considered "public cages or coops." Jails existed in ancient Egypt, Greece, and Rome but at the time were nothing more than unscalable pits, dungeons, suspended cages, and sturdy trees to which prisoners were chained while awaiting trial.

During the Anglo-Saxon feudal period in England, the countryside was divided into units of government originally known as "shires." Each shire had a *shire-reeve* (sheriff) as its chief law enforcement officer. The shire-reeve was appointed by the king and was charged with the responsibility of maintaining a jail. Each shire-reeve was required to establish a place to secure offenders until the next meeting of the king's court in that area. It appears that cities and municipalities also operated detention facilities. Two features of the early English jails are common elements in modern United States facilities: jails were the responsibility of the local government, and they were operated by the shire-reeve (sheriff).

Prior to the twentieth century, jails were often places of filth and disease. Jail fever, a form of typhus, was a common result of the unsanitary conditions of the jails. Generally, jails were poorly supported by local government. Many jailers were appointed for life and earned their living from the fee system, which provided payments to the jailer by jail residents or their families to maintain the facility. In some cases, individuals were required to pay an additional fee to be released. Items such as food, clothing, and toiletries were sold to the inmates by the jailers. In addition, it was a common practice for jailers to hire out jail inmates for manual work in the communities.

Such deplorable conditions helped bring about the establishment of certain basic rights that later appeared in the U.S. Constitution. The rights included:

- The 1628 Petition of Right, which assured the right to freedom before trial (Amendment XIV to the Constitution of the United States).
- The 1679 Habeas Corpus Act, which provided a remedy for illegal incarceration. (Amendment XIV to the Constitution of the United States).
- The 1689 English Bill of Rights, which outlawed the imposition of excessive bail. (Amendment VII to the Constitution of the United States).

7-1b Jail Standards

Although correctional standards existed for many years, it was not until the 1970s that guidelines for jails became necessary, primarily as the result of increasing liability incurred by jail authorities. In addition, during the 1970s most states established jail standards commissions or boards. Presently, jail standards have been established by the American Correctional Association, the American Bar Association, the National Sheriff's Association, the American Psychological Association, the American Public Health Association, and even the United Nations.

These standards vary by state. In many jurisdictions, the courts have become the chief enforcers of jail standards. Areas of concern to the courts are overcrowding, medical services, library services, available recreation, and the safety of inmates.

Box 7-1

New York City Challenges Jail Standards

In May, 1996, the City of New York filed a federal suit to strike down a 1978 agreement that forced the city to improve living conditions for prisoners.[1] The agreement resulted in the establishment of standards that still regulate almost every aspect of the city's 20,000 inmates' lives, covering everything from how often the jailhouse windows should be washed (four times a year) to how many prisoners should be held in a dormitory room. Similar suits are pending in federal courts in South Carolina and Iowa.

The city contends that enforcing the standards costs too much and that the city, not the courts, should decide how the jails are run. The city also argues that the Prison Litigation Reform Act, passed by the U.S. Congress in April 1996, has placed restrictions on what courts can require prison systems to do. Prisoner rights advocates contend that without the court decree, prisoners will have fewer rights and jail conditions would sharply deteriorate.

The present decree covers over 90 orders, stipulations, and work plans. It designates how much time inmates may spend in the law library and the hours they are to be locked in their cells. It regulates the prices in the jail barber shop, inmate access to telephones, and the minimum amount of cleaning fluids to be used in cleaning the floors.

7-1c Role of Jails

There are approximately 3,500 jails currently operating in the United States.[2] They represent the most widely used type of confinement in the country. Jail populations change daily as people are admitted and released. Currently, jails function as temporary local detention units that have only minimal concern for the identification and mediation of inmate problems. The major distinction between jails and prisons continues to be that jails are locally controlled and their residents have a shorter length of stay.

Generally, jails are used for two types of prisoners: those convicted of minor crimes and sentenced to short terms of confinement, and detainees who are awaiting trial and who either do not qualify for bail or cannot afford the bail set in their cases. Some have estimated that at least four times as many people pass through our jails annually compared to the number that are incarcerated in state and federal institutions.

Jails are usually operated by local governments, such as counties or cities. Jails differ from prisons in that prisons are administered, operated, and funded by the state or the federal government. Jails are used to punish persons convicted of minor offenses who are sentenced to confinement for a year or less whereas prisons are used to punish persons convicted of major crimes (felonies) and in most cases sentenced to one year or more. Jails differ from "lockups" in that **lockups** are generally operated by the police and are located in police stations or headquarters or at county sheriff's departments. A lockup is a temporary holding facility. Arrestees are usually held in a lockup for no more than 48 hours (excluding weekends and holidays). Lockups are also used to hold juveniles until their parents can be summoned or another placement can be arranged. Although there is extensive research on jails, there is little on lockups, despite the fact that there are over 15,000 being used in the United States.

As discussed above, jails perform a very broad role. Often new students of criminal justice are confused over the role of jails versus the role of lockup facilities and prisons. The Bureau of Justice Statistics has outlined eight important functions of jails. Jails:

1. receive individuals pending arraignment and hold them awaiting trial, conviction , and sentencing;
2. readmit probation, parole, and bail-bond violators and absconders;
3. temporarily detain juveniles pending transfer to juvenile authorities;
4. hold mentally ill persons pending their movement to appropriate health facilities;

5. hold individuals for the military, for protective custody, for contempt, and for courts as witnesses;
6. release convicted inmates to the community on completion of sentence;
7. transfer inmates to state, federal, and local authorities; and
8. relinquish custody of temporary detainees to juvenile and medical authorities.[3]

7-1d The Revolving Door

The **revolving door concept** refers to defendants who are arrested, remain in jail only long enough to become sober, then return to the streets, drink more, and return to jail. This concept is especially evident in cases involving the "common drunk." Several studies indicate that over 50 percent of the misdemeanor arrests are for drunkenness or offenses directly related to drinking. The police make over two million arrests per year for public drunkenness. A high percentage of all misdemeanor convictions are for alcohol-related offenses. The typical sentence is time in jail. The Bureau of Justice Statistics estimates that approximately 50 percent of the individuals serving jail time as the result of a misdemeanor conviction would be treated in other types of facilities (i.e., hospitals, drug treatment centers, etc.), if such facilities were available.[4]

Most researchers agree that alcoholism is a major problem and the alcoholic is neither deterred nor cured by frequent trips to jail. The sheer number of cases involving drunks makes it necessary to establish alternatives to automatic jailing.

Box 7-2

Jail Facts

According to the National Coalition for Jail Reform's pamphlet, "Look at Your Jail," there are approximately 6,500,000 commitments to jail each year in the United States. Approximately 40 percent of those in jail are awaiting trial. About 600,000 mentally ill people go through our jails each year. The suicide rate for adults in jails is 16 times greater than for the general public. Approximately 70 percent of the jail inmates are incarcerated for nonviolent offenses. Approximately 35 percent of our jails are more than 50 years old. Jails are expensive: it costs an average of $18,000 to keep one person in jail for a year. It costs about $75,000 per bed to build a new jail.

7-1e Female Jail Inmates

Between 1990 and 2000, the number of adult females in jail increased at a higher rate than that of males. Approximately 12 percent of jail inmates are female and approximately 75 percent have dependent children. Although some of the larger urban jails have adequate facilities for females, most jails are small and lack sufficient space to separate female residents. In addition, because of their limited number, special services and programs for female residents are limited or nonexistent in most jails. For the most part, the needs of female residents in our jails have been ignored. Figure 7-1 depicts the ten-year growth of adult females in our nation's jails compared to adult males.

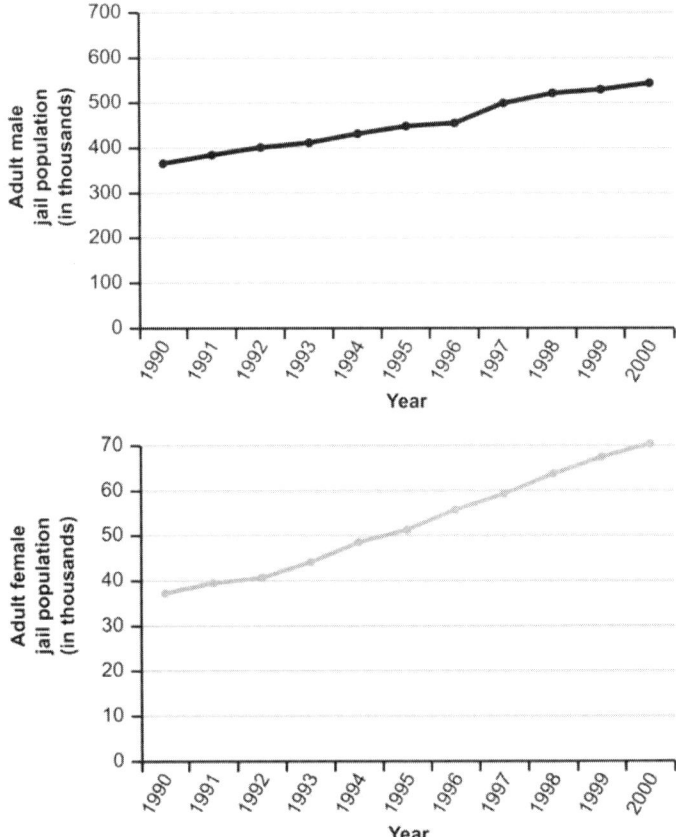

Figure 7-1
Jail Populations by Gender 1990–2000 (One-day count)
Source: Bureau of Justice Statistics, *Surveys in Correctional Populations in the United States, 1997* and *Prison and Jail Inmates at Midyear 1998; 1999; and 2000.*

7-2 Jail Procedures

Because jails vary greatly in size, organization, and facility type, it is impossible to make definitive statements regarding jail procedures. The basic operating procedures can generally be divided into five categories: intake, classification, orientation, court liaison, and release.

7-2a Intake

Intake or **booking** is the point of entry in jails. The intake process involves the transfer of responsibility for the arrestee from the law enforcement officer to the jail. The individual is booked and logged into jail records. Booking consists of a series of steps including verification of the arrest warrant, assignment of jail number, property check, fingerprinting, photography, and other preliminary identification processes. Normally at this stage in the process, the arrestee is permitted to make his or her traditional one telephone call. The intake process may also vary according to the time of day of the arrival. Frequently, the arrestee is agitated and uncooperative, or often under the influence of drugs or alcohol. The intake process is a high-stress period for many arrestees and special precautions should be taken to prevent suicides.

7-2b Classification

The **classification** process is concerned with the identification, categorization, and assignment of the inmate to various levels of security, programs, and work. The initial classification focuses on housing and any special needs. Factors that need to be considered in the classification decision include age, sex, type of offense, prior criminal history, special medical needs, and available jail space.

Some of the larger urban jails have temporary holding areas, single cells, multiple cells, dormitory type cells, sobering or detoxification units, observation cells, segregation cells, hospital wards, and individual rooms. In these large jails, it is easier to provide the proper classification and housing for residents. Most jails, however, are much smaller and many have only one type of cell for residents.

A frequent problem is the lack of verifiable information available on the inmate. Often the jail staff must rely on their own records, the data provided by law enforcement personnel, and the information obtained from the arrestee. Of particular concern is the ability of the jail staff to recognize arrestees who need special medical or mental health treatment.

7-2c Orientation

Because confinement in jail places a person in a dependant status, proper orientation is needed for individuals who have not been previously confined. The **orientation** process should inform the residents of jail rules and procedures. In addition, any special programs or other assistance that is available should be explained to the new residents. An effective orientation process can help relieve the stress and conflict present with new arrestees. Most jails provide standard informational handouts for new arrivals that explain the rules, regulations, and other procedures. Many arrestees have only limited reading ability and, thus, need special assistance in understanding the rules and facilities.

7-2d Court Liaison

The **court liaison** or court appearance process is critical to jail operations because jail residents make frequent and repeated court appearances. All jurisdictions require that a suspect be brought before a judge or a magistrate shortly after arrest. For example, most residents will make a court appearance within 24 hours of being arrested with subsequent appearances to follow. The liaison or court appearance process involves the suspect appearing before the judge for the purpose of being advised of his or her constitutional due process rights. The safe and timely delivery of jail residents to court requires detailed planning and a significant number of staff to supervise the process. Generally, jails are located in close proximity of the courthouse because of the required close working relationship. In some jurisdictions, judges hold initial hearings in the jail.

7-2e Release

The release process varies based on whether the release is on bail, completion of sentence, dismissal of charges, transfer to another institution, or some other form of release. It is also important that the jail staff are certain the proper resident is released. Accordingly, it is crucial to make positive identification of the releasee. In addition, any personal property that was taken from the arrestee is required to be returned to him or her on release.

7-3 State Jail Felony

Several states have created a new punishment category, the state jail felony. In 1994, for example, Texas designated 55 offenses as state jail felonies.[5] A **state jail felony** is more serious than a misdemeanor and less serious than a felony. The punishment range for a state jail felony is from 180 days to two years in a state-controlled jail. Generally people sentenced to confinement under a state jail felony are subject to mandatory community supervision on completion of confinement. There is no parole, no credit for good time, or special enhancement provisions. State jails are intended to be secure facilities built especially for the confinement of convicted state jail felons and to be less expensive to build and operate than current prisons.

Deferred adjudication may still be used with state jail felons. After a state jail felon is released from confinement, the judge must set a period of supervision that may generally range from two to five years. The judge may extend the period of supervision at any time up to one year after the period of community supervision has expired. Generally, a judge may impose any reasonable condition of community supervision on a state jail felon.

Box 7-3

Smoking in Jail

In 1996, New York City banned smoking in its 16 jails. The ban is part of a national trend sweeping the nation's jails and prisons. Prior to the ban, the city's jail commissaries were selling 8,000 packs of cigarettes a day. Cigarettes were not only used for smoking, but as a form of currency in a system which required inmates to wait as long as two weeks to be allowed commissary privileges. Cigarettes were also used to buy drugs and razors (the jails' weapon of choice). Inmates do not have access to any other nicotine products. In addition, gum is not allowed because it could be used to jam locking devices.

Several prisoner rights organizations have protested the ban on cigarettes. According to them, a cigarette helps inmates to relax, especially those addicted to nicotine and removal of cigarettes could lead to an increase in tensions and hostilities. The jail administrators contend that the ban is necessary for health and safety reasons and is also motivated by a growing concern over lawsuits regarding secondhand smoke.

At least 68 jurisdictions with 619 jails and prisons have instituted total or partial bans on smoking. Those jurisdictions include Los Angeles County jails and prisons in the states of Texas, North Carolina, West Virginia, Georgia, Indiana, and Nebraska. Since the ban, cigarettes have become a valued contraband. The going price in Los Angeles County jails in 1996 was $5 a cigarette. In Vermont, the contraband became such a problem that the officials rescinded the ban.[6]

7-4 Issues in Jails

There are many issues that jails face in the twenty-first century. In an era of dwindling budgets, many jail administrators are struggling to do more with less money. Like many correctional institutions in the United States, jails have not escaped the escalating inmate populations. In fact, jail overcrowding is one of the more serious issues facing jails today.

7-4a Overcrowding

Overcrowding has increasingly become a problem in jails. In 1990 there were 405,320 inmates housed in jails, and in 2000 there were 621,149, a 4.4 percent increase from 1990 to 2000. Table 7-1 presents the number of inmates held in local jails throughout the 1990s. Similarly, between July 1, 2000, and June 29, 2001, the number of persons held in local jail facilities grew 1.6 percent from 621,149 to 631,240.

TABLE **7-1** Inmates Held in Local Jails

Year	Number	Incarceration Rate (per 100,000)
1990	405,320	458
1995	507,044	601
1996	518,492	618
1997	567,079	648
1998	592,462	669
1999	605,943	691
2000	621,149	699

Source: Bureau of Justice Statistics, "Prison and Jail Inmates at Midyear 2001, In 2000," (Washington, DC: U.S. Department of Justice, 2001), 2.

The headlines of our nation's newspapers readily reveal the overcrowding problems that many jails face. For example, an Associated Press story in June 2002 quoted Pottawatomie County, Oklahoma, Sheriff Kurt Shirey as saying that the conditions in the Pottawatomie County Jail are deplorable.[7] The Pottawatomie County jail is among 49 across the state of Oklahoma that failed inspection last year by the Oklahoma Department of Health, and the sheriff reports that up to 80 inmates are housed in holding cells that were built to accommodate 35. In Crawford County, Arkansas, the sheriff blames overcrowding for a fight that broke out on June 12, 2002, in one of the jail's cell blocks. The sheriff reports that there were 47 inmates in a cell block designed for 24 persons.[8]

Overcrowding is blamed for two incidents in the Brunswick County Jail located in Bolivia, North Carolina. In the first incident, three inmates escaped and fled to Pennsylvania before police captured them. In the second incident inmates attacked a detention officer and brutally beat him. A consulting firm reports that the 24-year-old Brunswick County Jail is outdated and filled with too many inmates.[9] In Denver, Colorado, the jail was built to hold 1,350 inmates and currently holds 1,967. Denver jail officials have taken measures to reduce overcrowding, such as allowing inmates serving minor sentences, such as driving under the influence, to serve their sentence at home where they will be monitored by wearing an electronic ankle bracelet.[10]

One of the primary causes of jail overcrowding that has influenced police and correctional practices is a more punitive public attitude toward crime. Other causal factors are delays between arrest and final case disposition, the inability of many inmates to make bond, and mandatory jail time for non-violent offenders (e.g., offenders convicted of drunk driving, minor drug offenders, and second-offense property offenders). The results of overcrowded conditions in jails can be disastrous. For example, there is an increased level of violence among inmates, which is directed at weaker inmates or in some cases toward guards. There is also the possibility of lawsuits being filed by inmates and federal court injunctions that mandate the jurisdiction take immediate action to alleviate the overcrowded conditions.

Several jurisdictions have taken substantial steps to reduce jail overcrowding. The Sedgwick County Sheriff's Department in Wichita, Kansas, operates the largest jail in the state and has experienced overcrowded jail conditions for several years. In an effort to reduce overcrowding, the sheriff's department contracts with surrounding counties and cities to house overflow inmates.[11] In Galveston County, Texas, jail officials routinely divert many mentally ill arrestees directly to a mental health facility.[12] In San Diego, California, drunks are removed from the jail's drunk tanks and placed in a privately operated detoxification center.[13]

Many jurisdictions are experimenting with varying approaches, such as those discussed above, to reduce jail overcrowding. Approaches such as the ones discussed above appear to be the cheaper and more immediate solution in light of the cost to build new jail facilities. Building costs continue to be a deterrent to new jail construction and renovation. Jails that have built new and larger facilities find themselves at or beyond capacity soon after a new facility is opened. The attempts to build new jails to solve the problem of overcrowding have failed miserably and our nation's jails are still overcrowded.

Jail administrators will have to continue to be creative in their efforts to reduce jail overcrowding. Whether the innovation is through contracting with other jurisdictions to hold inmates or diverting mentally ill inmates out of the jail and into metal health facilities, these solutions are not only just short term, but also costly to county or city government.

7-4b Controversies

Some jails have come under scrutiny for their solutions to overcrowding. In 1995, an Arizona sheriff added tents in the desert for inmates to inhabit in an effort to relieve overcrowded conditions in the jail. The Maricopa County Arizona Sheriff's Office and Sheriff Joe Arpaio are well known for their tough stance on criminals and inmates. Sheriff Arpaio started "Tent City," a canvas incarceration compound in the Arizona desert that houses 1,200 convicted men and women. The sheriff is also credited with starting the nation's first male and female chain gangs. He is known as the sheriff who puts inmates in pink underwear and feeds them green bologna. The press has dubbed the sheriff as the "toughest sheriff in America." The sheriff maintains that the tents are a mechanism to relive overcrowding. Inmates at Tent City are required to maintain themselves at all times, including cutting one another's hair. The sheriff has also banned violent television programs in the jail, forcing inmates to watch shows like Lassie and Donald Duck rather than shows with more violent themes.[14]

The "In-Tents" section of the Tent City jail is one of five such sections and has been very controversial. There are 29 tents of male working inmates, 10 tents of female working inmates, and one control tower of non-working fully sentenced male inmates in this section. The tent compound includes a sixty-foot observation tower with a pink vacancy sign that is manned around the clock. The average population in the tents is about 1,000 inmates. Three detention officers are typically assigned to supervise the yard. Temperatures in desert jail soar to well over 100 degrees in the summer. The tents are not air conditioned.[15]

There have been numerous lawsuits filed against the sheriff that allege that Sheriff Arpaio nurtures an environment that encourages detention officers to abuse inmates. So far the total bill for jury awards and settlement is approximately $15 million. The federal government has been investigating reports of brutality in Sheriff Arpaio's jails.

7-4c Jail Suicides

Inmates confined in jails have among the highest rates of suicide in the United States. According to the Bureau of Justice Statistics over 400 jail inmates commit suicide each year. The typical jail suicide victim is a young, single male arrested for a crime involving alcohol or is presently under the influence of alcohol. Generally, the victim takes his life within three hours of incarceration.

A recent report in the *Los Angeles Times* reveals that in California more jail inmates are killing themselves then ever before, and some experts believe that it is because mentally ill people are inappropriately being held in jails.[16] In 2001, 38 inmates in California jails committed suicide, most by strangulation, usually with jail bedding but sometimes with socks or even shoelaces. One inmate managed to hold a plastic bag over his head until he suffocated.[17] The death total was a sharp rise over the 23 suicides recorded by California jail officials in 2000. It also surpassed the previous high of 37, recorded nearly 20 years ago before sweeping reforms were adopted to identify suicidal arrestees and keep them under close supervision. Records filed with the California Department of Justice by counties where suicides occurred reveal the inmates who committed suicide to be young and old, educated and jobless, and accused of crimes from petty theft to murder. Most were awaiting trial. The suicide rate for the 73,000 county jail inmates in California is 52 per 100,000. By comparison, the 33 state prisons had 21 suicides in a population of 157,493, or 13 per 100,000 prisoners.[18]

The high rate of suicides in jails may be attributed to a variety of factors. One explanation is the type of inmates housed there. For example, many inmates are awaiting trial and it may be their first experience with incarceration, which some inmates are unable to handle. The Bureau of Justice Statistics reports that 36.2 percent of deaths in local jails were attributed to suicides, while only 4.9 percent of the deaths in state correctional facilities were attributed to suicide. Another possible explanation for the large number of jail suicides may be the fact that jails typically serve an at-risk population. Many inmates housed in jails have serious drug and alcohol addiction problems or a serious mental illness. In some cases, suicides may occur because jail personnel failed to prevent them. One example of this occurred in St. Louis, Missouri. St Louis county officials suspended several jail officers, including a supervisor, after they admitted to taking almost no suicide prevention measures before suspected serial killer Maury Travis hanged himself. Jail logs revealed that jail officers missed more than half the checks that are supposed to be made every 15 minutes on someone considered to be a suicide risk. Records showed that Travis went unchecked for more than an hour on five occasions and once for more than two hours during his stay of a little more than two days in jail.[19]

There have been a number of studies examining jail suicides. In Ohio, researchers examined 228 cases of suicide among jail inmates occurring between 1975 and 1985. The total of 94 percent of all suicides were men, 78 percent were white, and the average age was 28. The estimated suicide rate for males in Ohio jails during the study was 3.1 per 100,000 inmates. The most frequent method of suicide in jails was hanging (98 percent). Over 40 percent of offenders had been arrested for alcohol-related crimes, and these cases were significantly more likely to commit suicide within the first 24 hours of incarceration than other cases. Among those committing suicide within the first 24 hours after admissions, intoxicated inmates committed suicide significantly more quickly than others.[20] Similarly, in Texas, researchers examined data on 107 suicides and found that hanging accounted for 103 (96 percent) of the suicides and extraordinary circumstances (e.g., electrocution by means of rewiring an electric hospital bed) contributed to 3 of the 4 non-hanging suicides.[21]

A study of suicides in the Sacramento County, California, jail found that there was a high percentage of mentally ill inmates among those attempting suicide, and a significant number of these inmates had experienced hallucinations or delusions.[22] Other research has revealed that the characteristics of suicide in jail facilities such as nature of offense, intoxication, method/instrument, isolation, and length of incarceration have remained virtually unchanged overtime.[23]

Strategies for reducing the number of suicides in our nation's jails have drawn a considerable amount of debate. Due to the transient nature of lockup and jail populations, long-term strategies such as counseling or other programs may not be feasible. Two themes are prevalent throughout the literature pertaining to suicide prevention in jails. The first is reducing the opportunity for suicides to occur. Opportunity-reducing techniques are more appropriate for institutions that are faced with helping inmates through temporary periods of despair.[24] This is accomplished by better monitoring of suicidal inmates and more visible cell areas to enable consistent and frequent observation. The second theme centers on training jail personnel to better recognize a potential suicidal inmate. This includes enhanced inmate screening and better communication among staff members.

CASE

Paul PATZIG, Administrator c. t. a. of Estate of Annette M. Patzig, Deceased, Appellant, v. Joseph O'NEIL, Commissioner of Police of the City of Philadelphia, (and others) and City of Philadelphia. (D.C. Civil Action No. 76-1287)

United States Court of Appeals, Third Circuit. (577 F.2d 841)

Parents of individuals who committed suicide after being arrested brought action against city and city police employees, alleging violations of the Civil Rights Act as well as independent state law claims. The United States District Court for the Eastern District of Pennsylvania, Charles R. Weiner, Jr., granted the defendants' motion for directed verdict at end of plaintiffs' case, and plaintiffs appealed. The Court of Appeals, Garth, Circuit Judge, held that: (1) arrest for drunken driving at 4:30 A.M. on Saturday followed by confinement for five hours pending arraignment before magistrate did not, without more information, constitute deprivation of due process rights; (2) it was not unreasonable for city police to hold arrested individual for arraignment; (3) plaintiffs failed to establish violation of their daughter's Eighth Amendment rights; (4) evidence concerning whether arresting officer had probable cause to make warrantless arrest presented jury question; (5) where arresting officer was never served, he could not be held liable for false arrest, and (6) case would be remanded to district court for its consideration concerning exercise of pendent jurisdiction with regard to state law claims against city.

Affirmed in part, reversed in part, and remanded.

OPINION OF THE COURT

GARTH, Circuit Judge.

This appeal involves various civil rights claims and pendent state law claims arising out of the arrest, custody and subsequent suicide of Annette Patzig. The district court granted the defendants' motion for a directed verdict at the end of the plaintiffs' case. We affirm as to all defendants except the City of Philadelphia. As to the City, we reverse, limiting our reversal solely to the Patzig's false arrest claims.

On February 21, 1975, the decedent Annette Patzig, accompanied by two friends (Christine Conan and Cynthia Slough), visited a private night club in Philadelphia, arriving at 11:30 P.M. Patzig, according to Conan's testimony, had two drinks. Conan drank heavily and became intoxicated.

Patzig's other friend, Slough, was injured during the course of the evening and was rushed to a hospital. Patzig and Conan, upon learning this fact, left the club in Patzig's automobile in search of Slough. Patzig was driving the car. At trial, Conan testified that the decedent was sober at the time she left the club, and was able to drive.

Because the two girls did not know to which hospital Slough had been taken, they drove to several center city hospitals. At each one Patzig went into the emergency room to inquire about Slough. Again, according to Conan, Patzig was able to walk and talk normally. It should be noted, however, that during this time, Conan remained in the back seat of the car, lapsing in and out of consciousness.

At 4:30 A.M. Patzig, while driving the wrong way on a one-way street, was arrested by Officer McMullen of the Philadelphia Police Department on a charge of drunken driving. Conan testified that Patzig did not appear intoxicated at the time of her arrest. Patzig and Conan were taken to the local police station, and later, at 5:55 A.M., were transported to the Police Administration Building. At 6:07 A.M. Patzig was given a Breathalyzer test, the results of which were not conclusive. The test showed a blood alcohol level of 0.06%. A police surgeon administered a medical examination shortly thereafter (at 6:15 A.M.), and found that Patzig was sober and able to operate a motor vehicle as of the time of the examination. There was other testimony that Patzig did not appear to be intoxicated while in police custody.

Patzig was nevertheless detained in a cell with two other women pending arraignment before a magistrate. The cell had only one metal rack which could be used as a bed or bench. Because her two cellmates were using the rack, Patzig was required to sleep on the tile floor.

During the early part of her confinement, decedent manifested disturbance at her arrest, but exhibited no unusual behavior. During several cell checks by police matrons she was seen either standing or sleeping on the floor. Sometime between 9:00 A.M. and 9:40 A.M. (there is conflicting evidence as to this), Patzig was allowed to make a telephone call. After her call, she refused to return to her original cell. Patzig was then taken by a matron and a police officer to a cell near the end of the cell corridor. The cell to which she was taken was situated between vacant cells. Patzig was the sole occupant in this cell. There was testimony that she was isolated in this manner because she was creating a disturbance.

Patzig then began to act hysterically, shouting, flushing the toilet, and banging the bars of the cell. A police matron attempted to quiet her, failed, and left her alone. Patzig continued to act in this manner for approximately 30 minutes. She then became quiet. At 10:00 A.M., a matron found Patzig hanging by her belt. She was later pronounced dead.

The autopsy revealed a blood alcohol level of 0.0% at the time of death. Extrapolating from this datum and the result of the Breathalyzer, a medical expert concluded that Patzig's blood alcohol level at the time of arrest was 0.085% to 0.09%. The autopsy also indicated the presence of barbiturates in her blood. There was testimony that the decedent was in the habit of taking large doses of barbiturates, which can cause the same clinical symptoms as alcohol intoxication.

Patzig's parents instituted the present lawsuit, alleging violations of the Civil Rights Act, as well as pendent state law claims. The defendants included the Philadelphia Police Commissioner, as well as various police supervisors, police officers and police matrons (some of whom were identified by name and others of whom were listed as John Doe's). Additionally, the plaintiffs joined the City of Philadelphia, alleging jurisdiction under 28 U.S.C. 1331 and asserting an implied cause of action under the Fourteenth Amendment.

The constitutional violations alleged by the plaintiffs can be distilled into three essential claims:

> First, that Patzig was arrested without probable cause in violation of her right against unreasonable search and seizure; second, that the delay in taking Patzig before a magistrate abridged due process; third, that the treatment Patzig received while in custody constituted cruel and unusual punishment . . .

After the plaintiffs had presented their evidence, the district court granted the defendants' motion for a directed verdict under Fed.R.Civ.P. 50(a), and entered judgment against the plaintiffs This appeal followed . . .

> Because this is an appeal from a directed verdict for the defendant, we must examine the record in a light most favorable to the plaintiff, and review the specific evidence in the record and all inferences reasonably capable of being drawn therefrom. We must determine whether, as a matter of law, the record is critically deficient of that minimum quantum of evidence from which a jury might reasonably afford relief. . . . [I]f the evidence is of such character that reasonable men, in the impartial exercise of their judgment may reach different conclusions, the case should be submitted to the jury.

The plaintiffs' second (due process) and third (cruel and unusual punishment) constitutional claims are clearly without merit. The district court did not err by directing a verdict as to these claims . . .

> An arrest for drunken driving at 4:30 A.M. on a Saturday, followed by confinement for five hours pending arraignment before a magistrate does not, without more issues, constitute a deprivation of due process rights. . . . Many times arraignments are not until the next morning and are nonetheless held sufficiently prompt. . . . Delay between arrest and arraignment from 4:30 P.M. to 10:30 P.M., during which time the defendants held plaintiff in custody and allegedly interrogated her . . . is not considered per se a violation of her civil rights.

. . . Given this positive Breathalyzer test, it was not unreasonable for the Philadelphia police to hold Patzig for arraignment. Moreover, during the period after her arrest, the police were processing her, and were administering tests, the results of which might have been exculpatory. Given the necessity for the time of arrest and processing and testing Patzig, there was no unnecessary delay in bringing her before a magistrate.

Insofar as plaintiffs allege that Patzig was subjected to "cruel and unusual punishment," we note that "while it is questionable whether the Eighth Amendment's prohibition . . . is applicable to a pretrial detainee, the most accepted view being that the amendment's proscription applies only after conviction. The due process clause, however, protects pretrial detainees from abusive treatment. . . . In order to establish a constitutional violation under the Eighth Amendment, it is necessary that there be a deliberate indifference to the prisoner's needs . . .

A reading of the evidence before the district court reveals that police personnel may have acted negligently, perhaps even callously, but such actions do not amount to the "intentional conduct characterizing a constitutional infringement." More is needed than a naked averment that a tort was committed under color of state law.

. . . The judgment of the district court will be affirmed insofar as it grants a directed verdict in favor of the defendants as to the due process and "cruel and unusual punishment" claims.

[Note: Regulations called for two women per cell, if possible. Cell checks were required every 15 minutes. The matrons made checks only every 30 minutes. The belt had never been taken from her as required by regulations.]

What do you think?

1. Should the city be held responsible for her suicide?
2. If plaintiffs could establish that, had the matrons followed regulations, then Annette could not have committed suicide, should the estate receive damages?
3. Do the jail administrators have a duty to prevent jail suicides?

7-5 Jail Designs

7-5a Traditional Jails

Jails of the past were designed to provide optimum security, with thick bars and walls that separated the guards from the inmates. First-generation jails are usually rectangular in design, with corridors leading to either single- or multiple-occupancy cells arranged at right angles to the corridor. With a few exceptions, most of the jails of the eighteenth and nineteenth centuries were of the linear/intermittent surveillance type. In other words, guards make rounds every 15 minutes or so (intermittent) by walking around the rectangle cell block via a cat walk while observing inmates.

These jails were designed with the premise that most inmates are violent and needed to be controlled and watched at all times. The problem with these jails is that the very architecture is notorious for limiting the staff's visibility and access to many of the confinement areas. In a linear/intermittent jail, inmates have intervals between patrols to make escape preparations, fashion weapons, assault other inmates, and so on. Because destruction of fixtures and furnishings also occurs with regularity during unsupervised intervals, it is necessary to install expensive vandal-proof housing materials. The paradox here is that this type of jail perpetuates the inmate misconduct that it was designed to control. Many of the traditional jails are still in existence today due to the costs to build more contemporary designed structures.

7-5b Direct-Supervision Jails

Today, the state-of-the-art jail is designed as a direct-supervision or **new-generation jail.** The **direct-supervision jail** is designed in a podular fashion that centers on the concept of proactive and participative philosophy.[25] Direct supervision is an innovative concept of jail management that represents a unique departure from traditional jails; physical boundaries are replaced with behavioral boundaries. The direct-supervision jails, through a combination of architectural design, classification philosophy, inmate ground rules, and officer deployment, effectively control inmate behavior.

Architectural design in direct-supervision jails is based on open, self-contained living units. These units can be dormitory and celled units. Proper design of the direct-supervision jails enhances supervision, increases perimeter security, and effectively divides inmates into manageable groups. Direct supervision places the correctional officers' station within the inmates' living area or pod. The officer can interact and speak to the inmates on a regular basis.

In direct supervision jails, classification of inmates determines the level of supervision an inmate will need. New inmates are carefully screened and those who are mentally ill, violent, or for any reason cannot follow the rules of the housing units are placed in a more structured environment. Each housing unit then has a population that is able to follow rules while ensuring an atmosphere that promotes positive interaction.

Officer deployment is an important part of direct-supervision jails. In the traditional jail, inmates spend a great deal of time without officer supervision. In direct supervision, officers spend a great deal of time with the inmates. Officers spend much of their shift supervising inmate activities and managing the housing unit. Officers are expected to treat inmates fairly and follow disciplinary procedures within established rules and regulations.

Several studies support the efficacy of direct supervision jails. The National Institute of Corrections surveyed 12 new-generation jails. The survey revealed that respondents universally agreed that direct-supervision management is effective for managing prisoners; increasing staff morale; and reducing violence, vandalism, and graffiti. Improved staff morale produces improved attitudes and treatment of prisoners; decreased staff-prisoner conflicts; staff discussions; visitors' comments; decreased staff tension; less sick leave; improved institutional cleanliness and orderliness; reduced staff misconduct and confrontations with management; and enhanced active staff involvement in participatory management. The respondents also noted that cost savings were achieved for plumbing fixtures, lighting fixtures, control stations, walls and gazing, furniture, cell doors, frames, and hardware.[26]

Another study that evaluated a large new-generation jail revealed support for the effectiveness of the jail style. Inmates and staff at the new-generation jail were much more satisfied with the physical facilities. Staff perceived it as more secure, though they reported only limited advantages in safety and security. Violence and disciplinary problems were substantially lower.[27] Similarly, research on the new-generation jail in Sonoma County, California, found that inmate-on-inmate assault rates were reduced by 50 percent. The overall rate of all criminal disciplinary actions had also been reduced by 50 percent and disciplinary isolation had declined by one-third.[28]

Summary

Prior to the twentieth century, jails were often places of filth and disease. Jail fever, a form of typhus, was common in the jails. The causes of jail fever were attributed to the unsanitary conditions of the jails. Generally, jails were poorly supported by local government. Many jailers were appointed for life and earned their livings from the fee system. The deplorable conditions helped bring about the establishment of certain basic rights that later appeared in the U.S. Constitution.

Generally, jails are used for two types of prisoners: those convicted of minor crimes and sentenced to short terms of confinement, and detainees who are awaiting trial and who either do not qualify for bail or can not afford the amount of bail set in their cases. It is estimated that at least four times as many people pass through our jails annually than the number that are incarcerated in state and federal institutions.

Most jails are operated by local governments, such as counties or cities. Jails differ from prisons in that prisons are administered, operated, and funded by state or federal governments. Jails are used to punish people convicted of minor offenses, who are sentenced to confinement for a year or less.

Presently, there are jail standards established by the American Correctional Association, the American Bar Association, the National Sheriff's Association, the American Psychological Association, the American Public Health Association, and even the United Nations. The standards vary by state. In many jurisdictions, the courts have become the chief enforcers of jail standards. Areas of concern to the courts are overcrowding, medical services, library services, available recreation, and the safety of inmates.

There are approximately 3,500 jails in operation in the United States. They represent the most widely used type of confinement in the United States. Jail populations change daily as people are admitted and released. It appears that jails will remain basically temporary local detention units that have only minimal concern for the identification and mediation of inmate problems. The major distinctions between jails and prisons continue to be that jails are locally controlled and their residents have a shorter length of stay.

Many jails are old and overcrowded. Jail populations more than doubled from 1986 to 1999. In 1990 the nation's jails were running 108 percent of capacity. Court-ordered caps on jail populations are common. Jail overcrowding is a factor in inmate-on-inmate assault as well as inmate-on-guard assaults. Some jails have reached the point where it is impossible to accept new inmates. Jail administrators and sheriffs have increasingly contracted services with other cities and counties to house inmates.

Inmates confined to jails have among the highest rates of suicide in the United States. Over 400 jail inmates commit suicide each year. The typical jail suicide victim is a young, single male arrested for a crime involving alcohol or is presently under the influence of alcohol. Generally, the victim takes his life within three hours of incarceration. The high rate of suicides in jails is attributed to the type of inmates housed there. For example, many inmates are awaiting trial and it may be their first experience in an incarcerated environment, which some inmates are not able to handle.

New-generation jails or direct-supervision jails are the newest evolution in jail design. Direct supervision places the correctional officers' station within the inmates' living area or pod. Direct supervision offers many advantages, including effective control and supervision of inmates; improved communication between staff and inmates; safety of staff and inmates; improved classification and orientation of inmates, and staff ownership of operations. Studies support the efficacy of new-generation jails.

Discussion Questions

1. Discuss the role and purpose of jails in our present correctional system.
2. How do jails differ from prisons?
3. Jail standards have caused some local jurisdictions to spend a significant percentage of their budget upgrading jails. Should communities be required to take money from other needed areas to upgrade their jails?
4. What duties should a jail administrator have concerning the safety and well being of jail inmates?

Chapter Quiz

True/False

1. Prior to the twentieth century, jails were often places of extreme cleanliness and sterile environments.
2. From their earliest beginnings, jails were always strongly supported by local government.
3. Jails are the mostly widely used type of confinement.
4. The revolving door concept refers to defendants who are arrested, remain in jail for a period of time, are released, and do not return.
5. Jails have not experienced the issue of overcrowding that prisons have.

Multiple Choice

1. Which of the following is NOT a factor in jail overcrowding?
   a. a more punitive public attitude
   b. delays between arrest and final case disposition
   c. the inability of many inmate to make bond
   d. many homeless persons commit crimes to stay in jail

2. Direct supervision jails have been referred to as
   a. old generation jails.
   b. new generation jails.
   c. linear observation jails.
   d. first generation jails.
3. Which of the following statements is NOT true regarding jails?
   a. Jails are generally operated by local governments.
   b. Jails are used to punish persons convicted of minor offenses.
   c. Jails have not experienced overcrowding like prisons.
   d. Jails house persons waiting for trial.
4. _____ is the point of entry in jails.
   a. Classification
   b. Intake
   c. Orientation
   d. Release
5. Studies of jail suicides have found that persons were more likely to commit suicide
   a. after 40 hours in jail.
   b. within the first 24 hours.
   c. within the first month.
   d. within the first six months but after two months.

Endnotes

1. Donatella Lorch, "New York Files Suit over Rules for Jails" *The New York Times*, 31 May 1996: B3.
2. Bureau of Justice Statistics, *Prison and Jail Inmates at Midyear 1999* (Washington, DC: U.S. Department of Justice, 2000), 7.
3. Bureau of Justice Statistics, *Profile of Jails* (Washington, DC: U.S. Department of Justice, 1990).
4. Bureau of Justice Statistics, *Prison and Jail Inmates at Midyear 1999*.
5. Ken Anderson and John Bradley, *Texas Sentencing* (Bulverde, TX: Omni Publishing, 1996).
6. Joyce Purnick, "Disappearing in Legal Maze of Jail System," *The New York Times*, 7 July 1996: A17.
7. Justin Juozapavicius, "Two-Thirds of State's Jails Fail Inspection," (Oklahoma City, OK: *The Associated Press, State and Local Wire*, June 22, 2002)
8. David Hughes, "Overcrowding Spawns Fight in County Jail," *Arkansas Democrat Gazette*, 21 June 2002: B-6.
9. "Dangerously Overcrowded," *The Myrtle Beach Sun News*, 21 June 2002: C1.

10. "Denver's Jail Crowding Prompts Home Sentencing for Some Inmates," *The Associated Press,* 20 June 2002.
11. Personal communication with Lt. Greg Etter, Sedgwick County Sheriff's Department, Wichita, Kansas, 26 June 2002.
12. Andy Hall, *System Wide Strategies to Alleviate Jail Crowding* (Washington, D.C.: National Institute of Justice, 1987).
13. Ibid.
14. Curtis Rist, "Sheriff with a Vengeance," *People Weekly* 46 (October 7, 1996): 131–132.
15. Barry Graham, "Star of Justice," *Harpers* 302 (1811, April 2001): 59–67.
16. Lindsay M. Hays and Joseph R. Rowan, *National Study of Jail Suicides: Seven Years Later* (Alexander, VA: National Center on Institutions and Alternatives, 1988).
17. John Johnson, "Suicides Reach Record Pace in State," *Los Angeles Times* June 16, 2002.
18. Ibid.
19. Heather Ratcliffe, "Three at County Jail are Suspended Over Suspect's Suicide; Officials Admit that Little Was Done to Prevent Travis From Killing Himself," *St. Louis Post Dispatch,* 20 June 2002: A-1.
20. Mark S. Davis and Joshua E. Muscat, "An Epidemiologic Study of Alcohol and Suicide Risk in Ohio Jails and Lockups, 1975–1885," *Journal of Criminal Justice* 21(3): 277–283.
21. William E. Stone, "Means and Cause of Death in Texas Jail Suicides, 1986–1988," *American Jails* 4 (1, 1991): 50–53.
22. David Lester and Bruce L. Danti, *Suicide Behind Bars: Prediction and Prevention* (Philadelphia: The Charles Press, 1994).
23. Lindsay M. Hayes and Joseph R. Rowan, *National Study of Jail Suicides: Seven Years Later* (Alexandria, VA: National Center on Institutions and alternatives, 1988).
24. Christine Tartaro, "Reduction in Suicides in Jails and Lockups through Situational Crime Prevention: Addressing the Needs of a Transient Population," *Journal of Correctional Health Care* 6 (2): 235–263.
25. Herbert R. Sigurdom, Billy Wayson, and Gail Funke, "Empowering Middle Managers of Direct Supervision Jails," *American Jails,* (Winter, 1990), p. 52.
26. Raymond W. Nelson, "Can Cost Savings Be Achieved by Designing Jails for Direct Supervision Inmate Management?" *Proceedings from the First Annual Symposium on New Generation Jails,* (Washington, DC: National Institute of Corrections, Jail Center, 1986), 13–20.
27. James L. Williams, Daniel G. Rodeheaver, and Denise W. Huggins, "A Comparison Evaluation of a New Generation Jail," *American Journal of Criminal Justice,* 23 (2, 1999): 223–246.
28. Patrick G. Jackson, "Detention in Transition: Sonoma County's New Generation Jails," (Washington, DC: A report by the National Institute of Corrections, Jail Center, 1992).

Chapter 8

Doing Time

Mark C. Ide

Key Terms

cleared count	individual counseling	prison argot
commissaries	institutionalized personality	put down
gang associates	lock down	script
group counseling	Megan's law	shakedowns
HIV/AIDS	prisonization	train

Outline

8-1 Prisonization
8-2 Inmate Social System
    8-2a Prison Subculture
8-3 Gangs in Prison
8-4 Prison Routine
    8-4a Classification
    8-4b Shakedowns
    8-4c Sexual Activity
    8-4d Inmates and Guards
    8-4e Controlled Movement
    8-4f Counts

8-5 Special Issues in Doing Time
    8-5a AIDS
    8-5b Mental Health Issues
    8-5c Sex Offenders
Summary
Discussion Questions
Chapter Quiz
Endnotes

Learning Objectives

After studying this chapter, the reader will be able to:

- Explain the concept of prisonization.
- Explain the inmate social system.
- Describe the role inmate gangs play in prisons.
- Define the term "prison argot" and explain the role it plays in prison.
- Outline the inmate code.
- Describe the methods used to control inmate movements.
- Explain the importance of classification.

> Every man who gets whipped for a sin claims that other men have done more, and been whipped less.
>
> —E.W. Howe, 1911

This chapter is designed to provide the reader with some understanding of what a prisoner experiences in "doing time day-to-day." Much of the material in this chapter was obtained from personal interviews with prisoners in California and Texas prisons that took place from April 1997 through August 2000. When an offender is confined, the major deprivations he or she experiences include loss of liberty, loss of outside links, moral rejection, deprivation of material amenities, sexual frustration, and loss of identity.[1] And, as Dostoyevski noted, the prisoner learns patience.

Most offenders will admit that they committed the crime for which they were incarcerated, and most will admit that they made a mistake. This does not mean, however, that they feel they should be in confinement. When discussing confinement as a correctional tool almost all offenders will point out the injustices in the system. They will cite examples of people who committed more serious crimes but were not confined because of special treatment or special status. Most prisoners have the "Why me?" attitude when discussing their situation.

8-1 Prisonization

Prisonization is the term used to indicate the taking on of the folkways, mores, customs, and general culture of prison life. It is the process of assimilation into prison life. During the process of prisonization, inmates become socialized as prisoners. Every person who enters prison undergoes prisonization to some degree.[2] Prisonization begins almost immediately on arrival to the first institution or reception center. The first step in the prisonization process is the integrative step where a person leaves his or her individualism and becomes an anonymous figure in a subordinate group. An inmate number replaces the name. The prisoner no longer chooses what clothes he or she wears, but wears the clothes of a subordinate group. The prisoner soon learns that the warden and the correction officer's rank is all-powerful. The prisoner begins to use prison slang or argot and learns to eat in haste. Many inmates may experience abnormal sexual behavior for the first time in their lives, while others may not.

The offender going through prisonization forms an **institutionalized personality.** This personality type is characterized by moving like a robot in routine patterns, losing any initiative, living on a day-to-day basis, forgetting the past, and avoiding the future. The offender begins to look forward to simple diversions from the dullness of prison life, such as the next meal, a TV program, or the next movie that will be shown in the institution. Often, when these small diversions are withheld from the offender, a violent reaction occurs. During an interview, an inmate who had assaulted a guard justified the assault because the guard would not allow him to have a piece of cake as dessert after the evening meal. Apparently the guard felt that the offender had already received his dessert and was attempting to obtain a second one. The inmate stated that he had waited all day for a piece of cake. The inmate, who had a lengthy criminal record, was convicted of assaulting the guard and received an additional 50-year prison sentence for the assault. In almost all jurisdictions, it is required by statute that prisoners who are convicted for criminal offenses committed in prison will have their new sentence "stacked" or "tacked on the end" of their present term (i.e., served consecutively and not concurrently).

During the prisonization process, the offender learns to speak prison argot. **Prison argot** is a language that is unique to prison. The offender learns prison argot much the same way as a person who moves to a foreign land learns to speak the local language. Table 8-1 presents some of the more common terms or slang used by prisoners. The prison language, however, differs among institutions much the same way dialect differs among various regions in some countries.

Inmates are issued I.D. cards at the reception center. It is a rule infraction for an inmate not to have the proper I.D. card on him or her at all times. Offenders are not allowed to have money in their possession. Offenders who have money with them when they are committed are required to surrender their money at the reception center. They may exchange their money for items at the commissary or have it deposited in their inmate trust fund. In most cases, the inmate's prison number is his or her trust account number. Family members or other persons who want to send money to a prisoner must send the money to the institution to be deposited in the inmate's trust fund. In some states, the inmates are allowed to establish bank accounts but may not have any blank checks in their possession. Since they are not allowed to possess money, inmates find other items to use instead of money (known as **script**). For example, a popular item that is used by many inmates are bags of coffee. Coffee is highly desired in prison and many inmates use hot tap water in order to prepare coffee, likewise inmates are required to purchase coffee outside of what they receive with meals through the prison commissary. Prior to their banning, cigarettes were popular as "script."

TABLE 8-1 Prison Slang

Term	Definition
Croaker	Doctor
Screws	Guards
Right guys	Inmates who obey the inmate code and oppose prison staff
Square johns or straights	Inmates who obey prison regulations and do not adhere to inmate code
Merchants	Inmates who yield power by selling scarce goods and contraband
Outlaws	Inmates who are aggressive and rely on force
Squealers	Inmates who are informants
Wolves	Homosexuals who are prone to prey on others
Fangs	Inmates who passively accept homosexual advances
Fish	New inmates
Hard time	Doing your time day for day without hope of early parole
Script	Items used as a substitute for money in prison
Shank	Knife or blade
Bos	What inmates call staff [spelled backwards is sob (son of a bitch)]
Chill out	Calm down
Hack	Correctional officer
Dr. Feelgood	The psychologist
Waste	To kill someone
Roll-over	To become an informant
Phone off the hook	A correctional officer is within hearing distance
Clicking	When several inmates physically assault or manipulate a weaker inmate
Hogging	When one inmate is forced to fight another inmate until one of the two succumbs
To take off the count	To kill
Crew	The gang
New boot	An inmate new to prison
Steel	Knife
Run	A cell block
Touch	To beat another inmate
Punk	Weak inmate who is the property of a stronger inmate
Ride with an inmate	A new or weaker inmate who pays protection
Hochecking	When number of inmates approach another inmate ordering him to provide money or sex for protection

Commissaries are stores within the prison where items not furnished by the institution may be purchased. The inmate uses his or her I.D. card to make commissary purchases. Those charges are then deducted from the inmate's trust fund. Access to the commissaries is often restricted from use by rule-violating inmates. Generally there are two types of purchases made at the commissaries—regular and special. Regular purchases are those that happen frequently, such as buying candy and soft drinks. Regular purchases are generally limited to about $60.00 per month in most states. Special purchases are items that are generally bought once, such as radios, fans, and clothing. Special purchases must be approved by a staff member. While it is a violation for inmates to purchase items for other inmates or to trade items purchased at the commissary, inmates regularly trade items in an active underground economy.

All states have some type of personal cleanliness and grooming standards. For example, Texas requires inmates to shower one time each day, brush their teeth daily, and male inmates must be clean shaven. Male inmates are issued one disposable razor each week. No beards, mustaches, or hair under their lips is allowed. Hair must be kept trimmed up to the back of their necks and heads and neatly cut with no block style, Afro, natural, or shag haircuts allowed. Female inmates cannot have extreme haircuts or mohawk or "tailed" haircuts.

Each inmate is assigned a bunk in a cell or dormitory and cannot change bunks without permission. Each inmate is also assigned a locker. Inmates may not use lockers or bunks not assigned to them. They are prohibited from hanging towels, blankets, clothing, and other personal items in their living area in a manner that blocks an officer's view of any area. We offer parts of the following narrative that was gleaned from an interview conducted by one of the authors at the Federal Correctional Institution at Bastrop, Texas. Notice how this account resembles a sort of homecoming for the inmate.

> Joe Acosta arrived at the Federal Correctional Institute, in Bastrop, Texas, one May morning to begin serving a sentence for possession and transfer of a controlled substance. Joe, a seasoned veteran of prison life, immediately looked around for old friends whom he had served with before. He found several. They discussed old times and compared this "country club" to some of the state prisons that they had served in. To the observer, it was an experience very similar to those encountered by the soldier or marine being transferred to a new base and looking for old friends he had served with before on other military bases. The defendant in one of the leading U.S. Supreme Court decisions involving constitutional rights was named Acosta. When Joe was asked if he was the defendant in that case, he stated that no, it was his uncle.[3]

In the early 1980s, one of this book's authors taught a criminology class for college credit to offenders in a federal correctional institution. As the class discussed the various theories on why individuals committed crimes, the prisoners' responses were very similar to those of regular students in university criminology classes. Taking the discussions one step further after an offender had explained his favorite criminologic theory, I asked the offender if that was why he committed his crime. Invariably, the student responded with comments explaining that while he agreed with a certain crime causation theory, it did not apply to him because . . . and he would then attempt to neutralize or rationalize his conduct.

8-2 Inmate Social System

From numerous interviews regarding the informal chain of command in prisons, it appears that, like any large group, there are inmates who are leaders and inmates who are followers. Generally the social backgrounds of the leaders are not much different from those of the followers. The inmate leaders, however, have usually served more time in prison and are more frequently in prison for violent crimes than the followers. It was rare that a first-time, nonviolent inmate was labeled a leader.

The concept of a separate inmate social system was first discussed by Sykes and Messinger in 1960.[4] They suggested that prisoners have a pervasive value system and that this value system takes the form of an explicit code of behavior. In recent interviews with prisoners in Texas and California prisons, it appears that almost 40 years later, prisoners still abide by these maxims. Often violation of the code will result in retaliatory action by fellow prisoners. In some cases, it appears that while the prisoners assert these maxims vocally, they violate them when it is to their advantage and the chances that other prisoners will know of their violations are minimal. As Sykes and Messinger noted, the actual behavior of the inmates ranged from full adherence to the maxims to deviance of various types. The maxims are listed below:

1. Don't interfere with inmate interests.
   This is accomplished by not "ratting" on a convict, not being nosey, not talking too much, keeping off a man's back, and not putting an inmate on the spot. The value involved in this maxim is that of being loyal to your class/inmates (group).
2. Minimize emotions.
   Don't lose your head. Play it cool. Minimize emotional friction and ignore the minor irritants of confinement.

3. Don't exploit your fellow inmate.
   One inmate should not take advantage of another inmate. This is accomplished by not selling favors, repaying debts, and not being a racketeer.
4. Be tough; be a man.
   Inmates should be able to take prison life. When confronted with aggressive behavior, stand tall. Don't start fights, but don't run from one that someone else started.
5. Don't trust the screws.
   Guards and other correctional officers are not to be trusted. In conflicts between a correctional officer and an inmate, the correctional officers are always wrong. Don't be a sucker and work with the hypocrites.

Box 8-1

Standing Tall

Arthur Glenn was serving a ten-year sentence in a Houston County, Texas, correctional institution in. While serving time, he was indicted and convicted of assaulting another inmate with a dangerous weapon. For this offense, his third felony conviction, he received the minimum sentence of 25 years. Arthur insisted that he hit the other offender in self-defense. It appears that Arthur came up to the victim from behind and hit him in the head with a lock swinging from the end of a rope. To Arthur, this was self-defense. The victim had stolen some items from Arthur and had bragged about it. Arthur told the jury that he had no alternative but to take protective action against the victim. According to him to fail to take the action would have left him a marked person and everybody would take what they wanted from him.

8-2a Prison Subculture

Social scientists have been interested in the social world of prison for some time. Just as society has norms and customs so does the inmate society behind bars. Inmates within the confines of prison develop their own customs, norms, and culture. This phenomenon is known as the prison subculture. Not only do prisons have their own set of customs, norms, and cultures, but they also have their own language. This language is referred to as prison argot, meaning the language or slang of prison. For example, the use of the word "snitch" or "rat" is common argot used by inmates to describe someone who is an informer to the authorities. Please refer to Table 8-1 for examples of prison slang.

In 1940, sociologist Donald Clemmer conducted early research on prison culture. Clemmer's research was groundbreaking in the sense that he described an elaborate and formal organizational structure of the prison subculture.[5] Other studies support Clemmer's findings of a prison subculture rooted in power, influence, and organization, with a language of its own and a distinct set of customs and cultures.

Most studies on inmate subcultures consider prisons a contained and isolated institution. They tend to focus on prisoners being subject to numerous restrictions within a very coercive environment, cut off from the outside world.[6] Later studies have challenged these assumptions, asserting instead that preprison and extraprison influences have a significant impact on the prison social culture. Later studies criticize both sets of assumptions and consider them unrealistic and no longer applicable to today's prison conditions.[7] According to the latest studies, if an inmate social code does exist, it is unlikely that black and white inmates would be equally committed to the same values. Prison populations contain a variety of racial and ethnic groups that range in solidarity and function and are not homogeneous. Accordingly, the inmate code of conduct is different for each racial and ethnic group. The groups or cliques range from a group of offenders who share common interests to tightly knit organizations in which the members cooperate in rackets, thefts, and violence. Often the cliques share leisure hours together and protect each other from attacks.[8]

Prison subculture is passed down from one inmate to another. New inmates find that they must quickly begin to conform to the prison subculture if they want to fit in, and in some cases survive, in the harsh environment of prison. When new inmates learn appropriate attitudes, behaviors, and norms of prison life, they begin to adapt to the process of prisonization. This process leads to the adoption of the folkways, mores, customs, and general culture of the prison inmates.[9]

Box 8-2

Put Down

The slang term "**put down**" eloquently describes the emotional effect of being put in prison. It is hard to realize just how humiliating ("put-down") prison life can be even in well-run institutions. Accordingly, sooner or later, the prisoner must lose his spirit, or he must rebel.[10]

8-3 Gangs in Prison

Have prison gangs replaced the inmate social system? Prior to the 1960s, the inmate social system was dominated by a few powerful inmates. These leaders, primarily white, used their power to stabilize the inmate social system. Prison staff allowed the leader-inmates to rule in exchange for the assurance that the prison population remained stable and controlled. In several states, such as Texas, the leader-inmates became all-powerful under a builder-tender system (the process of allowing some inmates to supervise other inmates), until a federal court ruled in 1990 in the case of *Ruiz v. Estelle* that the state could not allow inmates to supervise other inmates.[11] In *Ruiz*, Justice Wayne Justice ruled that the use of building tenders (inmates) who worked for the staff and maintained order through fear and intimidation was unconstitutional. There were some strong opinions regarding the removal of building tenders (BTs). Some examples are as follows:

> "Getting rid of BTs, turnkeys, and countboys was a good thing because in the old days it was a simple matter for them to "cross out" (lie about the inmate to a staff member) somebody they didn't like."

> "In a way, they were a good thing. They kept the noise down and the blacks in line."

> "It was bad when the BTs were here because they stole your property and they also ran protection scams. The "greys" [guards] never did nothin' about it neither."

According to criminologist Paige Ralph, the traditional accommodations between inmate leaders and prison staff were disrupted and replaced by gangs. Ralph concludes that the prison gangs of today are highly organized enterprises with a deadly profit motive.[12] She also points out that the civil rights movement of the 1960s allowed inmates to become more assertive to the point they seemed almost militant in their manner of seeking redress from the courts. The judicial intervention, for example the removal of building tenders, was intended to make prisons safer and more humane but it actually created a vacuum that allowed gangs to develop. According to Ralph, the presence of gangs in prison provides protection, a way to "beat the man," and access to illicit goods and services. In addition, the gang offers solidarity and brotherhood, thereby providing social and psychological support for its members. As one gang member stated: "As long as a man's a brother, you ain't gonna let nothing happen to him. If he has a problem, then you have a problem. If you have a problem, then he has a problem."

The latest data in California (2001) reveals that there are 100,000 gang members in prison who were responsible for over 200 homicides and thousands of stabbings during an eight-year period in the 1990s.[13] These gang members are getting out of prison at a rate of about 3,000 per month. In 2001, there were some 30,000 veteran gang members released from prison and back on the streets in California. In addition, approximately 7 percent of the California total offender population are "gang associates." **Gang associates** are "wannabe" gang members and others who actively support gang activity. According to the latest estimates, associate gang members, since they are not official gang members, are not locked down and thereby account for 70 percent of the criminal activity of the prison gangs in California prisons. Texas recently estimated that 92 percent of the homicides and 80 percent of the prison assaults are gang related.[14]

Accordingly, many studies show that gang members and associate members adhere more enthusiastically to the gang's code of conduct than to those of the institution. The most common punishment for breaking a gang rule is death. The leading prison gangs include the Black Guerrilla Family, Texas Syndicate, Mexican Mafia, and the Aryan Brotherhood. There are also street gangs like the Bloods, Crips, Vice Lords, Hells Angels, Skinheads, and Latin Kings who have infiltrated prisons. A 1992 survey by the American Correctional Association identified 1,153 different prison gangs in the United States.[15]

Before accepting a person as a gang member, sponsorship is mandatory. Every member must meet certain requirements and generally a period of internship is necessary. The Aryan Brotherhood, for example, requires that the recruit go through a six-month indoctrination during which he learns the rules and conduct code. During that period he is tested by the members in certain situations to see how he reacts. At first, he will not be allowed to attend gang meetings. If successful, after the indoctrination, the individual is accepted as a full-fledged gang member. Only after the member has been accepted can the inmate identify himself as a member with a tattoo or patch. Most institutions have an administrator whose duties include the monitoring of gang activity. These individuals screen inmate mail and look for other signs of gang membership in order to identify those prisoners with gang affiliation.

Prison gangs have increasingly become a concern of prison guards and administrators. These concerns focus on solutions to effectively dealing with prison gangs, protecting vulnerable prisons, and improving the general safety for corrections staff. Prison gangs vary from loosely organized to extremely organized and structured groups. Prison gangs spread from one prison to another when inmates are transferred to several prisons.

One particular problem with prison gangs is that they continue to operate their criminal enterprise while in prison. For example, federal prosecutors say that for more than 12 years, a group of gang members inside California's toughest prison "Pelican Bay" ordered associates on the outside to commit murder and steal and sell drugs despite one of the most stringent security systems in the country. On April 24, 2001, a 31-page indictment unsealed in San Francisco federal court revealed that 13 prison gang members were accused of orchestrating a reign of terror across the state over the past 19 years, including arranging at least five murders throughout the region.[16]

In Utah, prison officials are attempting to find a system for dealing with rising prison gangs. With Utah's prison population expected to grow by 324 inmates in 2002, prison officials are scrambling to head off weapons problems and possible gang retaliations while trying to deal with limited bed space and resources. According to Utah prison officials, Latino and white supremacist gangs have been feuding for some time and there has been a growing hostility between these two gangs.[17]

With the prevalence of gangs in prisons, the personal safety of corrections staff is an increasing concern. In the twenty-first century, prisons are receiving younger and often more violent inmates. Many of these inmates, who specifically single out correctional staff to victimize, are affiliated with prison gangs, called security threat groups.[18]

Prison gangs constitute a persistently disruptive force in correctional facilities because they interfere with correctional programs, threaten the safety of inmates and staff, and erode the quality of life. It is imperative that correctional administrators ensure training is provided to all prison staff in gang identification and recognition, as well as characteristics of gangs. If corrections staff are made aware of the issues centering on gangs, violent contact between inmates gang members and staff may be reduced. Furthermore, prison officials should review the lessons learned from the past when dealing with prison gangs, both good and bad. Finally, standard operating procedures should be reviewed and enhanced with various methods in dealing with prison gangs and improving the safety of the work environment.

8-4 Prison Routine

8-4a Classification

The degree of freedom that an offender has in prison and the privileges that he or she gets are based largely on security classification. The purposes of classification include:

- To systematically identify inmates as to their needs regarding training programs, security, and/or treatment
- To assign offenders to minimum, medium, or maximum security institutions or supervision levels on the basis of their predicted likelihood of recidivism, escape, or disciplinary infractions
- To assign offenders to appropriate treatment approaches on the basis of psychological, developmental, and/or personality characteristics

The courts have held that any classification criteria used by the correctional institutions must be rational and reasonable. In most jurisdictions, classifications are accomplished by classification boards appointed by the warden. The classification criteria cannot be arbitrary or capricious. The courts have also held that prisoners cannot be reclassified in retaliation for the exercise of a constitutional right, such as filing lawsuits and grievances. While a state has no duty to protect individuals who are not in state custody, they have a duty to protect inmates taken into custody and held against their will. Accordingly, one aspect of classification procedures should be to protect the prisoner from himself or herself and from others.

Recently, the courts held that institutions may segregate HIV-positive inmates from the general population. Other court cases have held that the failure to segregate HIV-positive inmates also does not violate the Eighth

Amendment rights of the noninfected offenders. Accordingly, it appears that the state may or may not segregate HIV-positive inmates from the general population.

8-4b Shakedowns

All prisoners are subject to **shakedowns** or cell searches. Prisoners have no Fourth Amendment rights regarding "a reasonable expectation of privacy." Accordingly, prisoners' possessions are subject to being searched without the necessity for a warrant or probable cause. The officers must, however, respect the inmate's property and cannot recklessly destroy property in the search process. For example, in one search conducted in an Illinois prison, the officer doing the search destroyed a magazine belonging to the prisoner. The prisoner successfully sued in court to be reimbursed for the cost of the magazine ($3.00). The court also awarded the lawyer who handled the case for the prisoner $5,000 in legal fees.

Searches may not be used to single out and harass any particular person. Since inmates have proved to be ingenious at finding unsuspected hiding places, the searches may be very detailed. Body searches can range from frisk (an external pat-down of the body) to internal body-cavity searches. Generally there are three types of searches:

- Routinely at predetermined, but unannounced, times
- Randomly at undetermined and unannounced times
- Based on information or reasonable suspicion

8-4c Sexual Activity

A 1968 study of American prisons stated that virtually every slightly-built young man admitted to prison is approached by a homosexual within a day or two of his admission. Since correctional institutions are designed to deprive the offenders of sexual activities, and generally all prisons are a single-sex environment filled with young offenders with active sex drives, homosexuality exists. Many are overwhelmed and are repeatedly gang raped. Others enter into a housekeeping arrangement with an individual who, in exchange for being his "woman," is protected by the tormentor. According to the study, only the toughest and most hardened young men escape penetration of their bodies.

8-4d Inmates and Guards

What is the relationship between inmates and guards? While maxim five noted earlier states not to trust the screws, many observers have commented on the relationships between guards and inmates. Victor Hassine, an inmate in a Pennsylvania correctional institution noted that he was surprised to discover that there was no open hostility between guards and inmates. He also noted that often many guards and inmates went out of their way to establish relationships with each other and that inmates often befriended guards in hopes of obtaining extra privileges such as special shower time or the overlooking of some minor infraction. He noted that, in many cases, there were unwritten agreements between the two, whereby the inmates got what they wanted by being friendly and nonaggressive, while the guards ensured their own safety by not strictly enforcing the rules. He concluded that most guards are assaulted for attempting to enforce some petty rule. Hassine noted that for the most part, inmates exploited the guards' desire for safety, and the guards exploited the inmates' needs for autonomy.[19] Subsequent interviews with prisoners in both California and Texas prisons support Hassine's conclusions.

8-4e Controlled Movement

In addition to being isolated from the outside world, segregation is used within institutions to isolate offenders from each other. The justification for segregation is based on the premise that segregating offenders from each other minimizes the offenders' opportunities for disruptive behavior. In addition, it restricts their opportunities to plan escapes and deal in contraband. One aspect of segregation is the controlled movement of offenders. The degree of movement allowed within the institution depends largely on the institution's security classification. Two frequently used methods to control movement are very similar to those used in many of our schools—individual passes and group movement.

Probably the most controlled movement institution in the United States is the U.S. Penitentiary at Marion, Illinois.[20] At Marion, if an offender refuses to move as directed, a five-man unit in riot helmets and flack jackets approaches him. Each man on the team is assigned a body part—such as an arm or a leg. They take him down, chain him, and carry him to the desired location. Most offenders are locked in their cells for 22 hours each day. Until 1990, the inmates' food came in cellophane wrappers. The cellophane wrappers were banned because the offenders were melting the cellophane and fashioning it into crude blades.

External movement of offenders from one institution to another is normally accomplished by the use of prescheduled movements. For example in Texas, the state uses a "train" to move prisoners from one location to another. The **train** is a nickname for the scheduled bus network used whereby prisoners are transported by several busses to the desired location.

8-4f Counts

A significant portion of each day in prison is taken up by the mandatory counts. A count is the determination by physical sighting of the precise location of all offenders in an institution. A **cleared count** means that all offenders have been physically accounted for. In maximum-security institutions, count is taken about every two hours. In other institutions it is taken at least three times each day. Any time a count does not match the number of offenders on the official roster, a "lock down" is instituted until a satisfactory recount is made or it is determined that an offender is missing. A **lock down** is a situation where all offender movement is stopped, and no one is allowed to enter or leave the institution until the lock down is lifted. If an inmate is missing or a discrepancy still exists after a recount, emergency search procedures are instituted.

8-5 Special Issues in Doing Time

8-5a AIDS

In light of the prevalence of sexual activity in prison there is a growing concern for the number of inmates who have contracted Human Immunodeficiency Virus (HIV). At the beginning of 2000, correctional officials reported that 24,607 state inmates and 1,150 federal inmates were HIV positive. Of those known to be HIV positive in all U.S. prisons, 6,642 were confirmed Acquired Immune Deficiency (AIDS) cases, while 17,718 either showed symptoms of HIV infections or were without symptoms but tested positive.[21]

Not all persons who test positive for HIV have full-blown AIDS. If the individual tests positive for HIV, a series of blood tests must be taken to determine if the person has **HIV/AIDS** infection. It appears that HIV individuals without AIDS symptoms can spread the infection even if they never develop full-blown AIDS. Generally, it is spread through heterosexual or homosexual sexual activity and blood-to-blood contact, such as drug-needle sharing. Casual contact does not transmit HIV.

AIDS is a fairly recent disease, first discovered in the United States in 1981. It is caused by the HIV that damages the body's immune system destroying the body's ability to fight off germs and leaving the body susceptible to certain diseases that generally do not occur in individuals with healthy immune systems. The diseases, such as PCP pneumonia and certain cancers, are usually fatal. Recent research has provided new information on the virus and new drug treatments have been effective at slowing its progress. In light of the prevalence of sexual activity in prison there is a growing concern for the number of inmates who have contracted HIV.

There are three major concerns in dealing with prisoners who test positive for HIV: preventing the spread of the virus to others, protecting employees who deal with infected prisoners, and the legal rights of infected prisoners. Offenders with AIDS need special treatment and medical needs. Offenders who test positive for HIV, but present no symptoms also create a special problem because they may spread the virus. Those offenders, however, have privacy rights claims regarding who may be notified regarding their condition. One issue that administrators must face is whether HIV/AIDS-infected individuals should be segregated from the general institution population. Another issue is whether all prisoners should be subjected to mandatory HIV testing. Most states currently test inmates on their request or upon clinical indication of need. Approximately 16 states test all incoming prisoners. Five states test all prisoners being released from an institution.[22]

8-5b Mental Health Issues

Another major problem facing correctional institution directors is the handling of the mentally ill offender. While there are conflicting opinions regarding the relationship between mentally ill persons and involvement in criminal behavior, research indicates that a large segment of the population in correctional institutions has serious mental problems. One study concluded that about 10 percent of prisoners have severe or significant psychiatric disabilities. To handle the most seriously mentally disabled offender, most states have at least one prison that has special treatment programs and facilities for these offenders.

Other correctional institutions have either a full- or part-time psychological service team that works with offenders. Many institutions and parole authorities require a psychological profile of offenders under their care. Accordingly, a good portion of the psychological resources are used to administer and interpret standardized psychological tests.

Mental health professionals in correctional institutions generally provide counseling and crisis-intervention services. Counseling approaches use either individual or group counseling. **Individual counseling** is one-on-one counseling and is generally part of a larger treatment program and frequent visits. The high ratio of offenders to counseling personnel makes it difficult in most situations to conduct any extensive individual counseling programs.

Group counseling is a planned activity with three or more clients present for the purpose of solving personal and social problems. While most professionals would prefer to do individual counseling, group counseling allows the mental health teams to provide more service to more offenders. Group counseling is also practical because there is an availability of offenders with similar types of problems. Group counseling, in most institutions, focuses on personal and social needs. It is different from group therapy, which is generally concerned with deep-seated psychological problems and needs to be directed by highly trained mental health professionals.

8-5c Sex Offenders

State prisons hold about 93,000 convicted sex offenders. The number of convicted sex offenders has increased about 46 percent in the past five years. It is estimated that for every sex offender in prison, there are two out in the communities on parole or probation. Therapy for sex offenders is the popular, though controversial, solution. There is, however, substantial evidence that therapy does not work. For example, a 1993 Canadian study by R. Karl Hanson of the Solicitor General's Office found that approximately 42 percent of imprisoned child molesters are later reconvicted for violent or sexual crimes. The study also concluded therapy did not change the reconviction rate, despite the fact that therapy programs generally accept only those persons considered "treatable."

In 1996, the United States had more than 2,000 known sex-offender treatment programs, more than triple the approximate 640 in 1986. Some of the treatment programs are based in prisons. In the communities, individual practitioners, private clinics, and nonprofit agencies run programs. Even the Salvation Army offers limited therapy services at some of its facilities. The "sex-offender treatment" industry now has its own associations, holds conferences, and publishes books and a professional journal. Some therapists even advertise their services on the Internet. The Association of Treatment of Sexual Abusers, headquartered in Beaverton, Oregon, has seen its membership grow from 25 in 1986 to over 1,000 members in 1997. Safer Society, a major publisher on this subject matter, has annual sales of textbooks, workbooks, and videotapes of about $500,000 a year.

One of the problems in sex-offender treatment programs is the lack of definite certification guidelines. Currently only one state (Washington) requires sex-offender treatment providers to pass a certification test to practice in the field. Texas maintains a registry of treatment providers. Elsewhere, just about anyone can "hang out a shingle" (attempt to offer sex-offender treatment programs).

The sex-offender treatment programs generally differ sharply from traditional psychotherapy. Therapists often do not guarantee confidentiality to clients in order to help parole and probation officers determine if the offender has violated the terms of his release. Often parole and probation officers steer offenders to programs that cooperate with law enforcement. Jerome Miller, of the National Center on Institutions and Alternatives in Washington, DC, claims that this high level of cooperation makes therapists a "part of the crime-control industry."[23]

Most states have some form of sex-offender registration law that requires convicted sex offenders to register when they move into a community. Sex offender registration laws are often called "**Megan's laws,**" after Megan Kanka, who was raped and strangled by a known sex offender.

In 1994, Jesse K. Timmendequas confessed to strangling and raping Kanka when she was seven years old. She had just finished the first grade. Timmendequas, a slight man with dirty blond hair and a nervous preoccupation with himself, lived across the street from Kanka. He had pleaded guilty twice before to sexually assaulting small children. In 1981, a judge had labeled him a "compulsive, repetitive sexual offender." After he had served more than seven years for the 1981 crime, he was released. He and two other convicted child molesters had quietly moved into a neighborhood of split-level homes, where people tended to take good care of their children. Before the killing, he appeared to the neighbors as pleasant and had helped an elderly man move furniture. His classmates in high school considered him "one of those quiet kids." A therapist stated that: "He would pout and then go hide. He spent a lot of time in bed."

The cases against him, stemming from the assaults in 1979 and 1981, were handled routinely in the legal system, with plea bargains authorized in both cases. One prosecutor justified the plea bargain and was reluctant to take the case to trial, claiming that child victims make poor witnesses.

Timmendequas' first known case occurred in 1979 when he was 18 years old and his victim was five years old. He told police that he just wanted to look at her vagina. But the little girl stated that he smelled her and touched her. For that offense he pleaded guilty to attempted aggravated sexual assault. The judge in that case concluded that, "While he certainly has mental or psychiatric problems, these seem to be of the type which can be dealt with best in an outpatient setting." He was given a suspended sentence on the condition that he seek counseling. Later cited for violating the terms of his suspended sentence, he served nine months in the Middlesex County Adult Correctional Center.

His second known case occurred in 1981, only months after he was released from the correctional center. The victim, who was seven years old at the time, was found unconscious in the woods near her neighborhood home. Examination revealed that sexual contact had occurred. There were blue marks on her neck where she had been choked and her stomach had black and blue marks on it. He was charged with five felonies and attempted murder. As the result of his plea bargain, all charges except the attempted murder were dropped. The judge imposed the maximum 10-year sentence and stated that he "constituted a danger to the public at large and to young children in particular." At that time, a 10-year sentence in New Jersey really meant six years and eight months with credit for good behavior. He was sent to Avenel, New Jersey's center for sexual offenders. Avenel's therapeutic approach to sexual offenders has been criticized for years by officials who claim that they "coddle" offenders. Supporters contend that therapy helps some child molesters and rapists, who are destined to return to the streets, gain enough insight to control themselves. Both sides admit that sex-offender treatment programs are particularly frustrated by the many offenders who participate in treatment. Individuals who were at Avenel at the time say that Timmendequas never seemed engaged in therapy.

Megan's death has since become a part of the national consciousness. Many states have passed laws named for her, requiring that communities be notified when sex offenders move in. On May 17, 1996, President Clinton signed a federal "Megan's Law." The Random House Webster's College Dictionary added Megan's Law as a new term in the language. Megan's mother speaks often around the country, lobbying for the law and warning parents to take care of their children.

Public records in New Jersey and interviews with people who knew Timmedequas, including psychologists, detectives, lawyers, a judge, and other professionals who dealt with him picture him as the type of sex offender who defies efforts at rehabilitation.[24] One of his earlier victims, who was attacked in 1981, described the turmoil she felt years later. When she heard he was accused of killing Megan, she said she "wanted to kill him herself" and "that they didn't stop him the first time."

Under Megan's Law, when an individual is released from prison, the warden has a duty to notify him or her of the requirement to register with the local authorities. If the individual moves or intends to reside in a new location for a period of time (normally about seven days) he or she must register with the local law enforcement agency. In most states, at the time that he or she registers, the individual must submit a photograph and fingerprints. Except for certain identifying data on the registration form, the information is available to the public.

One of the issues involved in Megan's Law is whether it may be applied to people already convicted before the state act was passed. A sex offender who completed his sentence before the enactment of the statute argued that it was a violation of his constitutional rights to require him to comply with the statute. The U.S. Court of Appeals for the Third Circuit held that the purpose of the statute was not to punish the plaintiff, but to safeguard the public. Accordingly, the registration requirement can be explained only in terms of helping law enforcement agencies keep tabs on certain offenders and that the impact of the registration was not significant enough to brand it punishment.[25]

The New Jersey statute in question is typical of notification statutes. Under it, all people who complete sentences for certain crimes involving sexual assault must register with local law enforcement agencies. The registrant must provide certain identifying information to the local agency in the municipality in which he or she lives. He or she must confirm the address every 90 days and notify the agency if he or she moves. In addition, when the offender moves, he or she must notify the law enforcement agency in his or her new municipality. The prosecutor in the county in which the offender lives must determine whether the registrant poses a low, moderate, or high risk of re-offense. Under Tier I (low risk), notification is the only requirement. Under Tier II (moderate risk), the prosecutor must ensure that schools, licensed day-care centers, summer camps, scout organizations, and other child-care organizations are notified. Notification is not shared with the public under Tier II. Under Tier III (high risk), the law enforcement agencies are required to notify members of the public who are likely to encounter the registrant. Notification of individuals and organizations under Tiers II and III include the registrant's name, a recent photograph, his physical description, offense, address, place of employment or schooling, and a description and license number of his or her automobile.

Summary

When an offender is confined, the major deprivations he or she experiences include loss of liberty, loss of outside links, moral rejection, deprivation of material amenities, sexual frustration, and loss of identity. Prisonization is the term used to indicate the taking on of the folkways, mores, customs, and general culture of prison life. It is the process of assimilation into prison life. During the process of prisonization, inmates become socialized as prisoners. Every person who enters prison undergoes prisonization to some degree. During the prisonization process, the offender learns to speak prison argot. Prison argot is a language that is unique to a prison. The offender learns prison argot much the same way as a person who moves to a foreign land learns to speak the local language.

All states have some type of personal cleanliness and grooming standards. Generally, no beards, mustaches, or hair under the lip are allowed. Hair must be kept trimmed up to the back of the neck and head and neatly cut with no block style, afro, natural, or shag haircuts allowed. Female inmates cannot have extreme haircuts or mohawk or "tailed" haircuts. Each inmate is assigned a bunk in a cell or dormitory. Inmates cannot change bunks without permission. Each inmate is also assigned a locker and may not use lockers or bunks that are not assigned to them.

The concept of a separate inmate social system was first discussed by Sykes and Messinger in 1960 who suggested that prisoners have a pervasive value system and that this value system takes the form of an explicit code of behavior. Often the violation of the code will result in retaliatory action by fellow prisoners. In some cases, it appears that while the prisoners assert these maxims vocally, they violate them when it is to their advantage, and the chances that other prisoners will know of their violations are minimal.

Prior to the 1960s, the inmate social system was dominated by a few powerful inmates. These leaders, primarily white, used their power to stabilize the inmate social system. They were allowed to rule by the prison staffs in return for stability and control. The traditional accommodations between the inmate leaders and prison staffs were disrupted and replaced by gangs. The prison gangs of today are highly organized enterprises with a deadly profit motive. The civil rights movement of the 1960s allowed inmates to become more assertive to the point where they seemed almost militant in their manner of seeking redress from the courts. That judicial intervention intended to make prisons safer and more humane, but actually it created a vacuum that allowed gangs to develop. The gangs offer solidarity and brotherhood, thereby providing social and psychological support for its members.

Correctional institutions are designed to deprive the offenders of sexual activities. For the most part, prisons are a single-sex environment filled with young offenders with active sex drives, often perpetuating homosexuality.

In addition to the separation from the outside world, segregation is used within institutions to isolate offenders from each other. The justification for segregation is based on the premise that segregating offenders from each other minimizes the opportunity for disruptive behavior. In addition, it restricts their opportunity to plan escapes and deal in contraband. One aspect of segregation is the controlled movement of offenders.

A significant portion of each day in prison is taken up by the mandatory counts. A count is the determination by physical sighting of the precise location of all offenders in an institution. When count is "cleared," this means that all offenders have been physically accounted for. In maximum-security institutions, count is taken about every two hours. In other institutions it is taken at least three times each day.

In light of the prevalence of sexual activity in prison there is a growing concern for the number of inmates who have contacted human immunodeficiency virus (HIV). Prison officials have to take the necessary precautions to prevent the spread of HIV, which can ultimately lead to AIDS. There are major concerns in dealing with prisoners who test positive for HIV: preventing the spread of the virus to others; protecting employees who deal with infected prisoners; and the legal rights of infected prisoners. Offenders with AIDS need special treatment and medical supervision.

Another major problem facing correctional institution directors is handling the mentally ill offender. While there are conflicting opinions regarding the relationship between mentally ill persons and involvement in criminal behavior, research indicates that a large segment of the population in correctional institutions have serious mental problems. Prison officials must increasingly ensure that the resources are available so that they can deal with a growing population of inmates who experience mental illness.

State prisons hold about 93,000 convicted sex offenders. The number of convicted sex offenders has increased in our nations prisons. It is estimated that for every sex offender in prison, there are two out in the communities on parole or probation. Therapy for sex offenders is the popular, though controversial, solution. There is, however, substantial evidence suggesting that therapy is not effective. Sex-offender treatment programs generally differ sharply from traditional psychotherapy. Therapists often do not guarantee confidentiality to clients to help parole and probation officers determine if the offender has violated the terms of his release.

Discussion Questions

1. Explain the concept of prisonization.
2. How is life in prison different from life in the "free world"?
3. Analyze the relationships between inmates and guards.
4. Explain the purpose of "counts."
5. Why are inmates' movements controlled?
6. Explain the concepts behind the inmate social system.
7. Why did gangs develop in prison?
8. What can be done to reduce the gang problem in prisons?

Chapter Quiz

True/False

1. Prisonization is a term used for folkways, mores, customs, and general culture of prison life.
2. In prison slang, a "screw" is an inmate who has snitched on another inmate.
3. There is usually no precise chain of command among inmates in the prison culture due to the large number of inmates usually incarcerated in prison.
4. Most studies on inmate subcultures consider prisons as contained and isolated institutions.
5. Prison gangs have been decreasing in recent years.

Multiple Choice

1. According to Paige Ralph, the traditional accommodations between inmate leaders and prison staff were disrupted and replaced by
   a. a chain of command among inmates.
   b. prison gangs.
   c. pecking order among inmates.
   d. prison associations.
2. Which one of the following is NOT considered a purpose of prison classification?
   a. to identify inmates as to their needs regarding training programs, security needs, and/or treatment needs
   b. to identify and prioritize offender needs
   c. to assign offenders to appropriate treatment approaches on the basis of psychological, developmental, and/or personality characteristics
   d. to identify those inmates that may need additional time to exercise in the prison yard with the purpose being to prevent prison violence

3. Which one of the following statements is NOT true pertaining to prison shakedowns or cell searches?
   a. All prisoners are subjected to cell searches.
   b. Prisoners have no Fourth Amendment rights regarding "a reasonable expectation of privacy."
   c. Prisoners generally do have an expectation of privacy only in their prison cells.
   d. Searches may not be used to single out or harass any particular person.
4. One of the problems that has been cited in sex-offender treatment programs is that
   a. there are a minimal amount of sex-offenders actually doing time in prison.
   b. it is difficult to encourage inmates to attend sex-offender treatment programs while in prison.
   c. Sex offender treatment programs lack definite certification guidelines.
   d. It is difficult to determine who needs treatment.
5. The offender going through prisonization forms a
   a. type A personality.
   b. institutionalized personality.
   c. non-routine work habit.
   d. futuristic outlook.

Endnotes

1. Leon Radzinowicz and Marvin Wolfgang, *The Criminal in Confinement* (New York: Basic Books, 1971). While this reference is over 30 years old, it appears that modern offenders face the same deprivations.
2. Donald Clemmer, *The Prison Community* (New York: Holt, Rinehart and Winston, 1968).
3. Personal conversation with Cliff Roberson, April 1989.
4. Gresham M. Sykes and Sheldon L. Messinger, "The Inmate Social System," *Theoretical Studies in the Social Organization of the Prison* (New York: Social Science Research Council Pamphlet No. 15, 1960).
5. Donald Clemmer, *The Prison Community* (New York: Holt, Rinehart and Winston, 1966).
6. Richard W. Snarr, *Corrections*, 3rd. ed. (Madison: Brown & Benchmark, 1996).
7. Neal Stover and Werner Einstadter, *Analyzing American Corrections* (Belmont, CA: Wadsworth, 1988).
8. James B. Jacobs, *New Perspectives on Prisons and Imprisonment* (Ithaca, NY: Cornell University Press, 1983).

9. Anthony Scacco, *Male Rape: A Casebook of Sexual Aggressions* (New York: AMS Press, 1982).
10. James B. Jacobs, *New Perspectives on Prisons and Imprisonment* (Ithaca, NY: Cornell University Press, 1983).
11. 503 F. Supp. 1265 (S.D. Texas, 1980).
12. Paige H. Ralph, "From Self-Preservation to Organized Crime: The Evolution of Inmate Gangs," *Correctional Contexts: Contemporary and Classical Readings* (Los Angeles: Roxbury, 1997).
13. Terry McCarthy, "L.A. Gangs are Back," *Time* 158 (9, September 3, 2001): 46–49.
14. Salvador Buentello, "Combating Gangs in Texas," *Corrections Today* 54 (5 July 1992): 58.
15. G. Camp and C. Camp, *Prison Gangs: Their Extent, Nature and Impact on Prisons* (Washington, DC: U.S. Department of Justice, 1985).
16. Susan Sward, Bill Wallace, and Pamela Podger, "Prisoners Charged with Ordering Crimes," *The San Francisco Chronicle,* 24 April 2001: A-5.
17. Pat Reavy and Derek Jensen "Prison Gangs on the Rise in Utah," *The Deseret New News,* 18 March 2001, p. A01.
18. Terry L. Stewart and Donald W. Brown, "Focusing on Correctional Staff Safety," *Corrections Today* 63 (6, 2001): 90–93.
19. Victor Hassine, *Life Without Parole: Living in Prison Today,* 2nd ed. (Los Angeles: Roxbury, 1999).
20. Christopher Dickey, "A New Home for Noriega?" *Newsweek* 15 January 1990: 66–69.
21. Laura M. Maruschak, *Bureau of Justice Statistics, HIV in Prisons and Jails, 1999* (Washington, DC: United States Department of Justice, 2001), 1.
22. Bureau of Justice Statistics, *HIV in Prisons and Jails, 1999.* (Washington, DC: Bureau of Justice Statistics, 2001).
23. *The Wall Street Journal,* 24 May 1996, 1.
24. *The New York Times,* 26 May 1996, B6, Col. 1.
25. *Artway v. Attorney General of New Jersey,* CA3, decided April 12, 1996.

Chapter 9

Institutional Procedures

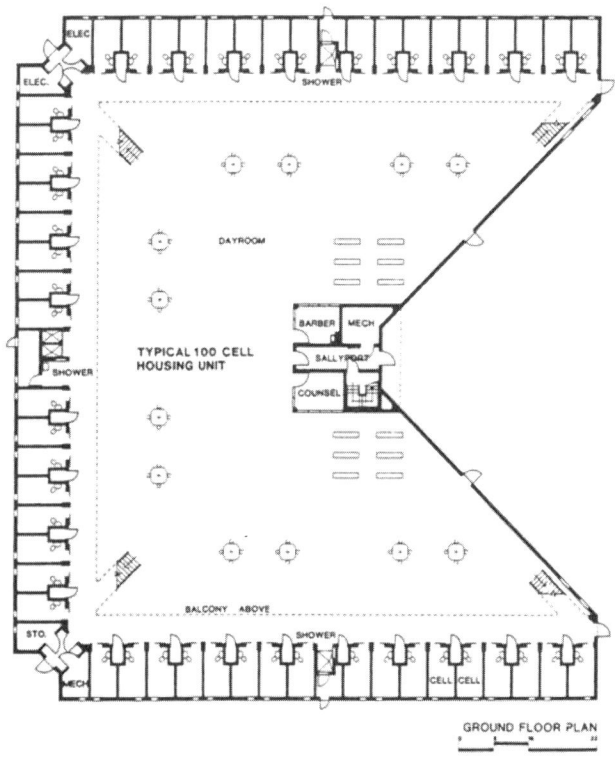

A typical housing unit with single occupancy cells.

Key Terms

aftercare	discharge	parole services
custody designation	flat time	segregative classification
diagnostic facilities	mandatory supervision	supervised release

Outline

9-1 Why Prisons?
  9-1a Diagnostic Process
  9-1b Inmate Orientation Process
  9-1c Custody Levels
  9-1d Discipline
  9-1e Disciplinary Hearing
      Procedures
  9-1f Grievances
9-2 Rules of Conduct
9-3 Release from Confinement
9-4 Release on Parole
9-5 History of Parole
9-6 Good-Time Credit
9-7 Supervised Release
9-8 Parole Today
9-9 Parole Services
9-10 Revocation of Parole
9-11 Discharge from Parole
9-12 Costs of Prisons
Article—Is Further Prison Expansion
  Worth the Costs?
Summary
Discussion Questions
Chapter Quiz
Endnotes

Learning Objectives

After studying this chapter, the reader will be able to:

- Explain the inmate orientation process.
- Identify the various classifications used for offenders in prison.
- Describe the discipline system for state institutions.
- Explain the grievance system for offenders.
- Analyze the requirements for "rules of conduct."
- List the types of release from state penal institutions.
- Analyze the factors involved that attribute to prison building costs.
- Describe the history of parole.
- Compare and contrast the differences between adult and juvenile parole.
- Explain the "due process" rights involved in parole revocation.
- List and define the methods that are used to discharge an offender from parole.

9-1 Why Prisons?

The following questions should be examined regarding prisons.

- What purpose do prisons serve?
- What purpose should prisons serve?
- Under what conditions should prisoners be held?
- What rights and privileges should prisoners forfeit?
- What should prisoners be obliged to do?[1]

Historically prisons were organized on the principles of order and regularity. Each prisoner was isolated in a cell and the rule of total silence was strictly enforced. By the 1900s, the institutions tended to model themselves on the outside community and afforded the inmates the opportunity to mix with other prisoners and to work in groups. It was also during the early 1900s that prisons began to specialize in certain corrective techniques, such as vocational and educational programs for inmates.

Box 9-1

Assaults on Prison Guards Increase

In 1990, there was one assault on a prison guard for every 321 inmates. In 1996, there was one assault for every 171 inmates. In 1998, 35.4 percent of the total assaults committed in prisons were committed against guards. Some prison officials believe the demise of early release and curtailment of parole causes inmates to believe that they have nothing to lose by being belligerent. Other officials believe that the increase is due to the fact that prisoners, many of them repeat offenders, have become more hardened.[2]

9-1a Diagnostic Process

Defendants convicted of felonies are often ordered to **diagnostic facilities** within the state department of corrections for diagnostic and treatment services prior to being sent to prison. In many states, defendants may be retained in the diagnostic facilities for a period not to exceed 90 days. During that stay, defendants are examined and a report of the diagnoses and recommendations are submitted to the court. Time spent in confinement at a diagnostic facility is generally credited to the defendants as part of their confinement term.

9-1b Inmate Orientation Process

Inmates of state prisons/correctional institutions are generally first sent to a diagnostic unit or a reception center. The main function of these reception and diagnostic centers is to receive and process inmates. Inmates who do not speak English or only limited English are identified in order to receive the necessary type of language assistance while in the orientation process and later when assigned to a regular prison unit.

Inmates' money and property are taken from them. A receipt is made for each inmate's money and property. Inmates are given a physical examination by the medical staff. The medical staff inquires about the inmates' medical histories. Any special medical needs of the inmates will be noted in the inmates' records. Urgent medical care is given and inmates are housed according to security needs. Each inmate is generally given psychological testing. Inmates experiencing psychological problems are generally referred for further testing. Additionally, inmates are tested to determine their educational needs.

Inmates are also given sociological interviews. During these interviews, the inmates are asked questions about their criminal history, social history, institutional history, educational history, employment history, family history, military history, drug and/or alcohol histories, and any other pertinent information. The interviews should verify information in their records. Inmates are advised that they may be subject to disciplinary actions for giving untruthful information during the interview process. A summary of all information collected on each inmate will be used to help classify him or her.

The orientation process includes providing inmates with information regarding the department's policies, programs, educational services, rules, classification procedures, disciplinary procedures, and other inmate activities and programs. They are generally fingerprinted and the prints are sent to the state department of public safety and the FBI.

Most states use classification committees to determine the first unit to which an inmate will be assigned. Inmates do not have a right to choose their unit assignment. The committees make their decisions based on all information collected, the inmate's safety needs, the inmate's security needs, and the inmate's treatment needs. In most states, the committees also recommend the inmate's custody level, good-time earning category, housing assignment, and job assignment.

Inmates undergo classification before they are assigned to a unit. Classification means putting inmates who are alike together. Generally states use segregative classifications and custody levels. **Segregative classification** is the process of determining where inmates will be assigned within the institution or in which institution the inmate will serve his or her sentence. Segregative classifications are assigned to inmates based on age and previous incarceration. A typical segregative class system is as follows:

I—first offender, age 17–21 years of age

IA—first offender, age 22–25 years of age

IB—first offender, 26 years of age or older

II—second offender, 17–21 years of age

IIA—second offender, 22–25 years of age

IIB—second offender, 26 years of age or older

IIC—multiple offender

9-1c Custody Levels

After the inmates spend a couple of weeks going through the diagnostic process, the inmates are assigned custody levels. A **custody designation** does two things. It tells how much supervision the inmate needs and with whom and where he will live. The inmate's custody depends on how he or she behaves. If the inmate does not follow rules, the inmate will be given a restrictive custody designation and watched closely. If the inmate behaves, he or she will be given a less restrictive custody designation. There are five custody groups:

1. Maximum. Also referred to as administrative segregation. It is used on inmates who must be separated from the general population because they are dangerous, either to other inmates or staff, or they are in danger from other inmates. These inmates leave their cells, for the most part, only for showers and limited recreation.
2. Close. This level is used for inmates who have serious and/or long disciplinary records. Close custody inmates generally live in cells. They cannot work outside the security area without armed supervision.
3. Medium. This level is used for inmates who live in cells and may work outside the security fence with armed supervision. In some states, especially with female inmates, medium custody inmates live in dormitories.

4. Minimum (in). This level refers to inmates who can live in dormitories or cells inside the security fence. They can work outside the fence under direct armed supervision.
5. Minimum (out). This level allows inmates to live in dorms outside the security fence. They may also work outside the security fence with little supervision.

9-1d Discipline

Inmates confined to institutions are required to obey a lengthy list of policies. When an institution employee observes an inmate commit an infraction, the employee is generally required to submit a disciplinary report. Infractions include numerous violations of institutional rules, for example, fighting with other inmates, having contraband, such as weapons, in the cell, and failing to return to their cells when instructed to do so. The inmate receives notice of the report with written notification of the charge and a hearing date. At the hearing, the hearing officer receives the evidence presented by the institutional division and any that is presented by the inmate. The formal rules of evidence do not apply to these hearings. At the hearing, the hearing officer decides whether or not the inmate committed the infraction. Possible punishments include loss of time credited for good conduct or participation credit, solitary confinement, extra work, loss of certain privileges for stated periods of time (recreation, commissary, television, access to personal property, or contact visits), and other reprimands. Generally, the inmate may appeal the hearing officer's finding and/or punishment to the unit warden.

9-1e Disciplinary Hearing Procedures

American Bar Association's (ABA) Standard 23-3.2 relating to the Legal Status of Prisoners provides:

(a) At a hearing where a minor sanction is imposed, the prisoner should be entitled to:
  (1) Written notice of the charge, in a language the prisoner understands, within 72 hours of the time he or she is suspected of having committed an offense; within another 24 hours the prisoner should be given copies of any further written information the hearing officer may consider.
  (2) A hearing within three working days of the time the written notice of the charge was received.
  (3) Be present and speak on his or her own behalf.

(4) A written decision based upon a preponderance of the evidence, with specified reasons for the decision. The decision should be rendered promptly and in all cases within five days after conclusion of the hearing.
(5) Appeal, within five days, to the chief executive officer of the institution, and the right to a written decision by that officer within 30 days, based upon a written summary of the hearing, any documentary evidence considered at the hearing, and the prisoner's written reason for appealing. The chief executive officer should either affirm or reverse the determination of misconduct and decrease or approve the punishment imposed. Execution of punishment should be suspended during the appeal unless individual safety or individual security will be adversely affected thereby.

(b) At a hearing where a major sanction is imposed, in addition to the requirements of paragraph (a), the prisoner should be entitled to have in attendance any person within the local institution community who has relevant information, and to examine or cross-examine such witnesses except when the hearing officer(s):
(1) Exclude testimony as unduly cumulative; or
(2) Receive testimony outside the presence of the prisoner pursuant to a finding that the physical safety of a person would be endangered by the presence of a particular witness or disclosure of his or her identity.

(c) Disciplinary hearings should be conducted by one or more impartial persons.

(d) Unless the prisoner is found guilty, no record relating to the charge should be retained in the prisoner's file or used against the prisoner in any way.

The Supreme Court has approved a distinction between disciplinary proceedings that may result in the imposition of major punishments such as loss of good time and solitary confinement and minor punishments that affect only privileges.[3] Regarding the requirement that the person or persons conducting the hearing be impartial, the courts have held that no hearing officer should have been involved in the circumstances or investigation of the alleged violation.

When the misconduct involves the violation of a prison rule and criminal misconduct, there is no formal bar to disciplinary action and referral of the matter to criminal courts. The drafters of the standards contend that it is preferable administrative policy to refrain from pursuing both actions concurrently. Many states, like Texas, as a matter of routine, pursue both avenues. In one recent Texas case, a prisoner lost three years' worth of good-time credit at a disciplinary hearing for assaulting a correctional officer and was then prosecuted in the local district court for assault of a peace officer.

9-1f Grievances

Most state prisons and local jails have grievance procedures for inmates who feel that they have been mistreated or have not received proper credit. Generally the inmate must file a written claim on an approved form. In most states, if the grievance is denied and the inmate has exhausted his or her administrative remedies, the inmate may file a petition with a district or superior court.

The ABA standards provide:

(a) Correctional authorities should authorize and encourage correctional employees to resolve prisoner grievances on an informal basis whenever possible.

(b) Every correctional institution should adopt a formal procedure to resolve specific prisoner grievances, including any complaint arising out of institutional policies, rules, practices, and procedures, or the action of any correctional employee or official. Grievance procedures should not be used as a substitute appellate procedure for individual decisions reached by adjudicative bodies, for example, parole, classification, and disciplinary boards, although a complaint involving the procedures or general policies employed by any correctional adjudicative body should be subject to grievance procedures.

(c) Correctional authorities should make forms available so that a grievant may initiate review by describing briefly the nature of the grievance, the persons involved, and the remedy sought.

(d) The institution's grievance procedure should be designed to ensure the cooperation and confidence of prisoners and correctional officials and should include:
  (1) Provisions for written responses to all grievances, including the reasons for the decision;
  (2) Provision for response within a prescribed, reasonable time limit. A request that is not responded to or resolved within 30 working days should be deemed to have been denied;
  (3) Special provision for responding to emergencies;
  (4) Provision for advisory review of grievances;
  (5) Provision for participation by staff and prisoners in the design of the grievance procedure;

(6) Provision for access by all prisoners, with guarantees against reprisal;
(7) Applicability over a broad range of issues; and
(8) Means for resolving questions of jurisdiction.

Courts have held that the right to petition for redress of grievances is a First Amendment right.[4] It appears that common sense would also indicate that as many disputes as possible between prisoners and administrators should be worked out informally. In addition, an effective grievance procedure should reduce the number of cases filed in court involving inmate complaints. As a general rule, before filing a court action regarding the conditions of confinement, the prisoner must exhaust his or her administrative remedies, namely the formal grievance process. By filing a grievance, the inmate provides the institution with an opportunity to correct any wrongs without resorting to court action.

9-2 Rules of Conduct

The American Bar Association's Joint Task Force on the Legal Status of Prisoners contains the following standard rules of conduct:

(a) Correctional authorities should promulgate clear written rules for prisoner conduct. These rules and implementing criteria should include:
(1) A specific definition of offenses, a statement that the least severe punishment appropriate to each offense should be imposed, and a schedule indicating the minimum and maximum possible punishments for each offense, proportionate to the offense; and
(2) Specific criteria and procedures for prison discipline and classification decisions, including decisions involving security status and work and housing assignments.

(b) A personal copy of the rules should be provided to each prisoner upon entry to the institution. For the benefit of illiterate and foreign-language prisoners, a detailed oral explanation of the rules should be given. In addition, a written translation should be provided in any language spoken by a significant number of prisoners.[5]

The authors of these standards feel that many prison rule books contain ambiguities and that correctional officers often believe that publications of this sort provide sufficient guides for ascertaining violations. According to the authors, prison regulations should be concise. The courts have held that due process requires a schedule of penalties for violation of penal rules and that the punishment must bear some proportionality to punishable misconduct, measured in some objective fashion. Disproportionate penalties will be struck down by the courts, both within and without prison walls.[6] When challenging a prison rule for a disproportionate penalty, however, the prisoner must "demonstrate disparities in punishment that are not reasonably related to legitimate state interests."[7]

9-3 Release from Confinement

In most states, there are three ways an inmate may be released from confinement: parole, mandatory supervision, and discharge. Parole is the discretionary release of an inmate from prison when he or she completes a prescribed portion of his or her sentence and the parole board agrees that the release will not increase the likelihood of harm to the public. Parole is discussed in the next section. **Mandatory supervision** is the release of an inmate from prison when he or she completes a prescribed portion of his or her sentence. For example, an inmate could receive a sentence of confinement for two years with two years of mandatory supervision when released. Mandatory supervision differs from parole in that the defendant is informed when sentenced as to the release date, whereas a parole date must be approved by a parole board. Not all states use mandatory supervision. Once released, the inmate is on mandatory supervision and under the close supervision of his or her parole officer as long as the inmate follows the conditions of his or her supervision. Should the inmate violate the conditions of supervision, the inmate may be returned to confinement. **Discharge** is the outright release of the inmate after he or she serves his or her entire sentence minus any participation or good-time credit given. An inmate who serves his or her time, often referred to as serving the sentence **flat time,** is not subject to any form of supervision. Table 9-1 presents statistics on parole.

9-4 Release on Parole

Parole is the conditional release of a defendant from a correctional institution prior to the completion of his or her term of confinement. In theory, the defendant is released from the correctional institution at a time when he or she can best benefit from the release and continued supervision after release. Parole is a conditional release of the defendant to the community under supervision of a parole officer.

TABLE **9-1 Parole Points of Interest**

- As of December 31, 2000, 725,500 adults were on parole.
- Nearly all offenders on parole (97 percent) had been sentenced to incarceration of more than one year.
- In 2000, women made up about 12 percent of the parolees.
- At the end of 2000, more than 652,000 adults, or more than 12 in every 320 adults, were under state parole supervision.
- State inmates released from prison as a result of a parole decision dropped from 39 percent of all releases in 1990 to 24 percent in 1999.
- Forty-two percent of state parole discharges in 1999 successfully completed their term of supervision, relatively unchanged since 1990. Forty-three percent were returned to jail or prison and 10 percent absconded.

Source: Probation and Parole Statistics (Washington, DC: Bureau of Justice Statistics, 2000), pp. 1–4.

Parole is often used incorrectly to refer to the release of any defendant from custody. It differs from probation in that probation usually requires little or no confinement and probation is administered by the courts on a countywide basis. Parole is generally administered by a statewide agency on a statewide basis. Normally parole is granted only after the defendant has served a significant portion of his or her confinement. Probation is considered a pre-institutional procedure. Parole, on the other hand, is considered a continuation of the correctional process. Unlike probation, a person on parole has already completed a portion of his or her term of confinement. Release is conditional and may be revoked if the terms of parole are violated.

In many states, the term **aftercare** is used in lieu of parole for juvenile cases. To many social-service providers, the concept of juvenile aftercare is more acceptable than the use of the phrase juvenile parole. In this text, the two terms are used interchangeably. It appears that about half the states use "aftercare" and the other half use "parole."

The word parole is taken from the French, meaning "a word of honor given or pledged." It was first used by the military to release prisoners of war who promised to refrain from attempting to escape or to forbear from taking up arms against their captors. Presently, it generally means a conditional release on good behavior from a correctional institution.[8]

The parolee usually requires more supervision than a person on probation. The parolee has been confined and must readjust to society. In addition, the parolee may be bitter toward society, or remorseful and resentful of his or her period of confinement.

9-5 History of Parole

Parole in America can be traced back to the houses of refuge that were established in the latter part of the nineteenth century. Parole is, however, more English and European than American. It was first used by the English to offer a conditional release from prison for those prisoners who agreed to work for a certain period of time to regain their freedom. Parole, unlike probation, was originally motivated by economic pressures rather than humanitarian concerns. Parole provided employers with cheap labor and relieved the British government from having to pay the expenses of imprisonment. Box 9-2 presents a brief history of the origin of parole.

Box 9-2

Alexander Maconochie and Sir Walter Crofton

The concept of parole is often credited to England's Alexander Maconochie and Ireland's Sir Walter Crofton.

Alexander Maconochie was born in Edinburgh, Scotland. After a distinguished career in the British navy, he was appointed the first Professor of Geography at University College in London. Later, he became involved in studying prison conditions at the Tasmania Island penal colony. In 1838 and 1839, he published *Thoughts on Convict Management* and *Supplement to Thoughts on Convict Management.* He wrote that the proper object of prison discipline is to prepare men for discharge: to reform prisoners and prepare them to separate with advantage both to themselves and to society after their release. Maconochie devised five ideas to serve the rehabilitation purpose:

1. Sentences should not be imprisonment for a period of time, but for the performance of a determined and specified quantity of labor. Time sentences should be abolished and task sentences should be substituted.
2. The quantity of labor a prisoner must perform should be expressed in a number of marks that he must earn, by improvement in conduct, frugality of living, and habits of industry, before he can be released.
3. While in prison, a prisoner should earn everything he receives, all else should be added to his debt of marks.
4. When qualified by discipline to do so he should work in association with a small number of other prisoners, forming groups of six or seven, and the whole group should be answerable for the conduct and labor of each member of the group.

5. In the final stage of the prison term, the prisoner should be given a proprietary interest in his own labor and be subject to a less rigorous discipline.

Sir Walter Crofton used Maconochie's ideas in the Irish Prison System. Idea 5 (above) developed into the concept of conditional release, i.e., parole. The gradual approximation to freedom in every successive stage of discipline—from maximum security to trustee to conditional release or parole.[9]

9-6 Good-Time Credit

In colonial America, criminals were sentenced to prison for stated periods of time and were not released until the term had expired. Good-time credit was not used until 1817, when New York passed the first good-time law. The good-time law allowed for a reduction in the fixed term based on the prisoner's cooperative good conduct and behavior while in prison. Other states soon passed similar statutes that were firm and straightforward. Generally, the good-time laws permitted the prison term to be reduced by one-fourth for terms of five or less years. The prisoner would need to obtain a certificate of good behavior from the principal confinement keeper to obtain the credit. By 1916, all states had adopted some form of good-time statutes.

In recent years, there has been a trend by states to require that inmates serve a longer period of time before they are eligible for parole. Traditionally, inmates were eligible after serving 25 percent of their time. Several states now require inmates to serve at least 30 percent of their time before being eligible for parole. In some states an inmate is required to serve more time before being eligible for parole if the crime involved the use of a dangerous weapon. The federal government has abolished the use of parole, instead using what is currently called "supervised release."

9-7 Supervised Release

As noted above, the federal government now uses **supervised release** in lieu of parole. Under the Federal Sentencing Guidelines, the judge is required to order a term of supervised release to follow imprisonment when a sentence of imprisonment of more than one year is imposed. In addition, the judge may order a term of supervised release to follow imprisonment in any other case.[10] It appears that the judge may consider the need for a term of supervised release to facilitate the reintegration of the defendant into the community in cases where the supervision is not mandatory. It can also be used to enforce a fine, restitution order, or other condition of release. If the defendant is convicted under a statute that requires a term of supervised release, the term shall be at least three years but not more than five years.

The terms of the supervised release shall include a condition that the defendant not commit another federal, state, or local crime. In addition, the defendant may not possess illegal controlled substances during the period of release. Other conditions that the court may impose include conditions that are related to the nature and circumstances of the offense and the history and characteristics of the defendant. The court may also impose conditions to afford adequate deterrence to criminal conduct, to protect the public from further crimes of the defendant, and to provide the defendant with needed educational or vocational training, medical care, or other correctional treatment in the most effective manner.

Supervised release may be revoked and the defendant returned to confinement. If the defendant is convicted of a crime of violence, involving a controlled substance, firearm possession, or any federal or state felony offense, the court must revoke the defendant's supervised release. If the defendant commits a misdemeanor or violates other conditions of release, the court may revoke the defendant's release.

Another method used to gain freedom is petitions for pardons. Because some of the early laws mandated long sentences, juries would frequently petition the governor to grant pardons. In some cases, pardons were used to make more room in the overcrowded prisons. It is important to note that prison overcrowding is an old and continuing problem with our correctional systems.

9-8 Parole Today

Most defendants, after release from institutions, return to the communities from which they came. Generally, defendants are released from confinement long before the expiration of their maximum period of commitment. In some states, the defendant must serve a minimum time before being released. In nine states, the judge who committed the defendant must agree to the release before the defendant may be released early. The problem with this latter practice or requirement is that often the committing judge is too busy with other cases and does not have sufficient time to review the case and make a viable recommendation as to the release decision. In addition, because no new presentencing investigation reports are prepared, the judge may act on dated or incomplete information. For these reasons, judicial involvement in the early release decision has been eliminated in most states.

Most experts assign two goals to parole: protection of society and the proper adjustment of the defendant back into society. Presently, it appears that the most important goal is the protection of society. Some scholars see the two goals as conflicting ones, pitting society against the defendant. A better approach appears to be the concept of protecting society by rehabilitating the defendant.

Parole includes the objective of assisting the parolee in integration into the community. Therefore, the defendant must be assisted in coping with the problems faced upon release and aided in his/her adjustment to the status of being a parolee. To be a permanent benefit to society, parole agencies must assist in the development of the defendant's ability to make good decisions that are behaviorally acceptable to the community.

The functions of the institution include classifying the defendant's readiness for release and the risk factors to society upon release of the defendant. The duty of the parole officer is, among other things, to assist in the rehabilitation and reintegration of the defendant into the community and to reduce the likelihood of the defendant committing further criminal acts.

9-9 Parole Services

Parole services consist of the various programs and components of the criminal justice system necessary to facilitate the goals and purposes of parole. Parole services include the classification tasks performed at the institution, counseling sessions, and the education classes provided by the institution. Prior to release, pre-parole investigations are conducted to obtain the necessary background information to devise parole plans for the defendants. Parole services continue until the defendants are released from parole.

In most states, parole services are administered by the state agency that is also responsible for the correctional institutions. There are, however, no clear-cut organizational patterns as to who makes the early release decision. In some states, the decision is made by the parole board, in others by an adult correctional agency, a lay board, or the correctional institution staff. In addition, in many states, the state officials have delegated the decision-making authority to local agencies.

The President's Commission on Corrections' report called for a maximum active caseload of 50 probation cases per officer or counselor.[11] Although there is no empirical justification noted for the figure of 50, it does appear to be a reasonable number. Unfortunately, most parole officers have caseloads so large that routine contact is conducted only through the telephone. Many persons have advocated that reducing the caseload sizes would result in greater success in rehabilitating the defendants. Research indicates that the problems of rehabilitation are more complex, and reducing the caseload size alone is not sufficient to make the system more successful.[12]

9-10 Revocation of Parole

Generally it is the function of the paroling agency to revoke a defendant's parole. The U.S. Supreme Court case *Morrissey v. Brewer,* involved two parolees in Iowa who were originally sentenced for forgery.[13] About six months after being released on parole, their parole was revoked for violation of parole conditions. The two parolees appealed the revocation decision on the grounds that their paroles were revoked without a hearing and that the lack of a hearing deprived them of their due process rights. The Supreme Court held:

> The liberty of parole, although indeterminate, includes many of the core values of unqualified liberty and its termination inflicts a "grievous loss" on the parolee and often on others. It is hardly useful any longer to try to deal with this problem in terms of whether the parolee's liberty is a "right" or a "privilege." By whatever name, the liberty is valuable and must be seen as within the protection of the Fourteenth Amendment. Its termination calls for some orderly process, however informal.

The Court then stated that the "orderly process" included these minimum standards of due process:

- Written notice of the claimed violations of parole
- Disclosure to the parolee of the evidence against him
- Opportunity to be heard in person and to present witnesses and documentary evidence
- A hearing before a neutral and detached hearing body
- A written statement by the fact finders as to the evidence relied on and the reasons for revoking parole

The Court also held that, before requiring a parolee to face a revocation hearing, there should be a preliminary hearing conducted to determine if there is probable cause or reasonable grounds to believe that the parolee has committed acts that would constitute a violation of parole conditions. Although *Morrissey v. Brewer* dealt with adult paroles, it appears that the requirements are also applicable to juveniles.

9-11 Discharge from Parole

In many states, the defendant may be released or discharged from parole at any time after the defendant's release from the institution. Most states require defendants to be on parole for a minimum time, usually one year, before they may be discharged. To be effective, enough time is needed to work on the defendant's long-range needs and to help him or her achieve independence from the criminal justice system.

The release from parole may also be conditional. In some cases, the release is automatic after a certain period of time. After discharge, most juveniles are left to their own devices and are no longer supervised by the system. The decision to discharge the defendant from parole may have many pitfalls. For many defendants, survival in the community was possible only because of the assistance of their parole officer or counselor. Once this crutch is removed, the parolee may regress into the behavioral and attitudinal modes that were the underlying causes of the previous encounters with the law.

What due process rights should a parolee have when revocation of his or her parole is being considered? Does the following court decision provide adequate guidance in answering this question?

CASE
Morrissey v. Brewer U.S. Supreme Court, **408 U.S. 471 Decided June 29, 1972**

Two Iowa convicts whose paroles were revoked by the Iowa Board of Parole filed *habeas corpus* petitions in the United States District Court for the Southern District of Iowa, alleging that they were denied due process because their paroles were revoked without a hearing. The District Court denied the petitions on the ground that due process did not require a pre-revocation hearing, and the United States Court of Appeals for the Eighth Circuit affirmed . . . The United States Supreme Court reversed . . . In an opinion by BURGER, Ch. J., expressing the views of six members of the court, it was held that the minimum requirements of due process in revoking paroles include (a) written notice of the claimed parole violations; (b) disclosure to the parolee of evidence against him; (c) opportunity to be heard in person and to present witnesses and documentary evidence; (d) the right to confront and cross-examine adverse witnesses (unless the hearing officer specifically finds good cause for not allowing confrontation); (e) a neutral and detached hearing body such as a traditional parole board, members of which need not be judicial officers or lawyers; and (f) a written statement by the fact finders as to the evidence relied on and reasons for revoking parole.

The court further held that a preliminary hearing officer's determination that there is probable cause to hold a parolee for the parole board's final decision on parole revocation warrants the parolee's continued detention pending the final decision; but the court expressly permitted the question whether a parolee is entitled, in a parole revocation proceeding, to the assistance of retained counsel or to appointed counsel if he is indigent.

BRENNAN, J., joined by MARSHALL, J., concurred in the result on the ground that due process also requires that the parolee be allowed the assistance of retained counsel at his revocation hearings.

DOUGLAS, J., dissented on the grounds that a parolee who does not commit a new offense should not be arrested or jailed until his parole is revoked, and that a parolee is entitled to counsel in parole revocation proceedings.

Mr. Chief Justice BURGER, delivered the opinion of the Court.

We granted certiorari in this case to determine whether the Due Process Clause of the Fourteenth Amendment requires that a state afford an individual some opportunity to be heard prior to revoking his parole.

Petitioner Morrissey was convicted of false drawing or uttering of checks in 1967 pursuant to his guilty plea, and was sentenced to not more than seven years' confinement. He was paroled from the Iowa State Penitentiary in June 1968. Seven months later, at the direction of his parole officer, he was arrested in his home town as a parole violator and incarcerated in the county jail. One week later, after review of the parole officer's written report, the Iowa Board of Parole revoked Morrissey's parole, and he was returned to the penitentiary located about 100 miles from his home. Petitioner asserts he received no hearing prior to revocation of his parole.

The parole officer's report on which the Board of Parole acted shows that petitioner's parole was revoked on the basis of information that he had violated the conditions of parole by buying a car under an assumed name and operating it without permission, giving false statements to police concerning his address and insurance company after a minor accident, obtaining credit under an assumed name, and failing to report his place of residence to his parole officer. The report states that the officer interviewed Morrissey, and that he could not explain why he did not contact his parole officer despite his effort to excuse this on the ground that he had been sick. Further, the report asserts that Morrissey admitted buying the car and obtaining credit under an assumed name, and also admitted being involved in the accident. The parole officer recommended that his parole be revoked because of "his continual violation of his parole rules."

The situation as to petitioner Brewer is much the same. Pursuant to his guilty plea, Brewer was convicted of forgery in 1966 and sentenced to a maximum term of 10 years. He was paroled November 14, 1968. In August 1969, at his parole officer's direction, he was arrested in his home town for violation of his parole and confined in the county jail several miles away. On September 13,

1969, on the basis of a written report by his parole officer, the Iowa Board of Parole revoked Brewer's parole and Brewer was recommitted to the state penitentiary, located about 250 miles from his home, to complete service of his sentence. Petitioner asserts he received no hearing prior to revocation of his parole.

The parole officer's report, with respect to Brewer, recommended that his parole be revoked because he had violated the territorial restrictions of his parole without consent, had obtained a driver's license under an assumed name, operated a motor vehicle without permission, and had violated the employment condition of his parole by failing to keep himself in gainful employment. The report stated that the officer had interviewed Brewer and that he had acknowledged to the parole officer that he had left the specified territorial limits and had operated the car and had obtained a license under an assumed name "knowing that it was wrong." The report further noted that Brewer had stated that he had not found employment because he could not find work that would pay him what he wanted. He stated he would not work for $2.25 to $2.75 per hour and that he had left the area to get work in another city.

After exhausting state remedies, both petitioners filed *habeas corpus* petitions in the United States District Court for the Southern District of Iowa alleging that they had been denied due process because their paroles had been revoked without a hearing. The State responded by arguing that no hearing was required. The District Court held on the basis of controlling authority that the state's failure to accord a hearing prior to parole revocation did not violate due process. On appeal, the two cases were consolidated.

The Court of Appeals, dividing 4 to 3, held that due process does not require a hearing. The majority recognized that the traditional view of parole as a privilege rather than a vested right is no longer dispositive as to whether due process is applicable; however, on a balancing of the competing interests involved, it concluded that no hearing is required. The court reasoned that parole is only "a correctional device authorizing service of sentence outside the penitentiary," the parolee is still "in custody." Accordingly, the Court of Appeals was of that view that prison officials must have large discretion in making revocation determinations, and that courts should retain their traditional reluctance to interfere with disciplinary matters properly under the control of state prison authorities. The majority expressed the view that "non-legal, non-adversary considerations" were often the determinative factors in making a parole revocation decision. It expressed concern that if adversary hearings were required for parole revocation, "the full panoply of rights accorded in criminal proceedings," the function of the parole board as "an administrative body acting in the role of *parens patriae* would be aborted," and the board would be more reluctant to grant parole in the first instance—an apprehension that would not be without some basis if the choice were between a full scale adversary proceeding or no hearing at all.

Additionally, the majority reasoned that the parolee has no statutory right to remain on parole. Iowa law provides that a parolee may be returned to the institution at any time.

In its brief in this Court, respondent asserts for the first time that petitioners were in fact granted hearings after they were returned to the penitentiary. More generally, respondent says that within two months after the Board revokes an individual's parole and orders him returned to the penitentiary, on the basis of the parole officer's written report it grants the individual a hearing before the Board. At that time, the Board goes over "each of the alleged parole violations with the returnee, and he is given an opportunity to orally present his side of the story to the Board." If the returnee denies the report, it is the practice of the Board to conduct a further investigation before making a final determination either affirming the initial revocation, modifying it, or reversing it."

The State asserts that Morrissey, whose parole was revoked on January 31, 1969, was granted a hearing before the Board on February 12, 1969. Brewer's parole was revoked on September 13, 1969, and he was granted a hearing on October 14, 1969. At these hearings, the State tell us—in the briefs—both Morrissey and Brewer admitted the violations alleged in the parole violation reports.

Nothing in the record supplied to this Court indicates that respondent claimed, either in the District Court or the Court of Appeals, that petitioners had received hearings promptly after their paroles were revoked, or that in such hearing they admitted the violations; that information comes to us only in the respondent's brief here. Further, even the assertions that the respondent makes here are not based on any public record but on interviews with two of the members of the parole board. In the interview relied on to show that petitioners admitted their violations, the board member did not assert he could remember that both Morrissey and Brewer admitted the parole violations with which they were charged. He stated only that, according to his memory, in the previous several years all but three returnees had admitted commission of the parole infractions alleged and that neither of the petitioners was among the three who denied them.

We must therefore treat this case in the posture and on the record respondent elected to rely on in the District Court and the Court of Appeals. If the facts are otherwise, respondent may make a showing in the District Court that petitioners in fact have admitted the violations charged before a neutral officer.

Before reaching the issue of whether due process applies to the parole system, it is important to recall the function of parole in the correctional process. During the past 60 years, the practice of releasing prisoners on parole before the end of their sentences has become an integral part of the penological system. Rather than being an *ad hoc* exercise of clemency, parole is an established variation on imprisonment of convicted criminals. Its purpose is to help individuals reintegrate into society as constructive individuals as soon as they are able, without being confined for the full term of the sentence imposed. It also serves to alleviate the costs to society of keeping an individual in prison. The essence of parole is release from prison, before the completion of sentence, on the condition that the prisoner abide by certain rules during the balance of the sentence. Under some systems, parole is granted automatically after the service of a certain portion of a prison term. Under others, parole is granted by the discretionary action of a board, which evaluates an array of information about a prisoner and makes a prediction on whether he is ready to reintegrate into society.

To accomplish the purpose of parole, those who are allowed to leave prison early are subjected to specified conditions for the duration of their terms. These conditions restrict their activities substantially beyond the ordinary restrictions imposed by law on an individual citizen. Typically, parolees are forbidden to use liquor or to have associations or correspondence with certain categories of undesirable persons. Typically, also they must seek permission from their parole officers before engaging in specified activities, such as changing employment or living quarters, marrying, acquiring or operating a motor vehicle, traveling outside the community, and incurring substantial indebtedness. Additionally, parolees must regularly report to the parole officer to whom they are assigned and sometimes they must make periodic written reports of their activities. The parole officers are part of the administrative system designed to assist parolees and to offer them guidance. The conditions of parole serve a dual purpose: they prohibit, either absolutely or conditionally, behavior that is deemed dangerous to the restoration of the individual into normal society. And through the requirement of reporting to the parole officer and seeking guidance and permission before doing many things, the officer is provided with information about the parolee and an opportunity to advise him. The combination puts the parole officer into the position in which he can try to guide the parolee into constructive development.

The enforcement leverage that supports the parole conditions derives from the authority to return the parolee to prison to serve out the balance of his sentence if he fails to abide by the rules. In practice, not every violation of parole conditions automatically leads to revocation. Typically, a parolee will be counseled to abide by the conditions of parole, and the parole officer ordinarily does not take steps to have parole revoked unless he thinks that the violations are serious and continuing so as to indicate that the parolee is not adjusting properly and cannot be counted on to avoid antisocial activity. The broad discretion accorded the parole officer is also inherent in some of the quite vague conditions, such as the typical requirement that the parolee avoid "undesirable" associations or correspondence. Yet revocation of parole is not an unusual phenomenon affecting only a few parolees. It has been estimated that 35–45 percent of all parolees are subject to revocation and return to prison. Sometimes revocation occurs when the parolee is accused of another crime; it is often preferred to a new prosecution because of the procedural ease of recommitting the individual on the basis of a lesser showing by the State.

Implicit in the system's concern with parole violations is the notion that the parolee is entitled to retain his liberty as long as he substantially abides by the conditions of his parole. The first step in a revocation decision thus involves a wholly retrospective factual question: whether the parolee has in fact acted in violation of one or more conditions of his parole. Only if it is determined that the parolee did violate the conditions does the second question arise: should the parolee be recommitted to prison or should other steps be taken to protect society and improve chances of rehabilitation? The first step is relatively simple; the second is more complex. The second question involves the application of expertise by the parole authority in making a prediction as to the ability of the individual to live in society without committing antisocial acts. This part of the decision, too, depends on facts, and therefore it is important for the board to know not only that some violation was committed but also to know accurately how many and how serious the violations were. Yet this second step, deciding what to do about the violation once it is identified, is not purely factual but also predictive and discretionary.

If a parolee is returned to prison, he usually receives no credit for the time "served" on parole. Thus, the returnee may face a potential of substantial imprisonment. We begin with the proposition that the revocation of parole is not part of a criminal prosecution and thus the full panoply of rights due a defendant in such a proceeding does not apply to parole revocations. Parole arises after the end of the criminal prosecution, including imposition of sentence.

Supervision is not directly by the court but by an administrative agency, which is sometimes an arm of the court and sometimes of the executive. Revocation deprives an individual, not of the absolute liberty to which every citizen is entitled, but only of the conditional liberty properly dependent on observance of special parole restrictions. We turn, therefore, to the question of whether the requirements of due process in general apply to parole revocations. As Mr. Justice Blackmun has written recently, "This Court now has rejected the concept that constitutional rights turn upon whether a governmental benefit is characterized as a 'right' or as a 'privilege.' " *Graham v. Richardson*, 403 U.S. 365 . . . Whether any procedural protections are due depends on the extent to which an individual will be "condemned to suffer grievous loss." *Joint Anti-Fascist Refugee Committee v. McGrath*, 341 U.S. 123 . . . The question is not merely the "weight" of the individual's interest, but whether the nature of the interest is one within the contemplation of the "liberty or property" language of the Fourteenth Amendment. *Fuentes v. Shevin*, 407 U.S. 67 . . . Once it is determined that due process applies, the question remains what process is due. It has been said so often by this Court and others as not to require citation of authority that due process is flexible and calls for such procedural protections as the particular situation demands. "[C]onsideration of what procedures due process may require under any given set of circumstances must begin with a determination of the precise nature of the government function involved as well as of the private interest that has been affected by governmental action." *Cafeteria and Restaurant Workers Union v. McElroy,* 367 U.S. 886, 895 ... To say that the concept of due process is flexible does not mean that judges are at large to apply it to any and all relationships. Its flexibility is in its scope once it has been determined that some process is due; it is a recognition that not all situations calling for procedural safeguards call for the same kind of procedure.

We turn to an examination of the nature of the interest of the parolee in his continued liberty. The liberty of a parolee enables him to do a wide range of things open to persons who have never been convicted of any crime. The parolee has been released from prison based on an evaluation that he shows reasonable promise of being able to return to society and function as a responsible, self-reliant person. Subject to the conditions of his parole, he can be gainfully employed and is free to be with family and friends and to form the other enduring attachments of normal life. Though the State properly subjects him to many restrictions not applicable to other citizens, his condition is very different from that of confinement in a prison. He may have been on parole for a number of years and may be living a relatively normal life at the time he is faced with revocation. The parolee has relied on at least an implicit promise that parole will be revoked only if he fails to live up to the parole conditions. In many cases, the parolee faces lengthy incarceration if his parole is revoked.

We see, therefore, that the liberty of a parolee, although indeterminate, includes many of the core values of unqualified liberty and its termination inflicts a "grievous loss" on the parolee and often on others. It is hardly useful any longer to try to deal with this problem in terms of whether the parolee's liberty is a "right" or a "privilege." By whatever name, the liberty is valuable and must be seen as within the protection of the Fourteenth Amendment. Its termination calls for some orderly process, however informal.

Turning to the question of what process is due, we find that the State's interests are several. The State has found the parolee guilty of a crime against the people. That finding justifies imposing extensive restrictions on the individual's liberty. Release of the parolee before the end of his prison sentence is made with the recognition that with many prisoners there is a risk that they will not be able to live in society without committing additional antisocial acts. Given the previous conviction and the proper imposition of conditions, the State has an overwhelming interest in being able to return the individual to imprisonment without the burden of a new adversary criminal trial if in fact he has failed to abide by the conditions of his parole.

Yet, the State has no interest in revoking parole without some informal procedural guarantees. Although the parolee is often formally described as being "in custody," the argument cannot even be made here that summary treatment is necessary as it may be with respect to controlling a large group of potentially disruptive prisoners in actual custody. Nor are we persuaded by the argument that revocation is so totally a discretionary matter that some form of hearing would be administratively intolerable. A simple factual hearing will not interfere with the exercise of discretion. Serious studies have suggested that fair treatment on parole revocation will not result in fewer grants of parole.

This discretionary aspect of the revocation decision need not be reached unless there is first an appropriate determination that the individual has in fact breached the conditions of parole. The parolee is not the only one who has a stake in his conditional liberty. Society has a stake in whatever may be the chance of restoring him to normal and useful life within the law. Society thus has an interest in not having parole revoked because of erroneous information or because of an erroneous evaluation of the need to revoke parole, given the breach of parole conditions . . . And society has a further interest in treating the parolee with basic fairness: fair treatment in parole revocations will enhance the chance of rehabilitation by avoiding reactions to arbitrariness. Given these factors, most States have recognized that there is no interest on the part of the State in revoking parole without any procedural guarantees and all that is needed is an informal hearing structured to assure that the finding of a parole violation will be based on verified facts and that the exercise of discretion will be informed by an accurate knowledge of the parolee's behavior.

We now turn to the nature of the process that is due, bearing in mind that the interest of both State and parolee will be furthered by an effective but informal hearing. In analyzing what is due, we see two important stages in the typical process of parole revocation.

(a) Arrest of Parolee and Preliminary Hearing. The first stage occurs when the parolee is arrested and detained, usually at the direction of his parole officer. The second occurs when parole is formally revoked. There is typically a substantial time lag between the arrest and the eventual determination by the parole board whether parole should be revoked. Additionally, it may be that the parolee is arrested at a place distant from the state institution, to which he may be returned before the final decision is made concerning revocation. Given these factors, due process would seem to require that some minimal inquiry be conducted at or reasonably near the place of the alleged parole violation or arrest and as promptly as convenient after arrest while information is fresh and sources are available . . . Such an inquiry should be seen as in the nature of a "preliminary hearing" to determine whether there is probable cause or reasonable ground to believe that the arrested parolee has committed acts that would constitute a violation of parole conditions . . .

In our view, due process requires that after the arrest, the determination that reasonable ground exists for revocation of parole should be made by someone not directly involved in the case. It would be unfair to assume that the supervising parole officer does not conduct an interview with the parolee to confront him with the reasons for revocation before he recommends an arrest. It would also be unfair to assume that the parole officer bears hostility against the parolee that destroys his neutrality; realistically the failure of the parolee is in a sense a failure for his supervising officer. However, we need make no assumptions one way or the other to conclude that there should be an uninvolved person to make this preliminary evaluation of the basis for believing the conditions of parole have been violated. The officer directly involved in making recommendations cannot always have complete objectivity in evaluating them. *Goldberg v. Kelly* found it unnecessary to impugn the motives of the caseworker to find a need for an independent decision maker to examine the initial decision.

This independent officer need not be a judicial officer. The granting and revocation of parole are matters traditionally handled by administrative officers. In *Goldberg,* the Court pointedly did not require that the hearing on termination of benefits be conducted by a judicial officer or even before the traditional "neutral and detached" officer; it required only that the hearing be conducted by some person *other* than one initially dealing with the case. It will be sufficient, therefore, in the parole revocation context, if an evaluation of whether reasonable cause exists to believe that conditions of parole have been violated is made by someone such as a parole officer other than the one who has made the report of parole violations or has recommended revocation. A State could certainly choose some other independent decision-maker to perform this preliminary function. With respect to the preliminary hearing before this officer, the parolee should be given notice that the hearing will take place and that its purpose is to determine whether there is probable cause to believe he has committed a parole violation. The notice should state what parole violations have been alleged. At the hearing the parolee may appear and speak in his own behalf; he may bring letters, documents, or individuals who can give relevant information to the hearing officer. On request of the parolee, persons who have given adverse information on which parole revocation is to be based are to be made available for questioning in his presence. However, if the hearing officer determines that the informant would be subjected to risk of harm if his identity were disclosed, he need not be subjected to confrontation and cross-examination.

The hearing officer shall have the duty of making a summary, or digest, of what occurs at the hearing in terms of the responses of the parolee and the substance of the documents or evidence given in support of parole revocation and of the parolee's position. Based on the information before him, the officer should determine whether there is probable cause to hold the parolee for the final decision of the parole board on revocation. Such a determination would be sufficient to warrant the parolee's continued detention and return to the state correctional institution pending the final decision. As in *Goldberg,* "the decision-maker should state the reasons for his determination and indicate the evidence he relied on . . ." but it should be remembered that this is not a final determination calling for "formal findings of fact and conclusions of law." 397 U.S. at 271; 25 L.Ed.2d at 300. No interest would be served by formalism in this process; informality will not lessen the utility of this inquiry in reducing the risk of error.

(b) *The Revocation Hearing.* There must also be an opportunity for a hearing, if it is desired by the parolee, prior to the final decision on revocation by the parole authority. This hearing must be the basis for more than determining probable cause; it must lead to a final evaluation of any contested relevant facts and consideration of whether the facts as determined warrant revocation. The parolee must have an opportunity to be heard and to show, if he can, that he did not violate the conditions, or, if he did, that circumstances in mitigation suggest that the violation does not warrant revocation. The revocation hearing must be tendered within a reasonable time after the parolee is taken into custody. A lapse of two months, as the State suggests occurs in some cases, would not appear to be unreasonable.

We cannot write a code of procedure; that is the responsibility of each State. Most States have done so by legislation, others by judicial decision usually on due process grounds. Our task is limited to deciding the minimum requirements of due process.

We have no thought to create an inflexible structure for parole revocation procedures. The few basic requirements set out above, which are applicable to future revocations of parole, should not impose a great burden on any State's parole system. Control over the required proceedings by the hearing officers can assure that delaying tactics and other abuses sometimes present in the traditional adversary trial situation do not occur. Obviously a parolee cannot relitigate issues determined against him in other forums, as in the situation presented when the revocation is based on conviction of another crime.

In the peculiar posture of this case, given the absence of an adequate record, we conclude the ends of justice will be best served by remanding the case to the Court of Appeals for its return of the two consolidated cases to the District Court with directions to make findings on the procedures actually followed by the Parole Board in these two revocations. If it is determined that petitioners admitted parole violations to the Parole Board, as Iowa contends, and if those violations are found to be reasonable grounds for revoking parole under state standards, that would end the matter. If the procedures followed by the Parole Board are found to meet the standards laid down in this opinion that, too, would dispose of the due process claims for these cases.

We reverse and remand to the Court of Appeals for further proceedings consistent with this opinion.

Reversed and remanded.

9-12 Costs of Prisons

Building and running prisons are very expensive. Prison construction costs are usually expressed as cost per prison bed and are attained by dividing total costs by the number of available beds. During 1998, the average cost of the 35 new prisons that were opened was $28,912,516. In 1996, the average cost per bed to build a maximum-security prison was about $80,000. The cost to build medium-security prisons was more than $60,000 per bed and about $35,000 per bed to build a minimum-security prison. There is a wide range in construction costs across the United States. This range is caused by the variation of construction costs in different regions of the nation: land costs vary, some systems use prison labor to help offset the costs, the amount of space allotted per prisoner in different prison designs varies, and accounting methods differ in each state. Regarding accounting methods, in some states architectural fees and insurance costs are included, while they are excluded in other states. In addition, construction costs usually do not include finance charges, which could triple the initial costs. In addition to the construction costs, the long-term operating costs are also staggering. It costs approximately $25,000 per year, per bed to keep prisoners confined. As you can see, prison bed space is expensive for taxpayers and takes up a considerable portion of the federal and state revenues. Table 9-2 presents some statistics on the growing expense of prisons.

TABLE **9-2 Points of Interest—Prison Costs**

- Between 1990 and 2001, there was a 5.8% growth in the prison population.
- In 2001, there were 1.96 million inmates in prisons and local jails.
- When prison operating expenditures were divided by the average number of inmates incarcerated during 1996, the nationwide average annual cost to house each state inmate was $20,100, and each federal inmate, $23,500.
- Since 1990, state prison expenditures have been increasing about 11% per year.
- Since 1990 federal prison expenditures have been increasing about 17% per year.
- Per resident spending for state prisons increased each year an average of 7.3% between 1985 and 1996, about twice the 3.6% annual average rise in spending for state education.
- The highest average annual operating cost per state inmate occurred in Minnesota, (37,800) and the lowest in Alabama (8,000).
- Approximately 1.3 billion, or 6% of state prison expenditure in 1996, went for new construction, renovations, major repairs, land, or building purchases.
- Prison operations accounted for about 80% of all state correctional expenditures in 1996.

Source: James J. Stephan, *State Prison Expenditures, 1996* (Washington, DC: Bureau of Justice Statistics, 1999), 2–16. Allen J. Beck, Jennifer C. Karberg, and Paige M. Harrison, *Prison and Jail Inmates at Midyear 2001* (Washington, DC: Bureau of Justice Statistics, 2002), 2–16.

ARTICLE—
Is Further Prison Expansion Worth the Costs?[14]

In recent decades a primary response to crime has been to expand prison populations, which in 1993 exceeded 4.5 times the figure 25 years ago. State and federal governments have established longer sentences and mandatory minimum sentences, assuming that such action would reduce crime by deterring and incapacitating criminals.

Perhaps the most important question in penology today is whether further prison expansion is worth the expense. Cost-benefit analysis of imprisonment has been tried in the past, but it is suspect due to the questionable assumptions used. Much new information is now available, however, permitting reasonably firm estimates.

This article first compares the direct and measurable costs and benefits. The latter are mainly savings to victims from crimes not committed because prison populations were expanded; these include the value of items that would have been stolen and the pain victims would have suffered from violent crime. The direct costs are the expenses of building and operating prisons. I also outline the potential costs and benefits that cannot be quantified or cannot be attributed to changes in prison populations and crime rates.

Direct Benefits

The first step in determining the direct benefits is to estimate how many crimes are avoided when prison populations expand. Lack of adequate data here has long been a major stumbling block to making cost-benefit calculations. This year, however, two major research efforts independently reached nearly the same conclusions with different research procedures. W. Spellman, a researcher who authored *Criminal Incapacitation*, using prisoners' accounts concerning the volume of crime they committed, concluded that increasing prison and jail populations by one percent reduces index crime by 0.12 percent to 0.20 percent, with a best estimate of 0.16 percent. Marvell and Moody, conducting econometric analysis of crime rates and prison populations, concluded that each 1 percent increase in state prison populations reduced crime by at least 0.16 percent in 1971 to 1989. The reduction reached 0.21 percent in the period after 1976. The Spellman estimates are a little lower probably because they pertain to prison plus jail inmates, whereas Marvell and Moody studied prison populations only. Spellman's estimate, in addition, is limited to the incapacitation effect, and Marvell and Moody include deterrence and other crime-reduction effects of imprisonment.

Marvell and Moody also studied the average impact per additional state prisoner, producing an estimate of nearly 21 crimes averted per year. When broken down by crime type, each additional inmate leads to, on average, 0.06 fewer rapes, 0.63 fewer robberies, 6.10 fewer burglaries, 12.65 fewer larcenies, and 1.11 fewer vehicle thefts. There is no discernible impact on homicides and assaults.

The most obvious and easily calculated benefit of crime reduction is avoiding economic loss to potential victims. The Department of Justice publishes two estimates of victims' losses, one from the National Crime Survey (NCS) and the other from the Uniform Crime Reports (UCR). The NCS includes the value of stolen property, medical expenses, and pay loss for worked missed. The NCS figures lead to an estimate of $13,000 saved per additional prisoner in 1994 dollars. The UCR figures produce a higher estimate, $21,000, because citizens tend to report crime more often when the loss is greater and because the NCS excludes commercial crimes, which involve greater property loss for robbery and burglary (but not larceny). As a rough estimate, I take the average of the two measures, or $17,000 direct costs to victims saved per additional prisoner for index crimes. In addition, I add $2,000 for fraud and forgery which are not index crimes, for a total of $19,000.

This is probably an underestimate, although not seriously so. The UCR measure includes only costs of items stolen. The NCS excludes costs incurred after the interview date (which took place sometime between the crime and six months later), and many victims probably did not know the cost of medical care paid directly by their insurers. Medical costs, however, are only a small portion of total costs even for violent crime. The estimates might be higher if I could include victimless crime, such as gambling and drug offenses, but the impact of prison expansion is probably small because many other people are available to provide the illegal services, taking the place of those imprisoned.

Also not included are costs associated with psychological injuries, such as pain and suffering, which are difficult to measure but which are important and should be included if possible. The civil courts routinely give monetary damages for psychological injuries, and recent studies have used data for damage awards to estimate the costs of psychological injury in crimes. The results are rough averages of $51,000 for each rape, $17,000 for each robbery, and $700 for each burglary. These translate into $3,000 avoided for rape for each additional prisoner on average (0.06 times $51,000), $11,000 for robbery, and $4,000 for burglary.

In all, the calculable direct benefits from crime reduction total to some $37,000 per additional prisoner, about half for monetary loss and half for psychological injury.

Direct Costs

The best estimate of prison operating and construction costs per prisoner is $22,920 to $26,245 per year in 1989 dollars. Taking the average and adjusting for inflation leads to a rounded estimate of $30,000 in 1994 dollars. If the inmates were not imprisoned, they would most likely be on probation, so I must subtract the cost of supervising a probationer, which Cavanagh and Kleinman, in their book *A Cost Benefit Analysis of Prison Cell Construction and Alternative Sanctions,* estimate to be $1,000 per year (again after converting into 1994 dollars and rounding). The net costs, therefore, are $29,000 per prisoner.

Additional Putative Benefits

There are several other possible benefits to the crime-reduction impact of expanding prisons, but they are not included here because they apparently have little or no causal connection with crime reduction or because one cannot estimate the cost savings.

An important potential gain is alleviating the financial burden of the criminal justice system. In 1990, federal and state justice system expenses totaled $74 billion, or nearly $2,000 per index crime and $40,000 for crimes avoided per additional prisoner. Nongovernment crime costs for insurance and private security are probably even greater. The potential indirect costs savings, therefore, approach $100,000 a year per additional prisoner. But this cannot legitimately be considered a crime-reduction gain for the simple reason that, to the best of my knowledge, there is no reason to believe that such costs undergo a net decline because prison expansion reduces crime (for example, P. A. Langan and Moody, in their research on prison population, concluded that crime rate changes have little effect on prison populations).

Crime entails losses other than loss to victims: suffering by victims' families, increased fear of crime by acquaintances, loss to the victims' employers for sick leave, and commercial declines in high-crime neighborhoods. The latter is not truly a cost of crime because it means that other areas receive commercial gains, and the remaining potential benefits from crime reduction are too nebulous to calculate.

Other Putative Costs

More imprisonment also entails "downstream" costs that some try to attribute to the imprisonment. A prisoner's loss of legitimate earnings, which has been estimated to average some $10,000 a year, is not properly a cost because the loss typically means a job opening for someone else.

Prisoners' dependents are often on welfare, which costs the government another $10,000 or so per prisoner. Most of this is not properly a cost of imprisonment because (a) the dependents may be on welfare even if the prisoner were on the street, and (b) to the extent that additions to welfare result from the prisoner's loss of legitimate employment, the imprisonment provides employment opportunities for some whose families would otherwise be on welfare. On the other hand, welfare costs that result from loss of illegal income are true costs of increasing imprisonment. That is, when crime reduction through more imprisonment reduces theft losses, it also reduces criminals' incomes and perhaps causes some dependents to go on welfare. I have no basis for estimating, however, how often this happens and what portion of the welfare expenses can be considered a cost of imprisonment.

There are several other indirect costs that cannot be measured with information currently available. These include suffering by prisoners and relatives resulting from the imprisonment, relatives' costs for visiting and telephoning inmates, and the possible "crime-school" effect of imprisonment.

Conclusions

Prison populations appear to be near an equilibrium point from a cost-benefit viewpoint. The most readily measured benefit, reduced monetary loss to victims, is some $19,000 per additional prisoner per year. This is substantially less than the most readily measured cost, $29,000 for prison operation and construction, less probation supervision costs. But reduction in psychological costs to victims, estimated to be worth $18,000 per prisoner, raises the benefits to $37,000. For all practical purposes, given the uncertainties involved, especially for psychological costs, there is no indication that the direct calculable costs ($29,000) and benefits ($37,000) of imprisonment differ appreciably.

Additional costs and benefits that are not quantified, such as suffering by victims' and inmates' relatives also appear to be roughly balanced. Potentially the most important benefit, reduction in overall criminal justice expenses, and a major potential cost, inmates' loss of earnings, cannot be included because there is little to suggest that they are truly benefits and costs in practice.

This leads one to ask what might make the incarceration strategy more worthwhile. Criminals vary greatly in the amount of crime they commit, and there is growing evidence that many of the most active criminals remain on the streets, while prisons contain large numbers of criminals less adept at evading capture. Surveys of inmates suggest that the vast majority of crimes are committed by a small percent of criminals who tend to have much lower apprehension rates than others. Reducing crime by expanding prisons is unlikely to be very cost-effective unless accompanied by greater efforts to imprison the most active criminals. Lawmakers, therefore, should seek to improve police effectiveness as a way to make better use of prisons.

Summary

The prisons of the 1830s were organized based on the principles of order and regularity. Each prisoner was isolated in a cell and the rule of total silence was strictly enforced. By the 1900s, institutions tended to model themselves on the outside community and afforded the inmates the opportunity to mix with other prisoners and to work in groups. It was also during the early 1900s that the prisons began to specialize in classifying inmates (i.e., high risk, moderate risk, low risk). Generally, a defendant who is convicted of a felony may be ordered to a diagnostic facility within the state department of corrections for diagnostic and treatment services. The orientation process includes providing inmates with information regarding the department's policies, programs, educational services, rules, classification procedures, disciplinary procedures, and other inmate activities and programs.

Most states use classification committees to determine the first unit to which an inmate will be assigned. Inmates do not have a right to choose their unit assignment. The committees make their decisions based on all information collected: the inmate's safety needs, the inmate's security needs, and the inmate's treatment needs. After the inmates spend a couple of weeks going through the diagnostic process, the inmates are assigned custody levels. A custody designation does two things: it tells how much supervision the inmate needs and with whom and where he will live.

Inmates confined to institutions are required to obey a lengthy list of policies. When an institution employee observes an inmate commit an infraction, the employee is generally required to submit a disciplinary report.

In most states, there are three ways an inmate may be released from confinement: parole, mandatory supervision, and discharge. Parole is the discretionary release of an inmate from prison when he or she completes a prescribed portion of his or her sentence and the parole board agrees that the release will not increase the likelihood of harm to the public.

Parole is often used imprecisely and incorrectly to refer to the release of any defendant from custody. It differs from probation in that probation usually requires little or no confinement and probation is administered by the courts on a countywide basis. Parole is generally administered by a statewide agency on a statewide basis. Normally parole is granted only after the defendant has served a significant portion of his or her confinement. Probation is considered a preinstitutional procedure. Parole, on the other hand, is considered a continuation of the correctional process.

Parole in America can be traced back to the houses of refuge that were established in the latter part of the nineteenth century. Parole is, however, more English and European than American. It was first used by the English to offer a conditional release from prison for those prisoners who agreed to work for a certain period of time to regain their freedom. Parole, unlike probation, was originally motivated by economic pressures rather than humanitarian concerns. Parole provided employers with cheap labor and relieved the British government from having to pay the expenses of their imprisonment.

In recent years, there has been a trend by states to require that inmates serve a longer period of time before they are eligible for parole. Traditionally inmates were eligible after serving 25 percent of their time. Several states now require inmates to serve at least 30 percent of their sentence before being eligible for parole.

Discussion Questions

1. Differentiate between probation and parole.
2. How does the historical development of parole differ from that of probation?
3. What are the major goals and objectives of parole?

4. What factors should be considered in releasing the youth in society?
5. Explain the significance of the *Morrissey v. Brewer* case.

Chapter Quiz

True/False
1. The orientation process includes, but is not limited to providing inmates with information regarding the department's policies, rules, and educational services.
2. Classification committees determine to which group an inmate will be assigned.
3. Inmates, while incarcerated, in prison usually have no grievance process in situations where they feel they have been mistreated.
4. The latest data from the "parole points of interest section" in this chapter reveals that parole boards have been increasing in large numbers across the United States.
5. The word "parole" is taken from the Germans.

Multiple Choice
1. The concept of parole is often credited to
    a. England's Alexander Maconochie and Ireland's Sir Walter Crofton.
    b. America's August Vollmer and O. W. Wilson.
    c. England's Robert Morrissey and Alexander Maconochie.
    d. France's John Locke and Francois-Marie Arouet Volaire.
2. Generally it is the function of the _____ to revoke a defendant's parole.
    a. prison
    b. paroling agency
    c. judge
    d. parole officer
3. Which one of the following are segregative classification decisions based on?
    a. age and previous incarceration
    b. marriage and family status on the outside
    c. drug offenders vs. crime against person offenders
    d. rehabilitation potential of the inmate
4. Which of the following custody levels is used for inmates who have serious and/or long disciplinary records, and those inmates who cannot work outside the security area without armed supervision? These inmates usually live in cells.
    a. minimum (out)
    b. maximum
    c. minimum (in)
    d. close

5. The conditional release of a prisoner from a correctional institution prior to the completion of his or her term of confinement is referred to as _____.
   a. probation
   b. early release
   c. parole
   d. time served

Endnotes

1. Norval Morris and David J. Rothman, *The Oxford History of the Prison: The Practice of Punishment in Western Society* (New York: Oxford, 1995), ix.
2. *Victoria Advocate*, June 22, 1996, p.5A.
3. *Hughes v. Rowe*, 449 U.S. 5 (1980).
4. *Nickens v. White*, 622 F.2d 967 (8th Cir. 1973).
5. ABA Standards for Criminal Justice, Legal Status of Prisoners, Standard 23-3.1.
6. *Weems v. United States*, 217 U.S. 349 (1910).
7. *Rhodes v. Robinson*, 612 F.2d 766 (3d Cir. 1972).
8. Robert M. Carter and Leslie T. Wilkins eds., *Probation, Parole, and Community Corrections* (New York: John Wiley, 1976).
9. John V. Barry, "Captain Alexander Maconochie," *Victorian Historical* 27 (June 1957): 5.
10. United States Sentencing Commission, Guidelines Manual, Section 5D1.1 (Nov. 1994).
11. Presidents Commission on Law Enforcement and Administration of Justice, *Task Force Report: Corrections,* (Washington, DC: GPO, 1976), 60.408 U.S. 471 (1972).
12. George M. Camp and Camille G. Camp, *The Corrections Yearbook: 1993* (South Salem, NY: The Criminal Justice Institute, 1994)
13. President's Commission on Law Enforcement and Administration of Justice, *Task Force Report: Corrections,* (Washington, DC: GPO, 1976), 60.408 U.S. 471 (1972).
14. Thomas B. Marvell, "Director Justice Research, Williamsburg, Virginia," *Federal Probation* 58 (4 December, 1994).

Chapter 10
Juvenile Corrections

Spencer Grant/PhotoEdit

Key Terms

adjudicatory hearing
child-saving movement
diversion
halfway houses
juvenile detention centers
non-secure facilities
parens patriae
reception/diagnostic centers
secure facilities
shelters

Outline

10-1 History of Juvenile Justice
10-2 Establishment of Juvenile Court
10-3 Present Role of Juvenile Justice
10-4 Juvenile Diversion
10-5 Waiver of Juvenile Court Jurisdiction
10-6 Juvenile Trials
10-7 Disposition
10-8 Institutionalization
10-9 The Right to Treatment
10-10 Types of Cases Handled by the Juvenile Courts
10-10a Violent Youths
10-10b Property Cases
10-11 Types of Institutions
10-12 Conditions of Confinement in Juvenile Facilities
10-13 Disproportionate Minority Youth Confinement
10-14 Group Home Programs
10-15 Juvenile Release Decisions
10-16 Parole
Summary
Discussion Questions
Chapter Quiz
Endnotes

Learning Objectives

After reading this chapter, the reader will be able to:

- Explain the development of juvenile corrections.
- Trace the development of juvenile court.
- Analyze the impact of the *Gault* decision on juvenile justice.
- Analyze the present role of juvenile justice.
- Identify the critical steps in the waiver of juvenile court jurisdiction.
- List the criteria for juvenile diversion programs.
- Differentiate between juvenile trials and adult criminal trials.
- Explain the juvenile's right to treatment.
- List the types of trials handled by juvenile court.
- List the problems involved in juvenile corrections.
- Explain the conditions of confinement in juvenile institutions.
- Describe the steps involved in the release decision in juvenile institutions.
- Analyze the effectiveness of group homes.

The primary and controversial issues in juvenile justice include:

- Whether the juvenile's needs or rights are paramount to society's needs for security.
- What is the proper scope of authority for juvenile justice?
- What processes should be used to adjudicate and make disposition of juvenile offenders?
- What reforms are necessary to improve juvenile justice?

10-1 History of Juvenile Justice

At common law, children over 14 years of age were treated as if they were adults. Children under the age of seven were considered incapable of committing crimes. Children between the ages of seven and 14, were "presumed" incapable of committing crimes. However, the state could, by establishing the maturity of the child in question, hold him or her accountable as an adult. Even when formally treated as adults, however, children were rarely punished as harshly as adults by the criminal courts.

In early English history the doctrine of *parens patriae* was developed. According to this doctrine, the king could intervene in family life to protect the child's estate from dishonest parents or guardians. **Parens patriae** can roughly be defined as the duty of the state to act as a parent in the interest of the child. This principal expanded and now includes the right of the state to intervene to protect child welfare against parental neglect, incompetency, and abuse.[1]

The Reform Movement of the nineteenth century also developed a concern for children in general. A **child-saving movement,** which was directed at children in need or in trouble, grew out of this general concern. The *child savers* attempted to save children by using houses of refuge and reform schools. These institutions were based on the contemporary idea that children's environment made them bad and that removing the youths from poor homes and unhealthy associations and placing them in special homes, houses of refuge, or schools would cause the children to give up their bad and evil habits and would in fact reform the children.[2]

10-2 Establishment of Juvenile Court

The influence of the child savers prompted the development of the first juvenile court in Cook County, Illinois, in 1899. The Illinois Juvenile Court Act set up an independent court to handle criminal law violations by children under 16 years of age. The court was also given responsibility for supervising care of neglected, dependent, and wayward youths. The Juvenile Court Act also set up a probation department to monitor youths in the community, and it directed juvenile court judges to place serious offenders in secured training schools for boys and industrial schools for girls. The purpose of the act was to separate juveniles from adult offenders and to provide a legal framework in which juveniles could get proper care and custody.

By 1940, every state in the United States had established a juvenile justice system. The juvenile justice systems were normally created as divisions of family court. As the juvenile court movement spread throughout the United States, it provided for the use of a quasi-legal type of justice. The main concern of the juvenile courts was the best interest of the child. Accordingly, the courts did not adhere strictly to legal doctrine, protect constitutional rights, or conduct their proceedings according to due process requirements. The general theory was that these were not criminal courts, and the youths did not have rights as if they were being tried in an adult criminal court.

For many years, the stated goals of the juvenile justice system were to prevent juvenile crime and to rehabilitate juvenile offenders. In the 1980s, an additional goal was imposed on the juvenile courts to protect society.

Our early reform schools were generally punitive in nature and were based on the concept that rehabilitation could only be achieved through hard work. In the 1950s, the influence of therapists, such as Carl Rogers, promoted the introduction of psychological treatment in juvenile corrections. By 1960, group-counseling techniques were standard procedure in the vast majority of juvenile institutions. Box 10-1 presents one of the main cases to be decided in this area.

Just as the due process revolution affected prisoners' rights and defendants' rights, the U.S. Supreme Court also drastically altered the juvenile justice system. In a series of cases, it established that juvenile delinquents are protected under the due process clause of the U.S. Constitution and therefore have constitutional rights in juvenile proceedings.

As a result of the influence of constitutional requirements in juvenile proceedings, the distinction between adult and criminal juvenile justice systems is much less now than it was 40 years ago.

Box 10-1

In Re Gault, U.S. 1, 18 LEd. 2d. 527, 87 S.Ct. 1428 (1967)

FACTS. Jerry Gault, a 15-year-old boy, was taken into custody on June 8, 1964 by the sheriff of Gila County, Arizona. He was arrested based on a complaint of a woman who said that Jerry and another boy had made an obscene telephone call to her. At the time, Gault was on a six-month probation, having previously been declared a delinquent for stealing a wallet.

Based on the verbal complaint, Gault was taken from his home. His parents were not informed that he was taken into custody. When his mother appeared in the evening, she was told by the superintendent that a hearing would be held in juvenile court the following day.

The next day, the police officer who had taken Gault into custody filed a petition alleging Gault's delinquency. Gault, his mother, and the police officer appeared at a judicial hearing before a judge in his chambers. Mrs. Cook, the complaining witness, was not at the hearing. Gault was questioned about the telephone calls and was sent back to the detention home. He was released a few days later.

On the day of Gault's release, his mother received a letter indicating that a hearing would be held on his delinquency status a few days later. When the hearing was held, the complainant, Mrs. Cook, was still not present. There was no transcript or a recording of the proceedings. At the hearing, the juvenile officer stated that Gault had admitted making the lewd telephone calls. Neither the boy nor his parents were advised of any of his rights, including the right to be silent, the right to be represented by counsel, or the right to a due process hearing. At the conclusion of the hearing, the juvenile court committed Jerry as a juvenile delinquent to the state's industrial school in Arizona for the period of his minority, i.e. six years.[3]

This, in effect, meant that Gault got six years for making an obscene phone call. Had he been an adult and convicted of the same crime, the maximum punishment would have been no more than a $50.00 fine and/or 60 days in jail.

Attorneys on behalf of Gault filed a writ of *habeas corpus* with the Superior Court for the State of Arizona. The request for the writ was denied. The decision was appealed to the Arizona Supreme Court and that was denied. The denial by the Arizona Supreme Court was then appealed to the U.S. Supreme Court. The U.S. Supreme Court in a far-reaching decision, agreed that Gault's constitutional rights were violated. The Supreme Court indicated that at the very minimum, notice of charges is an essential right of the due process of law, as is the right to confront witnesses and to cross-examine them, the right to counsel, and the privilege against self-incrimination.

continues

Box 10-1 (continued)

Several items not answered by the court in reversing the Arizona's determination of delinquency were whether Gault had a right to a transcript, or whether there was a right to an appellant review.

The significance of the Gault case is that it established that a child in a delinquency adjudication proceeding has procedural due process constitutional rights as set forth in the constitution. Note: This case was confined to rulings at the adjudication stage of the judicial process.

10-3 Present Role of Juvenile Justice

Our juvenile justice system is independent from, yet interrelated with, the adult criminal justice system. The juvenile court system developed on the concept of parens patriae. Starting in the 1960s, the concept was modified to one of procedural due process and in the 1980s to one of controlling chronically delinquent youths. It appears that the juvenile system will continue to evolve as we hunt for a more efficient system.

What is the present role of our juvenile justice system?

1. To provide a social welfare program designed to assist and act as the wise parent
2. To protect the constitutional rights of children
3. To rehabilitate delinquents
4. To protect society from violent youths

10-4 Juvenile Diversion

The most common screening out of juveniles after they have been processed into the court system is through the use of diversion. **Diversion** has been very popular in the juvenile justice system since it was recommended by the President's Commission on Crime in 1967. There are several reasons for the growing popularity of diversion: it helps to reduce the increasing caseload; it provides more flexibility than the juvenile justice treatment programs currently in existence; and it costs less per capita than the use of institutionalization of juveniles.

10-5 Waiver of Juvenile Court Jurisdiction

Prior to the first juvenile court established in Illinois in 1899, juveniles were tried for violations of law in adult criminal court. Today, most statutes provide that juvenile court shall have primary jurisdiction over children under the age of 17. There are provisions in all state statutes, however, stating that the juvenile court can waive jurisdiction and allow the juvenile to be tried in adult criminal court in cases involving serious crimes. The transfer of juveniles to criminal court is often based on statutory criteria. The two major criteria for waivers are the age of the child and the type of the offense alleged in the petition. For example, many jurisdictions require the child to be at least 15 before he/she may be tried as an adult. The nature and effect of the waiver is significant to the juvenile. Accordingly, the United States Supreme Court has imposed several procedural protections for juveniles in the waiver process. The first major 1966 court decision in this area was that of *Kent v. United States*.[4] This case challenged the provisions of the District Court of Columbia, which stated that the juvenile court could waive jurisdiction after a full investigation. The Supreme Court held that the waiver proceeding is a critically important stage in the juvenile process, and therefore, the juveniles must be afforded minimum requirements of due process of law.

Consistent with the minimal requirements, the following conditions are considered necessary before a valid waiver may occur:

1. A hearing must be held on the motion to waiver.
2. The child is entitled to be represented by counsel at the hearing.
3. The attorney representing the juvenile must be given access to all records and reports considered by the court in reaching a waiver decision.
4. The court must provide a written statement of the reasons for the waiver decision.

In most states, prior to 1975, if a juvenile was charged with a serious offense, there would be an adjudication hearing to determine whether the juvenile had committed the offense. If the court found that the juvenile committed the offense, there would be a hearing to determine whether a waiver of juvenile court jurisdiction should be entered and the juvenile tried in adult criminal court. In 1975, however, the case of *Breed v. Jones* held that jeopardy attaches when the juvenile court begins to hear evidence as to whether the juvenile committed the offense. Therefore, if an adjudication hearing is held prior to the waiver hearing, the juvenile cannot be waived to adult criminal court because that would constitute double jeopardy.[5] After the *Breed v. Jones* case, the courts of all the states were modified to establish a waiver hearing first. Then if it was determined that the juvenile should be retained in the juvenile court system, a hearing on the adjudication phase would take place.

10-6 Juvenile Trials

Juvenile courts receive about 1.8 million delinquency cases each year.[6] The trial process in juvenile court is referred to as the **adjudicatory hearing.** It is in this hearing that the court determines whether or not the juvenile committed the offenses alleged in the petition. During the adjudication process, the juvenile has the constitutional right to a fair notice of the charges, the right to be represented by counsel, the right to be confronted by and to cross-examine witnesses, and the privilege against self-incrimination. Additionally, by adjudicating the juvenile a delinquent, the juvenile court must use the standard of proof beyond a reasonable doubt.

At the conclusion of the adjudicatory hearing, the court is required to enter a judgment either sustaining the petition (i.e., finding that the accused committed the crimes alleged in the petition) or dismissing the petition. Once the juvenile has been adjudicated a delinquent, the court must make a determination as to the disposition of the child.

10-7 Disposition

At the separate disposition hearing, the juvenile court should look at the record of the delinquent, the family background, the needs of the accused, and the safety of the public. A juvenile court judge has broad discretion in determining the disposition of the juvenile. Some of the standard dispositions are dismissal of the petition, suspended judgment, probation, placement in a community-treatment program, or commitment to a state agency that is responsible for juvenile institutional care. This latter disposition is basically a commitment to a reformatory or other state institution for juveniles. In addition, the court has the power to place the child with parents or relatives under extensive or moderate supervision. It can make dispositional arrangements with private youth-serving agencies, or it can have the child committed to a mental institution.

As in adult criminal court, probation is the most commonly used formal sentence for juvenile offenders. In fact, many states require that before a youth may be sent to an institution, the youth must have failed on probation unless the juvenile has been charged with a serious felony.

Probation may include placing the child under the supervision of the juvenile probation department for the purposes of community treatment.

The conditions of probation are normally spelled out in the state court's order. There are general conditions that all delinquents are required to obey, such as to obey the law, to stay away from other delinquents, and to attend school. There are also special conditions of probation that may require the child to participate in certain training, treatment, or education programs.

10-8 Institutionalization

The most severe disposition that a judge may make at a juvenile court hearing is the institutionalization of the juvenile. In most states, this means that the child can be committed to a juvenile detention facility until he or she is 21 years of age. Unlike that of most adult courts, the disposition of commitment to an institution is an indeterminate sentence.

Many professionals involved in delinquency and juvenile law have questioned the practice of committing juveniles to institutions. Deinstitutionalization of juveniles has been attempted by using small residential facilities, operated by juvenile care agencies, to replace the larger state schools. The success of deinstitutionalization of juveniles is still being debated by scholars and professionals.

10-9 The Right to Treatment

Although it has not directly stated that juveniles have a right to treatment while incarcerated, it appears that the Supreme Court is leaning in that direction. The Court of Appeals for the Seventh Circuit indicates that *Nelson v. Heyne* (1973) upheld the constitutional right to treatment for institutionalized juveniles under the Fourteenth Amendment; and recent decisions by the U.S. Supreme Court seem to indicate that juveniles do have a right to receive treatment if committed to a juvenile institution.

10-10 Type of Cases Handled by the Juvenile Courts

10-10a Violent Youths

Law enforcement agencies refer approximately two-thirds of all youth arrested to a court with juvenile jurisdiction for further processing. As with law enforcement, the court may decide to divert some juveniles from the formal justice system. United States courts with juvenile jurisdiction handle an estimated 1.8 million cases in which the juvenile was charged with a delinquency offense, an offense for which an adult could be prosecuted in criminal court.[7]

From 1987 through 1996, the juvenile courts saw a disproportionate increase in violent and other personal offense, weapons, and drug offense cases. Personal offenses rose from 16 percent to 22 percent of delinquency cases, aggravated assault rose from 3 percent to 5 percent, simple assault rose from 9 percent to 12 percent.[8] The courts are more likely to file petitions in cases involving violent offenses than in any other type of cases.

10-10b Property Cases

Property offenses are a major part of the juvenile crime problem. However, property offenses committed by juveniles actually declined from 1987 through 1996, (60 percent to 50 percent). Specific property crime decreases include burglary (11 percent to 8 percent), and larceny-theft (28 percent to 24 percent). Approximately 30 percent of all juvenile arrests are based on property offenses. Shoplifting was the most common offense for youths under 15 years of age. Burglary was the most common property offense for older youths. Female offenders are more likely to be involved in shoplifting. Males are more likely to be involved in burglary.[9]

Approximately 25 percent of the youths arrested for property offenses are detained. Juveniles involved with motor vehicle thefts were most likely to be detained awaiting disposition of the case. Table 10-1 depicts juveniles in residential placement and those offenders granted diversion in the United States for violent crimes, property crimes, and drug and alcohol offenses.

TABLE 10-1 Juveniles in Residential Placement—United States

Offense	Total	Committed	Detained	Diversion
Homicide	1,514	1,146	366	0
Sexual Assault	7,511	6,147	1,121	51
Robbery	8,212	6,795	1,395	3
Aggravated Assault	9,984	7,815	2,112	30
Burglary	12,222	9,696	2,475	15
Theft	6,944	5,316	1,581	27
Auto Theft	6,225	4,632	1,551	24
Arson	1,126	879	240	6
Drug Trafficking	3,106	2,436	657	6
Weapons Violation	4,023	2,928	1,074	3
Alcohol Offense	328	195	126	6

Source: Melissa Sickman and Yi-chum Wan (2001). *Census of Juveniles in Residential Placement Databook.* Available Online at: http://www.ojjdp.ncjrs.org/ojstatbb/cjrp.

10-11 Types of Institutions

Currently, juveniles who have been adjudicated as delinquent and committed may be held in one of six types of facilities.

- Detention centers
- Shelters
- Reception/diagnostic centers
- Training schools
- Ranches or camps
- Halfway houses or group homes

Juvenile detention centers are short-term, secure facilities that hold juveniles awaiting adjudication, disposition, or placement in an institution. **Shelters** are also short-term facilities that are operated like detention centers, but are non-secure with a physically unrestricted environment. **Reception/diagnostic centers** are also short-term facilities that are used to screen youths for assignments to appropriate levels of custody and institutions.

Training schools are generally long-term secure facilities that are used only for adjudicated delinquents. *Ranches, forestry camps,* and *farms* are long-term, non-secure facilities used for adjudicated juveniles. **Halfway houses** or *group homes* are non-secure facilities that are used to help integrate youths back into the community. They may be either long- or short-term facilities.

As you may have discerned from the above, there are two levels of security: secure and non-secure. **Secure facilities** are characterized by their locks, bars, and fences. Movement is typically restricted in a secure facility. **Non-secure facilities** are characterized by their lack of bars, locks, and fences, and generally permit a greater freedom of movement for youths within and around the facility.

10-12 Conditions of Confinement in Juvenile Facilities

In a recent study of conditions of confinement in U.S. juvenile detention and correctional facilities, conducted by ABT Associates for the Office of Juvenile Justice and Delinquency Prevention (OJJDP), institutional crowding was found to be pervasive. Thousands of juvenile offenders, more than 75 percent of the confined population, were housed in facilities that violated one or more standards related to living space (facility design capacity, sleeping areas, and living unit size). Increasingly, the percentage of confined juveniles living in facilities where the daily population exceeds design capacity has created many problems for juvenile correctional administrators. Crowding was found to be associated with higher rates of institutional violence, suicidal behavior, and greater reliance on the use of short-term isolation.

The study, required by Congress in its 1988 amendments to the Juvenile Justice and Delinquency Prevention Act, was the first such nationwide investigation of conditions in secure juvenile detention and correctional facilities. Using nationally recognized correctional standards as a gauge, researchers assessed how juvenile offenders' basic needs were met, how institutional security and resident safety were maintained, what treatment programming was provided, and how juveniles' rights were protected.

The study included surveys mailed in 1991 to all 984 public and private juvenile detention centers, reception and diagnostic facilities, training schools, and ranches in the United States. In addition, experienced juvenile correctional practitioners conducted two-day site visits to a representative sample of nearly 100 facilities in the fall of 1991. These facilities held about 65,000 juveniles on the date of the 1991 Children in Custody census, or about 69 percent of the juveniles confined on that date in the United States. During 1990, these facilities received nearly 690,000 admissions, including readmissions and transfers of juveniles from other facilities.

Based on standards conformance and related outcome measures, researchers concluded that serious and widespread problems existed in the areas of living space, health care, institutional security and safety, and control of suicidal behavior. In important areas of treatment, rehabilitation, and education, the evaluation demonstrated the need for more rigorous assessment of how facilities were meeting juveniles' needs in these areas.

Juvenile detention centers, like adult jails and prisons, provide juvenile inmates with opportunities to engage in recreational activities.
Spencer Grant/PhotoEdit

The study found several areas in which conditions of confinement appeared to be generally adequate: basic needs such as food, clothing, hygiene, recreation, and accommodations. An important overall finding was that, generally, conformance to existing standards does not guarantee adequate conditions for juveniles in custody. For example, although more than 90 percent of juvenile detention facilities conformed to the fire inspection requirement, more than half of the 30 detention centers visited had at least one unmarked fire exit in a sleeping area. Two-thirds did not have fire escape routes posted. In some facilities, fire exits were blocked.

In many cases the standards only require the existence of policies, procedures, or programs, without stipulating performance measures or desired outcomes. Thus, interpretation of standards conformance is problematic. Over the 12 months prior to the mail survey, researchers estimated that:

- Juveniles injured 6,900 staff and 24,200 other juveniles.
- 11,000 juveniles committed 17,600 acts of suicidal behavior, with 10 suicides in 1990.
- More than 18,600 incidents required emergency medical care.
- More than 435,800 juveniles were held in short-term isolation (one to 24 hours) and almost 84,000 were isolated for more than 24 hours.
- 9,700 juveniles escaped from custody.

In 1999, OJJDP officials, ABT researchers, juvenile correctional experts, and youth advocates from across the country assembled in Washington, DC, to discuss the findings. While there was general concurrence about the findings, some experts speculated that facility conditions had deteriorated since 1991, citing substantial state and local budget cuts, resulting in staff reductions, staff turnover, and strain on facility program and maintenance budgets.

Compounding these pressures are demographic shifts that already show a steady growth in the juvenile population at risk. Concern was voiced that problems of crowding and related conditions will not only persist, but will increase, to the serious detriment of juveniles for whom rehabilitation is still a hope. They were especially concerned about the impact on minority youth. According to the OJJDP 1999 National Report on Juvenile Offenders, between 1987 and 1997, the minority populations in detention and correctional facilities grew from 53 percent to 67 percent of the confined population.

10-13 Dispropotionate Minority Youth Confinement

In light of the OJJDP report that reveals increases in the number of minority youth confined in public and private juvenile facilities, a further examination of this problem is necessary. While research findings are not completely consistent, data available for most jurisdictions across the country show that minority (especially black) youth are over-represented within the juvenile justice system, particularly in secure facilities. These data further suggest that minority youth are more likely to be placed in public secure facilities, while white youth are more likely to be housed on private facilities or diverted from the juvenile justice system.[10]

There is substantial evidence that minority youth are often treated differently from majority youth within the juvenile justice system. Research suggests that race/ethnicity does make a difference in juvenile justice decisions in some jurisdictions at least some of the time.[11] Because juvenile justice systems are fragmented and administered at the local level, racial/ethnic differences exist in some jurisdictions but not in others.

Some research has found that when racial/ethnic effects do occur, they can be found at any stage of processing within the juvenile justice system.[12] Across numerous jurisdictions a substantial body of research suggests that disparity is most pronounced at the beginning stages. The greatest disparity between majority and minority youth court processing outcomes occurs at intake and detention decision points. Existing research also suggests that when racial/ethnic differences are found, they tend to accumulate as youth are processed through the justice system.[13]

To more effectively grasp this growing problem of disproportionate minority youth confinement in the juvenile detention facilities we have prepared the following points taken from the OJJDP Census of Juveniles in Residential Placement, 1997.

- Nationally, minorities accounted for 34 percent of the juvenile population in 1997.
- Minorities accounted for 67 percent of juveniles committed to public facilities nationwide, a proportion nearly twice their proportion of the juvenile population.
- Minorities accounted for 62 percent of juveniles detained nationwide.
- Minority proportions were somewhat lower for youth committed to private facilities than to public facilities.
- In seven states, the minority proportion of the total population of juveniles in residential placement was 75 percent or greater: California, Connecticut, Delaware, Louisiana, New Jersey, New Mexico, and Texas.

- Non-Hispanic black juveniles accounted for more than 6 in 10 juveniles in residential placement for drug trafficking and more than 5 in 10 in residential placement for other drug offenses.

10-14 Group Home Programs

As noted earlier, one type of institution used in juvenile corrections is the group home. A group home is a long-term juvenile facility in which residents are allowed extensive contact with the community, such as attending school or holding a job.[14] The report below, which appeared in the Federal Probation journal in 1993, discusses the problems that the group home treatment programs are experiencing.[15]

> The report noted that significant changes have occurred in the juvenile justice system in the last several decades. Due to recent emphasis on rehabilitation, reform, and above all, concern for the welfare of young offenders, the juvenile justice system has employed a wide variety of options in treating young offenders. Optimism about rehabilitation and dissatisfaction with the traditional "lockup" in detention homes has caused many to consider residential treatment and the rehabilitation of juveniles in family-type centers rather than conventional incarceration. The popular trend, therefore, has been deinstitutionalization. Due to this dominant philosophy, group home treatment programs, one of oldest options in treating young offenders, gained a special momentum during the 1960s and 1970s. The availability of federal dollars, the rising concern of numerous child-care institutions, and above all, the dissatisfaction with detaining juveniles have resulted in the proliferation of group homes as a viable alternative and supplement to juvenile institutions.[16]
>
> Unlike many alternatives for juveniles, group homes have been recognized for providing a family-type atmosphere where the youths and house parents (counselors and case workers) often establish the same warm and intense ties that one would hope to find in healthy families. Stewart and Associates, by tracing 906 juvenile offenders in a three-year period, recorded that such a family-type atmosphere has a significant impact on the recidivism rate of juvenile offenders. Group home treatment programs, as they found, are particularly effective when first-time offenders are referred to such programs. Similarly, Gaier and Sarnacki suggested that group home treatment is an effective approach in interrupting delinquent behavior, because it is designed to alter the delinquent's environment and provide a meaningful family-type setting. According to Murray and Dox, institutions have a greater "suppression" rate on subsequent arrests than do group home treatment programs.

Group home treatment programs are also recognized for their cost efficiency in providing a workable alternative for unruly and delinquent children. At the time that most local governments are pressed with budgetary concerns, group home treatment programs are viewed as a promising alternative. One recent investigation by the Office of Juvenile Justice Delinquency Prevention regarded group home treatment programs as a viable option in saving the juvenile justice system from budgetary problems. The investigation further revealed that group home treatment programs have been appealing to juvenile court judges due to both their effectiveness in treating young offenders and their cost efficiency.

Treatment

The group-home treatment program in this study was established in the mid-1970s by a local juvenile probation officer due to his dissatisfaction with the local juvenile court's referral of the majority of unruly and delinquent children to state facilities. The program began by housing a few unruly, disturbed, and runaway children in the 1970s, later accepting juveniles with various problems and backgrounds in the 1980s. The program started with a few hundred dollars donated by local businesses and grew to have an operational budget of over $350,000 in the late 1980s. Despite the rapid growth in a short period, the program solely functions on donations and charitable contributions by citizens and local businesses without relying on local or state funds.

The treatment program rests on providing a therapeutic community, elevating children's self-esteem, reducing stress, and providing group orientation. The program offers community service projects (helping senior citizens, beautifying the community, etc.), assists in obtaining employment, organizes athletic activities, and helps residents with educational and vocational programs. Overall, the program focuses on building a positive attitude and respect for others. In particular, being in a position to provide service to others enables the juvenile to help rather than hinder.

Conclusions

Treatment of juveniles in the community and rehabilitation of young offenders in a group home setting has become a hotly debated subject. The recent "get-tough-on-crime" policy, coupled with the national concern regarding the drug problem, has motivated many decision makers to re-evaluate the juvenile justice process. During the last few years, a number of states have moved toward more stringent and punitive measures to deal with young offenders. Motivated by the increasing number of serious offenses committed by juveniles and the ineffectiveness of community treatment programs in reducing recidivism, proponents of stiffer sentencing have proposed the departure from the rehabilitative efforts and the re-implementation of punitive measures. In such debates, group home treatment programs have been attacked frequently for their leniency and their inability to punish and change young offenders.

Some scholars believe that the entire juvenile justice system is becoming tougher. A few states have already revised their juvenile justice system, reflecting more concern for retribution and deterrence than for rehabilitation and reform. In Washington, for instance, the entire juvenile justice code has been revised to include detention and determinate sentencing. By dropping the family court's jurisdiction over status offenders, the Washington legislatures have explicitly noted that the aim of the new legislation is primarily the protection of citizens and community through tougher sentencing rather than the welfare of juvenile offenders. Throughout the 1990s other states followed the same path. California, Colorado, Delaware, Florida, and New Mexico have adopted legislation that focuses more on retribution and deterrence than concern for juveniles. It is believed that the remaining states will adopt more punitive measures in dealing with young offenders, especially the violent and recurring offenders, before the turn of this decade.

Many believe that this recent development will undermine the entire rehabilitative effort. Recent concern for punishment will ultimately jeopardize the existence of community treatment programs, and in particular, group home program facilities. Proponents of stiffer punishment, however, believe that nothing will be lost. A high recidivism rate, in their view, is an indication that group home programs have failed to live up to their intent.

The findings reported in *Federal Probation Journal*, however, suggest a different outlook. The analysis of sample cases revealed that the productivity or success of group homes could be maximized if certain factors are taken into consideration. First, it was found that group home programs would be highly effective in the rehabilitation and reform of young offenders if such an option is considered in the early stages of delinquent behavior. Precisely, group home programs are most effective (77 to 80 percent) if juveniles are dispositioned to such treatment programs immediately following the first or second delinquency act. Conversely, they are least effective (33 to 15 percent) when group home facilities were considered after five or more delinquent acts.

Secondly, the "get tough" approach against young offenders may not reduce the number of repeated offenses committed by this group. Records indicate that group home programs are the least effective when the child has served a period of time in state detention facilities prior to his or her referral to a group home program. In comparison, those previously placed on probation had a higher rate of success in group home programs. These findings lead to arguments that suggest that the re-implementation of determinate sentencing and the application of punitive measures by confining juveniles to detention facilities may result in a higher rate of recidivism and ultimately the elevation of offenses committed by juveniles. Hence, in the long run, we can conclude that such an approach will cause a dramatic increase in the population of adult felons, because the juvenile justice system will have failed to serve its clientele properly. On face value the "get tough" approach may appear promising, but it may also cause unexpected results.

Finally, to depart from a productive alternative that has proven to be effective in reforming young offenders while reducing the costs of the juvenile justice system is premature. In light of the war on drugs and the substantial cuts to juvenile justice system budgets in favor of efforts to combat drug traffickers, it does not seem logical to revoke an alternative that has proven to be cost effective. Group home treatment programs could become productive if they are used properly. To maximize their success and reduce the rate of repeated offenses by juveniles, this option must be made a priority rather than considered an option after dissatisfaction with other alternatives in the juvenile justice system.

10-15 Juvenile Release Decisions

Unlike the adult parole process, most juveniles' release times are not determined at the post-sentencing hearing. Generally, the juvenile's length of commitment is determined by the youth's progress toward rehabilitation. In some jurisdictions, progress is measured by a token system that awards a specific number of points for various actions.

Although there is a general agreement that youths should be released as soon as they are ready, there are no valid measures to determine if a juvenile has been successfully rehabilitated or has undergone a real change of attitude. The criterion used to determine if the juvenile has been successfully rehabilitated and thus should be released is generally whether or not the juvenile conforms to institution rules or causes problems. Thus, by appearing to have been reformed, the youth receives the earliest release date. Accordingly, the youth's conduct and behavior in the institution may be based solely on the desire to please his supervisors to obtain release.

The question of when to release the youth depends on predictions of the youth's future behavior. The policy considerations that are required to be evaluated before the youth is released include:

- Has the youth been reformed?
- Is it unlikely that the youth will commit another serious offense?
- Was the youth's behavior acceptable during his or her confinement?
- Does the youth have a home or other place, such as a group home, to live?
- Will suitable employment, training, or treatment be available for the youth on release?
- What is the youth's own perception of his or her ability to handle reintegration into the community?
- Is the seriousness of the youth's past offenses and the circumstances in which they were committed sufficiently severe so as to preclude release?

10-16 Parole

Most juveniles, after release from institutions, return to the communities from which they came. Generally, juveniles are released from confinement long before the expiration of their maximum period of commitment. In some states, juveniles must serve a minimum time before being released. In nine states, the judge who committed the juvenile must agree to the release before he/she may be released early. The problem with this latter practice or requirement is that often the committing judge is too busy with other cases and does not have sufficient time to review the case and make a viable recommendation as to the release decision. In addition, because no new presentencing reports are prepared, the judge may act on dated or incomplete information. For these reasons, judicial involvement in the early release decision has been eliminated in most states.

Most experts assign two goals to parole: protection of society and proper adjustment of the youth. Presently, it appears that the most important goal is the protection of society. Many see the two goals as conflicting ones involving society versus the youth. A better approach appears to be the concept of protecting society by rehabilitating the youth.

Parole includes the objective of assisting the parolee in integration into the community. Therefore, the youth must be assisted in coping with the problems faced upon release and to adjust to the status of being a parolee. In order for the parolee to be a permanent benefit to society, parole agencies must assist in the development of the youth's ability to make good decisions that are behaviorally acceptable to the community.

Summary

At one time, according to common law, children over 14 years of age were treated as adults. Children under the age of seven were considered incapable of committing crimes. For children between the ages of 7 and 14, it was presumed that they were incapable of committing crimes, however the state could, by establishing the maturity of the child, hold him or her accountable as an adult. Even when formally treated as adults, children were rarely punished as harshly as adults were punished by the criminal courts.

In early English history the doctrine of parens patriae was developed. According to this doctrine, the king could intervene in family life to protect the child's estate from dishonest parents or guardians. The parens patriae doctrine allows the juvenile court to assume parental responsibility over wayward children, with a rehabilitative emphasis. This principal expanded and now includes the right of the state to intervene to protect child welfare against parental neglect, incompetency, and abuse.

Our juvenile justice system is independent of, yet interrelated with, the adult criminal justice system. The juvenile court system was developed based on the concept of parens patriae. Starting in the 1960s, the concept was modified to one of procedural due process and, in the 1980s, to one of controlling chronically delinquent youths. It appears that the juvenile system will continue to evolve as we search for a more efficient system.

Some juveniles are transferred from juvenile court to adult criminal court. The transfer of juveniles to adult criminal court is often based on statutory criteria, and the two major criteria for waivers are the age of the child and the type of the offense alleged in the petition. If they are found guilty in adult criminal court they enter the adult system of prison or probation. As in adult criminal court, probation is the most commonly used formal sentence for juvenile offenders. In fact, many states require that before a youth may be sent to an institution, the youth must have failed on probation, unless the juvenile has been charged with a serious felony.

Juveniles who are adjudicated as delinquent may be sent to one of six types of facilities: detention centers, shelters, reception/diagnostic centers, training schools, ranches and camps, and halfway houses and group homes. The juvenile's length of commitment to any of these facilities is generally determined by the youth's progress toward rehabilitation. The criterion used to determine if a juvenile has been successfully rehabilitated is typically whether the juvenile conformed to the rules and regulations of the institution while confined.

Parole may include placing the child under the supervision of the juvenile department for the purposes of community treatment. The conditions of the parole are normally spelled out in the state court's order. There are general conditions that all delinquents are required to obey, such as to obey the law, to stay away from other delinquents, and to attend school. In addition, there may be special conditions of probation that require individuals to participate in certain training, treatment, or education programs.

Discussion Questions

1. Explain the differences between juvenile corrections and adult corrections.
2. Summarize the history of juvenile justice.
3. What reforms are necessary to improve juvenile justice?
4. When should a juvenile be tried as an adult? Why?
5. How do juvenile trials differ from adult trials?

Chapter Quiz

True/False

1. In the old common law doctrine, children over 14 years of age were treated as if they were adults.
2. The *parens patriae* doctrine afforded juveniles the right to an attorney or the right to have their parents notified upon arrest.
3. The *child savers* attempted to save youth by using corporal punishment.
4. The Gault case established that juveniles do not have due process rights.
5. There has been no evidence to suggest that minorities are treated different in the juvenile justice system as is currently experienced in the adult court system.

Multiple Choice

1. The trial process in juvenile court is referred to as the
    a. jury trial.
    b. adjudicatory hearing.
    c. bench trial.
    d. *Parens patriae* hearing.
2. *Parens patriae* can be roughly defined as
    a. an adjudicatory hearing in juvenile court.
    b. a jury trial procedure in juvenile court.
    c. rights that juvenile has while in custody.
    d. the duty of the state to act as a parent in the interest of the child.
3. Which case below established that a child in a delinquency adjudication proceedings has procedural process constitutional rights?
    a. *Miranda vs. Arizona*
    b. *In re Gault*
    c. *In Parens patriae*
    d. Juveniles are not afforded rights under the constitution

4. Which crime category makes up a major part of the juvenile crime problem?
   a. violent crimes
   b. property offences
   c. drug offences
   d. status offences
5. Which one of the following statements is NOT accurate regarding group home programs?
   a. They are long term in nature.
   b. They allow juveniles much contact with the community.
   c. They are not very cost efficient as an alternative for unruly and delinquent children.
   d. They allow juveniles to attend school and hold jobs.

Endnotes

1. Ralph Weisheit and Diane Alexander, "Juvenile Justice Philosophy and Demise of Parens Patriae," *Federal Probation* (December 1988): 56.
2. Anthony Platt, *The Child Savers* (Chicago: University of Chicago Press, 1969).
3. *In re Gault*, 387 U.S. 1, (1967).
4. 383 U.S. 541 (1966).
5. 421 U.S. 519 (1975).
6. 491 F.2d 1430 (7th Cir., 1974).
7. Howard N. Snyder and Melissa Sickmund, "Juvenile Offenders and Victims: A National Report," U.S. Department of Justice, Office of Justice and Delinquency Prevention, A National Report, 1999.
8. Ibid., 144.
9. Barbara Allen-Hagen, "Conditions of Confinement in Juvenile Detention and Correctional Facilities," *Office of Juvenile Justice and Delinquency Prevention, Fact Sheet #1*, April 1993.
10. Snyder and Sickmund, "Juvenile Offenders and Victims," 51.
11. Ibid., 52.
12. Carl Pope and William Feyerherm, *Minorities in the Juvenile Justice System*. Final Report (Washington, DC: Office of Juvenile Justice and Delinquency Prevention, 1991).
13. Ibid.
14. John N. Ferdico, *Criminal Law and Justice Dictionary* (St. Paul: West, 1992.)
15. Bahram Haghighi and Alma Lopez, "Success/Failure of Group Home Treatment Programs for Juveniles," *Federal Probation* (September 1993). Citations and references have been omitted.
16. Ibid.

Chapter 11

Women and Corrections

Mark C. Ide

Key Terms

Butler v. Reno
Civil Rights Act
cottage system
differential justice
disparate treatment
Dothard v. Rawlinson
Equal Pay Act
gender roles
Girl Scouts Beyond Bars (GSBB)
glass ceiling
reformatory movement
sexism
Title VII

Outline

11-1 Women's Prisons in the United States
11-2 The Early Years
   11-2a Separate Quarters
   11-2b Women's Reformatories
   11-2c Racial Disparities
   11-2d The End of the Reformatory Era
11-3 Women Offenders
11-4 Issues
   11-4a Substance Abuse Treatment
   11-4b Parenting Programs
   11-4c Educational Programs
   11-4d Mental Health Programs
   11-4e Medical Treatment
11-5 Women Correctional Officers
11-6 Problems Facing Women Correctional Officers
   11-6a Job-Related Issues
11-7 History of Women in Corrections
11-8 Progress of Women in the Correctional Field
11-9 Affirmative Action Goals
Summary
Discussion Questions
Chapter Quiz
Endnotes

Learning Objectives

After studying this chapter, the reader will be able to:

- Explain the methods of confinement of women in the early United States prison system.
- Explain the problems that prison administrators historically faced when incarcerating female inmates.
- Explain the concept of the "cottage system."
- Identify what led up to the reformatory movement for women.
- Describe the historical disparate treatment of African American female inmates.
- Describe the historical nature of women offenders.
- Describe the contemporary nature of women offenders.
- Identify the current problems facing prison administrators involving women inmates.
- Explain the significance of parenting programs and why they are important for women inmates.
- Identify the problems facing women correctional officers.
- Analyze the historic criticisms of women correctional officers.
- Explain the advantages of women correctional officers.
- Analyze the history of women employed in the correctional field.

11-1 Women's Prisons in the United States

This chapter discusses an increasingly important issue in corrections: women offenders and women working in the correctional system. First we begin the chapter with a discussion of women's prisons and women offenders; we then devote the second half of the chapter to women working in the correctional field.

Historically, women were confined in separate quarters within the confines of men's prisons. They were for the most part exposed to the same conditions as male prisoners including overcrowding, filth, inmate violence, and unsanitary conditions.[1] In some prisons women were actually confined with men and guarded by male guards, leaving them directly vulnerable to acts of aggression by men. In 1819, the managers of the New York Society for the Prevention of Pauperism described the women's quarters at the Bellevue Penitentiary as "a great school of vice and desperation, replete with prostitutes, vagrants, lunatics, thieves, and those of a less heinous character." What shocked them as much as the indiscriminate mixing of "every kind of female convict" was the lack of attention paid to these outcasts by the more fortunate of their sex.[2]

Prison administrators of the past faced the perplexing problem as to what actually to do with women offenders. There were not a large number of female offenders and those that did offend were usually handled with more lenience when compared with men. Because of the small number of female offenders, there weren't many prisons designed specifically to accommodate women so they were housed either separately in men's quarters or directly with men. In some cases women were kept in total isolation for their personal safety.

Women that were isolated for their safety while in prison were deprived of many of the privileges enjoyed by male inmates such as visitation, exercise, and social interaction and affiliation with other inmates. Once again, it's important to point out that during the early history of American prisons the majority of inmates convicted for crimes and incarcerated were male. The data in Table 11-1, which captures New York criminal convictions from 1830 to 1900, further illustrates this point. Notice the number of females convicted is relatively small compared to male inmates.

TABLE 11-1 New York Criminal Convictions Rates 1830–1900

Courts of Special Sessions

Five Year Period	Courts of Record Male	Courts of Record Female	County Male	County Female	City Male	City Female	Sum of All Courts Male	Sum of All Courts Female	% Change Male	% Change Female
1838–32	166.72	13.97	—	—	—	—	—	—	—	—
1833–37	150.35	10.28	—	—	—	—	—	—	—	—
1838–42	165.06	13.83	297.74	49.34	131,83	35.60	594.63	98.77	—	—
1843–47	164.52	9.21	324.45	55.63	189.09	41.17	678.06	106.01	+14.03	+7.33
1848–52	145.33	8.89	332.66	52.20	267.74	65.10	745.73	126.19	+9.98	+19.04
1853–57	142.57	9.50	477.78	97.10	544.74	230.60	1165.09	337.20	+56.23	+167.22
1858–62	137.23	12.75	678.76	174.41	1376.17	905.20	2192.16	1092.36	+88.15	+223.95
1863–67	143.80	16.09	663.18	211.97	1819.65	1126.93	2626.63	1354.99	+19.82	+24.04
1868–72	153.57	10.38	1176.49	238.68	2228.72	1281.98	3558.78	1531.04	+35.49	+12.99
1873–77	208.64	12.86	1717.63	356.23	2492.57	1157.87	4418.84	1526.96	+24.17	-.27
1878–82	176.79	9.32	1464.19	309.90	2857.92	1187.55	4498.90	1506.77	+1.81	-1.32
1883–87	134.63	7.29	2846.71	655.70	2944.64	1151.24	5925.24	1814.23	+31.72	+20.41
1888–92	150.09	7.08	2729.30	449.82	2594.58	965.75	5473.65	1422.65	-7.63	-21.58
1893–97	155.43	8.06	2599.69	292.00	2785.17	1015.83	5540.29	1315.89	+1.21	-7.50
1898–1902	137.07	8.13	—	—	—	—	—	—	—	—

Source: New York Secretary of State, *Convictions for Criminal Offences, 1830–1899*
Note: Figures represent five-year average conviction rates per 100,000 adults.

11-2 The Early Years

The eighteenth century was an important turning point in America's response to crime. Crime was on the rise, especially in large urban cities that were part of the industrial revolution slowly emerging in America. With the rise of big manufacturing and industrialization, many cities experienced a significant population growth along with increases in crime.

In the 1880s both men and women were confined in the Walnut Street Jail in Philadelphia, and they were not segregated by gender.[3] Women were typically incarcerated for relatively small or minor offences such as begging, larceny, vagrancy, and prostitution.[4] The Walnut Street Jail eventually evolved into the first separate system for male and female inmates. Male and female prisoners were kept in isolation from one another with the exception of performing manual labor during the day. Female prisoners were separated and isolated from the male prisoners for their personal safety; however, the isolated conditions and the fact that female prisoners were virtually cut off from all forms of interaction and social affiliations were in their own sense abusive.

Women early in the history of America were regarded as more pure than men, thus, when women committed relatively minor offenses they were looked upon in a more serious light.[5] To prison administrators women inmates were of great concern and created many dilemmas regarding how best to accommodate them. On the one hand administrators believed female inmates had to be separated in order to prevent sexual mischief and other violence, but on the other hand there were far too few women in prisons to fill a wing of cells.[6] It was common for women prisoners to be locked in large rooms above the guard shack or the mess hall within the confines of a male prison, and left entirely to themselves, vulnerable to attacks from male guards, and secluded from the main population.

11-2a Separate Quarters

By the mid-nineteenth century the increasing rates of women offenders prompted a move to provide them with prison quarters of their own. Women's quarters were often small buildings erected in the corner of the prison yard and fraught with neglect.[7] Prisons across the United States developed a tradition where female facilities received care inferior to that given to their male counterparts. The further the women were removed from the general population, the more they were cut off from prison guards and other prison personnel who only left the main male prison quarters to visit the female housing area in emergencies.[8] In time, matrons were hired to supervise women inmates, and sewing machines and laundry buckets were supplied for their employment. When the female inmate populations outgrew their quarters, many states began to construct female prison departments that were located in close proximity to the male penitentiaries. Through this process, custodial prisons for women began to evolve.[9]

11-2b Women's Reformatories

The **reformatory movement** officially began in 1870 following the historic conference of the National Prison Association. One of the outcomes of the conference was that rehabilitation should be the undercurrent of both men's and women's correctional institutions. Many women's prisons began to appropriately reflect the rehabilitation model by shedding the harsh fortress-type structure of prisons and moving toward a cottage look. It was the underlying thought that the **cottage system** would be more conducive to rehabilitation. The New York Reformatory for Women at Albion is one example of the cottage plan:

> The idea of family life, each cottage with its own kitchen, its pleasant dining-room adjoining, which matrons and girls used in common, and living or sitting room in the second story, where family assemble for diversion.[10]

The Indiana Women's Prison was the first separate prison for women. It was founded by a Quaker couple and opened in 1873. In 1877 Massachusetts built an all-female state reformatory. About this time the progressive women's reformatory at Bedford Hills, New York, was founded by an American Quaker. The women's reformatory at Bedford Hills is an example of the cottage design. The progressive movement advocated many changes in the state of women's prisons and it was instrumental in making significant improvements.

By the late-nineteenth century, nearly all states had opened separate prison units for women. The reformatory movement lasted from about 1860 to 1935 and produced about 21 institutions.

Women's reformatories were modeled on a domestic venue rejecting much of the punishment orientation of the male custodial prison environment. Moreover, the late-nineteenth century women's prison reformers adopted the philosophy of rehabilitation almost exclusively. Nicole Hahn Rafter eloquently describes the new women's prison movement:

> Unwalled institutions, women's reformatories architecturally expressed their founders' beliefs that women, because more tractable, required fewer constraints than men. Rejecting large congregate buildings, women's reformatories came to adopt the "cottage" plan, holding groups of twenty or so inmates in small buildings where they could live with a motherly matron in a familial setting.[11]

Women's reformatories encouraged femininity, sexual restraint, genteel demeanor, and domesticity.

The new reformatories were also staffed by women with the objective to correct women's moral behavior. The typical inmate confined to a reformatory was described as a young, white girl of working-class background, and her crime was typically little more than sexual independence. In many instances women were sentenced to the reformatories for various sexual misgivings, including pregnancy outside of marriage and unlawful sexual intercourse.

11-2c Racial Disparities

Not all women received the benefits of the reformatory model of incarceration with its emphasis on rehabilitation. Some women who were placed in the custodial prisons, mostly African American women, suffered from filthy conditions and the harshness of prison violence inflicted by male guards. African American women were sentenced to custodial prisons even in light of their offenses being petty in nature. Judges justified these racist practices by alleging that African American women were not as morally developed as white women.

African American women were, as a matter of routine, sentenced by judges to custodial prisons, including the atrocious custodial plantation prisons of the South while white girls who committed the same offenses were sent to reformatories. It is well documented that in many cases judges outright refused to send white women to the custodial prisons while almost always sentencing African American women to custodial prisons.[12] Social scientists have referred to these practices as differential justice. **Differential justice** is a term used to suggest that whites are dealt with more leniently when compared with African Americans, whether at time of arrest, indictment, conviction, sentencing, or parole.

Before 1865, African American women entered the prisons of the Northeast and Midwest in numbers grossly disproportionate to their representation in the general populations of these regions.[13] It is clear that racism continued to powerfully influence prisoner populations in the United States after the Civil War. The proportions of African Americans, including African American women, continuously swelled in the prisons of the Northeast and Midwest. However, racist criminal justice practices were most obvious in Southern states. For years after the Civil War, previously white prisons of the South became engorged with newly freed African Americans, while whites were routinely screened out of Southern prisons.[14] The mentality of many Southern states was that African American female offenders were not as worthy of the same chivalry extended to white females.[15] A North Carolina report of 1922 described one institution as being so horrible that the judge refused to send white women to this jail, but African American women were sometimes sent.[16]

11-2d The End of the Reformatory Era

By 1935, the women's reformatory movement had all but ended and it was at this time that reformatories began to merge with custodial prisons. The reformatory movement had, for the most part, achieved its goals of reform, particularly in those states in the Northeast and Midwest, and it produced a few reforms, although slow and resistant, in the South and West. Evidence of the "cottage system," which was advocated during the reformatory movement, is still evident in many state prisons.

As women offenders, over time, were sentenced to prison for more serious crimes and began to offend in larger numbers than in the past, there was a gradual shift back toward the custodial philosophy of incarceration. The 1960s and 1970s brought renewed interest in the treatment of women inmates in the prison system, largely as a result of civil rights legislation and by protests from women's and feminist advocacy groups.

Since the 1980s, the number of women incarcerated in the U.S. prison system has increased, largely due to the war on drugs. Female minorities have been adversely affected by the war on drugs largely because of the disparity in sentencing in crack cocaine versus powder cocaine. The media have also played a role in the sensationalizing of crime and the war on drugs, which increased the public's fear and demand for tougher sentences. Subsequently, since the 1980s, we have witnessed a period of massive retrenchment of social services and a punishment-oriented prison system for not only male offenders but also women offenders.

Construction of women's prisons increased after 1973 and more prisons were built for women than for men. For example, about 60 new women's prisons were built from the 1970s through the 1990s. Likewise, there were more prisons built to accommodate women than there were for men between 1973 and 1998.

11-3 Women Offenders

The number of women incarcerated in state and federal prisons in the United States has grown substantially. Since 1990, the female prisoner population has doubled. For the one-year period of 2000 to 2001, the number of women under the jurisdiction of the state or federal prison authorities grew from 93,681 to 94,336, an increase of 0.7 percent.[17] In 2000, there were known to be an annual average of about 2.1 million violent female offenders. Three out of four violent female offenders commit simple assault and an estimated 28 percent of violent female offenders are juveniles.[18]

In 1998 about 3.2 million women were arrested in the United States for various crimes. An estimated 4 in 10 women who commit violent crimes are under the influence of alcohol and/or drugs at the time the crime was committed. Since 1990, the number of female defendants convicted of felonies in state courts has grown at more than twice the rate of increases for male defendants. In 2001, Texas had the most women offenders incarcerated (13,328) followed by California (10,926). Alaska incarcerated the fewest women offenders (328) followed by Montana (321).[19] As the twentieth century came to a close, about 950,000 women were under the care, custody, or control of correctional agencies, a rate of about one out of every 109 adult women. Figure 11-1 depicts the number persons under the correctional supervision and compares male and female custody data from 1986 to 1997. As you examine Figure 11-1 note the significant increases in the number of incarcerated females compared to the increases of male inmates.

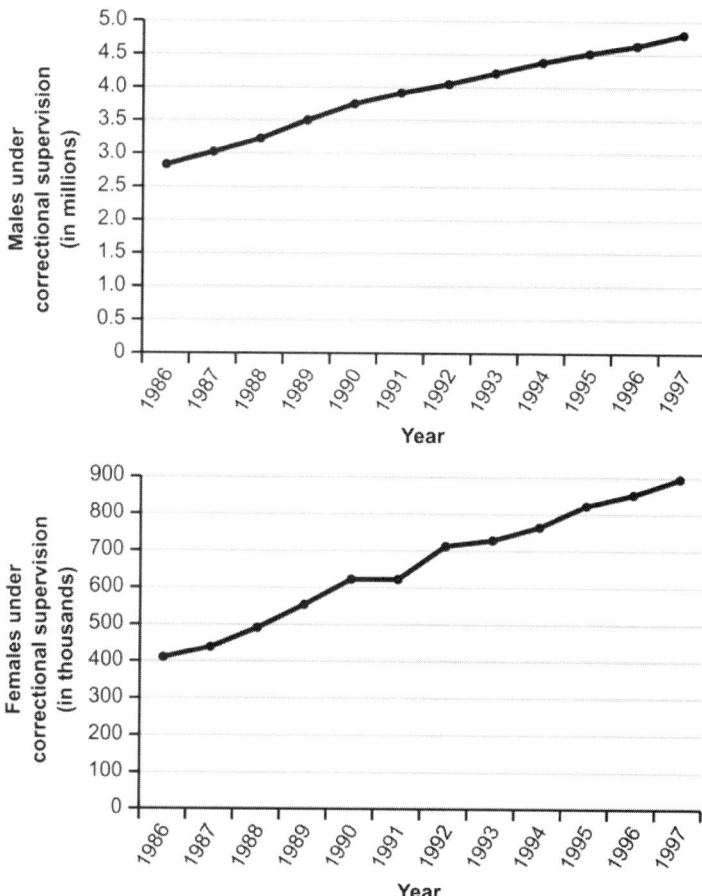

Figure 11-1
Number of Persons under Correctional Supervision by Gender from 1986 to 1997
Source: Bureau of Justice Statistics, 1997.

When demographics are taken into account, black and white offenders accounted for nearly equal proportions of women committing robbery and aggravated assault; however, simple assault offenders were more likely to be white.[20] The racial and ethnic composition of the general population aged 10 or older varies slightly when males and females are compared. For example, black females outnumber black males by nearly 1.9 million, accounting for more than a quarter of the total difference in the number of males and females in the general population. Minorities disproportionately compose a slightly higher percentage of the female prison population when compared with the male minority prison population.

According to the Bureau of Justice Statistics, since 1993 both male and female rates of committing murder have declined. Rates of committing murder in 1998 were the lowest since statistics were first collected in 1976. The estimated rate for murder offenses by women in 1998 was 1.3 per 100,000, about one murder for every 77,000 women. The male rate of murder offenses in 1998 was 11.5 per 100,000, about one murder for every 8,700 males.[21] In 1996 the average sentence and time served for women were shorter than for males with equivalent offenses.

Among violent female offenders, 53 percent committed the offense while alone, and 40 percent were with others, all of whom were female. When compared with male offenders, 47 percent were alone, and 51 percent with other males when the offense occurred. About 8 percent of violent female offenders committed their offense together with at least one male offender; by contrast, about 1 percent of male violent offenders committed the offense in the company of a female offender. Table 11-2 presents data on violent female offenders.

TABLE **11-2** Characteristics of Violent Female Offenders (1999)

Offense (%)	Race of Female Offenders		
	White (%)	Black (%)	Other (%)
Violent Offenses	55	35	11
Robbery	43	43	14
Aggravated Assault	45	46	10
Simple Assault	58	31	10

Source: Bureau of Justice Statistics, December 1999

11-4 Issues

Even given the increases of women incarcerated in the U.S. prison system, women make up a relatively small portion of the nation's prison population. Women incarceration rates tend to be much lower than men—51 out of 100,000 women versus 819 out of 100,000 men.[22] However, the numbers of women in the nation's jails and prisons appear to be growing at a faster rate than the numbers of men. In light of these increases there are a number of special concerns that center on women inmates. Simply put, the needs of women in prison are quite different than the needs of men, in part because of women's disproportionate victimization from sexual and/or physical abuse and for their responsibility for children.[23]

Many women who enter prison have suffered from either sexual or physical abuse and prison administrators should be prepared to provide adequate counseling and support for these women. Women offenders are also more likely than men to have become addicted to drugs, to have mental illness, and to have been unemployed before incarceration.[24]

Many incarcerated women have children and some are pregnant when they enter prison. A National Institute of Justice report revealed that women under the supervision of justice system agencies were mothers of an estimated 1.3 million minor children, that is, children whose mothers are either in prison or on probation or parole. This is important because studies have shown that children whose family members have been imprisoned are at a greater risk to be imprisoned than other children.[25]

The U.S. Bureau of Justice Statistics survey of state prison inmates reported some important findings that illustrate the special needs that women inmates pose for prison officials:

- More than 43 percent of women inmates (but only 12 percent of men) said they had been physically or sexually abused before their admission to prison.
- Women serving a sentence for a violent offense were about twice as likely as their male counterparts to have committed their offense against someone close to them.
- More than two-thirds of all women in prison had children under the age of 18, and among them only 25 percent (versus 90 percent for the men) said their children were living with the other parent.
- Women in prison used more drugs and used those drugs more frequently than men. About 54 percent used drugs in the month before their current offense, compared with 50 percent for the men.[26]

It is important that prison officials provide the same services for females as they provide for male inmates. The different circumstances, together with the general rise in the number of incarcerated women, point to the need for different management and operational approaches as well as different programming to ensure parity and to provide interventions that reduce recidivism.[27] Unfortunately, this has not always been the case.

In 1995 the U.S. District Court in the case of **Butler v. Reno** ruled in favor of a group of federal female inmates who sued the federal prison system. The female plaintiffs made their argument based on gender discrimination by the Federal Bureau of Prisons. The lawsuit alleged that female inmates were denied access to facilities, materials, and other programs that were available for male inmates but not for female inmates. The U.S. Court in the District of Columbia stipulated an order of settlement in which the parties were in agreement that the Federal Bureau of Prisons would provide comparable programs for female inmates. A few of the programs included maintaining similar staff-inmate ratios, providing work within the prison, comparable health care to male inmates, educational programs, parent–child programs, and recreational opportunities.

11-4a Substance Abuse Treatment

The increased presence of women in U.S. prisons has been accompanied by a growing recognition that a substantial proportion of these women enter the system because of their involvement with drugs. During the last decade, both drug offenses by women and the proportion of female offenders who are substance abusers increased significantly. This population of offenders continues to increase despite the increase in deterrents and tough crackdowns on drug offenders. In 1994, 67 percent of women inmates entering the prison system tested positive for drugs.[28] Lifetime prevalence rates of alcohol abuse and drug dependency disorders also reveal that female arrestees are more likely than male arrestees to be diagnosed with substance abuse disorders.[29]

The unique needs of women inmates, along with the increased drug abuse and drug-related arrests of female offenders, have prompted changes in correctional programming for this population. Prison officials now have to ensure that women inmates have the treatment and medical and mental health services to assist those who have substance abuse problems. Drug and alcohol abuse continues to be the most common disorder among female offenders and many prisons are offering drug education. In many cases the first time a female offender goes through any type of detoxification period is in a jail or prison.

11-4b Parenting Programs

Recall that a majority of female inmates are mothers, and as such have many special program needs. The Bureau of Justice Statistics reports that about 78 percent of female inmates have children, most of whom are under the age of 18.[30] With each mother having an average of 2.5 children, there are now close to a quarter-million children whose mothers are incarcerated.[31] One of every four adult women in prison is pregnant at the time of incarceration or has given birth at some point during the previous year.[32] When a mother with children is sent to prison the impact on the family structure can be devastating. Moreover, the socialization and stigma on the part of the children can create dysfunction.

Studies have consistently shown that the absence of women from the family is far more devastating on children than the absence of men. Mothers play a significant role in the development of the physical and emotional health of their children. From birth, mothers are often the ones who encourage the first smiles, words, and steps from their babies. Mothers are traditionally the ones who provide the unconditional love babies need to develop strong relationships with others. For incarcerated mothers, developing and maintaining any type of meaningful relationships with their children is difficult.

The ability of a mother developing a healthy relationship with her children has particularly been devastating on African American mothers. Reports indicate that the criminal justice control rates for young African American women have increased significantly. One sentencing project study reports that from 1989 to 1994, the number of incarcerated African American women increased some 78 percent, at a rate greater than any other demographic group. This was more than double the increase for African American men and for white women and more than nine times the increases for white men.[33]

The disturbing disparity in the number of young African American women has prompted many to call for reform in sentencing laws that may be biased toward African American women, particularly mandatory drug law sentencing guidelines. Mandatory sentencing requires judges to impose a specified length of sentence for certain crimes or categories of offenders taking away almost all discretion from the judge during sentencing. Most states and the federal government have now established some form of sentencing guidelines. Studies at the federal and state levels indicate that African Americans and Hispanics are more likely than whites to be given mandatory sentences or receive enhanced sentences under habitual offender laws.[34] The problem here is that a large percentage of these inmates have children, exemplifying the importance of parenting programs for incarcerated women.

In the past, parenting programs have not been prevalent in U.S. prisons. The increase of incarcerated women has prompted many prisons to implement parenting skills programs. Recent studies have found that approximately 84 percent of prison systems offer incarcerated women some form of parenting programming.[35]

Prison administrators face a number of challenges when developing programs aimed at maintaining ties between incarcerated mothers and their children. In many cases, the prison environment and distance discourage visits from children and their guardians. Moreover, agency visiting policies, which in large part are designed for male facilities, may place limitations on what can be done specifically for visitation in women's institutions, especially when wardens are not allowed to modify policies and practices to meet the needs of incarcerated women.

There are some innovative prison programs that have minimized the effects that incarceration has on the children of incarcerated women. For example, two states (Nebraska and New York) operate nurseries for children. Both of these programs stress the development of nurturing behavior by the mother and provide parenting classes for women to learn and practice positive child-rearing skills. The Nebraska program also includes overnight visits for older children.[36] It is programs such as these that must continue to be implemented and expanded if we are to ensure that a disproportionately large number of children whose mothers are incarcerated receive the most appropriate nurturing possible in light of the incarcerated state of their mothers.

The Bedford Hills, New York, Correctional Facility houses a nursery, where babies of women involved in the prison programs are cared for until they are one year old. When there is certitude that mother and baby can live together, an extension to 18 months is granted. The nursery promotes parenting skills and serves the infant living at the institution and the inmates' children living outside the prison. Approximately 75 mothers are involved with the Children's Center at one time and over a one-year period it serves 700 women. Most women are involved in the program from 1 to 5 days each week. The purpose of the program is to help inmates learn to be mothers with a special focus on meeting the women's mental health needs. Other focus areas are relationships with family, transition to the community, and parenting.

Some facilities have camps for children and their mothers to encourage bonding. The Pocatello Women's Correctional Center in Idaho sponsors a camp for women who have gone through the facility's parenting program. The camp is an excellent example of cooperation and collaboration between the facility and a variety of other agencies and groups, including the local hospital, churches, and the university, which have formed partnerships to ensure program success.[37]

One other program that deals with the issue of separation of mothers from their children is the 1994 Family Unity Demonstration Project that was passed by Congress as part of the Violent Crime Control and Law Enforcement Act. This project was designed to house eligible female offenders and their children under seven years of age in residential facilities that were not within the confines of a jail or prison and that would prove a safe and stable environment for children. Eligible parents for the program include nonviolent offenders with no history of abusing or neglecting a child, facing or sentenced to a term of not more than seven years, who acted as a primary caretaker of the child prior to incarceration or had just given birth and were willing to assume this role. The goal of the Family Unity Demonstration Project is laudable, but moot because Congress never funded the project.[38] The paradox here is that funding for additional prisons continues to escalate while programs with the objectives of rehabilitation and the prevention of recidivism are not deemed important.

The National Institute of Justice sponsors an innovative program titled: **Girl Scouts Beyond Bars (GSBB),** which is currently operating in 11 jurisdictions. The GSBB originated in a Maryland women's prison, met much success, and is being replicated in several other states including Arizona, Delaware, Florida, Kentucky, New Jersey, and Ohio.

The GSBB program entails Girl Scout daughters visiting their mothers in prison on a regular basis. During the twice-a-month visits they work together with their mothers on Girl Scout projects and engage in a variety of general interactions. Topics range from aerobics to math and science activities to arts and crafts. The frequency and regularity of these visits by these girls are much greater than for other inmate mothers whose daughters are not in the GSBB program. The cost of transporting the girls to the prison facility are borne partly by the appropriate Girl Scout councils and charitable organizations, with the National Institute of Justice providing funding for start-up and demonstration projects.[39]

The following data are offered to further illustrate the need and urgency for women offenders to maintain and strengthen ties with their children:

- 25 percent of women admitted to prison are pregnant or have recently delivered a child.
- 74 percent of women in prison have children, compared to 64 percent of men.
- Incarceration of a mother disrupts the family considerably more than incarceration of a father.
- 25 percent of incarcerated women's children live with grandparents and 10 percent are in foster care.
- 90 percent of incarcerated women have contact with their children while in prison, compared to 80 percent of incarcerated men.
- More than 50 percent of incarcerated women with children under 18 never have visits from their children.
- The majority of women believe they will have responsibility for their children upon release.[40]

Some research has focused on attitudes of female inmates toward the idea of allowing children in the prison environment. These studies have found that women in prison, regardless of whether they personally have children, respond favorably to the presence of children. It was revealed that many women made an attempt to clean up their language and behavior when children were present, and that they enjoyed playing and talking with the children.[41]

11-4c Educational Programs

Educational programs for incarcerated women are important. If incarcerated women are given the opportunity to complete their basic high school studies, take a few college courses, or learn a new vocational skill, their chances of gaining employment when released from prison improve significantly.

Although correctional education has a long history and was established with the first prison in 1798, educational programs have not always been seen as a priority in prison budgets. On the average, more females than males participate in educational programs in the federal system. In 1996, 47 percent of female inmates, compared to 29 percent of male inmates, participated in one or more educational programs while in prison.[42]

The federal prison system is very innovative in their approach to offering educational programs for inmates. The Federal Bureau of Prisons (BOP) has mandated a general educational development program for its facilities. Inmates who enter the BOP system without a high school diploma or general equivalency diploma (GED) are required to attend literacy classes for 120 days or until they achieve a GED. A recent BOP study concludes that participation in prison educational programs greatly reduces the likelihood of recidivism.

Vocational programs are also important in the sense that they provide the opportunity for women inmates to learn a new job skill. A Bureau of Justice Statistics survey in 1991 found that female inmates were significantly less likely than male inmates to be employed at the time of arrest (47 percent females employed versus 68 percent males).[43] There is an increasing need to provide women inmates with job skills and good work habits. This is especially important because when many female inmates are released from prison, they most often fall into the role of providing support for their families.[44]

The American Correctional Association has deemed the education of inmates an important goal for United State's prisons. Many correctional agencies are striving to become nationally accredited institutions. As part of their accreditation, the prison is required to initiate and maintain educational and job training programs for inmates. With standards for national accreditation of correctional institutions it is now appropriate that institutions make available to inmates programs that (1) provide a program to improve communication skills; (2) provide general education; (3) provide basic academic skills; (4) provide GED preparation; (5) provide vocational training; (6) provide postsecondary education; and (7) provide other educational programs as dictated by the needs of the population.[45]

It has been suggested that standards should require that academic and vocational programs be recognized, certified, or licensed by the state department of education or other agencies having jurisdiction.[46] Because of the discrimination that women still suffer in our society it is important that they have the opportunity for educational and vocational pursuits while incarcerated which may assist them with employment opportunities upon their release.

11-4d Mental Health Programs

Women inmates, as a whole, have higher rates of mood disorders and substance abuse or dependency when compared to the general population. Studies have found that women in prison who are treated for substance abuse disorders, personality disorders, anxiety disorders, and mood disorders have reduced recidivism rates.[47] Treatment of drug and alcohol abuse and post-traumatic stress disorder are the most common disorders among female inmates followed by borderline personality disorder.[48] The borderline personality disorder is experienced in the individual most often by her emotions overwhelming her cognitive functioning and thinking.[49]

Mental health screening is not only a requirement, but also an essential aspect of the prison classification system. One study found a clear connection between the size of the inmate population and the frequency of mental health screening.[50] For example, 12 states with more than 1,000 incarcerated women reported screening all of the female inmates for mental disorders. States with 500 to 999 incarcerated women reportedly screened 91 percent of the female inmates, states with 100 to 499 reportedly screened 62 percent.[51]

Currently there is a lack of adequate programs that fully address the mental health needs of women inmates. The problem with nurturing and sustaining sound mental health programs in prisons is that they are not appropriately funded. Nevertheless, prison officials should offer the proper mental health services needed to effectively treat women offenders. Programs should include treatment for substance abuse, general and specific mental health issues, and treatment programs dealing with other forms of abuse, including domestic and sexual abuse. Mental health programs that focus on empowering women offenders and developing a personal sense of responsibility on the part of the inmates offer promising hope in reducing recidivism. Empowering programs are designed to focus on the woman's strengths and not her weaknesses, and to provide a vast amount of peer support.

11-4e Medical Treatment

Women inmates pose unique medical needs when compared to males. For example, women often need gynecological examinations and prenatal and postnatal care. Historically, most prison health care programs have been designed for largely a male clientele and are usually operated by an all male medical staff. We cannot underscore enough the importance of the unique medical needs of women, especially urban minority women whose needs are usually more intensive and difficult than those of their male counterparts. Behavior that often leads to incarceration, such as intravenous drug use, violence, and prostitution, places women inmates at high risks for HIV, tuberculosis, and hepatitis.[52]

Women offenders, especially minority women, have the highest rates of HIV infection and associated tuberculosis, far exceeding rates for male offenders.[53] Consider a recent report in New York that reveals mortality among incarcerated women remains more than twice that of women in the same age group in the community.[54] In 1997 an estimated 2,220 women serving time in state prisons were HIV positive, about 3.5 percent of the female inmate population. The percentage of the female inmate population that was HIV-positive peaked in 1993 at 4.2 percent.

What further exacerbates the problem of providing appropriate health care to female inmates is that most of them have rarely received medical or dental care prior to incarceration. Health problems that have previously gone untreated have grown more serious. For example, the health problems facing African Americans are complicated by the evidence that they receive less medical care than do whites with similar medical conditions. Studies presented by the American Medical Association in 1994 reported that African Americans and whites receive different levels of health care. In addition, studies of Medicare patients found that African Americans and low-income people of all races received less care than affluent whites.[55] In part, this may be one factor for a substantial number of prison inmates, both male and female, having a higher level of medical needs than the general population.

The medical needs of the female inmate population are expected to increase over the next decade. Furthermore, the increase of elderly female prisoners, longer prison sentences, and a greater number of inmates entering into the prison system with infectious diseases will continue to make health care a priority of prison administrators. These problems are further complicated by the rising cost of health care in general, and the associated cost for prescription medication for inmates. All of this comes at a time when prison administrators are pressured to reduce operating costs and do more with less.

There is an abundance of literature addressing the unique needs of women inmates. Many correctional authorities and experts have presented recommendations aimed at improving the quality of life for incarcerated women. We conclude this section with a number of recommendations made by some corrections experts. As you will note, many of these recommendations were underscored in our previous discussion on the unique needs of women in prison.

1. Institute training programs that would enable imprisoned women to become literate.
2. Provide female offenders with programs that do not center on traditional gender roles; programs that will lead to more economic independence and self-sufficiency.
3. Establish additional programs that would engender more positive self-esteem for imprisoned women and enhance their assertiveness and their communications and interpersonal skills.
4. Establish additional programs that would allow imprisoned mothers to interact more with their children and assist them in overcoming feelings of guilt and shame for having deserted their children. In addition, visitation areas for mothers and children should be altered to minimize the effect of a prison-type environment.
5. Allow imprisoned mothers to spend more time with their children outside of the prison as an alternative to mother/child interaction behind prison bars.
6. Provide imprisoned mothers with training to improve parenting skills.
7. Establish more programs to treat drug-addicted female offenders.
8. Establish a community partnership program to provide imprisoned women with employment opportunities.
9. Establish a better classification system for incarcerated women, one that would not permit less hardened offenders to be in the same area with hardened female offenders.

10. Provide in-service training (sensitivity awareness) to assist staff members (wardens, correctional officers) in understanding the nature and needs of incarcerated women.[56]

11-5 Women Correctional Officers

Women correctional officers have suffered from the same social obstacles that are found in many other male-dominated professions such as policing and firefighting. Discriminatory employment practices against women by correctional agencies have restricted women to jobs that involve the processing and maintaining custody of female and juvenile prisoners.

As we settle into the twenty-first century, women still face discrimination and hostile environments in the corrections field and some have made the indictment that little has changed in the opportunities for women in the correctional field and that the glass ceiling is still in place. The phrase **glass ceiling** refers to the invisible barrier blocking the promotion of a qualified worker because of gender or minority membership.

In August 2002, 15 female prison guards in Hartford, Connecticut, filed lawsuits against officials of the State Department of Corrections, claiming that prison administrators did not do enough to stop sexual harassment by male co-workers. The female officers are also accusing male guards of watching pornographic movies while on duty and that one female guard was asked to work as a prostitute for a male guard's prostitution ring. It is also alleged that the department of corrections is brimming with men who regularly and routinely sexually harass, intimidate, and retaliate against the department's female employees.

11-6 Problems Facing Women Correctional Officers

Is sexual harassment and intimidation common for women corrections officers or are cases such as the one in Connecticut isolated? It is undeniable that women do have a problematic environment in the corrections profession. Women correctional officers suffer and have suffered discrimination and **disparate treatment** as they forge an identity into the correctional field. Gender inequity in the workplace is deeply ingrained and makes it difficult for women to overcome many traditional obstacles. Research is clear that women who enter male-dominated occupations almost unanimously face discrimination in hiring, promotion, assignment polices, opposition, and sexual harassment from male co-workers, as well as inadequacies in job training and socialization.[57]

11-6a Job-Related Issues

Some argue that women cannot perform the physical demands of the corrections officer job. These arguments, which are most often made by male correctional officers, go something like this: "Women are too small and weak to come to my aid which makes them vulnerable to inmate assault, and I'll have to risk my neck to bail them out more often."[58] Other objections to female guards are that women are too timid, afraid, emotional, and naive to handle inmates effectively. However, these objections are without merit and women have clearly demonstrated courage and presence of mind under pressure to perform in critical situations just as well as their male co-workers.[59] These objections may in part be explained by the presence of the traditional gender roles that society identifies for women. **Gender roles** are society's expectations of the proper behavior, attitudes, and activities of males and females.[60] For example, toughness has traditionally been seen in the United States as masculine and desirable only in men, while tenderness has been viewed as feminine. Additionally, the support role has traditionally been identified with men while women were viewed as the dependent person who stayed home and performed domestic duties.

Some argue that male inmates may sexually attack women officers and that women officers working in men's housing units would spark romantic involvement with staff and inmates.[61] Once again, these concerns are without merit and may be used as a ploy to keep women out of the corrections field.

It is encouraging that the majority of correctional agencies in the twenty-first century recognize that gender is not a factor in an officer's job performance in the prison environment. The archaic thought that the most effective corrections officer is the one that has brute size and strength is without much support or merit. Brute size and strength is neither a requirement nor a predictor of effective job performance in a correctional institution. The more important attribute is likely the ability to think clearly in stressful situations, and perhaps more importantly, the ability to communicate both interpersonally and verbally. This is evident in the correctional officer training curriculum, which entails a significant amount of classroom hours covering interpersonal communications skills and verbal communication skills. Highly effective correctional officers possess enthusiasm, good communication skills, good judgment, a sense of humor, self-direction, and knowledge of the job and system.

There is some evidence that suggests that female correctional officers actually have a positive effect on the prison environment. For example, it is believed that male prisoners are less likely to become hostile and aggressive toward female officers compared to male officers. Studies also reveal that male inmates claim that women officers treat them better and that a woman's presence substantially improves the prison environment.[62] Some of the earliest research on women working in adult male correctional institutions has pointed out several advantages.

1. The presence of females adds a degree of normalcy to an unreal environment for incarcerated males.
2. Men are more careful in behavior and personal grooming. Females foster self-imposed social control among male inmates.
3. The presence of women relieves boredom and creates feelings of pleasantness.
4. Allowing females to work in corrections makes men feel that the administration trusts them more, and they respond more positively.
5. Tensions are relieved; the presence of women constitutes a release valve.
6. Male inmates seem to appreciate education more and work harder to achieve under a female teacher.
7. Females are a connection with the outside. They evoke positive memories of other women outside.
8. The presence of women aids inmates in retaining their masculine identity. They are treated more as individuals, and given care, understanding, and respect.
9. Women provide a boost in morale.
10. Many inmates develop new images of women as professionals. Some have never been around well-adjusted females.[63]

Because of the disparate treatment and perhaps sexism practices by male guards and inmates alike, women have not been able to fully and routinely fill existing guard roles in male prisons.[64] **Sexism** refers to the ideology that one sex is superior to the other. The lack of an established female guard role model for women exacerbates this problem. In order to conceptually understand the problem that women face in fully evolving into the correctional occupation, we turn to a brief examination of their history in the field.

11-7 History of Women in Corrections

Prior to 1972, the practice of hiring only men to work as prison guards was common and usually unquestioned. Similarly, women were excluded from most jobs in the criminal justice profession and women that were employed in the field were assigned to menial job tasks and duties. For example, police departments usually used women police officers to supervise female arrestees, handle juvenile matters, and perform many clerical duties. Women probation officers were restricted to supervising only female and juvenile offenders. In prisons, women were only employed in all women's institutions, where an inmate's isolation from men was considered necessary for rehabilitation.[65]

Historically, few women have held executive positions in the corrections field. In 1793, Mary Weed became the first known female correctional administrator in the United States. She was the appointed warden of the Walnut Street Jail in Philadelphia. Mary Weed was known for her humane administration over men and women inmates alike, which contrasted the prevailing brutal and harsh treatment that inmates usually received.[66] The historical records reflect that during Mary Weed's tenure was the only time a warden was not accused of malfeasance in office or misappropriation of funds.[67] It should be pointed out that Mary Weed was a correctional administrator during a time when women in the corrections field were almost unheard of. In fact, before 1861, women correctional workers were almost non-existent.

Women slowly gained authority over public institutions that housed women offenders, and by the end of the eighteenth century, women began to increasingly, (however in small numbers) be employed in the growing field of corrections. Women became administrators and jail matrons in women's prisons as well as juvenile detention facilities.[68] In the late eighteenth and early nineteenth centuries, women were able to enter the corrections field only if they emphasized womanly qualities.[69] Middle-class women held the professional jobs of reforming women from the lower classes. The prevailing thought at the time was that women from the middle class possessed an inherently emotional and sympathetic nature that prepared them to work as professional role models for fallen women.[70]

As you will recall previously in the chapter, by around 1900 separate women's prisons were a reality in many states. This success was partially due to their increasing resemblance to men's prisons and the reliance on programs that conformed to the middle-class gender stereotypes.[71] From 1900 to 1920, progressive women reformers tried unsuccessfully to drop sexual distinctions and to diversify training. Although reformers did not specify new categories of work for women in corrections, their strategies reinforced culturally emphasized images of femininity, which limited women's work opportunities.[72]

The disparate treatment of women in the corrections field continued for many years. From the 1930s to 1970s, women primarily worked as probation and parole officers for women offenders only.[73] Women were also allowed to work as volunteers and as clerical staff in correctional institutions but were rarely allowed to supervise male inmates. During this time period, women's work in corrections was usually characterized by tedious jobs that entailed many long hours and low pay. According to corrections experts, women prison matrons became second-class citizens in prison systems that were usually planned and carried out exclusively around the demands of men's prisons.[74]

Some women, however, made laudatory strides in the corrections field in spite of the prevalence of discrimination and disparate treatment. In 1863, Edna Mahan, superintendent of the New Jersey Reformatory for Women was the first women to receive the American Correctional Association's achievement award.[75] Grace Oliver Peck, who chaired the Oregon's Institutions Committee and worked most of her career from around 1956 through 1976, successfully modernizing the entire Oregon correctional system.

11-8 Progress of Women in the Correctional Field

The progress and advancements of women in the corrections profession has only slowly come to light in the past two or three decades. The **Equal Pay Act** of 1963 (EPA) prohibits discrimination in wages on the basis of gender for all employees and labor organizations. The **Civil Rights Act** of 1964 and 1970 prohibits race discrimination in hiring, placement, and continuation of employment for all private employers, unions, and employment agencies. **Title VII** of the Civil Right Act of 1964, as amended by the Equal Opportunity Act (EEOC) of 1972, prohibits discrimination based on race, color, religion, gender, or national origin for private employers with 15 or more employees, governments, unions, and employment agencies.

The first case involving women as correctional employees to reach the Supreme Court in 1977 was ***Dothard v. Rawlinson*** (433 U.S. 321). In this case, a 22-year-old female college graduate with a major in correctional psychology sought and was denied a job as a prison guard in the Alabama prison system because she did not meet the 120 pound weight or 5′2″ minimum height requirements. She attacked both those requirements as well as Alabama's Administrative Regulation 204 that established gender-based criteria for "contact positions" in maximum-security institutions. The Court summarized employment at the correctional facility at the time of the litigation as follows:

> [T]he Board of Corrections employed a total of 435 people in various correctional counselor positions, 56 of whom were women. Of these 56 women 21 were employed at the Julia Tutwiler Prison for Women, 13 were employed in non-contact positions at the four male maximum-security institutions, and the remaining 22 were employed at the other institutions operated by the Alabama Board of Corrections. Because most of Alabama's prisoners are held at the four maximum security male penitentiaries, 336 of the 435 correctional counselor jobs were in those institutions, a majority of them concededly in the "contact" classification. Thus, even though meeting the statutory height and weight requirements, women applicants could under Regulation 204 compete with men for only about 25% of the correctional counselor jobs available in the Alabama prison system.[76]

The Court also noted that when the height and weight restrictions are combined, Alabama's statutory standards would exclude 41.13 percent of the female population while excluding less than 1 percent of the male population. Because these requirements had a discriminatory impact in the women applicants, the Court concluded that plaintiffs had established a prima facie Title VII violation. The Board of Corrections produced no evidence to show that the height and weight requirements were job related, so they may not be applied.

The Court then turned to Regulation 204, which explicitly made sex a basis for prison assignments and was therefore a clear case of disparate treatment of a protected group. The Corrections Board, argued that the regulation was permitted by 703(e) of Title VII as a "bona fide occupational qualification" reasonably necessary to the normal operation of that particular business or enterprise.

Because of the impact of the *Dothard v. Rawlinson* court decision women began to be employed as corrections officers in larger numbers across the country. However, it should be recognized that this would not have been possible without a number of other legal decisions throughout the 1970s that further assisted women in entering in larger numbers into the corrections field.

Several commissions formed in the 1970s advocated increasing women's role in corrections. The Joint Commission on Correctional Manpower and Training recommended that opportunities for women in correctional work be expanded and that women be used to their maximum potential.[77] In 1976, the American Correctional Association adopted the following policy statement.

> The American Correctional Association adopts affirmative action as a commitment to an ongoing process which will ensure equal employment opportunities and employment conditions for minorities and women in correctional employment.

The National Advisory Commission on Criminal Justice Standards and Goals established the following standards:

> Correctional agencies should immediately develop policies and implement practices to recruit and hire more women for all types of positions in corrections to include the following:
>
> 1. Change in correctional agency policies to eliminate discrimination against women for correctional work;
> 2. Provision for lateral entry to allow immediate placement of women in administrative positions;
> 3. Development of better criteria for selection of staff for correctional work, removing unreasonable obstacles to employment of women; and
> 4. Assumption by the personnel system of aggressive leadership in giving women a full role in corrections.[78]

According to the 1998 edition of *The Corrections Yearbook* there has been notable progress in the increase of women employed as correctional guards in adult male facilities. The percentage of women employed in community corrections is significant, because women represent more than one-half of all employees in parole and probation agencies. Women currently comprise 21.7 percent of all correctional officers. The percentage of female correctional officers has increased from 16.5 percent in 1990 to 21.7 percent in 1998, and this percentage is expected to continue to increase.[79]

Women are also making a modest impact at the top level of U.S. Corrections. The American Correctional Association has had two women serve as their president in the 1990s. Also, Kathleen Hawk Sawyer was appointed Director of the Federal Bureau of Prisons on December 4, 1992. She is a career public administrator in the Federal Bureau of Prisons and the sixth Director of the Bureau since its establishment in 1930.

Although the progress of women in correctional career fields is grounds for optimism in many respects, there is still much work to be done to ensure that not only women but also persons of color have equal opportunities for employment and advancement in the correctional field. Women can perform all aspects of the job in corrections just as well as their male counterparts. Unfortunately, workplace discrimination continues to make it difficult for women who choose careers in nontraditional jobs, thus making it more likely for women to leave their jobs.

There are both the obvious and not so obvious manners in which women are treated differently in the workplace. For example some of the disparate treatment has been documented as:

- Lack of acceptance by male supervisors and co-workers.
- Not getting proper training and not being allowed to learn all aspects of the job.
- Being given tools and equipment that aren't sized for women, which may be complicated by unfamiliarity with tools.
- Being assigned the heaviest, dirtiest, or most menial tasks.
- Isolation on the worksite, including limited access to mentoring and to female role models.
- Limited access to support services such as child care, transportation, and counseling.

11-9 Affirmative Action Goals

Recruiting, hiring, and retaining female correctional officers is vital to a balanced and effective organization. Correctional wardens and administrators should ensure that both women and other underrepresented groups are actively recruited for correctional service. Correctional administrators may find it helpful to establish affirmative action guidelines and goals to seek out and employ females and minorities in the corrections field. Affirmative-action programs are mandated by several of the employment laws. Their intent is to undo the damage caused by past discrimination in employment.

Among the special employment groups included in affirmative-action programs are African Americans, Asians, the elderly, Eskimos, Hispanics, homosexuals, immigrants, individuals with AIDS, individuals with disabilities, Middle Easterners, Native Americans, religious groups members, war veterans, women, and youth.

We offer the following caveat to correctional authorities who are responsible for recruitment and selection not to interpret the lack of applications from female and minority groups as lack of interest. It could very well be the perception of the white-male–dominated profession that deters many female and minority applicants from applying for correctional positions. It could also be that the correctional institution does not have any women or minorities on staff, giving the impression that the institution is closed to these groups, subsequently clouding the institution with an air of suspicion. Instead, correctional administrators must reach out and actively target and recruit underrepresented groups.

The correctional agency should be marketed to potential recruits as an open institution that values the concept of cultural diversity and inclusiveness. This is accomplished by an active recruiting agenda. Not only should correctional employers use caution to avoid discrimination in the hiring process, in some instances they must actively seek out certain groups of people and make certain they have equal opportunities to obtain jobs.

Summary

Historically, because of the small number of female offenders, there was a lack of prisons designed specifically to accommodate the needs of women. Consequently, many female inmates were housed separately in men's quarters. Women prisoners were exposed to the same conditions as male prisoners, including over crowded and filthy and unsanitary conditions. Because women were isolated while in prison, they were deprived of many of the privileges enjoyed by male inmates, such as visitation, exercise, and social interaction and affiliation with other inmates.

By the mid-nineteenth century the increasing number of women offenders prompted a move to provide women with regular quarters of their own. These were often small buildings erected in the corner of the men's prison yard. Ironically, the further the facilities were moved away from male quarters, the more they were neglected.

The Women's Reformatory Movement began in 1870 during which time women's and men's prisons alike began to reflect the rehabilitation model. Furthermore, women's prisons developed a cottage look since this design was thought to be more conducive to rehabilitation. The New York Reformatory for Women at Abion was one example of a cottage plan facility.

The Indiana Women's Prison was the first separate prison for women and was founded in 1873. In 1877, Massachusetts built an all-female state reformatory. Also at this time, the Progressive Women's Reformatory at Bedford Hills, New York, was founded by an American Quaker.

The progressive movement advocated many changes in the state of women's prisons. By the late-nineteenth century, nearly all states had opened separate prisons for women. The progressive movement lasted from about 1860 to 1935 and produced about 21 separate women's institutions.

The new reformatories were staffed by women with the objective to correct women's moral behavior. The typical reformatory inmate was a young, white female of a working-class background. Not all women received the benefits of the reformatory model. Some women who were placed in custodial prisons suffered from filthy conditions and violence by male guards. African American women routinely received discriminatory treatment compared to white women even when they had committed minor offenses.

By 1935 the women's reformatory movement had essentially ended. The reformatory movement achieved its goals of reform—particularly in prisons in the Northeast and Midwest. Evidence of the cottage system is still evident today in many states, such as Bedford Hills in New York.

The number of women incarcerated in the United States has grown substantially in recent years. Since 1990, the female prison population has doubled. The number of women in the nation's jails and prisons appears to be growing at a faster rate than the numbers of men. In 1998, about 3.2 million women were arrested in the United States for various crimes. From 2000 to 2002, the number of women under the jurisdiction of the state or federal prison authorities grew from 93,336 to 94,336, an increase of 0.7 percent.

Women have unique needs while incarcerated compared to men. The unique needs of women, coupled with the increase in drug abuse and drug-related arrests of females has changed the emphases of correctional programming. Prison officials have to ensure that women inmates have access to the appropriate treatment, such as medical treatment specifically tailored for women's needs, mental health services, and drug- and substance-abuse treatment.

A majority of women offenders are mothers. One out of every four adult women in prison is pregnant at the time of their arrest. Prison officials will have to increasingly develop parenting programs to assist women inmates. This is important in light of the studies that reveal that the absence of the woman from the family is far more devastating on children that the absence of the man. To encourage family bonding, some prison facilities have developed special camps for children and their incarcerated mothers. Some prisons, such as the Bedford Hills, New York Correctional Facility, provide a nursery where babies of incarcerated women are cared for until they are one year old.

Educational programs for incarcerated women are important to ensure that women inmates are given the proper educational tools so that when they return to society they can become more competitive in the job market. Vocational programs are also important because they provide women inmates with an opportunity to learn a new job skill. Thus, the American Correctional Association has deemed education of inmates an important goal for United States prisons, not to mention an effective means to reduce recidivism.

Women correctional officers have suffered from many forms of discrimination and disparate treatment as they have forged an identity in the corrections field. The most contested topic has been that of working in male facilities. Until recently, female role models were in short supply, making it even more difficult for women to adapt to nontraditional roles.

Women in the correctional field have been strong advocates for better services and programs for both juvenile and female offenders. In 1793, Mary Weed became the first known women's correctional administrator. Mary Weed was well known for her humane approach to prison administration toward both male and female inmates. Research has revealed that there are many advantages of women working in adult male prison facilities.

From the 1930s through the 1970s women primarily worked as probation and parole officers for women offenders only. Women also worked as volunteers and clerical staff in correctional institutions and were rarely allowed to supervise men.

Civil Rights legislation throughout much of the 1960s and 1970s has assisted women in entering into nontraditional professions such as corrections. Title VII of the Civil Rights Act was extended in 1972 to cover government employees.

The first United States Supreme Court case involving women in corrections was *Dothard v. Rawlinson*. A strict adherence to that ruling, which agreed with the Alabama Department of Corrections exclusion of women from correctional officer positions in male institutions that involved inmate contact, could have precluded the widespread employment of women. However, the ruling was narrowly interpreted across the country as applying only to the particular situation in Alabama, and women began to be employed in larger numbers in many correctional systems.

Several commissions formed during the 1970s advocated the employment of women in corrections. The American Correctional Association adopted affirmative action as a commitment to an ongoing process to ensure equal employment for women and minorities. The National Advisory Commission on Criminal Justice Standards and Goals established standards that progressively advocated recruiting and hiring more women for correctional jobs.

The progress of women in the correctional field has been somewhat slow to develop. Notwithstanding, women have made much progress in the corrections field in the past few years. In 1998, the number of women correctional officers has increased from 16.5 percent in 1990 to 21.7 percent in 1998. Prison administrators should set affirmative action goals to recruit and retain not only larger numbers of females but also larger numbers of minorities. Furthermore, correctional authorities should market their institutions as valuing the concept of multicultural diversity.

Discussion Questions

1. Describe where women were incarcerated prior to women's prisons and the characteristics of such confinement.
2. Explain the Girl Scouts Beyond Bars program.
3. Explain why female correctional institutions began to resemble a cottage look.
4. Identify and explain the facts of the first case involving women correctional officers to reach the U.S. Supreme Court.
5. Explain some the special accommodations that female prisoners need.
6. Discuss some of obstacles that have limited women in forging an identity in the correctional profession.

Chapter Quiz

True/False

1. Historically, women inmates always had separate prisons in the United States.
2. Women offending levels have remained relatively the same for the past thirty years.
3. The women's reformatory movement officially began with the Civil Rights legislation of the 1960s.
4. Women's reformatories were modeled on a domestic venue rejecting much of the punishment orientation of the male custodial environment.
5. By law, women are prevented from working in adult male prison facilities.

Multiple Choice

1. The first separate women's prison in the United States was located in
   a. Massachusetts.
   b. New York.
   c. Indiana.
   d. California.
2. In the 1880s both men and women were confined in the Walnut Street Jail in Philadelphia. Women were typically incarcerated for
   a. murder, attempted murder and prostitution.
   b. burglary, vagrancy, and theft.
   c. assault, battery, and threats.
   d. begging, larceny, vagrancy, and prostitution.

3. The idea of family life, with a dining room, living room, and kitchen best describes which type of prison philosophy?
   a. The modern penitentiary
   b. The cottage plan
   c. Punitive incarceration model
   d. The Walnut Street Jail plan
4. During the reformatory movement the new reformatories were staffed by women with the objective to
   a. correct women's moral behavior.
   b. punish.
   c. reform especially minority women.
   d. teach parenting and home skills.
5. Which one of the following concerns regarding female inmates is not a recent concern of prison administrators and policy makers in the twenty-first century?
   a. AIDS
   b. Substance abuse
   c. The increasing number of women inmates with children
   d. Proper diets to ensure that women obtain needed nutrition

Endnotes

1. Nancy Kurshan, "Behind the Walls: The History and Current Reality of Women's Imprisonment." In Ellen Rosenblatt (ed.) *Criminal Justice: Confronting the Prison Crisis* (Boston: South End Press, 1996).
2. Estelle B. Freedman, *Their Sisters' Keepers: Women's Prison Reform in America, 1830–1930* (Ann Arbor: The University of Michigan Press, 1981).
3. Nicole H. Rafter, "Prisons for Women, 1790–1890." In Tonry and Zimring (eds.) *Punishment and Reform: Essays on Criminal Sentencing,* (Chicago: University of Chicago Press, 1983).
4. Joycelyn Byrne-Pollock, *Women, Prison, and Crime,* (Pacific Grove, CA: Brooks Cole, 1990).
5. Alexis M. Durham III, *Crisis and Reform,* (Boston: Little, Brown and Company, 1994).
6. Nichole Hahn Rafter, *Partial Justice* (2nd ed.), (New Brunswick, NJ: Transaction Publishers, 1990).
7. Ibid.
8. Ibid.
9. Ibid.

10. Barbara Owen and Barbara Bloom, "Profiling Women Prisoners: Findings from National Surveys and a California Sample," *Prison Journal* 75 (June 1995): 181–182.
11. Nicole Hahn Rafter, *Partial Justice,* 1990.
12. Ibid.
13. Ibid.
14. Ibid.
15. Ibid.
16. Ibid., 134.
17. United States Department of Justice, *Prison and Jail Inmates at Midyear 2001,* (Washington, DC: Bureau of Justice Statistics, 2001).
18. Janice Joseph and Dorthy Taylor, *With Justice for All: Minorities and Women in Criminal Justice,* (Upper Saddle River, NJ: Prentice Hall, 2003).
19. United States Department of Justice, *Prison and Jail Inmates at Midyear 2001.*
20. National Institute of Justice, *Research on Women and Girls in the Justice System* (Washington DC: NIJ, 2000).
21. Bureau of Justice Statistics, *Prison and Jail Inmates 1999,* (Washington, DC: BJS, 2000).
22. Merry Morash, Timothy S. Bynum, and Barbara A. Koons, *Women Offenders: Programming Needs and Promising Approaches* (Washington, DC: National Institute of Justice, 1998).
23. Ibid.
24. D. Leclair, *The Incarcerated Female Offender: Offender, Victim, or Villain?* (Boston, MA: Division of Corrections, Research Division, 1990).
25. Joycelyn Pollock, *Counseling Female Offenders* (Thousand Oaks, CA: Brooks/Cole, 1998).
26. Tracy L. Snell, *Women in Prison* (Washington DC: Bureau of Justice Statistics, 1994).
27. Ibid.
28. National Institute of Justice, *Drug Forecasting: 1994 Annual Report on Adult and Juvenile Arrestees* (Washington, DC: U.S. Department of Justice, 1995).
29. Bruce L. Levin, Andrea K. Blanch, and Ann Jennings, *Women's Mental Health Services: A Public Health Perspective* (Thousand Oaks, CA: Sage Publications, 1998).
30. Tracy Snell, *Women in Prison.*
31. United States Department of Justice, *Law Enforcement Assistance Administration: Task Force Report on Women* (Washington, DC: U.S. Department of Justice, 1995).
32. Ibid.
33. Nkechi Taufa, "The Impact of the Criminal Justice System on Women and Their Families," *Center for Research on African American Women Journal,* 2, no. 1, (2001): 11–13.

34. Janice Joseph, Zelma Weston Henriques, and Kaylene Richards Ekeh, "Get Tough Polices and the Incarceration of African Americans," in Janice Joseph and Dorthy Taylor, *With Justice for All: Minorites and Women in the Criminal Justice System,* (Upper Saddle River, NJ: Prentice Hall, 2003): 105–119.
35. Mary J. Clement, "Parenting in Prison: A National Survey for Incarcerated Women," *Journal of Offender Rehabilitation,* 19, no. 1, (1993): 89–100.
36. Claudia G. Dowling, "When Mom Can't Come Home," *Life Magazine,* September 1997.
37. Joann B. Morton and Deborah M. Williams, "Mother/Child Bonding: Incarcerated Women Struggle to Maintain Meaningful Relationships with Their Children," *Corrections Today,* 60, no. 7, (1998): 98–105.
38. Evett L. Simmons, "Women the Target: Children the Victims," *Center for Research on African American Women Journal,* 2, no. 1, (2001): 24–25.
39. Marilyn C. Moses, "Keeping Incarcerated Mothers and Their Children Together: Girl Scouts Beyond Bars," *National Institute of Justice, Program Focus,* October 1995.
40. Jackie Crawford, *The Female Offender: What Does the Future Hold?* (Laurel, MD: American Correctional Association, 1990).
41. Phyllis J. Baunach, "Critical Problems of Women in Prison," in *The Changing Roles of Women in the Criminal Justice System,* ed. Imogene L. Moyer (Prospect Heights, IL: Waveland Press, 1985).
42. Federal Bureau of Prisons, *Program Report,* (Washington, DC: U.S. Department of Justice, 1996).
43. Tracy L. Snell, *Women in Prison.*
44. Corrothers, Helen C., Bureau of Justice Statistics, *Prevention and Intervention: Stemming the Flow-Complex Challenges and Collaborative Solutions: Programming for Adult and Juvenile Offenders.* (Washington, DC: U.S. Department of Justice, 1998).
45. *Law Enforcement Assistance Administration: Task Force Report on Women,* 1995.
46. Ibid.
47. Linda A. Temlin, Karen M. Abram, and Gary M. McClelland, *Prevalence of Psychiatric Disorders among Incarcerated Women,* Archives of General Psychiatry, (53): 505–512.
48. Susan Baugh, Susan Bull, and Kathy Cohen, "Mental Health Issues, Treatment, and the Female Offender," in Ruth T. Zaplin, *Female Offenders: Critical Perspectives and Effective Interventions,* (Gaithersburg, MD: Aspen, 1998): 205–225.
49. Ibid.
50. Merry Morash, "Findings from the National Study of Innovative and Promising Programs for Women Offenders," *National Institute of Justice Research Project,* (Washington, DC: U.S. Department of Justice, 1996).
51. Ibid.

52. Mark K. Campbell, *Infection Control: Managing Exposure to Communicable Diseases, The State of Corrections* (Lanham, MD: American Correctional Association, 1993).
53. Phyllis H. Ross and James E. Lawrence, "Health Care Concerns for Women Offenders," *Corrections Today,* 60, no. 7, (1998): 128.
54. Ibid.
55. Marian S. Gornick et al., "Effects of Race and Income on Mortality and Use of Services among Medicare Beneficiaries," *New England Journal of Medicine,* no. 335, (September 12, 1996): 791–799.
56. Concetta C. Culliver, *Female Criminality: The State of the Art* (New York: Garland Press, 1993).
57. Lynn E. Zimmer, *Women Guarding Men* (Chicago: The University of Chicago Press, 1986).
58. Joann B. Morton, *Change, Challenges and Choices: Women's Role in Modern Corrections* (Lanham, MD: American Correctional Association, 1997).
59. Ibid.
60. Richard T. Schaefer, *Racial and Ethnic Groups* (Glenview, IL: Foresman/Little Brown Higher Education, 2000).
61. Joycelyn M. Pollock, *Sex and Supervision: Guarding Male and Female Inmates* (New York: Greenwood Press, 1986).
62. Lynn E. Zimmer, *Women Guarding Men*, 1986.
63. Gaylen W. Paul, *Impact of Female Correctional Officers in Adult All-Male Institutions* (Houston, TX: University of Houston, 1972).
64. Ibid.
65. Estelle Freedman, "Their Sisters Keepers: An Historical Perspective on Female Correctional Institutions in the United States: 1870–1900," *Feminist Studies,* 7, no. 2, (1974): 77–95.
66. Joann B. Morton, "Women in Corrections: Looking Back on 200 Years of Valuable Contributions," *Corrections Today,* (August 1992): 76–77.
67. Negley K. Teeters, *The Cradle of the Penitentiary: The Walnut Street Jail at Philadelphia,* 1773–1835, (Philadelphia: Temple University, 1955).
68. Estelle Freedman, "Their Sisters Keepers," 1974.
69. Nicole Hahn Rafter, *Partial Justice,* 1990.
70. Ibid.
71. Susan Ehrlich Martin and Nancy C. Jurik, *Doing Justice, Doing Gender: Women in Law and Criminal Justice Occupations,* (Thousand Oaks, CA: Sage, 1996).
72. Ibid.
73. Ibid.
74. Nicole Hahn Rafter, *Partial Justice,* 1990.
75. Joanne B. Morton, "Women in Corrections," 1992.
76. *Dothard v. Rawlinson,* 433 U.S. 321 (1977).

77. American Correctional Association, *Women in Corrections: American Correctional Association Monographs Series 1 Number 1* (College Park, MD: American Correctional Association, 1981).
78. The National Advisory Commission on Criminal Justice Standards and Goals, *Corrections: Task Force Report,* (Washington, DC: U.S. Government Printing Office, 1973).
79. *The Corrections Yearbook,* (South Salem, NY: Criminal Justice Institute, 1998).

Chapter 12
Capital Punishment

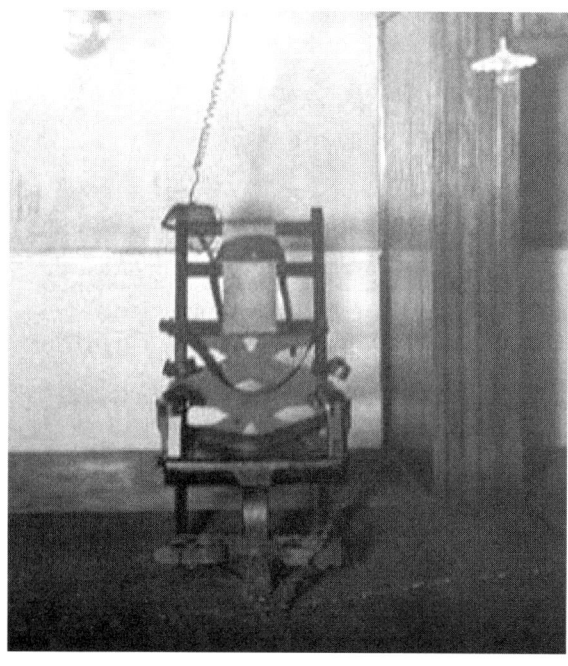

Electric chairs are used along with lethal injection, gas chambers, and firing squads to execute prisoners.

Key Terms

aggravating circumstances   capital cases   mitigating circumstances

Outline

12-1 Capital Cases
12-2 The Death Penalty and the Courts
    12-2a The Courts and Executing the Mentally Impaired
    12-2b Who Decides the Death Penalty?
12-3 Status of Capital Cases
12-4 Statutory Changes
12-5 Methods of Execution
    12-5a History
    12-5b Present Day
12-6 Automatic Review
12-7 Characteristics of Prisoners under Sentence of Death
12-8 Criminal History of Inmates under Sentence of Death
12-9 Is the Death Penalty Biased?
12-10 Is the Death Penalty Broken?
Summary
Discussion Questions
Chapter Quiz
Endnotes

Learning Objectives

After studying this chapter, the reader will be able to:

- Analyze the problems involved with the use of the death penalty.
- List the situations for which the death penalty may be imposed.
- Explain the procedural requirements for imposing the death penalty.
- Explain the history of the death penalty.
- List the arguments for and against the use of the death penalty.
- Analyze the characteristics of death row inmates.
- List the recent statutory changes in death penalty procedural requirements.
- Explain the methods of execution that have been used in the United States.
- Analyze the Eighth Amendment restrictions when considering the constitutionality of the death penalty.
- Explain the criminal history of inmates on death row.

12-1 Capital Cases

Capital trials are expensive to try and sensational to the press. As former Supreme Court Justice Felix Frankfurter stated: "When life is at hazard in a trial, it sensationalizes the whole thing almost unwittingly." Former Supreme Court Justice Robert H. Jackson, noting the problems with reviewing **capital cases,** stated that "appellate courts in capital cases, are tempted to strain the evidence and even, in close cases, the law, in order to give a doubtfully condemned man another chance." He also noted that the fear of mistake produces excruciating delays in executions. He concludes that the punishment is not only slow, it usually never comes. The President's Crime Commission in 1968 noted that the emotion surrounding a capital case "destroys the fact-finding process." Figures 12-1 and 12-2 illustrate how the numbers of people sentenced to death and people executed have fluctuated during most of the twentieth century.

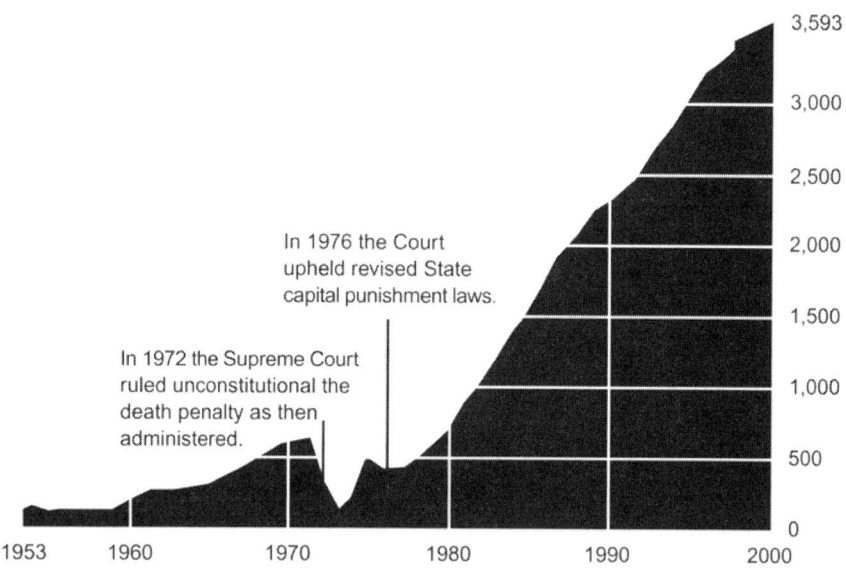

Figure 12-1
Persons under Sentence of Death, 1953–2000
Source: Bureau of Justice Statistics Bulletin, December 2001.

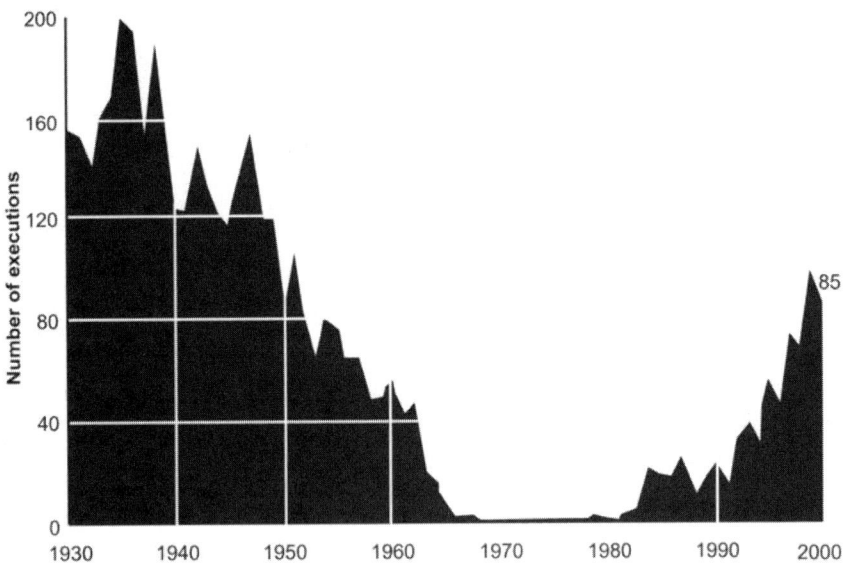

Figure 12-2
Persons Executed, 1930–2000
Source: Bureau of Justice Statistics Bulletin, December 2001.

The death penalty was the most common form of punishment in the seventeenth and eighteenth centuries. In England during that period, there were over 200 crimes for which the sentence could be imposed. In one famous case, a six-year-old boy and his dog were hanged for the murder of an infant. Presently, in the United States, capital punishment is typically authorized only for aggravated criminal homicide. However, at the federal level it can be used as a sentence for treason and the military may employ capital punishment in cases of desertion.

The last public execution took place in Owensboro, Kentucky, on August 14, 1936. Approximately 20,000 people gathered in that small Kentucky town to witness it. The holiday atmosphere that surrounded the event was normal in those days. Reform groups, upset that such solemn occasions were being transferred into circus-type events, pressured the states to require that executions take place behind prison walls and in private. The photo depicts one of the last public hangings. Since that date, executions have been conducted behind closed doors with only selected people allowed to observe.

Today, some people advocate the return to public executions. According to their arguments, if capital punishment deters crime, then why shouldn't all executions be seen by the largest possible audiences. In

This photo depicts one of the last public hangings in Anderson County, Texas in 1905.

1984, Texas inmate James David Autry petitioned the Texas Department of Criminal Justice to allow his execution to be televised. Twelve of the 44 television stations in Texas indicated that they would televise the execution if permitted. Twenty-six refused, and the others were either undecided or refused to state their position.[1]

As of 1995, approximately 77 percent of the people in the United States supported the use of the death penalty. In a Gallup Poll conducted in February 1999, 71 percent polled favored capital punishment. Similarly, a *Newsweek* poll taken in June 2000 found 73 percent supported the death penalty.[2]

The Death Penalty Information Center, however, contends that when the public is provided with alternative sentences, such as life imprisonment without any possibility of parole, that only a minority of people support the death penalty. The center contends that one reason the majority of the public supports the death penalty is the erroneous belief that criminals sentenced to life in prison are released after several years. According to the center, 33 states can impose life sentences without parole. In all other states, those who are sentenced to life are required to serve at least

20 years. It appears that the strongest argument used by people opposed to the death penalty is the prospect that innocent people may be executed. Other objections to the use of the death penalty include moral reasons, the argument that the death penalty is used arbitrarily, and that it is imposed in a racially discriminatory manner. Box 12-1 depicts the complexities of death penalty cases.

Box 12-1

Michael Owen Perry & Earl Washington, Jr.

Michael Owen Perry is on death row in the state of Louisiana. He will probably never be executed. Perry was convicted of killing five members of his family on July 17, 1983. Apparently Perry went to his grandmother's house and calmly shot his two sleeping cousins. He then walked across the backyard to his parents' house, where he killed his mother and two other people. He was found guilty of capital murder and sentenced to death. At his trial, the issue of his sanity was never raised.

While on death row, he was determined to be insane. The U.S. Supreme Court ruled that the state could not execute him until he regained his sanity and could therefore understand the nature and gravity of his punishment. In addition, the Louisiana Supreme Court ruled that the state could not forcibly medicate him in order to assist him in regaining his sanity for the purposes of executing him.

- Should it be cruel and unusual and thus a constitutional violation to execute a person who does not understand the nature and gravity of his punishment?
- Does it make sense to wait until an individual is sane before we kill him?
- What difference does it make if he understands the nature and gravity of the punishment if he is going to die immediately?

On January 14, 1994, in one of his last acts as governor, Virginia Governor Douglas Wilder commuted to life with the possibility of parole the death sentence of Earl Washington, Jr.

Washington had been convicted of murder committed during the course of a rape. Deoxyribonucleic (DNA) testing later established that he could not have been the rapist.[3]

Those who contend that the death penalty is unconstitutional typically base their legal argument on the cruel and unusual punishment clause of the Eighth Amendment to the U.S. Constitution. Those who support the death penalty point out:

Due Process—The due process clauses of the Fifth and Fourteenth amendments state that "... no person shall be deprived of life ... without due process of law. Thus, the two amendments imply that the Constitution does not forbid the death penalty.

Incapacitation—Supporters of the death penalty contend that the potential for recidivism is serious enough to require the ultimate incapacitation.

Deterrent—Supporters argue that the death penalty serves as a strong deterrent to keep individuals from committing serious crimes. (Note: Opponents argue that the death penalty is not a deterrent, because murder is not a crime normally committed by rational people.)

Proportional—Punishing criminals with the death penalty conforms to the requirement that the penalty be proportional to the crime.

Public Opinion—Supporters contend that the majority of the public supports the death penalty.

Those who argue against the death penalty use the following arguments to support their views:

Possibility of Error—There is a possibility of error and an innocent person could be executed.

Cruel and Unusual—The death penalty is a barbaric punishment and there is no place for it in modern society.

Discriminatory—The death penalty is most often used against minorities.

No Deterrent—The opponents argue that the death penalty does not deter others from committing serious criminal acts.

Rehabilitation—There is always the chance that a person might be rehabilitated.

12-2 The Death Penalty and the Courts

The U.S. Supreme Court has had very perplexing and complex experiences in the constitutional regulation of the death penalty. Prior to 1972, the Supreme Court placed virtually no constitutional restrictions on the imposition of the death penalty. Most state legislatures had rejected the automatic death penalty statutes. The juries were generally instructed that if they found the defendant guilty of a capital crime, they must then decide between death and life imprisonment. Juries had virtually unguided discretion. In most cases, little information regarding the defendant's character, background, and previous criminal record was presented.

In 1972, the U.S. Supreme Court decided *Furman v. Georgia*. This case held by a 5-to-4 decision that the capital punishment statute in Georgia was unconstitutional. All nine justices wrote separate opinions. Each of the opinions concluded that juries should not be given unguided discretion in imposing the death penalty. The decision, while providing no guidance regarding the use of the death penalty, clearly established that all states' death penalty statutes were unconstitutional.

In 1976, the majority members of the Supreme Court concluded in *Gregg v. Georgia,* that the authors of the cruel and unusual punishment clause did not intend to forbid capital punishment. They only intended to prohibit punishments not officially authorized by statute or not lying within the sentencing court's jurisdiction and any torture or brutal, gratuitously painful methods of execution.

As the result of the death penalty cases decided by the Court during the 1970s, the following guidelines or actions are considered necessary before a sentence involving the death penalty will be approved by the Court:

- The trial must be tried in separate phases. First, the question of the defendant's guilt must be established.
- At the same time guilt is established, the jury is also required to determine the existence of any special circumstances necessary for the imposition of the death penalty (e.g., murder for hire, murder committed to prevent arrest, prior conviction of murder, and murder committed by a prisoner serving a life sentence).
- If the defendant is found guilty of murder and one or more of the required special circumstances are determined to be present, further proceedings are held on the question of the penalty to be imposed.

Generally, special proceedings determine whether the defendant shall be sentenced to death or life imprisonment. After hearing the evidence at the special proceedings, the jury must weigh the evidence and determine if the **mitigating circumstances** outweigh the **aggravating circumstances.** If so, life imprisonment, rather than the death penalty, shall be imposed. In most states with the death penalty, the decision by the jury must be unanimous. If the jury fails to reach a decision, then life imprisonment is given. Mitigating circumstances are those circumstances that tend to reduce the severity of the crime (i.e., cooperation with the investigating authority, surrender, good character), whereas aggravating circumstances are those circumstances that tend to make the crime more serious (i.e., use of a deadly weapon, committing an offense against a law enforcement officer, taking advantage of a position of trust to commit an offense, etc.). Table 12-1 is a timeline showing significant Supreme Court decisions on the death penalty.

TABLE 12-1 Significant Supreme Court Decisions Involving the Death Penalty

Year	Case	Decision
1972	*Furman v. Georgia*	The U.S. Supreme Court overturned the death penalty in Georgia.
1976	*Gregg v. Georgia*	The death penalty is declared constitutional in Georgia.
1986	*Ford v. Wainwright*	The state is prohibited from executing the insane.
1987	*McCleskey v. Kemp*	The U.S. Supreme Court rejected the constitutionality of racial injustice of the death penalty.
1988	*Thompson v. Oklahoma*	The execution of juveniles under the age of 16 is prohibited.
1989	*Perry v. Lynch*	Mental retardation is no bar to capital punishment.
1989	*Stanford v. Kentucky*	Seventeen year olds can be executed.
1989	*Wilkins v. Missouri*	A 16-year-old can be executed.
2002	*Atkins v. Virginia*	It is unconstitutional to execute mentally retarded inmates.

12-2a The Courts and Executing the Mentally Impaired

Ramon Martinez-Villareal's IQ is between 50 and 60, and he can't read or speak in complex sentences. From his cell on Arizona's death row, he spends hours copying Bible passages he doesn't understand and gives them to his attorney.

Martinez-Villareal, who fatally shot two farm workers in 1982, has spent nearly two decades on death row and once came within eight hours of execution. But his attorneys say that a recent Supreme Court decision banning the execution of the mentally retarded appears to guarantee that he will live out a natural life in prison.

In a significant shift, the United States Supreme Court banned the execution of mentally retarded murderers. On June 20, 2002 the Supreme Court declared that executing mentally retarded murderers is unconstitutionally cruel, offering the possibility of reprieve to scores of inmates in the biggest shift in the court's stance on capital punishment in a quarter-century. Of the 38 states that have capital punishment, 18 bar the execution of retarded defendants. Although the legal definition of retardation used in those states varies slightly, most require an IQ under 70 and evidence that the person has difficulty navigating daily life. Legal experts say the most immediate challenges will come in the 20 states, including

Virginia and Texas that allow the execution of retarded defendants. The Supreme Court opinion, written by Justice John Paul Stevens, said that use of the death penalty in the case of mentally retarded persons is a violation of the Eighth Amendment.

Supporters and opponents of capital punishment agree that the practical implication of the court's ruling will be decided over the next several months and years by countless debates in courtrooms and state capitals. The high court's ruling that executing retarded killers violates the constitutional ban on cruel and unusual punishment will assuredly send defense attorneys scrambling to review files in death penalty cases. Likewise, prosecutors across the country are bracing for a flood of challenges by defendants in pending and even concluded capital cases. State legislators in the meantime are starting to think about how they will define retardation.

12-2b Who Decides the Death Penalty?

In *Ring v. Arizona* (decided June, 2002), the U.S. Supreme Court held that jurors, not judges, must make the crucial factual determinations that make a convicted murderer eligible for the death penalty. By a vote of 7 to 2, the Court held that Arizona's sentencing scheme for the death penalty was unconstitutional. In Arizona, and many other states, at the conclusion of the sentencing hearing, the judge was required to determine the presence or absence of the enumerated aggravating circumstances that would justify the imposition of the death penalty. Arizona's law authorized the judge to sentence the defendant to death only if there was at least one aggravating circumstance and "there are no mitigating circumstances sufficiently substantial to call for leniency."

Ring was convicted of shooting and killing a store clerk during a robbery. The judge agreed with the jury that Ring was the one who shot and killed the clerk. The judge found that he was a major participant in the robbery and that armed robbery was unquestionably a crime that carried with it a grave risk of death. The judge then determined the aggravating factors—that the crime was committed in the expectation of receiving something of "pecuniary value" and that the crime was committed "in an especially heinous, cruel, or depraved manner." The judge found one nonstatutory mitigating circumstance: his "minimal" criminal record did not "call for leniency."

On appeal, Ring's counsel contended that Arizona's capital sentencing scheme violated the Sixth and Fourteenth Amendments to the U.S. Constitution because it entrusted to a judge the findings of a fact necessary to raise the defendant's maximum penalty. The Court agreed and held that the right to trial by jury would be senselessly diminished if it did not include the fact finding necessary to put the defendant to death.

According to many researchers, the *Ring v. Arizona* case will result in fewer death sentences. At the time of the decision, there were about 40 other prisoners on death row in four other states, Colorado, Idaho, Montana, and Nebraska, which have systems similar to Arizona's.

The decision will probably affect the sentencing procedures in states, such as Alabama, Delaware, and Florida, where the juries give advisory verdicts, but the judges make the ultimate decision. Indiana had a similar system but changed to one where the jury makes the decision. One researcher concluded that in recent years in Alabama there were 83 cases where the judge overrode the jury recommendation for life and imposed the death penalty and only 7 cases where the judge imposed life imprisonment after the jury had recommended death.[4]

12-3 Status of Capital Cases

A review of the status of capital punishment for the year 2000 (the last year for which complete statistics are available) provides an overview of the numbers and demographics of those sentenced to death.[5] During 2000, 83 men and two women were executed. Of these, 49 were white, 35 were black and one was a Native American. The 85 people were under sentence of death an average of 11 years and five months before being executed. At the end of 1999, 37 states and the federal prison system held 3,593 prisoners under sentence of death, 1.5 percent more than at the end of 1999. All had committed murder. Of persons under sentence of death, 1,990 were white, 1,535 were black, 29 were Native American, 27 were Asian American, and 12 were classified as "other race." The 339 Hispanic inmates under sentence of death accounted for 11 percent of inmates with a known ethnicity. Fifty-four women were under a sentence of death.

Among inmates under sentences of death and with available criminal histories, 64 percent had a prior felony conviction, including 8 percent with at least one previous homicide conviction. Among those for whom legal status at the time of the capital offense was available, 39 percent had an active criminal justice status. Less than half of these were on parole, and one-quarter were on probation. The remaining one-quarter had charges pending, were incarcerated, had escaped from incarceration, or had some other criminal justice status.

Fourteen states executed 85 prisoners during 2000. The number of people executed was 1.5 percent fewer than in 1999. Recall that the prisoners executed during 2000 had been under sentence of death an average of 11 years and five months, about six months less than the average for inmates executed the previous year. Table 12-2 presents statistics on executions per state in 2000.

TABLE **12-2** Executions and Number of Prisoners under Sentence of Death per State in 2000

Status of Death Penalty, December 31, 2000					
Executions during 2000		**Number of prisoners under sentence of death**		**Jurisdiction without a death penalty**	
Texas	40	California	586	Alaska	
Oklahoma	11	Texas	450	District of Columbia	
Virginia	8	Florida	371	Hawaii	
Florida	6	Pennsylvania	238	Iowa	
Missouri	5	North Carolina	215	Maine	
Alabama	4	Ohio	201	Massachusetts	
Arizona	3	Alabama	185	Michigan	
Arkansas	2	Illinois	163	Minnesota	
Delaware	1	Oklahoma	129	North Dakota	
Louisiana	1	Georgia	120	Rhode Island	
North Carolina	1	Arizona	119	Vermont	
South Carolina	1	Tennessee	97	West Virginia	
Tennessee	1	Louisiana	90	Wisconsin	
California	1	Nevada	88		
		Missouri	79		
		23 other jurisdictions	462		
Total	85	Total	3,593		

Source: Bureau of Justice Statistics, December 2001.

California held the largest number of death row inmates (586) on December 31, 2000, followed by Texas (450), Florida (371), and Pennsylvania (238). Eighteen prisoners were in federal custody under a death sentence. Between January 1 and December 31, 2000, 27 state prison systems received 214 prisoners under the sentence of death. Forty-nine of the executed prisoners were non-Hispanic whites; 35 were non-Hispanic blacks; six white Hispanic, and one Native American. Eighty of the executions were carried out by lethal injection, and five by electrocution.

From January 1, 1977, to December 31, 1999, a total of 6,208 persons entered state and federal prisons under sentences of death, 49 percent of which were white, 41 percent were black, 8 percent were Hispanic, and 2 percent were of other races. During this 24-year period, a total of 683 executions took place in 24 states. Of the inmates executed, 337 were white, 246 were black, 49 were Hispanic, and 11 were other races. Also between 1977 and 2000, 2,312 prisoners were removed from a death sentence as a result of dispositions other than execution (resentencing, retrial, commutation, or death while awaiting execution). Of all people removed from under a death sentence, 52 percent were white, 36 percent were black, and 2 percent were other races.

2-4 Statutory Changes

Most states have revised their capital punishment statutes in the past seven years. Most of the changes involved additional aggravating circumstances, additional categories of victims permitting the application of the death penalty, and broadening of the law to allow a defendant to choose between two methods of execution. Examples of the changes include:

Alabama—Added to its list of capital offenses the use of any weapon from outside a dwelling or car to kill a person in that dwelling or car and use of a weapon from within a car to kill a person.

Colorado—Added to its penal code as aggravating factors the murder of two or more persons during the same criminal episode, and the intentional killing of a child under age 12.

Delaware—Added to its penal code as aggravating factors: the murder of a child age 14 or younger by a person at least four years older than the victim; the killing of a nongovernmental informant in retaliation for providing information concerning criminal activity to an investigative agency; and premeditated murder resulting from "substantial planning" for the commission of that murder itself.

Florida—Added new sections to, and revised an act relating to, death sentences. In specifying conditions of a sentence to life in prison without the possibility of release, the revision eliminates a previous stipulation of release if the offense was a capital felony. The stipulation was that the offender could be released after 25 years. Florida lawmakers also amended a statute making confidential any information that, if released, would identify the executioner.

Idaho—Amended its penal code to remove the requirement that the court determine whether the sentence of death is disproportionate to the penalty imposed in similar cases.

Illinois—Added to its penal code the aggravating factors of intentional killing ordered or committed by the leader of a drug trafficking organization and intentional murder involving the infliction of torture.

Indiana—Added murder by intentionally discharging a firearm into an inhabited dwelling or from a vehicle and murder during criminal gang activity.

New Jersey—Added as an aggravating factor the murder of a person younger than 14 years of age.

North Carolina—Amended its code of criminal procedure to allow, only by order of a judge, the admission of a defendant's juvenile record as evidence in either the guilt phase or to prove an aggravating factor at sentencing.

12-5 Methods of Execution

12-5a History

In pre-industrial societies, the death penalty was carried out by banishing the criminal to the wilderness where death was relatively certain. The effectiveness of banishment diminished as human skills and culture advanced and the chances of an individual surviving banishment greatly increased. Some of the ancient methods of execution included burning, hanging, stoning, boiling in oil, beheading, disemboweling, burying alive, throwing to wild beasts, crucifying, drowning, crushing, impaling, shooting, flaying alive, and being torn apart. The list, although long, is not exhaustive of the creative methods used to carry out death sentences. As noted in an earlier chapter, Socrates was forced to drink poison as his method of execution.

In Colonial America and in Early England, hanging was the most common form of execution. The use of a firing squad was the second most common. The preferred form in France and other European countries was by use of the guillotine, a beheading device consisting of a heavy blade that falls freely between two perpendicular grooved posts.[6] The use of the electric chair began in New York in 1890. On August 6, 1890, William Kemmler, a convicted murderer from Buffalo, was the first person executed in an electric chair at the Auburn Penitentiary in New York. The electric chair was hailed as a more humanitarian way to execute people. Many, however, claimed it was merely a promotional device for the developer of a New York electrical company.

Kemmler was strapped in a chair with leather straps. A headpiece was placed on his head and attached to electric wires. When voltage was transmitted through the headpiece, Kemmler's shoulders shot up. It appeared as though every muscle in his body went rigid. His face turned an intense red, then an ashen pallor. His eyes were glazed, pupils dilated. His right hand was clenched so tight that the nail had dug into the flesh. Spots appeared on his face. The electricity was shut off. His body sagged like a limp rag. They began to unstrap him from the chair. Suddenly, foam bubbled out of his mouth and a gurgling sound came from his throat. Quickly they replaced the headpiece and turned on the current again. He then sat up in the chair taut and then slumped. A wisp of smoke came from the top of his head.

In an unusual case, a convicted murderer (Francis) was sentenced to die in the electric chair. He was strapped in the chair and the execution began. The electrical system malfunctioned, however, and he was not killed when the current passed through his body. He then contended that to subject him to the process a second time was cruel and unusual punishment and thus a violation of the Eighth Amendment to the U.S. Constitution. By a five-to-four decision, the Supreme Court ruled against him and he was finally executed.[7]

Many, including Thomas Edison, advocated that the use of the electric chair was cruel and inhumane. In an effort to make execution more humane, the gas chamber originated. The first person to die in a gas chamber was Gee Jon, a Chinese immigrant worker convicted of murder. California executed him on February 8, 1924, using cyanide gas. Jon was fastened in a chair. As the gas was pumped into the chamber, his head suddenly sagged backward. He appeared to lose consciousness. His head continued to move, but became weaker each time. His eyes remained open. Six minutes later he was pronounced dead.

As a result of Supreme Court cases in 1970s, states were required to enact new capital punishment statutes. Some states, in order to reduce the opposition to capital punishment and make the passage of new laws easier, looked for ways to make execution more humane. The use of lethal injection gained favor. The first person to be executed by lethal injection was Charles Books. On December 6, 1982, in Texas, Brooks was strapped to a hospital gurney. His arms were strapped to boards that projected from each side of the gurney. A catheter needle was inserted into his left arm. The needle was attached to a clear plastic tube. First a saltwater solution flowed into his arm. Then sodium thieopental (a quick-acting barbituate) was used. Next Pavulon (a drug similar to the curare plant extract used by South Americans to dip their arrows in to paralyze their prey) was used. Finally, he was administered potassium chloride, which is often used by doctors to regulate the heart. Too much of it, however, will cause cardiac arrest. As the drugs began to take effect, Brooks moved his head and muttered something. He then yawned and wheezed. He opened and closed his hand several times. He was pronounced dead seven minutes later.

12-5b Present Day

Lethal injection is currently the predominant method of execution (36 states). Eleven states authorize electrocution; four states, lethal gas; three states, hanging; and three states, a firing squad. Eighteen states authorize more than one method: lethal injection and an alternative method, generally at the election of the condemned prisoner. However, six of these 18 states stipulate which method must be used, depending on the date of sentencing; one authorizes hanging only if lethal injection could not be given; one authorizes lethal gas if lethal injection can not be given; and one authorizes electrocution if another method cannot be given. In three states, the inmate is allowed to choose his or her method of execution.

The method of execution of federal prisoners is lethal injection. For offenses under the Violent Crime Control and Law Enforcement Act of 1994, the method is that of the state in which the conviction took place. Table 12-3 summarizes the methods of execution for each state in which capital punishment is legal.

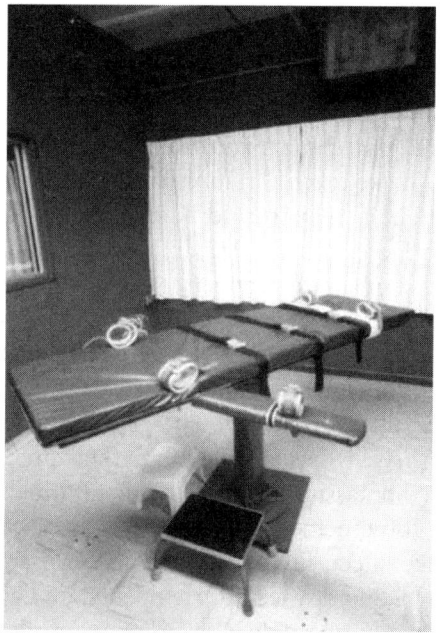

Prisoners are strapped to a gurney in preparation for lethal injection.
Mark C. Ide

TABLE **12-3** Methods of Execution by State, 2000

Lethal Injection	Electrocution	Lethal Gas	Hanging	Firing Squad
Arizona	Nevada	Alabama	Arizona	Delaware	Idaho
Arkansas	New Hampshire	Arkansas	California	New Hampshire	Oklahoma
California	New Jersey	Florida	Missouri	Washington	Utah
Colorado	New Mexico	Georgia	Wyoming		
Connecticut	New York	Kentucky			
Delaware	North Carolina	Nebraska			
Florida	Ohio	Ohio			
Georgia	Oklahoma	Oklahoma			
Idaho	Pennsylvania	Oregon			
Illinois	Tennessee	South Carolina			
Indiana	South Carolina	Virginia			
Kansas	South Dakota				
Kentucky	Tennessee				
Louisiana	Texas				
Maryland	Utah				
Mississippi	Virginia				
Missouri	Washington				
Montana	Wyoming				

Source: U.S. Department of Justice. Bureau of Justice Statistics. *Capital Punishment 2000* (Washington, DC: Author, 2001).

Box 12-2

The Death Penalty and the Eighth Amendment

Is the ban against cruel and unusual punishment embodied in the Eighth Amendment violated when the death penalty is imposed?

This question has plagued the courts for many years. What constitutes cruel and unusual punishment? Justice Thurgood Marshall stated in *Furman v. Georgia:*

> Perhaps the most important principle in analyzing "cruel and unusual" punishment questions is the one that is reiterated again and again in the prior opinions of the Supreme Court: i.e., the cruel and unusual language must draw its meaning from the evolving standards of decency that mark the progress of a maturing society. Thus, a penalty that was permissible at one time in our nation's history is not necessarily permissible today.[8]

12-6 Automatic Review

Of the 38 states with capital punishment statutes, 36 provide for review of all death sentences regardless of the defendant's wishes. Arkansas had no specific provisions for automatic review. Federal death penalty procedures do not provide for automatic review after a sentence of death has been imposed. While most of the 36 states authorize an automatic review of both the conviction and sentence, Idaho, Indiana, Montana, Oklahoma, and Tennessee require review of the sentence only. In Idaho, review of the conviction has to be appealed or forfeited.

In Indiana, a defendant can waive review of the conviction. The review is usually conducted by the state's highest appellate court regardless of the defendant's wishes. Alternatively, in Mississippi, the question of whether a defendant can waive the right to automatic review of the sentence has not been addressed; while in Wyoming, neither the statute nor case law clearly preclude a waiver of an appeal. If either the conviction or the sentence is vacated, the case could be remanded to the trial court for additional proceedings or for retrial. As a result of retrial or resentencing, the death sentence could be reimposed.

12-7 Characteristics of Prisoners under Sentence of Death

In December 2000, 38 states and the federal prison system held a total of 3,593 prisoners on death row, an increase of 53 (1.5 percent more) since the end of 1999. The federal prison system count remained unchanged at eighteen. Three states reported 39 percent of the nation's death row population: Texas (450), California (586), and Florida (371). California had an increase of 30, followed by North Carolina (13). Oklahoma and Texas had the largest decreases (12 and 10, respectively). Among the 38 states with prisoners on death row, 20 had more inmates than a year earlier, five had fewer inmates, and thirteen had the same number.

During 2000 the number of blacks under sentence of death increased by 20. The number of whites increased by 30, and the number of persons of other races (Native Americans and Asians or Pacific Islanders) rose from 65 to 68. The total number of Hispanics sentenced to death rose from 326 to 339 during 2000. Twenty-five Hispanics were received under sentence of death, six were removed from death row, and six were executed. Three-quarters of the Hispanics were incarcerated in three states: Texas (101), California (114), and Florida (32).

The number of women sentenced to be executed increased from 51 to 54. Eight women were received under sentence of death, and three were removed from death row and two were executed. Eight women were under sentence of death in 18 states. More than half of all women on death row at the end of 2000 were in Texas, California, North Carolina, and Pennsylvania.

The median level of education for death row inmates was the eleventh grade. Of inmates under a capital sentence and with reported marital status, nearly half had never married; somewhat more than one-fifth were married when they were sentenced; nearly one-fifth were divorced, separated, or widowed.

Among all inmates under sentence of death, about one-half were age 20 to 29 on December 31, 2000, and 13 percent were age 19 or younger. The median age was 38 years. Less than 1 percent were age 55 or older. The youngest offender under sentence of death was age 18; the oldest was 85. More than half of all inmates under the death sentence were age 20 to 29 when they were arrested for their capital offense; 13 percent were age 19 or younger; and less than 1 percent were age 55 or older. Eight jurisdictions do not specify a minimum age for which the death penalty can be imposed. In some states, the minimum age is set forth in the statutory provisions that determine the age at which a juvenile may be transferred to criminal court for trial as an adult. Thirteen states and the federal prison system require a minimum age of 18. Sixteen states indicate an age of eligibility between 14 and 17. Table 12-4 summarizes the minimum age requirements for the states in which capital punishment is legal.

TABLE **12-4 Minimum Age Requirement for Capital Punishment Sentence, 2000**

Age 16 or less	Age 17	Age 18	None Specified
Alabama (16)	Georgia	California	Arizona
Arkansas (14)	New Hampshire	Colorado	Idaho
Delaware (16)	North Carolina	Connecticut	Louisiana
Florida (16)	Texas	Federal System	Montana
Indiana (16)		Illinois	Pennsylvania
Kentucky (16)		Kansas	South Carolina
Mississippi (16)		Maryland	South Dakota
Missouri (16)		Nebraska	
Nevada (16)		New Jersey	
Oklahoma (16)		New Mexico	
Utah (14)		New York	
Virginia (14)		Ohio	
Wyoming (16)		Oregon	
		Tennessee	
		Washington	

Source: U.S. Department of Justice. Bureau of Justice Statistics. *Capital Punishment 2000* (Washington, DC: Author, 2001).

From 1977, the year after the Supreme Court upheld the constitutionality of revised state capital punishment laws, to 2000, a total of 6,208 people entered prison under sentence of death. During these 24 years, 683 people were executed, and 2,312 were removed from under a death sentence by appellate court decisions and reviews, commutations, or death. (An individual may have received and been removed from under a sentence of death more than once.)

Among individuals who received a death sentence between 1977 and 2000, 3,058 (49 percent) were white, 1,838 (40 percent) were black, 509 (8 percent) were Hispanic, and 44 (1 percent) were of other races. The distribution by race of the 2,995 inmates who were removed from death row between 1977 and 2000 was as follows: 1,564 whites (52 percent), 1,202 blacks (40 percent), 185 Hispanics (6 percent), and 44 persons of other races (1 percent). Of the 683 who were executed, 377 (55 percent) were white, 246 (36 percent) were black, 49 (7 percent) were Hispanic, and 4 (2 percent) were other races.[9]

12-8 Criminal History of Inmates under Sentence of Death

Among inmates under a death sentence, for whom criminal history information is available, 64 percent had past felony convictions, including 8 percent with at least one previous homicide conviction. Among those for whom legal status at the time the capital offense was reported, 39 percent were on probation or parole. Nearly one-half of those were on parole and one-fourth were on probation. The others had charges pending, were in prison, had escaped from incarceration, or had some other criminal justice status. Since 1988, data have been collected on the number of death sentences imposed on entering inmates. Among the 3,678 individuals received under sentence of death during that time, about one in every seven entered with two or more death sentences.

Among prisoners executed between 1977 and 2000, the average time spent between the imposition of the most recent sentence received and execution was slightly more than ten years. White prisoners spent an average of nine years and eight months, and black prisoners, ten years and eight months. The 85 prisoners executed in 2000 were under sentence of death an average of 11 years and five months. For the 683 prisoners executed between 1977 and 2000, the most common method of execution was lethal injection (518). Other methods were electrocution (149), lethal gas (11), hanging (3), and firing squad (2). Among prisoners under sentence of death at year-end 2000, the average time spent in prison was eight years.[10]

12-9 Is the Death Penalty Biased?

The death penalty is increasingly scrutinized by private and public groups. Many speculate that the death penalty is unequal justice in light of minorities being disproportionately sentenced to death. In February 1994, two months before his retirement from the Supreme Court, Justice Harry A. Blackmun articulated his personal conviction that capital punishment in the United States is not applied fairly and consistently and is therefore unconstitutional.[11]

For many years reports from around the country have found that a pervasive racial prejudice in the application of the death penalty exists. For example, since the 1950s, research is clear that the death penalty in some southern states fell disproportionately on African Americans who had been convicted of the rape of white women. Since 1930, 54.6 percent of the 3,859 persons executed for all crimes have been African American or other racial minority groups. More disturbing is that of the 455 executed for rape alone, 89.5 percent nonwhite.[12]

Most of the research centering on racial disparities in death penalty sentences concludes that in similar cases, defendants who kill white victims are much more likely to receive the death penalty than those who kill black victims.[13] The most convincing study of the racial breakdown of the death penalty was conducted by Professors David Baldus, George Woodworth, and Charles Pulaski. They studied more than 2000 murder cases in Georgia in the 1970s. These researchers found that defendants charged with killing white victims received the death penalty 11 times more often than defendants charged with killing black victims. Black defendants charged with killing white victims received a death sentence 22 percent of the time, while white defendants charged with killing black victims received the death penalty in only 3 percent of the cases.[14] Much of the disparity seemed attributable to Georgia prosecutors, who sought the death penalty in 70 percent of cases involving African American defendants and white victims, but only 19 percent of cases involving white defendants and black victims.[15] In 1997 these same researchers examined death penalty rates among all defendants in Philadelphia, Pennsylvania, between 1983 and 1993. The results of their study proved that the odds of receiving the death penalty in Philadelphia increased by 38 percent when the accused was black.[16]

In the fall of 2000, the U.S. Department of Justice (DOJ) released the results of an initial survey of federal death penalty prosecutions. The report shows that the federal death penalty, like its application in the states, is used disproportionately against people of color. Of the 18 prisoners currently on federal death row, 16 are either African American, Hispanic, or Asian. From

1995 to 2000, 80 percent of all the federal capital cases recommended by U.S. attorneys to the attorney general seeking the death penalty involved people of color. Even after review by the attorney general, 72 percent of the cases approved for death penalty prosecution involved minority defendants.

The DOJ study also revealed the influence that the race of the victim has in determining potential capital cases. U.S. attorneys recommended the death penalty in 36 percent of the cases with black defendants and non-black victims, but only recommended the death penalty in 20 percent of the cases with black defendants and black victims.

More recently, Maryland Governor Parris Glendening ordered a study into possible racial bias in the criminal justice system. Of the 13 prisoners on death row, nine (about 70 percent) are black in a state whose population is 28 percent black. In 12 of the 13 cases where the death penalty was imposed the victims were white. Although about three out of four murder victims in Maryland are black. Subsequently, Maryland's governor, in May 2002, declared a one-year moratorium on executions.[17]

12-10 Is the Death Penalty Broken?

Some criticize the death penalty on the grounds that evidence used to convict defendants in many death penalty cases is weak at best. In July 2002, a federal judge in New York declared the death penalty unconstitutional because it creates undue risk of putting innocent people to death. The judge concluded that execution is an indefensible sentence because, once carried out, it cannot be undone. With any other punishment, there are ways to redress errors. Not so with death. In the New York case, U.S. District Court Judge Jed Rakoff told federal prosecutors that they may not seek the death penalty for two drug dealers accused of murdering a government informant. He argued that the 1984 Federal Death Penalty Act should be set aside because so much more is known about mistakes that permeate the system.[18] Judge Rakoff further argued that imposing a death sentence using an inherently flawed system violates a very basic constitutional right.

DNA testing has proved conclusively that numerous innocent people have been convicted and sentenced to die. Several states have amended their death penalty laws and two, Illinois and Maryland, imposed moratoriums on capital punishment while they review their laws. In one capital case, a man was sent to death row after being defended by a court-appointed, alcoholic lawyer who slept through parts of the trial.

In January 2003, at a press conference condemning the capital punishment system as fundamentally flawed and unfair, Governor Ryan commuted all Illinois death sentences to prison terms of life or less, the largest such emptying of death row in American history. The governor acted just 48 hours before the end of his term and one day after he had pardoned four death row inmates outright. The governor was reported to have stated that "The legislature couldn't reform it, lawmakers won't repeal it, and I won't stand for it—I must act."[19] Illinois had executed 12 individuals since 1976 and had exonerated 13 death row inmates, one within 48 hours of the scheduled execution. Most cases that are eligible for the death penalty are plea-bargained to lesser offenses or lesser punishments. However, an innocent person is less likely to admit the crime and therefore, if wrongly convicted more likely to receive the death penalty.

The reaction to Governor Ryan's actions has been heated and mixed. For example a review of the letters to the *New York Times* editor after the story was published indicated a variety of opinions regarding his actions. One person from San Francisco stated that the miscarriages of justice will pique people's conscience and surely we can do better. An Illinois writer stated that he was shocked that he commuted all death row sentences to life or less. The writer stated that the governor's action was not a revelation but a politically motivated act intended as a defense to the governor's possible prosecution in a corruption scandal.[20] Many victims' organizations also criticized the governor's actions. The governor, while a state legislator voted for the present death penalty in 1977.[21] The governor had been investigated for his actions while serving in a different political office and 12 of his former staff members were indicted for alleged offenses that included using state money for political campaigns.[22]

The International Commission of Jurists, which represents judges and senior lawyers in 60 nations, said that it "thoroughly and emphatically" supported the decision of Governor Ryan. President Fox of Mexico, expressed his thanks to the governor as did the Pope. According to Amnesty International, the death penalty is either formally banned or has fallen out of use in 111 countries out of 195, and those using capital punishment are increasingly reluctant to do so. According to Amnesty International this leaves the United States in the company mostly of authoritarian nations such as China and Iran.[23]

In 2000, the governor appointed a commission that consisted of two prosecutors, two public defenders, a former federal judge, a former U.S. senator, and other prominent citizens, including novelist and attorney Scott Turow. He gave the commission only one instruction. They were to determine what reforms, if any, would make application of the death penalty fair, just, and accurate. The commission agreed that the present system was unfair and made numerous recommendations for changing it. The commission also, by a narrow vote, agreed that capital punishment should not be a punishment option.

During the same week that the Illinois governor announced his actions, the California governor despite a huge budget deficit, proposed building a $220 million state of the art death row for the state of California. The proposed unit would house about 1,000 inmates at the San Quentin Prison. The state averages more than 20 death sentences a year, but only about one execution.[24] Also that week, the U.S. Supreme Court in a 5-to-4 decision in the case of *Sattazahn v. Pennsylvania*[25] ruled that the U.S. Constitution's bar against double jeopardy didn't protect a murder defendant from being sentenced to death in a new trial after his first trial deadlocked over the sentence. The defendant was convicted by the first jury but they deadlocked on whether he should get the death penalty. In Pennsylvania in this case, the defendant receives a life sentence. David Sattazahn, however, appealed his case and a new trial was ordered. On the re-trial the court sentenced him to death. Justice Ginnsbury, in dissent, stated that "the Court's holding confronts defendants with a perilous choice." Now if the defendant does not receive the death penalty in a capital case, the defendant may hesitate to appeal no matter what errors were made in the trial. More than half the states and the federal government have similar statutes.

The peak year for executions in the United States since 1976 was in 1999. There were 98 executions that year compared to only 66 in 2001. In 2002 there were 71 executions, but fewer states (13) conducted executions in 2002 than in any year since 1993. Texas alone executed 33 people, and the next highest state was Oklahoma which executed seven. Outside of the South, where 61 were executed, only three states (California, Ohio, and Missouri) executed anyone.[26]

PRACTICUM

You are a probation officer in Broward County, Florida. You are assigned to develop a PSI (presentence investigation report) on the defendant. He has been found guilty of capital murder. The only possible punishments are the death penalty or life in prison. How would you answer the questions below? After you have answered the questions, read the following case. Does the case change your answers?

1. Should the requirements for PSIs be different in capital cases from non-capital cases?
2. Susan, a neighbor of the defendant, states that he raped her, but she has never reported this offense to anyone. He stated that he or one of his brothers will kill her if she tells anyone. Susan requests that her statement and any mention of the rape be kept secret from the defendant. You decide that this information should be included in your PSI. What do you do? Does the defendant have the right to be presented with this information?

CASE
GARDNER v. FLORIDA
430 U.S. 349, 97 S.Ct. 1197, 51 L.Ed.2d 393 (1977)

Justice Stephens announced the judgment of the Court and delivered an opinion, in which Justice Stewart and Justice Powell joined.

GARDNER was convicted of first-degree murder and sentenced to death. When the trial judge imposed the death sentence he stated that he was relying in part on information in a presentence investigation report. Portions of the report were not disclosed to counsel for the parties. Without reviewing the confidential portion of the presentence investigation report, the Supreme Court of Florida, over the dissent of two justices, affirmed the death sentence. We conclude that this procedure does not satisfy the constitutional command that no person shall be deprived of life without due process of law.

On June 30, 1973, Gardner assaulted his wife with a blunt instrument, causing her death. On January 10, 1974, after a trial in the Circuit Court of Citrus County, Fla., a jury found him guilty of first-degree murder. The separate sentencing hearing required by Florida law in capital cases was held later on the same day. The state merely introduced two photographs of the decedent, otherwise relying on the trial testimony. That testimony, if credited, was sufficient to support a finding of one of the statutory aggravating circumstances, that the felony committed by Gardner "was especially heinous, atrocious, or cruel." In mitigation, Gardner testified that he had consumed a vast quantity of alcohol during a day-long drinking spree that preceded the crime and professed to have almost no recollection of the assault itself. His testimony, if credited, was sufficient to support a finding of at least one of the statutory mitigating circumstances.

After the jury retired to deliberate, the judge announced that he was going to order a presentence investigation of Gardner. Twenty-five minutes later the jury returned its advisory verdict. It expressly found that the mitigating circumstances outweighed the aggravating circumstances and advised the court to impose a life sentence.

The presentence investigation report was completed by the Florida Parole and Probation Commission on January 28, 1974. On January 30, 1974, the trial judge entered findings of fact and a judgment sentencing Gardner to death. His ultimate finding was that the felony "was especially heinous, atrocious or cruel; and that such aggravating circumstances outweigh the mitigating circumstance, to-wit: none." As a preface to that ultimate finding, he recited that his conclusion was based on the evidence presented at both stages of the bifurcated proceeding, the arguments of counsel, and his review of "the factual information contained in said presentence investigation."

There is no dispute about the fact that the presentence investigation report contained a confidential portion that was not disclosed to defense counsel. Although the judge noted in his findings of fact that the State and Gardner's counsel had been given "a copy of that portion of the report to which they are entitled," counsel made no request to examine the full report or to be apprised of the contents of the confidential portion. The trial judge did not comment on the contents of the confidential portion. His findings do not indicate that there was anything of special importance in the undisclosed portion, or that there was any reason other than customary practice for not disclosing the entire report to the parties . . . expressly recognized by this Court.

. . . Five members of this Court have now expressly recognized that death is a different kind of punishment from any other that may be imposed in this country. . . . From the point of view of the defendant, it is different in both its severity and its finality. From the point of view of society, the action of the sovereign in taking the life of one of its citizens also differs dramatically from any other legitimate state action. It is of vital importance to the defendant and to the community that any decision to impose the death sentence be, and appear to be, based on reason rather than caprice or emotion.

. . . It is now clear that the sentencing process, as well as the trial itself, must satisfy the requirements of the Due Process Clause. Even though the defendant has no substantive right to a particular sentence within the range authorized by statute, the sentencing is a critical stage of the criminal proceeding at which he is entitled to the effective assistance of counsel. . . . The defendant has a legitimate interest in the character of the procedure that leads to the imposition of sentence even if he may have no right to object to a particular result of the sentencing process.

In the light of these developments we consider the justifications offered by the State for a capital-sentencing procedure that permits a trial judge to impose the death sentence on the basis of confidential information which is not disclosed to the defendant or his counsel.

The State first argues that an assurance of confidentiality to potential sources of information is essential to enable investigators to obtain relevant but sensitive disclosures from people unwilling to comment publicly about a defendant's background or character. The availability of such information, it is argued, provides the person who prepares the report with greater detail on which to base a sentencing recommendation and, in turn, provides the judge with a better basis for his sentencing decision. But consideration must be given to the quality, as well as the quantity, of the information on which the sentencing judge may rely. Assurances of secrecy are conducive to the transmission of confidences that may bear no closer relation to fact than the average rumor or item of gossip, and may imply a pledge not to attempt independent verification of the information received. The risk that some of the information accepted in confidence may be erroneous, or may be misinterpreted by the investigator or by the sentencing judge, is manifest.

If, as the State argues, it is important to use such information in the sentencing process, we must assume that in some cases it will be decisive in the judge's choice between a life sentence and a death sentence. If it tends to tip the scales in favor of life, presumably the information would be favorable and there would be no reason why it should not be disclosed. On the other hand, if it is the basis for a death sentence, the interest in reliability plainly outweighs the State's interest in preserving the availability of comparable information in other cases.

The State also suggests that full disclosure of the presentence report will unnecessarily delay the proceeding. We think the likelihood of significant delay is overstated because we must presume that reports prepared by professional probation officers, as the Florida procedure requires, are generally reliable. In those cases in which the accuracy of a report is contested, the trial judge can avoid delay by disregarding the disputed material. Or if the disputed matter is of critical importance, the time invested in ascertaining the truth would surely be well spent if it makes the difference between life and death.

The State further urges that full disclosure of presentence reports, which often include psychiatric and psychological evaluations, will occasionally disrupt the process of rehabilitation. The argument, if valid, would hardly justify withholding the report from defense counsel. Moreover, whatever force that argument may have in non-capital cases, it has absolutely no merit in a case in which the judge has decided to sentence the defendant to death. Indeed, the extinction of all possibility of rehabilitation is one of the aspects of the death sentence that makes it different in kind from any other sentence a State may legitimately impose . . .

Even if it were permissible to withhold a portion of the report from a defendant, and even from defense counsel, pursuant to an express finding of good cause for nondisclosure, it would nevertheless be necessary to make the full report a part of the record to be reviewed on appeal. Because the State must administer its capital-sentencing procedures with an even hand, it is important that the record on appeal disclose to the reviewing court the considerations that motivated the death sentence in every case in which it is imposed. Without full disclosure of the basis for the death sentence, the Florida capital-sentencing procedure would be subject to the defects that resulted in the holding of unconstitutionality in *Furman v. Georgia*. In this particular case, the only explanation for the lack of disclosure is the failure of defense counsel to request access to the full report. That failure cannot justify the submission of a less complete record to the reviewing court than the record on which the trial judge based his decision to sentence Gardner to death.

Nor do we regard this omission by counsel as an effective waiver of the constitutional error in the record. There are five reasons for this conclusion. First, the State does not urge that the objection has been waived. Second, the Florida Supreme Court has held that it has a duty to consider "the total record" when it reviews a death sentence. Third, because two members of that court expressly considered this point on the appeal in this case, we presume that the entire court passed on the question. Fourth, there is no basis for presuming that the defendant himself made a knowing and intelligent waiver, or that counsel could possibly have made a tactical decision not to examine the full report. Fifth, because the judge found, in disagreement with the jury, that the evidence did not establish any mitigating circumstance, and because the presentence report was the only item considered by the judge but not by the jury, the full review of the factual basis for the judge's rejection of the advisory verdict is plainly required. For if the jury, rather than the judge, correctly assessed Gardner's veracity, the death sentence rests on an erroneous factual predicate.

We conclude that Gardner was denied due process of law when the death sentence was imposed, at least in part, on the basis of information that he had no opportunity to deny or explain ...

THE CHIEF JUSTICE concurs in the judgment. JUSTICE WHITE, concurring in the judgment. "[W]e believe that in capital cases the fundamental respect for humanity underlying the Eighth Amendment, requires consideration of the character and record of the individual offender and the circumstances of the particular offense as a constitutionally indispensable part of the process of inflicting the penalty of death. This conclusion rests squarely on the predicate that the penalty of death is qualitatively different from a sentence of imprisonment, however long.... Because of that qualitative difference, there is a corresponding difference in the need for reliability in the determination that death is the appropriate punishment in a specific case.

Here the sentencing judge indicated that he selected Gardner for the death penalty in part because of information contained in a presentence report that was not disclosed to Gardner or to his counsel and to which Gardner had no opportunity to respond. A procedure for selecting people for the death penalty that permits consideration of such secret information relevant to the "character and record of the individual offender," fails to meet the "need for reliability in the determination that death is the appropriate punishment" which the Court indicated was required.... This conclusion stems solely from the Eighth Amendment's ban on cruel and unusual punishments ... my conclusion is limited ... to cases in which the death penalty is imposed. I thus see no reason to address in this case the possible application to sentencing proceedings—in death or other cases—of the Due Process Clause, other than as the vehicle by which the strictures of the Eighth Amendment are triggered in this case. For these reasons, I do not join the plurality opinion but concur in the judgment.

JUSTICE BLACKMUN, concurring in the judgment. In *Ring v. Arizona* (decided June, 2002), the U.S. Supreme Court held that juries, not judges, must make the factual determinations that makes a convicted murderer eligible for the death penalty. That case has raised a question regarding the legality of the procedures used by Florida as demonstrated by the Gardner case.

Given the judgments of the Court in *Woodson v. North Carolina,* 428 U.S. 280 (1976), and in *Roberts v. Louisiana,* 428 U.S. 325 (1976), I concur in the judgment the Court reaches in the present case.

JUSTICE BRENNAN. I agree for the reasons stated in the plurality opinion that the Due Process Clause of the Fourteenth Amendment is violated when a defendant facing a death sentence is not informed of the contents of a presentence investigation report made to the sentencing judge. However, I adhere to my view that the death penalty is in all circumstances cruel and unusual punishment prohibited by the Eighth and Fourteenth amendments. I therefore would vacate the death sentence, and I dissent from the Court's judgment insofar as it remands for further proceedings that could lead to its imposition.

JUSTICE MARSHALL dissenting. Last Term, this Court carefully scrutinized the Florida procedures for imposing the death penalty and concluded that there were sufficient safeguards to insure that the death sentence would not be "wantonly" and "freakishly" imposed. *Proffitt v. Florida,* 428 U.S. 242 (1976). This case, however, belies that hope. While I continue to believe that the death penalty is unconstitutional in all circumstances, and therefore would remand this case for resentencing to a term of life, nevertheless, now that Florida may legally take a life, we must insist that it be in accordance with the standards enunciated by this Court. In this case I am appalled at the extent to which Florida has deviated from the procedures upon which this Court expressly relied. It is not simply that the trial judge, in overriding the jury's recommendation of life imprisonment, relied on undisclosed portions of the presentence report. Nor is it merely that the Florida Supreme Court affirmed the sentence without discussing the omission and without concern that it did not even have the entire report before it. Obviously that alone is enough to deny due process and require that the death sentence be vacated as the Court now holds. But the blatant disregard exhibited by the courts below for the standards devised to regulate imposition of the death penalty calls into question the very basis for this Court's approval of that system in *Proffitt.*

JUSTICE REHNQUIST, dissenting. Had I joined the plurality opinion in last Term's *Woodson v. North Carolina,* I would join the concurring opinion of my Brother White in this case. But if capital punishment is not cruel and unusual under the Eighth and Fourteenth Amendments, as the Court held in that case, the use of particular sentencing procedures, never previously held unfair under the Due Process Clause, in a case where the death sentence is imposed cannot convert that sentence into a cruel and unusual punishment. The prohibition of the Eighth Amendment relates to the character of the punishment, and not to the process by which it is imposed. I would therefore affirm the judgment of the Supreme Court of Florida.

Summary

Individuals have been executed for their crimes from the earliest of recorded history. During the seventeenth and eighteenth centuries, the death penalty was the most common form of punishment. In England during that period, there were over 200 crimes for which it could be imposed. As of 2000, approximately 73 percent of the people in the United States supported the use of the death penalty. The Death Penalty Information Center, however, contends that when the public is provided with alternative sentences, such as life imprisonment without any possibility of parole, only a minority of people support the death penalty.

Those who contend that the death penalty is unconstitutional typically base their legal argument on the cruel and unusual punishment clause of the Eighth Amendment to the U.S. Constitution. Those who support the death penalty point out that the due process clauses of the Fifth and Fourteenth amendments state: "no person shall be deprived of life without due process of law." Thus, the two amendments imply that the constitution does not forbid the death penalty.

The U.S. Supreme Court has struggled through the years with many perplexing issues that center on the constitutional regulation of the death penalty. Prior to 1972, the Supreme Court placed virtually no constitutional restrictions on the imposition of the death penalty. Most state legislatures had rejected the automatic death penalty statutes. Juries were generally instructed that if they found the defendant guilty of a capital crime, they must then decide between death and life imprisonment. The juries had virtually unguided discretion. In most cases, little information regarding the defendant's character, background, and previous criminal record was presented.

In 1972, the U.S. Supreme Court decided *Furman v. Georgia*, which held by a five-to-four decision that the capital punishment statute in Georgia was unconstitutional. All nine justices wrote separate opinions. Each of the opinions concluded that juries should not be given unguided discretion in imposing the death penalty. The decision, while providing no guidance regarding the use of the death penalty, clearly established that all states' death penalty statutes were unconstitutional.

Recent Supreme Court decisions have placed further restrictions on the capital punishment. On June 20, 2002, the Supreme Court declared that executing mentally retarded murderers is unconstitutionally cruel, offering the possibility of reprieve to scores of inmates in the biggest shift in the court's stance on capital punishment in a quarter-century. Of the 38 states that have capital punishment, 18 bar the execution of retarded defendants. Although the legal definition of retardation used in those states varies slightly, most require an IQ under 70 and evidence that the person has difficulty navigating daily life. Legal experts say the most immediate challenges will come in the 20 states, including Virginia and Texas that allow the execution of retarded defendants.

There is an abundance of research that has made clear that the death penalty falls disproportionately on African Americans. Since 1930, 54.6 percent of the 3,859 persons executed for all crimes have been African American or other racial minority groups. What is more disturbing is that of the 455 executed for rape alone, 89.5 percent nonwhite. Most of the research centering on racial disparities in death penalty sentences has concluded, among all other things being equal, defendants who kill white victims are much more likely to receive the death penalty than those who kill black victims.

Discussion Questions

1. Should the death penalty be an authorized punishment? Justify your answer.
2. What safeguards may be imposed to prevent the death penalty from being discriminatorily applied?
3. Is the death penalty effective in crime prevention? Explain.
4. What are the general characteristics of individuals on death row?
5. Discuss the legal ramifications of imposing the death penalty.
6. Should executions be televised? Justify your answer.
7. Explain the court's rationale for holding that it was cruel and unusual to execute a person who does not understand the gravity of the punishment.

Chapter Quiz

True/False

1. Presently, in the United States capital punishment has been authorized for aggravated and nonaggravated criminal homicide.
2. Public opinion polls have shown that the general public is against the death penalty.
3. In 1976, the majority of the Supreme Court concluded in *Gregg v. Georgia,* that the authors of the cruel and unusual punishment clause did not intend to forbid capital punishment.
4. In pre-industrial societies, the death penalty was often carried out by banishing the criminal to the wilderness where death was relatively certain.
5. In early colonial America and the early England, a firing squad was the most common form of execution.

Multiple Choice

1. In 1972, the U.S. Supreme Court decided in _____ that the capital punishment statuette in Georgia was unconstitutional.
   a. *Gregg v. Georgia*
   b. *Furman v. Georgia*
   c. *Gardner v. Georgia*
   d. *Gains v. Georgia*
2. The last public execution took place in _____ on August 14, 1936.
   a. Houston, Texas
   b. Atlanta, Georgia
   c. Dallas, Texas
   d. Owensboro, Kentucky
3. Factors that tend to reduce the severity of a crime are called
   a. aggravating circumstances.
   b. mitigating circumstances.
   c. challenging circumstances.
   d. reasonable circumstances.
4. The most predominant method of execution today is
   a. electrocution.
   b. hanging.
   c. lethal injection.
   d. firing squad.
5. Research has revealed regarding disparities in who is sentenced to death that
   a. whites are disproportionately sentenced to death when compared to minorities.
   b. whites and minorities are sentenced to death at about the same ratios.
   c. minorities are disproportionately sentenced to death when compared to whites.
   d. none of the above

Endnotes

1. William Bailey, "Murder, Capital Punishment and Television," *American Sociological Review* 55(5, 1990): 628–633; "Public Executions," *Journal of Prison Discipline and Philanthropy* (July 1989): 117–123.
2. Jonathan Alter, The Death Penalty on Trial," *Newsweek,* 12 June 2000; Mark Gillespie, "Public Opinion Supports Death Penalty," The Gallup Organization Webpage, http://www.gallup.com, 24 February 1999.
3. Neil Walker, "Executive Clemency and the Death Penalty," *American Journal of Criminal Law* 22(1994): 245.
4. William Glaberson, "From Death, an Inmate Battles to Control his Case," *The New York Times,* 24 June 2002.

5. "Capital Punishment, 2000," NCJ–158023, February, 2001.
6. John N. Ferdico, *Criminal Law and Justice Dictionary* (St. Paul: West, 1992), 200.
7. *Louisiana ex rel. Francis v. Resweber,* 329 U.S. 459 (1947).
8. 408 U.S. 238 (1976).
9. Bureau of Justice Statistics Bulletin, *Capital Punishment 1999* (Washington, DC: U.S. Department of Justice, 2000), 1.
10. Ibid.
11. Marvin Wolfgang and Mark Riedel, "Race, Judicial Discretion, and the Death Penalty," *Annals of the American Academy of Political and Social Sciences* 407(1973): 119–133.
12. David Cole, *No Equal Justice: Race and Class in the American Criminal Justice System* (New York: The New Press, 1999).
13. Mark Tushnet, *The Death Penalty* (New York: Facts on File, 1994).
14. David Cole, *No Equal Justice*, 133; See also *McClesky v. Kemp,* 481 U.S. 279, 327 (1987) (Brennan, J., dissenting).
15. "Judge Takes Aim at Death Penalty," *Topeka Capital Journal* 9 July 2002, 4A.
16. David C. Baldus and George Woodworth, "Race Discrimination and the Death Penalty in the Post Furman Era: An Empirical and Legal Analysis with Recent Findings from Philadelphia," *Cornell Law Review* 83(1638, 1998).
17. Lori Montgomery, "Maryland Questioning Local Extremes on Death Penalty," *The Washington Post*, 12 May 2002, C01.
18. "Judge Takes Aim at Death Penalty," *Topeka Capital Journal,* 9 July 2002, 4A.
19. As reported by Jodi Wilgoren, "Governor Empties Illinois Death Row," *The New York Times,* 13 January 2003, A1.
20. Letters to the editors, *The New York Times,* 14 January 2003.
21. *The New York Times,* 12 January 2003, 2.
22. *Time,* 20 January 2003, 40.
23. *The New York Times,* 14 January 2003, A7
24. "National Briefing: West," *The New York Times,* 14 January 2003.
25. Decided January 14, 2003, Docket no. 01–7574.
26. *The Washington Post,* National Weekly Edition, 6–12 January 2003, 25.

Chapter 13

Prisoners' Rights

Prison guards conduct a search of a prisoner's cell.
Mark C. Ide

Key Terms

42 US Code 1983
deference period
deliberate indifference

hands-off period
Prison Litigation Reform Act
rights period

tort
writ of habeas corpus

Outline

13-1 Hands-Off Period
13-2 Rights Period
13-3 Categories of Involvement
    13-3a Due Process Rights
    13-3b Torts
    13-3c Conditions of Confinement
    13-3d Habeas Corpus
13-4 Prison Litigation Reform Act
13-5 Back to Basics
13-6 Historical Background of the "Cruel and Unusual" Clause
13-7 Significant Cases Involving Prisoners' Rights
    13-7a *Large v. Superior Court of County of Maricopa* 714 P2d 399 (1986)
    13-7b *Bounds v. Smith* 97 S.Ct. 1491 (1977)
    13-7c *Hutto v. Finney* 98 S.Ct. 2565 (1978)
    13-7d *Estelle v. Gamble* 97 S.Ct. 285 (1976)
    13-7e *Helling v. McKinney* 113 S.Ct. 2475 (1993)
    13-7f *Jones v. N.C. Prisoners' Labor Union* 97 S.Ct. 2532 (1976)
    13-7g *Meachum v. Fano* 96 S.Ct. 2532 (1976)
    13-7h *Vitek v. Jones* 100 S.Ct. 1254 (1987)
    13-7i *Turner v. Safety* 107 S.Ct. 2254 (1987)
    13-7j *Wolff v. McDonnell* 94 S.Ct. 2963 (1974)
    13-7k *Procunier v. Martinez* 416 U.S. 396 (1974)
    13-7l *McKune v. Lile* 536 U.S. 24 (2002)
13-8 Deliberate Indifference
    13-8a *Farmer v. Brennan* 511 U.S. 825 (1994)
13-9 *Warner v. Orange County Probation Department*, CA 2, No. 95-7055 decided 9/9/96, affirming 870 F.Supp. 69
Summary
Discussion Questions
Chapter Quiz
Endnotes

Learning Objectives

After studying this chapter, the reader will be able to:

- List and explain the three periods of court involvement in prisoners' rights.
- List and explain the four areas of prisoners' rights.
- Explain the importance of the *writ of habeas corpus*.
- Analyze the Prison Litigation Reform Act of 1994.
- Explain the "back to the basics" movement regarding prison conditions.
- Diagram the historical development of the "cruel and unusual" clause.
- List the prisoners' rights that the courts have recognized in court cases.
- Define the "deliberate indifference" requirement.
- Explain the importance of the *Warner v. Orange County* case.

Prior to the 1960s the courts stayed out of the area of prisoners' rights. In the late 1960s, the U.S. Supreme Court began to involve itself in this area and has since decided more than 30 cases on the subject. The court's involvement in prisoners' rights can be divided into three periods: the "hands-off" period (prior to 1964), the "rights" period (1964–1978), and the "deference" period (since 1979).[1]

13-1 Hands-Off Period

During the **hands-off period,** the courts rarely accepted a case involving the conditions of confinement or prisoners' rights based on the concept that prison administrators were best qualified to determine the appropriate conditions of confinement. While the courts apparently recognized that prisoners have constitutional rights, the courts felt that it was not their role to intervene to protect those rights. One theory to explain the reluctance of the courts to intervene during this period was that the courts perceived that intervention would usurp the proper functions of the legislative and executive branches of the government. A second reason given is that the courts felt they lacked the expertise necessary to protect prisoners' rights and therefore ran a risk of interfering with the proper functioning of the prisons. The third popular reason given was that most prisoners were confined in state institutions, and federal courts were hesitant to interfere in state governmental operations.

13-2 Rights Period

During the **rights period,** the courts became actively involved in prison administration. The movement started when the lower federal courts demonstrated a willingness to identify prisoners' rights and moved to protect those rights. In addition, the legal profession developed a cadre of public interest lawyers who were more willing to fight the system than in the past.

The current **deference period** is marked by the policy of the courts to defer to prison administrators' judgments unless constitutional violations are apparent. The present climate can be described as one in which prisoners will lose on most rights issues, while the courts stress the need to give deference to the expertise of correctional officials. The Federal Prison Litigation Reform Act of 1996 is designed to limit federal court intervention into prison administration.[2] This legislation is discussed later in this chapter.

13-3 Categories of Involvement

Prisoners' rights can be divided into four broad areas:

1. Right of access to the courts
2. Individual rights
3. Due process issues
4. Cruel and unusual punishment[3]

The general consensus is that the courts tend to favor inmates when the issue involves the right of access to the courts and favor the prison officials when the other three areas are involved. Included in Appendix A are excerpts from the American Bar Association's *Standards for Criminal Justice: Legal Status of Prisoners*. The standards are statements regarding what the law is, or should be, relating to the legal status of prisoners. Appendix B contains the national policies on corrections as ratified by the American Correctional Association. The two appendices should be reviewed by the reader to obtain a better understanding of the legal status of prisoners and our national policies on corrections.

13-3a Due Process Rights

Except for those cases brought by pretrial detainees regarding the conditions of their confinement, most due process rights issues concern procedural protections that must be afforded an inmate. For example, in most cases an inmate has no right to complain of the actions taken by prison officials, only that the officials failed to provide him with procedural due process before taking action. In this area, it appears that the Supreme Court generally holds that if a liberty interest is involved, such as the loss of good time, that prior to taking the action the inmate has a right to written notice, an opportunity to be heard, a written statement of the reasons for the decisions, and the right to be represented by a representative (not necessarily an attorney).

13-3b Torts

In most situations, prisoners challenging actions of prison officials do so by tort actions. A **tort** is a civil wrong or injury, other than a breach of contract, resulting from a violation of a duty. Most tort cases involving prisoners are filed under the Civil Rights Act, **42 US Code 1983.**

Less than 2 percent of the 1983 cases filed by inmates were successful in obtaining any redress. Despite this low rate of success, the number of cases filed each year continues to increase. It was estimated that approximately 50,000 suits were filed nationwide by prisoners in 1995. In 1993,

New York alone had over 10,000 filed against it. More recently, in 2001, there were about 58,805 suits filed by federal and state inmates. Of these, federal inmates filed 8,644 motions to vacate sentence and 4,440 *habeas corpus* petitions. The more prevalent petitions filed among state inmates were prison conditions. In 2001, state inmates filed a total of 10,395 petitions that centered on prison conditions and 20,446 *habeas corpus* petitions. Overall from 2000 to 2001 there was a 0.9 percent increase in the number of petitions filed by both federal and state inmates.[4]

13-3c Conditions of Confinement

Prisoners who are detained in pretrial confinement facilities may challenge the conditions of their confinement under the Fifth or Fourteenth Amendments' due process clause. Prisoners who have been convicted may challenge their conditions under the Eighth Amendment's prohibition against cruel and unusual punishments.

Box 13-1

Civil Rights Act Title 42, Section 1983, U.S. Code

Any person who, under color of any statute, ordinance, regulation, custom, or usage, or any state, or territory, subjects or causes to be subjected, any citizen of the United States or other person within the jurisdiction thereof to the deprivation of any rights, privileges, or immunities secured by the Constitution and laws, shall be liable to the party injured in an action at law, suit in equity, or other proper proceedings for redress.

13-3d *Habeas Corpus*

Traditionally, prisoners have filed *writs of habeas corpus* to attack the state court convictions. This writ, traditionally known as the "Great Writ," is a constitutionally protected writ designed to require the government to justify why the individual is being held in confinement. Under the process, the prisoner can file a writ in federal court alleging that he is being illegally held in confinement because his conviction was in violation of a state or federal constitutional right. If the writ involves only state issues, then the state courts make the final decision. If the writ is based on a federal issue (e.g., his conviction was based on the violation of a federal constitutional right) then the final decision makers are the federal courts. After the prisoner files the writ, the receiving court determines whether a writ should be issued. If the court issues a writ, then the warden (actually a representative from the attorney general's office) must come forward and justify the confinement. The justification usually consists of filing proof of the conviction, at which point the burden shifts to the defendant to establish the illegality of the conviction. Less than 1 percent of the writs filed are successful. The problem is that a vast number of writs flood the court system.

The writ is also the way that the death penalty from state criminal trials is traditionally attacked in federal court. In the past, convictions have been voided years after the defendants were found guilty. The process has also been used to delay the imposition of the death penalty. To eliminate this, in 1976, the U.S. Congress passed the Antiterrorism and Effective Death Penalty Act. This act establishes limitation periods for the bringing of habeas actions and requires that federal courts generally defer to state courts' determinations. Under the act, a habeas petitioner will normally have one year in which to seek relief. If the claim has been adjudicated in state court, relief will not be available unless the state court's adjudication resulted in a decision that is either contrary to, or involved an unreasonable application of, clearly established federal law as determined by the U.S. Supreme Court, or was based on an unreasonable determination of the facts in light of the evidence presented in the state court proceedings. The presumption of correctness accorded state courts' factual findings was also strengthened. Second or successive habeas actions presenting new claims must be dismissed unless the claim is shown to rely on a new, previously unavailable rule of constitutional law, or the factual predicate for the claim could not have been discovered previously through due diligence; and the new facts would be sufficient to establish by clear and convincing evidence that, except for the error, no reasonable fact finder would have convicted.[5]

13-4 Prison Litigation Reform Act

In an attempt to reduce federal involvement in the operation of state correctional systems, the U.S. Congress passed the **Prison Litigation Reform Act** in 1996. This act was an amendment to the 1994 Crime Bill.[6] Under this act, federal courts are instructed to extend no further than necessary prospective relief in prison overcrowding orders. The act sets two minimum conditions for the entry of prisoner release orders: first, a prior order of less intrusive relief must have failed; second, the prison official must have had a reasonable opportunity to comply with the previous order. One popular method used by federal courts was to order the correction of a problem, or in the alternative, to release the prisoners held under the conditions complained of in the case. In addition, a single judge may not issue a prisoner release order based on overcrowding. Any order issued must be approved by an appellate court or a three-judge federal court. The court, before issuing an order for relief, must find, by clear and convincing evidence, that overcrowding is the primary cause of the violation of a federal right and no relief other than an order releasing prisoners will remedy the violation. Prior to filing for a release order, the prisoner must first exhaust his or her state remedies. In addition, prisoners may not bring federal civil rights actions for mental or emotional injury suffered while in custody without a prior showing of physical injury. The award of attorney fees to successful prisoner litigators was also limited to only that which was directly and reasonably incurred in enforcing the relief.

13-5 Back to Basics

Starting in the mid-1990s, legislators decided that they were tired of "coddling" prison inmates and attempted to make prison conditions harsher for the inmates. A Mississippi senator stated, "We want a prisoner to look like a prisoner and to smell like one." In 1996, Mississippi banned individual televisions from inmate cells, banned air conditioning, prohibited weight-lifting equipment, and required inmates to dress in striped uniforms with CONVICT stamped on the back. Ohio, Wisconsin, and North Carolina have enacted similar legislation. California is now charging inmates $3 to initiate court actions and has banned R-rated movies. South Carolina has banned conjugal visits for minimum-security inmates, ending a 50-year tradition. New Jersey is considering legislation that would require inmates to work 10-hour days with no educational programs, no gyms, and no TVs. The U.S. Congress has eliminated educational grants for federal prisoners. Chain gangs are once again being used in some Southern states.[7] While the above perks may be considered rights by some, the courts have been deferring to the prison administrators regarding the new trend in making prison a harsher place. As one judge stated, "It appears that none of these types of measures will deter crime, but they do not infringe on any prisoner's constitutional rights."

13-6 Historical Background of the "Cruel and Unusual" Clause

Included in this section are excerpts for the U.S. Supreme Court case of *Ronald Allen Harmelin, v. Michigan* 501 U.S. 957 (1991) A review of the excerpts will provide the reader with a summary of the historical background of the "cruel and unusual" clause of the Eighth Amendment.

> [In this case, the defendant claims that his sentence was disproportionate and therefore in violation of the "cruel and unusual" clause of the Eighth Amendment. The Court denied his claim.]
>
> Justice Scalia announced the judgment of the Court . . .
>
> . . . There is no doubt that the Declaration of Rights is the antecedent of our constitutional text. (This document was promulgated in February 1689 and was enacted into law as the Bill of Rights.) In 1791, five state constitutions prohibited "cruel or unusual punishments," and two prohibited "cruel" punishments. The new federal Bill of Rights, however, tracked Virginia's prohibition of "cruel and unusual punishments," which most closely followed the English provision. In fact, the entire text of the Eighth Amendment is taken almost verbatim from the English Declaration of Rights, which provided "[t]hat excessive Baile ought not to be required nor excessive Fines imposed nor cruell and unusuall Punishments inflicted."
>
> Perhaps the Americans of 1791 understood the Declaration's language precisely as the Englishmen of 1689 did—though as we shall discuss later, that seems unlikely. Or perhaps the colonists meant to incorporate the content of that antecedent by reference, whatever the content might have been. Solem suggested something like this, arguing that since Americans claimed "all the rights of English subjects," "their use of the language of the English Bill of Rights is convincing proof that they intended to provide at least the same protection," . . . Thus, not only is the original meaning of the 1689 Declaration of Rights relevant, but also the circumstances of its enactment, insofar as they display the particular "rights of English subjects" it was designed to vindicate. . . . The Magna Carta provided that "[a] free man shall not be fined for a small offence, except in proportion to the measure of the offence; and for a great offence he shall be fined in proportion to the magnitude of the offence, saving his freehold . . .
>
> Most historians agree that the "cruell and unusuall Punishments" provision of the English Declaration of Rights was prompted by the abuses attributed to the infamous Lord Chief Justice Jeffreys of the King's Bench during the Stuart reign of James II. . . . They do not agree, however, on which abuses.

Jeffreys is best known for presiding over the "Bloody Assizes" following the Duke of Monmouth's abortive rebellion in 1685, a special commission led by Jeffreys tried, convicted, and executed hundreds of suspected insurgents. Some have attributed the Declaration of Rights provision to popular outrage against those proceedings.

But the vicious punishments for treason decreed in the Bloody Assizes (drawing and quartering, burning of women felons, beheading, disembowling, etc.) were common in that period—indeed, they were specifically authorized by law and remained so for many years afterwards. Thus, recently historians have argued, and the best historical evidence suggests, that it was not Jeffrey's management of the Bloody Assizes that led to the Declaration of Rights provision, but rather the arbitrary sentencing power he had exercised in administering justice from the King's Bench, particularly when punishing a notorious perjurer. Jeffreys was widely accused of "inventing" special penalties for the King's enemies, penalties that were not authorized by common-law precedent or statute.

The preamble to the Declaration of Rights, a sort of indictment of James II that calls to mind the preface to our own Declaration of Independence, specifically referred to illegal sentences and King's Bench proceedings. "Whereas the late King James II, by the Assistance of diverse Evill Councellors Judges and Ministers imployed by him did endeavour to subvert and extirpate the Protestant Religion, and the Lawes and Liberties of this Kingdome."

By Prosecutions in the Court of King's Bench for Matters and Causes cognizable onely in Parlyament and by diverse other Arbitrary and Illegall Courses." "[E]xcessive Baile hath beene required of Persons committed in Criminall Cases to elude the Benefit of the Lawes made for the Liberty of the Subjects. And excessive Fines have been imposed. And illegall and cruell Punishments have been inflicted. All which are utterly and directly contrary to the knowne Lawes and Statutes and Freedome of this Realme.

The only recorded contemporaneous interpretation of the "cruel and unusuall Punishments" clause confirms the focus upon Jeffreys' King's Bench activities, and upon the illegality rather than the disproportionality of his sentences. In 1685, Titus Oates, a Protestant cleric whose false accusations had caused the execution of 15 prominent Catholics for allegedly organizing a "Popish Plot" to overthrow King Charles II in 1679, was tried and convicted before the King's Bench for perjury. Oates' crime, "bearing false witness against another, with an express premeditated design to take away his life, so as the innocent person be condemned and executed" had, at one time, been treated as a species of murder, and punished with death. At sentencing, Jeffreys complained that death was no longer available as a penalty and lamented that "a proportionable punishment of that crime can scarce by our law, as it now stands, be inflicted upon him." The law would not stand in the way, however. The judges met, and, according to Jeffreys, were in unanimous agreement that "crimes of this nature are left to be punished according to the discretion of this court, so far as that the judgment extend not to life or member." *Ibid.* Another justice taunted Oates that "we have taken special care of you," ... The court then decreed that he should pay a fine of "1000 marks upon each Indictment," that he should be "stript of [his] Canonical Habits," that he should stand in the pillory annually at certain specified times and places, that on May 20 he should be whipped by "the common hangman" "from Aldgate to Newgate," that he should be similarly whipped on May 22 "from Newgate to Tyburn," and that he should be imprisoned for life. "The judges, as they believed, sentenced Oates to be scourged to death." Oates would not die, however. Four years later, and several months after the Declaration of Rights, he petitioned the House of Lords to set aside his sentence as illegal. "Not a single peer ventured to affirm that the judgment was legal; but much was said about the odious character of the appellant" and the Lords affirmed the judgment. A minority of the Lords dissented, however, and their statement sheds light on the meaning of the "cruel and unusuall Punishments" clause: "1st, [T]he King's Bench, being a Temporal Court, made it a Part of the Judgment, That Titus Oates, being a Clerk, should, for his said Perjuries, be divested of his canonical and priestly Habit . . .; which is a Matter wholly out of their Power, belonging to the Ecclesiastical Courts only. "2dly, [S]aid Judgments are barbarous, inhuman, and unchristian; and there is no Precedent to warrant the Punishments of whipping and committing to Prison for Life, for the Crime of Perjury; which yet were but Part of the Punishments inflicted upon him. "4thly, [T]his will be an Encouragement and Allowance for giving the like cruel, barbarous and illegal Judgments hereafter, unless this Judgment be reversed. "5thly, ... [T]hat the said Judgments were contrary to Law and ancient Practice, and therefore erroneous, and ought to be reversed. "6thly, Because it is contrary to the Declaration on the Twelfth of February last . . . that excessive Bail ought not to be required, nor excessive Fines imposed, nor cruel nor unusual Punishments afflicted."

Unless one accepts the notion of a blind incorporation, however, the ultimate question is not what "cruell and unusuall punishments" meant in the Declaration of Rights, but what its meaning was to the Americans who adopted the Eighth Amendment. Even if one assumes that the Founders knew the precise meaning of that English antecedent, a direct transplant of the English meaning to the soil of American constitutionalism would in any case have been impossible. There were no common-law punishments in the federal system, so that the provision must have been meant as a check not upon judges but upon the Legislature.

Wrenched out of its common-law context, and applied to the actions of a legislature, the word "unusual" could hardly mean "contrary to law." But it continued to mean (as it continues to mean today) "such as [does not] occu[r] in ordinary practice," "[s]uch as is [not] in common use."

The Eighth Amendment received little attention during the proposal and adoption of the federal Bill of Rights. However, what evidence exists from debates at the state ratifying conventions that prompted the Bill of Rights as well as the floor debates in the First Congress which proposed it "confirm[s] the view that the cruel and unusual punishments clause was directed at prohibiting certain methods of punishment."

13-7 Significant Cases Involving Prisoners' Rights

In this section, some of the significant cases involving prisoners' rights are discussed. Most cases are presented in summary form only. Two are presented as abridgements of the actual court opinions. The two opinions should provide the reader with an understanding of the form and substance of court opinions in this area.

13-7a *Large v. Superior Court of County of Maricopa* 714 P2d 399 (1986)

This case, decided by the Arizona Supreme Court, held that the forcible administration of anti-psychotic drugs to a prisoner for management and control rather than for treatment violated the prisoner's liberty interest protected by the due process clause. The court stated that the forcible administration of such dangerous drugs to a mentally ill prisoner in a nonemergency situation was unconstitutional.[8]

13-7b *Bounds v. Smith* 97 S.Ct. 1491 (1977)

In *Bounds v. Smith*, the U.S. Supreme Court made it clear that states were required to have law libraries to assist inmates in their efforts to petition the courts unless the states provided legally trained persons to assist the inmates.[9]

13-7c *Hutto v. Finney* 98 S.Ct. 2565 (1978)

In *Hutto v. Finney*, the Supreme Court held that given the harsh conditions of punitive isolation cells in the Arkansas prison system, inmates could not be placed in those cells for more than 30 days without violating the inmate's constitutional rights against cruel and unusual punishment.[10]

13-7d *Estelle v. Gamble* 97 S.Ct. 285 (1976)

The Supreme Court held in *Estelle v. Gamble* that an inmate cannot prove that inadequate medical care by the prison staff is cruel and unusual unless the inmate can also establish that the prison officials were deliberately indifferent to a serious medical condition.[11]

13-7e *Helling v. McKinney* 113 S.Ct. 2475 (1993)

In *Helling v. McKinney*, the Court held that the treatment a prisoner receives in prison, and the conditions under which he is confined, are subject to scrutiny under the Eighth Amendment. In this case, the prisoner was seeking an injunction prohibiting prison authorities from subjecting him to environmental tobacco smoke. Apparently, he shared a cell with an inmate who smoked five packs of cigarettes a day. In this case, the court stated that the prisoner should have been permitted to prove that his exposure to secondhand smoke was an unreasonable danger to his future.[12]

13-7f *Jones v. N.C. Prisoners' Labor Union* 97 S.Ct. 2532 (1976)

In *Jones v. N.C. Prisoners' Labor Union*, the Supreme Court held that a state may ban meetings of prisoners' unions and prohibit the unions from soliciting members and from making bulk mailings to members who are in prison.[13]

13-7g *Meachum v. Fano* 96 S.Ct. 2532 (1976)

In the *Meachum* case, the Court held that inmates have no due process rights to avoid transfer to another prison where conditions may be harsher. It appears that the state may transfer the prisoners, and it makes no difference if the transfer is for administrative or disciplinary reasons.[14]

13-7h *Vitek v. Jones* 100 S.Ct. 1254 (1987)

Unlike the *Meachum* case, the Court held in *Vitek* that a Nebraska state prisoner has a liberty interest to challenge his transfer to a state mental hospital. Accordingly, before the transfer of a prisoner from a correctional institution to a mental hospital, the inmate must be provided with appropriate procedural protection.[15]

13-7i *Turner v. Safety* 107 S.Ct. 2254 (1987)

In *Turner v. Safety,* the Supreme Court held that when a prison regulation impinges on an inmate's constitutional rights, the regulation will still be valid if the prison officials can establish that the regulation is reasonably related to legitimate penalogical interest. This approach is labeled as the "rational basis" approach. In addition, the Court placed the burden on the party (prisoner) whose rights have been violated to demonstrate that the government had no rational basis for doing what it did or did not do. In assessing the actions of the prison officials, the Court stated that four factors should be examined: (1) whether there is a rational connection between the prison regulation and the legitimate governmental interest put forward to justify it, (2) whether an alternative means of exercising the right exists in spite of what the prison has done, (3) whether striking down the prison officials' action would have a significant effect on fellow inmates or staff, and (4) whether there are ready alternatives available to the prison or whether the regulation appears instead to be an exaggerated response to the problem it is intended to address.[16]

13-7j *Wolff v. McDonnell* 94 S.Ct. 2963 (1974)

In *Wolff v. McDonnell,* the U.S. Supreme Court ruled that inmates have a liberty interest in good-time credits, and therefore good-time credits may not be denied without holding a hearing. In addition, the inmate should be (1) given notice of the alleged infraction, (2) given an opportunity to call witnesses, and (3) present documentary evidence, unless allowing these rights would be unduly hazardous to institutional safety or correctional goals. The inmate is also entitled to a written decision of the reasons for the action. The written decision should describe the evidence relied on to make the decision.[17]

13-7k *Procunier v. Martinez* 416 U.S. 396 (1974)

The *Procunier v. Martinez* case involved the censorship of outgoing mail. The Court stated that prisons could not censor outgoing mail that was viewed by prison authorities expressing "inflammatory views," unduly complained about prison administration, or was otherwise inappropriate. The court held that these standards were too broad and failed to exclude only material that posed a legitimate threat to the institution. Even restrictions on inmate correspondence that furthers an important or substantial interest of penal administration will nevertheless be invalid if the restriction is too broad. Accordingly, California prison regulations that authorize censorship of statements that unduly complain or magnify grievances, express inflammatory political, racial, religious, or other views are invalid.

The court stated that the decision by prison officials to censor or withhold delivery of a particular letter must be accompanied by minimum procedural safeguards. Accordingly, when mail is censored, the inmate sending the mail must be notified and given an opportunity to appeal to an official who was not involved in the original censorship decision. The court based their decision in this case on the First Amendment rights of the correspondents outside of prison as well as the rights of the inmates.[18]

13-7| *McKune v. Lile* 536 U.S. 24 (2002)

Prison rehabilitation programs that require inmates to reveal undisclosed crimes do not necessarily violate the constitutional right against compelled self-incrimination. In a 5-to-4 decision, the U.S. Supreme Court upheld a Kansas state prison system's Sexual Abuse Treatment Program, an 18-month-long rehabilitation program that has served as a model for a growing number of states in preparing convicted sex offenders for life outside of the prison. Under the program, inmates who choose to participate must acknowledge responsibility for any unreported sex crimes and pass a polygraph examination to ensure full disclosure. The inmates could face new prosecutions for the previously undisclosed crimes or possible perjury charges if they have previously denied in sworn testimony that they committed the crimes.

The decision written by Chief Justice Rehnquist essentially holds that an inmate's right against self-incrimination is limited while in prison. Justice O'Connor, whose vote was necessary to make the 5-to-4 decision, stated that she upheld the program because there were only "minor" consequences from a refusal to participate in the rehabilitation program. Justice Stevens writing in dissent stated "This is truly a watershed case. The plurality's policy judgment does not justify the evisceration of a constitutional right."

13-8 Deliberate Indifference

The courts have held that before prison administrators may be held liable for the violation of a prisoner's Eighth Amendment rights, the administrators must have acted with deliberate indifference. In the below case of *Farmer v. Brennan,* the U.S. Supreme Court attempts to define **deliberate indifference.**

13-8a *Farmer v. Brennan* 511 U.S. 825 (1994)

Dee Farmer, Petitioner v. Edward Brennan, Warden, et al. [June 6, 1994]

Justice Souter delivered the opinion of the Court.

A prison official's "deliberate indifference" to a substantial risk of serious harm to an inmate violates the Eighth Amendment. This case requires us to define the term "deliberate indifference" as we do by requiring a showing that the official was subjectively aware of the risk.

I.

The dispute before us stems from a civil suit brought by petitioner, Dee Farmer, alleging that respondents, federal prison officials, violated the Eighth Amendment by their deliberate indifference to the petitioner's safety. Petitioner, who is serving a federal sentence for credit card fraud, has been diagnosed by medical personnel of the Bureau of Prisons as a transsexual, one who has "[a] rare psychiatric disorder in which a person feels persistently uncomfortable about his or her anatomical sex," and who typically seeks medical treatment, including hormonal therapy and surgery, to bring about a permanent sex change. *American Medical Association, Encyclopedia of Medicine 1006* (1989); see also American Psychiatric Association, *Diagnostic and Statistical Manual of Mental Disorders,* 74–75 (3d rev. ed. 1987).

For several years before being convicted and sentenced in 1986 at the age of 18, petitioner, who is biologically male, wore women's clothing (as petitioner did at the 1986 trial), underwent estrogen therapy, received silicone breast implants, and submitted to unsuccessful "black market" testicle-removal surgery. Petitioner's precise appearance in prison is unclear from the record before us, but petitioner claims to have continued hormonal treatment while incarcerated by using drugs smuggled into prison, and apparently wears clothing in a feminine manner, as by displaying a shirt off one shoulder. The parties agree that petitioner projects feminine characteristics.

The practice of federal prison authorities is to incarcerate preoperative transsexuals with prisoners of like biological sex, and over time authorities housed petitioner in several federal facilities, sometimes in the general male prison population, but more often in segregation. While there is no dispute that petitioner was segregated at least several times because of violations of prison rules, neither is it disputed that in at least one penitentiary petitioner was segregated because of safety concerns.

On March 9, 1989, petitioner was transferred for disciplinary reasons from the Federal Correctional Institute in Oxford, Wisconsin (FCI-Oxford), to the United States Penitentiary in Terre Haute, Indiana (USP-Terre Haute). Though the record before us is unclear about the security designations of the two prisons in 1989, penitentiaries are typically higher security facilities that house more troublesome prisoners than federal correctional institutes. See generally *Federal Bureau of Prisons, Facilities 1990*. After an initial stay in administrative segregation, petitioner was placed in the USP-Terre Haute general population.

Petitioner voiced no objection to any prison official about the transfer to the penitentiary or to placement in its general population. Within two weeks, according to petitioner's allegations, petitioner was beaten and raped by another inmate in petitioner's cell. Several days later, after petitioner claims to have reported the incident, officials returned petitioner to segregation to await, according to respondents, a hearing about petitioner's HIV-positive status.

Acting without counsel, petitioner then filed a . . . complaint, alleging a violation of the Eighth Amendment. See *Bivens v. Six Unknown Fed. Narcotics Agents*, 403 U. S. 388 (1971); *Carlson v. Green*, 446 U.S. 14 (1980). As defendants, petitioner named respondents: the warden of USP-Terre Haute and the Director of the Bureau of Prisons (sued only in their official capacities); the warden of FCI-Oxford and a case manager there; and the director of the Bureau of Prisons North Central Region Office and an official in that office (sued in their official and personal capacities). As later amended, the complaint alleged that respondents either transferred petitioner to USP-Terre Haute or placed petitioner in its general population despite knowledge that the penitentiary had a violent environment and a history of inmate assaults, and despite knowledge that petitioner, as a transsexual who "projects feminine characteristics," would be particularly vulnerable to sexual attack by some USP-Terre Haute inmates. This allegedly amounted to a deliberately indifferent failure to protect petitioner's safety, and thus to a violation of petitioner's Eighth Amendment rights. Petitioner sought compensatory and punitive damages, and an injunction barring future confinement in any penitentiary, including USP-Terre Haute.

... The District Court denied petitioner's ... motion and granted summary judgment to respondents, concluding that there had been no deliberate indifference to petitioner's safety. The failure of prison officials to prevent inmate assaults violates the Eighth Amendment, the court stated, only if prison officials were "reckless in a criminal sense," meaning that they had actual knowledge of a potential danger. Respondents, however, lacked the requisite knowledge, the court found. [Petitioner] never expressed any concern for his safety to any of [respondents]. Since [respondents] had no knowledge of any potential danger to [petitioner], they were not deliberately indifferent to his safety. ...

II.

The Constitution "does not mandate comfortable prisons," *Rhodes v. Chapman,* 452 U.S. 337, 349 (1981), but neither does it permit inhumane ones, and it is now settled that the treatment a prisoner receives in prison and the conditions under which he is confined are subject to scrutiny under the Eighth Amendment. In its prohibition of "cruel and unusual punishments," the Eighth Amendment places restraints on prison officials, who may not, for example, use excessive physical force against prisoners. See *Hudson v. McMillian,* 503 U.S. (1992). The Amendment also imposes duties on these officials, who must provide humane conditions of confinement; prison officials must ensure that inmates receive adequate food, clothing, shelter and medical care, and must "take reasonable measures to guarantee the safety of the inmates." See *Hudson v. Palmer,* 468 U.S. 517, 526–527 (1984).

In particular, as the lower courts have uniformly held, and as we have assumed, "[p]rison officials have a duty ... to protect prisoners from violence at the hands of other prisoners—the protection [an inmate] is afforded against other inmates" as a "conditio[n] of confinement" subject to the strictures of the Eighth Amendment). Having incarcerated "persons [with] demonstrated proclivit[ies] for antisocial criminal, and often violent, conduct," *Hudson v. Palmer,* supra, at 526, having stripped them of virtually every means of self-protection and foreclosed their access to outside aid, the government and its officials are not free to let the state of nature take its course. ... Prison conditions may be "restrictive and even harsh," *Rhodes,* supra, at 347, but gratuitously allowing the beating or rape of one prisoner by another serves no legitimate penological objectiv[e] . . . any more than it squares with evolving standards of decency. . . . Being violently assaulted in prison is simply not part of the penalty that criminal offenders pay for their offenses against society.

It is not, however, every injury suffered by one prisoner at the hands of another that translates into constitutional liability for prison officials responsible for the victim's safety. Our cases have held that a prison official violates the Eighth Amendment only when two requirements are met. First, the deprivation alleged must be, objectively, "sufficiently serious," . . . a prison official's act or omission must result in the denial of "the minimal civilized measure of life's necessities." For a claim (like the one here) based on a failure to prevent harm, the inmate must show that he is incarcerated under conditions posing a substantial risk of serious harm.

The second requirement follows from the principle that only the unnecessary and wanton infliction of pain implicates the Eighth Amendment. To violate the Cruel and Unusual Punishments Clause, a prison official must have a sufficiently culpable state of mind. In prison-conditions cases that state of mind is one of "deliberate indifference" to inmate health or safety, a standard the parties agree governs the claim in this case. The parties disagree, however, on the proper test for deliberate indifference, which we must therefore undertake to define.

Although we have never paused to explain the meaning of the term "deliberate indifference," the case law is instructive. The term first appeared in the United States Reports in *Estelle v. Gamble,* 429 U.S., at 104, and its use there shows that deliberate indifference describes a state of mind more blameworthy than negligence. In considering the inmate's claim in *Estelle* that inadequate prison medical care violated the Cruel and Unusual Punishments Clause, we distinguished "deliberate indifference to serious medical needs of prisoners," from "negligen[ce] in diagnosing or treating a medical condition," holding that only the former violates the Clause. We have since read *Estelle* for the proposition that Eighth Amendment liability requires "more than ordinary lack of due care for the prisoner's interests or safety." While *Estelle* establishes that deliberate indifference entails something more than mere negligence, the cases are also clear that it is satisfied by something less than acts or omissions for the very purpose of causing harm or with knowledge that harm will result. That point underlies the ruling that "application of the deliberate indifference standard is inappropriate" in one class of prison cases: when officials stand accused of using excessive physical force. In such situations, where the decisions of prison officials are typically made in haste, under pressure, and frequently without the luxury of a second chance. An Eighth Amendment claimant must show more than "indifference," deliberate or otherwise. The claimant must show that officials applied force maliciously and sadistically for the very purpose of causing harm.

With deliberate indifference lying somewhere between the poles of negligence at one end and purpose or knowledge at the other, the courts of appeals have routinely equated deliberate indifference with recklessness. . . . It is, indeed, fair to say that acting or failing to act with deliberate indifference to a substantial risk of serious harm to a prisoner is the equivalent of recklessly disregarding that risk.

That does not, however, fully answer the pending question about the level of culpability deliberate indifference entails, for the term recklessness is not self-defining. The civil law generally calls a person reckless who acts or (if the person has a duty to act) fails to act in the face of an unjustifiably high risk of harm that is either known or so obvious that it should be known. . . . The criminal law, however, generally permits a finding of recklessness only when a person disregards a risk of harm of which he is aware. . . . We hold instead that a prison official cannot be found liable under the Eighth Amendment for denying an inmate humane conditions of confinement unless the official knows of and disregards an excessive risk to inmate health or safety; the official must both be aware of facts from which the inference could be drawn that a substantial risk of serious harm exists, and he must also draw the inference. This approach comports best with the text of the Amendment as our cases have interpreted it. The Eighth Amendment does not outlaw cruel and unusual "conditions"; it outlaws cruel and unusual "punishments." An act or omission unaccompanied by knowledge of a significant risk of harm might well be something society wishes to discourage, and if harm does result, society might well wish to assure compensation. . . .

13-9 *Warner v. Orange County Probation Department,* CA 2, No. 95-7055 decided 9/9/96, affirming 870 F.Supp. 69

Question: Can a probation department be held civilly liable for requiring attendance at a religion-based A.A. program as a probation condition?

Holding: Yes. Coerced attendance as condition of probation violated Establishment Clause.

Facts: The U.S. Court of Appeals for the Second Circuit held that a county probation department opened itself up to civil liability under 42 USC 1983 by recommending that a motorist who pleaded guilty to drunk driving be required to attend meetings of Alcoholics Anonymous as a condition of probation. The probation condition constituted coercion of religious activity in violation of the First Amendment's Establishment Clause.

The fact that the sentencing judge made the final decision about probation did not amount to a superseding cause relieving the probation department of liability. The majority also rejected the probation department's assertion of quasi-judicial absolute immunity. Individual probation officers might well be entitled to such immunity, but U.S. Supreme Court decisions strongly indicate that the department itself is not, the majority said.

Finally, it rejected the department's argument that the probation condition did not actually violate the Establishment Clause. The program had a strongly religious content, and the plaintiff was coerced into participating on pain of being imprisoned, it reasoned.

Judge Winter, dissenting, said the plaintiff waived his claim or consented to the probation condition by voluntarily participating in the program before being sentenced. The dissenter also said that the probation condition did not violate the Establishment Clause, as opposed to the First Amendment's Free Exercise Clause.

Plaintiff Robert Warner pleaded guilty to driving drunk and without a license. The Orange County, N.Y., Department of Probation ("OCDP") prepared a presentence report recommending probation with six special conditions, including the condition that Warner "attend Alcoholics Anonymous at the direction of [his] probation officer." The trial judge sentenced Warner to three years of probation, imposing the special conditions recommended by the OCDP.

Warner then brought suit against OCDP under 42 USC 1983, claiming that the probation condition forced him to participate in religious activity in violation of the First Amendment's Establishment Clause, and that OCDP was responsible, in part because it recommended the A.A. therapy to the sentencing court.

The district court found that the program Warner was required to attend involved a substantial religious component. For example, the "Twelve Steps" included instruction that participants should "make a decision to turn our will and our lives over to the care of God . . . "[a]dmit to God . . . the exact nature of our wrongs," be "entirely ready to have God remove all these defects . . . ," and "seek! through prayer and meditation to improve our conscious contact with God. . . ." Meetings frequently began with a religious invocation, and always ended with a Christian prayer. The district court awarded Warner declaratory judgment, nominal damages of one dollar, and attorney's fees, 870 F.Supp. 69, 56 CrL 1318 (DC SNY 1994).

It is clear that Warner's injury resulted from a custom or policy of Orange County, as opposed to an isolated instance of conduct. OCDP's recommendation was one of six standard probation conditions that it routinely submitted to sentencing judges in alcohol cases. OCDP argues that it is nonetheless not legally responsible because it was the judge's sentencing decision, not the Probation Department's recommendation, that caused the harm. Tort defendants, including those sued under Section 1983, are "responsible for the natural consequences of [their] actions." *Malley v. Briggs,* 475 U.S. 335,- 344 n.7 (1986). This includes "those consequences attributable to reasonably foreseeable intervening forces, including the acts of third parties." *Guiterrez-Rodriquez v. Cartagena,* 882 F.2d 553, 561 (CA 1 1989).

Under New York law, the determination of probation terms is a nondelegable judicial task. The probation department therefore argues that its role was purely advisory. *Malley* rejected a similar argument advanced by a state trooper who argued that he was shielded from responsibility for obtaining an allegedly illegal arrest warrant by his entitlement to rely on the judgment of the judicial officer in finding probable cause and issuing the warrant. The court said such reliance was not justified if "a reasonably well-trained officer in [the same) position would have known that his affidavit failed to establish probable cause and that he should not have applied for the warrant." 475 U.S. at 345.

The circumstances in *Malley* were more favorable than those here to the argument of exoneration by reason of the intervening decision of the judge. A police officer applying for an arrest warrant appears in a partisan role, whereas the probation officer is a neutral adviser to the court. The district court noted a high likelihood of court adoption of recommendations by the probation department. We review this determination for clear error, and find none. Given the neutral advisory role of the probation officer toward the court, it is an entirely "natural consequence," *Malley,* 475 U.S. at 344 n.7, for a judge to adopt the OCDP's recommendations as to a therapy provider without careful scrutiny.

Warner, following the advice of his attorney, sampled A.A. sessions prior to sentence and made no objection to their religious content at the time of sentence. However, this does not resolve the true issue of proximate cause, which is whether, when OCDP made its recommendation, it was reasonably foreseeable that the recommendation would result in the harm. Warner's failure to object was entirely foreseeable. Assuming his early visits made him aware of the full extent of the religious content of the A.A. therapy, it was not clear that Warner was aware at the time that the religious content gave him any legal basis to object, or that he had even told his lawyer about the religious content. Furthermore, even if aware of his rights, he might well have been afraid to annoy the sentencing judge by objecting to the standard recommendation of the probation department.

For the same reasons and others, Warner's conduct did not constitute consent. A defendant facing sentence may well undertake daily attendance at Mass in the hope of convincing the sentencing judge of his penitence. We do not see how such conduct, without more, could be construed as consent to a sentence of probation conditioned on daily attendance at Mass.

Nor can the actions of A.A. be considered to have broken the chain of causation. There can be no question as to the reasonable foreseeability of the religious nature of the program OCDP was recommending for Warner. OCDP is responsible for any resulting injury to Warner's First Amendment rights.

OCDP contends that even if its recommendation to the judge was a proximate cause of Warner's sentence, it is immune from liability. It claims that probation department sentence recommendations are so integral a part of the judicial process as to benefit from an absolute quasi-judicial immunity similar to that enjoyed by prosecutors. Were this suit brought against the probation officer, the claim for absolute immunity would likely have merit. See *Dorman v. Higgins,* 821 F.2d 133 (CA 2 1987), *Shelton v. McCarthy,* 699 F.Supp. 412 (DC WNY 1988). However, Warner sued only the department.

The county also argues that forcing Warner to attend Alcoholics Anonymous did not violate the First Amendment's Establishment Clause. We disagree. The Supreme Court has repeatedly made clear that "at a minimum, the Constitution guarantees that government may not coerce anyone to support or participate in religion or its exercise, or otherwise act in a way which "establishes a [state] religion or religious faith, or tends to do so." *Lee v. Weisman,* 112 S.Ct. 2649, 2655 (1992), quoting *Lynch v. Donnelly,* 465 U.S. 668, 678 (1984). The A.A. program had a substantial religious component; we have noticed that the meetings were intensely religious events. Neither the probation recommendation, nor the court's sentence, offered Warner any choice among therapy programs. If Warner had failed to attend A.A., he would have been subject to imprisonment for violation of probation.

Orange County argues that even if Warner was forced to attend the meetings, he was not required to participate in the religious exercises that took place. The county argues that, as a mature adult, Warner was less susceptible to such pressure than the children who were required to stand in respectful silence during a school prayer in *Lee v. Weisman,* 112 S.Ct. at 2658-59; it points out that the Supreme Court expressly questioned whether the obligation imposed by the school in *Lee* might have been constitutionally tolerable "if the affected citizens had been mature adults." *Id.* at 2658.

We do not find this argument convincing. Warner's exposure was more coercive than the school prayer in *Lee.* The plaintiff in *Lee* was subjected only to a brief two minutes of prayer on a single occasion. Warner, in contrast, was required to participate in a long-term program of group therapy that repeatedly turned to religion as the basis of motivation. And when he appeared to be pursuing the program with insufficient zeal the probation officer required that he attend "Step meetings" to reintensify his motivation. Warner was also paired with another member of A.A. as a method of enhancing his indoctrination into the group's approach to recovery from alcoholism. Failure to cooperate could lead to incarceration. The trial judge found that Warner's success in remaining aloof diminished his damages to a token of one dollar, the fact that Warner managed to avoid indoctrination despite the pressure he faced does not make the county's program any less coercive, or nullify the county's liability.

Dissent: Warner either waived his claim or consented to A.A. attendance because he voluntarily began attendance before any involvement by the probation office. Further, the sentence by the trial court was an independent, superseding cause. The invocation of the Establishment Clause, rather than the Free Exercise Clause, puts into play a principle that portends changes in our penal system that are not required.—Winter, J.

Summary

The constitutional rights of prisoners are summarized below:

Conjugal Visitation: No federal court has yet to hold that prisoners have a constitutional right to enjoy conjugal visits (family visits differ from conjugal visits in that family visits do not allow for intimate physical contact and conjugal visits do allow for such contact).

Mail: The courts have been active in protecting the rights of prisoners to receive and send mail, as noted in the *Martinez* case. Although access to mail is a "right," the courts have held that correctional administrators can place reasonable restrictions on prisoners in the exercise of that right if there is a compelling state need. Note: prison officials may not read mail addressed to, or received from, attorneys or government officials. They may, however, check that mail to ensure that it contains no contraband.

Religion: Prisoners have the right, within limitations, to exercise their religious customs or duties. The courts have, however, upheld restrictions on the exercise of the religious practices based on reasonable and substantial justification. The burden of justifying the restrictions is placed on the prison administrators.

Access to Courts: As noted earlier, the courts have continued to stress the right of prisoners to free access to the courts. Note: federal legislation discussed earlier in this chapter has attempted to limit the access. It will be interesting to observe whether the courts will uphold those laws.

Right to Medical Treatment: The courts have held that prisoners have a right to adequate medical treatment.

Discussion Questions

1. Explain the different periods of involvement by the courts in prison adminstration.
2. Classify prisoners' rights into four areas.
3. Explain the purposes of the Prison Litigation Reform Act of 1996.
4. Explain the importance of prohibition against cruel and unusual punishment.
5. What are the differences between the rights of prisoners who are in pretrial confinement and those who have been convicted?
6. Under what conditions may a prisoner sue for lack of health care?
7. Explain the significance of the *Warner* case.

Chapter Quiz

True/False

1. Historically, the courts have always been involved in the area of prisoners' rights?
2. Throughout history, the courts have always been concerned with conditions of confinement suits filed by inmates.
3. It was during the "rights period" that the courts took a hands-off approach to prison administration.
4. It is clear that inmates have no due-process rights while incarcerated?
5. *Habeas corpus* is usually filed by inmates who allege cruel and unusual punishment on the part of prison guards.

Multiple Choice

1. During the _____, the courts rarely accepted cases involving the conditions of confinement.
   a. rights period
   b. hands-off period
   c. Great Depression
   d. none of the above

2. What period in the history of U.S. prisons did the court become actively involved in prison administration?
   a. hands-off period
   b. prison reform period
   c. rights period
   d. reconstruction period
3. Which one of the following is NOT one of the four areas that prisoners' rights can be divided into?
   a. cruel and unusual punishment
   b. individual rights
   c. Due Process
   d. First Amendments rights
4. A writ filed by a prisoner which requires the government to justify why the individual is being held in confinement is called a
   a. *Writ of habeas corpus.*
   b. *Writ of certiorari.*
   c. *Writ of nolle prosequi.*
   d. None of the above
5. The courts have held that before prison administrators may be held liable for the violation of a prisoner's Eighth Amendment rights, the administration must have acted with
   a. deliberate neglect.
   b. deliberate liability.
   c. deliberate indifference.
   d. deliberate certiorari.

Endnotes

1. Jack E. Call, "The Supreme Court and Prisoners' Rights," *Federal Probation* 59(1 March 1995): 36–46.
2. 28 U.S.Code 3626, as amended.
3. Bureau of Justice Statistics, *Sourcebook of Criminal Justice Statistics—2001* (Washington, DC: U.S. Department of Justice).
4. Call, "The Supreme Court and Prisoners' Rights," 41.
5. 18 U.S.Code 3663A.
6. 28 U.S. Code 3626.
7. Richard Lacayo, "The Real Hard Call," *Time*, 4 September 1995, 31; Lincoln Coplan, "Uneasy Days in Court," *Newsweek*, 17 October 1994, 87.
8. 714 P2d 399 (1986).
9. 97 S.Ct. 1491 (1977).
10. 98 S.Ct. 2565 (1978).

11. 97 S.Ct. 285 (1976).
12. 113 S.Ct. 2475 (1993).
13. 97 S.Ct. 2532 (1977).
14. 96 S.Ct. 2532 (1976).
15. 100 S.Ct. 1254 (1980).
16. 107 S.Ct. 2254 (1987).
17. 94 S.Ct. 2963 (1974).
18. 94 S.Ct. 1800 (1974).

Chapter 14

Innovations in Corrections

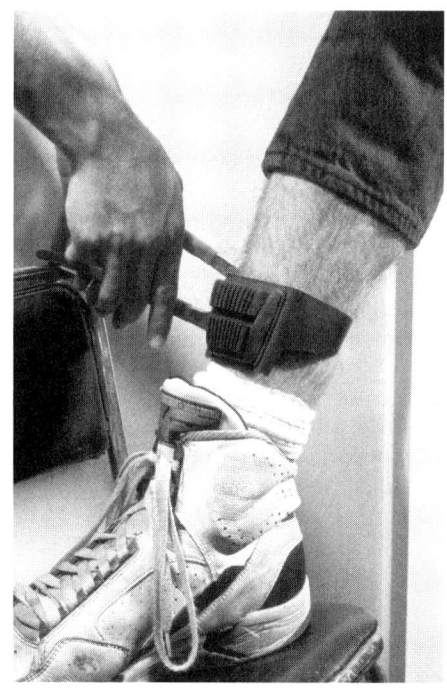

Tony Freeman/PhotoEdit

Key Terms

active electronic monitoring
day-reporting centers
electronic surveillance
home confinement
"lock them up" policy
passive electronic monitoring
supervised release

Outline

14-1 Alternatives to Confinement
    14-1a Electronic House Arrest
14-2 Other Innovations
    14-2a Mobile Intervention Supervision Team
    14-2b Operation Night Light
Article—Using Day-Reporting Centers As an Alternative to Jail
Article—Intensive Supervision: A New Way to Connect with Offenders
Article—Inmate Involvement in Prison Governance
Summary
Discussion Questions
Chapter Quiz
Endnotes

Learning Objectives

After studying this chapter, the reader will be able to:

- Explain the present "lock them up" policy.
- Analyze the use of electronic house arrest.
- Explain the advantages and disadvantages of home confinement.
- List the sanctions involved with the use of home confinement.
- Explain the history and present use of electronic monitoring.
- Analyze the controversy involving the duration of home confinement.
- List the legal issues involved in electronic monitoring and home confinement.
- Analyze the concept of using day-reporting centers as alternatives to jail.
- Explain the history of day-reporting centers.
- Explain the concept involved in "intensive supervision."
- Analyze the concept of "self-governance" in prisons.

14-1 Alternatives to Confinement

In a growing trend indicative of the politics involved in the crime problem, more and more states are trying to make prisoners pay for everything from filing lawsuits to their room and board. The number of inmates in state prisons has tripled since 1980. Our present **"lock them up" policy** is very expensive and robs the local communities and states of funds needed for schools, roads, and other government-funded services. The number of inmates incarcerated in the U.S. prison population has been increasing at alarming levels even in light of the decrease of violent crimes throughout much of the 1990s and the first years of the twenty-first century. This increase in population and the political pressures to tighten the budgets have led state officials to claim they are justified in going after even token payments from inmates, most of whom have little or no resources. In 1995, more than two dozen states passed laws intended to regain some of the costs of incarceration. For example, Arizona requires inmates to pay a utility fee if they have a television or other "major electrical appliance." Connecticut and Missouri have laws that force inmates to pay the expenses of their confinement. New Hampshire compels prisoners to repay the cost of state-provided lawyers. Texas takes part of an inmate's wages earned from any work program outside the prison.[1] In July 2002, the Massachusetts legislature was considering an "inmate fee bill." The inmate fee would help cover the cost of incarceration in Massachusetts prisons. The inmate fee would establish a sliding scale fee of $1 per day for first-time offenders, $5 per day for second offenders, and $10 per day for third-time offenders. The money would be taken from the inmate's canteen fund, cash on hand at the time of incarceration, or up to 25 percent of their earning while in prison.[2]

14-1a Electronic House Arrest

Electronic surveillance technology was first developed in the mid-1960s. It was not used with offenders until the 1980s. Since then, however, it has developed into one of the most popular intermediate sanctions used in the United States.[3] By January 1997, nearly 20,000 probationers and parolees were under electronic monitoring in the United States. It is estimated that more than one million people in the United States will ultimately be placed on some form of electronic monitoring in the future. Not only is the number of offenders placed on electronic monitor house arrest increasing, but the types of offenders are becoming more diverse. At first, it was used for offenders awaiting trial or sentencing and offenders released from institutional correctional facilities. In addition, it was first traditionally used for property offenders. Figure 14-1 presents the points in the criminal justice process at which electronic monitoring is used. The growing popularity of electronic monitoring has been due, in large measure, to the increasing demands to supervise offenders and protect communities effectively. Public support for the use of monitoring as an alternative to imprisonment is probably based on the public knowledge regarding the high cost of incarceration. The evaluations of electronic monitoring have been impressive. Many jurisdictions including Illinois, Oklahoma, Texas, and California have produced evidence of the successfulness of the program.

There are two types of electronic monitoring systems currently utilized. The **passive electronic monitoring** system is the process where offenders wear electronic devices that emit continuous signals to a receiver attached to the offenders' home telephone system. If the signal is broken, (for example, if the offender leaves his or her residence) the receiver communicates with a computer system, usually located at the local probation office, that the offender has violated the terms and conditions of his or **home confinement.** This information is documented in the computers hard drive and information can be readily retrieved.

Active electronic monitoring is the second type of electronic monitoring system utilized. With **active electronic monitoring** the offender wears devices that emit signals when plugged into the offenders' home telephone. A computer located at the probation office randomly calls the offenders' home telephone several times during the day. When offenders are called, they must answer their telephones within a specified number of rings. Once the offender answers the telephone he or she is greeted by a computer voice, at that time the offender must plug their bracelets into the devices. This will subsequently send a signal identifying the offender to the computer.

Electronic monitoring is an economic and effective way to keep track of inmates. For example, in July 2002, the division of corrections in South Carolina started an electronic monitoring program with the expectation of saving up to $50 a day for every inmate involved. The state charges each inmate up to $6 a day to participate in the program and saves the $44 a day it normally costs for keeping an inmate in prison. The South Carolina program allows offenders to return to the workforce, be more accountable by paying child support and restitution, and engage in intervention programs in their communities.[4]

Innovations in Corrections 399

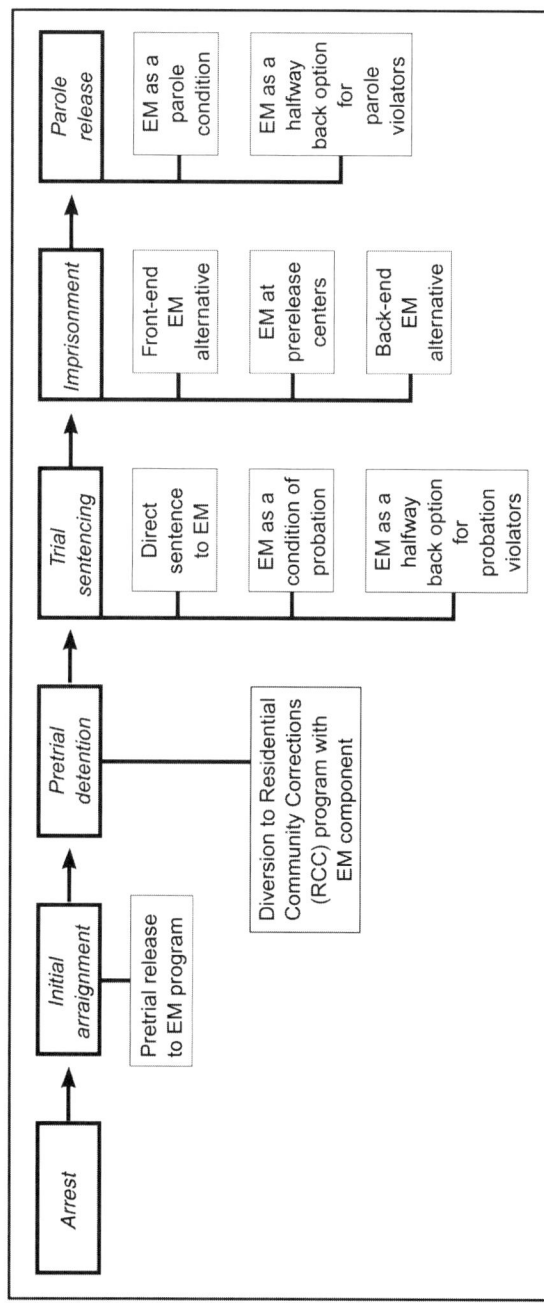

Figure 14-1
Key Decision Points at Which Electronic Monitoring Is Used

14-2 Other Innovations

14-2a Mobile Intervention Supervision Team

Recognizing a need for intensive supervision in the community of certain violent sexual and drug offenders, the Division of Community Corrections in Washington State initiated the MIST (Mobile Intervention Supervision Team). MIST is a community corrections field office currently located in Seattle, Washington. MIST's focus is that of providing intensive supervision of high-risk offenders after their release from prison. The **supervised release** program monitors only those offenders ordered to community placement by the court at the time of their sentencing. Each of the offenders is released under strict conditions of the supervision term of one to two years, usually including prohibitions against drug use and contact with victims, and requirements for completion of any treatment that is ordered. In addition, offenders must by employed, in school, or perform community-service hours.[5] The outcomes of the MIST program are impressive.

1. MIST officers personally have trained more than 100 police officers from four agencies to assist in the monitoring of offenders during curfew hours.
2. Through the partnerships developed with four local law enforcement agencies serving as community monitors, an average of 50 MIST offenders are being monitored by police officers at any given time.
3. Between September 1996 and June 1997, MIST had 2,261 offenders, of which 1,610 were available for prosocial activities (such as employment, life skill classes, and job search). Seventy-seven percent of the 1,610 offenders were involved in 32 hours or more of prosocial activities per week during this time period.
4. The use of alternative sanctions has saved more than one-half million dollars in jail beds. In a one-year period, MIST officers conducted 358 hearings. Of those hearings, 219 offenders were given alternative sanctions. A conservative estimate of jail beds saved, calculated at ten days saved per hearing, equals 2,190 days saved in one year. This number multiplied by $100 per day for a jail bed (a conservative estimate) equals $219,000 savings in a one-year period. In a two-year period, this would save $440,000. MIST has been in business for three years.[6]

14-2b Operation Night Light

Another innovative approach is Operation Night Light, which was implemented in Boston in the mid 1990s. Operation Night Light is a partnership between police and probation that provides the court with a tool to enforce the terms of probation in a meaningful fashion. The clear advantage to Operation Night Light is that it involves a collaborative effort between the police and probation. The police become increasingly more involved in community corrections while probation officers become more involved in addressing community problems.[7]

Operation Night Light is driven by knowledge acquired by practitioners. The project developed from a collaboration in 1992 between probation officers in the Dorchester District Court and Boston Police Officers in the anti-gang unit. Their success and innovation were recognized and pushed forward by executives in both police and probation. The recognition led to the establishment of Operation Night Light as a formal partnership between the Boston Police Department and the Office of the Commissioner of Probation for Massachusetts.[8]

Since the implementation of Operation Night Light in August of 1995, there have been no juvenile homicides involving firearms in the impacted areas. The data has shown a decline in assaults and homicides during the period in which Operation Night Light has operated.[9] According to officials involved in Operation Night Light, jurisdictions first must ensure that: (1) the need is critical, in terms of the serious juvenile crime, which in turn, will support this intrusive, high profile program; (2) there is a pre-existing positive relationship with local law enforcement, which will be critical to sustain the close working relationship; (3) that judicial support will be forthcoming; and (4) that community resistance is not anticipated. The Operation Night Light program is an example of coactive efforts between law enforcement and corrections, pairing one probation officer with two police officers to make surprise visits to the homes of high-risk probationers during the nontraditional hours of 7 P.M. to midnight, rather than from 8:30 A.M. to 4:30 P.M., which was previously the norm.

ARTICLE—
Using Day-Reporting Centers As an Alternative to Jail[10]

Growing prison populations, court-ordered capacity limits on jails and prisons, and tight government budgets have forced a return to correctional innovation and a renewed interest in community-based corrections programming. Among the newer innovations are several intermediate sanctions that serve as steps between the security and punishment of prisons and jails and the supervision without security offered by probation and parole. Intensive supervision, house arrest, and electronic monitoring are becoming accepted alternatives to incarceration.

Another intermediate sanction gaining popularity is day reporting. Day reporting can be defined as "a highly structured nonresidential program utilizing supervision, sanctions, and services coordinated from a central focus." Day reporting offers the punishment of confinement combined with the rehabilitative effects of allowing the offender to continue employment and receive treatment.

Offenders committed to day-reporting centers live at home and report to the center regularly, often daily. While at the center, the participant submits an itinerary that details his or her daily travels, destinations, and purposes. This schedule allows the supervision staff to monitor and control the client's behavior and is also a valuable tool for teaching responsibility to offenders. Clients are normally required to call in several times a day, and center staff also call the clients to verify their whereabouts. While at the center, the participants may be required to submit to drug testing and participate in counseling, education, and vocational placement assistance. Offenders are normally required to be employed in the community or be full-time students.

Day-reporting centers are a fairly recent innovation in community corrections programs, but like intensive supervision, house arrest, and other recent intermediate sanctions, they borrow from elements of more traditional correctional programming. Office visits, client interaction in a group setting, drug screening and treatment, and field work are all components of day reporting that have been used in probation and parole for years.

History of Day-Reporting Centers

Day-reporting centers started in Great Britain in the early 1970s as an alternative to incarceration for older petty criminals who were chronic offenders. The British Home Office originally asked Parliament to create the first day-treatment centers in 1972. At the same time, there was an independent movement by individual local probation agencies to open centers to provide group services to probationers. George Mair, the principal research officer of the Home Office Research and Planning Unit, traced the spread of day centers in England and Wales to prison overcrowding in the United Kingdom and to the interest of probation officials in supervising offenders in a group setting.

Frustrated by the inability to manage effectively the behavior of probationers in a traditional setting, officers were anxious to try working with groups of offenders. The Criminal Justice Act of 1982 formalized the existence of day treatment centers, and by the mid-1980s there were more than 80 centers in England and Wales. These programs differed greatly in staffing, target populations, programs and services offered, and hours of operation.

The first day-reporting center in America was opened in 1986 by the Hampden County, Massachusetts, Sheriff's Department. The center was implemented as an early release program for selected county jail inmates. This and other early day-reporting centers in the United States drew upon the 10 years of experience of the British centers. Day-treatment programs in use for juvenile offenders and deinstitutionalized mental patients also contributed to the accumulated knowledge about the concept. Additionally, day reporting was similar to a "living out" release option used by the Federal Bureau of Prisons that allowed inmates to spend prison time at home, after they had finished a residential phase of treatment at community correction centers.

Day-Reporting Center Operation

Like their British forerunners, American day-reporting centers are organized and operated in a variety of ways. Day-reporting centers differ in the offenders targeted to participate, criteria for selecting participants, operating agencies, services offered, violation policies, and even the goals of the center.

Day reporting is a concept that is adaptable to a number of different populations. Day-reporting centers are used to offer enhanced treatment and supervision to probationers or sentenced offenders not on probation, to monitor inmates released early from jail or prison, to monitor arrested people prior to trial, as a halfway-out step for inmates who have shown progress in community corrections or work release centers, and as a halfway-in step for offenders who are in violation of probation or parole.

Whatever the population selected, day reporting allows the treatment and supervision of arrested individuals and convicted offenders in a setting that is more secure than ordinary probation but less inhibiting and less expensive than incarceration. In performing this task, day-reporting centers fulfill three separate and distinct purposes: 1) enhanced supervision and decreased liberty of offenders; 2) treatment of offenders' problems; and 3) reduced crowding of incarceratory facilities.

Corbett asserted that this multiplicity of purpose also serves to satisfy goals of various correctional philosophies. The reduction of offender mobility and liberty supports a punishment philosophy and may act as a specific deterrent to future criminal activity. These restrictions also allow for a certain amount of incapacitation and, therefore, protection of the public. The ability to offer needed treatment to offenders assists in the correction or rehabilitation of offenders. Lastly, day reporting is significantly cheaper to operate than correctional institutions, allowing for greater cost effectiveness.

Differences in eligibility criteria are attributable to a variety of factors including the following: the orientation of the agency operating the center, the available population of offenders, the support of elected officials and judges, and the political climate of the community. Some programs place limits on the offenders they will accept based on type of offense, usually rejecting violent offenders. Besides the instant offense for which the offender is responsible, other eligibility variables may include the offender's gender, legal status, treatment needs, prior record, and residential stability. Program administrators must also ensure that the selected population exists in sufficient quantity to allow for program feasibility. If the desired population is too small, or unavailable for placement, the administration is faced with changing its eligibility criteria and selecting a different segment of offenders, thereby redefining the mission of the day-reporting center.

In discussing the effects of differing eligibility criteria, one cannot overlook the possible deleterious and costly effects of using day reporting, or any correctional program or sanction, when a less severe and less expensive alternative would be effective. The concept of net widening in corrections is a widely recognized and well-documented phenomenon. John Larivee, executive director of the Crime and Justice Foundation, which operates day-reporting centers in Massachusetts, lists three reasons that can account for the net-widening effect: unclear program goals, a mistaken belief that community corrections is soft on criminals, and a lack of support from public officials.

Judges and other involved decision makers must be convinced of the effectiveness of day-reporting centers and be willing to support them. If this support is not present, the center can expect continuing difficulty in securing participants, which may lead to taking inappropriate offenders who are easier to enroll, rather than serving the appropriate population that was originally identified. Corbett warned against the possible misuse of day-reporting centers to overtreat or widen the net and also the danger of overusing centers to maximize cost savings. This can lead to a loosening of standards and may damage programs that are required to accept clients who are dangers to the community or do not possess the motivation towards correction that is needed.

A day-reporting center's mission is often dependent on the type of agency that is offering the services. Day-reporting centers are operated by a wide range of government, public, and private agencies including residential community corrections centers, work release programs, jails, and treatment programs. These agencies obviously have different missions which, in turn, translate into diverse goals.

Day reporting is frequently operated on the site of a residential corrections facility such as a halfway house or work-release facility. The advantage to this arrangement is that facility staff members can use their normal down time to perform day-reporting duties. This sharing of staff between programs allows for a more cost-effective use of experienced, trained personnel. Among the services commonly provided by day-reporting centers are support, treatment, or referral for treatment, for offenders in such areas as substance abuse, mental health, education, vocational training, and job placement. In addition to these treatment services, most centers employ several tools of supervision to help monitor offenders' behavior. Centers commonly screen for use of intoxicants and illegal drugs and impose curfews and control over offenders' whereabouts and associates. Field work is normally less stringent and less frequent than with other intermediate sanctions, such as house arrest, but is still used along with telephone calls to monitor offenders' travel and verify employment and schooling. Additionally, centers normally enforce court-ordered fines, restitution, and family support and often assign community service.

Besides these common supervision and treatment services, some centers offer specialized services. Day-treatment centers in England frequently provide recreational and social services to their clientele, making the center not just a place of supervision but also a sort of offenders' club, where clientele can join with their peers, relax, and engage in socially acceptable pastimes. It is less common for American centers to provide this type of service, but some centers do provide recreational activities on site or in the community. Emergency or transitional housing is also provided by some programs. It would seem that providing housing to center clients would violate one of the key tenets of day reporting and could serve to blur further the line separating day reporting clients from residential services clients such as work releasees. One program that serves female offenders, who may be in a day reporting center program for child abuse, provides on-site day care for its clientele.

The goals of the day-reporting center and the philosophy of its parent agency will normally dictate the amount of flexibility in the center's violation policy. Centers that act as extensions of prisons or jails and espouse a philosophy of community protection will likely be less tolerant of program violations, such as using drugs or losing employment. Programs that place a priority on the rehabilitation and treatment of participants will be more likely to exercise a range of disciplines for violations of rules, rather than simply depending on incarceration of offenders. Jail and prison overcrowding may also affect violation policy, because many day-reporting centers operate to relieve overcrowding. Larivee warned against falling into the "more is better" trap: the more supervision, sanctions, and services imposed on the offender, the better the program. This results in an expensive, rigid program that no offender can successfully complete and no agency can possibly deliver.

Orange County's Experience

The Orange County, Florida, metropolitan area is one of the fastest growing areas in the country. Unfortunately, this growth has also led to growth in the jail population. Orange County has implemented a number of alternatives to incarceration to help control overcrowding. The jail has had a traditional pretrial release program for a number of years, which released selected offenders prior to their court obligations and also has administered a federally mandated population capacity release program. The Community Corrections Department of the Corrections Division has operated a work-release center for over 10 years. This 165-bed minimum security facility is primarily for sentenced county jail inmates but does service a small population of pretrial inmates. In 1989, the Community Corrections Department opened the Community Surveillance Unit, an electronically monitored home confinement program that currently monitors 150 pretrial and sentenced county inmates.

The latest attempt to help control overcrowding and provide treatment and community reintegration for inmates is a day-reporting center for 25 offenders. The center operates out of the existing work-release center and provides supervision and treatment to offenders who have been successfully complying with the work release or community surveillance programs. Participants are required to physically check in daily at the center and submit daily itineraries. Whereabouts are monitored by daily telephone calls and regular, random field checks. Clients are prohibited from using any illegal substances, and the center conducts drug and alcohol testing. All participants must be employed or be full-time students and must continue any treatment begun in work release or community surveillance. Failure to follow program conditions can cause the day-reporting center client to be returned to work release, community surveillance, or jail. The day-reporting center, which opened in May 1991, is staffed by a correctional surveillance officer who is assisted by work-release center staff.

Although it is too soon to know the long-term effects day reporting will have on the offenders who have participated in the program, the following statistics demonstrate that the program is meeting its goal to offer cost-effective treatment and reintegration into the community for selected offenders without endangering the community.

As of January 31, 1994, 224 offenders have participated in day reporting. The program has a success rate of 84 percent, and only one client has been rearrested while in the program. The new arrest was for a nonviolent misdemeanor offense. Over $136,000 in supervision fees were collected from clients to help offset the cost of the center. A study of the clients that successfully finished the day-reporting center program showed that eight percent of them were rearrested after completing the program. The amount of time between completing the program and rearrest averaged 7.5 months, with the shortest period being one month and the longest, 17 months. Of the seven re-offenders, four were arrested for new misdemeanors and three were accused of committing felony offenses. None of the seven were first-time offenders when accepted to the day-reporting center, and they had an average 7.2 prior arrests. Six of the seven committed the same offense for which they were in the day reporting center program. This may indicate that these individuals' criminal behavior was more deeply rooted and that the day-reporting center was not able to alter their criminality significantly. Future recidivism studies performed after a longer period of time will be needed to verify these results.

Preliminary indications are that Orange County's day-reporting center is an effective alternative to incarceration. Day reporting has helped relieve jail overcrowding and has provided treatment and supervision of offenders and at less cost to the community.

Discussion and Recommendations

In evaluating the effectiveness of day-reporting centers, it is important to consider not just program success rates but how day-reporting centers compare with incarceration in accomplishing treatment goals and in cost efficiency. English centers are operating effectively and are becoming a recognized aspect of probation supervision, evidenced by the continued spread of centers there. American centers in Massachusetts are reporting successful completion rates of 66 percent to 81 percent. These programs are also experiencing success in serving a population of prison-bound offenders and therefore saving tax dollars that would have been needed for prison beds. An important measure of success for any correctional program is the decreased recidivism of former participants. Unfortunately, because day reporting is a relatively recent development in community corrections programming, recidivism studies have not been conducted or at least not published in the professional journals.

Until recidivism is studied more comprehensively, two measures of success can be used to analyze day reporting: cost effectiveness and protection of the community. In assessing cost effectiveness, it is critical that the cost of centers is compared with the cost of incarceration. It is, therefore, equally important that day-reporting center clients be individuals that were incarceration bound. Day reporting, being an intermediate sanction that uses smaller caseloads than would be found in probation, will naturally not compare favorably with probation's costs. If offenders that would have been sentenced to probation are instead selected to be supervised by day reporting, the end result would be the costly widening of the net of social control. If, however, the offender was prison or jail-bound, the effect is to modify the offender's behavior at less cost than is required for incarceration.

Of course, cost effectiveness is a secondary concern to the safety of the community. No program will last long, no matter the cost savings, if it seriously threatens the well-being of the citizens. Community corrections is inherently political, and its very existence dependent on the approval, or at least the tolerance, of the community. Because community protection is of paramount importance to community corrections, a great deal of attention needs to be given to those treated in the community. Violent offenders and criminals whose crimes were particularly notorious are a significant risk to the operation of day reporting.

If not the violent or serious offender, then which of the offenders that populate our institutions should be selected? Perhaps we should take advice from the original English centers. These first programs were operated for petty criminals who were in danger of going to prison not for the heinousness of their crimes but rather from the sheer number of nonviolent crimes that they committed. Day reporting should be reserved for the offender whose behavior has not been corrected by probation and who has evidenced a need for greater structure in his or her treatment. This is the niche that day reporting will fill in a correction continuum that endeavors to apply the proper amount of control and treatment to ensure the correction of the individual.

Source: Reprinted with permission from *Federal Probation,* Vol. 58, No. 1, pp. 9–14, March 1994.

ARTICLE—
Intensive Supervision: A New Way to Connect with Offenders[11]

The essential challenge of supervision is to obtain sufficient knowledge about offenders' activities to be able to affect those activities. Even under the best of staffing circumstances, there will always be one probation officer to many offenders. More often than not, these offenders do not wish the officer to know what they are doing. How can a probation officer maximize his or her ability to track offender whereabouts and activities in a cost-effective manner?

Enter intensive supervision, Southern Florida style. Four years ago we were looking for a significant, immediate sanction for drug use in the occasional drug-user population. Dade County had the highest rate of cocaine use in the Southern District. Drug use was one of the most frequent violations leading to revocation and imprisonment. We believed an immediate consequence would deter occasional users from further use and would screen for drug-dependent users who could not stop using drugs on their own. Available consequences were inadequate; modifications of release conditions to add electronic monitoring or drug abuse treatment took too long. We also believed drug abuse treatment was not always indicated for occasional users, most of whom were not drug dependent, were unmotivated for treatment, or were often involved in drug trafficking. What else could we do with the resources we had?

We tried a new idea with a few offenders. We believe over the past four years we have developed this idea into a powerful method to control risk, a method which has many applications across populations and behaviors.

Intensive Supervision in Southern Florida

Offenders in the general supervision population in Dade County who test positive for cocaine or marijuana, the drugs of choice in the district, are placed in what we call intensive supervision. The case transfer occurs within 48 hours of a positive Emit test result. Because the Southern District of Florida has its own drug testing lab, in most cases offenders are transferred within four days of testing or within a week of the actual drug use.

Drug Use Issues

The offender is instructed to report to the office twice a week for drug testing. Networking with employers when necessary has revealed a surprising level of cooperation to allow the offender to report for testing. To our knowledge, not one single person has lost a job as a result of reporting.

Offenders are also required to report for a 16- to 20-hour drug abuse education program. This service is provided free of charge by two local hospitals to the community at large. It is available during evenings and weekends. The education program is not treatment. It is presented to the offender as information to use in making an informed decision about drug use and treatment. It differs from the traditional approach in which the probation officer tells the offender, "You have used drugs while under supervision, you have a drug problem." Or, "You need treatment."

Occasional, non-dependent drug users unmotivated for treatment are given an incentive: if they complete the education program, show no further drug use, and comply with intensive supervision instructions, they will not be required to enter treatment. Offenders who show continued drug use are referred for treatment. The Substance Abuse Subtle Screening Inventory (SASSI) is used as a screening tool in conjunction with behavioral observations.

Intensive Reporting

Offenders are told that, because of their positive drug test, they have been placed in intensive supervision. They are further informed that they will remain under intensive supervision for an unspecified period of time, depending on their future performance.

A detailed interview is conducted as to the circumstances surrounding the drug use, with the goal of obtaining an admission of drug use from the offender. The offender is informed that his or her reporting instructions are now changed: henceforth, the offender is to page the probation officer before every move from one location to another and upon arriving home. He or she is instructed to wait 15 minutes after paging the probation officer. If the officer does not respond within the 15 minutes, the offender is to call the officer's answering machine and leave a detailed message including name, time, present location, destination, and estimated time of return. Offenders are instructed that they are not to have caller ID or call return. By prohibiting caller ID and call return, the officer can return calls from home or any other location. Call forwarding is not allowed.

Incoming offenders are coached on how to report and conditioned to the procedure by initially returning pages and calls at an almost one-to-one frequency. Gradually, the frequency of response is dropped for those offenders who are employed, have no positive tests, and are otherwise stable. Sufficient response frequency is sustained to maintain the reporting behavior.

Supervision Advantages

The officer monitors the pager and the answering machine. Field contacts are made to verify location and activities. No longer is the probation officer looking for offenders who may or may not be where they are supposed to be. By recognizing the numbers on the pager and listening to the answering machine, the officer can pinpoint an offender's location any time and see the offender in the community. If the offender is not located at the last reported location, the officer immediately contacts significant others, locates the offender, and confronts him or her regarding inaccurate reporting. Failures to report are not charged as violations. Instead, they are used to inquire as to the offender's activities and reiterate the necessity of compliance. Failures to report also provide leads for further investigation.

Intensive reporting has a number of benefits for the officer and the offender:

1. Listening to messages gives us an unprecedented look at an offender's life-style: where the offender spends free time, how much time the offender spends at home. Subtle, and sometimes not so subtle, voice changes detectable in messages tell us the offender may be having a problem or may be under the influence of drugs or alcohol. Answering machines with date/time features provide immediate verification of the actual time of the message. Discrepancies between actual time and the time the offender reports are brought to the offender's attention every time they occur.

2. The procedure extends our presence in the offender's life. No longer can the offender easily predict when the officer will contact him or her. The combination of telephone and field contacts serves to reinforce the officer's presence. The probation officer can now multiply the opportunities for contact through use of the telephone, while remaining in control as to how much supervision to apply in each case.

   The extension of the officer's presence in the offender's life is not always negative; it is also positive. When an offender is complying, the officer responds to a message and positively reinforces the offender's adherence to a constructive schedule. We have found many offenders react positively to this kind of individualized attention. The rapport developed in this manner serves to increase cooperation on the part of the offender.

3. The intensity of reporting is not reduced when the officer is off duty. Daily, the officer chooses when to respond to pages or messages. When the officer is on leave, offenders continue to report as usual. During extended leave periods and on weekends, a secretary transcribes the

messages. The officer reviews the transcribed records upon return, and the records provide valuable information as to offenders' schedules and patterns of movement.

4. The procedure makes the offender take notice of his or her activities. Those who are involved in criminal activity have the most difficulty reporting and can be easily targeted for investigation. Impulsive offenders have to practice discipline: make a phone call, wait for an answer, leave a detailed message. Most offenders comply with the reporting instructions.

5. Depending on the offender's motivation to change, the reporting procedure either coerces or assists in the cessation of criminal associations. In either case, intensive reporting is a way to increase the probability that the offender will avoid the "people, places, and things" that trigger drug use and other dysfunctional behaviors.

Administrative Advantages

In a time of reduced resources, intensive supervision offers considerable advantages:

1. Whereas reporting demands are significantly increased, no action by a releasing authority is required, because the instructions are covered by the standard conditions of release. District judges were briefed before we began using this method and have extended their full support. There are significant savings in time and resources. No paperwork to modify release conditions need be prepared, mailed, handled, or signed by probation office staff, judges, or parole commission staff. No appointment of counsel, involvement by attorneys, or court time is involved in situations in which the offender might oppose a modification. Inquiring attorneys are advised that increased reporting instructions are based on probable cause of drug use as shown by a presumptive drug test. In four years, only one offender has formally, and unsuccessfully, challenged the instructions.

2. Intensive supervision also saves treatment funds and maximizes treatment resources. The testing protocol serves to screen offenders able to control their drug use from those who are drug dependent. Those whose drug use continues under the increased restrictions are placed in treatment. Offenders in denial are more likely to accept treatment when their failure to remain abstinent in intensive supervision is clearly remonstrated.

3. No outside contractor is involved. Equipment costs are minimal. There are no fees to collect. Virtually no additional paperwork is generated.

Requirements

In order to be effective, intensive supervision requires support in the following areas of personnel and equipment:

1. Intensive supervision requires probation officers who are attuned to field supervision. Willingness to insist consistently on compliance is crucial. Investigative training is important in that intensive reporting often uncovers information that requires follow-up. Unexplained assets or income, assets obtained by fraudulent means, and multiple identities are but a few examples of leads that are uncovered.
2. Intensive supervision requires management support. Any supervision program that demands a significant change in offender behavior patterns will generate complaints. Offenders will attempt to evade instructions by appealing to supervisors and top management. Positive supervisor involvement in the process increases the probability that the offender will remain compliant.
3. The third personnel requirement is caseload size not to exceed 25 offenders if the entire caseload is on intensive reporting. Because the program has no set duration, caseload size can be maintained by returning stable cases to general supervision to allow for incoming, unstable cases.
4. Equipment requirements are a 15-memory pager and an answering machine with remote message retrieval and date-time feature. A cellular phone for field work is highly desirable, but not essential.

Where Do We Go from Here?

At this time we do not know whether intensive supervision results in significant reductions in risk and noncompliant behaviors. When we began using this procedure, we did not simultaneously institute research to measure effectiveness. We have attempted to go back and examine some indicators, such as drug use, during and after intensive supervision. Uncontrolled variables (e.g., a lack of control groups matched or other characteristics or a lack of standardization in testing schedules after intensive supervision) preclude any conclusions. Prospective, controlled research is needed to determine whether this intensive supervision method makes a significant difference in compliance.

In a search for effective supervision, this procedure merits further examination and development. One obstacle to such development is lack of resources. Because intensive supervision does not require a special condition of release, it does not qualify for additional personnel. Its efficiency is its Achilles' heel.

In the technological area, the procedure can be improved in many ways. While we used the very limited technology we had, new voice-mail systems can increase effectiveness. Features such as ability to save messages can aid the officer in managing an intensive supervision caseload or even a few offenders placed under the reporting procedure. We will be exploring new telephone technology in the near future and welcome exchange of information in this area.

Intensive supervision can be successfully applied to other groups of high-risk offenders in addition to occasional drug users. Offenders placed in drug abuse treatment can certainly benefit. After all, what is the point of providing drug abuse counseling a few hours per week if the offender spends the rest of the time engaged in activities that are incompatible with treatment? The activities of offenders unwilling to obtain employment can be tracked. Too often we instruct offenders to "get a job," but fail to interfere with the job they already have: criminal activity. Follow-up on social service referrals can be improved by requiring immediate feedback from offenders as to whether they report for referral appointments. Activities of re-released supervision violators and violent offenders can be tracked from the first day of their release. This method can be used in conjunction with electronic house arrest to track the offender outside the home. Similarly, it can be used by halfway houses to track offender activities outside the facility.

Finally, although we do not supervise juveniles, we have discussed this method of intensive reporting with juvenile justice professionals. They see potential for improvement in the supervision of the juvenile population through this procedure. Juveniles, who are still amenable to adult direction, can be given such direction through this method. All of the supervision advantages discussed in the case of adults apply to juveniles.

Finding methods to provide improved, cost-effective supervision must be a priority if community corrections is to meet taxpayers' risk control demands. We believe this method offers a significant improvement over supervision techniques currently in use and welcome inquiries and ideas for improvement.

Source: Reprinted with permission from *Federal Probation,* Vol. 58, September 1994.

For those of us who have been involved in corrections for more years than we care to admit, it is difficult to think of a prison run by inmates. The basic concept discussed in the following article is controversial. However, in our search for a better method of dealing with crime, we cannot afford to overlook any possible solution.

ARTICLE—
Inmate Involvement in Prison Governance[12]

Few oxymorons sound to most people as silly and naive as that of prison democracy, and for good reasons. For one, one wants offenders punished, and democracy sounds like a reward. For another, few citizens are enchanted with what passes for democracy elsewhere, and one can conceive of the liabilities of representative governance enhanced, corrupted, and caricatured in prison settings.

How do we see democracy misfiring?

- We may feel the wrong people dependably get elected.
- To get elected, we see them making promises that we believe are not seriously intended.
- We feel that when political candidates get elected they start looking out for themselves and their sponsors instead of those who elected them.
- These perceptions make many of us cynical about politics.
- As people lose interest, they stop participating, which one suspects makes it easier for the wrong people to get themselves elected.

Time and again, prison politicians have been blamed for the demise of prison governance experiments, and with unseemly delight. Carefully documented worst-case scenarios have made it possible for penologists to indulge in 20/20 hindsight and discouraging extrapolations. Their jaundiced accounts, however, are only one side of the story. History can supply, if need be, scenarios that show that prisoner involvement can work. It need not create vehicles for the ascendance of self-appointed subcultural spokespersons who are oily, smooth, and psychopathic, or loud and angry and unconstructively obnoxious, or need participatory management widen the gap between prisoners and staff or corrections and the public.

Prisoner involvement, constructively envisaged, can be the very opposite of cynicism-enhancing game playing. It can be, as one Scottish prisoner put it to me, about becoming active instead of passive. It can be about creating community. It can be about prisoners having sound and practical ideas about improving life in the prison, about proposing these ideas and working hard to implement them. It can be about staff and prisoners working together, or as closely together as possible, about prisoners working together, and staff working together, to solve problems.

Prisoner involvement can enhance prison regimes by reducing the dependency of dependent prisoners, the alienation of alienated ones, and the ambivalence to authority of most others. It can help to motivate constructive involvements in civilian life through experiences in which the prisoner sees improvements as a result of actions he or she has taken in the quality of his or her institutional life and that of other prisoners.

Commitment and Trust

Prisons gain from prison democracy when prisoners become committed to the improvement of prisons. The development of this commitment, of course, hinges on the degree to which we can provide the prisoners with opportunities for involvement that make sense to them from their perspective, as well as making sense to us from ours.

Commitment also varies with the degree to which opportunities permit each prisoner to successfully display and rehearse skills along areas of his or her interest. For all participants, including prisoners, mindful activity is preferable to mindless activity, and it is satisfying to do something that one feels qualified to do. The same holds for the benefit of collaborative activity. Working with others allows for the exercise of interpersonal skills and can enhance the competence in the exercise of these skills. This, many prisoners and staff find useful. Collaborative activity also provides a respectable setting for people to interact with people they would ordinarily avoid. One can sneak up on offenders and subject them to constructive staff and peer influence at work. Persons who are sources of prison problems can even be enlisted in this way in the solution of prison problems. At minimum, those who have been enlisted to help solve a problem will be less likely to resist the implementation of solutions. Where prisoners and staff collaborate, problems can be solved in ways that are acceptable to prisoners and staff, and the resulting actions will make sense to prisoners and staff. But no one can argue that any of this is easy.

The principal impediment to initiating any experiment in prisoner involvement is the "them versus us" culture of prisons, which is shared, or rather, reciprocated, by prisoners and staff. Where a group of prisoners is convoked to consider involvement, one hears variations on themes such as "they don't trust us," and "we don't trust (expletives to taste)," and "we don't trust them to let us do anything," meaning, to trust us. Counterpart issues for staff are: "Can we trust offenders to behave responsibly without constant monitoring and supervision?"

Trust issues are related to the fact that even in the most benevolent prisons—there are such institutions—transactions between staff and prisoners are essentially parental. Prisoners request, demand, or protest. Staff members concede or refuse, circumscribe, delimit, monitor, and order prisoners about.

The transition from these sorts of transactions to adult-adult transactions is unbelievably difficult and strangely painful for both prisoners and staff. Among other things, prisoners must give up structure, the support inherent in dependence, and the luxury of blaming staff for every conceivable adversity; staff members must give up structure and prized assumptions about the immaturity, incapacity, and intrinsic untrustworthiness of prisoners.

To threaten to violate these vested assumptions of prisoners and staff invites expressions of anxiety from both groups to varying degrees. Anxiety is also evoked by the prospect of unknown challenges with which one feels one might be unable to cope. Then there is the prospect of hard work, which may not be unambivalently welcomed by some.

Anxiety, unfortunately, can be expressed in a variety of ways, and none of these is delicate, civilized, or attractive. This is especially true where anxiety translates into anger, and the change agent is at the receiving end of this anger. Such are stormy seas, and interventionists must reliably weather them at early stages of implementation. They must also deal with the next stage of the process, in which staff and prisoners wake up in the cold light of morning from their initial commitment and ask, "How can we undo it?"

A Prison Constitutional Convention

In the remainder of this article, I will summarize efforts to stimulate the inception of democracy in two Scottish prisons. One of these interventions was an intensive two-day convocation in an open prison, a prison without walls for prisoners who are on the last lap of long sentences. The prison contained some 70 prisoners and 37 staff members.

The person who designed the convocation in this prison was the regional director of the Scottish Prison Service responsible for the region in which the prison is located. Also involved was the prison's warden. Half the prisoners in the institution were present for the 2-day meeting and participated in it. So did 12 staff members—mostly uniformed officers.

The first day opened with a session in which the results of an opinion survey of staff and prisoners were presented to the group. A discussion of these findings was led by the head of the Research Branch of the Scottish Prison Service. The discussion highlighted perceived problems in the prison that could hypothetically benefit from remedial action. It also pointed out the fact that the climate of the prison is seen as a relaxed one, which would make it conducive to corroborative relationships.

The convocation was divided into task forces after a second presentation by the regional director about the Prison Service's commitment to the empowerment of officers and prisoners. The director stressed the opportunity offered to the prison to become a pioneering experiment in self-governance.

A staff group and three prisoner groups were first formed around the issue of assigning and taking responsibility. The officers dealt with the question, "What do we do that they can and should do for themselves?," while the prisoners considered, "What do they do that we can and should do for ourselves?"

During an ensuing plenary session, spokespersons for the groups explained their suggestions, which decorated the front of a dining hall and varied considerably in legibility. The reports also varied in content. The staff manifesto ranged from justificatory statements, (such as, "Why all the boundary rules? [Answer:] Protection of residents.") through cautious bids (such as, "Don't you trust us? [Answer:] Yes, given trust.") and concessions varying in generosity from making residents responsible for cleanliness and tidiness to letting them allocate the recreation budget and coordinate visiting arrangements.

One prisoner group brought a roster of requests for autonomy or discretion, and a second included new privileges in a laundry list. The third group, by contrast, offered several detailed, constructive proposals, some of which implied a strong task-oriented outlook and an uncompromising commitment to the Protestant ethic.

The group suggested that educational trips be organized by prisoner committees. It proposed a meeting between a town committee and a prisoner committee every month to improve relationships between prisoners and town folk with a view to enhancing (work and volunteer activity) placement schemes. It recommended a system of work allocation (for work on prison grounds) by a prisoner committee made up of skilled or experienced prisoners. The group also asked that "people with work or recreation skills (be) given the opportunity to pass on experience to others who are interested" and that "prisoners be consulted about job creation within the prison." They requested that prisoners be permitted to organize their own lunches for outside placements by being given a budget for the week to organize and supervise their own visits, by committee, and that they be allowed to run the inmate canteen with accounts available for inspection at all times.

The prisoners emphasized that all committees would have to be democratically elected, and they added a proposal for an open day for town folk to visit the prison and talk to prisoners and staff about the aim of the prison to improve relations, with the possibility of having town folk visit any time to see the jail working.

An idiosyncratic element in the report was mention of a vote of no confidence in the prison social worker, but not much was made of this passing reference in the discussion of the group's report. A concluding talk dealt with the need for meticulous detail and careful documentation in proposals to be drafted.

The second day opened with a speech by the prison's warden, who emphasized his receptivity to responsible proposals. The warden extended this offer to include proposals for the allocation of portions of the prison budget. The regional director also spoke, enjoining the group to be productive and offering support.

The next set of subgroups were asked to consider "the other side's" perspective, with officers considering the prisoners' views, and prisoners, those of the staff. The officers responded valiantly to this mandate, reviewing the impact on the inmates of minor rules and redundant security rituals and discussing the need for greater flexibility and open communication. Several of the staff showed remarkable empathy in characterizing prisoner reactions to frustrating prison routines.

No such empathy was forthcoming from the three prisoner groups, whose summarized reports were discursive and off the point. The discussion was similarly tangential and degenerated into attacks on the prison social worker. The rest of the reporting period was taken up with demands that the social worker be fired and the director's rejection of this demand. This dialogue sounded like a parent-child exchange, in which limits are tested and parents have to react to set boundaries.

The juncture proved to be a turning point in the intervention: a transmutation into attentiveness to business occurred in the next session, during which prisoners and staff dealt with the question, "What's in it for us?," presuming that the program were implemented.

The group of officers indicated that if they were freed of surveillance obligations and permitted to expand human service activities, this would make their jobs more interesting and worthwhile. They welcomed the opportunity to change from a custody role to a facilitator-counseling role and of enhanced "opportunity for interaction." They also recognized that their jobs would become more demanding and that training might be in order to ensure that they were qualified to do what was expected of them.

The officers discussed the risks and benefits of the impending changes for themselves as a group. To participate in a pioneering venture could advance one's career, but less so if the institution were seen as unrepresentative. Officers in other prisons might subject them to derision, and the public might become concerned about safety issues. A single escape could damage the program.

In response to the question, "What's in it for us?" the officers listed the following:

- Job satisfaction
- Free the staff to do other more worthwhile productive tasks
- The opportunity for more interaction
- A more demanding role for staff
- Because it is a pioneering project, (it can) further individual careers
- Gives staff opportunity to change from conventional role

One of the prisoner groups answered the same question with a counterpart list of benefits:

- The chance to get rid of the "them vs. us" attitude
- More relaxed community atmosphere
- More integration with staff (i.e., joint ventures with staff)
- Less boredom
- Less paranoia about release
- More rehabilitation factor
- Less bitterness against system on release

It should be obvious that the roster reflects commitment to collaborative activity and reintegration. The prisoners said they wanted to multiply joint activities with staff, including recreational activities. They saw the possibility of a useful bridging experience from the prison to the community. They saw activities as a way to reduce boredom and acquire and rehearse coping skills. The groups also saw value in improving the prison for future generations of prisoners.

Creating an Organization

To this point we had experienced dramatic movement, which included all night debates in prisoners' dormitories. It was now necessary to capitalize on this enthusiasm by designing the structure of the new governance machinery.

To this end, prisoner groups were tasked with listing desired interest groups or committees; a mixed prisoner-staff group was asked to deal with the overall organization and structure of governance.

The products of the groups turned out to be remarkably congruent. Joint staff-inmate committees were envisaged by the prisoners, except for groups representing housing units. These committees were envisaged as having responsibility for various functions, such as advising on culinary matters, running the commissary, coordinating visiting arrangements, and disbursing recreational funds. Each drafting group also suggested setting up a public relations committee to cement relations between the prison and the public.

In the overall structure, the committees were seen reporting to a council of six officers and four inmates, who in turn were to report to a managerial group comprising the warden and two senior officers. This system was set up to deal with budgetary and policy decisions at various levels. Also envisaged was a monthly community meeting that would include all prisoners and staff of the institution.

The convocation ended with the appointment of a prisoner-staff coordinating group charged with implementing the design, which was to begin at once. The prisoner representatives to this group were chosen among those who had played leading roles in the convocation.

The coordinating group went on to define its mission to include drafting a constitution. In this constitution, the prisoners and staff streamlined the organization that had been suggested, consolidating proposals from the various groups. The constitution also spelled out procedures for elections and committee deliberations. Excerpts from the documents read as follows:

1. The community council will consist of one executive committee and four subcommittees. The executive committee will be known as the council committee and will consist of four residents, one senior officer and one officer who have been duly elected to serve.

The four subcommittees will be known as:

1. House Committee
2. Visits and Family Welfare Committee
3. Sports and Recreation Committee
4. Public Relations Committee

Each subcommittee will consist of two residents and one officer who have been duly elected to serve. The executives reserve the right to increase the size of any subcommittee to look into different aspects of any changes or problems that may arise and also to co-opt anyone who has specialized knowledge to help to solve problems in the field.

Subcommittees
- Each subcommittee will meet at least once per week. Relevant time is to be allowed.
- Any issues that cannot be resolved at subcommittee level will be forwarded to the council committee.
- It will be the responsibility of each subcommittee to put forward reasoned arguments backed by relevant documentation, where appropriate, when forwarding issues to the council committee.

Council Committee
- It will be the duty of the council committee to review all proposals put forward by the subcommittees and to try to resolve all issues at council level. Any issues that cannot be resolved at council level will be forwarded to the governor (warden).
- The council committee will have access to relevant documentation, stationery and equipment in order to put forward properly formulated issues to the governor. The council committee will meet once every two weeks to discuss and resolve any issues put forward by the subcommittees.
- The council committee will meet once per month with the governor to update him on any relevant decisions taken and to put forward to him any issues they could not resolve.

Election of Committee
All officers and residents will be eligible to serve on the council committee or any of the four subcommittees.

- Notice for forthcoming elections and for willing candidates will be posted on the notice board at least seven days prior to the election. Anyone interested will put their names on the posted sheet. All candidates will be subject to a ballot with those attaining the highest number of votes being elected into office. If any positions are not filled from the notice board, then proposals will be accepted from the body of the hall. All officers and residents are eligible to vote.
- All committee members will serve for a period of three months, when they will be subject to re-election. If, during a term of office, anyone decides to drop out, the candidate with the next highest vote (relevant to the specific committee) will be co-opted until the end of that term.
- Any alterations or additions to the constitution can only be passed by a majority vote at an election.
- The council committee will have the right to call an extraordinary election by giving the appropriate notice.

Coordinator/Record Keeper

It was decided at the inaugural meeting that an election should take place for a coordinator/record keeper, whose post will include the duties of keeping the flow of information between the various subcommittees and the council. And also be responsible to the council for the preparation of proposals from all the committees to the governor. And of course the keeping of the records and decisions made for future reference. The post will be on the same terms as the posts on the council and subcommittees.

A month later the prison's newsletter reported results of elections to the committees and the council. The paper reported that "the Community Council held their first meeting last week" and pointed out that "the subcommittees meet every week and report to the Council who assemble on a fortnightly basis. . . . Minutes of each meeting are taken, then submitted to the coordinator who will keep a record of them."

Of course, this does not end the change process, and problems could still develop. The governance structure could be deemed superfluous and become underutilized. Fresh trust tests could be devised in the shape of proposals and demands that invite rejection. Personality conflicts could also arise that preempt serious business. New political entities in prisons are at first vulnerable, and they must be monitored and nurtured to ensure their survival.

A Grass Roots Mission Statement

It remains for me to describe a briefer experiment, which proved instructive but less conclusive. The target in this instance was a prison cellblock in a multipurpose prison, which functions as a detention facility for the west coast of Scotland. The cellblock contained long-term inmates and lifers in the midstage of their careers and is relatively new.

Twenty prisoners and three staff members participated in an afternoon meeting presided over by the principal officer of the cell block who was serving as acting warden. This officer is a respected staff member who volunteers as coordinator for the prison religious fellowship and has a loyal following among inmates.

Given the time available for the intervention, I proposed that the group draft a mission statement for the cellblock. Mission statements are taken seriously in Scotland, where quality management strategies are popular. The Prison Service has a mission statement, as do all prisons and autonomous special units. But no cellblock, in Scotland or elsewhere, has drafted a mission statement, and none has originated with a group of prisoners and officers.

I started the session noting that mission statements had traditionally been vapid public relations ploys, but that they have in recent times become embodiments of the central concerns of organizations, which guide and inform what they do and serve as reminders of what they stand for. This proved to become a problem when I cited the Prison Service mission statement, and the prisoners questioned whether this statement guided the agency's actions. (Rumors had circulated about impending cutbacks in furlough arrangements.)

Other objections from the group took familiar forms. One inmate reviewed a long and checkered prison career to document his reluctance to place trust in new initiatives. Another prisoner cited societal and systemic constraints to make a case for the proposition that local reform was futile. Other prisoners opined that mission statements should be drafted after more fundamental concerns had been addressed.

Eventually, the discussion drifted to mission statement planks that appeared to have some group support. Among these, one dealt with the desire to have the cell block operate as a community. Another dealt with the involvement of prisoners in decisions. A third suggested that rules be enforced with "flexible consistency." A fourth proposed that a climate be created to make family visits pleasant and profitable. Others dealt with the use of time, the planning of prison careers, and the control of serious drugs in the prison. This topic proved especially controversial and sparked a spirited debate.

The debate next turned to issues of a housekeeping nature and focused on assignments to double and single cells. The ostensible issue was the prioritizing of single-cell assignments, but the concern revolved around a specific individual and his assignment, with pressure to exact a decision in this matter becoming quite intense. The senior officer resisted the concerted campaign to force this issue, which presupposed the eviction of an inmate who was not present at the meeting.

At this stage the mission statement had to be tabled, but the group expressed satisfaction at the opportunity for what they saw as an open and honest exchange. This satisfaction was somewhat tempered when the prisoner on whose behalf cell assignment pressure had been exercised exploded in anger and left the meeting in a huff. It was subsequently resolved that the mission statement project would be resuscitated at a more strategic juncture.

I relay the second account with the first to point up the difficulties one encounters in pursuing the task of making prisons more normalized, humane, and participatory environments. Inmate cultures, and sometimes staff cultures, are obdurate, and having learned to fear, resent, and mistrust members of other groups, are apt to respond to trust bids with reluctant misgivings. The process of facing, surfacing, and disarming such resistance is slow, painful, and emotional. But given skilled and committed allies, such as my friends in the Scottish Prison Service, reform can eventually be achieved, and prisoners and officers can learn to work together to improve the settings in which they live and work.

Postscript

Whether American corrections is ready for this challenge is a difficult question. U.S. prisons are larger than those in Scotland. Our public appears more retributive. But inmate councils exist in American jurisdictions, and their role can be expanded, so can the involvement of prison staff in working with inmate councils. And in the U.S., functional prison units exist, which can serve as a setting in which community can be fostered.

Both American and Scottish correctional philosophies presuppose that offenders can be challenged to take responsibility for their lives upon release. This challenge, if it is taken seriously, is better met if prisoners are provided with opportunities to undertake responsibilities while in prison than if they are deprived of such opportunities. The point is to find acceptable ways for prisoners to shoulder and discharge responsibilities in the prison.

Source: Reprinted with permission from *Federal Probation*, Vol. 59, No. 3, June 1995.

Summary

In a growing trend that indicates how politically charged the crime problem has become, more and more states are trying to make prisoners pay for everything from filing lawsuits to their room and board. The number of inmates in state prisons has tripled since 1980. Presently, there are over one million state prisoners. This increase in population and the political pressures to tighten the budgets has led state officials to claim they are justified in going after even token payments from inmates, most of whom have little or no resources. In 1995, more than two dozen states passed laws intended to regain some of the costs of incarceration.

Electronic surveillance technology was first developed in the mid-1960s. It was not used with offenders until the 1980s. Since then, however, it has developed into one of the most popular intermediate sanctions used in the United States. It is estimated that more than one million people in the United States will ultimately be placed on some form of electronic monitoring. Not only is the number of offenders placed on electronic monitoring house arrest increasing, but the types of offenders are becoming more diverse. At first, it was used for offenders awaiting trial or sentencing and offenders released from institutional correctional facilities.

In sentencing jurisdictions throughout the country, judges are being faced with balancing such competing objectives as public safety, humaneness, and the assurance of offender accountability, while confronting accelerating increases in prison overcrowding and a political commitment to incapacitation and retributive justice.

Growing prison populations, court-ordered capacity limits on jails and prisons, and tight government budgets have forced a return to correctional innovation and a renewed interest in community-based corrections programming. Among the newer innovations are several intermediate sanctions that serve as steps between the security and punishment of prisons and jails and the supervision without security offered by probation and parole. Intensive supervision, house arrest, and electronic monitoring are becoming accepted alternatives to incarceration.

Discussion Questions

1. Describe some of the programs that states are attempting to use to reduce the high cost of prisonization.
2. Explain the advantages and disadvantages of home confinement.
3. What are the advantages to the use of electronic monitoring?
4. Explain the concepts behind the use of day-reporting centers.
5. Should inmates have a role in prison governance? Explain your answer.

Chapter Quiz

True/False
1. There is a general trend in many states to make inmates pay for filing lawsuits and their room and board.
2. Electronic surveillance has developed into one of the most popular intermediate sanction used in the United States.
3. Electronic monitoring has not been shown to be cost effective.
4. Researchers have determined that the length of a home confinement sentence can lead to a number of problems including "cabin fever."
5. One of the disadvantages of an intensive supervision program is that the costs tend to be astronomical and it minimizes treatment resources.

Multiple Choice
1. Which one of the following is NOT an administrative requirement of intensive supervision programs?
   a. Requires probation officers who are intoned to field supervision
   b. Requires management support
   c. Requires a 15-memory pager and an answering machine with remote message retrieval and date-time feature
   d. Requires an unlimited case load on the part of personnel

2. _____ is a concept that is adaptable to a number of different populations and used to offer enhanced treatment and supervision to probationers or sentenced offenders not on probation, to monitor inmates released early from jail or prison, and as a halfway step for offenders who are in violation of probation or parole.
   a. Intensive supervision centers
   b. Day-reporting centers
   c. Home confinement centers
   d. Electronic monitoring
3. Which are the two types of electronic monitoring systems currently being used?
   a. Home confinement and jail confinement
   b. Day-reporting centers and halfway houses
   c. Passive electronic monitoring and active electronic monitoring
   d. Intensive electronic monitoring and passive electronic monitoring
4. Regarding the successfulness of electronic surveillance technology, many communities including Illinois, Oklahoma, Texas, and California have produced
   a. no evidence of success.
   b. very minimal levels of success in such programs.
   c. evidence of success of the programs.
   d. The states listed above have not used electronic surveillance.
5. Day-reporting centers started in which country in the early 1970s?
   a. America
   b. Great Britain
   c. Australia
   d. West Germany

Endnotes

1. "State Prisons Go After New Source of Financing: Their Inmates." *The New York Times*, 9 July 1996, B-12.
2. "Proposal Would Levy Fees for Inmates' Incarceration," *Worcester Telegram and Gazette*, 16 July 2002, A6.
3. Michael P. Brown and Preston Elrod, "Electronic House Arrest: An Examination of Citizen Attitudes," *Crime and Delinquency* (July 1995): 332–346.
4. Jim Wallace, "Bracelet Program Beginning Monitoring Could Save Up to $50 a Day per Inmate," *Charleston Daily Mail*, 9 July 2002, 3D.
5. Tami J. Kampbell, "Mobile Intervention Supervision Team," In Edward E. Rhine (ed.) *American Correctional Association, Best Practices: Excellence in Corrections* (Lanham, MD: American Corrections Association, 1998), 79–83.

6. Ibid.
7. Bernard L. Fitzgerald and James Jordan, "Model for Police-Probation Partnership: Boston's Operation Night Light," In Edward E. Rhine (ed.) *American Correctional Association, Best Practices: Excellence in Corrections* (Lanham, MD: American Corrections Association, 1998), 92–100.
8. Ibid., 94.
9. James T. Jordon, "Boston's Operation Light House," *FBI Law Enforcement Bulletin* 67(8 August 1998): 1–5.
10. David W. Diggs and Stephen L. Pieper, *Federal Probation* 58(1 March 1994): 9–14. Mr. Diggs is manager of the direct supervision Department Orange County Corrections Division. Mr. Pieper is the Senior Superior of the Community Surveillance Unit in the Community Corrections Department of the Orange County Florida Division. Footnotes omitted.
11. Carol Freburger and Marci B. Almon. "Intensive Supervision: A New Way to Connect with Offenders," *Federal Probation* 58(3 September 1994): 23–25.
12. Hans Toch, "Inmate Involvement in Federal Government," *Federal Probation* 59(2 June 1995), 34–39. Footnotes and citations omitted. Mr. Toch is a Distinguished Professor of Criminal Justice at the State University of New York at Albany.

Chapter 15

Corrections As a Career Field

Mark C. Ide

Key Terms

codes of ethics
correctional officers
parole officers
probation officers
treatment strategies specialists

Outline

15-1 Parole and Probation Officers and Correctional Treatment Strategies Specialists
   15-1a Nature of Work
   15-1b Correctional Treatment Specialists
   15-1c Caseloads
   15-1d Changes in Work
   15-1e Working Conditions
   15-1f Training, Other Qualifications, and Advancement
   15-1g Job Outlook
Article—The Multifaceted Role of the Juvenile Probation Officer
15-2 Codes of Ethics
Article—Success in the Organization: A Primer for Probation Officers Seeking Upward Mobility
15-3 A Career As a Correctional Officer
   15-3a Federal Bureau of Prisons
   15-3b Kansas Department of Corrections
   15-3c California Department of Corrections
   15-3d Texas Department of Criminal Justice—Corrections Officer
   15-3e New York State Department of Corrections
Summary
Discussion Questions
Chapter Quiz
Endnotes

Learning Objectives

After studying this chapter, the reader will be able to:

- Analyze the corrections field as a career choice.
- Explain the meaning of the phrase "corrections is a growth industry."
- Explain the types of positions available in the corrections field.
- Describe the working conditions of correctional officers.
- Explain the training requirements for the various types of correctional officers.
- Analyze the employment outlook for the corrections field.
- Explain the multifaceted role of juvenile probation officers.
- List and explain the codes of ethics that apply to the corrections field.
- Analyze the requirements to be successful in the corrections field.

In this chapter, we will look at corrections as a career field. Included are discussions on parole and probation officers, the government occupational outlook for correctional officers, and the multifaceted role of juvenile probation officers. In addition, included in the chapter are the codes of ethics and a primer for probation (and parole) officers seeking upward mobility.

A distinction should be made early in this chapter between correctional staff and probation and parole officers. **Correctional officers** are prison or jail staff who manage inmates, while probation and parole officers supervise probationers and parolees in a variety of different settings and aftercare programs.[1] Thus, correctional officers manage and interact with incarcerated offenders while probation and parole officers interact with non-incarcerated offenders. Correctional treatment specialists may work with both incarcerated and non-incarcerated offenders.

According to the Bureau of Labor Statistics it is estimated that approximately 400,000 individuals are employed by correctional systems at the federal, state, and local levels. The demand for correctional employees has been increasing and probably will continue to increase in the foreseeable future. It is often stated that "corrections is a growth industry, thus there will always be a need for correctional personnel." Correctional employees represent both sexes and all ethnic groups. Since the work in corrections is varied, there are opportunities available for all types of skills and academic disciplines. Most researchers divide correctional employment into four main categories that cover a wide range of occupations and professions. They are:

- Custodial
- Treatment
- Administrative
- Support

Most individuals enter into corrections as correctional officers (COs). The correctional officers generally perform custodial roles in jails, prisons, and other institutions. The correctional officer position is not known for high entry-level pay. The typical correctional officer's entry pay is traditionally in the low $20,000 range. Figure 15-1 illustrates the process for applying and obtaining employment in the corrections field.

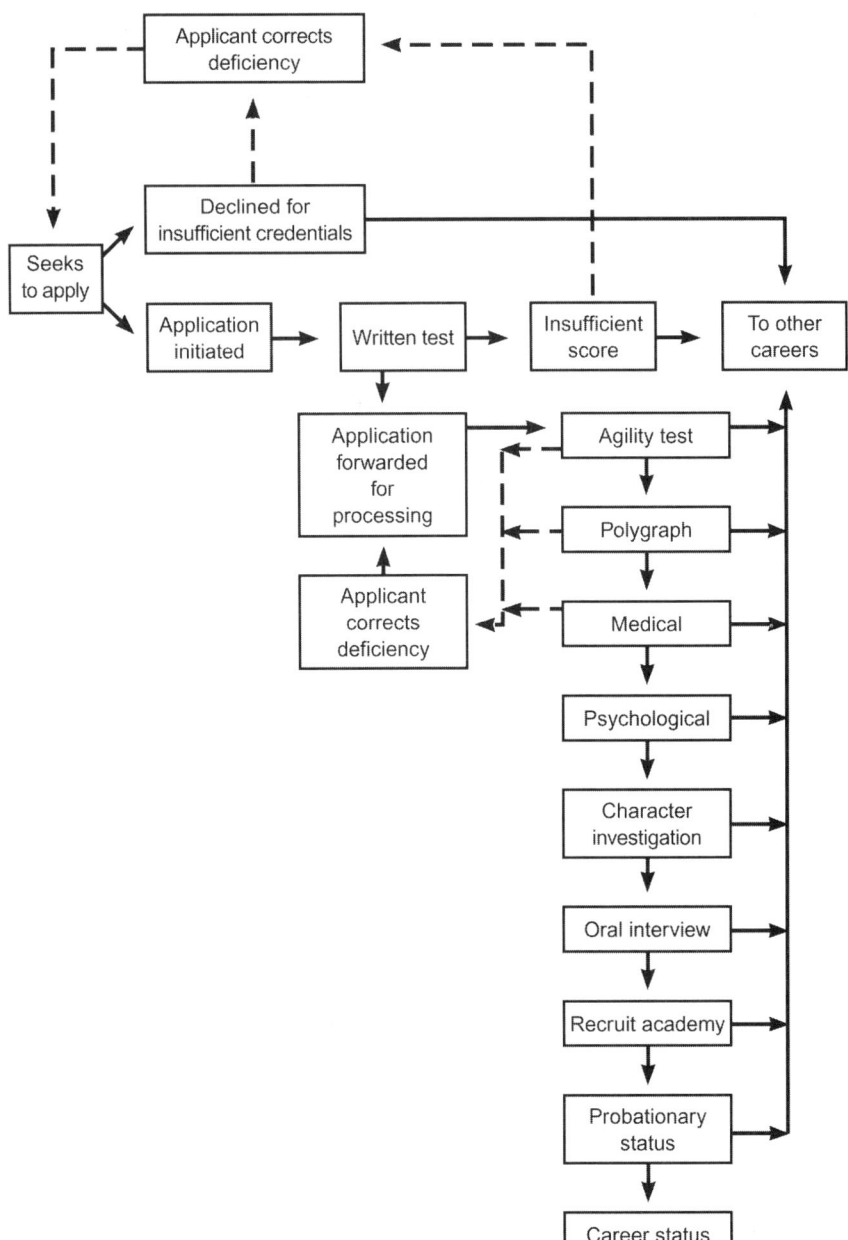

Figure 15-1
Corrections Employment Application Procedure

15-1 Parole and Probation Officers and Correctional Treatment Strategies Specialists

Many people convicted of crimes are placed on probation instead of being sent to prison. During probation, offenders must stay out of trouble and meet various other requirements. **Probation officers,** also referred to as community supervision officers in some states, supervise people who have been placed on probation. **Parole officers** perform many of the same duties that probation officers perform. However, parole officers supervise offenders who have been released from prison on parole to ensure that they comply with the conditions of their parole. In some states, the job of parole and probation is combined. Correctional treatment specialists work in correctional institutions or in parole or probation agencies. They are involved in planning educational and training programs with offenders as well as counseling offenders.

There are approximately 60,000 parole officers in the United States. Most are employed by state or county correctional departments. About 84,000 people were employed as probation officers and correctional treatment specialists in 2000. Probation officers generally work for the courts. Halfway houses and work-release centers also hire probation and parole officers.

Median annual earnings of probation and parole officers in 2000 were $38,150, with an average of between $30,270 and $49,030. The lowest 10 percent earned less than $25,010, and the highest 10 percent earned more than $59,010. In 2000, median annual earnings for probation officers and correctional officers and correctional treatment specialists employed in state government were $36,980; those employed in local government earned $40,820. Higher wages tend to be found in urban areas.

The regulations concerning requirements for parole or probation officers vary from state to state. Generally, the minimum educational requirement for becoming a parole or probation officer is a bachelor's degree in criminal justice, criminology, corrections, social work, or a related subject. A master's degree, as well as previous experience in the criminal justice system, is required in many cases. Some parole officer positions require fluency in a foreign language, most often Spanish. Personal qualities for parole or probation officers include patience, good communication skills, and the ability to work well with and motivate people.

One good method to gain the necessary experience for entry into the profession is by volunteer service with a rehabilitation center or some other social-service organization. Many of the agencies offer internships for students interested in a career in corrections. It is also helpful to contact local governmental agencies handling parole or probation and arrange informational interviews with parole or probation officers.

Generally, an individual enters the profession as a parole officer trainee before assuming the title of parole officer. New employees receive a majority of their training on the job. Advancement opportunities for parole officers to positions such as supervisors, administrators, and department heads are prevalent. Some parole officers assume supervisory positions as directors of specialized units.

The parole officer tries to help the parolee find housing, employment, job training, or formal education. In addition, the officer may try to help by referring the parolee to other specialists, such as a psychologist or a drug rehabilitation counselor, or to a halfway house. An officer is generally required to contact and talk with businesses that employ parolees. A great part of a parole or probation officer's job is ensuring that the defendant is upholding the parole or probation agreement.

Parole and probation officers usually work out of a government building, courthouse, social service agency, or correctional institution. Often they are required to travel to various settings, such as private homes, businesses, or schools, in order to conduct interviews and investigations. Typically they work 40 hours per week but overtime, as well as evening and weekend work may be necessary. Because of potential emergencies, some may be on seven-day, 24-hour recall status for part of their time. For more information regarding this career field, you may contact the American Correctional Association, 8025 Laurel Lakes Court, Laurel, MD 20707.

15-1a Nature of Work

Probation officers, parole officers, and correctional **treatment strategies specialists** work with criminal offenders, some of whom are dangerous. Good employment opportunities are expected for the future in these positions.

Many people convicted of crimes are placed on probation instead of being sent to prison. During probation, offenders must stay out of trouble and meet various other requirements. Probation officers supervise people on probation. Parole officers perform many of the same duties that probation officers perform. However, parole officers supervise offenders who have been released from prison to ensure that they comply with the conditions of their parole. In some states, the job of parole and probation officer is combined.

Probation and parole officers supervise offenders on probation or parole through personal contact with the offender and his or her family. Some offenders are required to wear an electronic device so that probation officers can monitor their activities. Officers may arrange for offenders to get substance abuse rehabilitation or job training. They also attend court hearings to update the court on the offender's compliance with the terms of his or her sentence and on the offender's efforts at rehabilitation.

Probation officers also spend much of their time working for the courts. They investigate the background of offenders brought before the court, write presentence investigation reports, and make sentencing recommendations for each offender. Officers review sentencing recommendations with offenders and their families before submitting them to the court. Officers may be required to testify in court as to their findings and recommendations.

Probation officers usually work with either adults or juveniles exclusively. Only in small, usually rural, jurisdictions do probation officers counsel both adults and juveniles. Occasionally, in the federal court system, probation officers may undertake the job of a pretrial services officer. Pretrial services officers conduct pretrial investigations and make bond recommendations.[2]

15-1b Correctional Treatment Specialists

Correctional treatment specialists work in correctional institutions (jails or prisons) or in parole or probation agencies. In jails and prisons, they evaluate the progress of inmates. They also work with inmates, probation officers, and other agencies to develop parole and release plans. Their case reports are provided to the appropriate parole board when their clients are eligible to be released. In addition, they plan educational and training programs to provide offenders with job skills, and counsel offenders either individually or in groups regarding their coping skills, anger management skills, and drug or sexual abuse. They usually write treatment plans and summaries for each client. Correctional treatment specialists working in parole and probation agencies perform many of the same duties as their counterparts who work in correctional institutions. Correctional treatment specialists may also be known as case managers or drug treatment specialists.

15-1c Caseloads

The caseload or number of cases a probation officer or correctional treatment specialist handles at one time depends on the counseling needs of the offenders and the risk they pose. Higher risk offenders and those who need a greater amount of counseling usually command more of the officer's time and resources. Caseload also varies by jurisdiction of the agency. Consequently, officers may handle from 20 to more than 300 active cases at one time.[3]

15-1d Changes in Work

The nature of the work of many probation officers and correctional treatment specialists has been affected by recent changes in the parole and probation system brought about by public debate on the proper role of prisons, probation, and parole. This has resulted in more community involvement on the part of probation and parole officers in many jurisdictions. Instead of requiring offenders to meet officers in their offices, many officers are going into the community to meet the offenders in their homes and at their places of employment or therapy. Probation and parole agencies also are employing the assistance of community organizations, such as religious institutions, neighborhood groups, and local residents, to monitor the behavior of many offenders. The ability to do this additional fieldwork is facilitated by telecommuting methods, such as the use of computers, phones, and faxes. Probation officers also may telecommute from their own homes. Other technological advances, such as electronic monitoring discussed in Chapter 14, also have assisted probation officers and correctional treatment specialists in supervising and counseling offenders.[4]

15-1e Working Conditions

Probation officers and correctional treatment specialists work with all types of criminal offenders. In the course of supervising offenders, they usually interact with many other individuals, such as family members and friends of their clients, who may be angry, upset, or difficult to work with. Workers may be assigned to fieldwork in high crime areas or in institutions where there is a risk of violence or communicable diseases. Probation officers and correctional treatment specialists are required to meet many deadlines, most of which are imposed by courts, which contributes to a stressful work environment. Although the high-risk stress levels can make these jobs very difficult at times, they also can be very rewarding. Many workers obtain personal satisfaction from counseling members of their community and helping them become productive citizens.

In addition, extensive travel and fieldwork may be required to meet with offenders who are on probation or parole. Workers may be required to carry a firearm or other weapon for protection. As discussed earlier, officers generally work a 40-hour week, but some may work longer. They may be on call 24 hours a day to supervise and assist offenders at any time. They also may be required to collect and transport offenders' urine samples for drug testing.[5]

15-1f Training, Other Qualifications, and Advancement

Background qualifications for probation officers and correctional treatment specialists vary by state, but a bachelor's degree in social work, sociology, human services, criminal justice, or related field from a four-year college or university is usually required. Some states also require one year of work experience in a related field or one year of graduate study in criminal justice, social work, or psychology to become a probation officer. Some employers may require previous experience or a master's degree in criminal justice, social work, or psychology, of applicants wishing to become correctional treatment specialists.

Applicants are usually administered written, oral, psychological, and physical examinations. Most probation officers and some correctional treatment specialists are required to complete a training program sponsored by their state government or the federal government. A certification test also may be required in some states during or after the completion of training.

Prospective probation officers or correctional treatment specialists should be in good physical and emotional condition. Most agencies require applicants to be at least 21 years old and, for federal employment, not older than 37. Those convicted of felonies may not be eligible for employment in this occupation. Familiarity with the use of computers often is required due to the increasing use of computer technology in probation and parole work. Candidates also should be knowledgeable about laws and regulations pertaining to corrections. Probation officers and correctional treatment specialists should possess strong writing skills due to the large number of reports they are required to prepare.

Most probation officers and correctional treatment specialists work as trainees for about six months. After successfully completing the training period, workers obtain a permanent position. A typical agency has several levels of probation and parole officers, and correctional treatment specialists, as well as supervisors. A graduate degree, such as a master's degree in criminal justice, social work, or psychology, may be helpful for advancement.[6]

15-1g Job Outlook

According to the U.S. Department of Labor, employment of probation officers and correctional treatment specialists is projected to grow faster than the average for all occupations through 2010. Despite recent decreases in the crime rate, vigorous law enforcement is expected to result in a continuing increase in the prison population. Overcrowding in prisons also has increased the probation population, as judges and prosecutors search for alternative forms of punishments, such as electronic monitoring and day-reporting centers. The number of offenders released on parole is expected to increase to create room for other offenders in prison. The increasing prison, parole, and probation populations should spur more demand for probation and parole officers and correctional treatment specialists.[7]

In addition to openings as a result of growth, many openings will be created by replacement needs, especially openings due to the large number of these workers who are expected to retire over the projections period. However, the job outlook depends on the amount of government funding allocated to corrections, and especially to probation systems.

ARTICLE—
The Multifaceted Role of the Juvenile Probation Officer[8]

An organization can, and should, set standards for ethical and professional conduct for all of the various aspects of the juvenile probation officer role. These standards represent a framework for the ideal juvenile probation officer. Only the juvenile probation officer can "flesh out" the established framework and, through his actions and demeanor fulfill this complex, multifaceted role. The probation officer is expected to fulfill many different roles, often "taking up the slack" after judges, attorneys, social agencies and parents and so on, have met what they see as their own clearly defined responsibilities in the case, and have expressed an unwillingness to extend themselves beyond these limits. Probation officers are all different in their individuality, but they share a strong, common concern for youth and the community.

A probation officer must balance many and sometimes conflicting roles, often within the same time frame. He or she must understand personal priorities, values and biases and how they coincide or conflict with those of the agency, resolving any conflicts in a manner that maintains credibility and effectiveness. The more the probation officer can be proactive in these roles, the less he or she will have to be reactive.

A short list of roles has been generated to stimulate thinking. Types of roles include diagnostician, agent of change, peace officer, and coordinator.

The Complete Juvenile Probation Officer [Many roles listed below.]

Cop—Enforces judge's orders
Prosecutor—Assists D.A./conducts revocations
Father Confessor—Establishes helpful, trustful relationship with juvenile
Rat—Informs court of juvenile's behavior/circumstances

Teacher—Develops skills in juveniles
Friend—Develops positive relationship with juveniles
Surrogate Parent—Admonishes, scolds juveniles
Counselor—Addresses needs
Ambassador—Intervenes on behalf of juvenile
Problem Solver—Helps juvenile deal with court and community issues
Crisis Manager—Deals with juvenile's precipitated crises (usually at 2 A.M.)
Hand Holder—Consoles juvenile
Public Speaker—Educates public re: tasks
P.R. Person—Wins friends/influences people on behalf of probation
Community Resource Specialist—Service broker
Transportation Officer—Gets juvenile to where he has to go in a pinch
Recreational Therapist—Gets juvenile to use leisure time well
Employment Counselor—Gets kids jobs
Judge's Advisor—Court service officer
Financial Advisor—Monitors payment, sets payment plan
Paper Pusher—Fills out myriad of forms
Sounding Board—Listens to irate parents, kids, police, teachers, etc.
Punching Bag—Person to blame when anything goes wrong, such as when a kid commits a new crime
Expert Clinician—Offers or refers to appropriate treatment
Family Counselor/Marriage Therapist—Keeps peace in juvenile's family
Psychiatrist—Answers question: why does the kid do it?
Banker—Juvenile needs car fare money
Tracker—Finds kid
Truant Officer—Gets kid to school
Lawyer—Tells defense lawyer/prosecutor what juvenile law says
Sex Educator—Facts of life, AIDS, & child support (Dr. Ruth)
Emergency Foster Parent—In a pinch
Family Wrecker—Files petition for abuse/neglect
Bureaucrat—Helps juvenile justice system function
Lobbyist—For juvenile, for department
Program Developer—For kid, for department
Grant Writer—For kid, for department
Board Member—Serves on a myriad of committees
Agency Liaison—With community groups
Trainer—For volunteers, students
Public Information Officer—"Tell me what you know about probation"
Court Officer/Bailiff—In a pinch
Custodian—Keeps office clean
Victim Advocate—Deals with juvenile's victim

15-2 Codes of Ethics

Every profession has its code of ethics. Accordingly, the codes of ethics of the American Correctional Association and the American Probation and Parole Association are set forth below. **Codes of ethics** serve as guidelines for professionals in the field. Because codes of ethics are not legislative enactments, there are no disciplinary actions associated with their violations. The codes provide us with a set of standards that we should strive to meet in our professional life.

Box 15-1

American Correctional Association Code of Ethics

Preamble: The American Correctional Association expects of its members unfailing honesty, respect for the dignity and individuality of human beings and a commitment to professional and compassionate service. To this end, we subscribe to the following principles:

- Members will respect and protect the civil and legal rights of all individuals.
- Members will treat every professional situation with concern for the person's welfare and with no intent of personal gain.
- Relationships with colleagues will be such that they promote mutual respect within the profession and improve the quality of service.
- Public criticisms of colleagues or their agencies will be made only when warranted, verifiable and constructive in purpose.
- Members will respect the importance of all disciplines within the criminal justice system and work to improve cooperation with each segment.
- Subject to individual's right to privacy, members will honor the public's right to know and will share information with the public to the extent permitted by law.
- Members will respect and protect the right of the public to be safeguarded from criminal activity.
- Members will not use their positions to secure personal privileges or advantages.

- Members will not, while acting in an official capacity, allow personal interest to impair objectivity in the performance of duty.
- No member will enter into any activity or agreement, formal or informal, which presents a conflict of interest or is inconsistent with the conscientious performance of his or her duties.
- No member will accept any gift, service, or favor that is, or appears to be, improper or implies an obligation inconsistent with the conscientious performance of his or her duties.
- In any public statement, members will clearly distinguish between personal views and those statements or positions made on behalf of an agency or the Association.
- Each member will report to the appropriate authority any corrupt or unethical behavior where there is sufficient cause to initiate a review.
- Members will not discriminate against any individual because of race, gender, creed, national origin, religious affiliation, age or any other type of prohibited discrimination.
- Members will preserve the integrity of private information: they will neither seek data on individuals beyond that needed to perform their responsibilities, nor reveal non-public data unless expressly authorized to do so.
- Any member who is responsible for agency personnel actions will make all appointments, promotions, or dismissals in accordance with established civil service rules, applicable contract agreements and individual merit, and not in furtherance of partisan interests.[9]

Source: Reprinted with permission of the American Correctional Association, Lanham, Maryland.

ARTICLE—

Success in the Organization: A Primer for Probation Officers Seeking Upward Mobility[10]

Each year a number of young college graduates, many quite talented, enter the probation profession eager to serve the courts, further the cause of justice, and help redirect the competent lives of errants. Some are successful and make significant contributions in the community corrections field. Still others, however, bring with them unrealistic expectations and unclear goals. As a result, they find the work unsatisfying and their careers blocked by a lack of opportunity for advancement. What is it that separates these two groups? Why is one group successful in finding satisfaction and opportunities for greater challenges while the other experiences burnout and disillusionment?

The difference between the successful and those less so in the field of community corrections is the same as it is in any other occupation. The successful possess certain traits that employers are seeking and that cause others in the field to look to them for leadership.

On occasions too numerous to recall we have been asked what characteristics we look for in candidates when filling supervisory and management positions in our respective organizations. Our responses, while not identical, tend to focus on several common characteristics which, for the purpose of this article, we have entitled *The Twelve "Cs"*. These qualities or characteristics, while applicable in community corrections, could apply in any organization or enterprise.

The Twelve "Cs"

Competent	Clear and Curious Mind	Composed
Committed	Compulsive	Competitive
Considerate	Cooperative	Consistent
Courageous	Communication Skills	Character

We hasten to add that these 12 characteristics are by no means inclusive of all the qualities we desire in employees, but they certainly are those we prioritize when we are engaged in the hiring process and selecting employees for promotions.

Competent

One of the first characteristics employers seek is competence. In addition to meeting the academic and experience requirements, people desiring greater responsibility must possess the intelligence and the heart for the job. Likewise, because the new position will require them to learn new techniques in dealing with people and will call upon them to use talents they did not fully exploit as a line officer, new supervisors must be trainable and willing to learn. The skills that made them competent frontline employees may not meet the demands of the new position.

Being competent includes having a vision, and that vision should be consistent with that of the organization to which they belong. In addition, they must be able to communicate that vision to their subordinates.

Finally, competent supervisors are those who exhibit control, particularly self-control. Charles Gandy, a prominent Texas attorney living in the Brazos Valley, is wont to say, "Don't start a fight you don't need to win." While it is frequently difficult to adhere to this admonition, good supervisors, nevertheless, should be expected to practice sufficient self-control to avoid unnecessary conflict.

Clear and Curious Mind

Supervisors must be endowed with clear and inquisitive minds—minds driven by common sense that are not only capable of recalling relevant data but analyzing it as well. They must be able to ferret out the wheat from the chaff and distinguish the minor issues from the big picture.

They must possess active minds that continue to absorb new information and subsequently translate that information into problem-solving strategies. Many years ago, far more than we wish to remember, International Business Machines, commonly known as IBM, initiated a practice of placing signs on the desks of its employees, and these signs contained a single word—"Think." The company's motive was obvious: it wanted its employees to be creative, to develop new strategies, and, as a consequence, to make the company more profitable. While this practice was implemented in a corporate setting, it is one which may be fittingly applied to entities in the criminal justice system. The ability to think strategically—considering an issue from different perspectives—is an essential quality for supervisors and managers.

Far too many employees attempt to attain advancement within their organization by working harder. Although hard work is admirable and should not be discouraged, those who work smarter rather than harder and are viewed as problem solvers tend to rise faster within the organization. Imagination and creative conceptualization are essential qualities sought in managers and supervisors. Management expert and prominent industrial leader Clarence B. Randall wrote of the importance of imagination in an administrator:

> He must be able to foresee what is likely to happen before it does. He must sense the significance of the forces that work about him and be able to evaluate their probable impact upon his decisions. Half a poet at heart, he must dream dreams and see visions. He must have the gift of building castles in the air without waiting for brick and mortar.

Evaluating the probable impact of forces around them requires supervisors to view problems in a variety of ways. Marlene Wilson points out:

> Too much valuable time goes into solving the wrong problems, and dealing with things that should have never been allowed to become problems, or dealing with the results rather than the causes of problems.

In addition, James Adams suggests:

> Few people like problems. Hence the natural tendency in problem solving is to pick the first solution that comes to mind and run with it. The disadvantage of this approach is that one may either run off a cliff or into a worse problem than the one started with. A better strategy in solving problems is to select the most attractive path from many ideas and concepts.

The key to problem solving is the ability to conceptualize as many solutions as possible from which to choose. Adams stresses:

> A good conceptualizer must be a creative conceptualizer. The mental characteristics which seem to make one creative not only are valuable in idea-having, but also better equip one to find and define problems and implement the resulting solutions.

It is also critical that supervisors be decisive. After analyzing available data from a global perspective, they must possess the ability to make a decision and be prepared to stick with it. In addition, the action plan they adopt should include incremental steps that will lead to the successful fulfillment of their objective.

Finally, a necessary and complementary component of a clear mind is good judgment, and particularly the exercise of good judgment under pressure. Academic achievement is a poor substitute for good judgment. During our careers we have seen many who appear academically suited for increased responsibility fail because of their inability to exercise sound judgment in decision-making situations.

Composed

Composure is an essential ingredient for success in an organization. Supervisors and managers must be self-assured and assertive, balanced with a good demeanor. This balance is important, for many people in supervisory positions, particularly those early in their careers, tend to become enamored with a sense of self-importance, and this can easily cause their downfall in an organization and with the external environment. Jesse E. Clark, who served as an assistant warden with the Texas Department of Corrections, a U.S. probation officer, and, at the time of his untimely death, U.S. district clerk for the Southern District of Texas, once told a group of young probation officers, "Don't take yourself too seriously because no one else does." A healthy sense of humor—even humor that at times is self-deprecating—can serve supervisors and managers well. In addition, supervisors must exhibit a mature demeanor. No one, and particularly subordinates, respects or likes people who appear to be immature.

Finally, a part of composure is appearance, and persons in supervisory positions should dress as well as their financial circumstances permit. Steve Robinson, director of the Texas Youth Commission, once made the observation that a well-dressed person with average intelligence will likely enjoy better career opportunities than a highly intelligent person who dresses poorly. While this may not be fair, it is, nonetheless, a fact of life: persons who dress well tend to command a greater degree of respect, and opportunities for advancement will come easier to them.

Committed

One of the more important qualities supervisors must possess is commitment—commitment to the employer, the agency, and the agency's mission. Truly committed supervisors, particularly those in agencies that deliver human services as probation departments do, view their position as their life's work, not just as a job. Former President Woodrow Wilson once said:

> You are not here merely to make a living. You are here in order to enable the world to live more amply, with greater vision, with a finer spirit of hope and achievement. You are here to enrich the world and you impoverish yourself if you forget the errand.

Commitment is also demonstrated through a sense of loyalty to the employer. A particularly favorite admonition used by Dr. George J. Beto, a clergyman, educator, and correctional administrator, which he drew from the writings of Edmund Burke, was "Don't bite the hand that feeds you." Found in that brief sentence is the message that one should be loyal to one's employer. This is particularly true of supervisors in an organization who are charged, to a great degree, with carrying out the agency's mission.

Probably one of the greatest correctional administrators was the late Joseph E. Ragen, who, while serving as warden of the Stateville and Joliet prisons in Illinois, presented his employees with the following homily:

> If you work for a man, in Heaven's name work for him. If he pays you wages that supply you bread and butter, work for him, speak well of him, and stand by him, and stand by the institution he represents.
>
> If put to a pinch, an ounce of loyalty is worth a pound of clearness; if you must vilify, condemn, or eternally disparage, resign your position.
>
> But as long as you are part of the institution, do not condemn it. If you do, you are loosening the tendrils that hold you to the institution, and with the first high wind that comes along, you will be uprooted and blown away, and probably you will never know why.

Warden Ragen's admonition is one that should be totally embraced by frontline employees who hope to succeed as supervisors and managers.

Finally, commitment is demonstrated through professional involvement. It is axiomatic that people who excel are usually involved in organizations that promote their profession. A cursory examination of community corrections leaders throughout the United States will show that most are active and contributing members of professional organizations. In addition to making a contribution to their profession and developing a sense of ownership, people in professional organizations establish relationships that, with time, serve to further their careers.

Compulsive

While this particular characteristic has some negative connotations, for the purpose of this article the term "compulsive" refers to the desire and ability to bring closure to an assignment, project, or issue. All too frequently supervisors have difficulty bringing closure to a particular initiative, and their inability to do so can cause irreparable harm to an organization. People who demonstrate that they can get things done, and done right, are a valuable asset to an organization.

Competitive

High energy and a competitive spirit are qualities sought after in supervisors. No supervisors will be successful if they are satisfied with the status quo, become just another member of a group, or lack the desire to be the very best. Another saying of Dr. Beto's was, "If you are not the lead cow, the scenery never changes." Supervisors should strive to see that the scenery always changes, not only for themselves but for their subordinates as well.

Two essential components of a competitive spirit are patience and perseverance. A perfect example of this is Abraham Lincoln, who sought public office on a number of occasions only to suffer disappointment. Because he never gave up hope and never lost sight of his objective, he persevered and was eventually elected president of the United States.

Cooperative

Competitiveness should not lead to a "win at all cost" mentality. Successful leaders are those who cooperate with others, negotiate compromise when necessary, and constantly seek mutual benefits in their interaction with others. They seek a balance between competition and cooperation. According to Stephen R. Covey:

> Competition has its place in the marketplace or against last year's performance—perhaps even against another office or individual where there is no particular interdependence, no need to cooperate. But cooperation in the workplace is as important to free enterprise as competition in the marketplace.

For an organization to be effective, its employees must cooperate with one another. Supervisors who can generate cooperation among employees will contribute significantly to the success of the organization and will quickly gain the attention of management. Too, people who consistently seek win/win relationships in all situations will realize the support of subordinates, peers, and management, and this support may well serve as the vehicle for advancement in the agency.

Considerate

People employed in probation and community corrections deal daily with people with problems. In addition to providing services to offenders and their families, probation personnel are called upon to address the needs of victims, law enforcement officers and court officials, colleagues, and employees of agencies charged with delivering human services. Many of these people are ill-equipped to handle their duties and responsibilities effectively, lack vision, are frustrated and unhappy with their stations in life, and feel overwhelmed by the demands of our complex society. Supervisors should be considerate when dealing with these people and should be sensitive to their problems. Consideration of the plight of others and a firm yet charitable nature will enhance the effectiveness of supervisors and managers.

Consistent

It is imperative that supervisors be consistent with those whom they supervise. According to Randall, when dealing with people and in making decisions, supervisors must "have one eye on what has gone on before and the other on what lies ahead." Hersey and Blanchard write:

> To be really consistent (in our terms) managers must behave the same way in similar situations for all parties concerned. Thus, a consistent manager would not discipline one subordinate when the person makes a costly mistake but not another staff member and vice versa. It is also important for managers to treat their subordinates the same way in similar circumstances even when it is inconvenient—when they don't have time or when they don't feel like it.

Supervisors and managers who fail to be consistent will not be able to provide clear direction to their staff. Equally important as being consistent in the manner we relate to others is that our actions be consistent with what we say. Kotter stresses:

> Few things can undermine the credibility of communication faster than a problem with consistency. People usually assume that actions do speak louder than words. As a result, one regularly finds in an effective leadership process a remarkable degree of congruence between the actions of key players and the messages they communicate.

Courageous

Closely related to consistency is courage, a quality that all successful supervisors possess. Quoting from Randall:

> Good ideas are not self-executing. They become effective only when there is behind them the driving force of a man who believes in them so fervently that he accepts all risks and surmounts all obstacles. Such high courage, upon which all industrial leadership must rest, has two sources: one is humility, the other is insight.

Courageous supervisors are driven by principles and are willing to take stands on critical issues, regardless of their popularity. In addition, courage is required of new supervisors because their role in the organization will have changed in that they will be responsible for directing people who formerly were their peers. This newly assumed role will prove to be very challenging and frustrating to the supervisor. In *The Prince*, a treatise on power written in 1513 and printed posthumously in 1532, Niccolo Machiavelli provided the following words of caution to new administrators:

> It ought to be remembered that there is nothing more difficult to take in hand, more perilous to conduct, or more uncertain in its success than to take the lead in the introduction of a new order of things. Because the innovator has for enemies all those who have done well under the old conditions and lukewarm defenders among those who may do well under the new.

While Machiavelli's cautionary advice was written for Renaissance nobility, it is applicable today to anyone assuming a position of authority. New supervisors and managers in community corrections would do well to remember the potential pitfalls envisioned by this Italian political philosopher and statesman and act accordingly. They should also be prepared to develop new friends among their co-workers because their relationships will change within the organization.

Communication Skills

A key ingredient in the formula for successful supervision and management is the ability to communicate, both in the written and spoken word. It has been our observation that far too many people entering the probation profession cannot compose a decent sentence. In most cases, this inability to write is not entirely their fault. They are the products of a generation where reading is not stressed in the home, where the television, with its inane programs, dominates leisure time, and where our educational institutions place insufficient emphasis on the importance of reading and writing.

Effective leaders are able to communicate their vision in a way that it is easily and immediately understood and translated into action. People with good communications skills are able to develop consensus on issues, and this is particularly important for managers and supervisors. As Covey points out:

> When you can present your own ideas clearly, specifically, visually, and most important, contextually, in the context of a deeper understanding of their paradigms and concerns, you significantly increase the credibility of your ideas.

There is no substitute for a good command of the English language.

Finally, essential to communication skills is knowing when not to speak. Most problems encountered by people are caused by quick and ill-considered responses.

Character

Probably the most important quality supervisors can possess is character, or what James Q. Wilson refers to as a "moral sense" and what Sam S. Souryal simply calls "ethics." It is this quality that all ethical employers seek in candidates for management and supervisory positions. Again, quoting from Randall:

> Character—one of the greatest words in the English language—defies both analysis and definition. Yet, no talent for administration, however brilliant, can long endure in a man without it. The fine executive invariably possesses a code of values which he himself has established. They sprang from his ethical and spiritual life and hold him staunchly true. In the face of each new challenge which he inspires in his associates, he issues few commands. They will obey, but that is the not the relationship, They follow, with enthusiasm and zeal.

According to Covey, "Character is the foundation of win/win, and everything else builds on that foundation." If, in responding to those who have asked what characteristics we look for in a candidate for a supervisory or management position in our organization, we were able to mention one quality, it would be character. It is all-important because the person with character is the person with integrity, credibility, and a moral sense, and whose presence in an organization can do nothing but enhance it.

In summary, probation officers possessing the qualities described in this article are in an excellent position to become the future leaders of the criminal justice system and are the type of leaders that are sorely needed. [Footnotes omitted.]

Source: Reprinted with permission from *Federal Probation*, Vol. 60, No. 1, pp. 55–56, March 1996.

15-3 A Career As a Correctional Officer

Correctional officers are the largest part of the correctional workforce. Most United States correctional institutions routinely have vacancies for correctional officer positions. Correctional officers work within a correctional facility and enforce the regulations governing the operation of the correctional institution. Correctional officers serve as both a supervisor and counselor of inmates. The following discussion will profile a few select correctional institutions so that the reader may understand the qualifications and salary ranges of correctional officers in various areas throughout the United States.

15-3a Federal Bureau of Prisons

Employment requirements for correctional officers with the Federal Bureau of Prisons include: (1) must be U.S. citizen; (2) be less than 37 years of age (although for some hard-to-fill positions an age waiver may be granted); (3) successfully complete an employee interview; (4) pass a physical examination; and (5) pass a field security investigation. Correctional officer candidates must hold a bachelors degree. Other requirements include successful completion of in-service training at the Federal Law Enforcement Training Academy at Glynco, Georgia.

Federal correctional officers are appointed at GS-5 level, while six months or more of graduate education in criminal justice or any social science may qualify the applicant for the GS-6 level or higher. A correctional officer may be advanced to the next higher pay-grade level after six months of satisfactory service.

Benefits include: (1) participation in the Federal Employees' Retirement System; (2) paid annual leave; (3) paid sick leave; (4) low cost health and life insurance; and (5) paid holidays. Other benefits naturally accrue from what the Bureau describes as "strong internal merit promotion practices" and "unlimited opportunities for advancement in one of the fastest-growing government agencies.[11]

15-3b Kansas Department of Corrections

Employment requirements for the corrections officer with the Kansas Department of Corrections include: (1) must have a high school diploma or equivalent; (2) must have no felony or domestic violence convictions; (3) must pass screening for alcohol and drugs; (4) successful employment and background check; (5) passing score on Corrections Officer Video Test, which assesses aptitude for the job; and (6) have a valid driver's license.

Corrections officers for the Kansas Department of Corrections start out as Corrections Officer I at up to an annual salary $22,609. Correctional Officer II has an annual salary of up to $24,918.

Benefits with the Kansas Department of Corrections include: (1) health insurance; (2) dental insurance/life insurance; (3) retirement benefits; (4) personal/sick/vacation leave; (5) paid holidays; (6) promotional opportunities; (7) and tax-deferred investment opportunities.[12]

15-3c California Department of Corrections

To be eligible for appointment as a State of California Correctional Officer, candidates complete each of the following components: (1) passing a written test; (2) passing a peace officer psychological examination; (3) passing a vision test; (4) passing a physical ability test; (5) passing a background investigation pre-screening interview; and (6) passing a pre-employment medical examination.

After successfully completing the exam process, candidates are placed on a list in the order of their final scores. Applicants will be contacted for appointment based on their rankings. Assignment to one of the state's 33 prisons is based on departmental need. However, whenever possible, candidates are assigned to an institution close to their home.

The California Department of Corrections is very competitive with other law enforcement agencies and offers one of the highest salaries for correctional officers in the United States. The monthly salary after completing the academy is $2,809 a month or $33,708 annually and tops out at $4,573 a month or $54,876 annually.

Benefits include: (1) health insurance; (2) dental insurance; (3) vacation leave; (4) holiday credits; (5) and employees may be eligible for special educational and physical-fitness incentive pay. Upon permanent appointment as a correctional officer, individuals are enrolled into the Public Employees Retirement System.

The California Department of Corrections has one of the finest correctional officer training programs in the United States. The Richard A. McGee Correctional Training Center annually prepares about 2,400 cadets to become correctional officers. After graduation from the academy, the new correctional officers are assigned to one of 33 prisons throughout California.

The sixteen-week residential training facility seeks to instill the skills and experience needed to function in a prison setting and to build *esprit de corps* (teamwork) among the cadets using a combination of academic instruction, physical fitness training, use of force awareness, group interaction, and communication skills. The curriculum consists of 640 hours of training and ranks among the top three correctional training academies in the country. Motor skills training may include: (1) firearms training; (2) chemical agents; (3) impact weapons; and (4) arrest and control techniques. The classroom instruction may include courses such as laws of arrest, constitutional rights of law, rules and regulations, rights of confined, disciplinary procedures, cell and person searches, transportation, prison gangs, and crime victims.[13]

15-3d Texas Department of Criminal Justice— Corrections Officer

The Texas Department of Criminal Justice has over 100 prison units throughout the state and employs approximately 25,000 correctional officers. The correctional officer eligibility criteria are as follows: (1) must be a U.S. citizen, or an alien authorized to work in the United States; (2) must be 18 years of age; (3) must have a high school diploma from a state-accredited school or state-issued GED (4) must not be on active duty from the military, unless on terminal leave; (5) must never have been convicted of a felony; (6) must never have been convicted of a drug-related offense; (7) must never have been convicted of an offense involving domestic violence. Corrections officer candidates must also pass a written test and a drug screen.

Benefits for correctional officer in Texas include: (1) uniforms and equipment furnished at no cost; (2) laundry of uniforms furnished at no cost; (3) group life and health insurance; (4) dental programs; (5) free meals while on duty; (6) vacation leave and sick leave; (7) paid holidays; and (8) retirement benefits. The starting salary for Corrections Officer I is $1,716 a month and after one year is $2,036 a month or $24,432 annually.[14]

15-3e New York State Department of Corrections

Correction officer positions are located throughout the state of New York in various facilities of the New York State Department of Corrections system. Correctional officer recruits are required to satisfactorily complete all requirements of a 12-month training program before advancement is made to correctional officer. As part of the program, recruits will attend the correctional services training academy for a minimum of seven weeks of formal training. Paid training at the academy includes academic courses in such areas as emergency response procedures, interpersonal communications, legal rights and responsibilities, security procedures, and concepts and issues in corrections.

While in the academy, recruits also receive rigorous physical training to develop fitness, strength, and stamina. To physically qualify, it is necessary to perform seven sequential job-related tasks in two minutes and 15 seconds or less. Failure in any of the tasks will result in failing to meet the agency qualification standards and, accordingly, being dismissed from the academy. The test is administered during the final week of the training program at the academy.

Candidates who successfully complete the academy training and their probation period will earn 16 college credits toward a post-secondary degree. Upon completion of academy training, new corrections officers are assigned to facilities based on staffing needs of the department, and can only be assigned to facilities for which no reassignment list exists.

After completion of 26 full, biweekly payroll periods, correctional officers make an annual salary of $32,432. The benefits package includes health insurance, dental insurance, leave benefits, retirement package, and other options such as payroll deduction savings and loan feature and consumer buying power features. Annual leave, sick leave, workers compensation leave, and holiday observances compensation benefits are also available.[15]

Summary

It is estimated that approximately 400,000 individuals are employed by correctional systems at the federal, state, and local levels. The demand for correctional employees has been increasing, and probably will continue to increase in the foreseeable future. For this reason, it is often stated that "corrections is a growth industry." Correctional employees represent both sexes and all ethnic groups. Because the work in corrections is varied, there are opportunities available for those with all types of skills and academic disciplines. Most researchers divide correctional employment into four main categories: custodial, treatment, administrative, and support. These categories cover a wide range of occupations and professions.

Most individuals enter into corrections as correctional officers (COs). The correctional officers generally perform custodial roles in jails, prisons, and other institutions. The correctional officer position is not known for high entry-level pay.

Correctional officers are charged with overseeing individuals arrested, awaiting trial or other hearing, or convicted of a crime and sentenced to serve time in a jail, reformatory, or penitentiary. They maintain security and observe inmate conduct and behavior to prevent disturbances and escapes. Many correctional officers work in small county and municipal jails or precinct station houses as deputy sheriffs or police officers with wide ranging responsibilities. Others are assigned to large state and federal prisons where job duties are more specialized. A relatively small number supervise illegal aliens being held by the Immigration and Naturalization Service before being released or deported.

There are approximately 60,000 parole officers in the United States. Most are employed by state or county correctional departments. Probation officers generally work for the courts. Halfway houses and work release centers also hire probation and parole officers.

Median annual earnings of probation and parole officers in 2000 were $38,150, with an average of between $30,270 and $49,030. The lowest 10 percent earned less than $25,010, and the highest 10 percent earned more than $59,010. In 2000, median annual earnings for probation officers, correctional officers and correctional treatment specialists employed in state government were $36,980; those employed in local government earned $40,820. Higher wages tend to be found in urban areas.

The juvenile probation officer is expected to fulfill many different roles, often "taking up the slack" after judges, attorneys, social agencies, parents, and so on, have met what they see as their own clearly defined responsibilities in the case, and have expressed an unwillingness to extend themselves beyond these limits. Juvenile probation officers are all different in their individuality, but they share a strong, common concern for youth and the community.

A probation officer must balance many and sometimes conflicting roles, often within the same time frame. He or she must understand personal priorities, values, and biases, and how they coincide or conflict with those of the agency, resolving any conflicts in a manner that maintains credibility and effectiveness. The more the probation officer can be proactive in these roles, the less he or she will have to be reactive.

Discussion Questions

1. Explain what a new correctional employee can expect during his or her first year on the job.
2. What types of duties can career correctional personnel expect to encounter during their careers in the field?
3. What steps may be taken to enhance corrections as a career field?
4. Explain the role that professional codes of ethics should play in our professional career.
5. What is the difference between those who are successful in corrections and those who are not?

Chapter Quiz

True/False

1. The majority of parole officers are employed by state or county correctional departments.
2. In general, probation and parole officers must possess a four-year college degree in an area such as criminal justice, criminology, corrections, social work or related subject.
3. It is not a good idea to have volunteer service or other experience prior to applying for a job in probation and parole.
4. According to the U.S. Department of Labor employment of probation officers and correctional treatment specialists is projected to slow down in the next five years.
5. A parole officer would typically supervise a defendant who in lieu of going to prison is sentenced to probation by the court.

Multiple Choice

1. Most researchers divide correctional employment into four main categories that cover a wide range of occupations and professions. Which one of the following is NOT one of these four areas?
   a. custodial
   b. treatment
   c. administrative
   d. outpatient
2. When a person is convicted of a crime and has his or her prison sentence waived as long as they do not commit another crime and follow the terms and conditions set down by the court, this is called
   a. parole.
   b. probation.
   c. correctional treatment.
   d. retribution.
3. The nature of the work of many probation officers has changed in recent years because of
   a. changes in the parole and probation system brought on by public debate over the proper role of prisons, probation, and parole.
   b. reductions of probation and parole staff.
   c. the changing nature of crime.
   d. new job requirements.
4. The presentence investigation report which is prepared for the judge is usually written by the
   a. parole officer.
   b. probation officer.
   c. court clerk.
   d. court bailiff.

5. _____ supervise offenders who have been released from prison to ensure that they comply with the terms and conditions of their early release from prison.
   a. Probation officers
   b. Parole officers
   c. Police officers
   d. Correctional treatment specialists

Endnotes

1. American Correctional Association, *The State of Corrections* (Laurel, MD: American Correctional Association, 1995).
2. United States Department of Labor, *U.S. Government's Occupational Handbook* (Washington, DC: U.S. Department of Labor, 2000).
3. Ibid.
4. Ibid.
5. Ibid.
6. Ibid.
7. Ibid.
8. National Center for Juvenile Justice, *Juvenile Probation Officer's Deskbook* (Washington, DC: U.S. Department of Justice).
9. Adopted August 1975 at the 105 Congress of Correction and revised August 1990 at the 120th Congress of Correction.
10. Dan Richard Beto and Elvin Brown, Jr., *Federal Probation* 60(1 March, 1996): 50–56. Mr. Beto is the Director of the Correctional Management Institute of Texas at Sam Houston State University in Huntsville, Texas. Dr. Brown is the Director of the Montgomery County Department of Community Supervision and Corrections in Conroe, Texas.
11. Federal Bureau of Prisons Website: http://www.bop.gov/.
12. Kansas Department of Corrections Website: http://docnet.dc.state.ks.us/.
13. California Department of Corrections Website: http://www.cdc.state.ca.us/.
14. Texas Department of Criminal Justice Website: http://www.tdcj.state.tx.us/.
15. New York Department of Correctional Services http://www.docs.state.ny.us/.

Appendix A

National Policies on Corrections As Ratified by the American Correctional Association

Correctional Policy on Classification

Introduction:

Classification is a continuing process basic to identifying and matching offender needs to correctional resources. This continuing process involves all phases of correctional management.

Statement:

Classification should balance the public's need for protection, the needs of offenders, and the efficient and effective operation of the correctional system, a correctional agency should:

 A. Develop written classification policies that establish criteria specifying different levels of security, supervision, and program involvement; establish procedures for documenting and reviewing all classification decisions and actions; describe the appeal process to be used by individuals subject to classification; and specify the time frames for monitoring and reclassifying cases;

B. Develop the appropriate range of resources and services to meet the identified control and program needs of the population served;

C. Base classification decisions on rational assessment of objective and valid information, including background material (criminal history, nature of offense, social history, educational needs, medical/mental health needs, etc.) as well as information regarding the individual's current situation, adjustment, and program achievement;

D. Train all personnel in the classification process and require specialized training for those directly involved in classification functions;

E. Use the classification process to assign individuals to different levels of control on the basis of valid criteria regarding risk (to self and others) and individual needs, matching these characteristics with appropriate security, level of supervision, and program services;

F. Involve the individual directly in the classification process;

G. Assign appropriately trained staff to monitor individual classification plans for progress made and reclassification needs;

H. Objectively validate the classification process and instruments, assess on a planned basis the degree to which results meet written goals, and, as needed, refine the process and instruments; and

I. Provide for regular dissemination of classification information to all levels of correctional staff and to involved decision-makers outside of corrections as an aid in the planning, management, and operation of the correctional agency.

Correctional Policy on Health Care for Offenders

Introduction:

Correctional facilities and other correctional agencies that, either by law or as part of their stated mission, provide health care to accused and adjudicated offenders must provide health services that are appropriate and that reflect contemporary standards for health care. To ensure accountability and professional responsibility, these services should meet the policy guidelines set forth below and the health care standards of the American Correctional Association.

Statement:

Health care programs for offenders include medical, dental, and mental health services. Such programs should:

A. Be delivered by qualified health care professionals;

B. Provide to offenders, upon their arrival at a facility or at the beginning of their participation in a correctional program or service, both oral and written information concerning access to available health services;

C. Provide continuous, comprehensive services commencing at admission, including effective and timely screening, assessment and treatment, appropriate referral to alternate health care resources where warranted, and, if necessary, referral at discharge for continuing health problems;

D. Establish a system to identify and treat emergencies quickly and effectively;

E. Establish a formal program to treat and manage inmates with communicable diseases;

F. Provide appropriate health care training for all correctional staff and continuing education opportunities for professional health care providers;

G. Establish health education programs to encourage offenders to participate in their own health maintenance and in the prevention of communicable disease; and

H. Provide a medical records system for documentation of care and information sharing, consistent with privacy, confidentiality, and security concerns, to enhance continuity of service and professional accountability.

Correctional Policy on Employment of Women in Corrections

Introduction:

The American Correctional Association has a long-standing commitment to equal employment opportunity for women in adult and juvenile corrections.

Statement:

Women have a right to equal employment. No person who is qualified for a particular position/assignment or for job-related opportunities should be denied such employment or opportunities because of gender. Therefore, correctional agencies should:

A. Ensure that recruitment, selection, and promotion opportunities are open to women;

B. Assign female employees duties and responsibilities that provide career development and promotional opportunities equivalent to those provided to other employees;

C. Provide all levels of staff with appropriate training on developing effective and cooperative working relationships between male and female correctional personnel; and

D. Conduct regular monitoring and evaluation of affirmative action practices and take any needed corrective actions.

Public Correctional Policy on Employment of Ex-Offenders

Introduction:

Obtaining and maintaining employment is a primary step toward assuring the successful transition of offenders to law-abiding citizens in the community. The cooperation of government, business, industry, and volunteer agencies and organizations is essential in making employment opportunities available. In helping to implement this philosophy, correctional agencies should demonstrate their willingness to employ qualified ex-offenders.

Statement:

Ex-offenders should be given equitable consideration for employment. Correctional agencies should:

A. Implement and promote programs that will help offenders to prepare for, seek, and bold gainful employment in the community;

B. Develop and implement policy permitting qualified ex-offenders to be employed in correctional agencies in capacities that preserve the security and public safety mission of those agencies; and

C. Support legislation that will ensure that equal employment opportunities for ex-offenders are restored.

Correctional Policy on Correctional Research and Evaluation

Introduction:

Research and evaluation, and the use of the findings that result from such efforts, are essential to informed correctional policy, program development, and decision-making.

Statement:

Correctional agencies have a continuing responsibility to promote, initiate, sponsor, and participate in correctional research and evaluation efforts, both external and internal, in order to expand knowledge about offender behavior and enhance the effectiveness and efficiency of programs and services. To encourage and support these research and evaluation efforts, correctional agencies should:

A. Establish clearly defined procedures for data collection and analysis that ensure the accuracy, consistency, integrity, and impartiality of correctional research projects;

B. Conduct regular and systematic evaluation of correctional management, programs, and procedures and implement necessary changes;

C. Review and monitor correctional research to ensure compliance with professional standards, including those relating to confidentiality and the protection of human rights.

D. Prohibit the use of offenders as experimental subjects in medical, psychological, pharmacological, and cosmetic research except when warranted and prescribed for the diagnosis or treatment of an individual's specific condition in accordance with current standards of health care;

E. Make available to others the information necessary for correctional research and evaluation, consistent with concerns for privacy, confidentiality, and security;

F. Involve and train appropriate correctional staff in the application of correctional research and evaluation findings; and

G. Encourage the dissemination of correctional research and evaluation findings.

Correctional Policy on Legal Issues and Litigation

Introduction:

Adherence to law is fundamental to professional correctional practice. This entails avoiding litigation through sound management, effective use of the adversarial process to resolve issues that are litigated, and professional compliance with judicial orders.

Statement:

Problems addressed through litigation, such as inadequate and insufficient facilities, services, procedures, and staffing, can often be remedied through professional correctional practice, supported by government officials and the public with the necessary capital and operational resources. To achieve sound management of legal issues, correctional agencies should:

A. Use the standards and accreditation process of the American Correctional Association and the Commission on Accreditation for Corrections as a method to develop and maintain professional practice:

B. Consult frequently with legal counsel to remain informed of current developments in the law and to anticipate and avoid emerging legal problems;

C. Train staff about legal issues and responsibilities and provide them with legal representation when appropriate;

D. Attempt to resolve potential legal problems through dispute resolution techniques such as administrative grievance procedures;

E. Negotiate and settle litigation when agreements can be developed consistent with professional correctional practice;

F. Litigate, when no professionally reasonable alternative is possible, with the best legal and correctional expertise available and with full preparation and development of the case; and

G. Implement court orders in a professional manner.

Correction Policy on Information Systems

Introduction:

Timely and accurate information is a basic requirement for effective management of organizations. Such information forms a basis for sound decision-making and provides for accountability in operations and program results.

Statement:

For correctional managers to function effectively, they must have accurate and timely information. The design of correctional information systems must reflect combined efforts of both correctional professionals and information system specialists. To meet the diverse needs of a correctional agency, information systems should be designed that will support the management processes of the agency as their primary function, support service delivery functions by providing data relevant to their efficiency and outcome, and provide sufficient flexibility to support relevant research and evaluation.

To promote development of effective information systems, correctional agencies should:

A. Clearly define the desired scope of the systems consistent with a realistic assessment of anticipated resources and technologies;

B. Involve and train correctional managers in all stages of system development and operation to ensure managers' needs are met;

C. Prepare detailed and carefully monitored development plans to ensure systems are designed and implemented in a timely and cost-effective manner;

D. Require that the system include formal evaluation procedures to ensure the quality of system input and output;

E. Cooperate with correctional, law enforcement, and other public agencies to provide for mutual sharing of information, consistent with legitimate concerns for privacy, confidentiality, and system security;

F. Ensure appropriate information needs of the public are met, consistent with legal requirements; and

G. Advocate provision of resources to implement and update advanced information system technologies.

Correctional Policy on Design of Correctional Facilities

Introduction:

The effectiveness and efficiency of correctional staff in maintaining security and delivering services can be either enhanced or limited by the physical plants in which they operate. Quality design has long-term cost and program advantages in assisting a correctional system to accomplish its mission.

Statement:

Correctional architecture is unique, involving the design of facilities that are functionally and environmentally supportive of the needs and activities of a confined society. The design of such facilities is a multi disciplinary process. To improve the design quality and operational adequacy of new and renovated correctional facilities, correctional agencies should:

A. Define operations of correctional facilities prior to design, including written specifications of the facility's mission and functional elements, basic operating procedures, and starting patterns so the design can fully support intended correctional operations;

B. Select architects and engineers on merit, as demonstrated by either successful completion of prior correctional projects, or by successful completion of other projects combined with access to recognized correctional expertise;

C. Design correctional facilities through a multi disciplinary process that directly involves correctional professionals, criminal justice planners, architects and engineers, and that also seeks the contribution of other groups and disciplines who have an interest in the facility's design, including those involved in the faciltiy's day-to-day operations;

D. Ensure that facility designs conform to applicable codes and nationally approved professional standards and that they encourage direct interaction in supervision of offenders, consistent with staff safety;

E. Ensure facility design is sufficiently flexible to accommodate changes in offender population and in the facility's mission, operating procedures, and staffing;

F. Maintain project oversight to assure that design objectives are met;

G. Recognize the need for early selection of key staff who will be responsible for initial operation of the facility so they can participate in the design and construction process; and

H. Engage in an ongoing process of research and evaluation to develop, improve, and recognize the most successful design features, equipment technologies, and operating procedures.

Correctional Policy on Purpose of Corrections

Introduction:

In order to establish the goals and objectives of any correctional system, there must be a universal statement of purpose that all members of the correctional community can use in goal setting and daily operations.

Statement:

The overall mission of criminal and juvenile justice, which consists of law enforcement, courts, and corrections, is to enhance social order and public safety. As a component of the justice system, the role of corrections is:

A. To implement court-ordered supervision and, when necessary, detention of those accused of unlawful behavior prior to adjudication;

B. To assist in maintaining the integrity of law by administering sanctions and punishments imposed by courts for unlawful behavior;

C. To offer the widest range of correctional options, including community corrections, probation, institutions, and parole services, necessary to meet the needs of both society and the individual; and

D. To provide humane program and service opportunities for accused and adjudicated offenders that will enhance their community integration and economic self-sufficiency and that are administered in a just and equitable manner within the least restrictive environment consistent with public safety.

Correctional Policy on Private Sector Involvement in Corrections

Introduction:

Although most correctional programs are operated by public agencies, there is increasing interest in the use of profit and nonprofit organizations as providers of services, facilities, and programs. Profit and nonprofit organizations have resources for the delivery of services that often are unavailable from the public correctional agency.

Statement:

Government has the ultimate authority and responsibility for corrections. For its most effective operation, corrections should use all appropriate resources, both public and private. When government considers the use of profit and nonprofit private sector correctional services, such programs must meet professional standards, provide necessary public safety, provide services equal to or better than government, and be cost-effective compared to well-managed government operations. While government retains the ultimate responsibility, authority, and accountability for actions of private agencies and individuals under contract, it is consistent with good correctional policy and practice to:

A. Use in an advisory and voluntary role the expertise and resources available from profit and nonprofit organizations in the development and implementation of correctional programs and policies;

B. Enhance service delivery systems by considering the concept of contracting with the private sector when justified in terms of cost, quality, and ability to meet program objectives;

C. Consider use of profit and nonprofit organizations to develop, fund, build, operate, and/or provide services, programs and facilities when such an approach is cost-effective, safe, and consistent with the public interest and sound correctional practice;

D. Ensure the appropriate level of service delivery and compliance with recognized standards through professional contract preparation and vendor selection as well as effective evaluation and monitoring by the responsible government agency; and

E. Indicate clearly in any contract for services, facilities, or programs the responsibilities and obligations of both government and contractor, including but not limited to liability of all parties, performance bonding, and contractual termination.

Correctional Policy on Offenders with Special Needs

Introduction:

The provision of humane programs and services for the accused and adjudicated requires addressing the special needs of certain offenders. To meet this goal, correctional agencies should develop and adopt procedures for the early identification of offenders with special needs. Agencies should also develop a plan for providing the services that respond to those needs and for monitoring the delivery of services in both confined and community settings.

Statement:

Correctional systems should assure provision of specialized services and programs to meet the special needs of offenders. To achieve this, they should:

 A. Identify the categories of offenders who will require special care or programs. These categories include:

   1. Offenders with severe psychological needs, mental retardation, significant psychiatric disorders, multiple handicaps, neurological impairments, and substance abuse;

   2. Offenders who are physically handicapped or chronically or terminally ill;

   3. Offenders who are elderly;

   4. Offenders with severe social and/or educational deficiencies, learning disabilities, or language barriers; and

   5. Offenders with special security or supervision needs, such as protective custody cases, death row inmates, and those who chronically exhibit potential for violent or aggressive behavior.

 B. Provide specialized services or programs for those offenders who are identified as being in need of special care or programs. Such services and programs may be provided within the correctional agency itself, or by referral to another agency that has the necessary specialized program resources, or by contracting with private or voluntary agencies or individuals that meet professional standards;

 C. Maintain specialty trained staff for the delivery of care, programs, and services;

 D. Maintain documentation of the services and programs provided;

E. Institute carefully controlled evaluation procedures to determine each program's effectiveness and the feasibility of its continuation or the need for adjustments; and

F. Provide leadership and advocacy for legislative and public support to obtain the resources needed to meet these special needs,

Correctional Policy on use of Appropriate Sanctions and Controls

Introduction:

In developing, selecting, and administering sanctions and punishments, decision makers must balance concern for individual dignity, public safety, and maintenance of social order. Correctional programs and facilities are a costly and limited resource; the most restrictive are generally the most expensive. Therefore, it is good public policy to use these resources wisely and economically.

Statement:

The sanctions and controls imposed by courts and administered by corrections should be the least restrictive consistent with public and individual safety and maintenance of social order. Selection of the least restrictive sanctions and punishments in specific cases inherently requires balancing several important objectives—individual dignity, fiscal responsibility, and effective correctional operations, To meet their objectives, correctional agencies should:

A. Advocate to all branches of government—executive, legislative and judicial—and to the public at large the development and appropriate use of the least restrictive sanctions, punishments, programs, and facilities;

B. Recommend the use of the least restrictive appropriate dispositions in judicial decisions;

C. Classify persons under correctional jurisdiction to the least restrictive appropriate programs and facilities; and

D. Employ only the level of regulation and control necessary for the safe and efficient operation of programs, services, and facilities,

Correctional Policy on Community Corrections

Introduction:

Correctional programs operating in a community setting are an integral part of a comprehensive correctional system. These include community residential facilities, probation, parole, and other programs that provide supervision and services for accused or adjudicated juveniles and adults. Responsiveness to the needs of victims and offenders and to protection of the public is essential to the success of community programs and services.

Statement:

The least restrictive sanctions and controls consistent with public and individual safety and maintenance of social order require that the majority of offenders receive services in a community setting. It is the responsibility of government to develop, support and maintain correctional programs and services in the community. A screening process to select offenders who can be safely maintained in the community is critical for placement in these programs. Those responsible for community corrections programs, services, and supervision should:

A. Seek statutory authority and adequate funding, both public and private, for community programs and services;

B. Develop and ensure access to an array of services, residential or nonresidential, that adequately address the identifiable needs of offenders and the community;

C. Inform the public and offenders of the reasons for community programs and services, the criteria used for selecting individuals for these programs and services, and that placement in such a program is a punishment;

D. Ensure the integrity and accountability of community programs by establishing a reliable system for monitoring and measuring performance in accordance with accepted standards and professional practice;

E. Recognize that public acceptance of community corrections is enhanced by victim restitution and conciliation programs; and

F. Seek the active participation of a well-informed constituency, including citizen advisory boards and broad-based coalitions, to address community corrections issues.

Correctional Policy on Correctional Industry

Introduction:

Correctional industry programs, whether operated by the public or private sector, aid correctional systems in reducing idleness, lowering costs, and providing opportunities for offenders to gain job skills, training, and economic self-sufficiency and to participate in programs of victim compensation and institution cost-sharing.

Statement:

Correctional industry programs. Operating under sound management principles and effective leadership, should:

A. Be based on statutes and regulations that support the development, manufacturing, marketing, distribution, and delivery of correctional industry products and services;

B. Be unencumbered by laws and regulations that restrict access to the marketplace, competitive pricing, and fair work practices except as necessary to protect the offender and the system from exploitation.

C. Provide evaluation and recognition of job performance to assist in promoting good work habits that may enhance employability after release;

D. Provide training and safe working conditions, for both staff and offenders, similar to those found in the community at large;

E. Assure that the working conditions in industry operated by public or private organizations are comparable with those in the industry at large, and that compensation to inmates is fair;

F. Recognize that profit-making and public service are both legitimate goals of an industry program;

G. Support reinvestment of profits to expand industrial programs, improve overall operations, maintain and upgrade equipment, and assist in the support of inmate training programs that enhance marketable skills, pre-release training, and job placement services; and

H. Integrate industry programs, public or private, with other institutional programs and activities under the overall leadership of the institution's chief administrator.

Correctional Policy on Use of Force

Introduction:

Correctional agencies administer sanctions and punishments imposed by courts for unlawful behavior. Assigned to correctional agencies involuntarily, offenders sometimes resist authority imposed on them, and may demonstrate violent and destructive behaviors, use of legally authorized force by correctional authorities may become necessary to maintain custody, safety, and control.

Statement:

Use of force consists of physical contact with an offender in a confrontational situation to control behavior and enforce order. Use of force includes use of restraints (other than for routine transportation and movement), chemical agents, and weapons. Force is justified only when required to maintain or regain control, or when there is imminent danger of personal injury or serious damage to property. To assure the use of force is appropriate and justifiable, correctional agencies should:

A. Establish and maintain policies that require reasonable steps be taken to reduce or prevent the necessity for the use of force, that authorize force only when no reasonable alternative is possible, that permit only the minimum force necessary, and that prohibit the use of force as a retaliatory or disciplinary measure;

B. Establish and enforce procedures that define the range of methods for and alternatives to the use of force, and that specify the conditions under which each is permitted. The procedures must assign responsibility for authorizing such force, assure appropriate medical care for all involved, and provide the fullest possible documentation and supervision of the action;

C. Establish and maintain procedures that limit the use of deadly force to those instances where it is legally authorized and where there is an imminent threat to human life or a threat to public safety that cannot reasonably he prevented by other means;

D. Maintain operating procedures and regular staff training designed to anticipate, stabilize, and defuse situations that might give rise to conflict, confrontation, and violence;

E. Provide specialized training to ensure competency in all methods of use of force, especially in methods and equipment requiring special knowledge and skills such as defensive tactics, weapons, restraints, and chemical agents; and

F. Establish and maintain procedures that require all incidents involving the use of force be fully documented and independently reviewed by a higher correctional authority. A report of the use of force, including appropriate investigation and any recommendations for preventive and remedial action, shall be submitted for administrative review and implementation of recommendations when appropriate.

Correctional Policy on Conditions of Confinement

Introduction:

Correctional systems must administer the detention, sanctions, and punishments ordered by the courts in an environment that protects public safety and provides for the safety, rights, and dignity of staff, accused or adjudicated offenders, and citizens involved in programs.

Statement:

Maintaining acceptable conditions of confinement requires adequate resources and effective management of the physical plant, operational procedures, programs, and staff. To provide acceptable conditions, agencies should:

A. Establish and maintain a safe and humane population limit for each institution based upon recognized professional standards;

B. Provide an environment that will support the health and safety of staff, confined persons, and citizens participating in programs. Such an environment results from appropriate design, construction, and maintenance of the physical plant as well as the effective operation of the facility;

C. Maintain a professional and accountable work environment for staff that includes necessary training and supervision as well as sufficient staffing to carry out the mission of the facility; and

D. Maintain a fair and disciplined environment that provides programs and services in a climate that encourages responsible behavior.

Correctional Policy on Crowding and Excessive Workloads

Introduction:

Overpopulation of correctional programs and facilities can negate the effectiveness of management, program, security, and physical plant operations and can endanger offenders, staff, and the public at large. High Population density within correctional facilities has been associated with increased physical and Rental problems, more frequent disciplinary incidents, higher rates of assault and suicide, and decreased effectiveness of programs and services. When the population of a correctional program or facility exceeds capacity, maintaining safe and reasonable conditions of confinement and supervision becomes increasingly difficult, and may become impossible, Excessive workloads in institutional and community corrections dilute effectiveness of supervision and support services and threaten public safety.

Statement:

The number of offenders assigned to correctional facilities and community services should be limited to levels consistent with recognized professional standards. Correctional agencies should:

A. Establish and maintain safe and humane population and workload limits for each institution and service program based on recognized professional standards;

B. Develop, advocate, and implement, in coordination with the executive, legislative, and judicial branches of government, emergency and long-term processes by which offender populations can be managed within reasonable limits;

C. Anticipate the need for expanded program and facility capacity by using professional population projection methodologies that reflect both demographic and policy-related factors influencing correctional population growth;

D. Advocate the full development and appropriate use of pretrial/adjudication release, probation, parole, community residential facilities, and other community services that are alternatives to assigning offenders to crowded facilities or that reduce the duration of assignment of offenders to such facilities; and

E. Develop, advocate, and implement plans for necessary additional facilities, staff, programs, and services.

Correctional Policy on Offender Education and Training

Introduction:

Many accused and adjudicated juvenile and adult offenders lack basic educational, vocational, and social skills necessary to enhance community integration and economic self-sufficiency. These deficiencies may interact with other socioeconomic and psychological factors to affect the life choices, made by offenders and may limit the legitimate financial and social opportunities available to these individuals.

Statement:

Education and training are integral parts of the total correctional process. Governmental jurisdictions should develop, expand, and improve delivery systems for academic, occupational, social, and other educational programs for accused and adjudicated juvenile and adult offenders in order to enhance their community integration and economic self-sufficiency. Toward this end, correctional agencies should:

A. Provide for assessment of academic, vocational, and social skills deficiencies of those under their jurisdictions;

B. Make available opportunities to participate in relevant, comprehensive educational, vocational, and social skills training programs and job placement activities that are fully coordinated and integrated with other components of the correctional process and the community as a whole;

C. Ensure programs provided are taught by certified instructors in accordance with professional standards and relevant techniques;

D. Provide incentives for participation and achievement in education and training programs;

E. Maximize use of public and private sector resources in development, implementation, coordination, and evaluation of education and training programs and job placement activities; and

F. Evaluate the efficiency and effectiveness of program performance based on measurable goals and objectives.

Correctional Policy on Juvenile Corrections

Introduction:

The juvenile corrections system must provide specialized care for young offenders in our society. Juvenile corrections, although sharing the same overall purpose as adult corrections, has significant different processes and procedures and requires specialized care, services, and programs.

Statement:

Children and youth have distinct personal growth and developmental needs and should be secure from any harmful effects of association with adult offenders. Juvenile corrections must provide a continuum of programs, services, and facilities for accused and adjudicated juvenile offenders that are separate from those for adult offenders. Services and care for the individual youth must be a primary concern, consistent with protection of the public and maintenance of social order. To achieve these goals, juvenile corrections officials and agencies should:

A. Establish and maintain effective communication with all concerned with the juvenile justice system—executive, judicial, and legislative officials, prosecution and diverse counsel, social service agencies, schools, police, and facilities—to achieve the fullest possible cooperation in making appropriate decisions in individual cases and in providing and using services and resources;

B. Provide a range of community and residential programs and services to meet individual needs, including education, vocational training, recreation, religious opportunities, family, aftercare, medical, dental, mental health, and specialized programs and services such as substance abuse treatment;

C. Involve the family and community as preferred resources and use the least restrictive appropriate dispositions in program planning and placement for juveniles;

D. Exclude from correctional systems all status offenders (those whose behavior would not be considered criminal if committed by adults);

E. Operate a juvenile classification system to identify and meet the program needs of the juvenile offender, while actively considering the public's need for protection; and

F. Support limitations on the use of juvenile records according to approved national standards, recognizing that the need to safeguard the privacy and rehabilitative goals of the juvenile should be balanced with concern for the protection of the public, including victims,

Correctional Policy on Female Offender Services

Introduction:

Correctional systems must develop service delivery systems for accused and adjudicated female offenders that are comparable to those provided to males. Additional services must also be provided to meet the unique needs of the female offender population.

Statement:

Correctional systems must be guided by the principle of parity. Female offenders must receive the equivalent range of services available to other offenders, including opportunities for individualized programming and services that recognize the unique needs of this population. The services should:

A. Assure access to a range of alternatives to incarceration, including pretrial and post-trial diversion, probation, restitution, treatment for substance abuse, halfway houses, and parole services;

B. Provide acceptable conditions of confinement, including appropriately trained staff and sound operating procedures that address this population's needs in such areas as clothing, personal property, hygiene, exercise, recreation, and visitation with children and family;

C. Provide access to a full range of work and programs designed to expand economic and social roles of women, with emphasis on education; career counseling and exploration of nontraditional as well as traditional vocational training; relevant life skills, including parenting and social and economic assertiveness; and prerelease and work education release programs;

D. Facilitate the maintenance and strengthening of family ties, particularly those between parent and child;

E. Deliver appropriate programs and services, including medical, dental, and mental health programs, services to pregnant women, substance abuse programs, child and family services, and provide access to legal services; and

F. Provide access to release programs that include aid in establishing homes, economic stability, and sound family relationships.

Correctional Policy on Staff Recruitment and Development

Introduction:

Knowledgeable, highly skilled, motivated, and professional correctional personnel are essential to fulfill the purpose of corrections effectively. Professionalism is achieved through structured programs of recruitment and enhancement of the employee's skills, knowledge, insight, and understanding of the correctional process.

Statement:

Correctional staff are the primary agents for promoting health, welfare, security, and safety within correctional institutions and community supervision programs. They directly interact with accused and adjudicated offenders and are the essential catalysts of change in the correctional process. The education, recruitment, orientation, supervision, compensation, training, retention, and advancement of correctional staff must receive full support from the executive, judicial, and legislative branches of government. To achieve this, correctional agencies should:

A. Recruit personnel, including ex-offenders, in and open and accountable manner to assure equal employment opportunity for all qualified applicants regardless of sex, age, race, physical disability, religion, ethnic background, or political affiliation, and actively promote the employment of women and minorities;

B. Screen applicants for job-related aspects of physical suitability, personal adjustment, emotional stability, dependability, appropriate educational level, and experience. An additional requisite is the ability to relate to accused or adjudicated offenders in a manner that is fair, objective, and neither punitive nor vindictive;

C. Select, promote, and retain staff in accordance with valid job-related procedures that emphasize professional merit and technical competence. Voluntary transfers and promotions within and between correctional systems should be encouraged;

D. Comply with professional standards in staff development and offer a balance between operational requirements and the development of personal, social, and cultural understanding. Staff development programs should involve use of public and private resources, including colleges, universities, and professional associations;

E. Achieve parity between correctional staff and comparable criminal justice system staff in salaries and benefits, training, continuing education, performance evaluations, disciplinary procedures, career development opportunities, transfers, promotions, grievance procedures, and retirement; and

F. Encourage the participation of trained volunteers and students to enrich the correctional programs and to provide a potential source of recruitment.

Correctional Policy on Probation

Introduction:

The vast majority of adjudicated adult and juvenile offenders remain in the community. Probation is a judicial decision that assigns the responsibility for supervision and control of these offenders to community corrections.

Statement:

Probation is a frequently used and cost-effective sanction of the court for enhancing social order and public safety, Probation may be used as a sanction by itself or, where necessary and appropriate, be combined with other sanctions such as fines, restitution, community service, residential care, or confinement. Agencies responsible for probation should:

A. Prepare disposition assessments to assist the court in arriving at appropriate sanctions. The least restrictive disposition consistent with public safety should be recommended;

B. Establish a case management system for allocating supervisory resources through a standardized classification process;

C. Provide supervision to probationers and, with their input, develop a realistic plan to ensure compliance with orders of the court;

D. Monitor and evaluate, on an ongoing basis, the probationer's adherence to the plan of supervision and, when necessary, modify the plan of supervision according to the changing needs of the offender and the best interests of society;

E. Provide access to a wide range of services to meet identifiable needs, all of which are directed toward promoting law-abiding behavior;

F. Assure any intervention in an offender's life will not exceed the minimal amount needed to assure compliance with the orders of the court;

G. Initiate appropriate court proceedings, when necessary, if the probationer fails to comply with orders of the court, supervision plan, or other requirements so the court may consider other alternatives for the protection and well-being of the community;

H. Oppose use of the probation sanction for status offenders, neglected or dependent children, or any other individuals who are neither accused nor charged with delinquent or criminal behavior;

I. Establish an educational program for sharing information about probation with the public and other agencies; and

J. Evaluate program efficiency, effectiveness, and overall system accountability consistent with recognized correctional standards.

Correctional Policy on Parole

Introduction:

Parole is the conditional release of an offender from confinement before expiration of sentence pursuant to specified terms and conditions of supervision in the community. The grant of parole and its revocation are responsibilities of the paroling authority. Supervision of the parolee is provided by a designated agency that ensures compliance with all requirements by the release, through a case management process. Because the vast majority of those incarcerated will eventually be released into the community, the public is best protected by a supervised transition of the offender from institutional to community integration. Parole offers economic advantages to the public, the offender, and the correctional system by maximizing opportunities for offenders to become productive, law-abiding citizens.

Statement:

The parole component of the correctional system should function under separate but interdependent decision-making and case supervision processes. Paroling authorities should seek a balance in weighing the public interest and the readiness of the offender to reenter society under a structured program of supervisory management and control. Paroling systems should be equipped with adequate resources for administering the investigative, supervisory, and research functions. Administrative regulations governing the grant of parole, its revocation, case supervision practices, and discharge procedures should incorporate standards of due process and fundamental fairness. To achieve the maximum cost-benefits of parole supervision, full advantage should be taken of community-based resources available for serving offender employment and training needs, substance abuse treatment, and other related services. The parole system should:

A. Establish procedures to provide and objective decision-making process incorporating standards of due process and fundamental fairness in granting of parole that will address, at a minimum, the risk to public safety, impact on the victim, and information about the offense and the offender;

B. Provide access to a wide range of support services to meet offender needs consistent with realistic objectives for promoting law abiding behavior;

C. Ensure any intervention in an offender's life will not exceed the minimum needed to ensure compliance with the terms and conditions of parole;

D. Provide a case management system for allocating supervisory resources through a standardized classification process, reporting parolee progress, and monitoring individualized parolee supervision and treatment plans;

E. Provide for the timely and accurate transmittal of status reports to the paroling authority for the use in decision-making with respect to revocation, modification, or discharge of parole cases;

F. Establish programs for sharing information, ideas, and experience with other agencies and the public; and

G. Evaluate program efficiency, effectiveness, and overall accountability consistent with recognized correctional standards.

Correctional Policy on Standards and Accreditation

Introduction:

Correctional agencies should provide community and institutional programs and services that offer a full range of effective, just, humane, and safe dispositions and sanctions for accused and adjudicated offenders. To assure accountability and professional responsibility, these programs and services should meet accepted professional standards and obtain accreditation. The use of standards and the accreditation process provides a valuable mechanism for self-evaluation, stimulates improvement of correctional management and practice, and provides recognition of acceptable programs and facilities. The American Correctional Association and the Commission on Accreditation for Corrections have promulgated national standards and a voluntary system of national accreditation for correctional agencies. The beneficiaries of such a process are the administration and staff of correctional agencies, offenders, and the public.

Statement:

All correctional facilities and programs should be operated in accordance with the standards established by the American Correctional Association and should achieve and maintain accreditation through the Commission on Accreditation for Corrections. To fulfill this objective, correctional agencies should:

- A. Implement improvement as necessary to comply with the appropriate standards specified or referenced in the following manuals and supplements:
    1. Standards for Adult Parole Authorities
    2. Standards for Adult Community Residential Services
    3. Standards for Adult Probation and Parole Field Services
    4. Standards for Adult Correctional Institutions
    5. Standards for Adult Local Detention Facilities
    6. Standards for Juvenile Community Residential Facilities
    7. Standards for Juvenile Probation and Aftercare Services

8. Standards for Juvenile Detention Facilities
   9. Standards for Juvenile Training Schools
   10. Standards for the Administration of Correctional Agencies
B. See and maintain accreditation through the voluntary process developed by the Commission on Accreditation for Corrections in order that, through self-evaluation and peer review, necessary improvements are made, programs and services come into compliance with appropriate standards, and professional recognition is obtained.

Correctional Policy on Victims of Crime

Introduction:

Victims of crime suffer financial, emotional, and/or physical trauma. The criminal justice system is dedicated to the principle of fair and equal justice for all people. Victims' rights should be pursued within the criminal justice system to ensure their needs are addressed.

Statement:

Victims have the right to be treated with respect and compassion, to be informed about and involved in the criminal justice process as it affects their lives, to be protected from harm and intimidation, and to be provided necessary financial and support services that attempt to restore them to their former position before the crime was committed. Although many components of the criminal justice system share in the responsibility of providing services to victims of crime, the correctional community has an important role in this process and should:

   A. Support activities that advocate the rights of the victims;
   B. Promote local, state, and federal legislation that emphasizes victim rights and the development of the victim service programs in local communities;
   C. Advocate funding and technical assistance to develop and expand victim service programs;
   D. Promote and advocate the development of programs in which offenders provide restitution to victims, and compensation and service to the community;

E. Promote active participation of victims in the criminal justice process, including the opportunity to be heard;

F. Promote the use of existing community resources and community volunteers to serve the needs of victims;

G. Cooperate in the development of training programs, designed for criminal justice officials, that promote sensitivity to victims' rights and identify community services; and

H. Operate those victim assistance programs that appropriately fall within the responsibility of the field of corrections.

National Correctional Policy on Employee Assistance Programs

Introduction:

The most valuable resource in any correctional agency is the staff employed by that agency. Corrections is a service delivery enterprise with people as its most important product. The employees who deliver those services should be afforded all reasonable assistance to allow them to do the best job possible.

Statement:

Employee assistance programs should be made available to all employees. The programs should address employee needs and requirements that will help ensure a high level of on-the-job performance. Correcitonal agencies should:

A. Establish employee assistance programs based on appropriate assessment of employee needs and desires;

B. Publicize program availability regularly and frequently in a variety of ways to ensure that all employees know not only what is available to them, but also how to access and participate in them;

C. Provide programs at no cost to the employee where possible. Where the employee must pay some or all of the cost of the program/service, it should be an amount that does not exceed what that person could reasonably be expected to pay;

D. Provide an employee in the central/main office of the agency who would be responsible for coordinating all employee assistance programs. Each facility or major organizational unit should have one person designated as the coordinator of employee assistance programs;

E. Ensure programs and services are provided either directly by the agency or by other public or private agencies to which the employee is referred for assistance;

F. Require the Employee Assistance Program Coordinator to report at least quarterly on the level of activity that has occurred. That information should be used to assess the needs for adding, deleting, or modifying specific employee assistance programs.

G. Ensure employee requests or referrals for assistance remain confidential, unless the employee expressly elects to waive confidentiality.

Appendix B

American Bar Association
Legal Status of Prisoners[1]

Standard 23-2.1. Access to the judicial process

(a) Prisoners should have free and meaningful access to the judicial process; governmental authorities should assure such access. Regulations or actions should not unduly delay or adversely affect the outcome of a prisoner's claim for relief or discourage prisoners from seeking judicial consideration for their grievances. Interests of institutional security and scheduling may justify regulations that affect the manner in which access is provided.

(b) To implement the principles in paragraph (a), the following standards should apply:

   (i) Access should not be restricted by the nature of the action or the relief sought. Prisoners should be entitled to present any judicially cognizable issue, including:

      (A) Challenge to the legality of their conviction or confinement;

      (B) Assertions against correctional or other governmental authorities of any rights protected by constitutional, statutory, or administrative provision or the common law;

(C) Civil legal problems; and

(D) Assertions of a defense to any action brought against them.

(ii) Judicial procedures should be available to facilitate the prompt resolution of disputes involving the legality, duration, or conditions of confinement. The doctrine of exhaustion of remedies should apply unless past practice or other facts have demonstrated the futility of the available process. An administrative process unable to reach a decision within [thirty] working days is presumptively unreasonable.

(iii) When directed by a court, prisoners' attendance at legal proceedings directly involving their interests should be assured by correctional authorities.

(iv) Prisoners should be allowed to prepare and retain legal documents. The time, place, or manner of their preparation may be regulated for purposes of institutional security and scheduling. Retention of legal documents may be regulated only for purposes of health and safety. Regulations covering the preparation or retention of legal documents should be the least restrictive necessary.

(v) Legal documents should not be read, censored, or altered by correctional authorities, nor should their delivery be delayed.

(vi) Prisoners' decisions to seek judicial relief should not adversely affect their program, status within a correctional institution, or opportunity for release.

Standard 23-2.2. Access to legal services

(a) Prisoners should have access to legal advice and counseling, and, in appropriate instances, will have a right to counsel, in connection with all personal legal matters, including but not limited to:

(i) Court proceedings challenging conditions of confinement, correctional treatment, or supervision;

(ii) Parole grant and revocation proceedings;

(iii) Hearings to determine the length of sentences to imprisonment;

(iv) Civil matters, to the same extent as provided to members of the general public who are financially unable to obtain adequate representation; and

(v) Institutional disciplinary, classification, grievance, and other administrative proceedings. This standard does not limit existing rights to representation in parole revocation proceedings or in cases arising under subparagraph (a)(i) or

(vi) Neither, however, does it require correctional and parole authorities to allow the representation by legal counsel of prisoners at parole grant and other institutional hearings except as provided by law.

(b) Legal assistance for postconviction proceedings challenging the legality of a prisoner's conviction or confinement should conform to the requirements of standard 22-3.1.

(c) Prisoners should be entitled to retain counsel of their choice when able to do so and, when financially unable to obtain adequate representation, to have legal assistance provided for them by responsible governmental authorities to the same extent that such assistance is made available to members of the general public with comparable legal needs. Governmental authorities should establish programs to assure that adequate legal services are reasonably available to prisoners.

(d) Legal assistance for prisoners should be rendered by persons authorized by law to give legal advice or provide representation. When legal assistance is rendered by a person who is not an attorney, such counsel substitute should be trained by an attorney or educational institution and should receive continuing supervision by an attorney. Prison regulations should not restrict a prisoner's attorney in the selection of those assisting him or her.

(e) The relationship between a person providing legal assistance under paragraph (d) and a prisoner should be protected by the attorney-client privilege. Correctional authorities should facilitate confidential contact and communication between prisoners and persons providing legal assistance to them.

(f) Correctional and parole authorities should regulate by rule the roles of all persons who participate in institutional hearings.

Standard 23-2.3. Access to legal materials

(a) Correctional authorities should make available to prisoners educational services pertaining to their legal rights even when they have access to legal services. Printed materials outlining the recognized grounds for postconviction relief and the resources available to any person to pursue legal questions, specially prepared for prison inmates and written in terms understandable to them, are most desirable. Alternatively, an adequate collection of standard legal reference materials related to criminal law and procedures and cognate constitutional provisions should be part of a prison library.

(b) Prisoners should be entitled to acquire personal law books and other legal research materials. Any regulation of the storage of legal material in personal quarters or other areas should not unreasonably interfere with access to or use of these materials. The retention of personal legal materials may be regulated and restricted in accordance with standard 23-1.1.

Standard 23-3.1. Rules of conduct

(a) Correctional authorities should promulgate clear written rules for prisoner conduct.
These rules and implementing criteria should include:
  (i) A specific definition of offenses, a statement that the least severe punishment appropriate to each offense should be posed, and a schedule indicating the minimum and maxim possible punishment for each offense, proportionate to offense; and
  (ii) Specific criteria and procedures for prison discipline and classification decisions, including decisions involving security status and work and housing assignments.

(b) A personal copy of the rules should be provided to each prisoner upon entry to the institution. For the benefit of illiterate and foreign-language prisoners, a detailed oral explanation of the rules should be given. In addition, a written translation should be provided in any language spoken by a significant number of prisoners.

Standard 23-3.2. Disciplinary hearing procedures

(a) At a hearing where a minor sanction is imposed, the prisoner should be entitled to:

  (i) Written notice of the charge, in a language the prisoner understands, within [seventy-two] hours of the time he or she is suspected of having committed an offense; within another [twenty-four] hours the prisoner should be given copies of any further written information the tribunal may consider;

  (ii) A hearing within [three] working days of the time the written notice of the charge was received;

  (iii) Be present and speak on his or her own behalf;

  (iv) A written decision based upon a preponderance of the evidence, with specified reasons for the decision. The decision should be rendered promptly and in all cases within [five] days after conclusion of the hearing; and

  (v) Appeal, within [five] days, to the chief executive officer of the institution, and the right to a written decision by that officer within [thirty] days, based upon a written summary of the hearing, any documentary evidence considered at the hearing, and the prisoner's written reason for appealing. The chief executive officer should either affirm or reverse the determination of misconduct and decrease or approve the punishment imposed. Execution of the punishment should be suspended during the appeal unless individual safety or individual security will be adversely affected thereby.

(b) At a hearing where a major sanction is imposed, in addition to the requirements of paragraph (a), the prisoner should be entitled to have in attendance any person within the local prison community who has relevant information and to examine or cross-examine such witnesses except when the hearing officer(s):

  (i) Exclude testimony as unduly cumulative; or

  (ii) Receive testimony outside the presence of the prisoner pursuant to a finding that the physical safety of a person would be endangered by the presence of a particular witness or by disclosure of his or her identity.

(c) Disciplinary hearings should be conducted by one or more impartial persons.

(d) Unless the prisoner is found guilty, no record relating to the charge should be retained in the prisoner's file or used against the prisoner in any way.

(e) Where necessary, in accordance with standard 23-1.1(b), or (c), pending the hearing required by paragraph (b), correctional authorities may confine separately a prisoner alleged to have committed a major violation. Such preheating confinement should not extend more than [seven] days unless necessitated by the prisoner's request for a continuance or by the pendency of criminal investigation or prosecution as provided in standard 23-3.3(b).

(f) In the event of a situation requiring the chief executive officer to declare all, or a part, of an institution to be in a state of emergency, the rights provided in this standard may be temporarily suspended for up to [twenty-four] hours after the emergency has terminated.

Standard 23-3.4. Classification

(a) The initial classification of a prisoner according to security risk status and job or other assignment should be accomplished informally within [thirty] days of the prisoner's arrival at the place of classification.

(b) The prisoner should meet with a properly trained representative of the classification committee. The committee representative should:

   (i) Explain the classification process, the options the prisoner may have, and the relevant criteria; and

   (ii) Seek to develop a classification consistent with the needs of the prisoner and the institution; and

   (iii) Submit such classification to the classification committee and the prisoner.

(c) The classification of a prisoner should be reviewed by the classification committee at least every [six]-month period;

(d) Each decision of the classification committee should explain the considerations and factors that led to the committee's decision. The prisoner should receive a copy of the committee's written decision.

(e) If the classification committee or the prisoner rejects a classification (or if the prisoner is dissatisfied with the committee's periodic review), the prisoner should be given a prompt hearing before the classification committee if a request is made within [five] days of receipt of the classification decision.

(f) At a classification hearing, the prisoner should be entitled to:

 (i) Timely discovery of any written information the committee may consider, and

 (ii) Be present and speak on his or her own behalf.

(g) In any classification decision, the presence of a detainer based on a charged, but as yet unproven, criminal offense or parole violation should not be considered if the detainer has been pending for more than [six] months without formal action by the responsible authority after demand by the prisoner. All other detainees may be considered by the committee, but the mere presence of any detainer should not be given conclusive weight in deciding the prisoner's security classification.

Standard 23-5.1. Care to be provided

(a) Prisoners should receive routine and emergency medical care, which includes the diagnosis and treatment of physical, dental, and mental health problems. A prisoner who requires care not available in the correctional institution should be transferred to a hospital or other appropriate place for care.

(b) Personnel providing medical care in the correctional institution should have qualifications equivalent to medical care personnel performing similar functions in the community.

(c) If an institution operates a hospital, it should meet the standards for a licensed general hospital in the community with respect to the services it offers.

Standard 23-5.3. Medical examinations

(a) Upon admission to a correctional institution a prisoner should receive an examination by a person trained to ascertain visible or common symptoms of communicable disease and conditions requiring immediate medical attention by a physician.

(b) A sentenced prisoner should receive a thorough physical (including an appropriate evaluation of apparent mental condition) and dental examination in accordance with accepted medical practice standards:

  (i) Within two weeks of admission to the correctional institution;

  (ii) Not less than every two years thereafter; and

  (iii) Upon release from confinement if the most recent examination was given more than one year earlier.

(c) A person detained in a correctional institution who is not a sentenced prisoner should be afforded a thorough physical and dental examination upon request when the person is confined for more than two weeks.

Standard 23-6.2. Visitation; general

(a) Home furlough programs should be established, giving due regard to institutional and community security, to enable prisoners to maintain and strengthen family and community ties.

(b) Subject to the provisions of standard 23-1.1, correctional authorities should accommodate and encourage visiting by establishing reasonable visiting hours, including time on weekends and holidays, suited to the convenience of visitors.

(c) Subject to the provisions of standard 23-1.1, institutional visiting facilities should promote informal communications and afford opportunities for physical contact. Extended visits between prisoners and their families in suitable accommodations should be allowed for prisoners who are not receiving home furloughs.

(d) Prisoners should be able to receive any visitor not excluded by correctional authorities for good cause. A prisoner may have the exclusion of a prospective visitor reconsidered through a grievance procedure. All visitors may be subjected to nonintrusive forms of personal search.

(e) Visitation periods should be at least [one] hour long, and prisoners should be able to cumulate visitation periods to permit extended visits. Visits with attorneys, clergy, and public officials should not be counted against visiting periods, and should be unlimited except as to time and duration.

(f) Where resources and facilities permit, correctional authorities are encouraged to facilitate and promote visitation by providing transportation or by providing guidance, directions, and assistance as to available travel to visitors arriving in local terminals.

Standard 23-6.5. Religious freedom

(a) Prisoners' religious beliefs should not be restricted or inhibited by correctional authorities in any way.

(b) Prisoners should be entitled to pursue any lawful religious practice consistent with their orderly confinement and the security of the institution.

(c) Correctional authorities should provide prisoners with diets of nutritious food consistent with their religious beliefs. Prisoners should be entitled to observe special religious rites, including fasting and special dining hours, on major holidays generally observed by their religion, subject to standard 23-1.1.

(d) Prisoners should not be required to engage in religious activities.

(e) Correctional authorities should not maintain any information (other than directory information) concerning a prisoner's religious activities.

(f) Modes of dress or appearance, including religious medals and other symbols, should be permitted to the extent they do not interfere with identification and security of prisoners.

(g) Even while being punished, prisoners, should be allowed religious counseling.

(h) Resources and facilities made available for religious purposes should be equitably allocated according to the proportions of prisoners adhering to each faith.

Standard 23-7.1. Resolving prisoner grievances

(a) Correctional authorities should authorize and encourage correctional employees to resolve prisoner grievances on an informal basis whenever possible.

(b) Every correctional institution should adopt a formal procedure to resolve specific prisoner grievances, including any complaint arising out of institutional policies, rules, practices, and procedures or the action of any correctional employee or official. Grievance procedures should not be used as a substitute appellate procedure for individual decisions reached by adjudicative bodies, for example, parole, classification, and disciplinary boards, although a complaint involving the procedures or general policies employed by any correctional adjudicative body should be subject to grievance procedures.

(c) Correctional authorities should make forms available so that a grievant may initiate review by describing briefly the nature of the grievance, the persons involved, and the remedy sought.

(d) The institution's grievance procedure should be designed to ensure the cooperation and confidence of prisoners and correctional officials and should include:

  (i) Provision for written responses to all grievances, including the reasons for the decision;

  (ii) Provision for response within a prescribed, reasonable time limit. A request that is not responded to or resolved within [thirty] working days should be deemed to have been denied;

  (iii) Special provision for responding to emergencies;

  (iv) Provision for advisory review of grievances;

  (v) Provision for participation by staff and prisoners in the design of the grievance procedure;

  (vi) Provision for access by all prisoners, with guarantees against reprisal;

  (vii) Means for resolving questions of jurisdiction.

Endnote

1. Selected Standards from the American Bar Association's *Standards for Criminal Justice: Legal Status of Prisoners* (formally approved, February 1981). Reprinted by permission of the American Bar Association.

Glossary

42 US Code 1983: A major legislation instrument by which an employee may sue an employer for civil rights violations based on the deprivation of constitutional rights. It is the most versatile civil rights action and is also the most often used against criminal justice agencies.

A

Active electronic monitoring: A device worn by a person on probation that emits signals when plugged into the offenders' home telephone. A computer at the probation office randomly calls the offenders' home telephone system several times during the day to ensure the offender is home.

Adjudicatory hearing: The juvenile court proceeding that is equivalent to a trial in adult court.

Aftercare: The term used in lieu of parole for juvenile cases.

Aggravating circumstances: Those circumstances that tend to make the crime more serious (i.e., use of a deadly weapon, committing an offense against a law enforcement officer, taking advantage of a position of trust to commit an offense, etc.).

Alternative sentencing: Use of nontraditional programs in lieu of fines and custody.

American Correctional Association: The oldest and largest international correctional association in the world. American Correctional Association serves all disciplines within the corrections profession. The ACA provides professional development, certification, standards and accreditation as well as consulting to corrections officials.

American Jail Association: A national nonprofit organization dedicated to supporting those who work in and operate our nations jails. The AJA focuses exclusively on issues specific to the operation of local jails.

Arraignment: First stage of the trial process, at which the indictment or information is read in open court and the defendant is requested to respond thereto.

B

Blood feuds: Blood feuds are actions taken by the victim's family or tribe as revenge on the offender's family or tribe.

Booking: The initial point of entry in the jails, also known as intake, and involves the transfer of responsibility for the arrestee from the law enforcement officer to the jail.

Boot camps: Rehabilitative programs based on the military boot-camp routine.

Butler v. Reno: Court decision ruling that women's prisons are entitled to have the same facilities, materials, and programs as men's prisons.

C

Capital cases: Those cases in which the government seeks the death penalty.

Career criminals: Those persons who make, or attempt to make, a living committing crime.

Child-saving movement: A movement which was directed at children in need or trouble and attempted to save children by using houses of refuge and reform schools.

Civil Rights Act: The 1964 act that prohibits discrimination based on race, color, sex, ethnicity, national origin, and religion.

Classification: A process for determining the needs and requirements of individuals confined and for assigning them to housing units and programs in light of individual needs and existing correctional resources.

Cleared count: As the result of a head count, the precise location of all prisoners are accounted for.

Code of Draco: Early Greek code that used the same penalties for both citizens and slaves and incorporated many of the concepts used in primitive societies (e.g., vengeance, outlawry, and blood feuds).

Code of Hammurabi: Early code of laws involving criminal punishments.

Codes of ethics: Guidelines for professionals in the field which are not legislative enactments, and there are no disciplinary actions associated with their violations. The codes provide us with a set of standards that we should strive to meet in our professional lives.

Commissaries: Stores within the prison where prisoners are allowed to make purchases.

Community service programs: A sentencing alternative that allows the defendant to stay in the community and use community services as rehabilitative tools.

Consent decrees: Used in delinquency cases. These decrees are court orders that are agreed to by the youth and accepted by the court. Consent decrees remove the need for an adjudicatory hearing and it is similar to a plea bargain in adult court.

Correctional officers: Officers who generally perform custodial roles in jails, prisons, and other institutions.

Correctional subsystem: Corrections is part of the larger criminal justice system, which includes the police, courts, and corrections.

Cottage system: The cottage system represented the new rehabilitation model for women's prisons around 1870s. The new prison shed the harsh fortress-type structure and moved toward a cottage look.

Court liaison: The jail process that is responsible for the safe and timely delivery of jail residents to court.

Custody designation: The designation that tells how much supervision the inmate needs and with whom and where he will live.

D

Day-reporting centers: Highly structured non-residential programs utilizing supervision, sanctions, and services coordinated from a central focus.

Deference period: The period of time (since 1979) when the courts were more conservative in getting involved with prison administration.

Deferred adjudication: A form of probation that is used without a finding of guilt in which the defendant pleas guilty and agrees to defer further proceedings.

Deliberate indifference: The categorization of an act performed with reckless disregard to the consequences or to the victims.

Determinate sentence: Fixed periods of confinement that convicted offenders must serve in a correctional institution.

Deterrence: A punishment viewpoint that focuses on future outcomes rather than past misconduct and is based on the theory that creating a fear of future punishments will deter crime.

Diagnostic facilities: The centers that first receive and process inmates who are confined in state penal institutions.

Differential justice: A process where whites are dealt with more leniently than African Americans, whether at the time of arrest, indictment, conviction, sentencing, and/or parole.

Direct-supervision jail: Also known as "new generation jail," this jail design centers on the concept of proactive and participative philosophy.

Discharge: To liberate from confinement or supervision, such as a discharge from prison, probation, or parole.

Disparate treatment: Treating one group differently than another, such as with minority groups.

Disposition hearing: The proceeding in juvenile court that is similar to the sentencing phase of an adult criminal trial.

Disproportionate minority confinement: A phenomenon of disproportionate representation of minorities in the United States corrections system when compared to whites, which could indicate systemic bias in criminal justice policy.

Diversion: Removal of the defendant from the normal path of the criminal justice process to an alternative path (for example, a treatment program).

Dothard v. Rawlinson: The first case involving women correctional officers. In this case, a 22-year-old female college graduate was denied a job as a prison guard because she did not meet the weight and height requirements. The court ruled that this requirement had a discriminatory impact on women applicants.

E

Electronic surveillance: Use of electronic devices to signal supervising probation departments when offenders on home incarceration leave their premises, thus violating the conditions of their sentence.

Emergency overcrowding provisions: Regulations that allow early release of prisoners based on systematic provisions to relieve overcrowding.

Equal Pay Act: An act prohibiting discrimination in wages on the basis of gender for all employees and labor organizations.

F

Flat time: When an offender serves his or her sentence day for day with no early release.

G

Gang associates: "Wannabe" gang members or individuals who actively support gang activity without being gang members.

Gender roles: Society's expectations of the proper behavior, attitudes, and activities of males and females.

Girl Scouts Beyond Bars (GSBB): National Institute of Justice–sponsored program in which girl scouts visit their mothers in prison on a regular basis. During the visits they work together with their mothers on Girl Scout projects and engage in a variety of other activities.

Glass ceiling: The invisible barrier blocking the promotion of a qualified worker because of gender or minority membership.

Good-time guidelines: Statutes that give prison administrators the power to release inmates prior to the expiration of their sentences based on the administrator's judgment that the inmate had shown good behavior and thereby deserved early release.

Group counseling: A planned activity with three or more offenders present in a counseling session for the purpose of solving personal and social problems.

H

Halfway houses: Group homes that are non-secure facilities that are used to help integrate the youths back into the community.

Hands-off period: Practice of the courts to avoid involvement in correctional matters.

HIV/AIDS: AIDS (Acquired Immune Deficiency Syndrome) and HIV (Human Immunodeficiency Virus) are prevalent in many prisons. AIDS is the final and most serious stage of HIV disease, in which the signs and symptoms of severe immune deficiency have developed.

Holy inquisition: A court set up by the Church of Rome to inquire into cases of heresy.

Home confinement: The concept of home confinement is relatively ambiguous; it may range from evening curfew, to detention during all nonworking hours, to continuous incarceration at home.

I

Ideology: The belief system adopted by a group and consists of assumptions and values.

Incapacitation: A punishment viewpoint that holds that while the prisoner is in confinement, he is unlikely to commit crimes on innocent persons outside of prison.

Incarceration: Sanction that requires a defendant to serve a term in a local jail, state prison, or federal prison.

Individual counseling: One-on-one counseling sessions between offenders and court-appointed counselors.

Informal probation: A form of probation whereby the defendant agrees to comply with the terms of the probation, but no formal court order or action is taken nor is a finding entered in the case. If the defendant completes the terms of the probation, then the case is dismissed.

Institutionalized personality: The personality type developed by prisoners that is characterized by moving like a robot according to a routinized pattern, losing any initiative, living on a day-to-day basis, forgetting the past, and avoiding the future.

Intake: The formal entry into jails, also known as booking (*see* booking).

Intensive supervision probation: Probation for offenders who are too antisocial for the relative freedom afforded by regular probation, yet not so seriously criminal as to require incarceration.

Intermediate sanctions: Punishments, such as house arrest, electronic monitoring, and boot camp, that are more restrictive than traditional probation but less so than incarceration.

J

Jail therapy: The act of placing the probationer in jail and without holding a hearing, releasing the probationer after a short stay.

Jails: Confinement facilities that are used to punish persons convicted of minor offenses and who are sentenced to confinement for a year or less, and to detain individuals awaiting trial.

Juvenile correctional facility: A secure facility designed to house juvenile offenders.

Juvenile detention centers: Short-term, secure facilities that hold juveniles awaiting adjudication, disposition, or placement in an institution.

L

Lock down: A condition where all prisoner movement is stopped.

"Lock them up" policy: "Just deserts" model of justice in which many believe the offender must be incarcerated as punishment for their crime. The emphasis is on incapacitation of the offender.

Lockups: A temporary holding facility that is generally operated by the police and is located in a police station or headquarters.

M

Mandatory prison terms: Statues that require the courts to impose mandatory prison terms for convictions of certain offenses or for certain defendants.

Mandatory supervision: The release of an offender from prison with supervision when he or she completes a prescribed portion of his or her sentence.

Megan's Laws: Sex offender registration laws.

Misdemeanants: Individuals convicted of minor crimes (misdemeanors). Their sentences are to jails for periods normally not to exceed one year, fines, community service, and/or attendance at some type of behavior modification course.

Mitigating circumstances: Those circumstances that tend to reduce the severity of the crime (i.e., cooperation with the investigating authority, surrender, good character).

N

New-generations jails: A popular architectural design used in many newly constructed prisons that fosters the interaction between inmates and staff.

Non-secure facilities: Facilities lacking bars, locks, and fences permitting more freedom for juveniles.

O

Orientation: The process of providing inmates with information regarding the department's policies, programs, educational services, rules, classification procedures, disciplinary procedures, and other inmate activities and programs.

P

Parens patriae: A legal doctrine that says the state must provide parental-like protections to those who are unable to care for themselves; applied to convicts when popular ideology holds that criminals have shown themselves unable to act like adults.

Parole: The discretionary release of an inmate from prison when he or she completes a prescribed portion of his or her sentence and the parole board agrees that the release will not increase the likelihood of harm to the public.

Parole guidelines: Procedures designed to limit or structure parole release decisions based on measurable offender criteria.

Parole officers: Officers who supervise offenders who are released from prison on parole or on mandatory supervision. Parole officers generally work under the supervision of the state parole board.

Parole services: Various programs and components of the criminal justice system necessary to facilitate the goals and purposes of parole.

Passive electronic monitoring: A process in which offenders wear electronic devices that emit continuous signals to receivers, which are attached to the offenders home telephone system.

Penal servitude: The use of hard labor as punishment, which was generally reserved for the lower classes of citizens.

Penitentiary: Prison or place of confinement and correction for persons convicted of criminal acts; originally a place where convicts did penance.

Plea: Response to a criminal charge. Traditional pleas are guilty, not guilty, nolo contendere, and not guilty by reason of insanity.

Presentence investigation (PSI) report: Report prepared by the probation department for a judge; contains information about the offense, the offender, and the history of prior offenses and may include a recommendation of a sentence.

Presumptive sentence: A sentence suggested by the legislative body based on certain factors regarding the crime and the criminal.

Pretrial diversion: A form of probation that is granted prior to trial in which the defendant agrees to waive time and to complete a program or process.

Prison: Federal or state penal institution in which offenders serve sentences longer than one year.

Prison argot: The language of the prison subculture.

Prison Litigation Reform Act: This act was an amendment to the 1994 Crime Bill. Under this act, federal courts are instructed to extend no further than necessary prospective relief in prison overcrowding orders.

Prison privatization: Private organizations who contract with state and local governments to run correctional facilities.

Prisonization: The process by which prisoners learn the rules of socialization into the prison culture and is seen by many as a criminalization process whereby a criminal novice is transformed from a prosocial errant to a committed predatory criminal.

Probation: The conditional release of a defendant based on a promise by the defendant to abide by certain rules.

Probation officers: Officers who supervise probationers and generally work under the supervision of the court system.

Professional criminals: Persons of respectability and high social status who commit crime in the course of their occupations.

Put down: The emotional effect of being put in a prison.

Q

Qualified immunity: Protection against being held individually responsible, when the prison institution or organization correctional officer works for violates an individual inmate's rights.

R

Reception/diagnostic centers: The centers that first receive and process inmates who are confined in state penal institutions.

Recidivism: The repeating of criminal behavior.

Reformatory movement: A movement initiated around the late 1800s that advocated the rehabilitation of inmates.

Regular probation: The release of a convicted offender under conditions imposed by the courts for a specified period of time.

Rehabilitation: The view that punishment should be directed toward correcting the offender.

Reintegration: A process that stresses adaptation to the community by requiring the offender to participate in programs which are aimed at providing job skills, personal skills, and motivational skills or to refine these skills all done in a community setting.

Restitution: A sanction imposed by an official of the criminal justice system requiring an offender to make a payment of money or service to either the direct or a substitute crime victim.

Retribution: Based on the ideology that the criminal is an enemy of society and deserves severe punishment for willfully breaking its rules.

Revocation of probation: Procedure whereby probation is revoked, usually as a result of program violation.

Revolving door concept: Refers to offenders who are arrested, remain in jail or prison only long enough to dry out, then return to the streets, re-offend and then land back in jail or prison. This concept is especially evident in cases involving the common drunk.

Rights period: The period of time (1964–1978) when the courts became actively involved in the administration of prisons.

Risk management: Psychological assessment of offender's dangerousness and/or potential to harm self or others while on probation, parole, in community corrections program, or in a penal institution.

S

Script: Items or goods used as currency in a prison.

Secure facilities: Remanding a juvenile to a facility that is equivalent to a prison for adults.

Segregative classification: Assignments of inmates based on age and previous incarceration.
Sentence: An authorized judicial decision that places some degree of penalty on a guilty person.
Sentencing guidelines: Guidelines designed to structure sentences based on the offense severity and the criminal history of the defendant.
Sexism: Unfair discrimination on the basis of sex. It ranges from the blatant to the covert, such as when a token woman is appointed so that an employer appears to be committed to a policy of equal opportunities.
Shakedowns: A prison procedure where inmates and their cells are searched at random to ensure against contraband.
Shelters: Short-term facilities that are operated like detention centers, but are non-secure with a physically unrestricted environment.
Shock incarceration: Sentencing offenders to short periods of time in prison with following periods of time on community supervision; the idea is to make offenders realize what prison is like and to avoid their future return to prison.
Shock probation: Probation that is designed to give defendants a "taste of the bars" before placing them on probation.
Split sentencing: Sentences that include both time in an institution and a period of time on community corrections.
State Department of Corrections: The department of a state with designated authority to administer and run the state correctional facilities.
State jail felony: A relative new crime classification that is more serious than a misdemeanor and less serious than a felony.
Supervised release: A form of release from custody in which the offender is placed under the supervision of either a probation officer or a parole officer.

T

Technical violations of probation: Those probation condition violations that do not involve criminal misconduct (for example, failing to maintain employment).
Three strikes legislation: Law that states that an individual receives a life sentence after committing any three felonies.
Title VII: This broadly based act established a federal policy requiring fair employment practices in both the public and private sectors.
Tort: A private or civil wrong or injury, other than a breach of contract, resulting from a violation of a duty and for which courts will provide relief in the form of damages.
Train: The bus network used by states to transfer prisoners from one external unit to another.
Treatment strategies specialists: Correctional treatment specialists work in correctional institutions (jails or prisons) or in parole or probation agencies. In jails and prisons, they evaluate the progress of inmates. They also work with inmates, probation officers, and other agencies to develop parole and release plans.

Trials by ordeal: Practices used by the early churches as substitutes for trials, whereby the accused was subjected to dangerous or painful tests in the belief that God would protect the innocent and the guilty would suffer agonies and die.

Truth in sentencing laws: These laws require offenders to serve a substantial amount of their sentences, usually 85 percent of said sentence.

U

UNICOR: The Federal Prison Industries, Inc. that is wholly owned by the federal government with the mission to support the Federal Bureau of Prisons through the gainful employment of inmates in work programs.

V

Values: Beliefs about what is moral and desirable.

W

Wergeld: The acceptance of money or property as atonement for wrongs.

White-collar criminals: The traditional name for professional criminals.

Writ of habeas corpus: The writ, traditionally known as the "Great Writ" that is a constitutional protected writ designed to require the government to justify why the individual is being held in confinement.

Index

Page numbers in *italics* identify an illustration. An italic *n* next to a page number indicates information that appears in an endnote. An italic *t* next to a page number identifies information that appears in a table. Page numbers 493–502 indicate the glossary.

A

ABA. *See* American Bar Association (ABA)
Absent mothers, impact of, 308–309
ABT Associates, 285, 287
ACA. *See* American Correctional Association (ACA)
Accountability, prison privatization, 13–14
    Accreditation, ACA policies on, 479–480
Accused, adjudication of, 4–5
ACLU (American Civil Liberties Union), 18
Acquired Immune Deficiency Syndrome (AIDS). *See* HIV/AIDS
Active electronic monitoring, 398, 493
Adams, James, 441–442
Adjudication procedures
    in criminal justice enterprise, 4–5
    deferred, 83, 125, 198, 495
    hearing, 88, 282, 493
Administration. *See* Correctional officers (COs)
Administration of Justice Task Force Report on Corrections, 10
Adult inmates. *See* Inmates
Advocate, probation officer as, 170
Aesthetic view of retaliation, 35
AFDC (Aid to Families With Dependent Children), 54
Affirmative action and female correctional officers, 323–324
African American inmates. *See* Race and ethnicity
AFSCME-Corrections United, 18
Aftercare, 251, 493
Age
    in correctional subsystem, 25
    death penalty, 351, 351*t*
    elderly offenders and inmates, 105–106, 110–118, 315
    incarceration rates, 41, 41*t*
    See also Juvenile corrections
Aggravating circumstances, 340, 493
AIDS. *See* HIV/AIDS
Aid to Families With Dependent Children (AFDC), 54

AJA (American Jail Association), 8, 18, 493
Alabama, 139, 321, 343, 345
Alaska, 304
Albuquerque Journal, 13
Alcatraz Island website, 18
Alcohol and alcoholism
    diversion, 127–128
    elderly offenders, 105
    misdemeanors, 194
    probation origins, 158–159
    suicide in jail, 203
    treatment for, 54–55, 308
    Warner v. Orange County Probation, 386–390
Alien offenders, 107–108
Alternative sentencing, 125–151
    ABA standards on, 67
    about, 126–127
    article, 140–150
    attitude change, 133–134, 137–139
    community service, 140–150
    defined, 83, 493
    diversion, 127–128
    evaluation of effectiveness, 132, 139–140
    recidivism, 139–140
    rehabilitative programming, 134–137
    shock incarceration/probation, 129–134
Alternatives to confinement, 395–424
    articles, 402–423
    day-reporting centers, 402–408
    electronic house arrest, 397–398, *399*
    inmate involvement in prison governance, 413–423
    intensive supervision, 408–413
    mobile intervention supervision team (MIST), 400
    Operation Night Light, 401
American Bar Association (ABA)
    disciplinary hearing procedures, 246–248
    grievances, 248–249
    jail standards, 192

503

legal status of prisoners, 483–492
prisoner's rights, 370
probation standards, 165
rules of conduct, 249–250
standards on sentencing alternatives, 67
American Civil Liberties Union (ACLU), 18
American Correctional Association (ACA)
  affirmative action in, 322
  careers in corrections, 8, 432
  code of ethics, 438–439
  defined, 493
  educational programs for women, 312–313
  jail standards, 192
  National Policies on Corrections, 455–482
  prisoner's rights, 370
  prison gangs, 225
  website, 8
  women correctional officer's award, 320
American Jail Association (AJA), 8, 18, 493
American Probation and Parole Association, 438–439
American Psychological Association, 192
American Public Health Association, 192
Amnesty International, 355
Ancient history, historical view of corrections, 25–28
Antisocial attitudes and incarceration, 138–139
Antiterrorism and Effective Death Penalty Act (1976), 372
Application process for correctional employment, 429, *430*
Architectural designs of jails, 208–209
Argot, prison, 218, 219*t*, 223, 499
Arizona
  boot camps, 136
  death penalty decision, 342–343
  emergency overcrowding provisions, 79
  facilities for elderly inmates, 115
  Girl Scouts Beyond Bars (GSBB), 311
  jail overcrowding, 201
  payments by inmates, 397
  probation population, 161
  shock incarceration/probation, 160
Arkansas, 115, 131, 199, 350
Arkansas Democrat Gazette, 13
Arouet, Francois Marie (Voltaire), 29
Arpaio, Joe, 201
Arraignment, 5, 493
Arrest, gender bias in, 106, 107
Articles
  accountability, and prison privatization, 13
  community service, 140–150
  costs of prison expansion, 268–271
  day-reporting centers, 402–408
  elderly offenders, 110–118
  guiding probationary philosophies in 21st century, 172–182
  inmate involvement in prison governance, 413–423
  intensive supervision, 408–413
  probation officer advancement, 439–447
  rehabilitation, 49–56
Asian American inmates. *See* Race and ethnicity
Association of Treatment of Sexual Abusers, 232
Atkins v. Virginia, 341*t*
Attitude change and alternatives to incarceration, 133–134, 137–139
Attorneys, in criminal justice system, 4, 127

Auburn Penitentiary, NY, 346–347
Augustus, John, 158–159
Automatic review in capital cases, 350
Autry, James David, 337

B

Baldus, David, 353
Bank robbing as federal crime, 108
Beccaria, Cesare, 29–30, 31*t*
Bedford Hills Correctional Facility, NY, 302, 310
Bench trial, 5
Benefits, of prisons, 268–269, 270
Bentham, Jeremy, 31, 33
Beto, George J., 443, 444
Bias
  in capital punishment, 339, 353–354
  correctional employment practices, 316, 320–321
  gender, in criminal justice, 106–107
  gender bias in corrections, 106–107, 309–310
  See also Disproportionate minority confinement
Black inmates. *See* Race and ethnicity
Blackmun, Harry A., 353
Blood feuds, 25–26, 494
Booking, 196, 494
Books, Charles, 347
Boot camps, 129–133, 138, 494
BOP. *See* Federal Bureau of Prisons (BOP)
Bounds v. Smith, 377
Branding, as punishment, 28
Breed v. Jones, 281
Broker, probation officer as, 170
Brokerage ideology of probation, 173
Builder-tender system, 224–225
Building costs of correctional facilities, 9, 11, 195, 200, 266–271
Bunk, in prison, 220
Bureau of Justice Statistics
  crimes and substance abuse, 54–55
  criminogenic needs, 135
  incarceration rate, race and ethnicity, 40, 41
  jail functions, 193–194
  job opportunities in, 9
  National Crime Victimization Survey (NCVS), 75–76
  noncitizen inmates, 107–108
  number of correctional employees, 429
  on probation, 161, 169
  as resource, 18
  sentencing guidelines, 73
  suicide in jail, 202
  tougher sentencing, 6–7
  truth in sentencing laws, 70
  violent crime and drug use, 104
  women inmates' special needs, 307, 308
Bureau of Prisons (BOP). *See* Federal Bureau of Prisons (BOP)
Burke, Edmund, 443
Bussing prisoners, 230
Butler v. Reno, 307, 494

C

California
  boot camps, 138
  career criminals, 99
  death row, 344, 350, 351, 356

Index **505**

   electronic monitoring, 398
   funding choices, 11
   gender bias in criminal justice, 107
   good-time guidelines, 77
   harsher treatment, 373
   incarceration rate, 40
   juveniles, alternative sentencing, 288, 291
   location of confinement, 44
   new-generation jails, 209
   noncitizen inmates, 107
   overcrowding, 200
   presentence investigation (PSI) reports, 81
   prison gangs, 225, 226
   suicide in jail, 202, 203
   three strikes legislation, 36, 43, 73–75
   women offenders, 304, 351
California Department of Corrections, 449–450
California Penal Code, Section 1170 (a), 48
Capital punishment, 333–363
   automatic review, 350
   bias in, 353–354
   capital cases, 335–339, 494
   criticism of, 354–356
   execution, 336–337, 346–349
   Gardner v. Florida, 357–361
   prisoner characteristics, 350–352
   status of, 343–345
   statutory changes, 345–346
   See also Death penalty
Career criminals, 99–100, 494
Case load for probation officer, 169
Cases
   Atkins v. Virginia, 341t
   Bounds v. Smith, 377
   Breed v. Jones, 281
   Butler v. Reno, 307
   Dothard v. Rawlinson, 320, 321, 496
   Estelle v. Gamble, 378
   Farmer v. Brennan, 381–385
   Ford Pinto case, 109
   Ford v. Wainwright, 341t
   Furman v. Georgia, 340, 341t, 349
   Gagnon v. Scarpelli, 166
   Gardner v. Florida, 357–361
   Gregg v. Georgia, 340, 341t
   Harmelin, Ronald Allen v. Michigan, 374–377
   Helling v. McKinney, 378
   Hutto v. Finney, 377
   Jones v. N.C. Prisoner's Labor Union, 378
   Large v. Superior Court of County of Maricopa, 377
   McCleskey v. Kemp, 341t
   McKune v. Lile, 380
   Meachum v. Fano, 378
   Mempa v. Rhay, 166
   Minnesota v. Murphy, 182–184
   Morrissey v. Brewer, 166, 256, 257–266
   Nelson v. Heyne, 283
   Patzig v. O'Neil, 204–207
   Perry v. Lynch, 341t
   Procunier v. Martinez, 379–380
   Richardson et al. v. McKnight, 14
   Ring v. Arizona, 342
   Ruiz v. Estelle, 224
   Sattazahn v. Pennsylvania, 356
   Stanford v. Kentucky, 341t
   State v. Fuller, 182–184
   State v. Imlay, 182–183
   State v. Utah, 82
   Thompson v. Oklahoma, 341t
   Turner v. Safety, 379
   Vitek v. Jones, 378
   Warner v. Orange County Probation, 386–390
   Wilkins v. Missouri, 341t
   Wolff v. McDonnell, 379
Casework-type ideology of probation, 173
Categories of involvement, prisoner's rights, 370–372
Cell, in prison, 220, 228
Censorship of mail, 379–380
Census of Juveniles in Residential Placement (OJJDP), 287–288
Center on Juvenile and Criminal Justice, 18
Chief probation officer (CPO), 171
Childcare and female inmates, 306–307, 308–312
Child molesters, 232–235
Children in Custody census, 286
Child saving movement, 277–278, 494
   See also Juvenile corrections
Chinese proverb on punishment, 38
Church. *See* Theological view
Cigarettes in jail, 198
Cigarette smoking, 198, 378
Citation, juvenile, 86–87
Citizen response to crime, 3–4
Civil death, 27
Civil Rights Act (1964), 320, 370–371, 494
Civil War era, 303
Clark, Jesse E., 442
Classification of inmates
   ABA standards for, 488–489
   ACA policies on, 455–456
   defined, 196, 494
   historical view of, 49
   HIV-positive, 227–228
   in jail, 196, 209
   at orientation, 244–245
   in prison, 227–228
   for probation, 158
   segregative, 500
Cleanliness in prison, 220
Cleared count, 230, 494
Clemmer, Donald, 223
Close custody, 245
Cocaine, crack and powder forms, 42–43, 73, 103
Code of Draco, 28, 494
Code of ethics, 438–439, 494
Code of Hammurabi, 27, 494
Codification of punishment, historical, 27–33
Cohen, Mark A., 76
Collaboration, inmate and official. *See* Inmate involvement in prison governance
Collective incapacitation, 36
Colombian drug cartels, 105
Colorado, 200, 291, 343, 345
Commissaries, 219–220, 494
Community-based corrections
   ACA policies on, 467
   articles, 402–413
   cost of incarceration vs., 180–181
   day-reporting centers, 402–408
   electronic house arrest, 397–398, *399*
   facilities in correctional enterprise, 7
   intensive supervision, 408–413

mobile intervention supervision team (MIST), 400
Operation Night Light, 401
and probation, 157
and reintegration, 10
Community planner, probation officer as, 170
Community service
  article on, 140–150
  community service investigation, 144–145
  defined, 141
  evaluation of effectiveness, 140, 149–150
  judicial and correctional philosophy, 142
  offender eligibility and selection for, 142, 146–148
  organizational issues, 143–144
  origins, 141
  programs, 494
  as sentencing alternative, 140, 145–146
  supervision function, 148
  trends in, 141
Community service investigation, 144–145
Comprehensive Crime Control Act (1984), 141, 142
Conditions
  on discharge from parole, 257
  of incarceration, 371, 470
  living, and prison violence, 100–101
  of probation, 163
  working, for probation officers, 434
Conduct, rules of, 249–250, 486
Confidentiality, as probationer right, 164
Confinement. *See* Alternatives to confinement; Incarceration
Connecticut, 288, 316, 397
Consent decrees, 88, 494
Conservative ideology, 33, 50, 51, 53, 56
Constitution. *See* U.S. Constitution
Construction costs of correctional facilities, 9, 11, 195, 200, 266–271
Control
  ACA policies on use of force, 469–470
  ideology of, and probation, 176–177
  institutional discipline, 136–137, 246, 466
  sense of, and rehabilitation effectiveness, 135
  See also Supervision of offenders
Correctional clients, 97–120
  about, 98–99
  article, 110–118
  career criminals, 99–100
  drug offenders (*See* Drug offenses)
  elderly inmates, 105–106, 110–118, 315
  federal inmate (*See* Federal institutions and inmates)
  female criminal (*See* Female inmates)
  Ford Pinto case, 109
  gender bias, 106–107
  Hemparian's study of violent criminal, 102
  juvenile offenders (*See* Juvenile corrections)
  noncitizen offenders, 107–108
  nonviolent offenders, 74–75, 130, 194
  prisonization, 99, 217–221, 499
  prison violence, 100–101
  professional criminal, 103
  See also Inmates
Correctional enterprise, 6–7
  See also Criminal justice enterprise
Correctional facilities. *See* Facilities, correctional
Correctional industry, ACA policies on, 467

Correctional officers (COs), 427–452
  about, 429
  ACA policies on, 458, 475–476
  accountability, and prison privatization, 13–14
  application process, 429, *430*
  assaults on, 243
  caseloads, 433
  contemporary, 8–9
  defined, 494
  ethical code, 438–439
  and inmate relations, 229
  job outlook, 435–436
  nature of work, 432–433, 434
  preparation for, 8
  and prison gangs, 226–227
  qualifications and job descriptions, 448–451
  statistics, 431
  training, qualifications and advancement, 435
  treatment strategies specialists, 429, 431–436, 501
  working conditions, 434
  See also Female correction officers; Inmate involvement in prison governance; Parole officers; Probation officers
Correctional subsystem, 7, 25, 495
Correctional treatment strategies specialists, 429, 431–436, 501
Corrections, beginnings and philosophical underpinning, 23–58
  about, 24–25
  article, 49–56
  contemporary crime and offenders, 39–44
  historical view of corrections, 25–33
  locations of confinement, 44–47
  philosophical approaches, 47–48, 142, 172–182
  purpose of criminal sanctions, 33–37
  purpose of punishment, 37–39
  rehabilitation, 49–56
Corrections, introduction to, 1–19
  about, 2–3
  careers in corrections, 8–9
  correctional enterprise, 6–7
  criminal justice enterprise, 3–6
  overview of text book, 14–17
  resources, 17–18
  trends and challenges, 3, 9–14
The Corrections Yearbook, 111, 322
COs. *See* Correctional officers (COs)
Costs
  facility construction, 9, 11, 195, 200, 266–271
Costs, correctional
  community service, 140, 149–150
  contemporary trends, 11, 12
  of prisons and prison expansion, 11, 266–271
  of probation, 171, 180–181
  social programs, 54
Cottage system, 301, 302, 495
Counts in prisons, 230
Court appointed counsel, 4
Court liaison, 197, 495
Court referral. *See* Community service
Courts
  adjudication procedures, 5
  capital punishment, 339–343, 350
  deference period, 369, 495
  hands-off period, 369, 496
  jails as liaisons with, 197
  juvenile, establishment of, 278

and probation, 157, 159
right period, 369, 500
sentencing guidelines, 72, 73
See also Cases; Rights of prisoners; U.S. Supreme Court
Covey, Stephen R., 444, 446, 447
CPO (chief probation officer), 171
Crime. *See* Offenders and offences
Crime control model, 10–11
Crime rate, 74, 76, 268–271
See also Statistics, U.S.
Criminal Incapacitation (Spellman), 268
Criminal Justice Act of 1982, England, 403
Criminal justice enterprise, 3–6
   adjudication procedures, 5
   citizen response to crime, 3–4
   corrections, 5–6
   electronic monitoring in, 398, 399
   pretrial prosecution, 4
   sentencing, 5
Criminals. *See* Correctional clients; Inmates; Offenders and offences
Criminal sanctions. *See* Sanctions
Criminogenic needs and rehabilitation, 134–135
Criminology research. *See* Research
Criteria for granting probation, 161–162
Crofton, Walter, 252–253
Crowding. *See* Overcrowding
"Cruel and unusual" clause of Eighth Amendment, 339, 374–377
"Cs" in probation officer advancement, 439–447
Custody, 246
Custody designation
   defined, 245, 495
   and institutional types, 284–285
   levels of, 245–246
   and privatization, 12–13
   and sentencing, 6

D

Daily Texan, 47
Dangerousness, as punishment guiding principle, 38–39
Davis, Richard Allen, 73
Dawson, Robert, 34
Day-reporting centers
   defined, 402, 495
   history of, 402–403
   operation of, 403–405
   in Orange County, FL, 405–407
   recommendations, 407–408
Day-reporting centers, article on, 402–408
Death penalty
   conflicting views of, 339
   and courts, 339–343
   death row population, 344, 350–356
   DNA testing, 354
   execution, 336–337, 346–349
   vs. life imprisonment, 339–341
   and mental health, 338, 341–342
   public support for, 337–338
   as sentencing choice, 5
   states without, 344*t*
   and U.S. Supreme Court, 335, 339–343, 341*t*
   writ of *habeas corpus*, 372
   See also Capital punishment

Death Penalty Information Center, 337–338
Decrees, consent, 88, 494
Defendant, adjudication procedures, 5
Deference period, 369, 495
Deferred adjudication, 83, 125, 198, 495
Deferred adjudication probation, 125
Delaware, 115, 288, 291, 311, 343, 345
Deliberate indifference, 380–385, 495
Demographics of incarcerated population, 40
   See also Statistics, U.S.
Dependency proceedings, juveniles, 85–86, 87
Detection, by probation officer, 171
Detention centers, juvenile, 283, 284, 285, 498
Detention facilities, 9
Detention hearings, juvenile, 85–86
Determinate sentencing, 6, 68, 71, 495
Deterrence
   Beccaria on, 29, 30
   by boot camps, 137
   as criminal sanction purpose, 35–36
   death penalty, 339
   defined, 35, 495
   in liberal ideology, 34
Deterrence theory of punishment, 35–36
Diagnostic facilities, 243–244, 495
Differential justice, 303, 495
Dilulio, John J., 76
Direct-supervision jail design, 208–209, 495
Discharge, 247, 250, 495
Disciplinary hearing procedures, 246–248, 487–488
Discipline, institutional, 136–137, 246, 466
Discretionary to adult court, Uniform Juvenile Court Act, 89–92
Discrimination. *See* Bias
Disparate treatment, 316, 495
Disposition hearing, 88–89, 282, 495
Disproportionate minority confinement, 40–44
   criticism of enforcement model, 48
   defined, 40, 495
   drug offenses, 42–43
   incarceration rates, 40–42
   juvenile corrections, 288–289
   street gangs, 43
Diversion, 127–128, 280, 496
DNA testing and death penalty, 354
Doing time
   about, 217
   AIDS, 230
   exchange rates, 145–146, 179
   gangs in prison, 224–227
   inmate social system, 221–223
   mental health issues, 231–232
   prisonization, 217–221
   prison routine, 227–230
   "put down," 224
   sex offenders, 232–236
   standing tall, 222
   time served, 107–108, 193, 352
   See also Release
DOJ (U.S. Department of Justice), 139, 353–354
Domestic abuse and women offenders, 306–307
Dothard v. Rawlinson, 320, 321, 496
Draco, Code of, 28, 494
Drug abuse
   and diversion, 127–128
   treatment for, 54–55, 135, 308
   See also Alcohol and alcoholism

508 Index

Drug criminal, 103–105
Drug offenses
    disproportionate minority confinement, 42–43, 73
    as federal crime, 108
    federal institutions and inmates, 44–46
    mandatory prison terms, 71
    mobile intervention supervision team (MIST), 400
    noncitizen inmates, 107
    offenders as corrections client, 103–105
    in overall convictions, 44, 66–67t
    women incarcerated for, 304
Drug Treatment Alternatives to Prison (DTAP), NY, 128
DTAP (Drug Treatment Alternatives to Prison), NY, 128
Due process rights, 166–167, 339, 370
Duke of York (later, James II, King of England), 32, 33

E

Earned time, 77
Economics. *See* Costs, correctional
Edison, Thomas, 347
Education
    ACA policies on inmate, 472
    for correctional careers, 8–9, 431, 435
    female client programs, 312–313
    probation officer as educator, 170
    in rehabilitation model, 49, 53–54
    state-level funding choices, 11
    vocational training, 49, 53–54, 285, 312, 472
EEOC (Equal Opportunity Act of 1972), 320
Eighth Amendment of U.S. Constitution, 100–101, 339, 349, 374–377
Elderly offenders and inmates, 105–106, 110–118, 315
Electrocution/electric chair, 346–347, 348, 349t, 352
Electronic house arrest, 397–398, 399
Electronic monitoring (EM), 397–398, 399
Electronic surveillance, 397–398, 399, 496
Elmira Reformatory, 49
EM (electronic monitoring), 397–398, 399
Emergency overcrowding provisions, 68, 79, 496
Employee assistance programs, ACA policies on, 481–482
Employment in corrections. *See* Correctional officers (COs)
Enabler, probation officer as, 170
Enculturation, prison, 223
Enforcement model, 48
Enforcer, probation officer as, 171
England
    community service origins in, 141
    criminal law reform, 31
    day-reporting centers, 402–403, 405
    death penalty history, 336
    history of parole, 252–253
    jail development, 191
    juvenile corrections and *parens patriae*, 277
English Anglican Code (1718), 33
English Bill of Rights (1689), England, 191
English Penitentiary Act (1799), 32
English Prison Service (EPS), 37–38
English Statement of Purposes, 37–38
EPA (Equal Pay Act of 1963), 320, 496
EPS (English Prison Service), 37–38
Equal Opportunity Act of 1972 (EEOC), 320

Equal Pay Act of 1963 (EPA), 320, 496
Estelle v. Gamble, 378
Ethics, code of, 438–439, 494
Ethnicity. *See* Race and ethnicity
Evaluation of effectiveness
    alternative sentencing, 132, 139–140
    community service, 140, 149–150
    diversion, 128
    rehabilitation, 50–53, 135
    shock incarceration/probation, 132–133, 160–161
Evaluator, probation officer as, 170
Exchange rates for time served, 145–146, 179
Execution (death), 336–337, 346–349
    See also Capital punishment
Execution of sentence, suspension of, 83
Ex-offender employment, ACA policies on, 458
Expiatory view of retaliation, 35
"Eye for an eye" concept, 34–35

F

Facilities, correctional
    ACA policies on design, 461–462
    architectural designs, 208–209
    community-based, 7
    costs of construction, 9, 11, 195, 200, 266–271
    detention, 9
    for elderly inmates, 105, 115
    for juvenile, 284–285
    panoptical prison, 31
    security level, 12–13, 285, 500
    women's separate quarters, 299, 301
    See also Jails; Juvenile correctional facilities; Prisons
Family Unity Demonstration Project (1994), 310–311
Farmer v. Brennan, 381–385
Farms, juvenile, 285
FBI, 74
Federal Bureau of Justice Statistics. *See* Bureau of Justice Statistics
Federal Bureau of Prisons (BOP)
    boot camps, 129
    correctional officers' requirements and training, 448
    day-reporting centers, 403
    educational programs for women, 312–313
    equal inmate programs and gender, 307–308
    on federal prisons, 11–12, 108–109
    female director of, 322
    historical view of medical model, 49
    mandatory sentencing laws, 71
    number of elderly offenders, 111
Federal Comprehensive Crime Control Act (1984), 141, 142
Federal Criminal Code, 160
Federal Death Penalty Act (1984), 354
Federal institutions and inmates
    average time served, 46
    correctional client, 108–110
    in correctional subsystem, 25
    drug crimes, 44–45
    execution method, 348
    immigration offences, 45
    incarcerated population in, 44
    job opportunities in, 9
    mandatory prison terms, 71
    prison overcrowding, 47
    prisons, 7

Federal policy. *See* Policy issues
Federal Prison Litigation Reform Act (1996), 369
Federal Prisons Industries, Inc. (UNICOR), 110, 502
Federal Probation Journal, 289, 291
Felons, 65, 66–67t, 80, 167, *168*
  See also Offenders and offences
Female correction officers, 316–324
  ACA policies on, 457–458
  affirmative action goals, 323–324
  benefits of, 318
  history of, 319–320
  problems facing, 316–318
  professional progress, 320–323
Female inmates, 297–316
  absent mothers, impact of, 308–309
  ACA policies on, 474–475
  as correctional client, 106
  on death row, 351
  educational programs, 312–313
  gender bias in criminal justice, 106–107
  history of, 300–302
  incarceration rate, 40
  issues in, 306–316
  in jail, 195
  medical treatment, 314–316
  mental health programs, 313–314
  parenting responsibilities, 306–307, 308–312
  in prison, 299
  racial disparities, 302–303
  reform movement, 301–304
  statistics, 304–305
  substance abuse treatment, 308
  witchcraft, in Middle Ages, 28, 29
Fifth Amendment of U.S. Constitution, 182–184, 380
Finances. *See* Costs, correctional
Fines, 5, 26, 145
Firing squad, 348, 349t, 352
First Amendment of U.S. Constitution, 249
First-generation jails, 208
Flat time, 6, 68, 71, 496
Fleisher, Mark, 54
Florida
  day-reporting centers, 405–407
  death row, 343, 344, 345, 350
  emergency overcrowding provisions, 79
  executions in, 344t
  funding choices, 11
  Girl Scouts Beyond Bars (GSBB), 311
  group home programs, juvenile, 291
  intensive supervision, 408–413
Force, ACA policies on use of, 469–470
Ford, Gerald, 101
Ford Motor Company, Pinto case, 109
Ford v. Wainwright, 341t
Forestry camps, juvenile, 285
42 US Code Section 1983, Civil Rights Act, 370, 371, 493
Foundation for People, CA, 143
Frankfurter, Felix, 335
Free will, 30, 31t, 33–34
Friedensgeld, 26
"Front door" program, diversion as, 127
Fuller, Matthew C., 183
Furman v. Georgia, 340, 341t, 349

G

Gagnon v. Scarpelli, 166
Gandy, Charles, 440
Gang associates, 225, 496
Gangi, Robert, 54
Gang rape in prison, 228
Gangs
  prison, 224–227
  street, 43
Gardner v. Florida, 357–361
Gas chamber, 347, 348, 349t, 352
Gault, Jerry, 279
Gee Jon, 347
Gender Bias Task Force of Texas, 106–107
Gender issues
  in correctional subsystem, 25, 106–107
  custody data, 304, *305*, 306
  incarcerated mothers, 309–310
  incarceration rate, 40
  in jail, 195, *195*
  and prison violence, 100
  See also Female inmates
Gender roles, 317, 496
General deterrence, 35
Georgia
  boot camps, 129, 138
  death penalty in, 340, 353
  facilities for elderly inmates, 115
  jail smoking ban, 198
  prison overcrowding, 47
Geriatric (elderly) offenders and inmates, 105–106, 110–118, 315
Girl Scouts Beyond Bars (GSBB), 311, 496
Glass ceiling, 316, 496
Glendening, Parris, 354
Glenn, Arthur, 222
Good-time credit, 253, 379
Good-time guidelines, 68, 77–79, 496
Governance. *See* Inmate involvement in prison governance
Grand jury, 4, 5
Greek codification, 27, 28
Gregg v. Georgia, 340, 341t
Grievances, 241–242, 248–249
Grooming in prison, 220
Group counseling, 232, 496
Group homes, juvenile, 285, 289–292
Guillotine, 346
Guilty, as plea, 5

H

Habeas corpus, 371–372
Habeas Corpus Act (1679), England, 191
Halfway houses, 285, 496
Hammurabic codes, 27, 494
Hands-off period, 369, 496
Hanging, 348, 349t, 352
Hanson, R. Karl, 232
Haparian, Donna Martin, 102
Hard labor, as punishment, 27
Harmelin, Ronald Allen v. Michigan, 374–377
Hassine, Victor, 229
Health care issues
  ABA on prisoner access to, 489–490
  ACA policies on, 456–457

for elderly inmates, 111–115
Estelle v. Gamble, 378
female inmates, 314–316
HIV/AIDS, 230–231
at inmate orientation, 244
See also Mental health issues
Helling v. McKinney, 378
Hemparian's study of violent criminal, 102
Heresy, in Middle Ages, 28, 29
Hispanic inmates. *See* Race and ethnicity
Historical view of corrections
  in ancient history, 25–28
  codification of punishment, historical, 27–33
  "cruel and unusual" clause, 374–377
  of day-reporting centers, 402–403
  death penalty, 336
  early reformers, 29–33
  female inmates, 300–303
  of jails, 191
  of juvenile corrections, 277–278
  in Middle Ages, 28–29
  of parole, 252–253
  probation, 158–159
  public sanctions, development of, 26–27, 33
  of rehabilitation and reform, 49
  women as correctional officers, 319–320
HIV/AIDS
  defined, 230, 497
  as health care issue, 230–231, 314
  inmate classification by, 227–228
Holy inquisition, 29, 497
Home confinement, 398, 497
Homosexual behavior in prison, 228
House arrest, electronic, 397–398, 399
Housing. *See* Facilities, correctional
Houston Chronicle, 78
Howard, John, 32, 33
Howe, E. W., 217
Hulks, as prisons, 32
Human Immunodeficiency Virus (HIV). *See* HIV/AIDS
Hutto v. Finney, 377

I

I.D. cards, prison, 218, 219
Idaho, 161, 310, 343, 345, 350
Ideology
  conservative, 33, 50, 51, 53, 56
  criminal sanctions, 33–34
  defined, 33, 497
  liberal, 33–34, 51, 52
  of probation, 173, 176–182
  radical, 33, 34, 51
  sanctions, 33–34
  "tough on crime" ideology, 52, 56
Illinois
  boot camps, 138
  death penalty, 345, 354–355
  electronic monitoring, 398
  first juvenile court, 278, 280
Immigrant offenders, 107–108
Immigration and Nationality Act (1990), 107
Immigration and Naturalization Service (INS), 107–108
Immigration offenses, 45
Immunity, qualified, 13–14, 500

Imposition of sentence, suspension of, 83
Incapacitation as sanction purpose, 34, 36–37, 339, 497
Incarceration
  antisocial attitudes and, 138–139
  conditions of, 371, 470
  cost of, 11, 12, 180–181
  defined, 497
  for offender incapacitation, 36–37
  pain of, and inmate attitude change, 133–134, 137–139
  prison population levels, U.S., 6–7, 7*t*
  and probation, 157
  rates of, 40–42, 41*t*, 306
  release from, 250, 251*t*
  as sentencing choice, 5–6
  shock probation, 160
  See also Alternatives to confinement
Indeterminate sentencing, 70
  See also Rehabilitation
Index crimes, 106
Indiana, 198, 345, 350
Indiana Juvenile Statutes, 89–90
Indiana Women's Prison, 302
Indictment, grand jury, 4, 5
Individual counseling, 232, 497
Informal probation, 88, 497
Information manager, probation officer as, 170
Information systems, ACA policies on, 461
Inmate involvement in prison governance, 413–423
  about, 412–413, 423
  commitment and trust, 414–415
  grass roots mission statement, 421–422
  organization creation, 418–421
  prison constitutional convention, 416–418
Inmates
  ACA policies on special needs of, 464–465
  characteristics, and capital punishment, 350–352
  in correctional subsystem, 25
  and guard relationships, 229
  intake, 87–88, 196, 497
  leadership by, 221, 224–225
  orientation process, 244–245
  in prison gangs, 224–227
  sexual activity, 228
  shakedowns, 228
  social system, 231–233
  transsexuality of, 381–385
  See also Alternatives to confinement; Classification of inmates; Correctional clients; Female inmates; Offenders and offences; Rights of prisoners
Innovations in corrections. *See* Alternatives to confinement
Inquisition, in Middle Ages, 28, 29
In Re Gault, 279–280
Insanity, not guilty by reason of, as plea, 5
INS (Immigration and Naturalization Service), 107–108
Institutional facilities. *See* Facilities, correctional
Institutional personality, 217, 497
Institutional procedures, 241–272
  about, 242
  article, 268–271
  costs of, 266–267
  custody levels, 245–246
  diagnostic facilities, 243–244

Index

disciplinary hearing procedures, 246–248
grievances, 248–249
inmate orientation process, 244–245
juvenile corrections, 283
Morrissey v. Brewer, 257–266
on prison expansion costs, 268–271
reasons for prisons, 243–249
release from confinement, 250
rules of conduct, 249–250
See also Parole
Intake, 87–88, 196, 497
Intensive probation, 125
Intensive supervision, 408–413
  advantages, 410–411
  application, 412–413
  drug use issues, 409
  in Florida, 408
  reporting, 409
  requirements, 412
Intensive supervision probation (ISP), 158, 175, 177–178, 180, 497
Intermediate sanctions, 127, 497
  See also Alternative sentencing; Alternatives to confinement
International Commission of Jurists, 355
Interviews at inmate orientation, 244
Involvement, prisoner's rights categories, 370–372
Iowa, 42, 115, 192
Isolation in solitary confinement, 377
ISP (intensive supervision probation), 158, 175, 177–178, 180, 497

J

Jackson, Robert H., 335
Jacksonian era penitentiaries, U.S., 49
Jail fever, 191
Jails, 190–211
  ACA policies on design, 461–462
  architectural designs of, 208–209
  basic operating procedures in, 196–197
  classification, 196
  construction costs, 9, 11, 195, 200, 266–271
  in correctional enterprise, 7
  court liaison/court appearance process, 197
  defined, 191, 497
  detention facilities as, 9
  direct-supervision design of, 208–209
  female inmates, 195
  history of, 191
  incarcerated population in, 5–6, 44
  intake, 196
  orientation, 197
  overcrowding, 199–201
  Patzig v. O'Neil, 204–207
  vs. prisons, 193
  and probation, 160
  release from, 197
  as revolving door, 194
  role of, 193–194
  smoking in, 198
  standard for, 192
  state jail felonies, 197–198
  suicide in, 194, 202–203
  traditional design of, 208
  See also Alternatives to confinement; Juvenile correctional facilities; Prisons; Release

Jail therapy, 164, 497
Jeffery, C. Ray, 39
Job opportunities. *See* Correctional officers (COs)
Johnson Foundation, 54
Joint Commission on Correctional Manpower and Training, 322
Jones v. N.C. Prisoner's Labor Union, 378
Judges
  adjudication procedures, 5
  death penalty decisions, 342–343
  National Conference on Corrections, 79–80
  pretrial services, 4
  probation-granting privilege of, 160
  sentencing by, 65, 80
  See also Sentencing
Judicial process, ABA on prisoner access to, 483–484
Juries
  capital cases, 339–341
  jury trial, 5
  juvenile lack of right to, 88
  sentencing by judge or, 65, 80
Jurisdiction of correctional subsystem, 25, 44–47, 197
  See also Federal institutions and inmates; State institutions and inmates
"Just deserts" concept, 35, 39
Justice, Wayne, 224
Justice Policy Institute, 11
Juvenile correctional facilities
  for confinement, 85–89, 285–287
  defined, 8, 497
  detention centers, 283, 284, 285, 498
  federal mandate for segregation of, 101–102
  group home programs, 289–292
  job opportunities in, 9
  juvenile detention centers, 285, 498
  types of, 284–285
  workers in, 8
Juvenile corrections, 275–294
  about, 277
  ACA policies on, 473–474
  aftercare, 251
  boot camps, 129, 130, 140
  in correctional subsystem, 25
  court establishment, 278
  death penalty, 351, 351*t*
  disposition hearing, 282
  disproportionate minority youth, 288–289
  diversion, 280
  as future career criminals, 99, 100
  group home programs, 289–292
  history of, 277–278
  institutionalization, 283
  institutional types, 284–285
  intensive supervision of, 413
  juvenile release decisions, 292–293
  in lockups, 193
  parole, 256, 293
  probation, 160, 161–162, 282
  and probation officers, 85–87, 433, 436–437
  property cases, 284
  In Re Gault, 279–280
  revocation of parole, 256
  shock incarceration/probation, 160
  treatment for, 278, 283, 290–291
  types of cases, 283–284
  violent youths, 283

Juvenile detention centers, 283, 284, 285, 498
Juvenile Justice and Delinquency Prevention Act, 286
Juveniles, judicial process for, 84–92
    adjudicatory hearings, 88
    citation, 86–87
    detention hearings, 85–86
    disposition hearings, 88–89
    indeterminate sentences, 70
    intake, 87–88
    juvenile court procedures, 84–85
    present role of justice system, 280
    transfer to adult court, 89–92
    venue, 87
    waiver of juvenile court jurisdiction, 89–92, 280–281

K

Kanka, Megan, 233–234
Kansas, 42, 200
Kansas Department of Corrections, 448–449
Kemmler, William, 346
Kentucky, 115, 311, 336
Kent v. United States, 281
Klaas, Polly, 73

L

Labor, U.S. Department of, 435–436
Large v. Superior Court of County of Maricopa, 377
Larivee, John, 404, 405
Las Vegas Review, 13
Latino inmates. *See* Race and ethnicity
Law libraries, inmate access to, 377, 486
Lawyers, in criminal justice system, 4, 127
Leadership, inmate, 221, 224–225
Legal issues
    ABA on prisoner's legal services and materials, 484–486
    ACA policies on, 460
    Beccaria on, 30
    codification of punishment, early, 27–28
    torts and prisoner's rights, 370–371, 501
    See also Cases
Length of time served, 107–108, 193, 352
Les salica, 26
Lethal injection, 347–348, 349*t*, 352
Liberal ideology, 33–34, 51, 52
Lincoln, Abraham, 444
Locational considerations for corrections, 25, 44–47, 197
Lock down, 230, 498
Locker, in prison, 220
"Lock them up" policy, 397, 498
Lockups, 193, 498
Lombroso, Cesare, 30, 31*t*
"Look at Your Jail" (National Coalition for Jail Reform), 194
Los Angeles Times, 202
Louisiana, 40, 131, 288, 338

M

Machiavelli, Niccoli, 446
Maconochie, Alexander, 252–253
Mahan, Edna, 320
Mail censorship, 379–380
Maine, 40, 115

Mair, George, 402
Mandatory sentencing and prison terms
    average time served, 46
    defined, 68, 498
    incarcerated mothers, 309–310
    sentencing guidelines for, 70–71
    state guidelines, 5
    three strikes legislation, 36, 43, 73–75, 501
    See also Sentencing
Mandatory supervision, 250, 498
Marijuana, 103
Marion Penitentiary, Illinois, 229
Marshall, Thurgood, 349
Martinez-Villareal, Ramon, 341
Maryland, 115, 138, 311, 354
Massachusetts, 302, 397, 401, 403, 407
Matching, in community service, 147
Maximum custody, 245
McCleskey v. Kemp, 341*t*
McKune v. Lile, 380
Meachum v. Fano, 378
Mediator, probation officer as, 170
Medical approach, 49, 50
    See also Rehabilitation
Medical treatment. *See* Health care issues
Medium custody, 245
Megan's Laws, 233–235, 498
Mempa v. Rhay, 166
Mental health issues
    and death penalty, 338, 341–342
    for female inmates, 313–314
    at inmate orientation, 244
    for juvenile offenders, 278
    Large v. Superior Court of County of Maricopa, 377
    and prison violence, 100–101
    rehabilitative programming, 134–137
    in serving time, 231–232
    special programs, 134–137, 313–314
    suicide in jail, 194, 202–207
    Vitek v. Jones, 378
    See also Health care issues; Treatment approach
Messinger, Sheldon L., 231
Methamphetamine, 103
Mexican inmates, 107, 108
Michigan, 12, 99, 115
Middle Ages, historical view of corrections, 28–29
Military-style training, boot camps, 129, 132–133, 136
Miller, Jerome, 233
Minimum custody, 246
Minimum security prisons, privatization of, 12–13
Minnesota, 40, 42, 68, 69*t*, 72
Minnesota v. Murphy, 182–184
Minors. *See* Juveniles, judicial process for
Misdemeanants and misdemeanors, 80, 142, 194, 498
Mission statement, prison governance, 421–422
Mississippi, 40, 44, 356, 373
Missouri, 202–203, 356, 397
MIST (mobile intervention supervision team), 400
Mitigating circumstances, 340, 498
Mobile intervention supervision team (MIST), 400
Model Penal Code, 80
Money
    for atonement and fines, 5, 26, 145
    script as prison, 218, 500
    surrendered at orientation, 244
Monitoring, electronic (EM), 397–398, *399*
Montana, 42, 115, 161, 304, 343, 350

Morrissey v. Brewer, 166, 256, 257–266
Mortality among inmate women, 314
Mothers, absent from home, impact of, 308–309
Murderers and prison violence, 101

N

National Advisory Commission on Criminal Justice Standards and Goals, 128, 165, 322
National Center on Institutions and Alternatives, 233
National Coalition for Jail Reform, 194
National Conference on Corrections, 79–80
National Corrections Reporting Program (NCRP), 46
National Crime Survey (NCS), 269
National Crime Victimization Survey (NCVS), 75–76, 104
National Household Survey, 103–104
National Institute of Corrections, 18, 209
National Institute of Justice, 72, 74, 307, 311
National Policies on Corrections, ACA, 455–482
National Prison Association, 301
National Prison Project, 47
National Report on Juvenile Offenders (OJJDP), 287
National Sheriff's Association, 192
NCRP (National Corrections Reporting Program), 46
NCS (National Crime Survey), 269
NCVS (National Crime Victimization Survey), 75–76, 104
Nebraska, 42, 44, 198, 310, 343
Nelson v. Heyne, 283
Nevada, 115
New-generation jails, 208, 209, 498
New Hampshire, 42, 138, 397
New Jersey, 115, 234–235, 288, 311, 346, 373
New Jersey Reformatory for Women, 320
New Mexico, 288, 291
Newsday, 45
Newsweek poll, 337
New York
    boot camps, 138
    death penalty in, 354
    emergency overcrowding provisions, 79
    funding choices, 11
    historic women's facilities, 299, 300*t*, 302
    incarceration rate, 40
    jail smoking ban, 198
    jail standards challenge, 192
    mortality among inmate women, 314
    parenting prison program, 310
    shock incarceration/probation, 130, 138
    torts, prisoner's, 371
New York House of Refuge, 102
New York Reformatory for Women, Albion, 301
New York State Department of Corrections, 450–451
New York Times, 355
Nolle prosequi, 4
Nolo contendere (no contest), as plea, 5
Noncitizen offenders, 107–108
Non-secure facilities, 285
Nonviolent offenders, 74–75, 130, 194
North Carolina
    death penalty in, 346
    death row, 350, 351
    harsher treatment, 373
    historic women's facilities, 302
    jail overcrowding, 200
    jail smoking ban, 198

North Dakota, 40
Not guilty, as plea, 5
Not guilty by reason of insanity, as plea, 5

O

Objectives of corrections. *See* Purpose of corrections
O'Connor, Sandra Day, 380
Offenders and offences
    atonement through money or property, 26–27
    committed by elderly, 110–111
    convictions in state courts by offense, 65, 66–67*t*
    crime, types of, 44–46
    felons, 65, 66–67*t*, 80, 167, *168*
    and parole revocation, 165–166
    pre-sentence report on, 5
    prison gang activity in, 228
    property offenses, 44, 46, 66–67*t*, 99, 284
    sentencing, 5–6
    types of, in correctional subsystem, 25
    See also Inmates
Office of Juvenile Justice and Delinquency Prevention (OJJDP), 18, 101, 285, 287–289, 290
Ohio, 12, 115, 203, 311, 356, 373
OJJDP (Office of Juvenile Justice and Delinquency Prevention), 18, 101, 285, 287–289, 290
Oklahoma
    boot camps, 129
    corrections overcrowding, 47, 199
    death row and executions, 344*t*, 350, 356
    electronic monitoring, 398
    incarceration rate, 40
    shock incarceration/probation, 160–161
Oklahoma Shock Incarceration Program (SIP), 160–161
Older (elderly) offenders and inmates, 105–106, 110–118, 315
"On Crimes and Punishment" (Beccaria), 30
Operation Night Light, 401
Opiates, 103
Oregon, 42, 130–131, 320
Orientation, inmate, 197, 244–245, 498
Outlaws, and societal sanctions, 26, 27
Overcrowding
    ACA policies on, 471
    correctional employment outlook, 435–436
    emergency provisions, 68, 79, 496
    jails, 199–201
    juvenile facilities, 285
    and Prison Litigation Reform Act, 372–373
    prisons, 46–47
    See also Alternatives to confinement

P

Pack, Grace Oliver, 320
Packer, Herbert, 34, 36–37
Pain of imprisonment and attitude change, 133–134, 137–139
Panoptical prison, Bentham's, 31
Parens patriae, 277, 498
Parenting and female inmates, 306–307, 308–312
Parole
    ACA policies on, 477–478
    aftercase, 251
    capital crimes, 352
    contemporary, 254–255
    defined, 68, 498

514 Index

as determinate sentencing, 6
discharge from, 247
good-time credit, 253
guidelines for, 499
history of, 252–253
juvenile corrections, 256, 293
release on, 250–254
revocation of, 256
services, 255–256
technical violations of, 165
truth in sentencing laws, 70
Parole officers
application process, 429, *430*
caseloads, 433
defined, 431, 499
ethical code, 438–439
job outlook, 435–436
nature of work, 432–433, 434
preparation for, 8
statistics, 431
training, qualifications and advancement, 435
working conditions, 434
Parole services, 255, 499
Parsimony, as punishment guiding principle, 38
Passive electronic monitoring, 398, 499
Patriot Bill (2001), 45
Patzig, Annette M., 204–207
Patzig v. O'Neil, 204–207
Peace (police) officer, 3, 4, 85–87, 401
Penal servitude, 27, 499
Penitentiaries, 32, 49, 499
Penitentiary Act (1799), English, 32
Penn, William, 32–33
Pennsylvania, 300, 344, 351, 353
Perry, Michael Owen, 338
Perry v. Lynch, 341*t*
Personality, institutional, 217, 497
Personal retaliation. *See* Retaliation
Petition of Rights (1628), England, 191
The Philadelphia Inquirer, 13
Philosophy of corrections, 47–48, 142, 172–182
Pintard, John, 102
Pinto case, Ford Motor Company, 109
Plea, 5, 499
Pocatello Women's Correctional Center, ID, 310
Police, 3, 4, 85–87, 401
Policy issues
ABA on legal status of prisoners, 483–492
ACA on, 455–482
elderly offender programs, 116
on juvenile offenders, 101–102
"lock them up" policy, 397, 498
on probation, 165
on sentencing, 72, 73, 253
Population. *See* Statistics, U.S.
Post-sentencing process, 6
Poverty and crime, 50, 53–54, 99
Power and prisonization, 217
Precedents, legal. *See* Cases
Pregnant inmates, 307, 308
Preliminary hearing, 4
Presentence investigation (PSI) reports, 71–72, 80–82, 499
Pre-sentence report, 5
President's Commission on Corrections, 255, 280
President's Commission on Law Enforcement, 10
President's Crime Commission, 335

Presumptive sentence, 68, 69*t*, 499
Pretrial diversion, 83, 125, 499
See also Community service
Prevention approach, 48
Prison argot (slang), 218, 219*t*, 223, 499
Prison constitutional convention, 416–418
Prisoner Activist Resource Center, 18
Prisonization, 99, 217–221, 499
Prison Litigation Reform Act (1996), 192, 372–373, 499
Prisons
average time served, 46
builder-tender system, 224–225
building boom in, 11
construction costs, 9, 11, 195, 200, 266–271
controlled movement in, 229–230
in correctional enterprise, 7
costs of, 266–271
counts in, 230
defined, 499
federal, 108–110
gangs in, 224–227
guard-inmate relations, 229
incarceration in, 5–6
vs. jails, 193
overcrowding in, 46–47, 79
population in, 11–12, 44
privatization of, 12–14, 467, 499
procedures in (*See* Institutional procedures)
routine in, 227–230
sexual activity in, 228
subculture in, 222–223
violence in, 100–101
See also Alternatives to confinement; Inmate involvement in prison governance; Jails; Juvenile correctional facilities; Release; Rights of prisoners
Private sector involvement, ACA policies on, 464
Privatization, prison, 12–14, 467, 499
Privileges in prison. *See* Classification of inmates
Probable cause, 4
Probation, 155–185
about, 156
ACA policies on, 476–477
agency for, 5, 143
article, 172–182
and capital crimes, 352
classification of, 158
conditions of, 163
and corrections philosophy, 172–182
and courts, 157, 159
criteria for granting, 161–162
deferred adjudication, 83, 125
defined, 157, 499
extent of, 161
functions of, 167, 169–171
future of, 171, 176–182
gender bias in, 106
history of, 158–159
intensive supervision probation (ISP), 158, 175, 177–178, 180, 497
juvenile corrections, 160, 161–162, 282
Operation Night Light, Boston, 401
philosophies for future of, 172–182
pretrial diversion, 83, 125, 499
probationers' rights, 164–167, *168*
probation offices, 170

reform-based probation ideology, 178–182
revocation of, 159–160, 164–167, 500
role of probation officer, 169–170
as sentencing choice, 5
State v. Fuller, 182–184
status of, 159–161
technical violations of, 164, 501
Texas Code of Criminal Procedure, 163
Warner v. Orange County Probation, 386–390
See also Sentencing; Shock incarceration/probation
Probation officers
advancement considerations, 439–447
application process, 429, *430*
article, 439–447
caseloads, 433
defined, 431, 499
ethical code, 438–439
job outlook, 435–436
juvenile corrections, 85–87, 433, 436–437
nature of work, 432–433, 434
preparation for, 8
and revocation of probation, 164–165
role of, 169–170
statistics, 431
training, qualifications and advancement, 435
working conditions, 434
Probation offices, 170
Procunier v. Martinez, 379–380
Professional criminals, 103, 499
Programming time, 77
Property
as atonement for crime, 26
offenses involving, 44, 46, 66–67*t*, 99, 284
surrendered at inmate orientation, 244
Proportionality of death penalty, 339
Prosecution and prosecutors, 4, 127
Protection from prison violence, 100–101
PSI (presentence investigation) reports, 71–72, 80–82, 499
Psychology/psychopathology. *See* Mental health issues
Public executions, 336–337
Public opinion of death penalty, 337–338, 339
Public order crimes, 44
Public sanctions, historic development of, 26–27, 33
Pulaski, Charles, 353
Punishment
ACA policies on, 466, 469–470
atonement through hard labor, 27–28
atonement through money or property, 26
Beccaria on, 29–30, 31*t*
Bentham on, 31–32
Chinese proverb on, 38
as correctional philosophy, 48
death penalty as cruel and unusual, 339
deterrence theory of, 35–36
early codification, 27–28
English Statement of Purposes (EPS) 37–38
guiding principles, 38–39
Lombroso on, 30, 31*t*
punitive elements in boot camps, 136–137
purpose of, 37–39
by retaliation, 25–26
See also Sanctions
Punitive elements
boot camp, 136–137
jail overcrowding, 200

probational philosophies, 174, 177
solitary confinement, 377
Purpose of corrections
ACA policies on, 463
diversion, 127
incapacitation, 34, 36–37, 339, 497
punishment, 37–39
for rehabilitation, 37
for retribution, 34–35
"Put down," 224, 499

Q

Quaker Code (1682), 33
Quakers, as prison reformers, 32–33
Qualified immunity, 13–14, 500

R

Race and ethnicity
in corrections employment, 302–303, 309–310, 323–324, 429
death penalty and executions, 343–345, 344*t*, 350–354
disproportionate minority confinement, 40–44, 41*t*
drug crimes, 42–43
enforcement model, 48
female inmates, 302–303, 309–310
health care for women inmates, 314
incarceration rates, 41–42, 41*t*, 309–310
juveniles in residential placement, 288–289
prison subculture, 223
street gangs, 43
women offenders, 305–306, 306*t*, 309–310
Radical ideology, 33, 34, 51
Rafter, Nicole Hahn, 302
Ragen, Joseph E., 443
Rakoff, Jed, 354
Ralph, Paige, 225
Ranches, juvenile, 285
Randall, Clarence B., 441
Rand Corporation study, 99–100, 180
Rapes in prison, 228
"Rational basis" approach to prison rules, 379
Reception/diagnostic centers, 285, 500
Recidivism
alternative sentencing, 132, 139–140
boot camp, 129, 132
day-reporting centers, 406–407
defined, 129, 500
deterrence theory of punishment, 36
probation, 176–177
shock incarceration/probation, 160–161
See also Evaluation of effectiveness
Reformatory movement, 49, 277, 301–304, 500
Reform-based probation ideology, 176, 177–182
Regular probation, 125, 500
See also Probation
Regular purchases, prison commissary, 220
Rehabilitation
alternatives to incarceration, 134–137
article, 49–56
in boot camps, 129–130, 137
contemporary views and efforts, 53–55
controversy over, 50–56
criminogenic needs addressed, 134–135
death penalty, 339

defined, 49, 500
as goal of criminal sanctions, 34, 37
historical view, 49
as indeterminate sentencing, 70
for juvenile offenders, 278
matching with high-risk offenders, 1
McKune v. Lile, 380
medical approach to, 50
model for, 10
and probation, 174, 176–182
punitive elements, 136–137
reasons for reaffirmation of, 55
responsivity, 134, 135
shock incarceration/probation, 134–137
theoretical issues, 50
"tough on crime" ideology, 52, 56
See also Treatment approach
Rehnquist, William, 380
Reintegration, 10, 500
Release
  from confinement, 250, 251*t*
  good-time credit, 253
  from institutional confinement, 250
  from jail, 197
  juvenile release decisions, 292–293
  mobile intervention supervision team (MIST), 400
  to parole, 250–254
  supervised, 253–254
Religious freedom, ABA on prisoner access to, 491
  See also Theological view
Research
  ACA policies on, 459
  career criminals, 99–100
  death penalty, 353–354
  elderly offenders and inmates, 111–116
  Hemparian's study of violent criminal, 102
  increasing incarceration, 11
  juvenile correctional facilities, 286–287
  prison subculture, 223
  probation, 177–178, 180
  rehabilitation programs, 50–53, 134–137
Residential placement, juveniles in, 284*t*, 288–289
Restitution, 5, 128, 500
Retaliation, 25–27, 34–35
Retarded defendants, execution of, 341–342
Retribution, 34–35, 500
Revenge, 26–27, 34–35
Revocation
  of parole, 256
  of probation, 159–160, 164–167, 500
Revolving door concept, jails, 194, 500
Rhode Island, 40, 42
Richardson et al. v. McKnight, 14
Riggs, Michael, 75
Right of confidentiality, probationer's, 164
Rights of prisoners, 367–386
  cases, 377–390
  categories of involvement, 370–372
  confinement conditions, 371
  "cruel and unusual" clause, 374–377
  deference period, 369, 495
  deliberate indifference, 380–385
  due process, 370
  habeas corpus, 371–372
  hands-off period, 369, 496
  movement toward harshness, 373
  Prison Litigation Reform Act (1996), 372–373
  probationer's, 164–167, *168*
  rights period, 369, 500
  torts, 370–371
Rights period, 369, 500
Ring v. Arizona, 342
Risk management, 127, 500
Rogers, Carl, 278
Roman Catholic church, crime as sin against, 26, 28–29
Ruiz v. Estelle, 224
Rules of conduct, 249–250, 486
Ryan, George, 354–355

S

Safer Society, 232
Salvation Army, 232
Sanctions
  ACA policies on purpose of correctional, 463
  Beccaria on, 30
  correctional philosophies, 48
  deterrence, 35–36
  ideology, 33–34
  incapacitation, 36–37
  Lombroso on, 30, 31*t*
  outlaws, 26, 27
  parole goals, 255
  public, historic development of, 26–27, 33
  purpose of, 33–37
  rehabilitation, 37
  retribution, 34–35
  vengeance principle, and the law, 26–27
  See also Punishment
San Quentin Prison, CA, 356
Sattazahn, David, 356
Sattazahn v. Pennsylvania, 356
Sawyer, Kathleen Hawk, 322
Scared Straight program, 132–133
Scottish prison constitutional convention, 416–418
Script, 218, 500
Search of probationers, 164
Secure facilities, 285, 500
Segregative classification, 245, 500
Selective incapacitation, 36
Sentencing, 63–94
  about, 65–68, 66–67*t*
  alternative sentencing, 83
  average time served, 46
  to community service, 140, 145–146
  contemporary trends in, 6–7
  in criminal justice enterprise (system), 5
  defined, 65, 501
  determinate (flat time), 6, 68, 71, 496
  drug crimes and race, 42–43
  economics of crime rate reduction, 76
  emergency overcrowding provisions, 79
  for felons, 80
  good-time policies, 77–79
  guidelines for, 68, 71–73, 82, 501
  indeterminate, 70
  mandatory prison terms, 70–71
  misdemeanants, judicial process for, 80
  National Conference on Corrections, 79–80
  National Crime Victimization Survey (NCVS), 75–76

presentence investigations, 80–82
presumptive, 68, 69*t*
to prison or jail, 5–6
suspended sentences, 83
three strikes legislation, 36, 43, 73–75, 501
truth in sentencing laws, 70
United States Sentencing Commission, 75, 77
See also Alternatives to confinement; Juveniles, judicial process for; Mandatory sentencing and prison terms; Probation
Sentencing Reform Act (1984), 72
Services, parole, 255–256
Sexism, 318, 501
Sex of inmates. *See* Gender issues
Sexual issues
abuse and women offenders, 306–307
gang rape in prison, 228
harassment of women correctional officers, 316
offenders, 28, 232–236, 380, 400
prison sexual activity, 228
sex offender registration, 233
transsexual inmates, 381–385
Shakedowns, 228, 501
Shelters, 284, 285, 501
Sheriff position, 191
Shirley, Kurt, 199
Shock incarceration/probation, 129–134
boot camps, 129–133
catalysts for change, 133
characteristics of, 129–130
defined, 501
evaluation, 132–133
profiles of selected programs, 130–131
Shock Incarceration Program (SIP), Oklahoma, 160–161
Shock probation, 160–161, 501
Sin, crime as, 26, 28–29, 35
SIP (Shock Incarceration Program), Oklahoma, 160–161
Slang, prison, 218, 219*t*, 223
Slavery, as punishment, 28
Smoking, 198, 378
Social systems
inmate, 231–233
poverty and crime, 50, 53–54
protection of juveniles, 280
radical ideology, 34
Societal sanctions. *See* Sanctions
Socrates, trial and death of, 27, 346
Solitary confinement, 377
South Carolina, 115, 160, 192, 373, 398
South Dakota, 42, 136
Special conditions of probation, 163
Special needs of inmates, ACA policies on, 464
Special programs
educational, 312–313
for elderly inmates, 105–106, 110–118, 315
juvenile aftercare, 251
juvenile group home programs, 289–292
mental health, 134–137, 313–314
parole services, 255–256
rehabilitation, 50–53, 134–137
Scared Straight program, 132–133
types of, in correctional subsystem, 25
vocational training, 49, 53–54, 285, 312, 472
for women inmates, 195, 307–316
See also Shock incarceration/probation

Special purchases, prison commissary, 220
Specific deterrence, 35
Spellman, M., 268
Split sentencing, 160, 501
Standard conditions of probation, 163
Standards, ACA policies on, 479–480
Standards for Criminal Justice: Legal Status of Prisoners (ABA), 370
Stanford v. Kentucky, 341*t*
State Department of Corrections, 9, 501
State institutions and inmates
average time served, 46
in correctional subsystem, 25
death penalty outlawed in, 344*t*
funding choices, 11
incarcerated population, 44
jail felonies, 197–198, 501
job opportunities in, 9
juvenile, definitions of, 101
mandatory sentencing guidelines, 5
Middle Ages, crime as sin against, 26, 35
prison operations, 7, 12
prison overcrowding, 47, 79
See also individual states
State v. Fuller, 182–184
State v. Imlay, 182–183
State v. Utah, 82
Statistics, U.S.
on correctional employees, 429
correctional officers by gender, 322
crime rate, 74, 76, 268–271
criminal offenses (2000), 3
death penalty and executions, 335, *335, 336,* 343–345, 344*t,* 350–355
demographics of incarcerated population, 40
elderly inmates, 111
federal inmates, 109
female inmates, 304–303
incarceration rate, 6–7, 11, 39–40
jail population, 39, 194
juvenile offenders, 283, 286, 288–289
mothers, incarcerated, 311
parole, 251*t*
percentage incarcerated, 180–181
prisoner's torts, 371
prison population, 39
public support for death penalty, 337–338
recidivism, 3
women offenders, 304, *305,* 306
See also Crime rate
Status of probation, 159–161
Statutory changes in capital punishment, 345–346
Stephen, Sir James, 35
Street gangs, 43
Stress in shock incarceration/probation, 133–134, 137–139
Subculture, prison, 222–223
Substance abuse. *See* Alcohol and alcoholism; Drug abuse
Subsystem, correctional, 7, 25, 495
Suicides in jail, 194, 202–207
Sumerian codes, 27
Supervised release, 253–254, 501
Supervision of offenders
in community service sentencing, 148
intensive supervision probation (ISP), 158, 175, 177–178, 180, 497

probation, 169, 177–182
  See also Incarceration
Surveillance, electronic, 397–398, *399*, 496
Suspended sentences, 83
Suspension of execution of sentence, 83
Suspension of imposition of sentence, 83
Sykes, Gresham M., 231

T

Tax evasion as federal crime, 108
Technical violations of parole, 165
Technical violations of probation, 164, 501
Telephone and electronic monitoring, 398
Tennessee, 115, 350
"Tent City" jail, Arizona, 201
Texas
  builder-tender system, 224
  career criminals, 99
  cost of incarceration per prisoner, 12
  death row and execution, 337, 344, 344*t*, 350, 351, 356
  on disciplinary hearing procedures, 247–248
  electronic monitoring, 398
  facilities for elderly inmates, 115
  gender bias in criminal justice, 106–107
  good-time guidelines, 78
  incarceration rate, 40
  inmate lawsuits and good-time guidelines, 78–79
  jail overcrowding reduction, 200
  jail smoking ban, 198
  juveniles in residential placement, 288
  lethal injection, 347
  location of confinement, 44
  noncitizen inmates, 107
  overcrowded facilities, 47, 79, 200
  payments by inmates, 397
  prison gangs, 225
  retarded defendants, execution of, 342
  sentencing by judge or jury, 65, 80
  sex offenders, 233
  state jail felonies, 197
  women offenders, 304
Texas Code of Criminal Procedures, 163
Texas Department of Corrections, 450
Texas Department of Criminal Justice, 78, 169
Theological view
  ABA on religious freedom, 491
  and community service, 147–148
  crime as sin against church, 26, 28–29, 35
  "eye for an eye" concept, 34–35
  "just deserts" concept, 35
  Quakers, as prison reformers, 32–33, 302
  of vengeance, 35
Therapy. *See* Treatment approach
Thompson v. Oklahoma, 341*t*
Thoughts on Convict Management (Maconochie), 252
Three strikes legislation, 36, 43, 73–75, 501
Time off for good behavior. *See* Good–time guidelines
Time served, 107–108, 193, 352
Timmendequas, Jesse K., 233–234
Title VII of Civil Rights Act (1964), 320, 321, 501
Torts and prisoner's rights, 370–371, 501
"Tough on crime" ideology, 52, 56
Traditional jail design, 208
Training, vocational, 49, 53–54, 285, 312, 472
Train (inmate bus), 230, 501

Transfers
  inmate, 378
  of juveniles to adult court, 89–92
Transsexual inmates, 381–385
Travis, Maury, 202
Treatment approach
  as correctional philosophy, 48
  at day-reporting centers, 403
  historical view, 49
  for juvenile offenders, 278, 283, 290–291
  to sex offenders, 232
  See also Mental health issues; Rehabilitation
Treatment strategies specialists, 429, 431–436, 501
Trends in corrections
  community-based corrections, 10
  contemporary crime and offenders, 3, 9–14, 39–44
  cost of incarceration per prisoner, 11, 12
  crime control model, 10–11
  "lock them up" policy, 397, 498
  movement toward harshness, 373
Trials
  adjudication procedures, 5
  juvenile, 282
  by ordeal, 28, 502
  pretrial diversion, 83, 499
  Socrates, trial and death of, 27, 346
Truth in sentencing laws, 70, 502
Turner v. Safety, 379
"Twelve Cs" in probation officer advancement, 439–447

U

UCR (Uniform Crime Reports), 269
Underground economy, prison, 220
UNICOR (Federal Prisons Industries, Inc.), 110, 502
Uniform Crime Reports (UCR), 269
Uniform Juvenile Court Act waiver of jurisdiction and discretionary transfer to adult court, 89–92
Union, prisoner's, 378
United Nations (UN), 192
United States Sentencing Commission, 75, 77
UN (United Nations), 192
U.S. Constitution
  First Amendment, 249
  Fifth Amendment, 182–184, 380
  Eighth Amendment, 100–101, 339, 349, 374–377
  See also U.S. Supreme Court
U.S. Department of Justice (DOJ), 139, 353–354
U.S. Department of Labor, 435–436
U.S. Immigration and Naturalization Service (INS), 107–108
U.S. Sentencing Commission, 72
U.S. Supreme Court
  "cruel and unusual" clause, 374–377
  death penalty, 335, 339–343, 341*t*, 352–354
  discrimination and women correctional officers, 320–321
  execution methods, 347
  on juvenile offenders, 278–280, 281, 283
  on noncitizen offenders, 108
  prisoner's rights, 370, 374–380
  probationer's due process rights, 166–167
  on protection from prison violence, 100–101
  retarded defendants, execution of, 341–342
  revocation of parole, 256

rights of prisoners, 369
See also Courts
Utah, Stephen Thomas, 82
Utah (state), 42, 226

V

Values, 33, 502
Van den Haag, Ernest, 53
Van Winkle, Gloria L., 75
Vengeance, 26–27, 34–35
Venue for juvenile proceedings, 87
Vermont, 44, 161, 198
Verri, Pietro and Alessandro, 30
Victims
    ACA policies on, 480–481
    impact statements by, 5
Violent Crime Control and Law Enforcement Act (1994), 47, 70, 310, 348, 349*t*, 372–373
Violent offenders
    assaults on guards, 243
    average time served, 46
    Hemparian's study of, 102
    noncitizen inmates, 107
    in overall convictions, 44, 66–67*t*
    in prisons, 100–101
    women as, 106, 304
Virginia, 79, 111, 115, 342, 344*t*
Visitation, ABA on prisoner access to, 490–491
Vitek v. Jones, 378
Vocational training, 49, 53–54, 285, 312, 472
Voltaire, 29
Voluntary, rehabilitation as, 135
Volunteer bureau and community service, 143
Volunteer work. *See* Community service

W

Waiver of jurisdiction, Uniform Juvenile Court Act, 89–92
Waiver of juvenile court jurisdiction, 280–281
Walnut Street Jail, PA, 300

Ward of the court, juveniles as, 84, 85
Warner v. Orange County Probation, 386–390
War on drugs. *See* Drug offenses
Washington, Earl Jr., 338
Washington (state), 42, 115, 139, 400
Washington Total Abstinence Society, Boston, 158–159
Weed, Mary, 319
Welfare, and prison costs, 270
Wergeld, 26, 502
West Virginia, 44, 198
Whipping, as punishment, 28
White-collar criminals, 103, 142, 143, 502
White inmates. *See* Race and ethnicity
Wilkins v. Missouri, 341*t*
Will, free, 30, 31*t*, 33–34
Wilson, James Q., 447
Wilson, Marlene, 441
Wilson, Pete, 73–74
Wilson, Woodrow, 443
Wisconsin, 42, 373
Witchcraft, in Middle Ages, 28, 29
Wolff v. McDonnell, 379
Wolfgang, Marvin, 36
Women as correctional officers. *See* Female correction officers
Women in corrections. *See* Female inmates
Woodworth, George, 353
Work by inmates, ACA policies on, 471
Writs of *habeas corpus,* 371–372, 502
Wyoming, 42, 102, 115, 350

Y

Yates, Donald, 42–43
Youth. *See* Juvenile corrections

Z

Zero crime rate, 76
Zimring, Franklin